Day 34. Looking north from Sulebu to an alpenglow on the Gjendealpene with Knutsholstind on the left and Torfinnstind on the right

Day 195. Lunch by the warm waters of Lyngvær with the iconic Torghatten, the mountain with a hole through it, in the distance

ISBN: 978-0-9550497-1-2
Bar code number: 9 780955 049712

Text, illustrations and maps © James Baxter 2012
Layout, maps, design and all photos by James Baxter.

First edition. Printed 2012
Printed and bound in Edinburgh

Published by:
Scandinavian Publishing
7 Findhorn Place
Edinburgh
EH9 2JR

If you should require any further information about Scandinavia I will be happy to help. Please email your comments or queries to:
james@scandinavianmountains.com

Day 183. On Fjetterstad beach on the remote west side of Lundøya with an abandoned small holding on Fjetterstadholmen island in the bay

Front cover: Day 180. Looking from Skarstad to the granite spires of Tysfjord with Stetind in the middle
Front End Paper: Day 39. Ploughing a track in the virgin snow in Veslådalen heading down to Gjende in Jotunheimen
Back End Paper: Day 189. A beach on the north side of Sandvær in Lurøy with the island of Aldra in the background
Back cover from top: 1. Day 76. On the plateau between Tarnasjon and Tjultrask **2.** Day 144. Vesterneset between Båtsfjord and Kongsfjord **3.** Previous tour. Skiing up Ruohtesjiegna in Sarek **4.** Day 183. The author James Baxter **5.** Day 160. Puffin at Gjesværstappen

NORWAY
THE OUTDOOR PARADISE

Written by
JAMES BAXTER

A SKI AND KAYAK ODYSSEY IN EUROPE'S GREAT WILDERNESS

Day 41. After five weeks in the mountains above the tree line it was a delight to return to the pine forests and old summer farms of Sjodalen

SCANDINAVIAN PUBLISHING
EDINBURGH

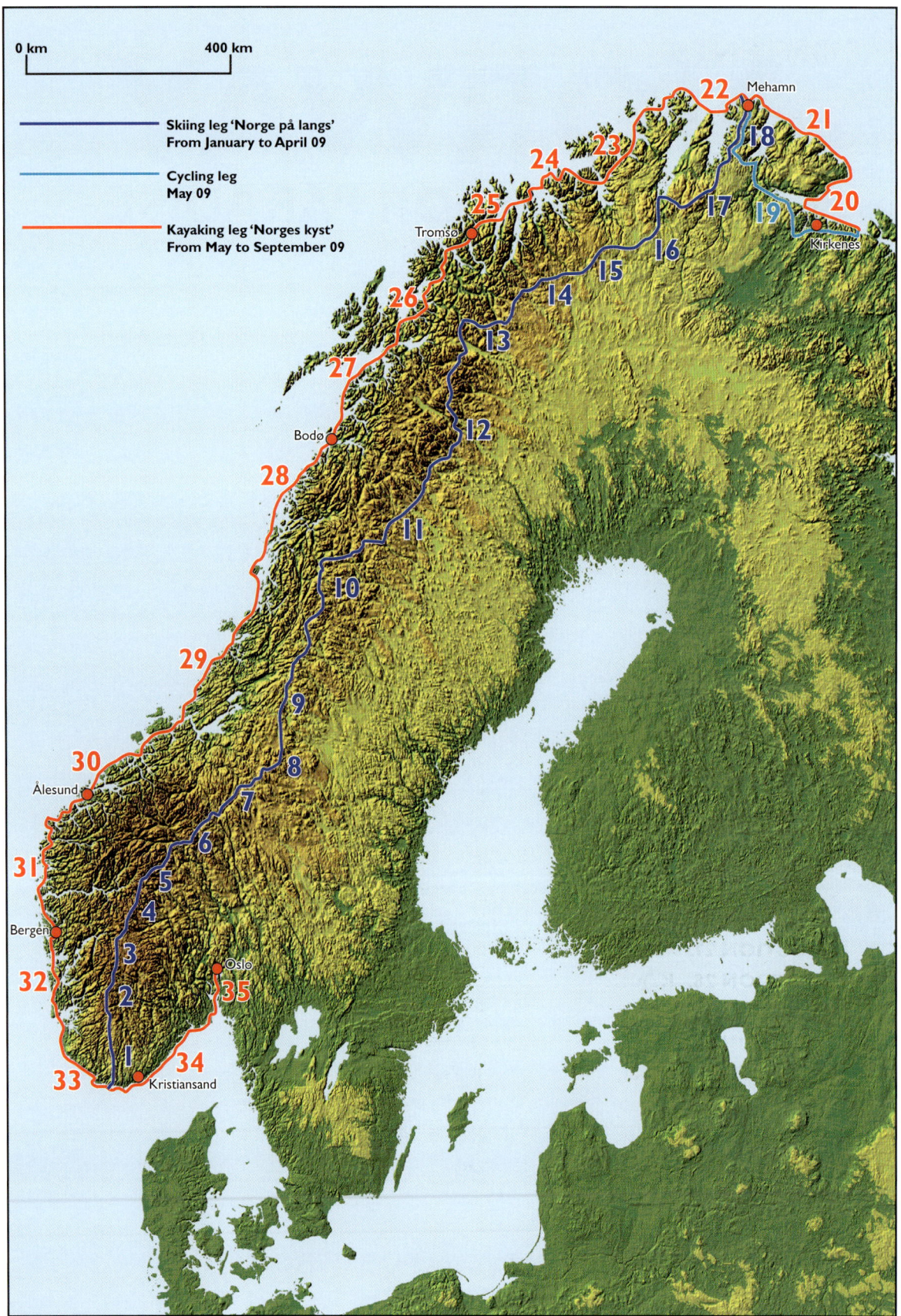

CONTENTS

THE PREPARATION			6
SECTION 1.	Ski	Lindesnes to Ljosland	14
SECTION 2.	Ski	Setesdalsheiane	24
SECTION 3.	Ski	Hardangervidda	42
SECTION 4.	Ski	Skarvheimen	52
SECTION 5.	Ski	Jotunheimen	60
SECTION 6.	Ski	Rondane	70
SECTION 7.	Ski	Upper Østerdalen	76
SECTION 8.	Ski	Sylan	88
SECTION 9.	Ski	Nord Trøndelag	94
SECTION 10.	Ski	Børgefjell and Hattfjelldal	110
SECTION 11.	Ski	South Kungsleden	120
SECTION 12.	Ski	North Kungsleden	136
SECTION 13.	Ski	Troms and Dividalen	148
SECTION 14.	Ski	North Finland	164
SECTION 15.	Ski	Reisadalen to Máze	168
SECTION 16.	Ski	Máze to Lakselv	176
SECTION 17.	Ski	Lakselv to Ifjord	184
SECTION 18.	Ski	Ifjord to Kinnarodden	192
SECTION 19.	Cycle	Mehamn to Grense Jakobselv	204
SECTION 20.	Kayak	Varangerfjord	216
SECTION 21.	Kayak	Østhavet	228
SECTION 22.	Kayak	Nordishavet	246
SECTION 23.	Kayak	Havøysund to Stjernsund	262
SECTION 24.	Kayak	Lopphavet	270
SECTION 25.	Kayak	Lyngen to Tromsø	280
SECTION 26.	Kayak	The Sounds of Troms	286
SECTION 27.	Kayak	Vestfjorden	298
SECTION 28.	Kayak	Helgelandskysten	316
SECTION 29.	Kayak	Folda and Frohavet	334
SECTION 30.	Kayak	The North West (Trondheim to Stad)	344
SECTION 31.	Kayak	North Vestlandet (Stad to Bergen)	366
SECTION 32.	Kayak	South Vestlandet (Bergen to Stavanger)	384
SECTION 33.	Kayak	The North Sea (Stavanger to Lindesnes)	396
SECTION 34.	Kayak	Sørlandet	410
SECTION 35.	Kayak	Oslofjord	430
THE EPILOGUE			440
LIMI VALLEY NEPAL			442

THE PREPARATION

Why Norway? Well, quite simply, Norway has the best nature in Europe! Arguably, regions of the Alps are more spectacular than the most dramatic mountain areas of Norway. The 2000 metre peaks of Scandinavia are second fiddle to the 4000 metre peaks of the Alps. But these are mere statistics and do not account for the higher latitudes which make for much more extreme climates. In the Alps the glaciers generally start at 2000 metres, while in Scandinavia they start at around 1000 metres, and the largest glacier in Europe, Jostedalsbreen, is about four times the size of the largest in the Alps. There are about 1600 of them in Norway and 300 in Sweden, and most of them are still grinding away at the higher mountains, shaping them into sharp peaks buttressed by serrated ridges. Like the Alps, the huge rivers of ice which drained the icefields have gone, leaving deep valleys. The valleys of Norway are equal to the biggest in the Alps, with Romsdal Valley boasting the highest vertical wall in Europe, the 1100 metre Trollveggen. On the west coast of Norway many of these valleys would be very much bigger than anything else in Europe, but they have been flooded by the sea to create dramatic fjords.

In addition to these treasures is the relatively untarnished and pristine wilderness. The Scandinavian Peninsula of Norway and Sweden has a land area of 750,000 km^2, well over three times the size of the United Kingdom, with just a fifth of the population, most of which is clustered around a few urban centres in the south, leaving the majority of this vast landscape in its unblemished natural splendour. While one can walk for a day or two in the Alps, Pyrenees or Scotland before meeting a busy road, ski resort or tourist development, one can go for a good week across flawless Scandinavian wildernesses without coming across any human intrusion, and when you meet it after a week it is very small scale and you are soon back into wilderness again for another week. You can really immerse yourself into the Scandinavian wilderness, while in all Europe's other wild places you have no sooner dipped your toe into it before you are interrupted.

I also have a long affinity and fascination with Norway. I lived there for four years at the beginning of the 1980s as a young man in my early twenties. As I travelled about I was gripped and fascinated by the landscape and yearned to get into it, especially in the winter. I had been downhill skiing in Scotland for a few years, which meant I could tolerate any weather and was happy careering down icy slides devoid of powdery snow. In fact skiing across frozen peat in a blizzard was the norm and I enjoyed it. However, I found that downhill skiing in Norway was not a passport into nature but something quite banal, like going to a football match. Any Norwegian worth their salt would go ski touring, as their parents, grandparents and ancestors had done for generations. It was something they learnt as young children, and as they grew up they honed their skills more and more, perhaps with an occasional deviation on to the downhill slopes as teenagers. I soon realized I had to go ski touring to really get into the winter wonderland. My Scottish downhill ski style had evolved to get me down slopes to the bottom of the lift in miserable conditions and had no finesse. What I lacked in style, I made up for in brute strength. However, this would not suffice for ski touring. Skill was paramount to control the longer, thinner skis, which were not attached at the heels, and I had none of this. I wanted to learn but had 20 years of catching up to do, which with doggish determination I set off into the forests around Oslo to do. It was an embarrassing experience. Families with toddlers whizzed around me as I gingerly snow-ploughed down gentle tracks. They would then look in amazement as I shot off out of control on the steeper sections, into the deep cushioning drifts and spruce trees beside the trails. At least once a day I would hear a child ask his parents if I might be Danish! After a whole winter, two pairs of broken skis and many hundreds of bruises, I was still eager. As winter came to an end around Oslo I thought I was ready for my first mountain trip. I bought the equipment and set off for a short week's trip down through the Skarvheimen. I found it much easier out of the forests on the open mountain and my brutish style was well suited to carrying a heavy pack. Over the next quarter century I made another 30 one or two week ski touring trips in the Norwegian and Swedish mountains, with about 10 of them being through Sarek, and mostly alone, when I could completely immerse myself into the winter wilderness. I was now more experienced than most Norwegians, but my style will always be clumsy compared to theirs.

When I made all my ski tours in Scandinavia there was always a start and a finish. I was curious to what was beyond the horizons of each one. Sometimes it would only be a few hundred kilometres or so to another area I had skied through previously. In the end, I had skied across so many of the mountainous areas in Norway that it looked like a dashed line on the map. I became more and more curious about the areas between the trips I had already skied, and slowly formulated a plan to join up the dashes. In the north, the dashed line stopped at Sarek and Abisko in the north of Sweden, and I thought about the great empty expanses of Finnmark which I had

THE PREPARATION

heard so much about. In the south, the dashed line stopped at Finse, and I thought about Setesdalsheiane and Hardangervidda. Areas which everybody has extolled the virtues of for decades when I visited Norway but I had never been to. Suddenly it seemed obvious to join up all the dashes and extend them so I could do one unbroken trip from the very south to the very north. I would really be able to immerse myself into this winter wonderland and see it transform and unfold through the entire winter as I skied over it. I knew a few people had already made this ski trip, and when I began to investigate I found that about 30 had already done it. It was something of a classic called 'Norge på langs', translated as 'Along the length of Norway'. Generally it seemed to take about 100 days from the south to the north and most people went from Lindesnes to Nordkapp. It was imperative to finish before the end of April as this was the time the snow and ice started to melt in an almost cataclysmic event called the 'Vårløsning' or the 'Spring loosening'. However, if I started too early there might not be enough snow on the southern mountains to ski across, and the streams, rivers and lakes might not have enough ice on them to cross easily and safely. The best time to start seemed to be in late December or early January when the days were still very short but hopefully winter had established itself. It would be naïve to think I could go in mid to late January and simply make up time by skiing longer distances each day. I had heard of a few people who thought they were up to this, and either injured their joints, tendons and muscles on the southern sections, or simply ran out of winter in the northern section and were left waist deep in soggy snow on the banks of a newly-thawed and roaring river they could not cross. The 1st of January seemed a nice round date to start and would give me about 120 days, which seemed adequate.

My next big decision was whether to pull everything on a sledge or carry it in a rucksack. It was not a question of what was best, but what was least worst. I knew the pitfalls of each well. With a sledge it is easy to take too much, and while crossing a flat lake you almost forget about it. However, when you get to the edge you are soon reminded it is still there as it hauls you back. There have been times when I have crashed with a sledge and it kept on going, grinding me into the snow, forcing snow into my shirt and up my nostrils. But where the sledge is at a real disadvantage is in the loose deep snow of a forest where you barely get enough purchase to force yourself through drifts, let alone a sledge that you have to weave through the trees and bushes. If this forest terrain is knobbly and gnarly with steep rises and falls it can be almost impossible to move; like being manacled to a millstone in a quagmire. The other disadvantage with a sledge is that you need snow. In the 2700 kilometres I had to ski there was bound to be some bare patches, and when I reached them I would be stuck. I would either have to carry the unwieldy contraption or just pull it across the stones and heather and hope to reach snow again before the base wore out. The alternative was a rucksack, but I would really have to limit its weight to a base of about 17 kilos with an additional kilo worth of food, fuel and maps per day. This would mean a maximum of 24 kilos for a week's section, and this would be the very maximum I could tolerate. I was wary though that it might grind my cartilage down, strain my sinews and I might get some terminal injury. I would have to be so strict with weight that the tent, sleeping bag and cooking equipment would have to be rated for the minimum performance I could get away with. Any superfluous comfort or excess safety features would have to be excluded. The week's supply of food would just be enough to survive on and I could not afford to take any tasty treats. Indeed, I would have to rely on resources stored on my hefty frame and gorge myself whenever I reached some civilization, and even then I would probably wither to supermodel proportions. Despite the physical strains of carrying a rucksack and lack of any comfort, I thought a rucksack would be better. It would give me much greater freedom to move in different terrain and it would allow me to move faster, especially when there was not much food in it. I wanted to do the entire trip under my own steam without having to resort to any external help. If I had a sledge and I came across a 10 or 20 kilometre bare patch, I would be very tempted to take a bus to detour round the problem, whereas with a rucksack I could tackle it.

I have been a kayaker since the age of 16, initially it was on the rivers of Scotland for three years. Then, after a pause of nearly 10 years I took it up again, but this time in the sea off the west coast of Scotland followed by a trip to New Zealand's South Island and another to Alaska. I occasionally took my kayak to Norway and did some shorter paddles on the south coast for a few years until I decided to try something more ambitious. In 2007 I paddled round the entire 310 kilometres of the Lofoten Islands. It took eight days altogether, and I was in awe during all of them. I had never seen such a concentration of alpine peaks and massive coastal architecture. Yet the whole of the Lofoten Islands were fringed in magnificent white beaches and superb birdlife and in one morning alone I saw over 100 sea eagles. I was hooked and did a few more shorter paddles in between my climbing trips.

I then heard about an account of the British Kayak Expedition in 1975 who kayaked from Bodø to Nordkapp and which spawned the infamous Nordkapp kayak, which I had tried out a few times. Later I came across two accounts by Swedes, Jim Danielsson and Barbro Lindman who in 1989 and 2005 respectively paddled the entire Norwegian coast from the Russian border in the Barents Sea all the way to the Swedish border. It seemed much of the Norwegian coast was like the Lofoten Islands. The seed of paddling the whole of the Norwegian coast was sown and it did not take long to start to grow, but it was an audacious plan. If I was to paddle the Norwegian coast then the summer months would be the best. Not only would it be warmer, but the weather would be more stable and I would enjoy very long daylight hours. May, June, July and August would be the optimum months. Jim and Barbro had taken well under 100 days to paddle the Norwegian coast and I thought I would take a bit longer than them.

Almost inevitably I thought of the ultimate Norwegian adventure. Why didn't I ski up and then paddle back down again in one great trip combining the classic 'Norge på langs' ski trip and the 'Norges kyst' kayak trip? If I left on 1st January I could ski up to the north, arriving on 1st May and could then paddle back south in the summer and get to Oslo around 1st September. That way I could really plunge myself into Norwegian nature and see every aspect of it from snow-covered winter mountains to bird-covered oceans, whose fingers pushed into the fjords. The more I thought about it the more convinced I became that this really was quite feasible. I would just have to link up the two trips. From the comfort of a study with an atlas and road-map in front of me it looked quite simple to ski the 300 kilometres from Kinnarodden, where the ski trip would finish, to the Russian border. I might be able to do it in a week! I would be able to do the whole skiing and kayaking expedition by just relying on my own steam power. This idea soon started to gather an almost unstoppable momentum and during most of 2008 it was constantly in my head, slowly being formulated. By the time I finally decided to do the expedition at the beginning of November, with just eight weeks to prepare everything, I had pretty much gone through every potential scenario in my head.

I had visited Norway a lot in 2002, 2003 and 2004, spending about a month there every spring and two months there every summer. During these nine months I spent the entire time focused on a mission to climb all the 2000 metre mountains in Scandinavia, of which there are 130 in Norway and 7 in Sweden. It was quite an undertaking and in total I had to walk or ski some 2500 kilometres and climb some 144,000 metres. About 20 per cent of the mountains were easy enough to ski up and down, 40 per cent were a long walk, 20 per cent involved crossing glaciers, 10 per cent were airy scrambles and the remaining 10 per cent involved climbing, but nothing more than a British V Diff on the easiest route. For probably half of the mountains on this project I was alone, but during holidays I was frequently joined by Arne Instebø and Tone Søvdsnes, two friends from Bergen. Two friends from Edinburgh, Gordon Bisset and Stuart Findlay, also came out to join me when I needed a climbing partner or someone on the other end of the rope to cross crevassed glaciers. During these three glorious springs and summers I endured virtually every type of mountain weather and spent a lot of time in cabins reading about the Norwegian mountains, their history, geology and the flora and fauna, and became a keen amateur naturalist. I knew most of Jotunheimen and Hurrungane like the back of my hand, and was so enamoured with it I wrote a well-received guidebook on the latter, called 'Hurrungane'. I could wax lyrical for months about these mountains, the transhumance farming culture, the mountain cabins, the meadows of summer flowers under the short mountain birch, and the towering ridges of abrasive gabbro above glacier-filled corries. It was during this project that I fell in love with the outdoors in Norway and I will always cherish the memories of this time. I was now a 'Norgesvenn'. Once the last mountain, Galdeberget, had been climbed with my trusty companion, Arne Instebø, there was a sense of loss and I needed another Norwegian outdoor project to fill the void. Skiing up and paddling down the length of Norway was the perfect project to fill this longing.

There were two big problems which I still had to overcome; how could I just take nine months off, and how could I get the kayak and all the kayaking equipment up to the Russian border? The first problem was solved when a friend offered to look after all my affairs for a small monthly fee. The business largely ran itself but it needed monitoring, and from time to time there would be some crisis to deal with. Johanna was the embodiment of Teutonic efficiency, extremely trustworthy, and I knew I could rely on her. The easiest thing to do was explain how everything worked, give her a checklist of things to do, access to my email and bank accounts and let her get on with it. After a couple of weeks she had the whole thing under control and I knew I could leave everything in her safe hands. The kayak was a more problematic issue and I was not even sure whether I wanted a fibreglass one, a plastic type or even a tough new thermoform design. I spent weeks poring through the catalogues. The thermoform designs were just too new and I could not get an opportunity to try out the Eddyline Falcon, which was the only suitable shape on the market at the time. Most of the plastic types were rotomoulded and just too flexible and I didn't consider any of them would be up to the job. However, Prijon kayaks, although plastic, are not rotomoulded but are made from high density thermoplastic, which is much stiffer and more durable. Barbro Lindman used a Prijon Kodiak for her paddle and she advised me to try one out. It was certainly tough, tougher than anything else I have come across, except the new thermoform kayaks, but I found the cockpit too high. So it was back to the tried and tested fibreglass ones.

Having seen some of the build quality on the otherwise excellent NDK Explorer, I was wary about getting lumbered with a lemon when I arrived at the Russian border. I found most of the Valley boats just too small for my 100 kilo frame. I liked the P&H Cetus, but then I came across the plans for the Tiderace Xplore X. I went down to have a chat with Dave Felton and Aled Williams about their boat, which was still on the drawing table. However, with Aled's design pedigree and Dave's organizational skills I took a chance and bought it off the sketch pad. It had everything I was looking for and they would beef up the vulnerable hull and keel, put both a rudder and skeg on it and supply it with Kajaksport hatches. Best of all they had ended their unhappy marriage with their Polish manufacturers and had moved their production base to Kokkola in Finland. I was acquainted with this Finnish manufacturer as it also made boats for Skim Kayaks which I had seen in Norway, and they were of a high quality. This solved the logistic problem of getting the kayak to the Russian border as I could simply give Dave everything I needed for the kayak leg of my expedition. He would then send it to Kokkola with the moulds and other equipment he was shipping over to them in a container. When my kayak was finished it could be filled with my gear and then sent by lorry freight to the north of Finland and just over the border to Kirkenes. I was putting a lot of faith in Dave and Aled, but if it all worked according to plan then everything would be easy, and the kayak big and solid enough to complete the journey. As a contingency I also got in touch again with Barbro Lindman, whose partner, James Venimore was the Prijon agent in Sweden, in case he needed to freight a Kodiak and the accessories up in a hurry.

With these two big problems out of the way I could now spend the next month evaluating and buying the equipment I would need for both the ski and kayak trips. The ski equipment would go in my rucksack with me to Norway and the kayaking equipment would go to Dave at Tiderace when it was all gathered together. As was the vogue, I also had to set up a website so I could post updates on to it. I had to work out how to do this with the minimum of fuss and make it interesting enough with interactive maps and a photo gallery. I contacted Richard Cross, a web-whiz I knew from a previous project, and he agreed to do it. We spent a day talking through how I would post the daily blog and pictures on the website 'www.skipaddlenorway.com' with my basic smartphone. Norway has extensive mobile phone coverage so this seemed the easiest option for updating the site once I had a monthly contract with a Norwegian mobile phone service. Richard set up a map to update my daily position when he received coordinates from a satellite GPS tracker I would carry and activate at the end of each day. He then set up a donation page for the educational charity in Limi Valley in Nepal which I would be collecting money for, and another page which would act as a gallery for the better images I took. Once the architecture of the website was set up I had to write text and supply pictures to fill and illustrate the empty pages. This alone took me about 10 days. Once it was finished there was a great relief. All I had to do now was start packing my equipment, but the deadline of the Christmas festive period was looming.

I had decided to get most of my camping equipment here in the UK before I left for Norway and then get my skis and boots over there just before I set off. Needlesports in Kendal stock a wide range of high quality outdoor gear, they were also close to Tiderace Kayaks and Knoydart in Penrith who would attend to all my kayaking needs. So, once I had pretty much established what I wanted I went down to Kendal and booked myself into a bed and breakfast for a couple of nights. I spent a day and a half at Needlesports and half a day at Tiderace and Knoydart. When I left to come back up to Edinburgh, my bank account had a massive dent in it, but I had everything I needed for both the ski and the kayak legs of my expedition. Needlesports were excellent and they allocated a staff member, Be Englebrecht, to deal with me. Often when I go into an outdoor shop I am approached by some newly-recruited staff who thinks the outdoors is all breathable membranes and hydration systems. Not so with Be, who not only knew about the equipment but was also aware of its flaws and limitations as he had great experience using it in Antarctica, the Himalayas and the high mountains of Europe. I must have tested Be's patience as I continually bounced ideas off him and changed my mind about the tent, sleeping bag, clothing systems and the cooking equipment. Be also had some superb tips from his time in Antarctica which I would never have considered. In the end I went for a Macpac Minaret tent, a Rab Summit 1100 sleeping bag rated to -30°C, a Rab Neutrino down jacket for comfort and to top up the bag if it was below -30°C. For ground insulation I bought a foam 'Karrimat', a Thermarest ProLite short and a 3mm sheet of lightweight foam which I cut to fit the entire bathtub groundsheet of the tent. To cook on I would risk a small gas burner, knowing I would have to heat the butane canisters in my bag, and I would use a single Jetboil pan with heat absorption fins. I thought long and hard about a petrol stove, but my neurotic obsession about weight overwhelmed the benefits and comfort of another half kilogram. For clothing I would use merino wool undergarments, then fleece mid-layers and Arc'teryx Theta Gore-Tex Salopettes as the bottom shell and a Patagonia fleece-lined 'soft shell' jacket made from a breathable but windproof weave of tight nylon fibres. Socks, as usual, were Bridgedale with some thin liners to absorb smell and ease friction and then some solid hefty warm socks over these. To carry all my equipment on the ski trip I bought a 90 litre X-Pod rucksack which only weighed 2.4 kg and was supremely comfortable.

When I had paid and put everything into the rucksack I left Kendal and went up to Penrith to pay for the kayaking equipment and to run over things one last time with Dave Felton. My usual presbyterian attire of damp fleece, neoprene boots, nylon salopettes and worn out paddling jacket was barely suited to temperate climates and certainly no match for the Arctic. I knew I had to get a drysuit. Dave steered me towards Kokatat's Gore-Tex Meridian drysuit and hooked me with a generous discount. I decided to go for one without a hood as it would just get in the way and spill water in the tent if I forgot to empty it. I would hopefully have all my skiing fleeces still intact to wear under the drysuit and would use my skiing balaclava to keep my head warm. I bought a new set of Epic Active Touring blades to use as my main paddle and relegated my smaller Nimbus Kiska 4 way splits as my spare pair or for when my tendons need a rest. I bought a neoprene spraydeck which I thought would help keep the cockpit warm. I decided not to buy a new life jacket but to remain faithful to my faded and bleached Delta Explorer. I also bought a solid foam paddle float which would be used as the final option if I could not roll without it, and make a nice pillow when camping. I decided not to take my helmet. On all my previous kayak expeditions, be them a day in Scotland or three weeks in New Zealand's Fiordland, I always carried a McMurdo Fastfind Personal Locator Beacon. This superb device could send a distress signal to a satellite and then to a national search and rescue centre with my GPS location. If I was drifting in currents the GPS would update my position as I moved to enable any potential rescuer to find me. It lived in the back pocket of my life jacket when I was on the water, and although I have never had to use it in 10,000 kilometres of paddling so far, it would be going with me. I had numerous drybags from previous trips so did not need to buy more. Once I had made all the purchases, I gave Dave a large hold-all to put everything in so he could ship it to Finland where the kayak was going to be made. In the hold-all were also various repair kits and a larger tent, my old faithful Macpac Olympus, so I could stretch out on my weather-bound days. There was more ringing of tills and another half metre of receipt before I was ready to drive back to Edinburgh and the run up to Christmas.

I still had to get my skiing equipment but could not obtain it until I was in Oslo. I was buying my skis and boots from a shop called Sportsnett. It was run by the well-known polar explorer, Sjur Mørdre, whom I spoke to a couple of times on the phone. He was extremely helpful, but advised me to forget the 75mm Nordic Norm Rottafella bindings I had been used to for the last 25 years and opt instead for the New Nordic Norm bindings, also manufactured by Rottafella. I was extremely sceptical as the New Nordic Norm looked too flimsy and I had heard of many cases of the metal bar in the sole of the ski boot, which attaches to this binding, breaking. The bar is at the front of the boot, under the sole and if one has to walk across boulders it can get bent or broken, rendering it useless. Sjur assured me this was not the case any more, as the bar's alloy had been changed to make it tougher and less brittle, and the bindings themselves were now excellent. If anyone's advice on skiing was to be heeded, it was Sjur's, so I went for the New Nordic Norm bindings. I now had to get the boots to match them, as the four pairs of ski touring boots I already owned were the 75mm Nordic Norm types, two of which were plastic and I loathed them with a passion. Sjur suggested either the Crispi Stetind or the very similar Alfa Skarvet. My only concern was that both boots were lined with Gore-Tex which I always think is a frivolous gimmick.

Leather is the best breathable membrane, if waxed properly, and the unnecessary Gore-Tex lining tends to retain some humidity. Besides I was planning to cover the entire boot in Berghaus Gore-Tex Yeti gaiters which I would attach permanently to the boot by gluing the gaiters rand to the sole of the boot and then staple-gun them into place. This would stop any snow entering the cuff or melting on the leather's surface.

I also chatted with Sjur about my choice of skis. I had three options; the normal waxing skis with full skins for sustained climbs, the relatively new skis with kicker skins attached to the middle third which could be removed to revert to traditional waxing skis, and waxless skis. I had also seen a lot of people using various Åsnes skis with their newly developed kicker skins. They all seemed to rave about them, and Sjur said this was the way to go as I would be making my own tracks most of the way. Ski skins are now strips of hairy material which stick on to the bottom of skis. They are covered in hairs which all point back to the rear of the ski and which dig into the snow while stepping forwards but slide over it while gliding forwards. Kicker skins attach to the middle third of the ski. If I was to go with normal skis, waxing them as I needed, and then attaching full skins for the longer sustained climbs this would give me more options and greater scope to match the conditions, but would add nearly 500 grams to my rucksack and cause more faffing about. Ski waxes are applied to the bottom of skis and they have varying stickiness to grip the snow. Waxless skis have a fish-scale pattern on the middle third of the base to grip the snow when you step forwards but slide over snow when gliding. However, waxless skis have a permanent loss of glide due to their design, which means a lot more double poling on gentle descents. In the end I went for the Åsnes Amundsen skis with the kicker skins as I could remove them and wax the skis for the flatter sections. Sjur said he would put the skis, kicker skins, bindings, both pairs of boots and the gaiters aside for me to try when I arrived in Oslo in a week's time.

The electronic gadgets I was taking on the trip had to be simple. I would not have much opportunity to repair or replace them. The smartphone I had was robust and had a solid slide-out keyboard which I could type on. As recharging of batteries might only occur every two weeks or so I bought another four batteries. As long as I kept my phone switched off, unless typing or updating the website, I could get three to four days out of each battery. Having had various cameras, from simple point and shoot to big fancy SLRs, I knew that SLRs were just not going to be worth the weight. I decided to buy two Canon Powershot A720 cameras which I knew to be superb. Furthermore they run off lithium AA batteries so I would not have to carry a charger. I would use one camera for the ski trip and the other for the kayak trip, keeping the first one as a spare in case of a watery grave as they are not waterproof. I had a Petzl head torch with LED bulbs, and an optional halogen one, that also operated on AA batteries. I had a GPS tracker device called a SPOT which sent a signal to a satellite and down to Richard's email and mobile phone with my location coordinates when I asked it to at the end of each day. This same device could also send an emergency signal to five mobile phones with my coordinates with a message saying I needed help if I was in trouble with broken bones or serious injury. I would take it both on the ski and kayak trips to update my position, but would use my more grown-up McMurdo Fastfind Personal Locator Beacon if I needed rescued on the kayak portion. This also operated on AA batteries. Finally, I had a small Garmin eTrex summit GPS. I did not have any Norwegian topographic maps loaded on to it but could use it to pinpoint my position on the paper maps I was carrying in the dark or in whiteouts. Both GPS devices also operated on AA batteries, which meant that when the batteries of one gadget ran low I could either replace them or pilfer them out of a less critical one.

I also bought a teenager's mini laptop which I thought I could carry in my rucksack on the ski trip and could take in a hatch on the kayak trip. I thought I would be able to update the website more efficiently and with better photos using it. It would also be useful for checking weather forecasts and I thought generally smoothing out the trip. It did not have any possibility of communicating with the outside world on its own but I could connect my phone to it and use the phone as a modem. This notebook had three spare batteries so I could use it for nearly 16 hours without recharging. It was not that heavy on its own at just a kilo, but with all the accessories and batteries it was well over two kilos. As soon as I began skiing I knew it was nowhere near worth its weight and it was only a matter of days before it was in a postal parcel back to Oslo. However, on the kayak leg of the expedition it was useful, but not indispensible, for processing photos, updating the blog and generally keeping in touch with the world and Johanna, who was looking after my affairs in Edinburgh.

As I was planning the expedition I knew one of my biggest quandaries would be with maps. I needed paper maps. Electronic maps and a gadget to view them would not suffice. However, I would probably need about 100 maps which would cost £1000 at least. However, a Norwegian friend, Ole Bjøråsen, whom I had bumped into a year previously on a ski tour trip through Sarek and had then teamed up with to ski the length of the Jostedalsbreen icecap for four days, had a full set which he kindly offered to lend me. He had skied 'Norge på langs' and had gone a slightly different route to the one I intended to go, but the maps were invaluable and I could sit in the evenings and pore over most of the route I intended to follow. A lot of Ole's maps were 1:100,000 which had been printed by independent publishers covering mountainous areas, rather than the standard 1:50,000 printed by the government. However, apart from the scale, all the information was identical, and it meant I would not have to carry so many maps. When I reached Oslo after Christmas I added some of my own maps to cover the missing segments and divided them up into six packages, five of which could be posted to various addresses as I approached them, and one that I took with me to the start at Lindesnes. For the kayaking leg I had decided that the 1:100,000 or 1:50,000 topographic maps were superfluous so decided to go with 1:350,000 scale maps. There were just five of them covering the entire Norwegian coast, and while they were essentially road maps they showed the coastline and islands in detail. However, I later changed my mind for the kayak trip and also bought a new GPS with the Norwegian maps loaded on to it. I felt I needed to see if some of the islands were indeed islands or were instead a peninsula with a narrow isthmus, or whether the new causeways which were being built across the narrows to some islands had bridges in them. I thought a GPS on the kayak portions might save me paddling into many dead-ends in the course of the entire coast, and I was right.

Over Christmas I had many loose ends to tie up and further equipment to test and modify, like sewing snow valances round the fringe of the Macpac Minaret tent to help with its stability in storms. After a few stressful days everything was ticked off my huge 'To Do' list and I felt confident I had done everything I could to make sure things ran smoothly in Edinburgh and that all my equipment was shipshape and Bristol fashion. I said my goodbyes, shouldered my rucksack and flew over to Norway on 28th December. Two good friends in Oslo, Hartmut and Øivind, had heard about my plans and had appointed themselves as my self-styled 'Support Team'. Hartmut was already abroad for Christmas and New Year and Øivind was going the day after I arrived, but he let me use his house in Asker as a base. I still had a few thing to do when I arrived in Oslo with just two days to spare. Firstly I had to go and get all the skiing equipment from Sjur Mørdre's shop. He was not there, but true to his word everything was set aside. I tried on the boots and the Crispi Stetind fitted like gloves and were extremely comfortable. It was a huge relief as the final piece of the equipment jigsaw finally fell into place.

The other thing I had to do was get a contract with a mobile phone provider. Telenor seemed to have the best coverage and offered a package which included unlimited data transfers for £50 a month with no minimum contract period. It was slightly expensive, but the unlimited data transfer was ideal for uploading the webpage blog and photos. The only trouble was I needed to pay a huge deposit as I did not have any recorded credit rating in Norway, and I also needed a Norwegian address. Luckily I already had a Norwegian bank account so I could transfer the money across to speed up the application. I gave Hartmut's address for Telenor to send the bills to, Hartmut would pay them and I would refund him. Despite the immediate bank transfer of the £200 deposit my application would still take up to a week to process and then activate the SIM card because administrative Norway was already shutting down for the New Year period. Until it was activated I had to use my UK provider, Vodafone, which was extortionate for data transfers.

On the night of 30th December I was at last ready to go. I had realized a week ago that the original rucksack I bought for the trip, the 90 litre X-Pod, was not big enough, so had resorted to a rucksack I already owned, which was an enormous 120 litre Bergans Viking II. While it was extremely comfortable, it weighed 4.5 kilos empty. It was now full and sat resolutely on Øivind's kitchen floor threatening me each time it caught my eye. When I finally wrestled it on to the scales I was shocked to see it was 28 kilos. I knew it was too much and could not work out how it had happened after I had been so neurotic about weight. It was not sustainable and would get the better of me sooner rather than later, and I pondered what I could eventually jettison. I would see initially how it went before a cull. I did still have access to my 90 litre X-Pod rucksack but it was back in the UK. I left my five packages of maps for Øivind to post to various places up the length of my route and then looked at timetables to get to Lindesnes tomorrow, on New Year's Eve.

The problem was all the public transport was running on the more limited holiday schedules and I had to take an 0600 train from Asker into Oslo to get the 0700 intercity bus to Kristiansand. Then I had to get another bus from Kristiansand to Vigeland in the early afternoon. When I arrived at Vigeland, public transport came to an expensive end, and I had no alternative but to take a £70 taxi ride for the final 27 kilometres to Lindesnes Lighthouse at the end of the road. The taxi driver seemed quite oblivious to what I was about to embark on and must have thought I was a naïve new-age hippy fool wanting to camp at Lindesnes Lighthouse at New Year instead of some rowdy joyous celebrations with friends into the early hours. As his tail-lights disappeared into the dusk I was left alone at Lindesnes. The buildings here were all empty and I only had the lighthouse's revolving light casting its beam through the very frosty air for company. I looked around for a place to pitch my tent on the frozen ground so I could curl up for the night and soon started to wonder why indeed I was not at some warm lively party with friends.

THE SKI: SECTION 1. LINDESNES TO LJOSLAND

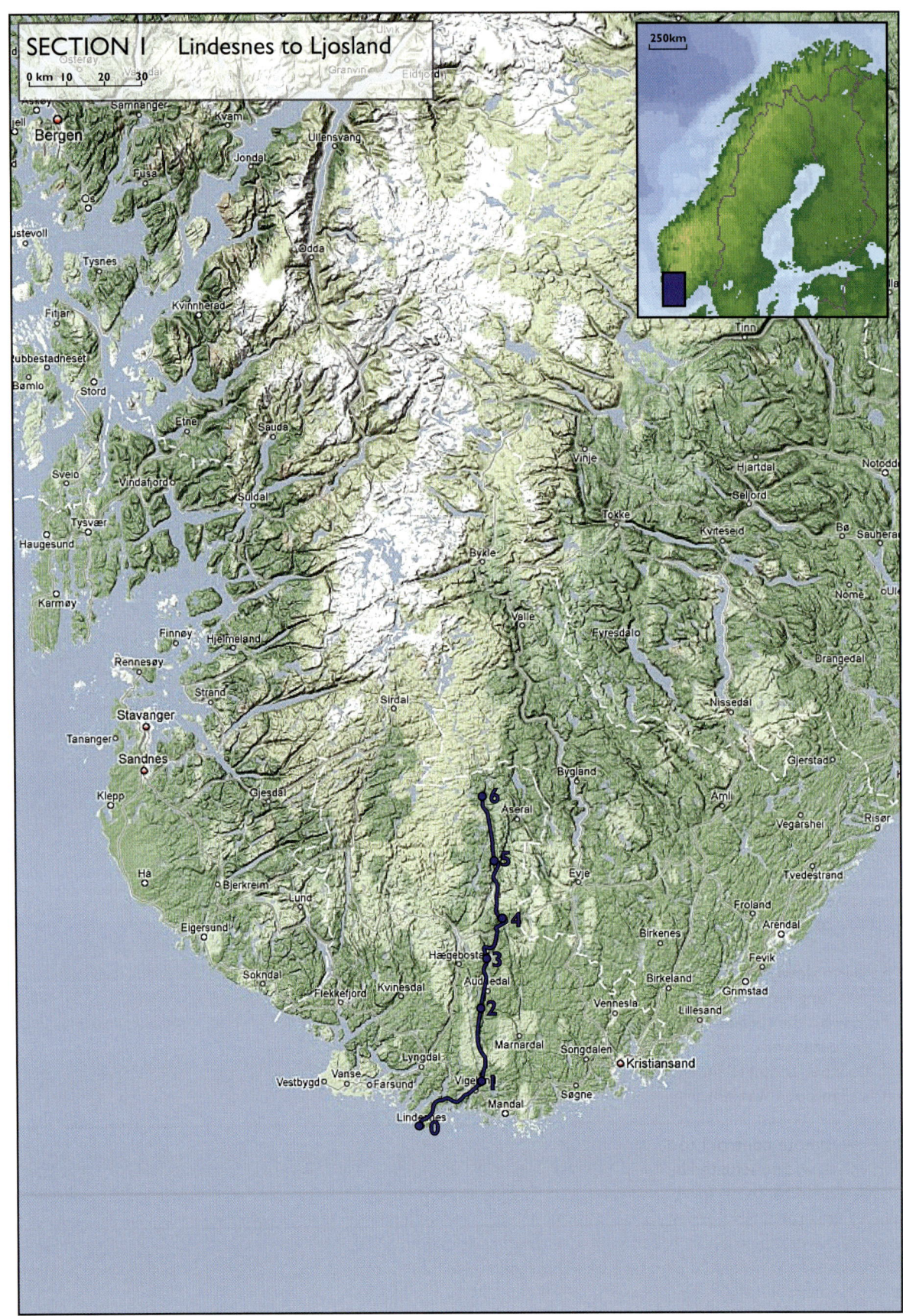

THE SKI: SECTION 1. LINDESNES TO LJOSLAND

It was a night filled with trepidation as I lay in my tent on the frozen ground. My stomach was tense as I anticipated some of the hardships, discomforts and dangers I might experience in the next eight months. The hardships and discomforts would mostly be due to the cold and wind during some of the gales I would have to weather. They would be the times I would just have to survive the best I could until things eased up. The dangers, however, could be life-threatening; falling through the ice and not being able to haul myself back through the hole, being consumed and encased in the frozen debris of an avalanche until my frozen, contorted form poked through in the spring thaw or being tumbled and dashed in my kayak against the jagged rocks by the force of the Arctic Ocean's unfettered and extremely cold fury. My safety lay in awareness. The more aware I

Day 1. Lindesnes Lighthouse watches over the sun as it sets for the final time in 2008

was of the dangers and the more I could anticipate an uncontrollable, life-threatening scenario unfolding then the safer I would be. My safety was entirely in the hands of my experience and knowledge of what could or might go wrong. Some of my library of awareness has come from books, some from the stories of fellow outdoorsmen, some from a half lifetime's worth of experience in the Scandinavian wilderness and some from dark thoughts where my imagination runs riot. With these I had good tools to avoid danger, and it would be up to me to use them properly and not take short cuts which laziness or impatience might tempt me to take. But despite knowing my safety would be in my own hands I was none the less filled with angst.

The four beams from Lindesnes Lighthouse, on the rocky promontory which is the most southerly point of mainland Norway, passed over the tent every 20 seconds. These beams were focused into rays of light by a large revolving glass prism lens which briefly illuminated the headland before casting a shaft of light far out into the cold, crisp, clear night above the still sea. I found comfort and reassurance in the regularity of the beams and it helped ease my anxiety. I was soon asleep with the alarm on my watch set for 0500. I woke well before at midnight, a bit bewildered as to where I was. There were waves of small, crackling explosions as midnight fireworks were set off from small villages further north on the Lindesnes peninsula. The sound was carrying well through the still night air and had woken me up as millions of kroners worth of fireworks were discharged into the sky. I imagined happy families and exuberant youths cheering as another barrage erupted into the night sky. For everyone, it was the celebration of a new year. For many, it was a party of contentment and togetherness, but for some it was the rites de passage to a new aspiration or ambition. I fell strongly into the latter camp; contentment and togetherness had been submerged by both angst and loneliness as I lay in the small tent kilometres away from anyone else. While the whole world was having fun I struggled to get back to sleep, the deadline of my 0500 start drawing closer with what felt like an impending dawn execution.

The alarm slowly started to penetrate my sleep and I was soon in a warm slumber wondering where I was. It did not take long for the reality to dawn on me. This was it. This was the start. Without any hesitation I sat up, made a hollow on the surface of my sleeping bag, poured a good handful of muesli into it and ate it with a bent spoon, my single item of cutlery. I then stuffed everything into sacks while dislodging showers of frozen condensation off the inner tent and finally emerged out into the crisp, frosty morning. It was just 0530 on 1st January, more often than not, I was not even in bed by this time on this day!

As if by remote control I took down the tent, packed my rucksack and took my first steps north at 0600. The pitch black was punctuated by the yellow light from the lighthouse which swept the horizon. I walked up the road with my head torch on for a couple of hours before there was the first hint of a dull orange glow in the south east. I felt surprisingly good. New boots always give cause for concern, but mine were surprisingly comfortable, even on the tarmac road. The rucksack was already starting to make its presence felt, and I could feel the 28 kilos, plus a couple more for the skis, starting to strain my shoulders. By the time it was getting light this was already giving me concern, and I was already thinking about what to jettison.

15

Day 1. Dawn breaks in the mid morning to reveal a late autumnal landscape over the bays

After pounding the tarmac road for three hours and seeing no one, daylight finally appeared. It revealed a very brown autumnal landscape. All the small brooks and rivulets were frozen in small bulbous contortions of clear ice. Icicles were hanging from rocks everywhere, as the water oozed out of the ground above overhangs, flowed down these sharp shafts of ice and froze before they could fall off the spike. Lindesnes peninsula juts out some 20 kilometres into the sea, so the climate here is tempered, but it was still minus 5 this morning. Just inland and away from the influence of the sea it would be a good 10 degrees colder. The road followed the convoluted coastline much of the way in and out of bays. Many of the bays were just freezing over, especially at the edges, and eider and mallard ducks abounded in each. There were farms along the flatter parts of the coastline, which were largely tidy small-holdings. No longer big enough to support a family, they are something to provide another income and also continue a rural way of life, of which Norwegians are so proud. With daylight almost fully up I approached a small industrial building where someone was putting up the Norwegian flag to hang limply over this cold clear morning. He saw the skis on my rucksack, and knowing it was 1st January jumped to a conclusion. "Nordkapp?" He asked, "Nearly," I replied in Norwegian trying to sound as sane as possible. "I am going to ski to Nordkinn. It's a little further." He wished me good luck and said "Any further than Nordkapp and you will be in the ocean!" as he secured the flag rope in a cleat. My first social event of the year showed me I was already on the fringe of society.

As I continued round the coast a few cars started to pass me. To their credit, a few stopped to offer me a lift. I explained why I could not accept as I wanted to do everything under my own steam, and they also wished me luck. About half way across one bay I heard a curious sound and looked behind me out to sea. It was a man in a small dinghy with an outboard engine crashing a path through the ice. The dinghy would ride up on to the ice and its keel would fold a groove in it as the boat collapsed back into the water. It noisily continued to crunch its way across the bay as the boatman bounced in the back. As I wandered along the frost-covered verge, with my skis forming a large A above my rucksack, I felt I was watching a kindred spirit. The boat soon disappeared round the headland leaving a two-metre wide channel of dark open water

Day 1. Boathouses in a frozen bay on the sea inlet just south of Vigeland

with fragments of ice floating on it, in an otherwise light grey surface and the oily stillness soon returned. By mid morning the sun had now ventured some 15 degrees above the horizon, but there was no warmth in it on this largely overcast day. My rucksack was becoming an overriding concern as the straps cut into my shoulders and even crushed my sternum until I had to stop by a litter bin in a lay-by. There were a few items which I already deemed as unnecessary, like a third Nalgene bottle, a third gas canister, a second foam mattress and some food. In all I managed to throw away about two kilos. I was a bit apprehensive at this stage about parting with them, but as the ski journey unfolded I became very ruthless about weight and even threw away my second Nalgene bottle, which I just used as a pee bottle when camping in the tent. My last remaining Nalgene bottle, used as a hot water bottle and then for a night time hot chocolate drink, just doubled up after a quick rinse!

I had been walking for some seven hours now and was getting weary. I still had a few kilometres to go to reach Vigeland at the neck of the Lindesnes peninsula. From Vigeland I would be in the main body of Norway and would gradually retreat from the sea. As I single-mindedly strove towards Vigeland, looking very out of place in my mountain wear and with skis on my rucksack, a car stopped and a young Norwegian with a mop of curly hair got out. Erik Moe was instantly likeable. He was also starting the same ski trip north and his girlfriend, Helene, was driving him to Lindesnes so he could start his epic tomorrow. He was full of enthusiasm and showed me his sledge, to which he had attached pram wheels so he could pull it along the road for the 120 kilometres to Ljosland Fjellstue where the road ended and apparently the snow started. With passion he explained he would carry 30 days' supplies on the sledge and make it all the way to Haukeliseter before restocking. Helene seemed to be more aware of the problems he might encounter than the infectiously optimistic Erik. I had intended to do this trip alone but it would be nice to do a few days with Erik and I hoped he would catch up.

I was glad to reach Vigeland. My feet were weary and my upper back sore from the 26-kilometre pounding along the tarmac. My poor feet had 140 kilos to contend with, my weight and that of my rucksack. I was pretty unfit, having had little time to prepare myself physically for the journey. I assumed I would just do the training on the job and hoped it would only take a couple of weeks before I would be in some sort of shape. I had high hopes for Vigeland. I had even started to dream of some cheap accommodation to rest my weary bones and a tasty meal to perk me up, but I was to be sorely disappointed. The petrol station was the only sign of life in the otherwise hibernating village. I had a lard-rich snack, realizing I would have to spend the night in my tent in the bitter cold. I prised myself from the comfort and warmth of the kiosk, shouldered my 26 kilos and

Day 1. After Vigeland the warming influence of the sea vanished and the frost in the Audnedal valley had built up into a thick layer

continued north for a couple of kilometres along the empty road beside the river. It was already starting to get dark and with the diminishing influence of the sea it was getting cold quickly. I passed some nice spruce woods; when I went into them I discovered a small, tent-sized flat clearing covered in soft spruce needles. Elsewhere the ground was frozen hard and white with accumulations of frost, but here I could get the tent pegs in. The tent was up by 1600 as darkness fell and I went straight into my sleeping bag. From the warmth of my sleeping bag I still had the task of writing up the first day's blog. I got out my mini laptop, put the day's photos on it, wrote up the blog and uploaded it using my phone as a modem. I was careful not to write too much as I did not want to set a precedent. None the less it took over an hour to write and a further hour to process the photos and upload them. It seemed so easy in theory, but on the tent floor with minus 10 outside and just slightly less cold inside it was an awkward and uncomfortable palaver. I would need to do it regularly as I hoped to build up a readership, but I knew it would become a profane chore on what I hoped would be a spiritual pilgrimage.

Day 2. The Audnedal river was starting to freeze over. At this place round platelets of ice were accumulating on the surface

I must have fallen asleep by 2000. Not only had it been a long day but it came after a long period where I was busy trying to organize many things and a lot of travel. I had had quite a few plates in the air until yesterday and it was quite stressful giving them all a good enough spin to last the next eight months. I did not wake for another 12 hours. When I did my body was tired and stiff, with aching muscles. It could not do another 30-odd kilometres today. It was cold, but crystal clear when I set off at 0930. There was no snow in the dry night, but the fields and trees had received yet another layer of frost and by now the ground looked like it was indeed covered in snow. I made my way up the quiet tarmac road beside the calm Audnedal river. Ice was forming in various places and bunches of slush were

Day 2. Father Christmas having a well-earned rest outside a house in the village of Vigmostad

slowly drifting down to form larger rafts. There was also a curious pool where there were many platelets of ice, like frozen lily leaves.

Despite the sun it was well below zero. I made quite good time and walked for three hours past beautiful farms to Vigmostad. Outside one farm, I passed an exhausted Father Christmas having a break on a chair outside the door. He seemed oblivious to the frost settling on him. A lot of the farmers were using the New Year break to collect timber from the surrounding forests. Their old reliable tractors were dragging either long spruce logs to season for timber or shorter bundles of more twisted birch logs to cut for firewood. Soon this area would be covered in deep snow and most activity beyond the immediate barns and outbuildings would be difficult until the spring thaw arrived in April. The surroundings were becoming more and more of a winter idyll as the frost got thicker and thicker and carpeted everything with sparkling crystals in the winter's sun. The vegetation was changing slightly; although there were plenty of birch and other small bare deciduous trees, like alder, along the river bank and in thickets on the valley floor, more and more spruce and pine trees were appearing. I pushed on through more pretty hamlets, like Tryland. The houses in their neat, tidy, frost-covered gardens looked enviably cosy inside. There was the smell of wood smoke all around these hamlets as it slowly welled up out of the chimneys into the still air.

Day 2. Many of the small farms in Audnedal valley were well prepared for the onset of winter

The little heat in the sun had long gone when it finally disappeared behind a low ridge during the mid afternoon. I was soon looking for a place to spend the night before the scorching cold of the approaching night started to descend. Just before I reached Vivlemo I spotted a campsite in the midst of some spruce. Here the ground was reasonably spongy with needles so I could get the snow pegs for my tent in. It was also near a brook which was surprisingly unfrozen. It sluggishly flowed down a deep mossy trench under the thick cover of the spruce forest which must have insulated it from the open skies. As the light faded during the late afternoon the temperature dropped rapidly to minus 10 again and the stars began to shine brightly in the green-tinged dusk between the tree tops. I settled into my sleeping bag again as it was too cold to stay up.

With the domestic chores of dinner out of the way I started on my blog again. I had problems with the battery on my mini laptop as it did not like the cold. I had to put it into my sleeping bag to warm it up before it worked properly, and after two hours I had uploaded the day's events. As I lay in my bag that night my bewilderment was starting to ease as I was becoming more familiar with my surroundings. I had managed the first two days quite well but it was obvious something had to happen with the rucksack weight. While I could walk along the

Day 2. At every overhang, water had welled up out of the ground then dribbled down forming large icicles, some 2 metres long

Day 3. My rucksack was about 26 kilos, and it was beginning to become an overbearing burden and make me feel like a donkey

road with 26 kilos in my rucksack for a few days like a heavily-loaded donkey, I would not be able to manage it for weeks without risking wear and tear to tendons and cartilage. It would also be impossible to ski with it in anything but the easiest terrain. The mini laptop and its accessories were two kilos, and would go back to Oslo at the next post office together with a few other items.

I woke early at 0700 and it was still pitch dark outside. As I lay in my warm sleeping bag, trying to muster the enthusiasm to get up, I heard loud erratic drips on to the tent. It was either raining or the frosts which had accumulated on the branches over the last week were now melting. Either way, the temperature was now above zero and must have climbed at least 10 degrees during the night. Perhaps a change to dry, cold, crisp weather was on the way and this high pressure, which had frozen southern Norway, was now making way for some fronts which would deposit the first of the winter's snows. With an effort I got up, breakfasted, packed my rucksack, then rolled up the wet tent and eventually left at 0900 just as daylight was appearing. It was a very overcast day and there was a warming mist, and it was this which was melting the frost on the trees.

It was a quick easy walk through Vivlemo and on to the large village of Konsmo where there was a shop open. I treated myself to a second breakfast here. It was just what I needed after the Calvinistic dried muesli I had eaten earlier. After Konsmo the road undulated through the increasingly pine-dominated forest until it came to the long frozen lake of Nedre Øydnavatn. By now the mist had burnt off and the weather had returned to one of the glorious winter's days to which I was getting accustomed, but the temperature had also dropped below zero again, despite the clear skies and

Day 3. The lake of Nedre Øydnavatn was covered in an unbroken sheet of ice across which some foxes had crossed

the sun. Although cars passed me occasionally, the road seemed almost deserted. It was also barely visible under the thick layer of frost and it really felt like I was walking on a track. My ski boots were proving to be extremely comfortable and my feet were coping well with the 20-odd kilometres a day I was now doing in the seven hours between dawn and dusk. The weight of my rucksack was still a burden and I was looking forward to the next post office where I was hoping to unload five kilos. I followed the road up the east side of Nedre Øydnavatn past a couple of well-kept hamlets for a good 7 kilometres and well over two hours. The lake had a complete covering of ice, and a couple of foxes had crossed it, leaving their footprints on the frost. It still looked far too suspect for me to contemplate skiing across. After two hours I reached the northern end of the lake where the short river from Øvre Øydnavatn lake, a bit further to the north, flowed into it. There was a campsite here where the grass beside the river was not too hummocky and

Day 3. I found a nice place to camp beside the frozen river and was in my sleeping bag before nightfall at 1600

the ice was thin enough for me to kick a hole in it for water. In fact it was quite an idyllic spot. I had the tent up quickly and retreated into it as it was getting dark. After supper and writing the blog I realized that I was starting to disconnect from the world I knew before and was starting to immerse my thoughts in this new frozen world of southern Norway. I had only spoken to Erik and Helene since I started and I had not really seen many people. Apart from the constant burden of my rucksack, my thoughts and observations were turning more and more to the natural things I saw around me, and the forests and valleys I was passing through.

Day 4. Looking across Øvre Øydnavatn with snow flurries sweeping over the lake

I had another late start the next day. It was difficult to get up early when it was cold and dark outside. My fingers were guaranteed to have a hard time packing up the tent in these temperatures and with last night's dusting of snow. My plan today was to walk the mere 17 kilometres to Sveindal. I was using the 1:400,000 road map for the walk up to Ljosland; the map intimated Sveindal was a large village, perhaps even with a post office to get rid of excess weight. My rucksack was really starting to take a toll on my shoulders and lower back and I was looking forward to Sveindal. As I walked along the frozen shore of Øvre Øydnavatn lake, flurries of snow came and went in the wintriest period of the tour so far. It did not last long and soon the weather was returning to the cold crisp high pressure. Before long the sun was out again, the skies cleared and the temperature was dropping. I made easy time passing a pretty hamlet beside the white frozen lake and continued on to the dormant village of Byremo. I did not stop here but continued up the quiet snow-covered road, pushing on to get to Sveindal and the hoped-for post office. The road now climbed steeply up through spruce forests to a junction. Here I turned east and descended into the frosty valley where Sveindal lay.

Day 4. Walking along the wintery road towards the pretty hamlet of Øvre Øydna on the way to Byremo

I thought I must have made a mistake, or that Sveindal was round the corner, but it was not. It was a tiny hamlet with just a few houses and most seemed semi-derelict. There were no facilities at all, let alone a post office. Before I knew it I had reached the crossroads and, turning left, was on the road north to Åseral, a day's march away. I left Sveindal downhearted and headed north until I could find somewhere to camp in the bitter cold, conscious that it would be dark again soon and that I did not want to be caught in the falling temperatures. The road followed a large torpid open river round a slow bend. Mist was rising from the river and hanging above it. It would soon be adding to the thick layer of snowy frost already coating everything in the valley. I was really searching for a campsite under trees which could offer me some protection from the cold. I could cope with camping in minus 20 but it was not much fun. Two kilometres north of Sveindal I spotted a potential site in mature spruce beside the river some 100 metres from the road. I left the road and headed through the spruce forest with my skis catching on all the lower branches as I headed down to the area I had seen.

Lo and behold, at the spot was a small rustic cabin totally hidden in the trees beside the river. A few of the windows were broken and the door was ajar so I went in. It was dry and had all the potential to be cosy as there was a rusting stove on a side wall. I patched the windows with plastic and swept up the broken glass with an old broom. There were some logs stacked outside in longer lengths and a rusty saw which just managed to get through them. I cut a few armfuls of wood and in the last light of dusk soon had a fire going. I then went down to the river and collected a bucket full of water. I could almost see the still water at the edge of the river getting a film of crinkly ice on it. By the time I returned to the cabin the fire was going well, and I wedged the door shut and settled in for the night. There were some half-burnt candles on a workbench and I lit them and then sat on a stool with my legs askew the fire trying to absorb as much heat as possible. Within an hour the fire was roaring and I had to retreat from it before my black fleece leggings melted on to me. It was a very cosy evening and I just went outside once to check the temperature. It was minus 16. It was the first time I had been inside this trip and the first time I could write and relax in the evening with the temperature well above freezing. After the previous four nights in the tent my sleeping bag was starting to get slightly damp but it quickly dried out in the cabin. It more than made up for the disappointment of Sveindal.

The next morning was bitterly cold and it was a luxury to get up in the rustic cabin without frozen condensation falling on me and to pack my rucksack without freezing hands. I returned to the road and then walked down a dark avenue formed by the tall forest where the sun was probably not going to penetrate for a month or two yet. I saw the river occasionally when the road passed near to it. The river was quite steep and it cascaded over the odd waterfall in places. These were now plastered with huge globules of ice and looked like giant candle sticks in an old tavern. I soon reached the sleepy hamlet of Kylland. It was nestled in the spruce forest where fields had been cleared. While it was basking in the sun, the bare birch trees were still thick with days of white hoarfrost. Beyond Kylland was a long lake called Øre. It was white and frozen and it stretched away to the north. At the far end, basking in

Day 5. Walking beside the frozen lake called Øre towards Åseral which lies in the valley at the head of the lake

the sun, I could just make out the village of Åseral. With the craggy pine-covered slopes on each side, it looked very picturesque. I walked for about two hours beside the lake with hardly a car passing me. Just before I reached Åseral one pulled up behind me and someone jumped out. It was Erik Moe again. I had not really chatted to anybody since I last saw him five days ago so it was good to see him. The pram wheels had broken off his sledge on the first day and his girlfriend, Helene, had come to the rescue. Last night they had ferried his belongings to Ljosland and they were now driving back to Vigeland so he could restart. It seemed like the wheels were also coming off Erik's attempt to ski the length of Norway, but he was still happy and good natured.

Day 5. The idyllic cabin I was allowed to use in Åseral, for which I will always be grateful

I reached Åseral in the early afternoon and it was basking in the sun. It was a very large village with about 300 houses and a large white Lutheran church which was visible from everywhere in the community. The southern counties of Norway have a reputation of being quite devout and religious. Alcohol, promiscuity and idleness are frowned upon in these Calvinistic, hard-working, rural communities. Åseral seemed such a community. It had prudently invested a lot of capital and time in constructing hydro-electric schemes. Maintaining the schemes now provided a few jobs, and the significant excess energy was sold by the council to provide good services and schools. It had everything I had hoped for; a shop with a post office attached and a nice 'kro', which is a smart café. I asked at the kro if there was any accommodation in the village. The nice lady who ran the kro said it was all closed for the winter. I must have looked downcast because then she delighted me by saying she had a small cabin on the outskirts of the village in the fringe of the forest, which I could use.

She gave me directions to walk to the cabin and then filled up a large container of water which she said she would take there by car. I walked the kilometre to the cabin and by the time I got there she had already lit the stove and had started to warm the place up. The cabin was absolutely perfect and quite idyllic. It was well insulated, and with the small Jøtul stove going and some candles lit, it was warm and cosy. I could fully unpack and sort out all my belongings to take to Åseral post office in comfort. I set aside the laptop, its accessories and some extra clothes to post to Oslo. I made a bundle of future maps to post to Finse, where I would be in a few weeks time. Finally, I fed a few superfluous items, like my lightweight 'crocs' shoes into the Jøtul. Then I headed back to Åseral post office to dispatch the two packages. I must have posted or burnt nearly five kilos. After posting the packages and chatting with some of the friendly people of Åseral I crunched my way over the frozen pavement and road to the kro for a meal. I was given an enormous helping of 'pytt i panne', a dish of diced meat, potato and other vegetables. It was minus 14 as I walked back to the cabin. It had been quite a hard trip so far, with the cold temperatures and the relentless weight of my rucksack sapping all my joy as I plodded along isolated and lonely roads from camp to camp. When I opened the door of the cabin I was filled with joy and a sense of well-being as the warmth enveloped me and I knew I could relax here for the night. I retired early, content and looking forward to my lighter rucksack for the last of the icy asphalt road to Ljosland Fjellstue.

Day 6. Walking along the road beside Brelandsvatn in snow flurries as I complete the final segment of road before Ljosland

I slept well in the small cabin, but when I woke there had been a change in the weather. The crisp, still minus 14 of last night was now a mere minus 1 and the trees swirled in the strong wind as the clouds raced across the sky. Having tidied the cabin I left as it was getting light at 0900. It was a delight to shoulder my lighter pack and those five kilos made all the difference. It was now a tad over 20 kilos and I felt I could cope easily with it. The road was deserted as I headed up the valley. Great granite crags rose on each side, their exfoliating granite buttresses covered in pine forests. Everywhere, small rivulets which flowed over the slabs had frozen into ribbons of white ice. It was an Alpinist's dream. As I reached the very small hamlet of Røysland a few snow flurries came. This did little to allay my fears as to just how bare the hillsides were of snow. There was plenty of ice, just hardly any snow and I was not optimistic for the mountains tomorrow, where it was imperative there was snow. When I reached the hamlet of Breland an hour further along the empty road, these snow flurries had joined into a heavy shower and there was a good five centimetres now lying on the road. I passed numerous cabins beside frozen lakes on this stretch, all looking very pretty in their forest clearings. After a quick six hours, during which I was barely troubled by my pack, I reached Ljosland at the end of the snow-covered tarmac road. Ljosland is a small farming hamlet at about 500 metres altitude in the upper reaches of the spruce and pine forests. There was a Fjellstue here where I hoped to spend my last night before I went into the mountains. A Fjellstue is a venerable part of the Norwegian outdoor culture. They are old mountain lodges where generations of people have initially ridden to, and now drive to, in order to start their mountain walking holidays. There are at least a hundred Fjellstue in Norway. Most are at least 100 years old and are crammed full with old artefacts and rose painted furniture. The cracked log walls ooze charm and exude warmth. Ljosland Fjellstue was not so old but still had the charm.

The young owner of Ljosland Fjellstue, Mikkel, allayed my fears and told me that there was plenty of snow in the mountain ranges immediately to the north. Getting to the first of the mountain cabins, called Gaukheihytta, would not be a problem on skis. It should take about seven hours. I was eager to get my new skis off my backpack tomorrow and see how they worked with the short 'kicker' skins. Indeed, I was eager to get into the wilderness of the winter mountains. It was necessary to have completed the last six days along the quiet roads, but it was not in the intended spirit of the tour. That would begin tomorrow with the demanding second section from Ljosland to Haukeliseter. I was pleased with myself so far and had some sense of achievement as I went to my room to have a shower. This shower was the first bit of hygiene this year, and came none too soon. I basked under the hot jets until I felt like my bone marrow was cooking. It was wonderful to be truly warm. I was the only guest at this large lodge and Mikkel kindly let me use the washing machine and drying room. He then cooked me a lovely meal which far exceeded anything else I had eaten so far this year, which was mostly a dull staple of dehydrated meals and mashed potato. It was a celebratory meal, as the first section was completed.

SECTION 1. Lindesnes to Ljosland.
6 days. 121 km. 35 hours. 1430m ascent. 820m descent.

THE SKI: SECTION 2. SETESDALSHEIANE

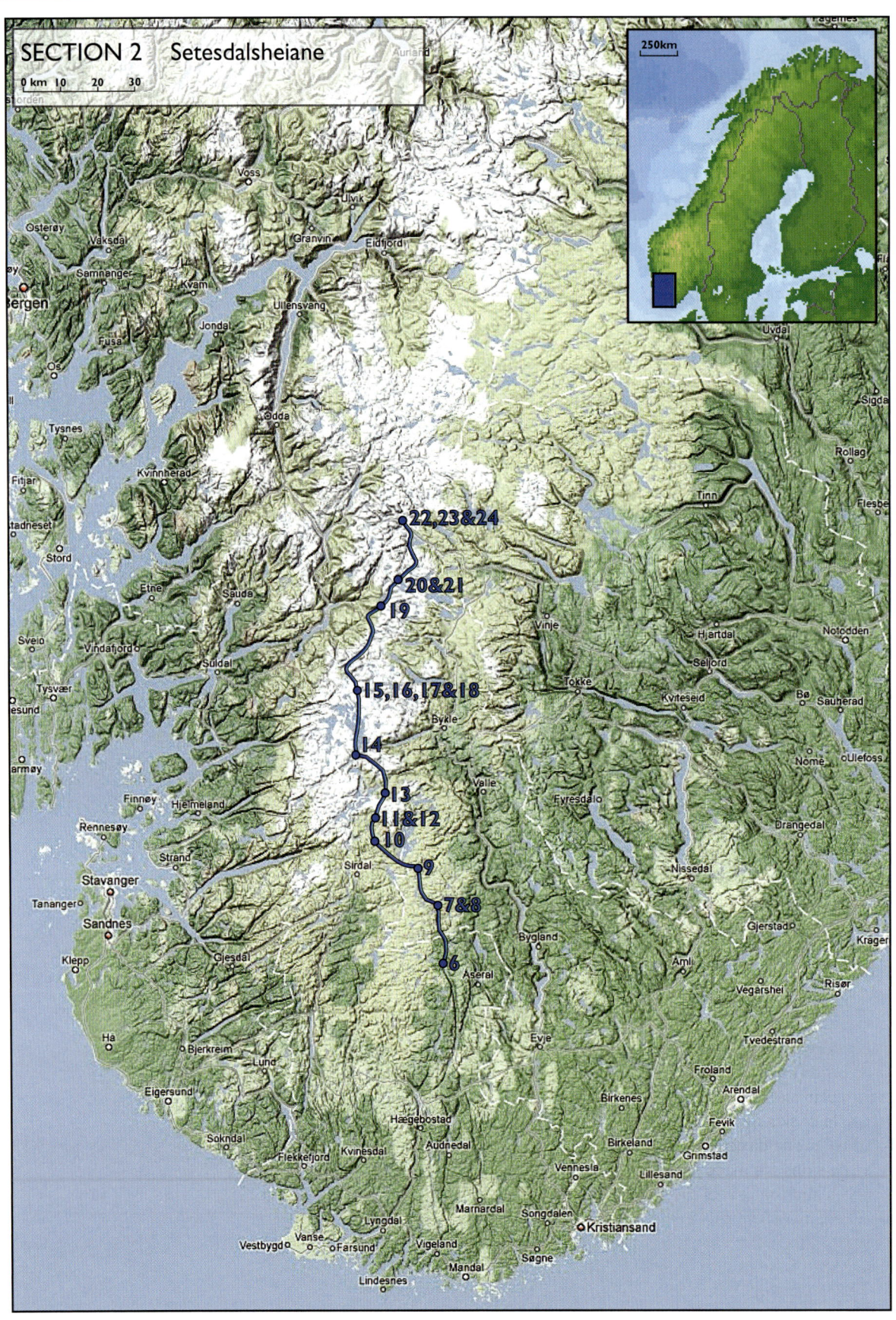

THE SKI: SECTION 2. SETESDALSHEIANE

After a wonderful Norwegian-buffet style breakfast and pleasant chat with Mikkel I was ready to set off. This was it. The walk along the icy road for the last six days was just the warm up. The expedition started in earnest as soon as I left Ljosland. I would climb up into the mountains and remain there for many weeks, staying in mountain cabins when I could, and in my tent when I could not reach a cabin. Initially there was a good network of cabins, especially in this Setesdalsheiane section, but as I went further north after Rondane they would get sparser. The cabins were extremely comfortable, well stocked with food and fuel, and would offer marvellous shelter and respite when the weather was foul. If I got caught out between cabins in bad weather I could either try and put up the small, solid tent or dig a snow-hole and wait in that until I could continue to the next cabin. It is no easy task putting up a tent in a gale and virtually impossible in a storm, so a snow-hole would be the more likely option. I would be pretty much entirely on my own, as virtually nobody ventures into the Scandinavian mountains in January or early February. I was both eager to get started and apprehensive, as there was no turning back after I had taken those first steps away from Ljosland up the track to Gaukheihytta cabin. Initially I had to ski uphill for a good hour to reach Langvatn lake.

There are two methods by which one can ski uphill, and naturally they both involve adhering to the snow. The first is ski wax, and the second fish-scales or ski-skins. Ski wax comes in many different compounds ranging from soft and extremely sticky chemical waxes, called klister, to hard and water-repellent polar waxes. The soft sticky end of the scale is used for old, wet, warmer snows in which the snowflakes have been transformed into globular grains of ice and the hard water-repellent waxes are for cold, dry snows where the snow crystals are still intact or have been broken up slightly by the rolling action of the wind. There is a skill in using wax which comes with the experience of previous mistakes. If you get it right, the wax will just stick to the snow sufficiently to give you enough traction on the trailing ski to step or kick forwards. If you get it wrong, at best

Day 7. After a week I at last had my skis on as I set off through the sunny upper forest to the north of Ljosland

it will be very tiring on the arms if the wax is too hard for the snow condition, and at worst it will be a complete disaster as dry snow crystals stick to the sticky wax and build up great clods of snow under the skis. In this hopeless latter case the sticky soft chemical wax has to be removed using a solvent, and something harder reapplied. To complicate matters more, the condition of the snow may change during the course of a day or even an hour and you might find the soft sticky klister wax you had on in the forest starting to ball up as you climb up on to the bare slopes, or conversely that you are continually slipping backwards as the wax you had on in the morning is now too hard if the day is warming up and the snow surface is changing. Wax is used in all competitions and events, where individuals and teams have scientific waxing specialists who can make the difference between a podium finish or a frustrating race, but in the mountain environment it is more of an art.

Fish-scales and ski-skins give traction not by sticking to the snow like wax but by digging into the surface of it. Fish-scales are a series of small ridges under the central third of the ski which are created by a long string of small wedges laid down on the underside of the ski. The ski slides along the snow while going forwards but the ridges on the small wedges dig into the snow to hinder it going backwards. These wedges are often small and semicircular and look like typical fish-scales. Ski-skins used to be made of seal skin and were strapped to the underside of skis. Seal hair lies nearly parallel to the underside of the skin, so skis glided well over the surface of the snow in one direction but in the opposite direction each hair would dig into the snow and provide traction. Today ski-skins are made from synthetic materials but work on the same principle. The front of the skin clips on to the ski and the rest of the skin attaches to the ski with a sticky glue which lives on the non-hairy side of the skin. There are a few variations; full length, full width and short skins which sit under the middle third of the ski. I had chosen to go with short skins which I intended to leave on permanently but could remove if necessary. The trouble with fish-scales and ski-skins is they tend to hinder a smooth glide but they save a lot of the palaver of getting the waxing wrong.

So at 0930 I attached the short skins to the bottom of my skis, placed the skis on the ground, clipped the bar on the underside of the front of each boot on to the ski bindings, shouldered my rucksack, picked up my ski-sticks and, after saying goodbye to Mikkel, slid my right ski along the ground in the first step northwards. I followed the small, snow-covered road for about a kilometre until a small track headed off to the north. The track was covered in about half a metre of frozen snow and climbed through birch trees, passing small private cabins for a good 2 kilometres until it arrived at a dam. It was one of the reservoirs which Åseral Community own. They are used to store the water until the electricity price is high in Norway or Europe, invariably in the winter time. Then they open the sluice gates and let the water flow down through the turbines. The water on the reservoir behind the dam was frozen to a depth of 40 centimetres, enough to drive a car on, let alone ski over. I had no hesitation in setting off across it, but just had to be careful where streams might flow in.

Day 7. Skiing across the frozen Øyarvatnet lake in the afternoon sun on firm snow

I quickly skied across the largely bare ice to the far end and then headed up through birch, juniper and pine forest. There were many fox trails and a few signs of ptarmigan. Generally the snow was firm, but occasionally yesterday's snow had blown into deeper soft drifts, which were harder work. The unmarked virgin route I took weaved a path between the trees in the sparse forest and along a row of interconnected lakes. It was a superbly cold, crisp day and when I passed pine trees the sun shone on them, giving them a warm green hue. I made good time up to a large lake called Øyarvatnet and skied along the east shore. At the north end of the lake were two short, steep slopes covered in thick, soft snow. I made heavy work ascending them in the deep snow and was a good half hour floundering around on each slope. It was difficult to wade up them; the short skins were proving to be totally inadequate on steeper slopes and I was exhausted when I got to the top. Luckily, these two final slopes were the only main hurdle of the day. At the top of them was the final lake of Gaukheivatnet and on the far side of it, behind an island covered in bare birch trees, was Gaukheihytta cabin. It was a gorgeous old log building with triple-glazed windows, a wood stove and bunk beds. I had a universal key which would let me into all the mountain cabins, including this one.

It was minus 11 outside and minus 4 inside the cabin. I quickly got a fire going from the store of dry birch wood in the adjacent wood shed. Soon the stove was roaring and I went out to collect two buckets of snow to melt. It did not take long for the temperature inside to creep up to zero and a bit beyond. I went to have a look at the larder. It was well stocked with non perishable food. I then settled down to a tin of peaches from the self-service larder shop. Suddenly there was a noise outside which heralded the arrival of three young Norwegians. I was very surprised to see them, as they were me. We stoked the fire well, lit a few candles and soon the cabin became warm and very welcoming. We chatted until the early evening, which felt like midnight as the sun had gone down at 1530, many hours ago. I retired into a cold unheated room off the main living room to sleep. As I lay in my sleeping bag I was pleased with everything so far. Apart from the two steep slopes, where the short ski-skins and my fitness had proved wanting, everything else was as I had hoped and expected. I looked forward to another 110 days of this, but knew there would be harder times.

Day 7. The end of the first day on skis was the locked cabin of Gaukheihytta on the right. Fortunately I had a universal key for it

The other three were up at 0700 and I followed them. The forecast that the dry, crisp, clear minus 14 of last night would deteriorate to a mild zero with strong winds and frequent snow showers seemed to have come true. Snow swirled around the lodge and it did not look very inviting outside in the pitch dark. The others ventured out for various tasks and came in covered in spindrift. They had to leave today and brave the weather for a few hours until they were down into the forest so they could return to their daily lives and appointments, but I had no urgency. I had done well in the past week to get here and thought my body, especially my legs and hips, needed a day of rest and food to build up worn tissue again. We said our goodbyes and I returned to my sleeping bag and listened to the wind with relish. It was great to have a day off. Initially I spent it poring over

Day 8. The poor weather at Gaukheihytta set the precedent for the next fortnight, but it meant I could have a rest day

my maps, trying to work out the best route north to Finse on the northern side of the great Hardangervidda plateau, which I assumed was still some three weeks away. I had been so rushed in my preparation for this trip I had not really had the opportunity to study the maps and work out a route before. There were a number of alternatives, but it seemed the most sensible one was not direct, but made a big detour to the west. This way I could follow a string of self-service cabins. It would mean I would only have to camp if I couldn't cover the distance to reach the next cabin or got caught out in a blizzard, both of which were very real possibilities. I would have to keep my four or five days' worth of dried provisions for any such emergency and otherwise live off the larders in the self-service cabins. The food in these larders is not cheap, but I would gladly pay a bit extra to avoid carrying it myself, and it was certainly a lot better than the dehydrated fodder I had in my rucksack.

I also had the time to read a little about Gaukheihytta and the area in a good supply of books in the cabin. Most were in Norwegian, which luckily I understand. The cabin was first built in 1868 and has been serving walkers, skiers, fishermen, and those looking after the animals on the summer farms in the surrounding mountains here for over 140 years. The original lodge still forms the core of the buildings. During its time it has had a number of hosts who spent Easters and the summers looking after and feeding guests. In the early days the lodge was supplied by horse and sledge, but in the 1970s this was replaced by snow scooter and freight sledge. Wood, food, vegetables, paraffin, and lamp oil all have to be brought in. The surrounding summer farms would previously have supplied some dairy produce in the summer months, but sadly these farms have all but disappeared from this region. Gaukheihytta cabin lies on the southern edge of a long plateau, scoured by ice sheets until recently. The area is riddled with small lakes in the hollows between granite outcrops and covered in hardy, twisted mountain birch and juniper. It seems remarkable life survives here in the winter, but fish thrive under the winter's ice and ptarmigan flourish on residual buds and berries. I spent an enjoyable and comfortable day recuperating and relaxing in the historic surroundings with the reassuring warmth of a stove and a well-stocked larder, and by the evening felt I was ready to move on.

I got up at 0700 in order to make the most of the daylight when it arrived in a couple of hours. It was still quite mild and overcast, but the wind was now negligible. I had breakfast, filled the wood basket and generally tidied the cabin and set off in the very early dawn at 0830. It was still dark enough to make it difficult to see where I was going. The snow was very damp and heavy and the fine crystals in its original structure were clumping together. I felt my way west across the frozen lake, then turned north west up a small rise and started

Day 9. I often had to leave in the early dawn to get the best out of the short days

Day 9. Øyuvsbu cabin appeared at the north end of a string of lake towards the end of a misty day

up the series of interconnected Monsvatnet. At one stage I looked back and the whole sky to the south was ablaze with the sunrise. Its orange colours were even reflected in the snow. I soon reached Søra Monsvatnet lake and skied up it. I crossed the stream which connected these lakes many times. In some places it was open, but shallow. As I skied, the mist came down, and before long I could only see for about 50 metres. I soon became confused and had to concentrate hard to find my way with my 1:100,000 topographic map. I even had to get my GPS out to confirm a position once. There were very few visible features, other than the broken lines of willow scrub which poked through the snow along the stream's bank, from which I could orientate myself. I continued to feel my way north with the mist playing tricks with my vision and skied over Nordra Monsvatnet lake. Slowly, the visibility improved and it did not take long to cross another two lakes, Sandvatnet and Øyuvsvatnet to reach the cabin. By the time I arrived the weather was much improved. Øyuvsbu cabin was again self service and I soon lit the stove, made myself comfortable and collected a couple of buckets of snow for the evening.

Just before arriving at the cabin I had passed some reindeer tracks. The animals which made them were probably part of the wild flock which still roam the Setesdalsheiane. This wild herd of about 3000 is the remnants of the original herds which migrated here from the Germanic Plains some 12,000 years ago as the ice started to retreat. At this time the Germanic Plains were becoming warm and forested and unsuitable for the reindeer. These first reindeer swam across what was then the narrow Norwegian Channel, which was a much narrower strip of water than the present Skagerrak that today separates Norway and Denmark. Alternatively, they could have wandered north across the land bridge between north Germany and south Sweden as the sea level was considerably lower then. Or they could have possibly done both, and then as the ice sheet which lingered between southern Norway and southern Sweden 9500 years ago melted, the flocks could have merged.

The next morning it was just below freezing in the pre-dawn darkness when I set off. By the time I reached the west end of Øyuvsvatnet lake I could just start to make out the shapes on the snow's surface in the diminishing darkness. I climbed the saddle leading over to the next lake called Håhellervatnet. I made heavy work of skiing down to the lake on the other side. I was not used to skiing with these skins on and the metal clips on the underside attaching the skins to the skis kept catching on the inconsistent surface of the snow. I would accelerate across the soft drifts and then grind to a halt as the metal clips dug into a patch of hard, bare, wind-polished icy snow. I fell a couple of times on this not-too-difficult descent. As I was picking myself up from one fall I noticed two skiers about a kilometre away on the lake I was heading for. They seemed to be coming my way. Perhaps they had seen me fall! We soon met. They were two very experienced Norwegians preparing for a trip to ski the length of Spitsbergen in a couple of months. One had skied the length of Norway just two years previously. We had a good 15-minute chat until the cold started to creep in.

Day 10. Crossing Håhellervatnet lake I had a chance encounter with two Norwegians preparing for an expedition to Spitsbergen

After crossing Håhellervatnet lake my route took me up Ramsdalen valley and down Anglaugdalen valley for 12 kilometres. The route followed a string of lakes and ascended to 1050 metres. These valleys were very barren and thick with snow. The lakes were frozen with what I estimated to be nearly metre-thick ice. I made slow progress along the valleys, which were so misty I had difficulty working out what was sky and what was land; navigation was difficult. Luckily the weather remained reasonably still as these exposed valleys were no place to be in bad weather. As I exited Anglaugdalen it got steeper. Given the poor visibility, lack of definition on the snow and my tiredness I fell another few times. In the end I removed my skis and waded down through the snow at a steeper section to save damaging anything in the inevitable fall. As I descended past some massive craggy buttresses the visibility returned and I put my skis back on. To the west were lower mountains which were also covered in snow and looked bleak. A couple of ravens, always very acrobatic birds, put on a fine show for me as they chased each other. Rounding a corner under a craggy knoll I crossed a snow-filled ravine, and on the other side down in the birch woods below me, Taumevatn cabin appeared.

As always, a cabin is a welcome sight at the end of a long day. It was a short ski through the upper birch trees and then I was at the cabin door. There were two men from Stavanger at the cabin. One of them, Hans, was a journalist, and both were very familiar with the Setesdalsheiane and gave me some good advice. We enjoyed a very sociable evening in front of the stove. When I filled in the hut book later I noticed the previous occupant, just a few days earlier, was Odd Eliassen. He had just had a small jaunt snow-holing in the Setesdalsheiane with a friend and stayed here on his way out. Here was a man you had to respect. Odd was now well into his 60s and yet he was still spending nights in snow-holes in these hostile and remote mountains. He is a well-known mountaineer in Norway and embodies the Norwegian ideal of accomplishment and capability with a down-to-earth and unboastful modesty.

It was snowing heavily when I got up before dawn. On Hans' advice I decided to just do a half day to Storevatn cabin, as continuing on to Kringlevatn cabin involved an exposed pass and the visibility and any wind would make it a formidable crossing. I had a relaxing breakfast with my companions and then we all set off about 1000, them down to the valley and me up the mountain. I did not know it at the time but they would be the last people I would see for a fortnight. It was still snowing heavily when I skied off through the trees down the short slope to Taumevatn lake. Luckily, the wind was quite gentle now and the snow was settling everywhere, and as I skied up through the birch forest it was a very wintry scene with the bare, twisted branches thick with new snow. I slowly weaved my way through the birch trees, cutting a deep slot as I climbed towards a pass

Day 11. It was an idyllic wintry scene as I made my way up through the quiet birch forest with thick flakes settling on the branches

at the south end of Storevatn. The going was slow as the snow was 30 centimetres deep, and it kept clumping up under my skins and even freezing to the rest of the ski. The great clods which formed had to be beaten off regularly, however, the winter postcard scene more than made up for it. By the time I climbed the pass to reach the south end of Storevatn lake the wind had increased significantly and visibility was down to about 100 metres. At least the weather, which was almost a blizzard, was directly behind me. I gingerly made my way over the lake for 2 kilometres hoping I was going in the right direction, until out of the whiteness the cabin emerged. It was a very unusual cabin covered in galvanized plates. I unlocked the door and went inside. It was freezing inside and the water that had been left in a steel bucket was frozen solid. I soon had the stove going and within two hours the cabin had warmed up. As I looked out of the frosted window pane I was glad I did not attempt the pass just beyond as there was a strong blizzard now, with a howling wind whipping spindrift into the air. The visibility was dreadful, and had I attempted to continue I would probably have had to have dug in somewhere, as it was just too wild to move and too bitter to remain exposed. With the hut shuddering as the gusts blasted it, I settled down to read in front of the stove for the evening.

The cabin at Storevatn was once part of a huge estate. A certain Mr Heiberg bought a lot of this mountain plateau some 100 years ago and built 30 hunting cabins on it. Storevatn is one such cabin. He charged rich

Europeans to come and hunt wild reindeer. His intention was not just carnage for the gentry, as Heiberg also wanted the wild reindeer and ptarmigan flocks to be restored to their mythical glory in his hunting reserve. To this end he introduced a system of wildlife management and preservation which he considered benevolent. Unfortunately it involved the brutal persecution of anything which jeopardized his reindeer and ptarmigan. He instructed his estate workers to exterminate all predators. Wolverine and fox were mercilessly poisoned, snared or trapped. Every owl, including snowy and eagle owls, and all eagles, falcons and hawks were also poisoned or snared on specially built cairns. The lists of the yearly cull of predators make shocking reading now. With the outbreak of the Second World War the clients dried up and Heiberg was forced to sell to the Norwegian State, who maintain the land to this day. The State has not been as good a custodian as I am sure Heiberg would have wished, although they did stop the persecution of predators. The State has allowed the building of three huge hydro-electric reservoirs in the midst of this land. These reservoirs are very important economically, but have completely interfered with the migration routes and calving areas of the vulnerable wild reindeer of the Setesdalsheiane. None the less, as long as there is no further encroachment, Heiberg's legacy is a very important one for the continued preservation of the Setesdalsheiane wilderness.

Day 12. The inside of the cabin at Storevatn was very comfortable with a stove, but the larder was largely just tinned mackerel

The forecast the next day was as predicted. When I got up at 0600 there was a blizzard of sleet. The temperature was just above freezing and the new wet snow was melting the old. Even in the dark I could tell visibility was poor. Just to emphasize the point, there was a huge roar as at least half a metre of snow slid off the cabin roof in an avalanche. I went back to bed, getting up occasionally, to make sure the weather had not improved, but it did not. I eventually surfaced mid-morning and lit the stove, knowing I would be here all day, as the visibility outside was terrible and down to just 10 metres in the gale force winds. With the fire going I settled down to a pile of books on this area which the organization who owned the cabin produced each year. These yearbooks of the Stavanger Turistforening made fascinating reading. I also pored over my maps again, fearful my progress was slowing. I peered outside frequently, worried about the amount of snow which was now falling. The Setesdalsheiane mountains are renowned for their changeable weather. They are greatly affected by the Atlantic weather systems with a lot of freeze and a bit of thaw in the winter months. The harshness of the climate here is such that the winter snows often have a layer of ice in them and the vegetation at the bottom is often covered in harder icy snow. This makes it much more difficult for the reindeer here to find food in the winter than their cousins further north and east. As a result, the reindeer of Setesdalsheiane are considerably smaller than the other wild herds in Norway.

I was up early and out by 0830. It was a hellish day in the gloom of dawn outside the cabin, but the wind had diminished since yesterday. Spindrift swirled around the cabin as I put my skis on without really thinking about what I was setting off in to. I thought I had to at least make some effort to try and get over Varebrodet pass and so reluctantly I pointed my skis up the hill and set off for the pass at 1150 metres. Visibility was just about 300 metres and the wind was a near gale, but I could expect that to increase as I climbed up to the notch. Mercifully, the wind was at my back as I climbed the first hill and entered the shallow valley which would take me all the way to Varebrodet itself. Visibility got much worse here, sometimes down to just 50 metres. I was forced to ski from one boulder to the next, using my compass to give me a rough sense of direction. The boulders were the only defining points in the white and they started to become friends. Occasionally, the visibility increased to a few hundred metres and I could get my bearings again in relation to the small tarns I was skiing over. Meanwhile the wind was buffeting me and blowing a sea of spindrift across the surface of the snow. A good hour after leaving the cabin I was finally climbing the final slopes and the cairn which marks the pass at Varebrodet appeared out of the white. Despite the heavy snowfall, the strong wind and the poor visibility, the ascent was reasonably incident free.

Day 13. In a white out any visual is a godsend and boulders become friendly, reassuring companions

The descent was quite different. The southerly winds of the last days had blown the snow off the south facing slopes and on to the north facing slopes, so the slope I was going down was absolutely plastered in snow. The boulders which were so vital for judging the lie of the land were now buried under a smooth sea of deep snow. I very gingerly stepped on to the featureless white slope, aware that once I started I was committed, as there was no chance I could really return up this slope in the deep snow with the gale in my face. I could see absolutely nothing except the tips of my skis. There was not the slightest feature I could focus on. I had to resort to making snowballs and throwing them five to ten metres in front of me and then carefully side step down to the indentation and repeat the process. It was slow and exhausting having to bend down with my rucksack on every ten metres to make snowballs. I moved very slowly with great caution for a good hour, in which time I probably only advanced half a kilometre. I was totally disorientated and confused, continually being buffeted by the wind as I gingerly shuffled forward. Suddenly, I was in the air and falling. About a second later I was sliding to a stop on a snowy shelf, with my skis akimbo. Below this shelf were another two metres of steep soft snow and then the bottom of the slope. I wriggled down to the debris of snow blocks at the bottom. On looking up I could see the lip of the cornice I had just stepped off about four metres above me. The broken edge and my path down the slope were the only visible features in the whiteness. I was lucky it was just a small cornice and also lucky it had a shelf on it. It could have been much worse; a fall off the side of a rocky ravine could have entailed a 10 metre fall on to rock. I was somewhat shaken by the plummet but had to either carry on or dig a snow-hole in this same drift. I decided to carry on, throwing another series of snowballs until I was confident enough to shuffle forward in the blinding white without their indentations in the snow ahead of me. Three more times I plummeted over an invisible drift which I could not see until I was half way down it. Luckily, none were more than three metres and they all had a very soft landing. None the less, the first second of each freefall was terrifying. After a good two hours of this frightening and cautious descent the boulders became more frequent and the wind diminished. Indeed, the further I descended, the further I could see, and soon the weather broke sufficiently to give me a longer view of about 50 metres. I was still cautious, however, and only just avoided going over a few more cornices.

With great relief I at last made it down to a flatter area where the land levelled off around some frozen tarns and there was a bit of willow scrub poking through. I checked my position on the old GPS I carried, and the coordinates it gave confirmed I was at Såvatn, which marked the end of the descent from Varebrodet. It had been a very interesting and demanding crossing which had tested my navigation skills to the limit. Most disconcerting was my inability to see the ground in front of me. Luckily, I was just following the valley floor and the unforeseen falls off the cornices and drifts were not as serious as they might have been on a mountain ridge. From here I skirted the east end of the huge Svartevatn lake, which everybody had advised me to stay off as it was a hydro-electric reservoir and the ice was known to be suspect in places. Keeping to the snow with willow scrub and birch trees poking through the surface I skied round the edge of the lake and then headed up through the sparse birch into the shallow open Brieidadalen valley. I then followed the frozen stream course for some 3 kilometres to Kringlevatn lake, during which time the blizzard continued to fluctuate from

Day 13. Kringlevatn cabin was a very welcome sight, even if I had to dig a large drift from the door to get in

gentle to almost violent. During a lull in the blizzard I saw Kringlevatn cabin some 500 metres ahead of me. It was a very welcome sight as I was now sure of some shelter and rest. I had not stopped all day. When I got to the cabin I found the door was completely covered by a two metre high snow drift. I got the shovel off my rucksack and spent an hour digging a massive hole with steps, to allow me a route to toss the snow away, so I could open the outward opening door. It was worth it; I was soon in the cabin and within an hour the cabin was warming, my damp clothes were drying near the fire, buckets of snow were melting. With just the roar of the wind in the chimney to remind me of the blizzard outside I went to the larder for my reward for today's testing effort.

Day 14. Heading north from Kringlevatn cabin into the wild barren Setesdalsheiane without a map cost me a wrong turn and a few hours

When I forced the door open on to the newly drifted but soft spindrift the next morning, the weather had changed completely. It was clear, frosty and rather cold, at minus 10. As usual I set off at first light, around 0845. The snow was in great condition with a firm base and a little frost lying on top like a silk scarf. As my ski stick tips twisted in the frozen base layer the snow squeaked. I made good speed across Kringlevatn lake and then up the stream bed on the north side, until the cabin disappeared from view. I then went through undulating country where there were lots of drifts and some of yesterday's dreaded cornices. At least I could see the cornices today, so I could nimbly skirt round them. After about 3 kilometres I ran out of map. There was a 5-kilometre section until I gained the next sheet. During this period I confidently followed a stream bed. I had so much confidence that I never referred to my compass or GPS. By the time I checked I was a good 45 degrees off course and had wrongly followed the U-shaped stream bed for a good 3 kilometres. Not checking with the compass is a mistake I have made too many times previously, but it usually happens when I have a nice downhill run and seldom on an uphill section like now. Let it be a lesson, but one I have had a few times now, to little avail! To rectify this I either had to climb over a ridge dividing the stream bed I was in and the one I should be in or go back. I chose to climb over the ridge.

On reaching the top of the ridge I had a remarkable view over the undulating Setesdalsheiane mountains. They are renowned for being ice scoured, bare, craggy, gnarly, rock outcrops but much of this was smoothed over by huge amounts of snow. A couple of ice-covered lakes stretched away into the distance to the south west and north of me. The way down the other side of the ridge was difficult. I descended one valley for a while but it became avalanche prone so I had to re-ascend my tracks and continue further westwards along the ridge. It seemed to end in a steep shoulder. I started to pick my way down the crags on the shoulder but it was convex and got steeper and steeper. I took my skis off and started to kick steps into the snow with the heels of my boots. As I descended it got more and more icy and I could not make a secure pocket for my heels any more. It was steep, and if I slipped here I would not be able to stop. I would go careering down through the icy snowfields and over the rocky outcrops like a rag doll and be dashed to pieces. Carefully, I turned and retraced my steps up the slope again. I tried another two places but they also just got too precarious and icy. Crampons would have made the difference, but I had none. In the end I had to back track a good kilometre along the top of the ridge in the direction I had come before I found a safe way down to Djupatjørn lake in the valley below. Once on the lake it was a short ski across it and up a side valley to reach Storsteinen cabin. As a consequence of my foolish and avoidable mistake and the predicament I ended up in on the dangerous icy slopes, the journey had probably taken three hours longer than it should have done and it was late dusk when I arrived. It was a nice cabin and within two hours I was warm, comfortable and fed. I needed the time to relax as the next day I planned a big day, aiming to ski the entire length of the ice-covered lake called Blåsjø, which I had seen earlier today from the ridge stretching away to the north.

I was up earlier than usual and was ready just after 0800. If I did not make it to Krossvatn cabin by nightfall at 1700, the price I would have to pay would be to camp. This was incentive enough not to dally. However, as I stood

Day 15. The sun rose and started to warm the air just as I reached the huge frozen Blåsjø lake

at the door of the cabin it was still pitch black outside and the temperature was minus 16. On the positive side it was crisp and clear and had all the promise of a good day. I eventually left at first light around 0830. I set off up Storsteindalen for a kilometre and then cut off north east up a snow-filled gully for 2 kilometres to reach the shores of Blåsjø. Just these 3 kilometres took nearly two hours and a fair bit of effort. It made me a bit anxious about the speed I was going. But the gully did have some tricky steep sections which slowed me up. Just before the lake I reached a small pass and got a wonderful view of the early morning sun on the mountain plateau to the east of the lake. Blåsjø lake is a vast reservoir built at the very top of the plateau. It has some eight dams at various points on its circumference, flooding the original numerous lakes and tarns which were previously here into an 80 square kilometre reservoir at about 1000 metres altitude. From here the water descends in stages to the sea, passing through 11 massive turbines and producing over 4,400,000 Megawatts hours per year, which apparently is enough to supply all of Stavanger's and Bergen's electricity. It cannot be denied that Blåsjø is an intrusion into nature, especially for the wild reindeer. Furthermore, its ring of bare sterile rock around the fringe is an eyesore while the reservoir is filling in the summer. It is, nevertheless, a very effective energy source per unit disturbance compared to the more naïve alternative energy sources, like wind turbines. Today while I skied across its surface I barely noticed it was a reservoir. There were lots of reindeer tracks on the lake but I saw no reindeer. The skiing was very good and the conditions great; there was even a small breeze behind me. I had taken the skins off and rubbed some blue ski wax under the middle section of my skis, and this seemed perfect. I was pushing with my back leg and then taking a long gliding stride with my forward leg. It was very satisfying to move so quickly with so little effort. I seemed to spend most of the time skiing into my long shadow which lay on the flat surface before me all day. It was a glorious day, and had I been going south, sunglasses would have been essential given the glare from the sun. I was in my element and for the first time since setting off from Lindesnes, 15 days ago, I was really enjoying myself as my skis slid over the silky snow with barely a noise. It took about three hours to ski the wonderful 15 kilometres across the snow-covered ice to the north end of the lake.

Day 15. All day I skied north into my shadow across the huge Blåsjø lake in wonderful sunshine

Now I had a choice. I could either do two sides of a triangle which was about 7 kilometres in total or risk the direct line of 4 kilometres. I was beginning to learn the hard way just how rugged these ice-scoured granite outcrops of the Setesdalsheiane are. It was an alien jumble of craggy knolls separated by a warren of clefts and ravines between them. In the past few days I had climbed many of these knolls just to find that the other three sides were steep slopes with cornices around the tops and outcrops on the slopes, leaving me no alternative but to ski back down my ascent route and try a different tack. It was a wintry maze, a nightmarish labyrinth of gnarly crests dissected by gorges and chasms where one could spend a huge amount of time and effort making little progress. I therefore decided to play safe and do the two sides of the triangle. Firstly I skied due east up the Pøyleåa stream bed for 3 kilometres. Even this simpler route was full of ups and downs between the tarns which spread out along the valley floor hemmed in between outcrops. Then after 3 kilometres I reached what looked like a fault line and turned north west for 4 kilometres until I reached Krossvatn lake. On each side of me up this corridor were gnarly outcrops dripping with snow cornices. It certainly vindicated my choice to take the longer route. As I reached Krossvatn lake it was starting to get dark. I still had 2 kilometres of shoreline to

Day 15. The hills along the edge of the Blåsjø lake were a warren of knarly outcrops separated by a maze of clefts and ravines

ski round to reach the cabin. It was nearly dark when I rounded a small peninsula and saw the welcome sight of the cabin before me. After digging out the door I went in. It was minus 5 inside, but after a couple of hours I had it warmed up a bit, but it was an open drafty cabin and would never get as cosy as the others had been. I was tired, as it had been a long day of nearly nine hours which I had done without a stop or even taking my rucksack off. However, it was the best day so far as I had been able to enjoy the wild, untarnished, snowscape in good weather for the first time.

I had been going for 15 days now, and while I had not had the best weather I had not been too unlucky. That changed when I woke on the 16th morning. When I looked outside I could hardly believe it. The clear, cold, calm weather of yesterday had deteriorated into a swirling, hissing blizzard. When I opened the cabin door it was nearly wrenched out of my hand. I was still tired from yesterday and I did not want to try and do the long day to Bleskestadmoen cabin in these conditions. So there was only one thing for it, and that was to go back to bed. By mid morning I had to go out and get some wood from the woodshed some 20 metres away. The blizzard was so violent I got dressed into my full weatherproof shell of salopettes and jacket. It was a maelstrom of spindrift outside. I was buffeted about by the very strong winds as I struggled between the cabin and the woodshed and back again. I put the wood inside and ventured out again with my wind meter and camera. The wind meter was measuring a steady 24 metres per second with one gust at 32 metres per second. These numbers can be doubled to get knots, so it was a force 10 or full storm. I was going nowhere, so I set about making the cabin a bit more homely. It was very draughty in the kitchen area which opened off the living room. There was no door, so I hung up an old blanket to divide the room and prevent the heat escaping. I cleaned out the stove, which was full of ash, and lit it. I then became quite house proud. I tidied up the books and kitchen utensils and swept the floors. I found an old radio, and by fashioning an aerial from a whisk and changing the batteries managed

Day 16. Even getting to the outhouse to get some wood for the stove was quite an ordeal in the storm

to get it going just in time to get a weather forecast. It did not make relaxed listening. It seemed the whole of southern Norway was getting battered by a large deep depression. There were huge snowfalls in the Telemark region and nearly all the mountain roads were closed due to 'uvær'. Uvær means 'unweather' and is used to describe particularly nasty weather. It seemed this uvær would be around for a day or two.

The storm lasted three days. On the second day it abated somewhat to a gale but it returned with a vengeance on the third day, when it was the most violent. I needed to go out to get some wood occasionally and when I ventured out on the third day I was really buffeted about. I measured the wind again and it seemed to be around 28 metres per second with a gust of 35 metres.

Day 17. Huge amounts of snow were falling and being driven by the gale and storm force winds for three days

That was a force 11 or violent storm. It was spectacular indeed. The air was completely full of spindrift being driven across the mountains in search of a cornice to settle behind. I had my goggles to protect my eyes but my exposed cheeks and nose were being sandblasted by the angular crystals. The visibility was down to just 10 metres, and that was where there was a reference feature like a hut or boulder. It was an awesome display of nature's crude authority and I was an insignificant spectator. Without these cabins my trip would be totally different. In the cabins I could recuperate, dry my equipment and stretch out, both mentally and physically. Even though this cabin was shaking in some of the gusts and the wind was humming in the chimney like a church organ, I felt quite secure. This cabin had probably seen a lot worse in its history and it was now hidden from

Day 18. I was lucky I had the space, warmth and comfort of the cabin while the storm raged outside for three days

the wind and partially buried by the snow drifts which had grown on the windward side. If it was not for the cabins I would have to camp in my tent or shelter in snow-holes and very quickly my clothing would get damp with condensation and contact with snow, and my boots would freeze stiff with frost; life would be hopelessly cramped and spent in a sleeping bag waiting for the next break. Later in the trip I would have to rely more on my tent as the cabins became much more scattered. But now I could enjoy their stoves, timber ambience and space. With these appreciative thoughts I settled down to three cosy candlelit afternoons and evenings in front of the stove at Krossvatn. Occasionally I would just go to the window or door and look out to gloat at my comfort and thank the stars I was not out in that storm.

During those three days I read many of the books on the cabin bookshelf. Most were old yearbooks of various mountain walking associations in Norway. The books held a wealth of information on nature, archaeology, cultural history, especially of the now vanishing summer farms, and suggested walks. I read a book on recent Norwegian mountaineers like Arne Randers Heen, the remarkable Arne Næss, and hero of Telemark and Royal mountain guide, Claus Helberg. As I looked into the embers on those evenings I also thought about the Norwegians. Norwegians first came to this wild land some 12,000 years or 500 generations ago. They followed the reindeer flocks as they migrated north away from the growing forests of the Germanic Plains to this land which was emerging from under the ice sheets. To survive, the earliest settlers had to be very resourceful and have great foresight. Through the 10 millennia since, the descendants of these first settlers honed their hunting skills and established a migratory transhumance existence, exploiting both fjord and mountain. Some 1500 years ago agriculture became more established, but hunting and gathering continued to be very important. This foresight and resourcefulness is really part of the cultural DNA. It has to be, as no mango is going to fall from the tree in these climes. If a happy-go-lucky Latin attitude meant firewood was not cut and stacked by November then it would be a miserable winter at best. It is in the Scandinavian genes to try and maintain an order over a harsh and sometimes unpredictable nature. Nothing is slapdash in Scandinavia, and Norway especially. Everything is done properly and everything is maintained and kept in good order. Sometimes this sensible attitude comes at the expense of jovial nonchalance though.

Against huge odds land was wrestled from the forests and farms were built. So substantial and well built were many of the farms that many still stand some 600 years later. This hard won land was part of the family soul; farm and family often shared the same name. It was nurtured and improved as it passed from generation to generation. Norway especially, and Sweden to a large extent, were until very recently predominantly rural societies. Rural families can trace their roots back to the mists of history and associate them with a farm or region and this gives them a tremendous sense of belonging. It is the reason why Scandinavians have such a comfortable sense of patriotism. By contrast, in most of Europe the industrial revolution resettled much of the population, who ended up in soulless urban congestions. These resettled industrial populations were completely disenfranchised from their rural cultural heritages, and the towns they settled in did not offer the same depth of comfort. All this explains much of the Norwegian and Swedish character today which is resourceful, full of foresight and until recently, hardworking. It explains why Norwegians and Swedes are such excellent engineers. They are world leaders in some fields and certainly punch well above their weight in all others. However, these admirable practical traits come at a price. Of course this is a generalization. But then everything in life is a generalization to some extent. We as humans are generalizers. We have to be to make sense of things. Without generalizations there would be mental chaos. We need generalizations as pegs to hang our thoughts on.

After three restful days the storm finally abated, and I was like a coiled spring ready to set off on the long day to Bleskestadmoen. I was up early but couldn't leave until there was enough light to see to ski, and it was 0830 before I could venture into the early dawn and ski down the short slope on to Krossvatn lake. There had been a huge dumping of snow and everything was white. The forecast said the fresh breeze would pick up to a gale in the evening so there was no time to dally. The breeze was at my back as I went up the line of lakes and streams in Vassdalen. After 3 kilometres I reached Gravetjøna lake, which had a valley coming into it from the north, under a craggy buttress. There was so much snow that even the vertical rock faces from this buttress were white with snow and spindrift which had been blasted on to it. It was this valley to the north that I had to take now. I noticed that the streams were open in a few places. I suppose when you get half a metre of snow it must depress the ice on the lakes by a centimetre or two and this squeezes the water into the streams. Going up this side valley was fantastic. The snow was new but already compacted by yesterday's wind, which would have rolled the snowflakes until they turned into more spherical crystals of spindrift with a small amount of air trapped in them. It was a great surface for skiing on, firm underneath with some loose snow on top. I made good time up the 10 kilometres of this valley across the three lakes of Kringlevatn, Midtvatn and Kaldevatn, which were each separated by a small gentle climb. As I skied across the uppermost lake, Kaldevatn, it remained cloudy with the low cloud being driven by the wind but there was the occasional flash of blue sky rushing overhead. I felt great. The easterly wind had started to pick up a bit and the surface of the snow was starting to flow in a river of spindrift. I passed a small snowbound hunter's cabin and then turned north west into Brudled valley.

Day 19. After leaving Krossvatn cabin I had a long ski up a valley with three lakes strung out along its floor

Initially I had to cross a couple of small, frozen tarns before I reached a saddle where the valley was squeezed between two mountains. I was keen to get over here before the gale swept in. As I approached the saddle the wind increased to a near gale and there were huge amounts of spindrift surging along the valley floor. Luckily it was behind me and it swept me along with it. As I approached the saddle I could see it was steep on the north side but fortunately there was a route down this glacier-formed crag on the west side. As I went down it I could look above me and see huge plumes of the spindrift being swept over a huge cornice and into the air. Luckily the visibility was good as this would not have been a cornice to ski off in a whiteout with its rocky 20-metre drop on the lee side. The descent was difficult because the snow surface fluctuated the whole time between soft accumulations of spindrift and a hard polished surface and I could not see where they changed, and the near gale bundled me along. The sky was reasonably clear and down in the valley below I could make out Krokvatnet lake. There were some old summer farms here at 900 metres which were in the upper limit of the birch woods. I reached them quickly after skiing across the bare ice of Krokvatnet lake. A raven, my only mountain friend of late, coped well with the gusts, and even showed off with some acrobatic displays. I was doing well. I just had a small valley to ski up and down again and I was home. I therefore took a rest amongst the bare birch which unfortunately offered no protection against the gale. I glanced at my watch, confident it would be midday. I could not believe it! The time was already 1530 and in an hour it would be dark. I still had a good 7 kilometres to go, and looking at the map they did not look easy. In addition, the gale was coming straight down the valley I now had to ski up.

Day 19. At Krokvatnet, with an hour of daylight left, the day suddenly became more challenging for the final push to Bleskestadmoen

I set off with urgency. The biscuits and partially frozen water in my bottle provided some extra vigour. The gale was hurling spindrift into my face and buffeting me about. My mild panic was causing my adrenaline-filled blood to surge through my veins, keeping any tiredness at bay. I made good time, and climbed out of the scant trees and reached the pass in the dusk. The wind now was a good gale and must have been 20 metres a second or force 9. I turned a slight corner and started to descend with the gale behind me, which I thought would be an advantage. However, it was so strong I had no control skiing. I got blown over twice, so decided to take my skis off and walk. Even walking I got blown over once, as I was heaved and shoved down the hard snow having to dig my heels in to stop myself sliding down the rather shallow slope. I walked for a good half hour until I had descended, sometimes quite steeply, the west side of the mostly invisible, cloud-covered hill called Moltenuten and entered the lower main valley of Bleskestadalen. This less exposed main valley was thick with the dark twisted shapes of the bare winter birch trees. The wind had now diminished a bit and there was spindrift dropping thickly out of the sky and settling on the boughs and on the deep snow of the forest floor. The problem was it was almost dark and I still had 2 kilometres to go to the cabin. I put my skis back on and dug out my head torch. It didn't punch very far into the dark and the spindrift was reflected back in a kaleidoscope of flashes. I could not see the terrain at all so just had to follow the arrow on my GPS which showed me the shortest, but not necessarily the easiest, way to the cabin. For a good hour and a half I wandered through the birch forest going steeply up and down, barely able to see the terrain more than five metres ahead of me. The uphill sections were especially hard as the snow was so deep and there were so many small branches and twigs under the snow which I kept collapsing on to. I had no idea of the terrain ahead but just had to keep wading through the snow as the metres to the cabin very, very slowly counted down on my GPS. I must have looked a sight wandering through the swaying forest in a strong wind with spindrift everywhere in the pitch black. The metres kept ticking down slowly but surely on my GPS read out and this kept me going as I struggled forward, using huge amounts of energy. Even the last 300 metres took about half an hour as there was a steep climb and drop, but at last, with 20 metres to go, I spotted the shape of a gable end. It was the cabin at Bleskestadmoen at long last. The cabin was a restored 'seter' or 'støl', which is a summer farm. Farmers from the fjords and large valleys brought livestock up here each summer for hundreds of years to graze on the lush pastures in the birch forests. In doing so they would also preserve the grass around the main farm which could be cut for hay and winter fodder. Sadly this practice is becoming rare now but the romance of it is still very much in people's hearts. It took two hours to warm the cabin up and get some snow melted on the stove. I was dog-tired from the long day and testing conditions and I was too exhausted to cook. I went to the larder and hungrily opened and attacked two tins of spam and two of tinned fruit. These provisions, with the accommodation fee, are paid for in an honesty box with your credit card in a Norway-wide system which is seldom misused. Full of food and in front of the hot stove I was glad I spent the extra two hours in persevering through the dark to reach the cabin rather than camp in the soft thick snow of the forest.

When I woke in the morning there was still quite a strong wind and it was snowing heavily. My body was tired after yesterday and I decided to have a rest day. As the morning wore on, however, I was getting more bored and the weather was improving. At 1030 the two weather trends crossed each other and I decided

Day 20. The cabin at Bleskestadmoen was a building which had been converted from one of the cluster of seters or summer farms here

to make a break for it. Crossing the open summer pastures beside the cabin and the other seters in the vicinity, I was saddened by the loss of the idyllic way of life which must have existed in these farms during the warm summer months. My sentimental nostalgia of happy bygone times was soon vanquished as I entered the deep snow of the forest and had to tread a route up through the trees. The journey through the forest was only about 4 kilometres yet it took nearly three hours. The snow was deep, soft and very taxing, and the terrain steep and gnarly. Drifts were everywhere and bogged me down. I tried to follow a stream but it kept leading me into dead ends of small frozen waterfalls. After much sweat and effort I eventually climbed out of the forest on to the easier bare mountainside where the snow was firmer. Now I could make good progress up to the dam on Sandvatnet lake. The visibility was now very poor and with Sandvatnet being a hydro-electric reservoir I had to follow its frozen shoreline; many of the lakes and waterways around here are regulated by hydro-electric power. These can cause unnatural currents which melt the underside of the ice. Hydro-electricity also causes the water in the reservoir to fall, and the metre-thick ice falls with it, except at the sides where it cracks into great sheets along the shore. Sometimes there are hidden cracks between these large sheets, and if you are very unlucky indeed they can be wide enough to fall through. I had to have my wits about me but it was a very easy pleasant ski along the edge of the lake. As I reached the middle of the lake I decided to cross and head up what I hoped would be a short cut to Holmavatnet and the next cabin.

Naustdalen valley was not long but quite steep and narrow. To make it worse there was a big open stream running at the bottom of the V-shaped floor where I wanted to be. This was obviously caused by releasing water from the higher reservoir of Isvatnet a few kilometres to the north, which swelled the stream to completely unnatural proportions. I had to traverse the steep side of the valley to keep away from this fast flowing open stream and any snow banks it may have undercut. After a kilometre and some difficulty I reached a frozen tarn. The water from the Isvatnet reservoir must have disgorged from a tunnel at the outflow of the frozen tarn. I wanted to cross the tarn to reach the west side of the valley and gingerly ventured across the ice. The crossing was short and nerve-wracking but I soon reached the other side, which was not as steep

Day 20. While crossing Sandvatnet lake the weather cleared to reveal a mountainscape plastered in snow

and less avalanche-prone than the east side. I went quite high to avoid the ravine below, and for once this did not lead into any difficulty, like steep corniced drifts. Soon I was at Holmavatnet lake and on the home stretch. On the other side of the lake there are archaeological remains of hunter's camps which are 8000 years old. These wild Stone Age nomads must have come up here in the summer months to hunt reindeer and fish. At the end of the summer they would have returned to the valley and forest by the coast where there was a plentiful supply of sea food. It was just 3 kilometres along the frozen shoreline to the cabin, but it was already getting dark. With a kilometre to go I had to get my head torch out and start using my GPS to home in on the cabin again. In the dark it seems a kilometre takes about an hour, and I did not arrive until 1800. There were two cabins. One was small and without a larder of provisions, but with wood and a large stove, and a much larger main cabin which was half buried in snow. The latter looked much more comfortable and probably had a good larder, but I would have been digging for at least an hour, probably two, to clear the huge snowdrift from where I could only guess, but could not be sure, the door might be, so I opted for the smaller one. Within an hour the cabin was like a sauna. I had melted enough snow for water and was basking naked in the heat as I cooked some of the dehydrated food I had been carrying in case I had to camp. It had been a good decision to go when I did from Bleskestadmoen. Had I stayed I would have been kicking myself when it brightened up in the afternoon, and despite the punishing struggle in the forest I had had a good day.

In the morning, despite two reasonably long days, I was disappointed when I heard the wind roaring outside. It was also snowing heavily and I think it had been all night. I had wanted to get to Haukeliseter today, but there was no chance of finding one's way in this blizzard. So it was back to bed. I got up again at 0900 and decided I needed to find a way into the other cabin and the treats in the larder. I dressed up for a wrestle with the blizzard and spindrift and waded across the deep snow for the 100 metres to the other cabin. I assumed the door was at the northern gable end. After half an hour of digging I had started to uncover the door, but it took another hour to have it completely cleared so I could open it. It was lucky I carried a spade, which was essentially to dig a snow-hole if needed, but seemed also to be worth its weight for excavating cabin doors. White with spindrift, I dusted myself down, went in and lit the stove. I then went back to the small cabin, packed, tidied up and migrated to the main cabin. It was already warming up. I soon collected snow for melting and by midday was ensconced. It was a wild day. I think it was snowing heavily in addition to the spindrift getting blown around, but there was no way to tell what was happening in the violent white turmoil. I restudied my map and decided to take a detour off the recommended winter route to Haukeliseter tomorrow. I would never have even considered this recommended winter route, had it not been marked on the map, as it goes through rugged terrain and a deep slot called Turistskardet.

A friend, Ole Bjøråsen, with whom I skied the length of Jostedalsbreen ice cap eight months previously, had also skied the length of Norway. It was at this same time of year, and just a year before. It was poor weather as he set off from Holmavatnet cabin towards Haukeliseter and he was skiing through Turistskardet. Suddenly and without warning, Ole was bundled about and then came to rest. He was completely encased and unable to move, as if set in concrete. He didn't know it, but he had just been buried to a depth of two metres in an avalanche. That is the depth of a good grave. Unable to move a finger and trapped with his skis, poles and rucksack still on, Ole thought he was dead and passed out. When he regained consciousness he found he had melted a small circumference around himself. Slowly, by bashing his head and scratching with his fingers, he managed to excavate some breathing room and free an arm. He then had to dig down, compressing snow to give him some more space to free his boots from his skis. He couldn't, so he undid the laces, and bootless, clawed and scratched his way to the surface. I can imagine the relief, when some nine hours later he emerged into the night. He put up his tent, collapsed into his sleeping bag, and spent a couple of days lying there, recovering from his ordeal. When his strength returned he had to dig down the two metres to retrieve his boots and skis. He then continued the 15 kilometres to Haukeliseter and reached it at the end of his strength. However, after a short break he continued north to reach Nordkapp, as planned, three months later. It is only because Ole is so tough, even by Norwegian standards, that he did not panic excessively and give up. Any lesser mortal would have been there until the spring melt. One of the main problems with a blizzard is the total lack of visibility and that you just can't see the dangers you are flirting with. The wind, even gale force, is a minor irritation compared to the lack of sight. Whatever the weather was, I would be giving Turistskardet a wide berth and going a slightly longer way via Ingelsvatn lake.

The next morning I looked out of the window at 0600 and, for the first time since putting my skis on in Ljosland ages ago, I saw stars. At last, maybe the weather was on the change. However, by the time I left at 0830 the weather was changing to the windy whiteness I was getting used to. Within a half kilometre of leaving the cabin I knew I was in for a hard day, and that I would be lucky to reach Haukeliseter lodge without camping. I was wading through a half metre of soft snow. It was even slow going back down the relatively steep slope to Holmavatnet lake! Luckily, the snow on the lake was more windblown and less airy, and therefore firmer. I skied to the north corner of the lake where there were a few private fishing and hunting cabins owned by locals. One of these cabins just had the eves and chimney poking out of the snow. There was a problem-free short climb up to Langevatn lake and I was lucky to pick an easy route. Occasionally it brightened up enough to see a kilometre or two. Looking back at my lonely tracks I surveyed the hills. In some 40 ski trips in Scandinavia I don't think I have ever seen so much snow. On crossing Langevatn lake the weather deteriorated and I could not make out where to go, so out came my compass. I reached the north shore and picked my way up the slope on the other side from boulder to boulder, slowly climbing to get to a saddle south west of Ingelsvatn lake. It was a whiteout at the top and my descent to Ingelsvatn lake was very difficult and timorous as the visibility was down to about two metres. I shuffled along on my skis, barely making progress. Occasionally I would spot a rare boulder, and using it as a reference, make for it. When I got a feeling of vertigo I would throw snowballs ahead and be reassured by the divots they made on landing. After an hour I had made the single kilometre down to the level lake without skiing off any cornice. Crossing this last lake was relatively easy as I followed the shoreline with its numerous reference points. At the north point of the lake I descended into a wide valley with a tarn. Again the visibility was terrible, and the wind was a good force 6 at least but was behind me. This poor visibility was costing me a lot of time.

At last, once I had descended a couple of hundred metres, the visibility improved. I then had a very pleasant gentle descent through a series of soft snow-filled smaller valleys and gullies until I made it right down beyond the tree line and spilled out on to Kjelavatn lake. Only now was I confident I would make the lodge at Haukeliseter. But it was already 1500 and I still had 7 kilometres to go. My confidence was misplaced as it was very heavy work ploughing a furrow through the deep snow, first across Kjelavatn lake, then up a frozen inlet, and finally across a frozen swampy forest. Luckily the forest was open and windswept so the snow was not that deep. None the less, I was making very slow progress and was getting frustrated as darkness started to fall. I was just starting to climb a slope to Ståvatn lake when I came across a line of twigs stuck into the snow about 30 metres apart. They are usually not put out until much later in the ski touring season and are route markers in case of bad weather. I was fortunate that Haukeliseter lodge put them out in its immediate vicinity earlier in order to cater for the odd hardcore ski tourer who ventured up here so early in the season. It was almost dark now but it was easy to follow the twigs for the last 2 kilometres. I approached the lodge about 1730 with the line of twigs and the lights from the building guiding me through the heavy snow showers and strong wind. I was very excited as I skirted round the mountainous pile of snow which the diggers had cleared from the lodge car park over the last two weeks. I took my skis off, and in triumph embedded them in a drift, then hung my ski sticks over them before going into the lodge.

The young guy at the desk almost did a double take when I came in. I was covered in spindrift and had to brush myself down. I approached the desk, removing my hood and balaclava, beneath which was a filthy, unshaven and weather beaten face. Yet my eyes and smile must have been glowing with the glint of victory. I had had the same clothes on for the last 16 days and they must have stunk beneath the wind and waterproof outer layer I had on. The heat of the reception area made my cheeks glow. I had not seen or spoken to anybody for a fortnight, so once the curious receptionist had engaged me in conversation I burst forth in an excited babble. I was shown a bunk room where I dumped everything. Soon I had peeled my filthy, sweaty, clothes off and was shaving in the shower. It was pure fantasy. I had to get back into my Gore-Tex salopettes and duvet jacket as this was all the clothing I had which was not filthy. Everything else went into the staff washing machine, which they kindly let me use. After a hefty meal I socialized for a good few hours with a very nice group of kiters who were staying here. Haukeliseter is a Mecca for young kiters who come and snowboard across Ståvatn lake while being pulled by up to 15 square metres of kite. I was hungry for conservation and social interaction and the kiters were interested in hearing my story about the last three weeks and my plans for the next 30 weeks despite my heavy English accent and broken Norwegian. Haukeliseter had a very good atmosphere; the staff could not have been more helpful and the other guests were an easy-going bunch. I had already decided to take tomorrow off to wash more clothes, eat, socialize and recuperate after the gruelling test Setesdalsheiane had given me. I had heard rumours that it was the toughest section on the whole trip, and had heard it described as a 'manndomsprøve', a test of mettle. It had certainly been a baptism of blizzard and ice where I had been a helpless ant creeping across a vast white wilderness. I slept well and contented.

Day 24. The characterful old buildings at Haukeliseter were a favourite haunt of Nansen, Amundsen and other great polar explorers

It was a joy to wake up at Haukeliseter and realize that I was to spend the rest of the day at this comfortable, warm, nourishing and historic lodge. Haukeliseter is one of the oldest tourist lodges in Norway, dating from the 17th and 18th Centuries. Its original old buildings, now gone, were initially a seter or summer farm. This old seter offered food and lodging for travellers and traders who had to cross these often inhospitable mountains between Setesdal in the east and the west coast. In the 19th Century it was expanded, and by 1888 the first of the present buildings was built. It was later acquired by the Stavanger Mountain Touring Club. It continues to offer hospitality to travellers today, as an arterial mountain road passes by its front door and the road is often closed in the winter for a day or two at a time. On those stormy days the lodge returns to its original role offering shelter, but now its focus is more on mountain walkers and skiers. Its old buildings are steeped in history and tradition, and the old logs of its stout walls have sheltered many famous explorers. Roald Amundsen used to stay here as he set off on trips across the Hardangervidda plateau to the north to train for his polar expeditions. Fridtjof Nansen, arguably one of the 10 greatest men of the 19th Century, who was not only a distinguished polar explorer but also a world statesman and the winner of the Nobel peace prize for humanitarian work, was also a regular visitor. Old wooden skis, wolf and bear skins, hundred-year-old farming utensils and all manner of mountain artefacts line its timbers. In the end I had to spend two days here as the weather was poor with heavy snowfalls, near gales and very poor visibility. The arterial road passing through Haukeliseter was closed for the two days while I relaxed here. The next stage of my journey was across the open windswept Hardangervidda plateau, which lay well above 1000 metres and would probably take a week to cross. I used my rest time to fully research my trip across this plateau, having found out that many of the cabins I had originally intended to use were locked. I decided on a new route of Hellevassbu to Litlos to Hadlaskard to Garden to Kjeldebu to Finse. If things went well it would mean I could stay in a cabin every night. I knew I would probably have to camp, but if I could avoid it, I would; camping is cramped, cold and difficult to get going the next morning. On the evening of my second rest day at the lovely Haukeliseter I heard the weather forecast for the next week. It was music to my ears and left me excited and eager to get started across the notoriously wild plateau.

SECTION 2. Setesdalsheiane.
18 days. 168 km. 70 hours. 4280m ascent. 3770m descent.

THE SKI: SECTION 3. HARDANGERVIDDA

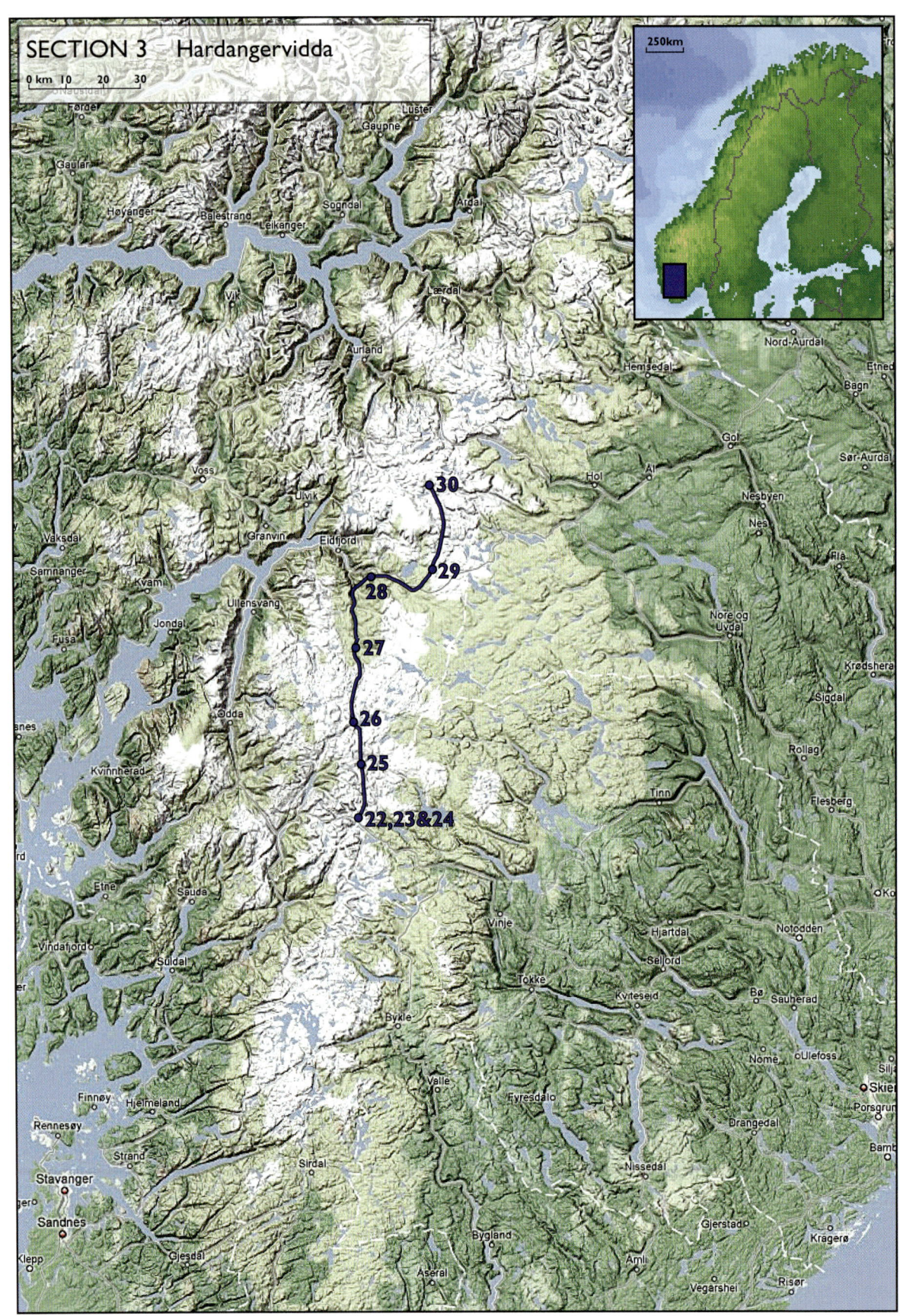

THE SKI: SECTION 3. HARDANGERVIDDA

After a huge breakfast at Haukeliseter I said my goodbyes to the friendly staff and set off at 0830. It was very misty and the visibility was just some 50 metres as I set off up the shin-deep virgin snow on the steep slope to the north. Haukeliseter was quickly enveloped by the familiar whiteness. It was a long, warm slog up and an hour later, when I reached the first lake, the sun was trying to break through the cover of mist and cloud and I could feel its warmth. However, it did not break through for another hour, when I was beginning to question where I was. Suddenly the great pointed peak of Vesle Nup burst out of the disorientating mist and soared into the blue sky ahead of me. I could at last confirm I was at the white smooth frozen expanse of Loftsdokktjønn lake and had an hour's climb up to the saddle to the west of the lofty Vesle Nup. I skied up with

Day 25. Looking south from the saddle by Vesle Nup back down my tracks into the mist and Haukeliseter with Setesdalsheiane beyond

the hot sun beating down on me and reflecting back off the snow, heating my face. When I got to the saddle the reward was tremendous. To the south I could see my lonely tracks disappearing back down the hill until they vanished into the layer of mist which was still filling the valley like a bath full of feathers. On the other side of this valley were the benign-looking Setesdalsheiane mountains which had given me such a challenge over the last three weeks. To the north was the crystal clear undulating plateau of the Hardangervidda with the nunatak of Nups Egga directly in front. It was a wonderful view under dark blue heavens.

Day 25. Looking north from the saddle by Vesle Nup to the sun-drenched, but wild and barren Hardangervidda plateau

After this climb I was rewarded with a wonderful five-hour ski through easy sunny terrain. The snow was loose and powdery and my skis flowed over the top of it quite easily, sinking only to my ankles. I followed an easy line of lakes and shallow open valleys from Mannevatn lake across Årmotsvatn lake and all the way up to Simletindvatn lake. Occasionally I passed into the shade where it was bitterly cold, perhaps minus 15. My eyebrows were covered in frost and my jacket hood was thick with ice crystals, but this was an insignificant price to pay to have the visibility. The anxiety I had in the morning about reaching the cabin was now replaced by euphoria as I sped over the lakes, homing in on Hellevassbu cabin at four kilometres per hour. If I could have conjured up some fantasy conditions and views this is exactly what I would have ordered. I passed many fox tracks as they crossed this vast empty plateau in the constant search for scarce food to help them survive over the winter. There were also a few tracks made by hare, lemming and ptarmigan which were the foxes prey. Generally lemmings stay under the snow pack throughout the winter in a network of grassy tunnels, but occasionally they venture on to the surface where they are very vulnerable. However, I did not see any, nor any sign of one which had lingered too long. Just as I reached Simletindvatn the mist came down again but now I knew I would make it to the cabin as it was only an hour away and I was used to poor visibility now. Soon the cabin appeared out of the whiteness. Luckily I did not have to dig much snow away from the door. There was a thermometer outside, which read minus 26 and dusk was still not upon me. It would be a cold night and I would be thankful I was not in my tent. I went into the cabin where another thermometer in the cooking area read minus 24. Sensibly the kitchen and living areas were divided into two halves by a wooden wall and wide doors. By closing the doors I could make a smaller room for the stove to heat. After fumbling around with the flammable birch bark, kindling and logs I got a fire going in the stove, collected some buckets of snow to melt for water, and started to thaw out tins from the larder for supper. In a couple of hours it was up to plus 25 in the cabin kitchen and my frosty clothes were drying beautifully.

Day 25. It was minus 24 inside the cabin at Hellevassbu when I arrived but it soon warmed up when I got the stove going

It was a relatively short day to Litlos cabin so I took my time the next morning and didn't leave until well after sunrise. As soon as I went outside I realized this was a mistake. Although it was windstill and just minus 10, a dense mist soon enveloped everything. I set off up the hill to traverse the slopes to the south of Buanuten and then go over the saddle between this mountain and Sandvikenuten mountain. Slowly I climbed in the dense whiteness. I was a bit lazy using my compass and my GPS was still packed in the rucksack. However, I soon reached the pass and I started down the north side of it to the small tarn. This ski down the other side of the pass was slow and careful as visibility was terrible. Still, at least I was making some progress, but the tarn took a long time coming. After a good hour I was suspicious I had gone past it in the whiteout and must be nearly at Øvsta Bjørnavatnet lake. I stopped and got my GPS out to see just how far it was. The coordinates on its reading confused me and I thought it wasn't working. When I referred the coordinates it gave me to the map it said I was still on the north shore of Nedre Hellevatnet. It took me a while to believe it, but in the end it dawned on me that the GPS was in fact right. I was furious with myself for being so stupid and lazy. Had I got the GPS out of my rucksack at the pass I could have saved myself making a total mess of the day so far. It now dawned on me that I had not gone over the pass at all, but over a shoulder on the south ridge of Buanuten, and had descended again on the same side I had ascended. After a good two hours of hard work I was 2 kilometres from Hellevassbu cabin. I was very disappointed and very angry with myself. This simple lapse of checking and the overconfidence in my sense of direction had cost me dearly, and I might be punished for this stupidity with a night in the tent.

Rather than retrace my descent to the pass I should have skied over, I went a different way. I climbed up again and this time went to the east of Sandvikenuten over another saddle. After much peering into the whiteness and endless cross-referencing with the map and GPS I eventually crossed the saddle and descended to Øvsta Bjørnavatnet lake where I intersected my planned route. I had wasted two hours on a day with no time to spare. I now had another pass to cross, the Tueslaet pass. This ascent was equally frustrating. I must have made endless detours as I fumbled about in the white. It was just impossible to go fast in the mist and without the reference of occasional boulders I was disorientated. The descent down the other side was worse still as it was the lee side and all the boulders had been covered. This constant whiteness was beginning to wear on my calm and I was tense I might take another wrong turn or go over an unseen cornice again. I eventually reached flat ground which I assumed was the Østre Tuevatnet lake. I confirmed it with the GPS, then turned west to Vestre Tuevatnet lake. When I reached this second lake the sun finally made it through the mist. My disgruntled mood suddenly vanished as a view opened up. It was marvellous to see something at last. My joy and relief was short lived as the mist soon returned, but it was worth having, even for 10 minutes.

Day 26. A slight break in the disorientating and confusing mist in which I took a wrong turning that cost me a good two hours

I crossed the lake and reached a wide shelf called Hardingslepa, which I skied along for 2 kilometres until it was time to descend to Kvennsjøen lake. I was a bit worried about the descent, but I need not have been as the mist cleared again to reveal a perfect slope to ski down. It was the best descent of the trip so far, and despite my tiredness I really enjoyed it and practised my turns all the way down to two small huts on the lake's edge which were half buried in the snow. Once I was on this lake I had much more confidence about reaching Litlos cabin,

Day 26. Only once did I get a view when the anxiety-inducing mist lifted for half an hour when I crossed Vest Tuevatnet lake

but then the mist returned with a vengeance and it was starting to get dark. I still had 5 kilometres to go and was cursing my relaxed start and stupidity this morning.

The mist was now so thick I could only see 10 metres. I got a bit lost again as there was an irritating air bubble in my compass housing which kept influencing the needle, and after another unnecessary diversion I had to get my GPS out again. Without it I would have been completely at a loss. Suddenly, I thought I was seeing things, as there was open water just in front of me. What the hell was going on now? Disconcerted and nervous, I retreated a bit and checked my position again. It must be the river between Litlosvatnet and Kvennsjøen lakes. I had seen it just in time before I stumbled towards it and crashed through the weak ice round the fringe. I made a deliberate detour, and after some uneasy minutes I felt I was on to firmer ice, and only then did I cross the narrow Litlosvatnet lake. I just had 2 kilometres to go now but it was totally dark and I would have to feel my way forward in the dark mist using my ineffective head torch and my GPS to home in. It is a very slow tentative procedure. After an hour I had only gone a kilometre, but suddenly the mist cleared to reveal a clear sky sparkling with shimmering stars and an unusually bright Venus. As I reached the cabin the sky was crystal clear and the constellations were bright and easy to identify. Even the shy North Star was shining quite proudly. I reached the cabin physically tired and mentally exhausted. Fumbling my way through the mist was very tense and taxing mental work. I soon had the stove warming up the room in the cabin and snow melting in the steel buckets. I could then relax and reflect on the mistakes, tensions and frustrations of the day.

Day 27. A cold dawn breaks over Skadvatn on the way from Litlos to Hadlaskard cabin

When I woke at Litlos the clear skies were still full of stars and there was a warm glow to the south. It was very cold outside, minus 23, when I set off at 0830. The drifts and fields of the recent heavy snowfalls were now becoming firm as the crystals were starting to merge and freeze together. On this cold morning the snow was very hard and my ski poles squeaked as they would do in a polystyrene block. Behind me was a uniform yellow hue across the southern sky as the sunrise approached, and in front of me to the north the whole sky turned a bluish purple colour – the colours of a crisp, cold, clear morning. The first rays of the sun appeared as I reached the north end of Skadvatn lake and there was instant heat in them on this bitter morning. I could tell it was going to be a perfect day for skiing and one was definitely overdue. Frost sparkled in the sun as my skis drove forward across the feathery frost on the snow's unyielding base. If I had been going south I would have needed glasses to avoid snow blindness. I headed for the large knoll of Brakanuten. It was fantastic being able to see what I was skiing across and I could nimbly skirt round snowdrifts and meander up smooth open gullies

Day 27. Just before the sun came up on this cold morning the sky turned a purple hue

Day 27. Looking back down to Skadvatn from the saddle to the east of Brakanuten shows the perfect snow conditions

without worrying where I was going. I had the luxury of planning my route from a kilometre away at least. It was marvellous skiing, almost spiritual in its rhythmic meditation. At the pass I took the short skins off as they were slowing me up slightly and it was mostly downhill now for the next 12 kilometres. I gently descended, making long glides across the sparkling feather-like snow with each stride. I passed many fox tracks and lots of signs of ptarmigan also. It seems in the bad weather these birds simply bury themselves up to their necks, and I observed many pockets in the snow with droppings in them where they must have sheltered. The foxes would have to use their keen sense of smell to sneak up on such a semi-buried ptarmigan without disturbing them.

Just before Åremot the nice descent ended in a short steep drop of about 40 metres. In this fine clear weather it was easy to see how I could get down from this obstacle. There was only one feasible route which did not have a cornice hanging over it. I had to take my skis off and dig my heels in to make steps in the steep hard snow. In poor visibility this would have been a nightmare; it would have been virtually impossible to find the only uncorniced spot and I may well have tumbled down the steep rocky slope. From the small hut at Åremot the route was initially quite easy as I could follow the frozen river, but after a couple of kilometres this river disappeared into a series of small rocky gorges with huge sculptures of ice hanging on the sides. I had to keep to the flatter slopes above the gorges to the east of the river. As I neared the cabin the gorges vanished and the valley opened into an area covered in boulders and willow scrub. Willow scrub loves wet places, so I suspect this is a marshy patch in the summer. I noticed how the snow was much icier here and how relatively little of it there was. It was almost as if it had received none of the recent heavy showers over the last fortnight. Hadlaskard cabin itself is a large old summer farm, or seter, which has been restored. It is made with huge lumber log walls which are protected by newer planks on the outside. On the inside these logs are exposed and have a warm old characterful charm. The logs fit perfectly into each other without a gap anywhere. It is great craftsmanship from perhaps a century ago, maybe more. So well do some of these log cabins fit together it is possible (and quite usual) to number the logs, disassemble them, transport and reassemble them somewhere else. It had been a lovely short day, and I had plenty of time to do all the cabin chores (get wood, light the stove and collect pails of snow to melt), and still had a couple of daylight hours remaining. I spent the whole evening in front of the stove in the cosy, candle-lit, ambience of this lovely building and pored over the books on the shelf.

It was very icy when I started the next morning and the further I went down the valley the less new snow there was covering the older, hard, icy snow which was occasionally polished by the wind. It seemed extraordinary that this valley had escaped the immense snowfalls of the last three weeks. With the skins off I was able to double pole down the frozen marshes and river bed. Just before Hedlo I came across some moose tracks. The moose had been nibbling the willow and birch, which were now forming into dense thickets which I did not want to become ensnared in. Moose belong more to the forests of the east rather than the fjord regions, which I was almost in, so I was surprised to see their tracks. The fast icy run continued to Viveli with a couple of more awkward sections of river to avoid. In some sections where it was flowing over small rapids, the river was open. In one of the adjacent frozen marshes there was a flock of about 200 willow grouse. Willow grouse are very closely related to ptarmigan but occupy the willow scrub zone. In winter they take on the same white camouflage as the ptarmigan and the two are impossible to tell apart from a distance. Viveli is a tourist lodge surrounded by a score of private cabins. The hamlet was deserted with all its roofs covered in deep snow. Luckily, there was a snow-scooter track which went from Viveli up through the birch forest to a roadhead in Berastøldalen. This was exactly the way I wanted to go and it saved me a long, hard struggle in the forest, where the snow was not so icy and would have been knee deep. After a couple of kilometres of this easier ascent the scooter track reached the roadhead.

This road had come up from the west coast at Eidfjord just a few kilometres in a series of precipitous hairpin bends for 900 metres until it reached this hanging valley at the treeline. I wanted to go in the opposite direction to the road which was east up Berastøldalen where there were a number of summer farms and newer leisure cabins scattered about the high open valley, which must have afforded good summer grazing for sheep and cattle from the farms in the deep slot of the main Eidfjord valley. Much of the high Berastøldalen was frozen marshes but as I climbed up it there seemed to be pasture under the layer of hard snow. I climbed on up between smooth rock outcrops with my skis clattering off the frozen icy surface as I reached the watershed. At this watershed I should have been able to see Hardangerjøkulen, a large round icecap which

Day 28. The birch-covered lower reaches of Berastøldalen, which is a hanging valley; to the left is the vast 800m descent to Eidsfjorden

sits on the northern section of Hardangervidda, but unfortunately it was too cloudy and the whole thing was shrouded. There was another small cluster of summer farms at the broad expansive watershed before the long descent to Garden. Unfortunately my legs were too tired to enjoy it and I was rather tense. I kept the skins on to slow me up as my shins and thighs were on fire with the effort needed to keep a controlled snowplough. Occasionally I tried to telemark turn but the metal skin clips caught the snow and sent me spilling on to the ground. Garden sits astride an arterial road which connects east and west Norway and is mainly made up of some 500 leisure cabins which stretch up and down the valley but do not intrude too harshly into the surroundings. There is a small shop in Garden which rented out some tiny log cabins. There was no-one there so I phoned the number in the window and a very outdoor-type lady soon arrived on skis being towed by a couple of huskies. She opened the shop for me which was just stocked with non-perishable food for the quiet winter months. She then showed me to a small cabin for the night. It only had an electric panel heater and I missed the raw radiating heat from a wood stove.

Day 29. Skiing along the valley between the cabins at Garden and Mauset which blended into the hillside

The barometer on my watch showed the pressure was 1020 mb and rising, and the snippets of weather forecast I could get were just fantastic. It seemed the good weather of the last days was going to become even more established. After having the best route to Kjeldebu cabin explained to me by the lady who ran the shop and cabins I set off at 0830. I was eager to get into the mountains above Garden to see the large icecap of Hardangerjøkulen which I would have to ski round for the next two days. Initially the route was a bit dull and it followed prepared ski trails which catered for the cabin owners up beside the frozen river. As the trail went up the valley it crossed the road and went through the village of Mauset with its 500 turf-roofed leisure cabins and an alpine ski slope. Beyond Mauset the ski trail re-crossed the road again, and then as the cabins petered out so did the trail. I was back to making my own trail through the firm snow of the scanty birch forest beneath the large dam until it climbed up through the last twisted birch trees where the valley levelled off. I was delighted to be heading away from the leisure cabins and birch trees and back into the wild white mountain wilderness as I veered north east now on to the plateau again. The snow conditions changed as accumulations of newer drifting snow started to cover the hard icy snow, and my skis, which had been noisily clattering across the surface for the last two days, fell silent, to my relief. My ankle tendons, tense and strained from digging the metal ski edges into the icy snow, could now relax. The grey overcast weather slowly emptied from the sky leaving it a dark blue above the bright white snow. I was soon in my element again pushing one foot in front on the other,

Day 29. I left the icy snow behind as I entered the northern half of the Hardangervidda plateau and came across fresh virgin snow

gliding whenever possible, across the increasingly sunny plateau. At the end of Sandtjørna lake I came across a line of branches or twigs stuck into the snow. These 'kvisters' are an ancient way of marking winter routes and are placed about 30 metres apart along the route. In the Easter time when ski touring is popular with many Norwegians, these kvistered routes are set up between many cabins. They are a blessing as even in poor weather, possibly up to a small storm, one can push on to a cabin if caught out. They have saved many lives in their time.

I liked this kvistered route because I knew the branches marked the most sensible route to Kjeldebu cabin. I could forget navigating and concentrate on the simply marvellous scenery. At last I was in skiing heaven. I had recently received many emails and comments from people wishing me well and saying how jealous they were. If only they knew the reality of it, especially during my time in Setesdalsheiane. However, this afternoon they would have had good reason to be jealous. The sun was out in full force and I was shedding clothes quickly as I rose up and glided down across the glistening white landscape. On one rise the Hardangerjøkulen ice cap appeared and I was stunned into admiration. It is a large, smooth, flat dome some 10 kilometres in diameter. This ice cap sat on top of a circle of cliffs and crags which rose up from the undulating plateau below it. Between these crags the occasional crevassed glacier flowed and tumbled down from the ice cap towards the surrounding plateau. These glaciers petered out above a series of moraine ridges on the plateau which showed its recent limits. Before I knew it, I crested a rise and below me lay the two Kjeldebu cabins. It was only 1400 and absolutely marvellous to arrive with such good time to spare. I leisurely lit the fire and melted snow and then basked in the comfort of the self-service cabin's main room. It

Day 29. The Hardangerjøkulen ice cap is about 10 kilometres across and feeds various glaciers which tumble down its slopes

was too cold to go outside and sit in the sun, so I sat inside with its rays heating me through the window like a lazy cat. It seemed January had kept her best to last. There were the wonderful green and orange hues of a very cold sunset and then I had a cosy evening in front of the fire reading outdoor magazines and enjoying the warm ambience of the cabin.

Hardangerjøkulen marked the end of one geological zone and the start of another. For the last month I had basically been crossing the very old basement rocks of the Baltica tectonic plate which were a billion years old. About 400 million years ago (MYA), this tectonic plate collided with another called Laurentia, which is roughly the North America of today. As these plates came together there was an arc of volcanic islands, a bit like the Aleutian islands of today, which got squeezed in between them. In this cataclysmic collision the margin of Baltica was pushed under the margin of Laurentia and the arc of volcanic islands, both of which rode up on

Day 29. I reached Kjeldebu cabin in the early afternoon which gave me plenty of time to relax later in the day

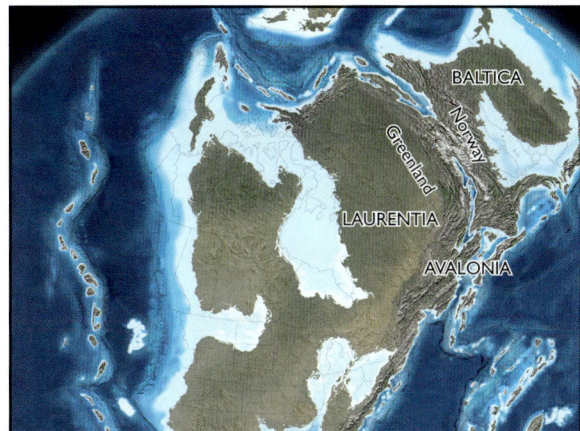

Geo Fig 1. 420 MYA Laurentia collides with Baltica and Avalonia and the volcanic island arcs are forced on to the continental crust

off into the oceans by erosion. Baltica and Laurentia have separated again as the Atlantic Ocean opened up between them. All that is now left of these once mighty Caledonian Mountains are the remnants of the thrust sheets or nappes along most of the western half of Norway and their counterparts on the east coast of Greenland. Over the next two months I would now be skiing through these nappes which still sit on top of the ancient basement rock of Baltica. Geologists have arranged these nappes into collections of layers called Allochthons, which are like groups of adjacent

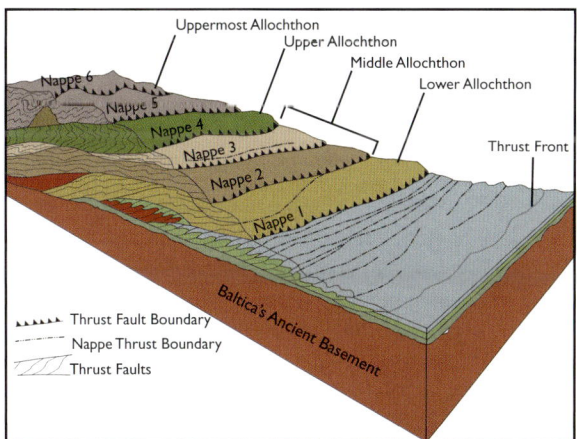

Geo Fig 3. The nappes are thrust, or smeared, long distances across the basement and each other, with the upper nappes being thrust the greatest distance, and in the Caledonian Orogeny nearly 300 km

softer sedimentary Lower Allochthon when I eventually venture further to the east. Hardangerjøkulen was the southernmost remnant of these nappes and it was in the Middle Allochthon, as was Hallingskarvet in the next section and Jotunheimen in the section after that.

I thought it would be a long day so was ready to go at 0800 the next morning. There was a slight breeze which was bitterly cold, but I was well-dressed for it. It was

to the fringe of Baltica, created the 10,000-metre high Caledonian Mountains. As this collision was happening over a 20-million year period, many of the rocks and sediments which were squashed between the two plates got smeared or thrust across the basement surface of Baltica under the mountains which had formed above. In many places these rocks were smeared or thrust with one type of rock on top of another in distinctive layers for a few hundred kilometres. Geologists call a layer of this rock a nappe. In the intervening 400 million years since this collision occurred much has happened and the 10,000-metre high mountains have been completely ground down to their stumps and carried

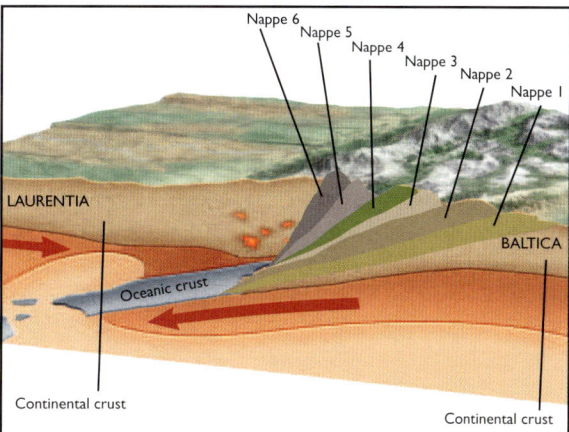

Geo Fig 2. In a continent-continent collision, rock is accreted on to the submerging continent in huge wedges, with the youngest (nappe 1) at the bottom and the oldest (nappe 6) at the top

playing cards spread out across a table. The nappes that were thrust furthest west are the underneath ones and these are collectively called the Lower Allochthon and the top nappes with the least thrusting are called the Upper and Uppermost Allochthons. I would mostly be skiing through the harder rocks of the Upper and Middle Allochthon with an occasional diversion into the

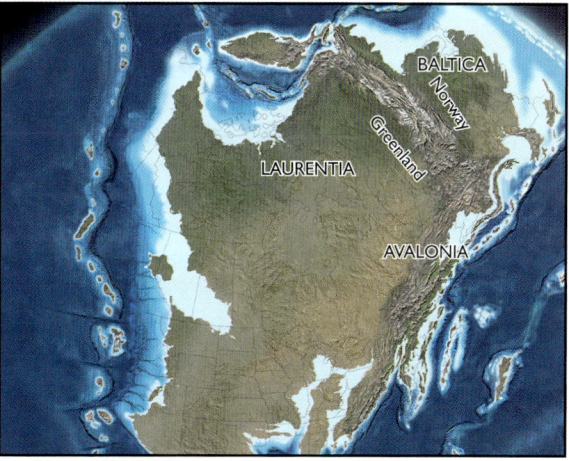

Geo Fig 4. 400 MYA Laurentia crumples into Baltica and Avalonia and the Caledonian Mountains are at their largest at 10,000 metres high

Day 30. The sun rises over the Hardangerjøkulen plateau on another cold morning as I skied from Kjeldebu to Finse

still dawn when I set off, but pretty soon the first rays of the new day were turning the mountain tops a golden orange. It had all the promise of a perfect day. I made very good time over the easy ground and after a couple of hours was at a junction where I could either go over Helvetes fjell, Hells mountain, or round an easier, but much longer way via Finnsbergvatnet lake. The latter route would have taken me past an archaeological site where Stone Age dwellers onwards have waited for migrating reindeer to cross a neck of water. When the reindeer were half way across they were ambushed by the hunters in small boats. Any trace of this, and the summer landscape it would have occurred in, would have completely vanished under these heavy winter snows, so there was no archaeological interest to go this way. I chose the route over Helvetes fjell as there were some old tracks which also went this way and it made it easier to force myself across the snow. The route over was very scenic and much easier than the map indicated. There were some wonderful views down to the plateau of Hardangervidda and also up to the Hardangerjøkulen icecap which I was skirting round. There were lots of hare tracks up here. The weather was now absolutely fantastic and it was completely windstill under a deep blue sky with the sun beating down. If I turned south I could feel the sun burning my face, but generally I was heading north. I climbed up to 1400 metres before descending the north side of the pass to Midnutevatnet lake down a long slope covered in virgin glistening soft snow in the bright warm sun. Yes, January really had kept its best to last and it was the best day this year.

Given the stunning conditions, and my continually improving level of fitness, I made very good time. It was just 1300 and I only had a couple of hours to go to Finse. The terrain was pleasant and easy. An hour

Day 30. As I climbed towards Helvetesnutane I got a great view of Hardangerjøkulen ice-cap and some of the ramparts on which it sits

before Finse I met some other skiers. They were heading to a cabin called Krækkja, where they would camp, as it was closed. We chatted a bit and then went our separate ways. The remaining hour to Finse was a delightful descent in the full sun. Finse itself marks the northern edge of Hardangervidda, the end of the third section. It had been very kind to me indeed, as Hardangervidda can be a notoriously vicious place in bad weather. As I made the last steps to Finse there was a long steep ridge towering over me called Hallingskarvet, and crossing it would be the next task tomorrow when I start to ski through Skarvheimen. Finse is a tourist village which has developed over the last 100 years round the train station, which other than on foot, is the only access. There is the large Finse 1222 Hotel and the Turistforening Lodge but the latter was still closed. Unfortunately the hotel was completely full as it was hosting a kiting weekend with 150 people attending. However, they managed to squeeze me into a small dormitory where there was a spare bed. I had hoped to

Day 30. From the pass just east of Helvetesnutane I got a fantastic view south over the vast expanse of the Hardangervidda plateau

Day 30. From the pass east of Helvetesnutane there was also great view north over the mountains of Skarvheimen and the next section

meet a couple of friends from Bergen, Tone and Greta, who were coming by train in a few hours, but as there was no room for them in this huge hotel they got off a few stops earlier to ski in a different area. I had a great shower and then picked up my maps for the next section from the post office at the train station, which was almost buried in snow. After a heavy supper and a chat to a few of the kiters whom I met a week ago in Haukeliseter, I had to write and do my washing in the hotel's private machine, which they kindly let me use. I had planned to spend a rest day here but still felt quite fresh and the weather forecast was absolutely perfect. I was also feeling a bit out of place in this busy hotel which was buzzing with the clichéd chat and flashy etiquette of the 150 kiters. It did not sit easily with the almost introspective peace and quiet of the last few weeks. I wanted to return to my pilgrimage through the wonderful Norwegian winter and the serene candle-lit evenings in front of a shimmering stove.

SECTION 3. Hardangervidda.
6 days. 130 km. 46.5 hours. 2960m ascent. 2830m descent.

THE SKI: SECTION 4. SKARVHEIMEN

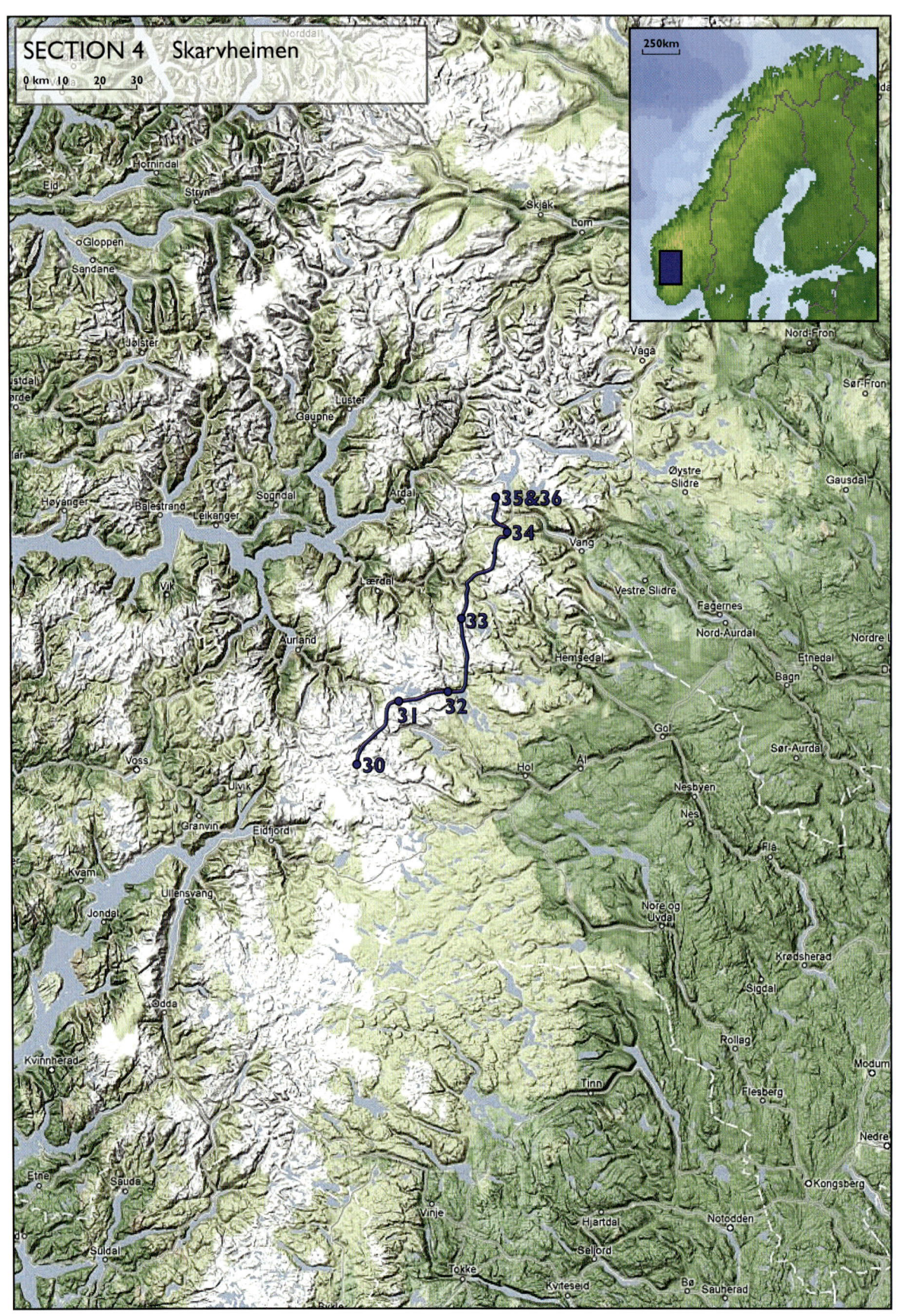

THE SKI: SECTION 4. SKARVHEIMEN

I was up early for an enormous breakfast – I must have eaten some 3000 calories. It was like the breakfast of a condemned man. I then set off as soon as possible as I assumed it would be a long day. It was minus 16 as I skied across the railway line and started to climb up Hallingskarvet ridge on the north side of Finse, towards the small Klemsbu hut near the ridge's crest. Hallingskarvet is a well-known landmark and mountain ridge in this region and is a hard-wearing remnant nappe, or rock group, from the Caledonian time 400 million years ago. It is this ridge which gives this mountainous area its generic name, Skarvheimen. This was not the best route, as the other side was a little steep, but I decided to risk it. The main problem was that the descent from Sankt Pål could be difficult and even avalanche prone. The map showed it was about 25

Day 31. After skiing down the slope from Sankt Pål in the left background I had a lovely ski across Ormsvatnet lake

degrees steep and the recommended winter route took a big detour to the west. As I reached Klemsbu hut the clothes were coming off fast. The chill of the morning was now replaced by the burning heat of the sun and when I finally got to the hut I was down to my wool vest. The views were fantastic. To the south, just beyond Finse, lay the huge dome of the Hardangerjøkulen ice cap in all its glory as an almost flat, slightly rounded,

Day 31. After Geiterygghytta I climbed up the slopes towards a saddle when I came across a herd of 50 wild reindeer foraging in the snow

dome of ice resting on a ring of steeper cliffs and crags. From the hut I continued up to Sankt Pål, a rounded hill on the crest of Hallingskarvet. I could enjoy the views from Sankt Pål in the windstill conditions and under the blazing sun. The descent down the north side of Sankt Pål was not a problem. In fact, it was a lot of fun. The steeper sections were easy to avoid as I sped down some 400 vertical metres descending diagonally across the remnants of small glaciers and snow fonns to reach the outlet of Ormsvatnet lake. By the time I reached the bottom, my muscles were burning with the pain of exertion. The north side was in the shade and considerably colder. From Ormsvatnet lake it was a very pleasant ski eastwards down the gentle valley to Geiterygghytta cabin. It was closed and had no self-service facilities.

I had suspected this and had decided to go all the way to Kongshelleren cabin today, which was another 12 kilometres. I felt fit now, and in these conditions I was not worried about getting to the cabin in the dusk. I passed Geiterygghytta and started straight up the hill to a saddle. It was an easy ascent treading between outcrops and keeping to the smooth, glistening snowfields. About half way up I came across a trampled road of reindeer tracks and then a bit beyond, a herd of about 50 animals. These were the wild Skarvheimen reindeer and were not used to human interaction unless they were being hunted, previously with arrows, and in the last few hundred years with guns. As soon as they saw me, some 500 metres away, they were off. Initially they seemed confused as to which way to go, but then they moved behind me. I then skied through the snowfield

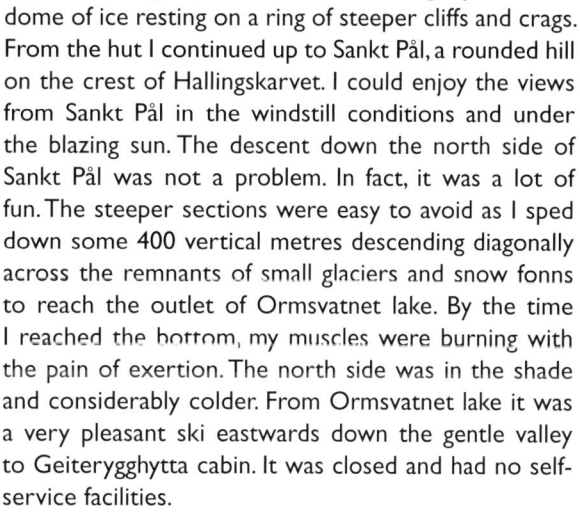

Day 31. It was a wonderful dusk as I skied the last 5 kilometres from Bolhovd mountain to Kongshelleren cabin

Day 32. Inside the cabin at Kongshelleren showing the stove, some of the larder and living area, the bunks are out of the photo to the right

where they had been resting. All the outcrops nearby had been scraped by their hooves, removing the snow to get to their favourite food, reindeer moss. This is a tennis ball sized fluffy bundle of cream-coloured lichen. With the reindeer gone, I carried on in the glorious weather, cresting a small saddle and then crossing a high open valley to another saddle at a prominent gap in the mountains to the east of Bolhovd mountain. As I reached the saddle, the sun set behind me and the smooth mountains to the north turned a shade of rose, then strong pink as the sun disappeared in a blaze of yellow and orange in a cloudless sky behind me. I still had 5 kilometres to go, but I knew it was flat and the clear evening would ensure the dusk light would linger long. The temperature fell quickly to minus 20, so all the clothes went back on again. For the last hour and a half I single-mindedly drove towards the cabin, not stopping. Indeed, I seldom stop at all now during the day except for the odd drink. At late dusk, just before my head torch would normally be put on, but with Venus and the crescent of moon already very bright in the near darkness, I reached Kongshelleren cabin. It was a pearl. Easy to heat, with a well-stocked larder, and once warm had a rustic and cosy ambience. It was only then I realized how tired I was. After a simple dinner I fell asleep in front of the fire, pleased with my effort and the day. When I woke I was too tired to do anything other than go straight to bed. It had been another magnificent day. In fact, today surpassed even yesterday as the best yet on the tour.

I had only planned a short day today to Lungsdalshytta cabin which was a mere 15 kilometres, with much of it downhill. So when I woke quite late at 0700, I treated myself to a lie-in for a further hour. It was nice to enjoy the cabin in the morning without rushing off. I was getting bored of porridge for breakfast so had a tin of ham and another tin of peaches instead. After I did my domestic chores at the cabin I was ready to go at 1000. It was yet another cracking day with just a few half-hearted clouds in the otherwise deep blue sky. There was a very small breeze which chilled the ears until the hat went on. I was sorry to leave Kongshelleren as it was so homely, and I turned to look back at it sitting in the sun in a vast snowfield. I had a lovely easy ski across Vestre then Austre Volavatnet lakes. The snow was fast, the sun was warming the right side of my face and my rucksack did not feel too heavy. At the end of the lakes was a small saddle where I stopped to take some photos and dress up a bit for a long downhill run in the shade. The descent down Vestre Lungsdalen was quite interesting. While most of it was big open bowls there were some steep narrow snow-filled gullies which connected them. The snow was soft and deep for most of this lovely descent. After about 5 kilometres of fun I finally arrived in the main valley of Lungsdalen which was more open and much shallower. Here I passed a small stone

Day 32. Looking back to the cabins at Kongshelleren. The cabin on the left is for living in while the one on the right is the outhouse

Day 32. At the east end of the Volavatnet lakes there was a wonderful descent into the valley ahead called Vestre Lungsdalen

Day 32. In the main Lungsdalen valley looking west back up my tracks as I approached the cabin in the early afternoon

shelter which I later found out was inhabited by an outlaw, Eivind, some 200 years ago. He sought refuge from his enemies in this area and had a few of these stone shelters to move between and evade capture. For 20 summers and winters he somehow managed to survive in these very harsh mountains. When I consider the conditions he must have endured over these 20 winters, I find it quite incredible he lasted so long. From this stone hovel there was a flat 3 kilometres in the blazing sun to Lungsdalshytta cabin. The main lodge was closed but there was a small self-service cabin beside it. After the usual tasks of melting snow and getting the fire going I was ensconced. Again, the cabin was small and cosy and took no time to heat. It was early afternoon and I was delighted to have some leisure time. There was a noise outside and I went to have a look. A local couple with a dog team of 12 huskies dropped in on a day's excursion from a village across the large Djupsvatnet lake. Their dogs were quivering with excitement to get going again and were straining at the sledge's snow anchor while we chatted.

That evening after writing, I thought a lot about my equipment. The terrain is getting flatter and less gnarly, and I now have to choose whether to ditch the rucksack and go for a sledge or not. In theory, this sounds a great idea, but pulks are cumbersome things, and a nightmare in difficult terrain like deep snow in woods, so I would stick with the rucksack. However, I would have another ruthless weight culling session. The first thing to go would be this comfortable, but heavy, 120 litre, 4.5 kilo Bergans rucksack and instead I would revert to my 90 litre X-Pod 2.2 kilo rucksack. I still had a long, long way to go, so it was worth the expense and hassle of getting it over from Edinburgh to shed 2.3 kilos. I decided another 2 kilos could be shed from the first aid and repair kits and some other items I thought I could do without. I would then be down to having a mere 17 kilos on my back as the basic weight. On top of this I would have to add about a kilo a day for provisions. As I headed further north I might have to have a week's worth of provisions which would take me up to 24 kilos which would diminish as I ate my way through the week. Towards the end of such a week it would be easy to ski for long days with under 20 kilos – as I would have to in the months ahead when the daylight increased.

The crimson and orange glow on the underside of the few clouds in the southern sky announced the dawn of yet another day full of promise. I had a slow breakfast, packed, tidied the cabin and set off reasonably late at 0900. As always, when it is clear in the morning it is also cold, and this morning it was very cold, at around minus 20. I could feel it coming through my gloves as I prepared, and had to put on my mitts before I set off. From the cabin there was a short run down to the large Djupsvatnet lake. I traversed down the slope and picked up quite a bit of speed, when I had a spectacular wipe-out. It must have looked quite comical, but luckily there was no-one around to see it. It was a soft landing in the deep powdery snow but as I ploughed head first into it, the snow found a way behind my glasses, into my shirt and even into my ears. It certainly refreshed me. I skied east across Djupsvatnet lake for a few kilometres until I got some telephone reception, then made a call to Øivind so he could get the X-Pod rucksack over from Edinburgh. A couple of kilometres later I reached the Mjolgedalen valley which came down from the north. This was the valley I had to follow for pretty much 14 kilometres to reach Bjordalsbu cabin, and it was stunningly beautiful. I had the sun on my back and the whole

Day 33. Looking back down Mjolgedalen valley to Djupsvatnet lake where Lungsdalen cabin lay

55

valley ahead of me was bathed in sunlight. Huge cornices hung from distant crags, waiting to extend further in the next gale, until their weight gets too much and they break off. There were some old ski tracks to follow, which made ploughing through 10 centimetres of snow much easier. I suspected that they belonged to two men who were also skiing the length of Norway, who had set off about a week ahead of me. Generally, the snow over the last few days had begun to consolidate and freeze into a firmer pack since the big falls, which had finished some 10 days ago. The few clouds of the morning sky had now vanished, to leave a dark blue sky over the white, untouched mountain wilderness.

Day 33. In the upper reaches of Mjolgedalen valley I came across some reindeer and wolverine tracks

As I entered a narrow part of the valley I came across some reindeer tracks and soon after, I noticed some wolverine tracks. Wolverine are remarkable animals, who belong to the Mustelid family, like stoats or pine martins, and like the other members of this genus they are supreme predators. Indeed, pound for pound, Mustelids are almost certainly the most formidable and bravest predators there are. Wolverines are the biggest land-based members of this family, and a large adult can weigh up to 25 kilos, making them very fearsome beasts. Wolverine easily kill reindeer. Their large fearsome paws support their weight well on snow and they can out run reindeer in soft deep snow. They are also very cunning beasts and will ambush reindeer from trees or crags by launching themselves on to the reindeer's back. Once they have clamped their vice like jaws with large teeth on to the reindeer they will not let go, no matter what the reindeer does. Eventually the reindeer will tire and the wolverine will bring it down and kill it. It is often thought wolverine kill for fun as they kill more than is necessary. While this is true, the wolverine does not waste the excess, but caches the carcasses in crevices or buries them in snow drifts. It will return to these caches when food is lean, possibly many months later in the winter. It has a remarkable memory and will dig straight down to the cache through many metres of snow to the exact spot without having to excavate needlessly. Unfortunately, wolverine will also take sheep in the summer, which for them are a ridiculously easy prey. So farmers and herders of domestic reindeer, mainly Lapps, hate the wolverine and persecute them mercilessly and have done for centuries. Although protected by law now, some illegal persecution continues. However, the wolverine is a very cunning animal and can often avoid hunters, even on snow scooters. Consequently they are very elusive and I have only seen one in 30 years and that was in north Sweden.

I passed a couple of lakes before reaching the crest of a shallow pass at 1620 metres, the highest I had been on the tour so far. From the pass there was a barely discernible descent past a couple of tarns to Øvre Bjordalsvatn lake. The sun was occasionally hidden by surrounding mountains and in the shade it was bitterly cold, easily cold enough to freeze my eyelashes together momentarily when I blinked. The cabin was just at the end of the lake and already in the shade. It was a beautiful cabin, better than I remembered from 25 years ago. Within half an hour I had lit the fire and started to melt enough snow for my stay. It took a while to warm the cabin up though as it was minus 12 inside when I arrived, but it was above zero after an hour or so. By early evening, when I went outside, the crystal clear night was a bitter minus 29. The constellations were plentiful. Cassiopeia (the distinctive 'W' shape

Day 33. The last part of the day involved skiing across Øvre Bjordalsvatn lake towards the cabin which was very cold on arrival

formed by five bright stars), pointed the way to the fainter North Star around which everything in the Northern Hemisphere revolved. The narrow crescent of the moon was filling again as new moon had recently passed. Returning to the warmth of the cabin and the stove was a delight. It had been yet another fantastic day, and like yesterday, I had time to enjoy it.

Day 34. The descent into the parabolic bowl on the north side of Breidstølen, and once out of the shade it soon warmed up.

I was up early at 0600 and ready to go after a breakfast of canned stew just after 0700. However, it was still pitch dark outside where it was also minus 21, with a bitterly cold south wind which cut through all my clothing. Eventually, by 0730 I could just see into the new dawn and set off knowing it would be a long day. The run down to Breidstølen was very pleasant, except for the bitter wind. Within an hour I had already gone 4 kilometres when the sun rose, turning the surrounding hills pink and then yellow. Soon the wind vanished and the warmth of the sun made me feel much more comfortable. The final descent to Breidstølen was down a wide snow-filled gully. It was a beautiful descent, swinging from one side to the other for a good half hour. I had dropped some 400 vertical metres and reached the icy valley floor, covered in willow scrub which poked through the snow pack. Breidstølen lodge was closed, as I suspected it would be, so I had to continue for 19 kilometres to Sulebu cabin, but it was still quite early. I took my gloves off to phone about the rucksack again and almost instantly my hands were stinging with cold. I started the climb to Sulebu cabin at 1100. It was a gentle ascent through the upper limits of the birch forest and then on to the wide expansive white mountain plateau. To the west there was a gash in this plateau which was so deep I could just see the top of it. This 1000-metre deep valley was Lærdalen, renowned for its precipitous sides. Just beyond Lærdalen was the end of a fjord some 30 kilometres away from me now. Indeed, the whole time on this trip so far I have never been far from the heads of fjords which cut numerous deep slots into these mountains.

The ascent eventually took me over a narrow saddle. On the other side of the saddle there was a wonderful descent into a south-facing bowl. This bowl was hot and I soon had to shed clothes. It was like a giant parabola which concentrated the sun's rays in the middle, which was where I was. I then rounded a significant craggy mountain called Masseringsnosi and turned north. I was on the home straight climbing up a gentle valley to a shallow pass. At the top of the valley I got a surprise. There, ahead of me in perfect view, some 40 kilometres to the north, was the Hurrungane massif. I had no idea I would be able to see these mountains from here.

The Hurrungane massif is perhaps the most alpine of all the mountains in Scandinavia. One of the mountains, Store Skagastølstind, the Matterhorn of Jotunheimen, was the birthplace for Norwegian mountaineering. It looked especially grand and impressive, even at this distance. Just across the other side of the massif was the equally imposing Austanbottstind, perhaps my favourite mountain in Scandinavia. The Hurrungane mountains are very dear to me; I spent several fantastic summers scrambling along their ridges and have also written a book on the area, so I was thrilled to see them. Some 6 kilometres in front of me was my final hurdle for the day, a long but easy climb to an obvious saddle between two mountains. I was tiring as I slowly clawed my way up. I was expecting another wonderful view on the other side. This view would be of the two massifs just to the north of lake Bygdin which were

Day 34. Looking north towards Hurrungane with Austanbottstind on the left and the darker point of Store Skagastølstind to the right

Day 34. Alpenglow over the Gjendealpene to the north of Bygdin lake from Sletmarkpiggen to Torfinnstind. Sulebu cabin is the bottom right

also in the Jotunheimen. As I neared the saddle the sun was setting so I blasted up the last 2 kilometres to catch the view before the sun vanished. I just made it and it was worth the hurry. The whole of the southern parts of the Gjendealpene, the craggy mountains between the lakes Bygdin and Gjende, were coated in a pink alpenglow off the setting sun. I paused here basking in one of the finest sunsets I have seen over my cherished Jotunheimen. After many photos the chill set in and I made the quick descent down the other side, crossing a lake and reaching Sulebu cabin just before I felt the need to dig out my head torch. It was a lovely small cabin and I soon had it warmed up and cosy. It had been another magnificent day. I am running out of complimentary superlatives to describe the weather. To have come across Hardangervidda and through most of Skarvheimen with one misty day in otherwise excellent weather is exceptional. I have been a lucky man indeed. There were some old visitor's books in the cabin and I found an entry I made on 20/03/84. It was the first night of my first ski trip, when I did Skarvheimen north to south.

From Sulebu I had the choice of going down to Tyinkrysset lodge for a night and then up to Fondsbu lodge. Alternatively, I could go to Slettningsbu cabin and then over the lake to Fondsbu. I had no reason to go to Tyinkrysset and thought I would prefer the peace of the isolated cabin to the noisy busy atmosphere of a ski resort, which might be like the Finse 1222 hotel. I decided to go to Slettningsbu cabin. I knew the route to Tyinkrysset was very short and assumed the one to Slettningsbu was also short and I felt no urgency. I was not really ready until 1100. It was far too late and I should have known better. Outside, it was minus 10 with snow showers and some mist and a slight breeze, but it was perfectly feasible to ski. How I had been spoilt over the last week with the spell of great weather. The way to Kyrkjestølen looked like it was marked with small branches or kvisters. The visibility was poor and I was glad for the twig markers which did indeed go all the way to Kyrkjestølen. They helped show me if the terrain was rising or falling as the enveloping mist was disorientating me, the undulating tundra almost indistinguishable from the sky. After a couple of hours the markers started to lead down to the birch forest in the valley below. It was quite steep in places, and not being able to see the snow well, I crashed once. Eventually the markers reached the valley floor where there was a collection of some 50 cabins, many of which were converted from old pastoral summer farms. There was also a small church. There was a major road which went through this hamlet, the main road between Oslo and Bergen but like the hamlet it was snowy and deserted. This road has historical connections and was a road once travelled by royalty some centuries ago. I crossed the snow-covered road with my skis still on and paused for a break in the minor blizzard by the church. I thought about camping here but it was only another 8 kilometres to go and I still had four hours of daylight. So, despite the weather I continued, knowing there would be no markers on the open plateau ahead. Initially I had to climb out of the north side of the valley. It was incredibly hard work. Despite the mild blizzard I was sweating with exertion as I climbed. Under the surface of the deep snow were juniper bushes. As I pressed down the juniper bush collapsed into a hole which I then had to step out of, so I made very slow progress. It took about two hours to ascend the short steep slope through the deep snow of the birch woods. The short skins were hopeless in this situation and I had by now made up my mind they were not the best solution. I think a waxless fish scale ski base would have been better and then I could use slightly heavier, full-length skis in situations like this.

Once I was up to Slettningen lake things got easier, but it was difficult to see in the near blizzard. It was now snowing heavily with a force 5 or 6 plastering the snow on to my windward side, building up a thick layer. With compass and GPS I slowly made my way across this lake and up the difficult featureless slope on the other side. I was running out of daylight and my GPS still said I had 3 kilometres to go. This would be another head torch finish. I climbed a final ridge in the very late dusk and started the descent down the other side virtually in the dark. I went over a small two-metre cornice which I just had not seen. After I dusted the snow off, I dug around the rucksack and got my head torch out. There was still 2 kilometres to go which would take at least two hours. It was a very surreal experience wandering about in the dark in a blizzard in the middle of winter. My world was limited to about three metres, and most of that was obscured by spindrift flashing in front of the meagre ray my head torch was producing. I thought about camping a couple of times, but my clothes were damp with sweat from the climb and my outer jacket was frozen stiff. Even my boots felt damp. All this would freeze solid and be somewhat unpleasant to get into again tomorrow morning. So I continued to the cabin, homing in metre by metre, being cautious and slow. The thought of a fire glowing in a shimmering hot stove and a larder with tinned food was my overriding consideration as I slowly homed in on the invisible cabin. Eventually, after a few disorientating events and stumbles I made out the cabin some 30 metres away, two hours after complete darkness had fallen. When I got to it I had to dig a large drift from the front door. Inside it was minus 8. The previous occupiers had left kindling, newspaper and matches beside the fire. This used to be the custom, but I have seldom seen it on this trip so far. After an hour the cabin was warming and I was looking into the flames with a tin of peaches. It had been worth the humiliating fumble around in the dark and near blizzard to get here. It had been a much harder day than I had anticipated, and in hindsight I should have gone to Tyinkrysset and avoided the steep climb from Kyrkjestølen.

Day 36. Slettningsbu where I spent a rest day recovering after a difficult afternoon and evening when I arrived in a blizzard after dark

When daybreak came at 0800 I was still in bed. I was tired, especially my legs. I got up to have a look outside, and to my disappointment it was a beautiful day. No excuses then. However, the angel perched on one shoulder and who was egging me on to Fondsbu was quickly questioned by the devil perched on the other. You're late, your legs are tired, your Achilles are sore, some vertebrae are aching and you're due a day off. It was a one-sided debate and I returned to bed after throwing some logs into the stove. I don't have any concerns as yet, the only problems I can foresee are my lower back or my heels. I have to take a little bit of care of them. I can always get to Nordkinn a day or two late, but with a ruptured Achilles tendon I won't be going anywhere. If my back deteriorated I could revert to a sledge and sacrifice some kilometres every day. I eventually got up at midday. When I did get up I cleaned out the stove and was amazed at how much more efficient it was without the extra ash clogging it up. Then I ate a few tins of meat and ham. I have lost a few kilos but am not too concerned about losing weight yet. I need some reserves for the north where supplies will be infrequent. I then spent the afternoon reading old walking magazines in the cabin and working out my route to Røros. I only left the cabin once, and that was to get another bag of wood from the outhouse. Sensibly the wood supplied to these cabins is silver birch, a wood with an enormous heat to weight ratio, compared to spruce. In addition, the bark of birch contains a lot of tar so it is easy to light. By the evening I felt well rested and even bored so was eager to get off tomorrow to the next place, which was Fondsbu lodge. I knew it would be closed and wasn't sure if it had some self-service facilities, or if I would have to camp. I enjoyed my leisure day at Slettningsbu cabin. It has been good for me to relax in its warm, candle-lit ambience. This was effectively the end of the fourth section, Skarvheimen, and tomorrow I start the fifth section, Jotunheimen, The Home of The Giants.

SECTION 4. Skarvheimen.
6 days. 109 km. 37 hours. 3270m ascent. 3030m descent.

THE SKI: SECTION 5. JOTUNHEIMEN

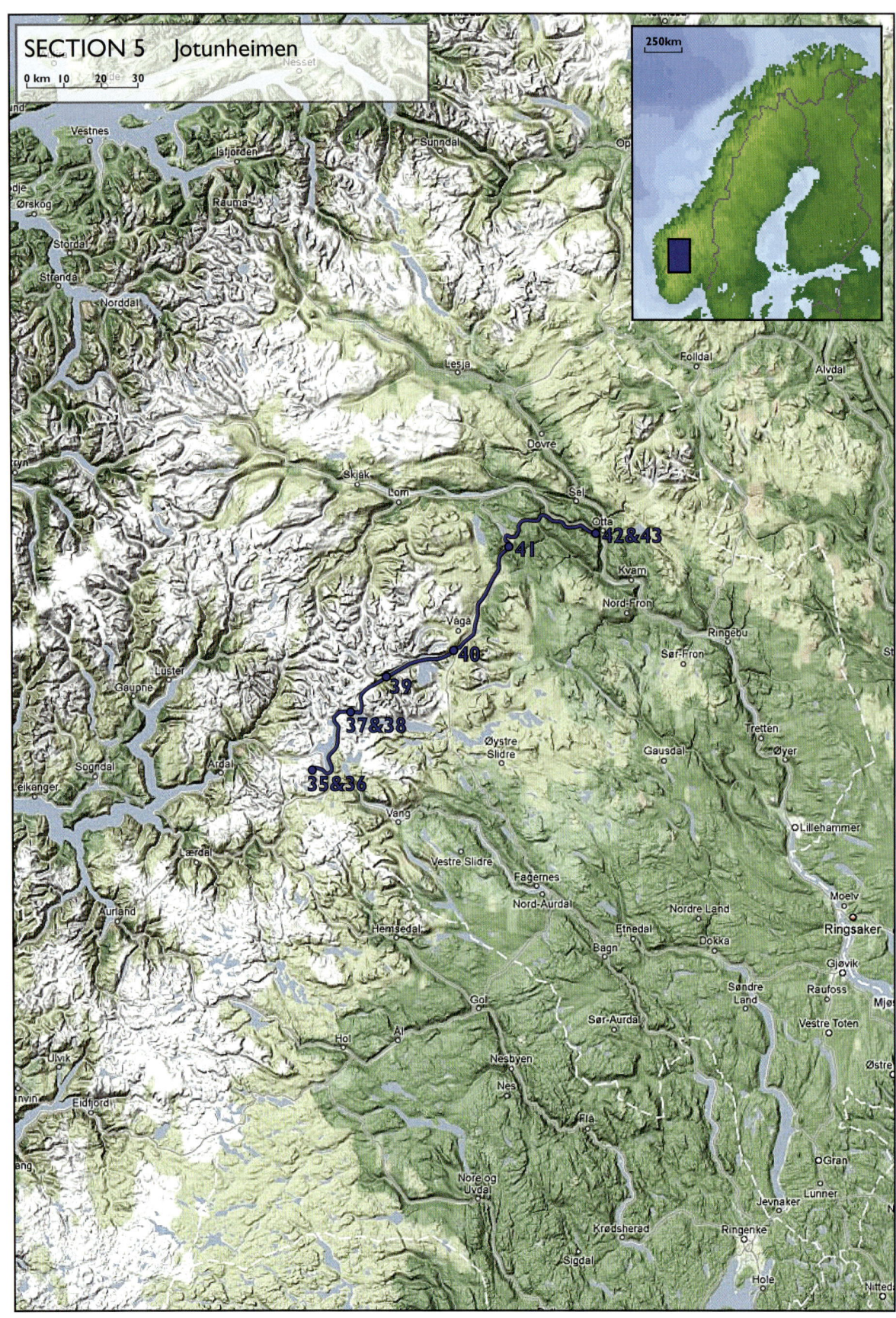

THE SKI: SECTION 5. JOTUNHEIMEN

It was snowing when I got up and the visibility was terrible. I could hardly see the outhouse some 25 metres away due to the snow and mist, luckily the wind was negligible. I did not feel in top form. I had an irritating cough and all my joints felt sore. I also felt a bit weak, as if I had some minor flu, but after yesterday's rest day I could not really afford to sit around another day. There was an unknown 3 kilometre section between Slettningsbu and Tyinstølen where the maps I had did not meet up, but I thought it would be easy to follow the compass and GPS. Before I left at 0930 I entered the location of Tyinstølen and Fondsbu lodge into my fiddly GPS. Tyinstølen was the first waypoint just 4 kilometres to the east. Outside, the visibility was as bad as ever on the knobbly terrain. I sometimes could not see the ground beyond my skis. I did not know if it was going up or down. In addition, there was a lot of deep snow. Progress was very slow at about a kilometre an hour and occasionally I had to throw snowballs again. Pretty soon I was off the map and into the uncharted area when I was confronted by a craggy ridge which loomed out of the mist. I could not go over so decided to go south rather than north to skirt it. It was easier to go south along what I thought was a lake. In retrospect this was a mistake as I had to keep heading south for nearly 3 kilometres, but if I had gone north I would have reached the steep slopes down to Tyinstølen in a short time. Instead of reaching the large frozen Tyin lake at Tyinstølen, I reached it at its very southern end some 3 kilometres to the south. This error cost me at least two hours, probably three. I was also still feeling weak and my joints were sore. It had been a bad morning. I should have stayed at Slettningsbu cabin and nursed my cold rather than flounder about the deep snow and mist wasting energy. In hindsight I also realized that going to Slettningsbu was a mistake, and I should have gone from Sulebu to Tyinkrysset. The detour to Slettningsbu had already cost me a rest day yesterday and now this morning I had squandered masses of energy by taking a very long detour. The chances of getting to Fondsbu lodge were fading rapidly and I would probably have to camp en route, a prospect I did not relish in my condition.

When I at last got out of these mountains I found myself on the road immediately below the very south end of Tyin lake. Just above me is an endless building project, which is a bit of an eyesore, where incongruous flats are being built which do not fit into the landscape, natural or cultural, at all. Usually when I passed here it was deserted, but now the owner of this project was here, overseeing some work and clearing snow. I chatted with him and he told me the lady who runs Fondsbu lodge was already there preparing to open in a week's time. I knew this lady, Solbjørg Kvålshaugen, from the days when I was climbing all the 2000-metre peaks, and we got on well. I gave her a ring with the last efforts of the battery. I asked if Fondsbu was open. "Not officially, but that's not a problem. We will be delighted to see you. The shower water is hot and you can have dinner with us. You're most welcome." My luck had completely changed. It was music to my ears. Not only did I not have to camp at Fondsbu but there was a warm welcome waiting. I still had 19 kilometres to go and it was well after midday, so I would arrive in the dark, but there was a marked track and this had been compacted by snow scooters so it should be easy, I thought. The route took me along the entire east side of Tyin lake. It was a great shame it was poor weather as this was one of the best views in Jotunheimen, especially towards the sharp pyramid of Uranostind and the tower of Falketind. It was a long ski with very little to see except for the private leisure cabins which dotted the shoreline. Most of these cabins were very tasteful and looked very picturesque with their log walls and grass roofs. I eventually reached Tyinholmen at the north end of the lake. It was dusk now but the moon was breaking through the mist and just shedding enough light. I was very tired though and both my Achilles tendons were sore, as were my hip joints. It would be another rest day tomorrow for sure, whatever the weather. I had a final 4 kilometres to go over a small rise and a final easy descent to reach Fondsbu lodge. From the top of the rise I could see the lights, it was a great relief and a welcome sight.

Solbjørg could not have been more helpful and I was soon in the shower. It was as much therapy as hygiene. After the shower there was a supper which far exceeded my expectations. Copious amounts of tender organic reindeer steak and heaps of fresh vegetables, all washed down by a very complimentary Italian red. Solbjørg (a well travelled and knowledgeable lady), the caretaker and myself, then spent the rest of the evening chatting about many topics, especially history. I eventually got to bed at midnight with my muscles and tendons still sore. It had been a very varied day, from the frustrating despair of being lost off the map and floundering about in whiteout conditions, then a long tiring ski, and finally the best evening of the year so far.

It was overcast and snowing lightly outside so I did not feel too guilty about a rest day. After breakfast I visited the library in Fondsbu and immersed myself in their books, including many that were newly published about the

Day 38. The Eidsbugarden hotel was built at the end of the 19th Century and has recently been restored to its former glory

Norwegian mountains. After a simple lunch the weather improved, and although it was still overcast some views appeared. I put my skis on and went for a short ski round the newly restored Eidsbugarden hotel and past some of the 100 or so leisure cabins at Eidsbugarden. The turf roofs of the cabins were heavy with snow and drifts covered some of the windows. One of the cabins here was once occupied by Aasmund Vinje, a well-known and respected political thinker and poet from the mid 19th Century. He was born in humble rural circumstances, but with the help of patrons and his own hunger to learn, he eventually graduated with a law degree and worked in the justice department. Norway at this time was ruled by, and indeed was part of, Sweden. Norway had also been subjected to Danish rule and its cultural influences and the official language of Norway, called Riksmål, was of Danish origin. Vinje belonged to a small but vociferous group of radicals who didn't like these political and cultural foreign dominances. He made frequent protests and his rebellious stance earned him further patronage among the patriotic but conservative Norwegians. Having spent a considerable time in Oslo, Vinje forgot about the Norwegian countryside he grew up in. However, on his way to write about and protest against the coronation of the Swedish King Charles in the Nidarosdomen Cathedral in Trondheim in 1860, he encountered the mountain region of Rondane. For him it was a road to Damascus moment and it reawakened his childhood appreciation of nature. Vinje also travelled in England and Scotland in 1862. He published a book on these travels in Edinburgh called A Norseman's View of Britain and the British. In it he dwelt on social injustices, especially the Highland clearances of the Scots peasant farmers, whom he warmed to.

Day 38. Aasmund Vinje's cabin at Eidsbugarden was where he found sanctuary in nature towards the end of his remarkable life

With his newly-awakened appreciation for Norwegian nature, Vinje spent a while looking for a perfect spot to immerse himself into it, and he eventually found a small spit of land at the west end of Bygdin lake. He borrowed some money from his patrons and built a small cabin that he named Eidsbugarden on this then deserted spot. He spent a couple of summers here, the first with friends, the second with the recent and only love of his life. During this period he wrote some significant Norwegian poems. It was Vinje who named this mountainous area Jotunheimen, The Home of The Giants. He wrote in Nynorsk, a mixture of Norwegian dialects, which created a new language, aiming to distinguish itself from the Danish-influenced Riksmål. Today, Vinje is considered one of the founding fathers of independent Norwegian culture. After a couple of years, Vinje suffered a tragic loss, when his only love died in childbirth and he passed away soon after with stomach cancer, probably encouraged by a broken heart. The cabin was taken over by a patron called Thomas Heftye who was the first leader of the newly-formed Den Norske Turistforening (DNT) which roughly

Day 39. Looking east down Bygdin lake from Eidsbugarden with Høystakkane crag on the very left below the mountain of Galdeberget

Day 39. Looking west from near Høystakkane toward the lodges and cabins at Eidsbugarden with the mountain of Falketind beyond

translates as The Norwegian Trekking Association. Heftye built the start of the current Eidsbugarden hotel around Vinje's cabin, and Fondsbu lodge was part of the outbuildings of the hotel until recently. Vinje had a very strong attachment to Eidsbugarden, so much so it is still associated with his ideals and cherished in current Norwegian culture through his poems. After pondering Vinje that afternoon, I earned my keep by helping Solbjørg and the caretaker carry boxes of drinks and kitchen equipment around to prepare for the lodge's opening. That evening, the meal was another delicious affair, with lots of stir-fried vegetables and a bottle of red wine – with further conversations about the history of Eidsbugarden and Norway in general. Tomorrow I would leave for Gjendebu cabin feeling well rested and nourished. I still had a lingering cough, but that is minor compared to how I felt when I arrived at Fondsbu lodge, just 24 hours previously.

After a great breakfast I set off at 0930 and headed east on to Bygdin lake. The snow was up to 30 centimetres deep which slowed me down a lot. But the weather was near perfect. I felt very good and my strength had returned. Initially I was going to go up the east side of a huge crag called Høystakkane where it was not too steep. As I skied down the lake I reconsidered this route, as it was up a sheltered bowl, where even more new snow might have blown and settled. So Instead I went up the west side following the ridge beside the Høystakka river. It was a bit steeper but the snow was firm and in many places the old snow from last week was still exposed. I think my gamble paid off as I got up quite easily. The weather was improving all the time but there was a bitter north breeze which cut straight through my fleece leggings. It was a small price to pay for the views and clarity. Behind me, the iconic Falketind, much loved by Vinje, rose into a sharp spite of steep rock covered in white snow. Below me, I could still see Eidsbugarden at the end of the flat expanse of white, which was the frozen Bygdin. In front of me, Galdeberget, the final and easy 2000-metre peak I did a few years

Day 39. Perfect weather in soft snow in the hanging valley to the north of Bygdin lake permitted me to have an euphoric ski

ago with my Bergenser friend, Arne Instebø. As I skied along the flat valley, more and more of the 'giants' of Jotunheimen appeared, most notably Snøhøltind and Slettmarkpiggen, one on each side of the valley, which I had also climbed with Arne. It was nostalgic to be back among these very familiar mountains. The ski up this high valley to the watershed between Geithøi and Rundtom was absolutely enchanting. I was floating across the perfect snow in stunning weather, leaving an almost mystical trail behind me, undulating down the smooth white slopes of the high valley. I took my time here absorbing the euphoric feelings which this immense grandeur of Jotunheimen inspired.

Day 39. Snøhøltind is one of my familiar 101 giants of Jotunheimen over 2000 metres and was plastered in deep snow when I went past

At the untouched watershed, buried under huge drifts and fields of virgin snow, I crossed over into Veslådalen

Day 39. Slettmarkpiggen is another of 101 giants in the Jotunheimen and had a vast glacier on the north side in the centre

valley. The huge Slettmarkbreen glacier almost flowed right into this valley, its bulbous front stopping just at the lip of the huge bowl it had carved on the north side of Slettmarkpiggen and Slettmarkhøe mountains. While further down Veslådalen the valley weaved between smooth spurs to the frozen Gjende lake. Its white unblemished surface fringed by the dark birch woods. At the east end of the lake was the snow-covered bulk of Besshøe and just beyond the famous Besseggen arête. The descent to the lake was lovely. I had taken off my skins and I glided down through the deep powder to the upper limit of the birch forest. Here, the terrain flattened a bit and I had to push one ski in front of the other. As the forest thickened, so did the traces of ptarmigan or willow grouse. Soon the most majestic of all the mountains in this area, Knutsholstind, 'a fine mountain for a lady' (the lady being Marie Sølfestdatter in 1881), showed its very lofty and steep pyramid-shaped summit. It was early dusk as I skied through the last of the birch trees to arrive at the cabin at Gjendebu. This place normally has a lodge, but when the lodge is closed a self-service cabin is made available. The cabin was poorly equipped but had a stove and a good larder. Getting wood was terrible as I had to wade through many hundreds of metres of thigh-deep snow to get to the wood shed and then drag the sack back. It got very cold, around minus 20, but the stove kept the cabin warm. As the full moon rose from behind a ridge and brightened up the sky, I could reflect on the best skiing day so far, as I melted snow and prepared a simple meal by candle light.

I was slow to get going and didn't leave the cabin until 1000. It was overcast with the occasional snow shower, and there was a gentle westerly breeze, which would thankfully be behind me. After closing the cabin I set off along the Gjende lake which is 19 kilometres long. The snow was deep and sometimes I didn't see my skis as they travelled beneath it without breaking the surface. It had all the potential of a long, slow epic slog up the entire length of the frozen lake.

Day 39. High up in Veslådalen, the conditions were magical and enchanting as I floated through the soft snow

There was the occasional flash of blue sky as I skied up the lake, especially over the east end and over Besseggen arête. Pretty soon these occasional flashes of blue combined into long periods. It was a spectacular sight to look down the frozen lake in its deep slot, flanked by dark mountains on each side, with Besseggen glowing in full sun. As I reached Memurubu lodge, which was closed for the winter, the wind started to get up a bit and soon was a strong force 6. The lake's surface was a flowing sea of spindrift, heading east at 15 metres a second. It was bitterly cold but at least I was not going into it. The further east I went, the firmer the snow became. Soon I was drawing level with the daunting Besseggen, which is a fabulous arête to the north of Gjende lake. This arête is a popular walk and has become something of a Norwegian rite-of-passage.

Day 39. Looking down the smooth Veslådalen, towards the woods where Gjendebu cabin lay, and then the flat Gjende lake beyond

In the summer, up to 40,000 people walk along its narrow rocky spine with the green waters of Gjende lake to the south and the blue waters of Bessvatnet lake to the north. Besseggen first became established in Norwegian culture in the 19th Century, when Henrik Ibsen included it in his story on Peer Gynt. In the story, Peer Gynt rode a reindeer along the ridge before they both fell off into the lake. It seems that the fictitious Peer Gynt is the only one who has ever fallen off. On the opposite side of the lake was Knutshøe. It is a steep crescent-shaped arête fringed by smaller lakes on the south side of Gjende. Many people suspect it was Knutshøe which Henrik Ibsen described as the arête by Gjende lake rather than Besseggen in the verse:

Day 40. Skiing along Gjende lake at Memurubu with the sharp Besseggen arête in the centre of the picture

"Have you ever chanced to see the Gendin-Edge?
Nigh on four miles long it stretches sharp before you like a scythe.
Down o'er glaciers, landslips, scaurs, down the toppling grey moraines,
you can see, both right and left, straight into the tarns that slumber,
black and sluggish, more than seven hundred fathoms deep below you."

Day 40 Knutshøe to the south of Gjende lake is a crescent-shaped arête which some believe is the *Gendin-Edge* to which Ibsen refers

Soon Gjendesheim lodge appeared, which is owned by the Den Norske Turistforening (DNT), and is one of their flagship lodges. I reached the end of the lake, passing the two summer passenger ferries hauled out of the water and sitting marooned in a snowfield being lashed by spindrift. The lodge was open, but not for business. I went in for a chocolate and a chat with the manager, Olav Gaute Vole, who I knew from some years ago. He phoned Bessheim lodge to arrange a room for me. There was still 5 kilometres to go. It was along a road that in the summer was a busy artery, but in the winter it was closed higher up on Valdresflya, so effectively it was a cul-de-sac now serving a few barely open lodges. It was deserted and, although snow-ploughed, it was still covered in snow. I skied down the middle of the road for the 5 kilometres to Bessheim lodge. It was a nice sunset and the bitter wind had now vanished because I was away from Gjende lake. I reached Bessheim at 1800 while it was still dusk. Bessheim lodge was originally a seter, or summer farm, for Storvik farm beside Vågå lake 40 kilometres to the north. It catered for the odd tourist in the mid to late 1800s. In 1890 a designated tourist cabin was built, and this characterful old timber building forms the kernel of the current lodge, which has been modernized and enlarged over its 120-year history. During this time it has been owned and managed by the same family, and the current hostesses, Kari and Ragnhild are the fifth generation. I was given a simple room with a shower and then a nice healthy Norwegian meal. In the evening I went into the rustic lounge to write in front of the open fire.

After breakfast at Bessheim I had to make a few phone calls as the rucksack I had ordered a week ago was stuck in customs. The officials were being rather pedantic and wanted a particular invoice for the tax calculation. I tried to get this invoice sent from the UK. When I did leave, it was a cold, crystal clear and crisp morning and the mercury was minus 23. I could feel the cold penetrating through my boots and gloves and stinging my exposed cheeks. Initially I crossed Øvre Sjodalsvatnet lake to the east side, where I'd been told there were some ski trails. I found them and they were very good. I skied north past a few cabins, their roofs thick with snow. The occasional pine tree added some green to the otherwise dark birch forest. Much was still in the shade, but in the sun everything shone with brilliance. I skied along the trail to the north end of the lake and then over a forested peninsula to the smaller lake of Nedre Sjodalsvatnet. The pines were becoming more plentiful now and the sun higher. The landscape was looking like a painting. I passed many more cabins, some over 100 years old and others more modern, but traditional. At the north end of Nedre Sjodalsvatnet I crossed the snow-covered and deserted main road and climbed to a collection of summer farms, unmatched for their idyllic setting. These centuries old summer farms are still working and are run by farmers from Vågå. They are two days walk from Vågå and the animals stay up here until the late autumn before they return to the valley. For this reason, the summer farms are substantial, and the barns have haylofts to feed the animals in the autumn and winter before they return to the main farms. They are well preserved because of the good quality pine logs, a dry climate in the rain shadow of Jotunheimen and the usual Norwegian attention to detail on maintenance. From these idyllic farms there was a beautifully prepared trail through pine forests to the lovely old tourist lodge at Hindsæter, surrounded by more gorgeous summer farms.

Day 41. Looking south from Bessheim towards Tjønnholstind which is another of the 101 giants over 2000 metres in the Jotunheimen

Day 41 A picture postcard cabin to the north of Nedre Sjodalsvatnet lake is still part of a *seter* or summer farm

Hindsæter lodge, a 110-year-old summer farm, seemed extremely well run and maintained. It was upmarket, but was busy with guests who were enjoying the ski trails the owners made daily in both directions in the forests. After a coffee at Hindsæter I continued north along the very beautiful Sjodalen valley in glorious sunshine. The pines glowed against the white snow. I was skiing through a postcard in an enchanted forest. After crossing an old log bridge the trail ended and I headed down to the snow-covered main road. Moose tracks were everywhere as they sought out buds and bark from birch trees. Once on the main road I skied along it for 10 kilometres. Only in Norway could I double pole on skis down the middle of a national road, in this case the Riksveg 51. On some downhill sections I was going a good 20 kilometres per hour. It was getting late but I had already booked a small timber cabin at Randsverk. The owner would be away until the early evening, but the key would be in the door and the electric heater on. Just before Randsverk a couple of moose crossed the road in front of me. They lumbered off into the pine forest, sinking in the snow on long ungainly legs, designed to move in deep snow. Having not seen many moose, I was very excited, and nearly careered into them. At dusk I reached Randsverk. It was another collection of summer and autumn farms. Every farm was a collection of timber barns and outbuildings. They were made out of big twisted logs, darkened with age and the sun. The houses smelt of ancient wood which had been preserved with Stockholm tar, a natural protective coating. Randsverk was a living museum. I found my cabin in the campground nearby, it was as expected. I made myself

Day 41. The *seters* or summer farms at Ormhaugen between Bessheim and Hindsæter were absolutely idyllic

at home and then went to meet Nina and Hans Petter Brag who ran the site. Nina opened the small shop for me and kindly gave me an elg salami for the next day, and numerous cups of coffee in their cosy house, while the kids did homework. When I returned to my cabin, silently walking along the soft frosty track, it was bitterly cold outside at minus 27, and it would get much colder yet. A huge full moon was just rising up through the pines like a giant yellow Christmas decoration. It had been a magnificent day, one of the best so far. It was wonderful to be in the comfortable pine forests, after the last five weeks of snow-covered barren mountain wilderness, where I was almost constantly well above the treeline of 1000 metres.

Day 41. The well run and historic Hindsæter lodge prepared ski trails through the tranquil pine forest in the valley above and below it

Day 41. I was able to ski down the middle of the Riksveg 51 main road as it was still covered in snow

It was very cold in the morning, minus 37 to be precise. The air was stinging my face and penetrating my trousers. I said goodbye to Nina and Hans Petter and set off up the snow-covered road for the 4 kilometres to Lemonsjøen. It was just after 0800 and very light now. The road was quite tedious and uphill all the way to Lemonsjøen lodge. At the lodge I left the road as advised and headed east to Slomma on prepared tracks. It was fantastic, skiing along the easy track among pine trees thick with snow. Slomma itself was a beautiful collection of summer farms overlooking a tarn. It was very pretty and in the bright sun looked idyllic. Just beyond Slomma was the old, rustic, picture-perfect Grønstulen summer farm. The prepared track stopped here but luckily there were some old compacted tracks in the deep snow where other skiers had been in the last 3-4 days. Their tracks now headed north over the east shoulder of Gråhøi hill. From the top of the shoulder I was out of the forest and could see over to the white rounded mountains of Rondane, the mountains of the next section. The view was crystal clear and they were perhaps 35 kilometres away. From the shoulder I dropped down the other side to Melingen lake. This descent was absolutely enthralling. If yesterday was skiing in a postcard, this was skiing through a fairytale. Amongst the pines were numerous old log cabins and summer farms basking in sunny clearings. Across the valley on the south-facing slopes, rising up from Melingen lake, were many more summer farms. This hidden valley was a Shangri-La and one of the prettiest sights I have seen in Norway.

Unfortunately, the time came to leave the valley when I reached Reiret. I now followed the icy road north east into the very cold, shaded Rinddalen. The road then became steep and clung to the side of the main Ottadalen valley as it went down numerous hairpin bends towards the large U-shaped valley floor. On one of these bends, quite far down, was an even smaller road, heading east which I took. This smaller road took me past some large farms and eventually down to the valley floor on the small road which went along the

Day 42. Between Lemonsjø and Slomma there were prepared ski trails through the enchanting forest for many kilometres

Day 42. After going over the shoulder of Gråhøi I had a wonderful descent past fairy-tale scenery and cabins to Melingen lake

south side of the River Otta. It was in the shade and bitterly cold. I walked along this road for 15 kilometres as there was a lot of grit and gravel in the snow beside the road. It was a change to walk and reminded me of the first days. I rejoiced at how much fitter I am now, as the 15 kilometres was now a breeze. This shaded south side of the road was not prime land because of the shade in all but the high summer months. None the less, there were some nice farms here. Some were quite grand, with avenues of hanging birch flanking the driveway. Everything was covered in a thick white frost. A good kilometre before Otta I reached the campsite, and the end of the Jotunheimen section. I was meeting a couple of friends here and they had already booked a very nice cabin and arrived almost at the same time as me. The friends, Hartmut and Øivind, were my self-styled support team. They arrived with red wine, lamb curry, long drinks and much humour. My new rucksack was still in customs, however. We had a long evening of curry, wine and chat. I could consume wine and long drinks without regard, as I was in the company of old friends, and tomorrow would be a day off in Otta.

I got up surprisingly early, and Hartmut cooked a fantastic breakfast; eggs, bacon, sausages – the full works. Øivind, ever the joker, had painted 'James Baxter Support Team' on to each side of his old faithful Mercedes, beside the picture advertising his 'Hebbe Lilles Galleri' in Asker, which exhibited and sold his range of comical light-hearted artwork. The support team drove into Otta while I walked the 2 kilometres. I visited the library to find out more about Otta's connection with Scotland. When I was here some five years ago the whole town was covered in Scottish flags and there were kilted men and bag-pipers in the square. I had an inkling that Otta's connection with Scotland was that the people of Gudbrandsdalen, the vast valley in which Otta lay, had a battle with a mercenary Scots army some 400 years ago.

Day 42. From the *seters* above Melingen lake I could see the forested Rinddalen valley to the left of the photo beyond Reiret

What I found out was that in 1612 Denmark controlled Norway. Sweden was at war with Denmark, in a conflict called the Kalmar war of 1611 to 1613. The war was caused by Sweden trying to find an alternative trade route to the Baltic which avoided the Skagerrak and the North Sea. They tried to establish a route through north Norway. The Danes, who were occupiers of Norway, retaliated and invaded Sweden, laying siege to the town of Kalmar. In turn the Swedes massacred 300 Norwegian conscripts, serving in the Danish army, who hailed from Otta and Gudbrandsdalen, at Ny Lödöse near Göteborg.

The Swedish King, Gustavus Adolphus, was looking for forces to bolster his weak army. With the permission of King James I of 'Great Britain', the Swedish King's agent, James Spens, contacted Andrew Ramsay to enlist Scots. Andrew appointed his brother, Alexander, to command the enlisted force. Many Scots were

Day 42. There was a great view from the *seters* above Melingen lake towards the mountains of the next section in the Rondane 35 km away

Day 43. The 'support team' of Øivind Jorfald and Hartmut Liste came to meet me in Otta with good food, long drinks and great humour

enlisted, with many pressed into service from the Lowlands by Alexander Ramsay, and from Caithness by George Sinclair, a laird in Caithness. However, James I of 'Great Britain' revoked this enlistment after protestations from his brother-in-law, the King of Denmark, whom these troops would be used against. Despite the main force being disbanded, a group of about 350 eager mercenary recruits sailed in two ships, one from Dundee under Ramsay, and one from Wick under Sinclair. They met in Orkney and then sailed to Norway, landing in Isfjorden in Romsdal. This Scottish mercenary army marched up Romsdalen to Dovre and then started down Gudbrandsdalen following the same route that plundering Dutch mercenaries had recently used. From Dovre they headed down Gudbrandsdalen en route to join the Swedish army and reached Otta on 26th August 1612. When they got to Kringen, however, they were ambushed by a local army of 500 locals who had prepared a trap. Oral history says two people followed the Scots on the other side of the river; a man who rode his horse backwards to distract the Scots and a woman, Priller-Guri, who blew a horn when the Scots reached the narrow ambush point.

When Guri blew her horn, the ambush was released, and huge rocks and logs came crashing down the valley side, crushing some of the Scots. They then shot at the poorly-armed Scots with crossbows and muskets and killed George Sinclair, who was at the head of the column on horseback. The locals then descended on the Scots with axes and scythes, and in the close combat more Scots were killed. About two hours after Guri sounded her horn, all but 134 of the original 350 Scots and 6 locals were dead. The 134 Scottish prisoners were taken to a barn near Kvam and locked inside while the locals decided what to do. The locals were angry about the recent massacre of the 300 Otta and Gudbrandsdalen recruits at the hands of the Swedish at Ny Lödöse. Furthermore, they did not want to take the prisoners to Akershus fort in Oslo, as it was harvest time and they did not want to squander the harvest. They were also full of adrenaline and were probably drunk on success and moonshine, so they took the prisoners out of the barn one by one and executed them. When there were just 18 left they came to their senses and stopped the slaughter. One of the survivors was the commander, Alexander Ramsay. He was sent to Copenhagen with three other officers and repatriated. The other fourteen were either sent as recruits to a Danish regiment or remained in the area and cleared land to become farmers. So, I was quite surprised to find out that the close connection between Otta and Scotland now, is a legacy of this macabre event. The hell-raising mercenary, George Sinclair, was buried outside the church yard at Kvam, as the locals refused to give him a Christian burial. However, in the 400 years since his burial he has now become something of a legend and his grave is a well-visited landmark and is revered. The clan Sinclair in Scotland, or their representatives, seem to be special guests at the annual celebrations, arranged by the largely Norwegian 'Sinclair's Club' in Otta.

While I was at the library, the librarian found out what I was doing and that I was Scottish and contacted a local journalist. He came to interview me after I had walked back to the cabin. We chatted for a good hour while he put together a piece for the Norddalen newspaper. One of the questions he asked was "As a Scot dare you come to Otta?" I spent ages sorting out my equipment and getting rid of the things I was unlikely to need. I managed to whittle away at least two more kilos of equipment in a ruthless clear out. I even cut my toothbrush in half and disposed of two of my three sewing needles. I was now down to about 19 kilos without provisions. It had been nice to have a rare unhurried day with friends among the weeks of mountain winter wilderness.

SECTION 5. Jotunheimen.
7 days. 131 km. 41.5 hours. 1670m ascent. 2850m descent.

THE SKI: SECTION 6. RONDANE

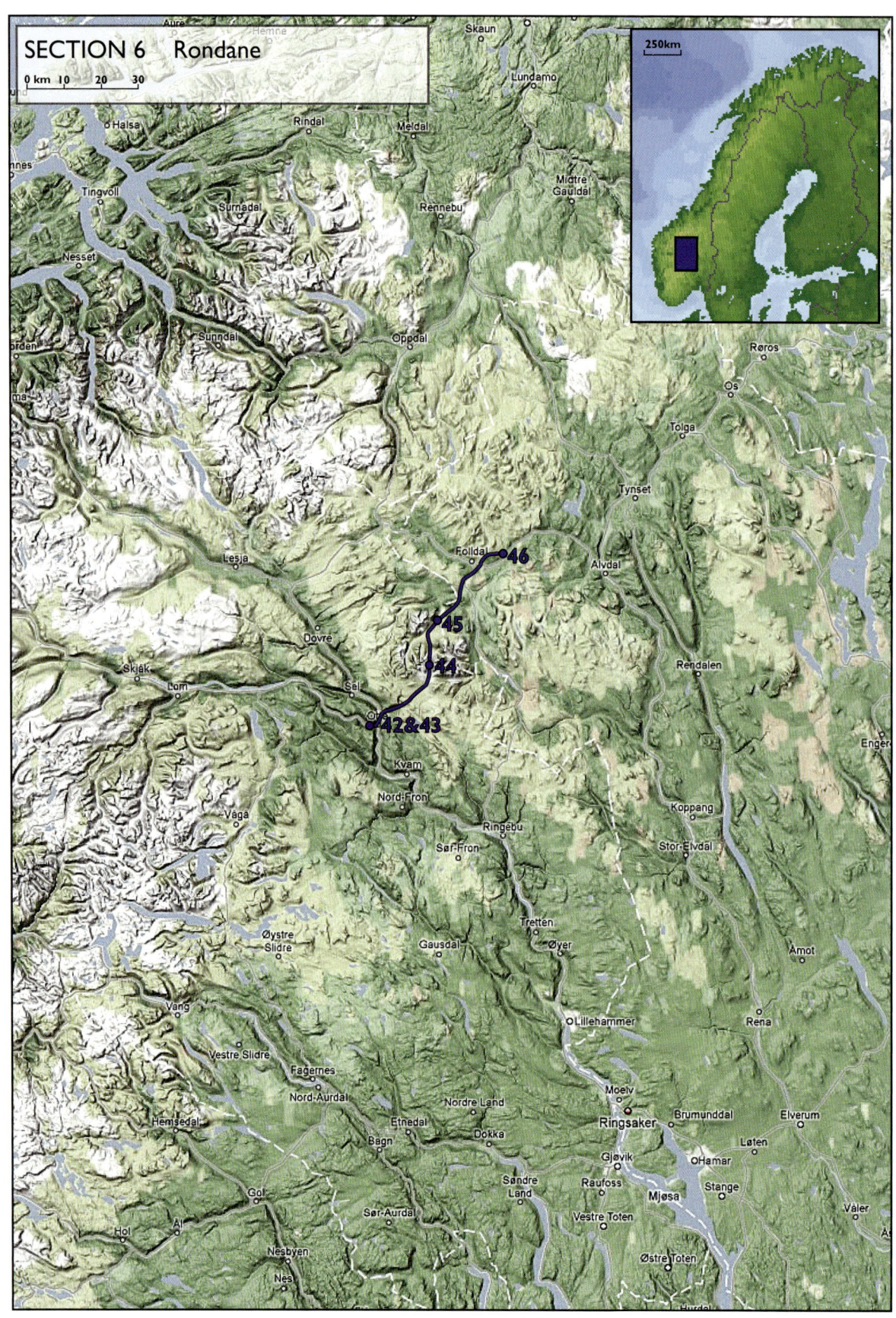

THE SKI: SECTION 6. RONDANE

Day 44. A typical cabin at Mysusæter nestled among the trees is a legacy of the summer farms once found here

I said goodbye to Hartmut and Øivind and then walked the 2 kilometres to Otta, where I started up the road to Mysusæter. I carried on up the hairpin bends through spruce forests until I climbed into the pines. As the hairpin bends finished, I passed some lovely farms at Rusten, perched on the lip of the valley overlooking Otta. There was plenty of farming activity at Rusten, where all the animals were in large barns for the winter. Eventually the road turned north east and headed over a spur to reach a plateau high above Uldalen valley. From my vantage point it looked cold, shaded and the forest track in it could well have been covered in deep snow. After an hour I reached Mysusæter, which once must have been a very pretty place. It was nestled in a large bowl in the upper reaches of the pine forest. Just beyond Mysusæter in most directions was the bare undulating plateau. This was the perfect setting for the summer farms of Gudbrandsdalen valley below, and would have provided unlimited summer grazing in an idyllic setting, with wonderful views westwards across Gudbrandsdalen valley to Jotunheimen. However, there have been a lot of cabins built here over the last 50 years. Many of these would have had some historical connection to the family summer farm, but many would have been built as leisure cabins. I skied north east up the shallow side of the bowl to the lip of the plateau. The quaint log cabins and the pine trees slowly petered out as I climbed through the deep snow for 2 kilometres. Here I reached the edge of the rim of the bowl where a magnificent view of the Rondane mountains suddenly unfolded. Their largely rounded shapes were completely white with deep snow. It was an easy ski for 5 kilometres across the treeless plateau and then another 5 kilometres skiing through the deepening valley into the heart of this mountain citadel. It was a very pleasant ski in the late sunny afternoon, and as there had been a few other skiers taking advantage of the good weather, I had firm tracks to ski on. As I entered Rondvassdalen and neared the lodge, the setting sun cast a wonderful rose-coloured alpenglow on to the mountains of Storronden and Rondslottet ahead of me. I could now feel the temperature plummeting.

Day 44. Skiing up through the last of the cabins and conifer trees above Mysusæter to reach the edge of the plateau

Day 44. Looking north from Mysusæter across the plateau to the mountains of Rondane

I was now to the east of Gudbrandsdalen valley. I always consider this valley to be a real divide in southern Norway. To the west, the weather is heavily influenced by the Atlantic weather systems, while to the east it is much more continental, drier and with more extreme temperatures. The vegetation is likewise divided, with the lowland pine and upper birch of the west being replaced eastwards with the mixed pine and spruce of the great forests of Scandinavia which extend around the Baltic Sea. To the east of Gudbrandsdalen the wildlife also changes, with moose replacing deer. Lynx, and very rarely wolf, become the supreme predators as the terrain becomes less suitable for wolverine. The occasional bear is also less rare in the eastern

Day 44. Approaching the mountains of Rondane with the easy 2000-metre peak of Veslesmeden in the centre of the picture

forests. Lemmings and ptarmigan also give way to mice and larger forest birds. The landscape also changes, with the mountains far more rounded to the east of Gudbrandsdalen than their heavily-glaciated, sharp, alpine counterparts to the west. This is because this rock type was much softer being of sedimentary origin. When the continents collided 420 million years ago the Caledonian Mountains where formed in the crumple zone (see page 49. Fig 1). The arc of Aleutian-like volcanic islands and the ocean floor was squeezed between the Laurentia and Baltica tectonic plates, with much of it riding up onto the ancient surface of the latter. These rocks were smeared across the Baltica's surface in layers which geologists call Allochthons. The lower and more easterly Allochthons were composed of the sedimentary rocks which had settled in a deep layer on the ocean floor. As the tectonic plates collided some of these sediments were forced up on to the rim of Baltica in a huge wedge or nappe. Then other rocks in the volcanic arc of Aleutian-like islands and some parts of the oceanic crust were also squeezed into wedges or nappes and forced up on top of this sedimentary nappe (see page 49. Fig 2). These immense nappes of the sedimentary layers, the volcanic islands and the oceanic crust were then bulldozed and smeared eastwards across the ancient surface of Baltica by the collision. The lower softer sedimentary nappes, or Lower Allochthon were bulldozed many hundreds of kilometres eastwards with the sediments at the leading edge until the continents stopped colliding. The harder upper nappes of the volcanic islands and the oceanic crust forming the Middle and Upper Allochthons were not bulldozed so far (see page 49. Fig 3). Jotunheimen was largely a hard wearing gabbro nappe of the Middle Allochthon, but the soft sedimentary mountains of Rondane were in the Lower Allochthon.

Day 44. As I arrived at Rondvassbu lodge there was a lovely alpenglow over Svartnuten crags and the highest, Rondslottet, in the middle

The rock type which formed this sedimentary nappe of which the mountains of Rondane are composed is called sparagmite. It was a layer which was thousands of metres deep but is greatly eroded now down to the remnant roots of the original nappe. Sparagmite is a mineral-sparse sedimentary rock which readily cracks to form flakes and blocks that create the characteristic scree slopes and boulder fields of Rondane. It means that the little rain which does fall here quickly drains from the surface through the blocks until it reaches the unfractured sparagmite below. It then drains under the blocks and surfaces in the streams in the valleys where the blocks have been removed. Because of the dry conditions found in the block fields of Rondane, and the deficiency of minerals in the sparagmite, there is very little nourishment for plant life, so vegetation in the Rondane is sparse. However, lichen does thrive in this environment, providing the wild reindeer of Rondane with valuable grazing habitats in a relatively intact mountain ecosystem. The reindeer in Rondane today are the remnants of the once vast wild herds which roamed Scandinavia. The first settlers from the Stone Age and up to medieval times hunted these reindeer by driving them into pit traps. I have previously seen a few pit traps in the summer as I wandered about the block fields in the valleys here. The pits were excavated out of the blocks and boulders and lined with slabs. They must have been labour intensive to build as they were some two metres deep. The pits were then covered with twigs and vegetation and the reindeer driven towards them. Reindeer which stepped on to them crashed through into the pits and were dispatched with spears. My fate as I approached Rondvassbu lodge was a lot more comfortable than the driven reindeer as it had just opened that afternoon. When the lodge opens, the self-service cabin beside it is locked, and is only reopened when the lodge closes at the end of the season in the autumn. Rondvassbu lodge was now managed by two young men from Otta. I was the first guest of the year and the only guest there that day, so was spoilt with a fantastic dinner.

Day 45. Looking south down Rondvassdalen valley with its open stream to Rondvatnet lake squeezed between high mountains

After the traditional buffet breakfast, which included pickled herring, I set off. It was overcast, with the odd snowflake and mist on the mountain tops, as I skied down on to Rondvatnet lake. It was much warmer than the previous days and the temperature had risen to minus 6. It was just some 4 kilometres up the length of the narrow lake lying in a deep slot between some of the biggest mountains in Rondane. Huge ice formations dripped from crags where seepages had frozen since November. At the north end of the lake there was some open water where the stream flowed in, which was very surprising given the recent bitterly cold week and the complete absence of any hydro-electric schemes. Beyond it was a valley full of piles of moraine debris. The snow was sparse in places here, especially on the north-facing side of these moraine mounds. I weaved a path between the mounds, glancing over my right shoulder from time to time to admire the magnificent north face of Rondslottet. It was a 700-metre near vertical wall cut by ice-filled gullies. I soon reached a gentle watershed and started down to the Dørålen valley through more mounds of snow-covered moraine. I kept well to the west of the stream in Bergedalen as it sliced a ravine through the moraine terraces and softer sparagmite rock on the valley floor. Through the mist, and over my left shoulder, I could just make out the very wild valleys and corries on the north side of the Smiubelgin massif. The three valleys of Smedbotn, Langholet and Verkilsdalen are some of the remotest in the Rondane, and are virtually only accessible up the flat valley floors as the side and head walls are so steep. These valleys are important reindeer calving areas in May. As I reached Dørålen valley I skirted round an area called Skranglehaugan. This remarkable area was a delta in an inland lake at the end of the last ice age. The lake was caused by a glacier damming the entire valley further downstream. There were a lot of ice bergs in this lake which grounded here in the delta. Masses of sediments were carried down the valley streams and deposited around the icebergs almost entombing them. When the glacial dam was breached at Jutulhogget and the lake drained in a few days, an event of Biblical proportions, the icebergs remained trapped in the sediments. They slowly melted, leaving large depressions in the sediments, and some 10,000 years later this area of well over a square kilometre forms a pockmarked landscape full of crater-like depressions. I was keen to avoid it as it would have been a very complicated area of deep holes ringed by cornices.

Day 45 From Bergedalen the skies slowly cleared to reveal some of the mountains, such as the easy 2000 plus metre Digerronden

When I reached the infant Atna river in Dørålen valley I had to cross it. It has carved a deep steep slot into the same deposits of this long gone 10,000-year-old delta. It was difficult to find a place to cross, due to the steep sides down from the terraces, and the climb up the other side looked bloodsome. I decided to try my luck by crossing the frozen Bergedalsbekken stream I was previously keeping to the west of, at its confluence and followed the south side of the river in Dørålen. This meant skiing along the lip of the terrace. However, this flat terrace was eventually squeezed between a steep hill and the river and I was eventually forced to cross. I had to traverse across a 45 degree slope where a slip would have meant a fast slide down to the river. I cautiously side slipped and side stepped the 40 metres down to the river and found a place, where the ice seemed quite solid, to cross. The climb on to the terrace on the north side was exhausting. The snow was thigh deep and my

Day 46. There was a magnificent sunrise over the cold morning as I skied down Dørålen valley

skis almost stood vertically in the snow as I tried to force myself up. I tried with the skis off but could barely move. It would have been very difficult with full skins, but with these inadequate short skins, it was hopeless. After much effort and cursing I eventually hauled myself up through the birch trees and snow to reach the lip. The whole crossing was just 100 metres and took over an hour. However, once up on the terrace on the north side it was a very simple 2 kilometre ski through sparse birch to the self-service cabin at Dørålseter. This area seemed to have a very small snowfall as it lay in a rain shadow from virtually all directions. Most of the snow which fell here was probably blown into the sheltered slot where the Atna river flowed and I had just finished floundering about in. The snow was so thin I could see the exposed ground was thick with lichen and reindeer moss, and the crimson leaves and the plump frozen purple berries of mountain bearberry which the local ptarmigan had so far failed to see. The cabin was large but had some small bedrooms and a snug, easy-to-heat kitchen and it did not take long to get settled. As I was getting ensconced in front of the stove, four others arrived with two dogs. It was the first time I had not been on my own in a self-service cabin for ages, and I was grateful for their company. They were young but very knowledgeable, and one of them was a geographer and could explain to me the formation of the terraces, moraines and especially Skranglehaugan. We chatted into the evening with the stove and candles making a cosy atmosphere.

With the encouragement of the other four in the cabin we all got up at 0600. It was very dark outside and about minus 10. By the time I managed breakfast, did the washing up, and had packed, it was already light but the sun had yet to rise. I skied down the terrace, above the river, on frozen snow for 3 kilometres, until the sun came up in a blaze of purple announcing its intentions for the day. To the south, the 600-metre north face of Høgronden looked particularly impressive. I continued across the stony moorland for another 5 kilometres with very little snow in places. Apparently the rainfall here

Day 46. The 600-metre north face of Høgronden rose above the surrounding tundra sparsely covered in snow

is less than half a metre a year and it is the driest place in Norway. I decided to take a chance and cut through the gap between the hills of Storkringla and Veslkringla. The sparse windblown snow was easily supporting my weight, as it was firm in the cold morning. This shortcut would save a good hour, but if the snow became loose and deep it could cost me many hours. The gamble paid off and I enjoyed a very fine ski through the upper pine forest. The light was superb and the green pines were almost luminous against the sunny radiant white background. After a good hour of skiing in this high pine forest some old ski tracks appeared. They led me down to a bridge over the Grimse river, as it flowed through a gorge encrusted with bulbous ice formations. After the bridge there was a short section of mature pine forest to reach the small farming settlement of Fallet. Ponies

Day 46. The lovely hamlet of Fallet was a cluster of old cabins and farm buildings with many adorned with hunting trophies

Day 46. The serene track through the quiet birch forest between Sletti and Folldal church was enchanting

wandered in the snowy fields and all the barns, houses and cabins were adorned in reindeer and moose antlers. It was a quick kilometre to the main road. I looked for an alternative route to ski, but there was none, and the snow in the forest was prohibitively deep and soft. I therefore skied along the edge of the quiet main road for 4 kilometres to the old wooden farm buildings at Sletti. Just beyond was a track branching off to the right. It was partly cleared, but there was a soft abundance of snow on top and it was wonderful to ski on. It went straight through the quiet core of the sunny pine forest. There were tracks of moose and fox everywhere again. I silently glided through this enchanting forest for an hour to reach the farming hamlet of Sandvoll by the Folla river and Folldal church.

There were some people about in the sunny afternoon, so I asked for the best way to Grimsbu. They said it was best to cross the river and main road and head up the hill on the north side of the valley above Krokhaug hamlet towards Moseng. Here I would find a prepared ski trail which contoured around the hill for 10 kilometres before descending to Grimsbu. It sounded good advice. The short climb beyond Krokhaug was hot in the afternoon sun. I found the wide ski trail and followed it through a magnificent pine forest above old farms. To the south of the valley were the high rounded mountains of Alvdal Vestfjell some 20 kilometres away. It was a very idyllic run through the woods, but I noticed I was tiring on the uphill sections. Folldal, which was the main valley I was now following, was once a copper mining centre. Operations continued here for a couple of centuries and the place is covered in museums from

Day 46. Looking across Folldal valley from the edge of the forest above Krokhaug with the mountains of Alvdal Vestfjell in the distance

the pioneer period. All mining here has stopped now because it is just not economical. After 7 kilometres contouring across the hillside the ski trail started a very pleasant and exhilarating descent down to Grimsbu for 3 kilometres. I had the luxury of being able to snowplough at will to slow my speed round blind corners in the forest as I was on a well used ski track. Soon Grimsbu village lay scattered in the snowy valley before me. I reached it still luxuriating in the newness of the pine forests and the interesting cultural landscapes hidden in the forest, like quaint cabins and traditional farms. Grimsbu had a small rustic wooden motel. What it lacked in charm it made up for in friendliness. I got a nice cheap room with a shower, and a fry-up of chicken. What was really useful was the local knowledge which the hard working hostess, Tove Rønning, could tell me about the route to Røros. There had very recently been a famous dog sled race along the valley called the Femundløpet. Forty teams with about 12 dogs per team had just completed a 600-kilometre race. I could follow their tracks and some prepared ski trails to the next overnight place of Savalen tomorrow. Thereafter there was an abundance of trails through quiet hamlets north of the Glåma river all the way to Røros.

SECTION 6. Rondane.
3 days. 77 km. 20.5 hours. 1590m ascent. 1180m descent.

THE SKI: SECTION 7. UPPER ØSTERDALEN

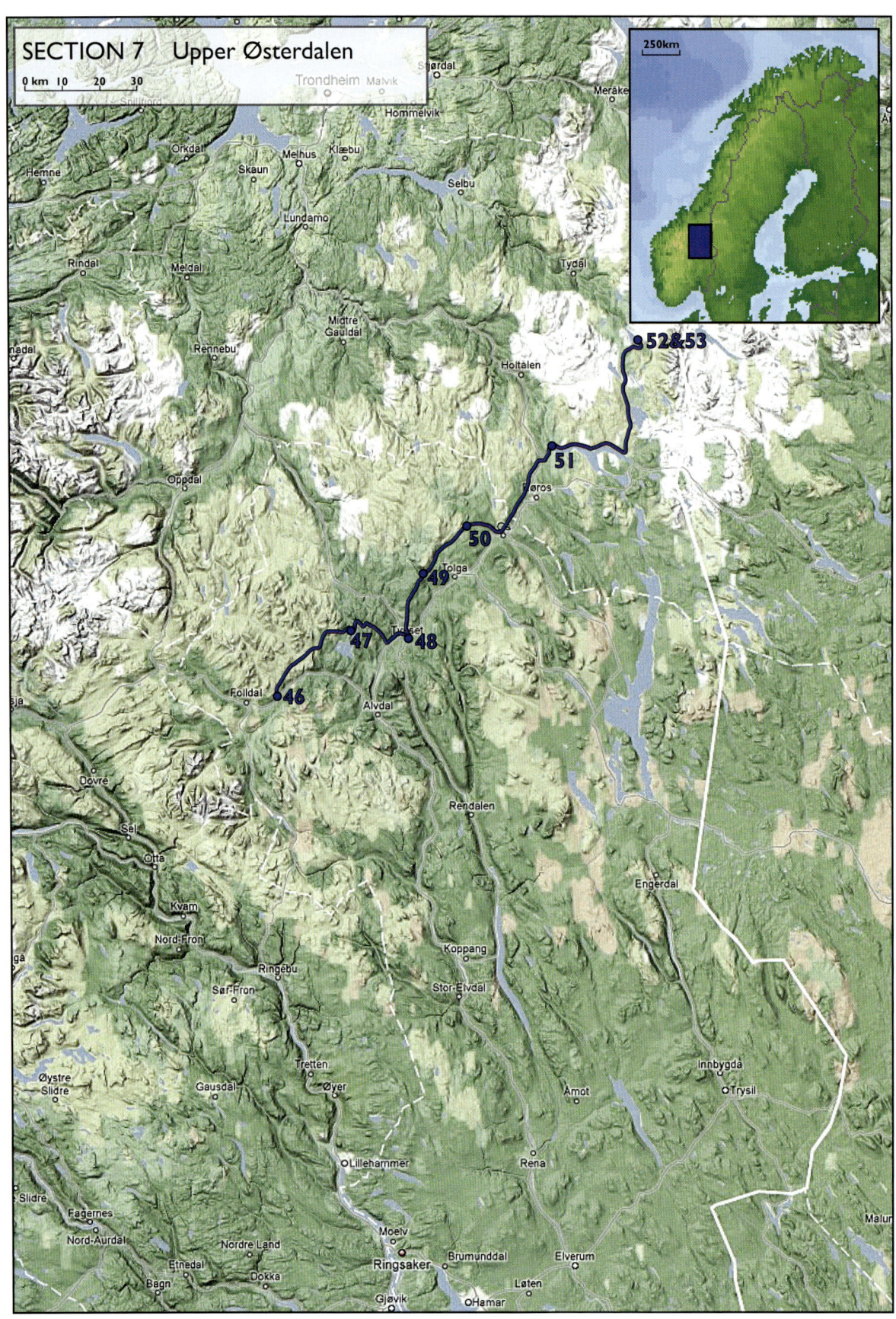

THE SKI: SECTION 7. UPPER ØSTERDALEN

I set off following Tove's directions to Savalen. It was a bit overcast and there was the odd snowflake in the air which was relatively warm at minus 12. The track from the road up to Gammelsætran was covered in deep snow and it was a very pleasant ski through the pine forests to the tree line where the summer farms were. It seemed many of these farms were still in use, and a few looked like they had modern dairy equipment. There was a clear view south down into the quiet main valley of Folldal from here. At Gammelsætran I came across signs of the recent Femundløpet dog sled race. The race is 600 kilometres and starts from Røros and goes in a large circle through Grimsbu before returning to Røros. It takes the fastest teams about 60 hours to complete the circuit. Each team would comprise a dog handler and 12 dogs. There was a fair amount of debris

Day 47. Looking back down to Grimsbu in Folldal over one of the summer farms at Gammelsætran where I found the dog sled tracks

and frozen turds left after the 500 dogs had run through, some 10 days previously. The trail was still quite compacted under the 20 centimetres of new snow, and it was quite easy to follow as foxes had wandered along it to see if any of the debris was worth eating. In this hard time of the year the foxes found the frozen turds worthy of some attention. I followed the trail east from Bjørnhøa and down into the birch trees again by a huge frozen marsh to the west of Einunnfjellet. Crossing the marsh I headed north passing some summer farms marooned and abandoned in the winter snows. These farms were waiting for the late spring to arrive when they would reawaken from their hibernation and host the grazing animals for the summer. Soon I reached the Einunna river where there was a small dam at Markbuli creating a frozen lake. I followed the dog trail north through the birch and the upper pines to the quaint summer farm at Sivillhaugsætra. Here the weather was getting very misty, and the snow knee deep, and I lost the dog sled race trail. I decided to abandon my original plans to go over Rødalshøa mountain, and instead decided to head east at once, down to the nearby leisure cabins at Kløftvangen. From this hamlet of cabins I could hopefully find a trail through the forest for 4 or 5 kilometres to Gardvika bay on the west side of Savalen lake. From here I thought it would be easy to follow the lake to the lodge at the north end. The first part of my new plan went well as I waded through the deep snow for the half hour to Kløftvangen. However, at Kløftvangen I could not find a trail heading east. Without a trail I would make little or no progress through this undulating forest with thigh-deep snow. I searched for a good hour to see if there was anything. Finding nothing, and conscious of the time, I reluctantly gave up and followed the only trail I could find. It seemed to go north east towards my original route over Rødalshøa so I took it.

It was a good trail and I made fast progress through the forest and up on to the bare mountain side. Here, as the last trees and the trail vanished by Stortjønna lake, I entered the misty mountain world which was virtually a white-out. Out came my compass and GPS, as I felt my way through the mist. As always when vision is poor, progress was slow, and I occasionally had to throw snowballs to make some reference points as I descended. Eventually, after a couple of hours, I had skied the 3 kilometres past Fjelltjørna lake and down the other side out of the mist and into a high-sided valley covered in deep snow, with willow scrub poking through. I now noticed that the light was starting to fade. Looking at my watch, I saw it was already 1700, and realized there was no chance of reaching Savalen lodge, and I would have to camp. The natural route initially seemed down Mogardsdalen valley into the forest and beyond. But, on closer inspection it looked like a ravine, and I might get trapped in the steep forest with thigh-deep snow. So instead, I erred on cautions side, and headed southwards in the wrong direction. This took me down a slope of deep snow into the birch and then pine forest. With a bit of luck I thought I might be able to make it to Bellsvikvangen before darkness fell. But the further I descended, the deeper and looser the snow became. It would be almost impossible to ascend this route, as I was up to my thighs. With fading light I continued down into the pine forest. The snow was still deeper here, almost to my waist, and progress was desperately slow, despite the descent. In the last light I spotted a mound where the snow seemed shallower and some blueberry bushes poked their tops through. It looked a good place to camp. I stamped the remaining snow with my skis on and then put up my tent in the pitch dark. There was so much loose snow about, some of my clothing was getting damp, especially my gloves. Within half an hour of stopping, I was in my sleeping bag and melting snow for my dehydrated supper. As it was still overcast it was not too cold and the thermometer read minus 16. I fell asleep soon after the meal as the sleeping bag warmed up.

Day 47. I could not make it to Savalen lodge and had to find a place to camp in the thigh-deep snow of the forest once darkness fell

The inside of the tent was covered in thick frost when I woke at 0700. It was minus 12 inside the tent and minus 19 outside. It could have been a lot worse. It was congested inside and each time I moved a shower of frost would land on my sleeping bag. If I had had a petrol stove I could have fired it up and blasted the frost through the inner tent. However, to save weight I was using a gas stove and it would not have been effective to evaporate frost from the inner tent. Perhaps the hardest single task on this trip is unzipping the sleeping bag to start the day. Once unzipped, everything then happened automatically, but making the initial decision to unzip the sleeping bag now rather than in another five minutes was a huge test of resolve. It took ages to eat breakfast, stuff the damp sleeping bag into its bag, roll up the tent and pack everything into my rucksack.

After a couple of hours I was at last ready to head off. I continued down through the forest in the waist-deep snow. Luckily, the slope continued down most of the time, but where it was flat I realized just how difficult it could be. At one flat 100-metre section I was almost stuck. The hopelessly inadequate short skins offered no purchase in this loose snow, and the skis just stood upright in the snow before me. I took them off, but I was equally hapless, as the snow was bottomless and too deep to wade through. Luckily, it was a short section, and I was soon heading down the slope again. At one point I disturbed about five female capercaillie which were gathered in a grand old pine tree. Soon, I came across some barely visible old ski tracks which were buried under half a metre of new snow. I followed them as they were firmer under the cover of recent loose snow. They led me past a very idyllic cabin in the forest and then to the old farms at Bellsvikvangen. These old farms were beside a forest track which had been partially cleared by tractor, and my wade through the impossibly deep forest was luckily over. I had only done perhaps 2 kilometres, most of it downhill, but it had taken two hours.

Day 48. The summer farmsteads at Bellsvikvangen were a welcome sight as I emerged from the waist-deep snow of the forest

Bellsvikvangen was a collection of some three or four summer farms. They were solid, old, rustic buildings, made from strong, massive spiralled pine logs. The spiralling on these pine logs is natural, and happens as the trees slowly age in the forest, making them stronger. These venerable old forest giants are called 'malmfuru' meaning 'iron pine' and are extremely durable as building materials. From these farms the cleared road headed north. I followed it for 3 kilometres and then headed east along another track to the very picturesque summer farm at Grasgodtvangen, which lay nestled in a serene clearing in the pines. From here it was a quick easy descent to Savalen lake. At the lake I got a clear view of Savalen lodge a kilometre to the north across the frozen surface. There are very few, if any, compliments I can say about Savalen lodge. It was a downhill ski centre with an eyesore of a large hotel. The spiritually bankrupt complex had a neon-lit indoor spa and even arranged Father Christmas competitions. I was glad I had spent the night camping in the woods, rather than have been thrust into the busy, bright, superficial atmosphere of Savalen lodge. I was rather at a loss of what to do next. I needed to continue as it was only midday and did not want to remain at Savalen. My next intended stop, Vingelen, was still some 30 kilometres away. I did not have a detailed map of this section and could not find out if there were tracks through the forest or not. The only information I could glean was from a helpful guest, but I felt I could not rely on it. He said he thought there were trails for the first half only, but after that I would have to slog through 15 kilometres of deep forest snow with an inevitable camp. He suggested a better option might be to ski down the road to Tynset and spend the night there. Then tomorrow take the ski trail along the old Pilgrims Route from Tynset to Vingelen. I was reluctant to do this but was terrified of the deep forest snow I might get stuck in if I went directly to Vingelen.

Day 48. A typical stabbur on a farmstead was where all the food was preserved and grain was stored in more traditional times

I set off down the road to Tynset and managed to ski more than half the way to Fåset before the snow got too gritty and I had to walk. The descent was fast and took me past some wonderful farms, especially in Fådalen. At Fåset the skis went back on again as I could now follow the old road to Tynset. It was cleared, but very quiet, and covered in snow. It was a good 8 kilometres, with farms and agriculture on the south of the road and pine forests to the north. Many of these all-year farms were large and traditional with many beautiful buildings including some fine stabburs. To add to the idyllic setting, snow was falling gently, while smoke from wood fires rose quietly from the chimneys. Of all the buildings found on old farms, one of the most distinctive is the stabbur. A stabbur is usually a two-storey log building, often taller than it is wide or long. The second storey is usually wider than the first, giving the building a top-heavy appearance. The stabbur was used as a food store. There was always a grain room with various bins to store cereals and flours. There was usually a salting room for preserving meat. Fish and meat were not smoked here because of the fire risk, and this was done in a separate, isolated building, but the smoked produce was normally stored in the stabbur. Stabburs were well constructed and often built on mushroom-shaped stone supports, like English straddle stones, to deter vermin and prevent dampness creeping into the stored foods. The stabbur was normally the only building in the farmstead which was locked, and the farmer's wife usually kept the key, which was seen as something of a status symbol. Every area in Norway has its unique design of stabbur, and some are very elaborate. Just before Tynset, this rural road through the old farmsteads came to an end but I could now follow a snow-covered cycle path all the way to the bridge over the arterial Glåma river, which is the longest river in Norway, to the campsite. At the campsite I got a very nice, reasonable cabin and did my chores – hang my tent and sleeping bag to dry, wash my clothes, shop for food and write. I also phoned a farmhouse at Vingelen to arrange accommodation for tomorrow night and find out about the snow conditions. I got lots of good advice. I found out later that there were tracks all the way from Savalen to Vingelen and I could have easily reached it by nightfall. Had I done that, I would have avoided the ski down the road from Savalen to Tynset, which made me feel a bit of an outdoor fraud.

It had snowed gently all night and there was about 10 centimetres of new snow lying on top of the considerable snow already lying. There was a ski trail on the opposite side of the street which went straight across the Glåma river under the bridge I had crossed yesterday. The trail then crossed the road, went through a few farms and up across some fields to reach the pine forest to the east of the very Lutheran looking white church. Once in the pine forest calm returned. Although it was only 2 kilometres from Tynset it was another world of peace and tranquillity. The ski trail I was now following went along an old track called Gammelallmannvegen. This track was once part of one of the much longer ancient pilgrim's roads which led from all over Scandinavia to the centre of Scandinavian

Day 49. Skiing along the old pilgrim's road through the quiet forest with only the sound of capercaillie flying off was enchanting

Day 49. One of the cabins near the summer farms beside Milskifttjønna lake would have been at least a century old

Christianity at Nidarosdomen cathedral in Trondheim. It felt very apt that I was following a pilgrim's route, as I often felt this tour was akin to a spiritual journey. The trail could not have been better. It was firm under the 10 centimetres of new snow which had softened all the hard edges. On each side of the forest track were old pines and the track seemed like an aristocratic avenue as it passed through them. The large pines were thick with huge helpings of light snow, resting on the twisted boughs and the huge bunches of green needles on the branches. It was a lovely scene. As I skied through this hushed fairytale, the only sounds were the clucking capercaillie which flew off as I disturbed them. The trail climbed gently for 3 kilometres, and the pines gave way to birch as I ascended. Soon it flattened off and I could get a good glide on my skis along the track. Before long the birch woods opened up as I approached Milskifttjønna lake. These birch woods would have previously been kept down by animals in the summer months nibbling shoots. In this way the pastures would have been kept clear. Now with less summer farms the pastures are being re-colonised by birch saplings again. There were quite a few cabins and summer farms up here and many showed signs they were in still in use through the summer. I passed through this quiet setting under its blanket of soft snow, imagining how idyllic it must have been here 50 years ago during the summer months, and probably still is. After the summer farms I was back into the birch woods. The snow was still falling, the flakes were large and they fell very slowly out of the still sky on to the postcard I was drifting through.

Before I knew it I was at Åsan, where the forest trail ended at a couple of cabins and a cleared forest track, which was covered in a thick dusting of new snow, started. I skied down the track until I got to the lower edge of the forest where land had been cleared for farming on the edge of Vingelen village. The more I skied towards the rural heart of Vingelen, the quainter it became. It seemed a wonderfully preserved community.

Day 49. When I reached Vingelen village I was in for an unsurpassed cultural feast with many gorgeous well-preserved old farmsteads

Most of the grand old farms had numerous buildings. Huge log barns and old houses with many windows dotted the landscape. Horses with massive hooves peered at me from barn doors or from the fields. Sledges for the horses were in farmyards. One horse and sledge passed me in the centre of the village, the lady driver under a mass of fur and sitting on a pile of reindeer skin. There was another grand white Lutheran church here. It was surrounded by many more old farms. I have not seen anything as historic, grand and as well preserved as Vingelen village in Scandinavia. The whole village was like a living museum. The only other place I have seen in Norway that could possibly match it would be Heidal in Gudbrandsdalen. I later found out that Vingelen village was one of the five National Park Villages in Norway, so it has recognised status and protection. The farm I wanted, Vingelsgaard, lay in

Day 49. There were many horse-drawn sledges in the village of Vingelen

Day 50. The old farmhouse at Vingelsgaard farm was over 400 years old

another cluster of old buildings to the north west of the church about a kilometre away. I skied along the road to these buildings. When I reached Vingelsgaard farm it was an absolute pearl of historic heritage. The farm was about 400 years old, like most of the other farms in Vingelen village. The two stabburs were also 400 years old, but apparently there were older buildings here before these were built, which went back into the mists of history 600 years ago. Like many old farms in Norway, this one was lovingly passed down from generation to generation in an unbroken chain dating back many centuries. The sense of belonging that such farmers have is quite unrivalled in today's world. The hosts explained a lot of the cultural heritage to me and it seemed that there are some 56 farms in Vingelen and at least half of them still had and used their summer farms at the edge of the forests around here before the bare mountain sides rose up. The two generations who ran the farm and the guest house could not have been more helpful and interested. They explained the most scenic route to Dalsbygda tomorrow and Røros the day after. Bjørn Vingelsgaard even arranged accommodation with his brother in Dalsbygda for me. It was a very warm welcoming end to an idyllic day, and although the landscape here was not dramatic in a spectacular way, it was a cultural landscape which filled me with euphoria and well being.

To make the day even more interesting, I had the company of another skier who was also skiing the length of Norway. He was Andre Spica and he had also been skiing for about 50 days. We had been in touch by text message occasionally, and when we discovered we were both near Vingelen, he decided to meet me here at Vingelsgaard. He burst into the guest house just a few minutes after I arrived with his contagiously good humour and chaotic manner. We had lots to talk about. Andre had skied with other people for much of his trip, and his recent companion, Bjørn, had finished a week ago, after Rondane, and he was now skiing for a few weeks with Morton. I had seen their tracks in Skarvheimen and in Rondane as I passed through these areas about a week after him. He was doing his journey with a sledge or pulk, which meant he was slower, but

Day 50. One of these two stabburs on Vingelsgaard farm dates from 1676 and is perfectly preserved.

could take more. He had a larger tent, a petrol stove, goose down boots, and everything he needed to make camping not only tolerable, but also enjoyable. Whereas I had spent about six nights camping, Andre had spent about 25 nights camping so far.

I started with a great farmhouse breakfast at Vingelsgaard and a further chat with the very nice hosts. I finally got under way at 0930. I skied down the road and passed close to the noble Lutheran church sitting on a knoll overlooking the village. After the church I headed north east along a small snow-covered country lane for 6 kilometres towards Røset. Not a car passed me as I skied along the quiet lane. Initially, I skied past lots of grand old farms similar to Vingelsgaard, but these slowly petered out as I left the village and there was just the occasional house beside the quiet snowy lane. As I skied along I suddenly had the company of an elghund dog, which came bouncing up the road beside me. Elghund dogs are used for elg (moose) hunting. The dogs have a keen sense of smell and are trained to find elg. When they find elg they either bark at it and try and keep it stationary until the hunters arrive, or drive it towards the hunters who are waiting in hides along the elg's migratory paths. Elghund dogs did have an aggressive reputation some 50 years ago when farmers kept them in barns on long chains

Day 50. The forest track through the forest was recently cleared by a convoy of 30 horses and sleds en route to the Rørosmartnan market

and only released them during hunts. Since then dog husbandry has changed and elghunds are now more often allowed into the household as family pets and their aggressive side has vanished. This elghund kept me company for 3 kilometres before it turned back. After 6 kilometres the lane ended in a forest track. This track served summer farms and continued through the forest for some 8 kilometres until it reached another lane on the other side which eventually went down to Dalsbygda. Normally this track past the summer farms would be deep with uncleared snow, but very recently there had been a convoy of some 30 horse-drawn sleds along this track. The horses and sleds had gone to Rørosmartnan, a 150-year-old winter market in the old copper mining town of Røros. The market was held in the winter because all the tradesmen who came here in the mid 1800s onwards brought their wares to sell on sledge and mid-February was the best time. These tradesmen came from all over the district and also from Dalarna in Sweden. They brought with them grain, preserved meat and fish, dairy products, tobacco, felt, moonshine, rope and ironmongery. Since the first Rørosmartnan market in 1854, it has grown from a farmer's market to a major festival, where the tradition of bringing some wares on horse-drawn sled has been revived, and nearly 100 sleds arrive each year now. The original wares are now largely replaced by handcrafts, textiles and speciality food, and much of this arrives by van nowadays. During the five days of Rørosmartnan market there continues to be a lot of folk music and dancing in the evenings, as many musicians also arrive for the festival. Indeed, the first Rørosmartnan market had about 2000 visitors and now there are around 100,000 visitors.

Day 50. There were some lovely old summer farms in this culturally rich landscape between Vingelen and Dalsbygda

As I skied along the track I could see some hay and fodder which had fallen off the sleds and was not yet covered by the falling snow. The track went past some 20 very idyllic summer farms, and various forests of birch, pine and spruce. It was a superb cultural landscape. The skiing on this track was very easy, as there was some new snow on the compacted under layer to lubricate a long glide. Eventually the track ended at Gruva where a country lane started again. Along this lane were some remote farms which were occupied through the winter, so the lane was cleared. It was very quiet along the peaceful lane past the farms with the occasional dog barking. As I rounded one corner, I caught up with Andre and Morten, who both had large pulks and were therefore a bit slower. We skied together, three abreast down the middle of the lane, all the way to Dalsbygda, chatting profusely about our experiences so far. It was nice to have company. Andre wanted to meet up again and continue together all the way north, but I had decided to do this trip alone and did not crave company as he did. In fact, I rather relished the loneliness of it and wanted to appreciate

Day 50. Morten and Andre skiing down the snow-covered road to Dalsbygda towing their sledges or 'pulks'

Day 51. Me at the ancient hamlet of Austgarden with the farms of Dalsbygda spread out in the valley behind me

the wintery nature without too much disturbance. We soon reached Dalsbygda, where Andre and Morten knew someone who had a cabin a further 8 kilometres towards Røros, which was part of a summer farm. I had already arranged to stay in Dalsbygda, so found my very cheap lodging and said goodbye. The snow was falling heavily now and the pretty village of Dalsbygda was hushed and subdued in the darkening light of the afternoon. I had to make a phone call to Øivind, in Oslo, to see what was happening with my X-Pod rucksack. Apparently it was still in customs and poor Øivind was becoming exasperated trying to extract it from the jobsworth officials.

It had been snowing during the night and everything was covered in fresh snow. In the lanes, this soft layer was lying undisturbed on the previous numerous layers of already compacted snow. At the edge of the village there was a steep track up through the fields, which led to a higher lane from Dalsbygda to Os, which I thought would be deserted. Just as I reached it, a journalist stopped her jeep, she interviewed me for a half hour, took some photos for the local Dalsbygda paper, and explained a little about the history of Dalsbygda, of which she was very proud. We had a great view back down to the farms and fields of Dalsbygda in the snow. Just beyond the area where we chatted was a hamlet of farms at Austgarden. The buildings here dated back some 600 years and you could see the history engrained in the sun-blackened logs. Apparently these fields were farmed as far back as 1000 years ago, but nothing remains of the original farmsteads which were ruined and had to be rebuilt after the Black Death devastated the area in 1351. After the living museum at Austgarden, I had a very pleasant ski along the road covered in new snow for another 6 kilometres, until it reached the descent to Os. Os was similar in character to Vingelen and Dalsbygda. It had

Day 51. One of the unoccupied summer farms beside the tranquil lane on the way to Orvos

a Lutheran church and many splendid old farms huddled together in a few tight hamlets which were loosely gathered around the heart of the village. After a fast descent down the snow-covered road to Os, I turned north east and went along a very quiet snowy lane for 10 kilometres on the west side of the frozen Glåma river. When I reached the bridge over the Glåma to Røros, I changed my plans and decided not to go to Røros after all. The town was in the middle of the Rørosmartnan festival and it would be very busy, and there would be absolutely no accommodation, so I would have to camp on the outskirts. The alternative was to continue along this snowy tranquil lane for another two hours to Orvos. The road north was much of the same quiet back lane with old farms and extensive woods. There was one with large riding stables with some 40 varied horses nervously running in snowy fields divided up with a maze of electric fences. In the woods I heard frequent woodpeckers and saw one. There were also a lot of traditional old farms along this lane, but many

Day 51. The tranquil lane to Orvos was deserted and the soft new snow lying on the compacted snow gave perfect skiing conditions

looked like they were empty for the winter. At Orvos the snowy lane ended at a busy road. I had to cut back south along this main road for a kilometre to cross the River Glåma again. Once I had crossed the river I could take another lane for a further two hours to the small town of Glåmos. This lane was much busier than I had anticipated, but I had to ski along it with cars passing frequently, or I had to wade through the deep snow of the woods, which would have been virtually impossible.

I reached Glåmos surprisingly quickly, conscious that it was getting late in the day. Glåmos was much more modern than the other villages I had enjoyed over the last three days. There was a shop here, where I enquired about accommodation, there was none. I therefore had to continue for another 3 kilometres to the west end of Aursunden lake and find a place to camp. The large Glåma river I had crossed and re-crossed over the last few days, and which is the longest river in Norway, had its birthplace here at the outflow of Aursunden lake. At the lake, the road veered north and I followed it, looking for a place to set up my tent. There were many leisure cabins tucked away in snow drifts in the birch woods with warm glows coming through the windows. I was a little envious as I skied past them trying to find a suitable place to put up my tent in the frequent snow showers. I reached a tolerable camp spot in the dusk, just where two young men with dogs were chatting in the approaching darkness. As I passed I also joined in their conversation. They were very friendly and had been at the Rørosmartnan market and festival all day. After a half hour's chat they suggested I pitch the tent and come up for coffee. They would have let me stay but were returning to Trondheim later that evening. I pitched the tent and went up to their beautiful, warm and cosy cabin. We carried on chatting. Their wives then suggested they return to Trondheim tomorrow instead of this snowy night. The boys, Lars-Erik and Robin, released from their driving responsibilities, enthusiastically opened beers and a bottle of moonshine and invited me to stay in the spare room. The poured me a 'kaffedoktor' (coffee doctor), a typical rural Norwegian drink. A traditional recipe for a kaffedoktor was to put a coin in a cup which was then filled with strong coffee until the coin disappeared, and then topped up with moonshine until the coin appeared again. Many a flagging Scandinavian has been revived by a kaffedoktor, and it was exactly what I needed after the 43 kilometres today. I was also quickly given pizza, beer and my damp clothes were soon hanging by the roaring fire. I was basking in their hospitality and generosity, and we chatted until the early morning with a few more kaffedoktors keeping me awake. Like most Norwegians, they were interested in the outdoors, and were fascinated to hear about my trip so far. I went to bed very grateful of the comfortable evening and their good company. Occasions like this confirm everything good about humanity.

After too little sleep, I got up a bit before 0800. Lars-Erik, Robin and the girls had already breakfasted and were cleaning up the cabin. Outside there was heavy snow and an easterly force 4. While they packed their cars I dug my half buried tent out of the snow, as it had been up all night, and packed my rucksack. Eventually at 0900 we were all ready to go; them to Trondheim and me towards Stugudal. I waved them off and thanked them again for their good company and kindness. My initial plan had been to go over the west shoulder of Storskarven into Gauldalen valley, which I could follow up to Kjølihytta cabin. However, I did not know if there were tracks in the forest sections of this route, and if there were no tracks, the snow would be prohibitively deep. In addition, the poor weather and visibility would mean the stages above the forest would be very difficult. I had no real option other than to ski along the road, which was thick with snow. Although I was not really getting into the wilderness by skiing along the road, I was rewarded by some fascinating traditional rural scenes. I rolled my balaclava down, pulled my jacket hood up, half closed my eyes and set forth. With some 10 centimetres of new snow on top of the compacted base on the road, the conditions were actually superb. The skis were gliding well and I was flying along at a good 5 kilometres per hour. I moved forward in a bubble of visibility that was at times just 50 metres. The smell of wood smoke heralded the arrival of a farm or cabin, long before I could see it in the near blizzard. There were quite a few farms along this stretch. Very few were old and most

Day 52. A self-portrait during a lull in the blizzard as I skied along the road by the north shore of Aursunden lake before Brynhildsvollen

seemed to have been built in the last 50 years. The buildings were quite modern with sharp edges and pragmatic doors for large modern farm implements. They did not sit well in the landscape, unlike the farms of Vingelen, Dalsbygda and Os which blended in. In the immediate vicinity around these more modern farm buildings there was a dearth of trees, which made them look bleak. Between the farms there were just birch woods with no pine or spruce trees, despite it being only 700 metres. Within the woods there were many leisure cabins, and the occasional older farm, which had been abandoned in favour of the newer buildings nearby. I skied from hamlet to hamlet along the lake for four hours, during which time I had covered the 19 kilometres to reach the hamlet of Brynhildsvollen. The traffic was minimal, with a car every 15 minutes.

At Brynhildsvollen there was a junction and another very snowy road, heading north for 34 kilometres across the windswept and partially treeless, frozen, moorland plateau to the village of Stugudal. The weather had improved slightly but it was still snowing and windy. It was just 1300 so I paused a bit before starting a gradual climb through birch woods to Rein lake. Here, I thought I could leave the road and head on to the lake. However, when I got to Rein lake an hour later, the snow was just too deep to contemplate leaving the easy skiing along the road, which was by far the best option to make faster progress. I was now starting to think it was feasible to go all the way to Stugudal where there was the Væktarstua lodge. It would be dark before I arrived, but as long as the weather did not deteriorate further, I could follow the line of the road. I carried on past quite

Day 52. The hibernating summer farms on the bleak birch-clad plateau at Storelvavollen were empty and waiting for summer's green arrival

a bleak landscape of thinning birch woods and occasional simple summer farms. The birch woods eventually petered out on each side, into scattered copses and then bare white mountain, which looked grey and uninviting in today's poor weather. After the collection of summer farms at Storelvavollen, the road climbed out of the thinning birch woods and past a couple of clusters of leisure cabins and on to the bare mountain. It was a tough climb for my weary thighs. It was more exposed here and the wind had caused a lot of drifting. A snow plough was trying to keep the road open for the occasional car. In fading light I skied down the other side of the plateau and back into the relative shelter of the birch trees again. The map I had showed there was a 5 kilometre ski trail from my vicinity at the upper limit of the birch trees all the way down through the small forested Tjønndalen valley to Stugudal. I wanted to get off the road so decided to follow it.

The ski trail was poorly marked and barely visible in the deep snow. I struggled along it for half a kilometre, falling twice when the lie of the land surprised me in the late dusk. Then I came to my senses, just before the point of no return, and retraced my track back to the road. I was way too tired to try and ski down this buried ski trail with a weak head torch. I would have fallen every 50 metres and would have had to camp in the forest. I made it back to the road as darkness fell and took off my skis and put on my head torch. It was still 10 kilometres to the lodge, which would take a good two hours. There was the occasional snow plough and car. It was a near blizzard again and there were huge amounts of spindrift flying off the steep banks on each side of the road. There would be no way any traffic could see me, but I could see it from a considerable distance and had about a minute's warning to climb up the high banks beside the road. I then waited until it had passed before I returned to the road to continue down. On one occasion, when a snow plough approached, I could not climb the bank I wanted to and had to climb up the wrong side. When the snow plough went past, it threw a huge shower of snow over me. On another occasion a jeep went past towing a trailer which was slewing and skidding from side to side, across the road between the banks of snow below me. It would have been a nice ski down the road, but I could not climb the steep banks at the side with my skis on, and it was far too dangerous to remain on the road. I don't think any of the 10 or so drivers saw me in the blizzard. At long last, I saw some lights from the village far below me appear out of the spindrift. I reached the lodge, white with spindrift, and very tired. It was very welcoming. They gave me a very reasonable room, and the hot water of the shower was soon stinging my chaffed areas under my arms and between my legs. Utterly invigorated by the shower, I went through to the dining room where there were the remains of a buffet. I assaulted it with the large implements I found, and gorged myself on a couple of heaped servings, showing little or no etiquette. After the meal, I went through to the closest thing you are going to get to a pub in rural Scandinavia, where there was a slightly redneck country dance band playing. I wanted to join in and chat to some of the locals from the village, but could barely keep my eyes open and had to crash out at 2200.

When I woke in the morning it was snowing heavily, I was tired after nearly 100 kilometres in two days and I needed to write and wash clothes. I had now finished the awkward section between the mountain areas of Rondane and Sylan. I called this section Upper Østerdalen. I had been a little apprehensive about this section as there seemed no obvious way, and there was a dearth of the wonderful self-service cabins which I had started to rely upon. However, now I had completed it, I have nothing but praise for it. For the entire section the weather had been poor and it had virtually snowed constantly for the entire six days. Had I been in the mountains, this would have been a real struggle, like I had endured in Setesdalsheiane. However, here in Upper Østerdalen it was barely noticeable as I skied along forest tracks and quiet snow-covered lanes. In fact the snowfalls had accentuated the beauty and tranquillity of the place and had made parts of this section seem like I was skiing through an enchanted fable. What it lacked in mountain landscape, it more than made up for in a cultural landscape. Perhaps after nearly six weeks of the high stern mountains I needed a more comfortable and reassuring landscape, so I was very content to ski through mature conifer forests with their calm reassuring protection and shelter. Also, after six weeks of relative loneliness, where even the twisted stunted mountain birch trees were becoming familiar friends, I was ready to ski past ancient farms and charming cottages whose cosy solace made me happy. Whatever the reasons, I absolutely loved the three days skiing from Tynset to Glåmos through the soothing and charming fairytale landscape. I had a lovely relaxing day at the lodge chatting with a few of the other guests. Two of the guests were an old couple, both in their 80s. Each day they made an effort to go 10 kilometres, whatever the weather. In the winter, it was on skis through the forest, and on foot in the summer. They were fitter than many 40-year-olds I had met recently. I also chatted to the owner, he was like most Norwegians and was justifiably proud of his heritage and the lodge. He told me that Thor Heyerdahl had spent the summer of 1948 here, when he took over the upstairs lounge with the fireplace and wrote Kon-Tiki. I also had the opportunity to prepare for the next stage, through the Sylan mountains to Storlien, which are at their most spectacular in Sweden. It was a bit longer going via Sweden, but I hoped the mountain views would reward me. The Sylan mountains are subject to sudden and severe storms, and there have been many tragedies over the years in these mountains. None can match the death march of the Karoliners some 300 years ago.

During the 17th Century, Sweden became a major European power. The whole of the Baltic Sea was almost a Swedish lake. Much of this empire was conquered by the feared soldiers of the Swedish army, called Karoliners. They were enlisted from throughout the Swedish empire, especially Finland. But Sweden and the Karoliners suffered a reverse of fortune and a crushing defeat at the Battle of Poltava in the Ukraine in 1709 and this weakened the empire. Sweden's enemies united against it in the Great Northern War. In 1718 the Swedish King, Charles XII, decided to invade Norway to use it as a bartering tool to sue for peace. The main force of 40,000 Karoliners, led by him, invaded south Norway, while another 10,000 Karoliners, under General Armfeldt, invaded mid Norway, to capture Trondheim. It was a disastrous invasion for the Swedes. Charles XII was killed in southern Norway, and the 40,000 troops there, which had been quite successful up to that point, retreated back to Sweden. Meanwhile, the remains of the 10,000 Karoliners in mid Norway were ineffectively laying siege to Trondheim and had run out of provisions. On hearing the news of the Swedish king's death, the poorly-equipped army started to retreat back to Sweden. The retreat went to Støren and then up Gauldalen to Haltdalen. It was Christmas and bitterly cold, and the remaining 6000 Karoliners were starving and exhausted. Normally well disciplined, they ravaged the farms for food and burnt many for warmth. They then crossed over the mountains in bad weather, losing a further 200 troops and reached the hamlets of Ås and Østby, just down the valley from Stugudal. Here, just 55 kilometres to the nearest hamlet in Sweden, the exhausted troops plundered to stay alive, taking food, clothing and firewood. On 31 December, 1718, there were just 5800 Karoliners who had survived the campaign, disease, and now the intense cold, and they started their infamous march for the farming hamlet of Handøl in Sweden.

The 5800 Karoliners had just made it up into the mountains by Øfjellet when an afternoon storm struck. They managed to get to the north end of Esandsjøen and camp in the blizzard, but by the next morning, a further 200 were dead. The storm continued the next day and made the retreat chaotic, with the troops scattering in the blizzard. The main force headed to the Swedish border and camped at Enaälven, while others blindly staggered about in the blizzard looking for a short cut to Handøl via Storulvån. The severe weather took its toll that day, and many of the draught horses died and all equipment had to be abandoned. The storm was still raging on the third day of the march as the first troops, led by Armfeldt, made their way to Handøl. The majority of the 2800 survivors arrived at Handøl over the next two days of January 3rd and 4th, leaving about 3,000 men frozen to death in the Sylan mountains. But the hamlet of Handøl was so overwhelmed and could not provide shelter, and a further 600 died here. The wretched frozen survivors had to continue down to the garrison at Duved, but another 100 died en route. Of the surviving 2100 soldiers, 600 were crippled for life due to frostbite and amputation. The 1500 who survived unscathed were mostly hardened Finnish recruits.

SECTION 7. Upper Østerdalen.
7 days. 190 km. 47.5 hours. 2850m ascent. 2870m descent.

THE SKI: SECTION 8. SYLAN

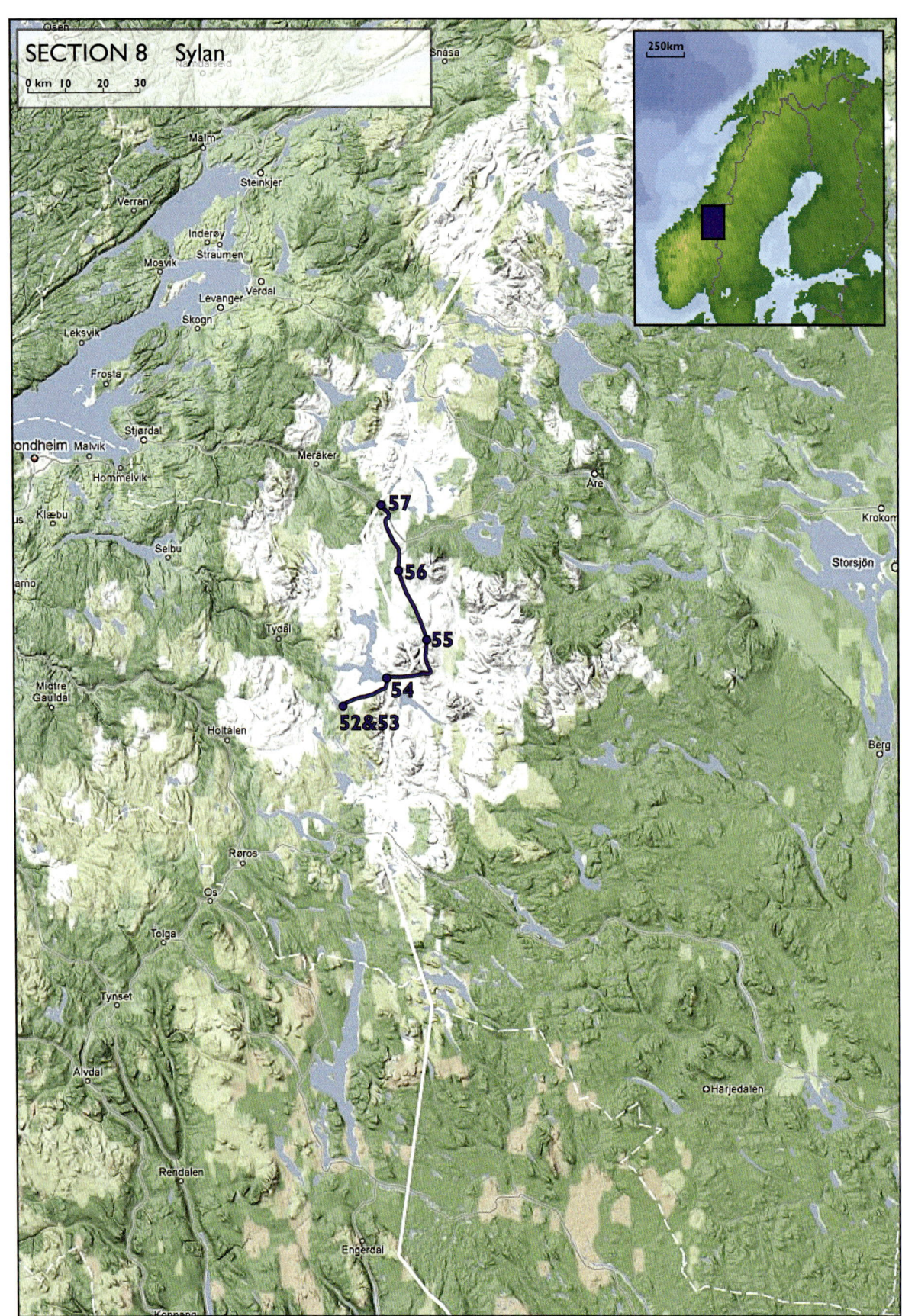

THE SKI: SECTION 8. SYLAN

It was about 18 kilometres up to Nedalshytta and it was still snowing. I had been a bit worried about the weather, especially the visibility, above the 1000-metre tree line, until I found out the whole route was marked by old wooden stakes. These stakes were put there to mark a rough track which was used to build a hydro-electric station here in the early 1950s. This track went round the north side of Skardsfjella and almost went all the way to Nedalshytta cabin. I left the lodge and went to the shop to get some provisions and then started up the track. The track went up through an area of leisure cabins for about 4 kilometres and had been cleared by tractor. The roofs of these mostly log cabins seemed to be turf but they were thick with snow. The cabins started to peter out as the track climbed to around 700 metres and the birch forest started to get thinner.

Day 54. The snow scooter trail helped me get through the upper birch forest from the cabins to the open wind-swept Skardsfjella mountain

The cleared track ended at the last of the cabins but there seemed to be a seldom-used snow scooter trail through the last of the trees and across some frozen marshes. I followed it for another 5 kilometres until the birch became twisted and dwarf, and the open mountainside started. Here the scooter trail vanished but it was a godsend through the birch, otherwise I would have made slow heavy progress in the deep snow of the birch woods. At the edge of the forest I met a young Swedish man. He was dressed completely in white with an old cotton jacket, now beige with wear, and white cotton over trousers. He was on old wooden skis pulling a wooden sledge. He looked as if he was from a bygone era. Most noticeable was the old rifle slung over his back which made him look like a character from the 'Heroes of Telemark'. We started chatting and he said he spent most of the winter in the high Sylan mountains hunting red fox on both the Swedish and Norwegian side. This year so far he had only managed to shoot two. At first I was a bit repulsed by this seemingly wanton bloodlust until he explained further. He was a fox hunter employed by both the Swedish and Norwegian wildlife departments to hunt and kill red fox in the Sylan mountains. The reason was that the Sylan mountains are one of the last bastions of the much endangered Arctic fox. Red foxes are more adaptable and as roads and cabins are built in the mountains they are expanding out of the valleys and forests to take advantage of new opportunities. As they invade the mountain territories of the vulnerable Arctic fox they compete with it for food, especially lemmings. The Arctic fox is almost completely reliant on lemmings and can only breed in lemming years when there is an abundance of the small rodents. This only happens every five years or so. The red fox is starting to establish itself in the mountains to their Arctic cousins' detriment. The only way to restore the balance is to keep the red fox in check and shooting is the most humane way. In addition to this the wildlife department in Norway had just released five Arctic foxes in the Sylan mountains to try and stem the declining population.

We chatted for a good half hour in the snow, until the cold began to creep into our boots and under our jackets, before carrying on; him into the forest down to Stugudal and me across the exposed mountainside. There were frequent heavy snow showers and the visibility was poor, but luckily there was the line of stakes to follow. They made a huge difference as it gave me confidence I was going in the right direction and I didn't have to check my map, compass and GPS all the time. After a couple of hours in the near white out, the line of stakes veered north and dropped down into the upper birch woods again. The weather also improved, and the visibility got much better. I could soon see the southern end of Nesjøen lake and the birch woods which surrounded it. As I entered the birch woods, ptarmigan which were sheltering under the surface of the snow took off, leaving a white hollow, with some droppings at the bottom. The cabin soon came into view on the other side of the open valley, high up in the birch trees. I crossed a bridge over the stream, where the track seemed to end and started to climb through the deep forest snow towards the cabin. This short climb proved to be quite difficult. It took me a good half hour to complete the half kilometre slog through the deep, loose snow, zig-zagging up and over the knolly terrain. During this climb the sun was out and I got very hot as I worked hard to forge a trench up to the cabin. As soon as I reached it and was inside, another heavy blizzard arrived. I had not been in a self-service cabin since Rondane about 10 days ago, and it was nice to be back in one. My usual cabin routine was made much easier, as this cabin had electricity. It was put in there as a concession when the hydro-electric station was built nearby,

Day 54. The view over the birch woods at the southern end of Nesjøen lake near Nedalshytta cabin

as compensation for the disturbance. There were electric heaters in addition to the wood stove. I lit the stove and put on the heaters, and within a short time the cabin was warm and cosy. After a few hours I noticed three people outside. I went to greet them and help them in. They were Dutch and had come from Sylarnas Fjällstation lodge where I hoped to go tomorrow. One can usually say that the Dutch are interesting, fun and pleasant people, and these three reinforced that generalization. The two men were orchestral conductors and the lady was a Boeing 737 pilot. They tried to do a Norwegian ski tour each year, and it was the Sylan mountains turn this year. Their English was as good as mine. The last time I spoke English was two weeks ago, so it was great to throw puns and jokes around. We settled down to a great evening with lots of humour, wit and craic. While I told them of my trip so far they fascinated me with their extraordinary careers.

The three Dutch and I all got up at the same time, had breakfast together, and set off at the same time, around 0830. While they headed north up Nesjøen lake to Storerikvollen cabin, I was going to take a tour into Sweden and head for Sylarnas Fjällstation. We would hopefully meet again tomorrow night in Blåhammarens Fjällstation. My journey took me through the deep snow of the upper forest initially and then on to the bare mountainside. The visibility was poor, and more than once I thought about turning back and going to Storerikvollen cabin with the Dutch. The reason I was coming this longer and much higher way was to ski through the heart of the Sylan mountains and soak up their views. If the weather remained like this it would be a wasted effort. The route was well marked with bleached wooden stakes across the flat treeless plateau. I continued to head into the snow showers towards the unseen Sylan mountains. The snow was soft and the going was quite slow as I sunk in well over my ankles with each step. It took a good two hours of trudging across this to reach the meaningless and abstract Swedish border on this white misty plateau. I carried on climbing very slowly with the wind and snow showers now behind me, and mist cloaking the mountains. Occasionally it cleared enough so I could get an obscured glimpse of the crags and snow fields on each side of the steepening valley. The wind was increasing the whole time and must have been a good force 4 when I entered Ekorrdörren, the deep valley to the south of the Sylan massif.

There was a small simple shed here. It was not suitable to spend the night in unless one was caught out in bad weather. I had lunch out of the bitter wind in the shelter and then prepared to climb the mountainside to the north. On the map it looked very steep, but in reality it was not that bad. The wind would be directly into my face though so I pulled the balaclava down over my nose and face and tightened up my jacket hood. I had abandoned my goggles as they were just not worth the weight and steamed up frequently, but I put on my sunglasses to protect my eyes against the driving snow and spindrift. On the climb the wind got stronger and stronger as I neared the pass. It must have been a force 7 at the top and I was being buffeted about. Due to the snowfalls of the last week there were huge amounts of spindrift swirling around. At times it was a maelstrom of white and I could barely see my skis. I slowly climbed through this, almost thankful for the markers. The markers here were not the subtle and unobtrusive markers of Norway, but permanent, unsightly, red

Day 55. As I skied into Ekorrdörren valley on the south side of the Sylan mountains, I just got rare glimpses of the valley sides

crosses which were over the top and unnecessary. It was the Swedish cradle to grave, multiple airbag approach to trail marking. The snow surface after the Ekorrdörren shelter was at last firm. I was no longer sinking into it and could make better time. Soon I reached the pass and the weather cleared momentarily. I snatched the odd view of some of the lower foothills and the base of the peaks, but nothing spectacular. The descent down the north side of the pass was gentle and pleasant. As I descended, the wind diminished from the force 7 to 4 and the spindrift settled down again, no longer chilling my cheeks and freezing on to my eyelashes. After an easy 4 kilometres, some dark shapes of the Sylarnas Fjällstation structures emerged out of the grey. It was a massive complex of buildings. Inside, it was much more spacious, comfortable and better organized than I had expected. I had a nice shower, dried clothes and even had a sauna, quite oblivious to the blizzard outside, unless I looked at the whiteness out of the steamed-up window. I thought of the poor army of Karoliners who had to struggle through something probably much worse than this 300 years ago, without the red cross markers or Gore-Tex clothing. There were about 20 other people staying in this enormous lodge, and in the evening a friendly group of Swedes invited me to join them for supper. I went to bed early, hoping I would get some views tomorrow as I headed north through the remainder of the Sylan mountains.

It was a reasonably short day and the usually accurate Norwegian weather forecast said it would clear up around midday for a short while. There seemed little need to rush off, so I lounged around in the early morning with spindrift still flying around outside. I eventually left mid morning when the wind had diminished, but there was no sign of the lingering mist lifting. Initially, the route to Blåhammarens lodge went gently downhill, but I had put far too much and too sticky a wax on the lower surface of the skis. The result was they kept balling up and I could not slide them at all, so I had to scrape most of the wax off. After that they were a dream with a good glide on the downhill section and sticky enough to grip the snow for the gentle uphill climbs. I was not the first to leave for Blåhammarens lodge, so there was already a good trail. I glanced behind me from time to time but the clouds still covered the mountains. Before long I was at a junction where one route headed down to Storulvån lodge and a roadhead, while the other route started a long sustained climb for 3 kilometres up the slopes of Enkälen. The mist seemed to be slowly lifting, and the plateau was now visible, but the mist still lingered on the mountains and the sky remained grey. I was feeling strong and fit when I started the ascent up Enkälen and my skis were still perfectly waxed. Quite quickly I caught up with two of the three other parties I could see ahead of me. All the time the weather was improving and there was the occasional flash of blue sky and bright sunny patches on the bland grey white slopes. There was a wonderful run down the north side of Enkälen to another small shed used for emergencies and lunch breaks. The first group of six were already inside eating their lunch, and I squeezed in. We were having a chat when the Swedes, who invited me to sit with them for supper last night, arrived 15 minutes later. They said the skies had cleared. We all rushed out and right enough the whole landscape was now basking in sun. I had not really seen the sun since the last day in Rondane some 10 days ago and it was wonderful to feel its warmth on my face again. I took some photos and set off for the final 8 kilometres to Blåhammarens lodge.

Day 56. After three days in the Sylan mountains, the weather cleared for a couple of hours to give me a great view of what I had just passed

I was the first now, so had to break trail in the variable snow; sometimes deep and loose, sometimes firm and compact. It was hot work in the still air with the sun beating down on my back. I soon had to stop and take off my jacket. It was marvellous to ski in the mountains in the sun again. Much of the final 6 kilometres was up a gentle slope. The skis were just gripping enough to stop me sliding back and prevent me wasting energy by using my arms and ski poles. Up and up the gentle slope I went, with the Sylan mountains clear behind and sunny slopes around me. Eventually I skied up a rise and there was Blåhammarens lodge about a kilometre in front of me. I glided across the easy firm snowfield and reached the lodge in the mid afternoon. It had been an easy, short day. I was just in time, as the predicted mist was already coming back in and there was the odd snow flake falling out of the greying sky. There had just been a two hour weather window for me to enjoy the Sylan mountains. At the

Day 56. Looking north from Blåhammarens down to the birch-filled Enaälven valley, and then the bare snowy hills beyond to Storlien

lodge the groups of Swedes who had followed me from Sylarnas Fjällstation soon arrived. While chatting with them the three Dutch also arrived from Storerikvollen cabin. It was good to see the Dutch again and they felt like long lost friends already. It had all the makings of a great evening. I sat with the Dutch for the sumptuous three-course dinner which the lodge provided. We had many lively conversations with lots of laughter right into the evening. It was a pleasure to be in their bright cheerful company. Meanwhile outside the weather had deteriorated to a blizzard again which made the warm candle lit evening inside all the more merry.

After a fine and sociable stay at Blåhammarens, it was time to move on. Everybody else ventured out into a blizzard for the short journey to Storulvån lodge while I had to plough a lonely furrow to Storlien on a seldom-travelled route. I waited a bit to see if the visibility would improve, as I could only see about 20 metres in the heavy snowfall. While waiting, I found out that Øivind had finally liberated my rucksack from customs and we could at last make some arrangements to post it. After waiting a while it seemed the weather was not improving and I had to bite the bullet and go out into it. I felt sure the weather would improve, as I descended from the hill Blåhammarens was situated on. Initially the route down the hill was impossibly thick with mist. It was also reasonably steep, so the skiing was difficult. I snowploughed to keep my speed down, as I could not make out the lie of the land, despite the copious red marker crosses. After a couple of kilometres, a small shed appeared out of the whiteness. As I had just started I skied right past it. Descending a bit further, the visibility slowly improved and I could soon make out the darker patches of the birch copses below, and the forest below them. The descent got a tad steeper, but with the improving view I could go faster. When I entered the birch forest the snow was a bit deeper

Day 57. The hushed birch forest in the Enaälven valley was covered in a thick blanket of soft snow which made it quite enchanting

and this slowed me down, which was great, as my leg muscles were burning with the previous hours snow ploughing. I weaved in and out of clumps of trees as I descended. Eventually this pleasant ski brought me down into the wide valley in the midst of a thick birch forest. Mercifully there was a trail through it but it was deep with new snow. Thick snow lay on the still branches of the birch trees and it was an enchanting calm scene. I slowly skied along this trail sinking deeply into the soft snow. After a kilometre I came to a suspension footbridge over the large frozen Enaälven river. It was near here the frozen Karoliners army spent the second night of their disastrous retreat. When they reached the Enaälven river they knew they had to follow it to reach the Swedish hamlet of Handøl. However, the valley is so flat here they could not tell which way the river flowed, so they had to hack holes in the thick ice to see which way the water moved.

Day 57. Luckily there was an old trail through the birch forest in the Enaälven valley which led to the bridge over the river

Day 57. On the way up Rundvalen I saw some of the narrow spruce trees which are typical of the Taiga-like interior forests of Scandinavia

After crossing the bridge I had to either wax my skis or put skins on for the long, shallow climb in loose snow. I went for the skins. The climb was relatively easy and the scenery very pleasant. There was the odd very thin pointed spruce tree and a smattering of pines which added life to the dull, leafless birch trees. Near the top of the climb, by Rundvalen, I met another skier. He was local and told me he had once seen a wolverine on this hill. From Rundvalen, it was a nice descent through the thickening spruce and pine forest to the village of Storvallen. The spruce were very thin and needle shaped as this allows them to shed snow easily so they are not damaged. Just before Storvallen village I had a simple fall and landed on my bum in a deep pile of soft snow, but broke my rucksack hip belt buckle in the process. I called into the empty youth hostel at Storvallen to enquire about accommodation in Storlien, and got some good information about the route north as well. Storlien was another 6 kilometres through an area of leisure cabins and spruce forest on the north side of the main road. There is little to commend Storlien. It is a border town with an alpine ski development and a cluster of ugly buildings. It was pretty down market as a resort, and was swarming with rudimentary Norwegians on snow scooters. I checked into a poor room above a pub, which was redeemed with a powerful shower. The pub did, however, serve a great meal. Half way through the meal, Andre Spica, who was also doing Norge på langs (The length of Norway) on skis, and who I had met a week ago, texted me to say he was camping in the town. He soon arrived at the pub for a meal and a beer. It was good to see him again and hear his good humoured stories. We laughed about the route gone and discussed the route ahead. We would no doubt meet again soon. Øivind and Hartmut, the trustees of my liberated rucksack, had also sorted out a place for me to rendezvous with it. It would be in about three days time at a hamlet called Sveet where there was a lady called Gudrun Olsen who would receive it from the post bus. She also had a small cabin there that I could use that night. My route to Sveet would largely be through Sweden.

SECTION 8. Sylan.
4 days. 74 km. 21.5 hours. 1830m ascent. 1870m descent.

THE SKI: SECTION 9. NORD TRØNDELAG

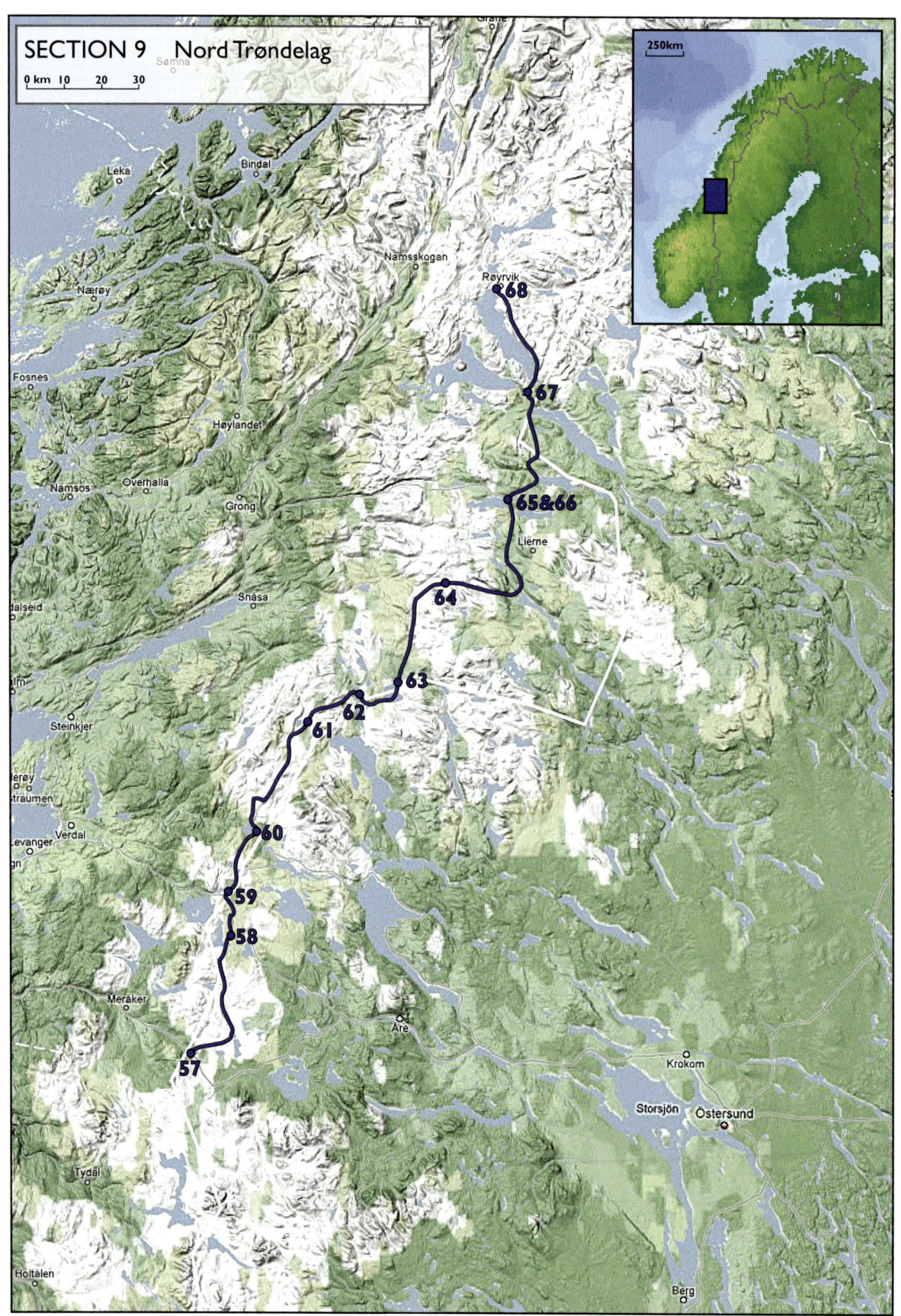

THE SKI: SECTION 9. NORD TRØNDELAG

Day 58. Above Storlien the wind started to whip up the spindrift into a river of ice crystals flowing over the exposed mountain side

It had been snowing all night in Storlien and the streets were deep in snow when I left. I skied back to the east end of town and then headed north on a ski and scooter trail. Within a kilometre the benign still weather at Storlien was replaced by a bitter north wind which picked up the loose snow. I skied up this deserted trail for a good 4 kilometres until I came to a small shelter. I was hopelessly dressed for this bitter weather so went in to put on more clothes out of the swirling spindrift. From the shelter I had a dilemma. I could go east down to Norder Rensjön and then follow the lake north to Rensjösätern private hunting lodge. Alternatively I could risk the shorter way, with no trail, across the exposed Flatrun mountain. With the increasing wind and decreasing visibility I decided to go the considerably longer way. The descent to the strait which separated Norder and Sönner Rensjön lakes was absolutely wonderful. The wind died down and the sun came out. The stark bare plateau, with a metre-high river of sharp spindrift flowing across it, soon vanished as I skied into the first of the birch. These hardy, twisted, deciduous trees in turn gave way to the taiga type forest of thin spruce trees with very sharp crowns. This type of forest covers vast tracts of north-west Sweden, Russia and Canada. When I reached the strait between the lakes, it was completely still and the sun was beating down on me. Turning north, I headed up Norder Rensjön lake with only the very occasional scooter bothering me. It was very quiet and peaceful. As I approached the north end, the apparition I had been told about appeared. Here in the barren wilds of Sweden was the hunting lodge of Rensjösätern. The lodge was built over 100 years ago for Oscar Dickson, a Swedish magnate of Scottish origin who was held in high regard at the end of the 18th Century. He was a sponsor of both Swedish and Norwegian polar expeditions including Fridtjof Nansen's. The most remarkable thing about the hunting lodge at Rensjösätern was it was pink.

Day 58. At Norder Rensjön I came across the first of the taiga type forests which covered the hills around this quiet sunny lake

I passed the lodge and stopped for a pause when three locals arrived on snow scooters. One of them was a know-all with the swagger of a Latino law enforcement officer. They told me the small shelter, or large shed, I was heading for and hoping to spend the night in, at Holmsjöstugan, was private and locked. This was not the information I had, but they told me with such confidence and authority that I believed them. However, they kindly phoned Skalstugan, which was a further 12 kilometres after Holmsjöstugan, and arranged a place for me to stay there. That left me another 20 kilometres to do today and it was already 1430, but it was a beautiful afternoon and as they were also going that way, I would have their snow scooter tracks to follow if it got dark. I set off up through the thinning birch trees and on to the bare slopes of Ugglan. After a sustained climb of 3 kilometres, I reached a junction with the main snow scooter route continuing to Medstugan. I had to turn north from here and continue over the undulating spine of Ugglan hill for a good 5 kilometres before I dropped down into the forests again. Something was happening to the weather, though, and the still blue skies had gone. The sun had disappeared and the wind had begun anew. Indeed, the three scooter tracks I was following were already filling with spindrift. By the time I reached the north end of this high ridge, just some 4 kilometres north of the junction, the wind was up to a force 6, it was snowing heavily, spindrift was everywhere, and the visibility was terrible. The scooter tracks I had hoped to follow had long vanished under the river of spindrift. It was quite remarkable just how quickly the weather was deteriorating. My progress slowed down hugely as I was caught out in a couple of deep snowfields where the snow was up to my knees.

As I descended down the north side of Ugglan I was being buffeted by the wind. I had hoped the wind would decrease as I descended from the mountain, but it increased to a force 7 and the spindrift was dense and thick. I lost the line of stakes which must have been buried in the deep drifts for many hundreds of metres, and in the poor visibility of just 50 metres I could not see where they re-emerged again. I could not ski across this snow but trudged through it. Eventually I descended down into the upper birch forest and by accident found the line of wooden stakes again. I followed them down into the birch trees, hoping for some protection from the wind and spindrift, but there was none. All the small, stocky, strong birch trees here were writhing and whipping in the wind and being blasted by the river of spindrift, which threatened to obscure them. Taking care to follow the bleached broken stakes I trudged through the deep snow in the thrashing woods. After a while I came to a sign which said 'Holmsjöstugan Privat'. I assumed it was indeed locked and did not want to detour for half a kilometre to find out. I decided to continue down to Skalstugan, which I had little hope of reaching in this growing gale, but thought if I could get down into the forest I had the possibility of putting my tent up, especially if I made the spruce forest. The next 4 kilometres were perhaps the hardest of the trip so far. The wind was a good force 8 or 9. I was being buffeted about wildly and was blown over a couple of times. Spindrift was flying everywhere in swirling maelstroms whipped up by the wind and it made a constant hiss against my clothing. I could hardly see 30 metres and frequently lost the line of bleached wooden post markers. The hardy birch trees looked like they were about to snap in the gusts. The snow was deep and difficult and I was frequently up to my knees. There was no chance of getting my map out to navigate and even using my GPS in these conditions was difficult. If I was forced to stop there was no way I would have contemplated putting my tent up. It would have been ripped out of my hands and blown away by the gale. I would just have had to have dug a hole in the snow and crawled into it. Slowly, step by step, I hoped I was edging towards the spruce forest, and the sight of the occasional marker post gave me confidence. In the twilight of dusk the first spruce trees appeared, and as I descended a bit further the spruce got taller and denser.

I was fortunate that I managed to follow the marker posts as I entered the spruce forest. Once I was in the forest I could just see in the twilight where the trail weaved a path through the tall thin trees. The wind had eased considerably now, on the floor of the forest, but I could see the tops of the spruces whipping in the wind. There were large dollops of snow from the last week which had settled all over the spruce branches. As the wind thrashed the trees about, this was all shaken from the branches and dispersed into the wind, so the air was still full of spindrift. I thought about camping here, but there was just 5 kilometres to go, and most of it seemed through the forest. It would have been difficult to keep the loose snow and huge amounts of spindrift out of the tent if I made camp in this deep snow. So I put my head torch on and continued down with its pathetic beam trying to punch a meaningful hole into the spindrift. The descent through the trees was quite difficult, as I could not judge the lie of the land. I was lucky the snow was up to my knees as this slowed me down enough so I did not go careering uncontrollably down the slope. None the less, I must have fallen a good five times. Getting up was arduous, as there was no hard surface to shove myself up from, and my arms just disappeared up to my shoulder in the bottomless fluff when I pushed down. At last I reached Skalsvattnet lake. I was worried about crossing its exposed surface, but the wind seemed to have dropped down to a small gale now, and the surface of the lake was reasonably firm. In addition, there was a snow scooter track across the lake marked with bamboo poles with a twist of reflective tape fastened to them. The head torch picked up these flashes and guided me across the lake. Once across, I was delighted to see the snow scooter track continued up a small forest-clad knoll for a kilometre, which made the ascent very easy. From the top of the hill I could see the orange lights of Skalstugan shining through the blizzard a mere half kilometre away. I was going to make it. I arrived at Skalstugan at 2000, which was a good two hours after nightfall. I took off my skis and ventured into the foyer, looking like a yeti, plastered white in spindrift. A few people came to the door and stared as I extricated my face and head from my balaclava and jacket hood. They seemed very surprised to hear I had come from Storlien, through what they described as a storm. It seemed the easier of the two options I had earlier, which was to carry on or camp in a snow-hole. Soon the manager, Elizabeth, came and ushered me through to the kitchen. Skalstugan was not open to the public, but belonged to a financial organization, and the guests were all private. In the kitchen, I was shown the food the staff had just served to the guests and told to help myself. They could not have been more helpful and pleasant, and they spoilt me with juices and, in addition to the large meal, desserts. Elizabeth then took me over to an old building where some of the staff stayed and where there was a vacant room. It was charicterful and rickety and there was also a shower downstairs. After a shower I crawled into my sleeping bag, thanked my good fortune that the men of the snow scooters had phoned Skalstugan and that the staff here were so friendly and hospitable. It turned out the man with the confident swagger was in fact a policeman, and he was also a friend of the helpful Elizabeth.

Elizabeth made sure I had a huge breakfast and then showed me round the main building. It had been built at the end of the 19th Century by a Scottish magnate called Tom Nickalls, who made his money on the American railroads. He was a keen sportsman and built Skalstugan as a hunting lodge. The architecture in the public rooms was very similar to that in the hunting lodges I had visited in Scotland, especially the roof beams. These rooms were adorned with hunting artefacts and solid furniture from a bygone era. When Tom Nickalls died in 1899, none of his many children, some of whom were famous rowers, wanted to inherit the hunting lodge in wildest Sweden, and so it was auctioned in London. It was bought in 1902 by K. A. Wallenberg, a sportsman and banking magnate from a well-known and respected Swedish family. He in turn left it to his nephew, Marcus Wallenberg, in 1932. In 1947 Marcus bequeathed it to a foundation he established at Skalstugan, which was now to serve as a country retreat for the more notable employees of Stockholms (later Skandinaviska) Enskilda Bank, (SEB). This bank was established by the Wallenberg family 150 years ago; the family is still associated with it. Indeed, the powerful and influential Wallenberg family has fingers in many business and political pies in Sweden today. After its establishment, the Skalstugan foundation acquired another 22,000 hectares in the area to form a large estate. One of the estate cabins was in fact, Holmsjöstugan, which I was told was locked yesterday by the policeman. Although private, I found out it has an emergency shelter attached to it which is always open, and I would have been entitled to use it last night after all, given the severe, and almost life-threatening, conditions. At midday I was ready to leave and said my goodbyes to the good-natured and happy staff and the well-liked and generous manager, Elizabeth.

Day 59. Skiing through the sun-kissed forest across fields of new glistening snow from Skalstugan lodge's ski trail to the road

Ignoring advice, I took one of the lodge's ski trails north for a couple of kilometres through very beautiful forest. The trail wound through copses of birch and spruce and across open glades of glistening snow. The weather was fantastic. It was windstill with a perfectly blue sky. How it had changed since yesterday evening! I revelled in the sun and enjoyed the mood it put me in. Where the trail doubled back in a circuit to the lodge again, it passed close to the road. I left the trail here and waded through the sparkling snow in the forest, under the hot sun, to reach the road. It was only some 7 kilometres to Norway along the road, which was covered in compacted snow and easy to ski along. Indeed, within an hour I had skied along the flat section and made the swift descent to Sandvika. To the west and north, spruce forests filled the valley and the white sun-drenched mountains of Norway rose beyond. I would ski in these mountains tomorrow. I skied down the road and passed right through the sleepy customs and border post without stopping until I got to Sandvika. From here it was a short ski along a road to the quaint self-service cabin at Innstua. I had to clear snow from the door to get in. Once inside I was surprised to see it had electricity. With the wall heaters on and the wood stove lit, it soon warmed up from the minus 10 it was when I first arrived. The cabin was very comfortable and furnished with traditional farmhouse furniture. It got very cosy by the time darkness fell and I had to light

Day 59. As I skied along the road in Sweden I could look across the valley to the border and beyond to the white mountains of Norway

Day 59. The cosy traditional cabin at Innstua was tucked away in a forest clearing covered in loose deep snow

the candles. The larder here was very sparse, though, and the dinner I had was dull.

I left Innstua cabin early, as I was sure the forest I had to ski through today had some difficult surprises to spring on me. It was a bit windy with the odd snow flake in the overcast air as I skied up the small road for 4 kilometres until I reached Breivatnet lake. Just before the lake was a cleared parking area and a sign pointing north, saying 'Veressjøen', which is another name for Veresvatnet. It looked like the ski trail I needed to find my way through the woods. There had been a lot of skiers this way recently, and even with the new snows of late there was a prominent ski trail through the forest of tall sharp spruce. I followed this trail for a good kilometre to a treeless clearing which was a frozen, snow-covered marsh. Here, the ski trail disappeared under newly-drifted snow. I found some old bleached posts I assumed were the trail markers. I followed them until they reached the forest and the trail reappeared as the snow had hardly drifted here between the trees. This alternation between a reasonable trail through the spruce trees and stretches of deep snow with no ski trail across frozen marshes continued for many kilometres. I soon climbed above the spruce forest on to a hillside covered in large pine trees. The trail vanished and I had to trudge through the deeper snow. It was slow going as my skis were constantly on an upward slope and with every step I had to press down some 25 centimetres of snow. However, the threat of bad weather had now receded; there was even some blue sky and I was now in extremely beautiful pine forests with some venerable, old, twisted giants. I continued to climb out of the trees on to a very broad ridge with a couple of lakes gouged into it. From here I got a marvellous view north across forests to large, rounded mountains in the distance. These mountains, which stretched out across the northern horizon, must have been about 1250 metres high. They were the Skjækerfjella mountains, which extend across the border with Sweden, where they are a national park. With the high rounded mountains and extensive pine forests, one could be forgiven for comparing it to the more rugged parts of the Scottish highlands after an extremely heavy snowfall.

Day 60. Skiing through the sparse pine woods to Veresvatnet lake and Sveet farm with the Skjækerfjella mountains in the background

The snow was much firmer above the tree line, as the wind had broken the loose snowflakes into icy crystals which packed together more tightly. I was not sinking in at all and could enjoy the section until I descended back into the pine woods again, where I had to work much harder in shin-deep snow. I managed to keep to the vague line of stakes which marked the summer track. I had hoped that by following them I would find some ski tracks to lead me down through the more difficult spruce forest far below me. However, there were none but the route remained manageable, especially as I was going slightly downhill. Once the trail rose over a small crest I got my first glimpse of Veresvatnet lake some 4 kilometres to the north. I skied through more of the open pine woods, past more magnificent trees, many with spiralled trunks which come with age. Just at the final descent where the pine woods gave way to dense spruce forest, I came across some very fresh snow scooter tracks. They didn't follow the stakes but descended to the lake anyway. I followed them down through the steep forest until I reached the lake, where the scooter tracks went off in another direction. I had to plough a deep furrow for a kilometre across the loose snow on the lake to get to Sveet farm. Here I met Gudrun Olsen, who had run a small summer campsite with a few simple cabins here for decades. She was now trying to hand it over to her son, or sell it, so she could enjoy her retirement. Although the cabins were in hibernation for

Day 60. Looking down past dense the spruce forest to the frozen Veresvatnet lake with Sveet farm on the very right of the photo

the winter, she had already warmed one up for me as she knew I was coming. Øivind had told her and had also posted my X-Pod rucksack to her after liberating it from the inflexible customs officials who had held it for nearly a month. I eagerly skied to the warm cabin and unwrapped my new rucksack. I transferred most of my belongings from my old rucksack and was delighted with the capacity and weight. I was now down from about 19 to 17 kilos, excluding provisions. The two kilo difference doesn't sound much but in reality was a huge change. I was pretty fit now, so with the lighter load I should be flying along, gobbling up the kilometres. I returned to Gudrun with my old rucksack to send back to Øivind on the post bus. Gudrun invited me in for coffee and cake. She takes a fair bit of interest in the Norge på langs winter skiers and summer walkers as they all have to pass through this bottleneck at Sveet. Apparently there were only some 20 people living in this very beautiful area around the Veresvatnet now. This surprised me, as I thought with the good farming it would be more. Most of the farms here only had cows and there were no sheep. The surrounding hills were divided up into grazing areas for domesticated reindeer, and sheep were not popular. This was just as well, because lynx were apparently common in the area and there were also some wolverine here, and either of these predators would have made short work of the relatively docile sheep. That evening I phoned Steinar Gaundal, the owner of Gaundal farm, some 40 kilometres to the north of Sveet and Veresvatnet lake, which was my next stop. He said he had a cabin I could use. He also gave me directions to get there, in the present conditions, but warned me the forests were heavy going with deep snow and told me to keep high and go over Seterfjellet. He then offered to drive his snow scooter from his very remote and roadless farm for 15 kilometres up through the forests in Ståggådalen and back again. This was so I would have a firm trail to ski along; otherwise, he explained, I had little hope of getting there in a day. I was very grateful for this help. That evening I ate some dried food I had been carrying since Lindesnes to reduce my rucksack's weight even further.

I was up well before there was the slightest glow of daybreak, but breakfast, packing and cleaning the cabin all took their toll on my early start, and I eventually left at 0700 when dawn was just breaking. It was snowing heavily when I shouldered my new pack and put on my skis. This was a bit disappointing, because if I was to make Gaundal today, I needed good visibility so I could ski quickly along the rounded ridges of the bare mountains. I skied along the road for 3 kilometres towards Vera, hoping the weather forecasters had not made a rare mistake. I found the track I was looking for which went up through the forest and would hopefully lead me up on to the firmer snowfields above the tree line. Surprisingly, the track was partly cleared for a short distance, and after that an old snow scooter track continued. This track went up the hillside through the forest roughly to where I wanted to go. I followed it, as it was firm under some 20 centimetres of new snow, and it was a better alternative to wading waist-deep through the loose forest. I did not look at my map until I reached the bare hilltop, but I was roughly where I wanted to be on the treeless flat summit of Reinsmyrhøgda. I could now hopefully ski north east across the mountain ridge to Klumpan and then Seterfjellet.

After just a kilometre I came to a ravine separating me from the rounded top of Klumpan. Bugger! There was no way across this ravine, called Vargtjønndalen, which was about 30-40 metres deep. When I looked east or west for a kilometre I could not see an easy way to cross. I opted to go west, as this looked more promising on my map. I had to detour for a kilometre before I got to the end of the ravine. Here, the sheer rocky sides eased off and became steep slopes. I cautiously skied down one slope to reach the small Vargtjønna lake on the ravine floor. The ski across this small tarn was difficult, due to the deep snow, but the climb up the other side was desperate. It took almost an hour of hard work to force a groove in the deep snow as I zig-zagged up the tree-clad slope. Once out of Vargtjønndalen ravine I still had another 2 kilometres of difficult terrain in deep snow. I skirted round other ravines and negotiated numerous knolls covered in steep drifts and cornices. It was very taxing and slow work. At least the snow had stopped and the sun was trying to break through. However, I

Day 61. Once I reached the summit of Reinsmyrhøgda, I hoped I was home and dry, but was shocked when I arrived at the hidden ravine

had wasted precious hours and energy in this wintery obstacle course. I assumed Andre Spica was half a day behind me, and he would inevitably follow my tracks into this trap. I tried to warn him, by sending a text message, but there was no signal. I guessed he would be cursing me later that day or the next. Once away from this gnarly terrain things got much better. The deep snow vanished as I climbed on to the windblown ridge of rounded tops which stretched north east. The Skjækerfjella mountains rose up out of the dark birch forests on either side of the ridge I was skiing along. These mountains are found in both Sweden and Norway. They seemed almost luminous white under the dark grey skies. I continued the lovely easy ski along the ridge to Hitre Seterfjellet and then up to Nordre Seterfjellet. Below me, to the west, was the wooded Lakadalen which I was advised to stay clear of. I could imagine what it would be like after my tangle with the ravine this morning, and felt quite smug up here on the firm snow. Once I reached the top of Nordre Seterfjellet it was time to head down into the forest where Steinar Gaundal said he would make a trail with his snow scooter. I glided down the open slopes in a long diagonal descent on the west side of Lakavassklumpen until I reached the valley floor. It was a glorious descent across the consistent snow to reach the valley, just at the watershed between Lakadalen and Ståggådalen. Steinar Gaundal had advised me to follow Ståggådalen by keeping to the treeless west side and avoiding the forest on the east.

I reached the watershed at 1430; time was ticking away. If Steinar had not made the scooter tracks, or I could not find them, I was resigned to camp. Suddenly, I saw a light flashing in the sparse birch woods. It was a snow scooter and it was coming directly towards me; Steinar Gaundal was coming to introduce himself and check that everything was OK. We chatted a bit and he told me if I followed his tracks I would do the 16 kilometres in three hours. What a service! He then headed off, back down the same tracks to his inaccessible farm, leaving an easy trail for me to follow. I took my ski-skins off and started to glide along his scooter tracks. They followed the very shallow descent of the flat, wide valley for 8 kilometres down to the confluence of Ståggåelva and Fiskløysa streams. There were fewer trees on

Day 61. Looking south west from Ståggåfjellet to some Skjækerfjella mountains and back up Ståggådalen which I had just skied down

the west side of the valley and the snow was firm, especially after the scooter had passed over it. On the east side of the valley was forest that looked like it would be fiendishly difficult to ski through. When I reached the confluence of the streams I was starting to tire. This morning's squandered efforts and my small breakfast were coming home to roost and my blood sugar level was dropping. However, there was still one last trick up the day's sleeve, which was Ståggåfjellet, a 100-metre climb up and over a long hill. The scooter tracks which Steinar had made entirely for my benefit were indispensable, and I would have camped there without them. It was about 1700 when I set off up the ridge and the sun had just set, but it was still light. The mountains which had been luminous white all day, now turned a remarkable deep blue. From the top of Ståggåfjellet I could make out the homestead of Gaundal. The descent to the valley was wonderful. Steinar had driven the scooter to give a long slow run for me. Soon I was whizzing towards the beautiful forest of old majestic pines below. A capercaillie flew from one of the trees. After crossing a frozen marshy delta where birch trees lined the natural levees on each side of the river, I arrived at the homestead. Steinar came out to meet me.

Day 61. The yellow Gaundal farmhouse and the red farm buildings were very well kept and comfortable, despite the extreme remoteness

The cabin he had for me was perfect, with an inside toilet and fridge. I chatted with him for a while and he asked if I was hungry. I was. He disappeared, then returned with 10 eggs, a loaf of bread, margarine, a litre of milk and on top of all that, a very lean and tender kilo of roasted elg (moose) fillet. After he left I fell upon this feast like a famished man with no manners. The dried food in my pack could be postponed for a less happy occasion. I then tidied up my stuff and went up to visit Steinar and his mother in the main house for coffee and cake. The Gaundal homestead is a remarkable place, and the Gaundal family has been associated with it since the 16th Century. Initially they hunted wild animals for their skins and meat, but many generations later they started keeping sheep. There are still a few sheep here today, but tourism is much more feasible. Steinar's whole farm is some 7500 hectares. There are lakes on it for fishing, and moorland and forest for hunting. The tourists who come here are mainly Swedish. They come at Easter to ice fish, and in the summer to fish and sometimes hunt. There are a lot of wolverine in the area, and also some bears. Between them they take about 10 sheep each summer. There are not a lot of lynx here as the terrain is apparently not gnarly enough. There are also a lot of elg and grouse in the forests. Steinar was a wildlife officer and he told me there was also the occasional Arctic fox passing through. But life here is remote and difficult. It is 26 kilometres to the nearest road. In the winter, these 26 kilometres are easily covered by snow scooter if the conditions are good. In the summer he has to use a small aeroplane to go the nearest town for supplies. He has built his own 13-kilowatt hydro-electric plant, some 4 kilometres away, at Grønlivatnet, and erected poles and cables to bring electricity to his house, sheep barn, henhouse and the few cabins for rent. Steinar's mother was 87 and still feisty. Remarkably she had brought up seven children in this far-flung outpost. Like most Norwegian farms, it was well cared for, and the cabin I was in was one of the best on the trip so far. I could not really have thanked Steinar enough for the food and the scooter tracks. It was a fascinating end to a great day and it was wonderful to arrive at such a unique place with such generous hosts.

I was still tired from yesterday's 11-hour ski without a break so did not get up until 0800. I then had the remainder of the eggs I had been given for breakfast. Afterwards, I chatted with Steinar and his mother for a good half hour. They showed me aerial pictures of their farm in the autumn. It looked stunning, resting in the golden fields and surrounded by the orange birch forest in its late fall colours. As I was about to ski off, up through the forest to the bare hillside, and eventually on to Holden cabin, Steinar volunteered to drive up through the woods on his snow scooter to make more tracks for me. This would save me at least an hour, possibly two, and a lot of hard work as it was about 3 kilometres to the forest's edge and firmer snow. I gratefully accepted, embarrassed at the superb hospitality he had shown me. Indeed, the hospitality and service at Gaundal was equal to Skalstugan a few days earlier, and that was second to none. The climb through the woods was short, and with the snow scooter tracks to follow, I made good time. Steinar's tracks ended at the tree line, but here, the snow was harder and easier to ski on. There was a line of old telegraph poles between Gaundal and Holden which carried the telephone wire. Apparently, the best route to Holden was simply to follow them. It was overcast, with the odd snowflake, but the visibility was good. As I climbed, the views got better, and the Skjækerfjella mountains I passed through yesterday were especially impressive. They were nothing like

Day 62. From the shoulder of Nordskardklumpen I got my first view of Gjevsjøen lake, surrounded by dark forest

Day 62. The descent to Holden farm, in a forest clearing at the end of Holden lake was wonderful, except for one small tricky section

Jotunheimen or Rondane; they were far more rounded, but spectacular, none the less, as their remoteness made up for their lack of height. When I was half-way, on the higher slopes of Nordskardklumpan, I got a wonderful panorama down the 30-kilometre-long white frozen Torrön lake, surrounded by a wide fringe of dark forest. As I skied a bit further over the smooth broad shoulder of Nordskardklumpan, the lake at Gjevsjøen, which was tomorrow's goal, appeared, and then Holderen lake also slowly rose from the snow-covered shoulder. Both these lakes were also surrounded by forest, and I was apprehensive about the deep snow I might have to wade through to reach them. It was an easy run down to the upper pine trees as I continued along the old telegraph poles, bleached light grey by decades of weather and sun. I could now make out the farm buildings at Holden, beside the unblemished white surface of Holderen lake. From here, the farm looked absolutely idyllic, in its clearing in the sunny pine forest.

Today's route had one last challenge. On the valley floor a stream had cut a path through the moraine. On the far side of this stream was a steep bank some 10 metres high. I went downstream for half a kilometre but found no way up it, so I retraced my furrow and went half a kilometre upstream and found a difficult and exhausting route though the deep snow up its almost impenetrable, steep side. This wild goose chase to find a way up the moraine took nearly an hour, and showed me just how impossible, even the smallest obstacles can be when the snow is deep and loose like this. After clearing the moraine I had a very pleasant ski through the stunningly beautiful and sunny pine forest. I had to make a small detour to a bridge which was marked on my map, as the river was surprisingly unfrozen and open in many places, making it difficult to cross. On the

Day 62. I had to cross the river over the summer bridge, as it was unfrozen and open despite recent temperatures of minus 30

other side of the river there were more big old pine trees, and I could see the frozen lake beyond them. Soon I could see the red farm and its old outbuildings appearing out of the forest. One of these outbuildings was the tourist association cabin. It was in a very pretty setting under the winter sun. The farm itself was as isolated as Gaundal, however, there was no one living here throughout the year, only occasionally in the summer. It was one of the most peaceful and idyllic spots I had seen on the trip so far. The outbuildings were all old log buildings. The self-service cabin was also old and it was very authentic inside, with cracked log walls, a large fireplace with a more recent and efficient stove, and simple old furnishings. It was one of the nicest and cosiest of the cabins to date. I got a fire going, melted some snow and then looked for the larder. It was not well stocked, but had some tinned peaches and stew. I wrote my blog while the temperature outside plummeted. I noticed that the cabin, although old and authentic, had some cold

Day 62. One of the old log farm buildings at Holden has been clad in rustic planks and converted to a cabin for walkers and skiers

Day 63. The old log cabin at Holden was very traditional and cosy but the stove struggled to heat the room due to some drafts

drafts, and the stove struggled to heat the room up as the mercury dropped to minus 23 outside.

I assumed the next day would be short, and as the weather was lovely, there was no rush, and I lingered at the cabin, enjoying its rustic charm and studying my map. I eventually left at 1030 in blazing sunshine. I decided not to go directly through the forest to Gjevsjøen, but to take the longer route down Holderen lake into Sweden. I reasoned that the forest would be impossibly slow in the deep snow, and I had a hunch there might be some snow scooter tracks if I went via Sweden. Snow scooters are not allowed in Norway with a few exceptions where it is a necessary part of running a business, like operating a rural farm, herding reindeer or servicing telecom masts. Even then the snow scooter can only be driven in connection with running that business. Norwegians are very law abiding, so there is little abuse of these regulations, especially in the south. In the more liberal Sweden, snow scooters have been allowed pretty much everywhere since their invention 50 years ago, except in some national parks and nature reservations. The genie is out of the bottle in Sweden and it will be very difficult to contain it now. Many Norwegians haul their snow scooters on trailers from Norway, then indulge themselves in Swedish nature, which increasingly irritates the Swedes. It was a very beautiful trip down the sunny Holderen lake. I was skiing south for the first time, and even with my glasses on the sun was blindingly bright and very warm. Somewhere down the short lake I crossed into Sweden and then a bit further on I came across a snow scooter trail. It went east towards the beautiful pine forest along the shoreline and then weaved through the big trees to Björkede farm. This farm was similar to Holden with a red farm house and many log outbuildings, and it was equally tranquil in the bright winter sun. There are Stone Age animal traps near here and some remains of an Iron Age settlement at Björkede farm itself, showing this was a worthwhile area to settle long before this lovely farm was built in the 18th Century. The farm overlooks an island in the frozen river between Gjevsjøen and Holderen lakes. The track from the farm goes over an old wooden bridge, crosses this wooded island, and then goes over another old wooden bridge before it vanishes into the forest for some 30 kilometres before it arrives at a tiny community at the south end of Torrön lake.

I crossed the two wooden bridges and the island in the frozen river and headed north east for 6 kilometres up the south side of the same river which drained Gjevsjøen lake. My route took me along a forest track buried under a metre of snow. There was a scooter track down the middle of it which made the ski easy and fast. As I skied through the pine trees in the sun it got warmer and warmer. I had to stop and strip down to my vest. There were masses of moose tracks in the forest. At the end of this easy, bright ski the track reached some old cabins on the edge of Gjevsjøen lake. The farm I was heading for was 7 kilometres across the lake and back into Norway, as the border runs across the lake. There were some old scooter tracks going to the farm, which was lucky. If I deviated from the barely visible scooter tracks, which were covered in spindrift, then I was up to my knees in deep snow as I sank right down to the hard ice on the lake's surface. Suddenly there was a bitter wind blowing, which blew the spindrift around in small tornado-like vortexes above the lake. On the far side, when I was back in the forest, the wind died and the warmth of the sun returned for the short ski up to the red buildings of Gjevsjøen farm. There are actually two farms at Gjevsjøen, but one is not used. The

Day 63. Björkede farm was well sited in a clearing in a pine forest beside a river and was accessed by two old wooden bridges

Day 63. Looking across Gjevsjøen lake to the farm's vicinity and one of the smaller mountains in the Blåfjella-Skjækerfjella National Park

active farm is run by Kristian Gjevsjø and his parents. It was very much like Holden and Björkede farms, with the farmhouse surrounded by masses of old log buildings. Even the huge barn was constructed of old logs. The farmhouse at Gjevsjøen was relatively new, however. Kristian knew I was coming because Steinar Gaundal had phoned him. He had already warmed up a small cabin for me, which was perfect. We chatted a bit, mostly about his 2.5 kilowatt windmill, and the two tonnes of batteries he had to store the power in. I settled in, unpacked and started writing my blog, when there was a knock on the door. I thought it was Kristian with some bread. I opened it to see the beaming smile of Andre Spica. He had made it from Gaundal in a day, which was quite a feat with his sledge in this deep snow. He was full of adrenaline after the hard ski, and had the glint of victory in his eyes at having caught me up. I was glad to see him. He soon spread his considerable equipment about the cabin. We chatted a lot about the route from Storlien where we last met, especially the Vargtjønndalen ravine north of Vera where he had optimistically followed my tracks into what he described as "hell". He got so frustrated in the difficult terrain there, he hoped that I had had to suffer a miserable bivouac on the mountain that evening! Because of his infectious good humour, I decided I would ski with him for a couple of days after all.

Andre managed to arrange a meal with the Gjevsjø family. It was fresh trout caught in the lake through the ice and also a large serving of roast elg. It was absolutely delicious and there was masses of it. After the meal we chatted with the family for a couple of hours. They had been here at the farm for over 200 years. They owned a vast tract of land with many thousands of hectares. They also had a few sheep, but like the Gaundals, made their living off tourists who came here to ice fish in the winter and to fish from a boat in the summer. There were also hunting groups who stayed to shoot ptarmigan and occasionally elg. There were many elg in the vicinity and each year the Gjevsjø family shot about five just for their own larder. Gjevsjøen lake was teeming with trout. Some of the photos in the farmhouse showed huge specimens of eight kilos with hooked lower jaws. Trout with these characteristics cannot survive on insects alone and have to metamorphose into predatory cannibalistic ferox trout, which primarily hunt and eat Arctic char but will also eat their lesser brethren. There is a national park, the third biggest in Norway, called Blåfjella-Skjækerfjella which safeguards this whole region on the Norwegian side of the border. On the Swedish side, there are two protected areas, called Skäckerfjällen Naturreservat and Svenskådalen Naturreservat which are adjacent to the Norwegian areas, and make this a vast wilderness. The whole area is characterized by high moorland, lakes and tarns, forested valleys with old-growth pines and spruce, and extensive marshes, which I had not seen as they were all frozen and covered with snow. It is also

Day 63. The main farm at Gjevsjøen had a new farmhouse, but all the outbuildings, barns and cabins were old log buildings

Day 64. Heading up through the fantastic pine forests on the way up to Seterlifjellet and the bare mountain plateau

one of the few remaining bastions of the rarer mammals like wolverine, lynx, bear, Arctic fox and, occasionally, even wolf. There was once talk of including the enclaves of Gjevsjøen and Gaundal farms into the protected areas which surround them on all sides, but this was met with strong opposition from the two families, especially Steinar Gaundal, who argued that they would effectively have to sell to the government and leave. It does not really seem necessary to include the farms in the national park as the cultural heritages at the farms are being well preserved.

Day 64. Andre hauling his sledge up the final slopes of Seterlifjellet past the last remaining vestiges of the birch scrub

Mrs Gjevsjø prepared Andre and me a super breakfast. It was quite a spread and included a large plate of waffles, fresh bread, eggs and good Swedish coffee. We then said goodbye to the family and set off around 0800 on a snowy, slightly overcast morning. It made a welcome change to ski with Andre. It was fun to have company and we chatted as we went up through the spruce trees to Livsjøen lake. We crossed the lake and then entered a pine forest as the sun came out. I find pine forests beautiful at any time but they were especially so this morning. The sun and the bright Nordic light made the trees stand proud in the brilliant white, almost luminous snow. We passed the small tarn of Setertjønna and started to climb out of the trees and up on to the bare hillside on Seterlifjellet. The sun was out now and the snow showers had stopped, but a slight breeze blew from the south east. There was some lingering mist in the high valley on the mountain moorland north of Seterlifjellet when we reached it an hour later. Here there was a string of lakes that we followed north for some 12 kilometres. Andre had a fancy GPS, far more sophisticated than mine, with the map already on it, and this made navigation very easy in the mist. The soft snow of the forest was soon forgotten as we sped from lake to lake across firm and fast snow. The mist was also lifting as the breeze increased and the mountains on this plateau were slowly unveiled. We skied side by side chatting continually and stopping for Andre to take photos and videos. It didn't seem to take long to ski across all the lakes and glide through the saddle between the cone-shaped mountains of Gauptjønnaksla and Finnhuva. The breeze, however, had now become a wind and rivers of spindrift were starting to flow across the snow's surface.

Day 64. On the mountain plateau near Urddalsfjellet the gale was blowing spindrift across the exposed plateau in a river of ice crystals

After we passed this saddle we turned north east and crossed a wide open valley, dominated by a shark's fin of a mountain called Lurusneisa. The wind had now become a small gale and was buffeting us about. We fought into the wind as we rounded the north side of Lurusneisa and reached the southern slopes of Urddalsfjellet. Due to the time of day and the increasing gale, we decided it would be madness to go over this mountain and camp as initially planned. We now thought it would be much better to pass to the south of it and hopefully find a sheltered camp in the trees of upper Fossdal. This meant a final hour battling into the gale over a shallow watershed. The bitter wind was cutting right through my fleece trousers and the end of my privates were already numb. However, my windproof salopettes were at the bottom of my rucksack and I could not get them out easily in this wind. I therefore had to put a more accessible thick woollen sock into my underpants to stop the wind cutting through my drafty trousers. With my chilled privates now thawing out in the sock, there was just a short descent into the twisted stunted birch trees in upper Fossdal. The birch trees offered very little in the way of a windbreak, but did reduce the force 8 gale down to a force 6 wind. We decided it would be tolerable to put the tents up here, despite the wind and the constant river of spindrift. Within half an hour we had our tents up, mine small and cramped and Andre's slightly more spacious. Despite burying the storm flaps sewn around my flysheet and anchoring the tent well, it still rippled and beat noisily in the wind. I heated water on my small gas stove for the dehydrated meal I keep for camping. When this was finished it was dark, so I found my earplugs to try and dull the noise of the flapping tent, so it did not irritate or worry me too much. I then zipped up the inner tent, tightened my sleeping bag hood, so I resembled an Egyptian mummy, and soon fell asleep on the thin mattress.

After a very blustery and noisy night, I woke to find the inner tent covered in frost on the inside. When I unzipped it I saw that it was also covered in fine spindrift which had been forced under the flysheet by the wind. To reduce condensation I had sewn storm flaps round the circumference of the tent, except the two end panels, one of which was the door. The spindrift was blown through this gap and I was paying for the mistake I had made some 10 weeks ago. Still, the tent held up well in the strong wind, despite this. The sleeping bag foot was damp, due to contact with the frosty inner tent. I boiled some water and put it in my plastic water bottles. I then put the water bottles inside my boots to thaw them out, while I had breakfast. Given the wind, the spindrift and also the mist on the mountains, both Andre and I were sceptical of going north over the rugged exposed plateau of Hykkelfjellet to Nordli. This area might be a maze of problems with corniced knolls and ravines. To risk going into this possible labyrinth in bad visibility would have been foolhardy. We decided instead to bail out and head down Fossdal. This initially meant going into the teeth of the strong wind, but we hoped that as we descended to the pine and then spruce forests the wind would diminish. This descent down the valley would take us through these forests and across frozen swamps. We would have to try and avoid the forest with its deep snow, and link up the exposed open expanses of the frozen swamps, where the wind would have packed the snow. We set off around 0830, having wrestled the tents down and packed everything in the driving spindrift. The gentle descent was quick and within an hour we were into the first of the conifers. We managed to link up the swamps and keep out of the forest by heading down the north side of Fossdal valley, and then, by the knoll of Litlklokklumpen, crossing to the south side. After about three hours, during which we were really very lucky not to get bogged down in deep forest snow, we reached a lake which was also called Holden. The 4 kilometre ski across the lake was horrible. The wind reappeared and the snow had a thin crust on it. Sometimes this crust supported me and then it suddenly collapsed and I was up to my knees. Andre fared a bit better as he was lighter and only had a light rucksack as the rest was on his sledge. It was a slow tedious trudge east across the lake with very limited views due to the poor weather. Eventually we reached the end of the lake by a tiny hamlet called Aunet. There was a road here which we planned to follow to the town of Nordli.

The road was much busier than either of us had anticipated, and it was hardly covered in snow. What snow there was at the side of the road had gravel embedded in it. I opted to take my skis off and put them on my backpack and walk. Andre had no option but to continue with his skis on and hope the gravel embedded in the ice and snow would not scrape a hole in his sledge, which weighed well over 60 kilos. We phoned the shop at Nordli to enquire about a cabin to rent which someone had tipped me off about. We got this arranged which cheered us up a bit. I cannot pretend that the next 20 kilometres were anything but dull and tedious. When we reached a point where the icy road descended, Andre disappeared ahead on his skis with his plastic sledge noisily bouncing along behind him. I was more cautious with my equipment and walked the whole way, not wanting to damage my skis or myself if I suddenly hit gritty sections and dived forwards on to the hard ice as my skis suddenly stopped. I eventually got to Nordli about half an hour after Andre, just as it was getting dark. He directed me to the cabin which our hosts, Astrid and Ragnar Monsen, had already warmed up. They were both very elderly and for decades had been renting out the few cabins they had to long distance walkers and skiers. Their visitor's book contained glowing reports. They told us the shop and Lierne Bakery at Nordli has a tradition of providing free coffee, cakes and pancakes to all the long distance walkers and skiers who pass through the town. We set off for it and were well plied with coffee and cakes at this community shop. Since leaving southern Norway the hospitality was hard to beat. I also bought some food to last me the next few days to Røyrvik before we returned to the Monsen's. Still full with cake, I was invited into Astrid Monsen's house and plied with waffles, homemade strawberry jam and more coffee. I suppose rural people the world over are more thoughtful than their urban counterparts, and the Monsen's were no exception. That afternoon Andre decided to take a break from his trip. He had had an erratic journey from the south so far, with a few diversions and pauses, and had even skipped a section. He arranged for a friend to come and pick him up that evening for a couple of days respite. I had a stricter regime to follow, and was a bit irritated by his lack of consistency and short attention span. I suspect Andre also knew the bottom of his sledge had taken a beating on the road, and there was potentially another 50 kilometres of it over the next two days.

It seemed ages since my last rest day in Stugudal some two weeks ago. I had covered a lot of kilometres since then, and as I also had a considerable amount of writing to catch up on I thought I deserved a rest. I also had a few nagging problems to sort out. I desperately needed a shower and had to wash my clothes. I needed to sew a parting seam on my Berghaus yeti gaiters, which I was annoyed about, as they are one of their flagship products. I also needed to look at my maps to plan where I was going to go after Børgefjell which I hoped to pass in a week or so. By mid afternoon I had done the writing and sauntered into Nordli. It really was a friendly place, where people had time to stop and ask questions. At the shop and petrol station, everybody was interested in chatting, giving advice and generally being helpful. It was a charming small community and a great place to wander around. I asked the owners of the petrol station for a route north and they advised me to take the 'Flyktningsløype' or escape route used in the war to flee to Sweden as far as Kvelia. Then I should follow the small lane to Tunnsjø senter. At that point a customer interrupted and said she could organize a cabin for me, just beyond Tunnsjø senter, at her son's farm. She gave him a quick ring and it was arranged that I could rent a cabin on Nynes farm tomorrow. The day after that I could ski down the huge Limingen lake all the way to Røyrvik, and the start of Børgefjell. This all made perfect sense and fitted in with my plans. I returned to the cabin where Mrs Monsen had washed my clothes and gave them to me to dry. After hanging them up in the warm cabin I had the luxury of a late afternoon siesta. In the evening I went back to the Monsen's house to pay and was offered more coffee. They told me spring comes late here, as the frozen Laksjøen lake acts like a deep freeze. Once the ice has gone the leaves unfold very quickly and the place erupts into a lush green paradise around mid May. When I returned to my cabin in the bitter evening air, I saw six roe deer in their garden, feeding on scraps of bread which had kindly been put out on the snow to help them through the hard winter.

Day 67. Skiing through the forest from Nordli to Kvelia I followed the tracks which had been prepared for the Flyktningerennet ski race

It was only 10 kilometres to Kvelia along the road but there was a ski trail which was 12 kilometres. This trail was part of the Flyktningerennet ski race which was scheduled to take part in a week's time. The 44-kilometre Flyktningerennet ski race attracts nearly 2000 skiers every year now, and was first run in 1950. The race follows the route escaping Norwegians took during the Second World War from Nordli to Gäddede in Sweden. The trail for this race was already prepared and it went through the woods near to Kvelia, so it made perfect sense to take it. After just 100 metres I met another skier who was being pulled by his eager dog. The pair were out for an early morning training ski. We chatted for a good 10 minutes and he confirmed the route to me again. I must say again what a friendly place I found Nordli to be, and how everybody seemed so easy going and helpful. The wind was quite strong, up to a force 6 but it barely troubled me in the spruce forest. The wide ski trail which had been prepared for the race meandered through the trees, rising and falling over knolls and crossing flat exposed marshes. Where the trail crossed these open marshes the wind blew unhindered, and it had a bitter bite on this cold morning. Where the trail climbed to the upper edge of the forest near the tree line, I saw a few ptarmigan. After a very pleasant two-hour ski I descended to Harrbekkvollen farm. I had to leave the prepared ski trail here, as it continued east across Kvesjøen lake and then into Sweden. I needed to go north along a farm track and then a quiet road for a couple of kilometres to Kvelia. Just before Kvelia I passed a magnificent farm beside the road called Oppgården. This farm was built in the mid 19th Century and was a stunning example of a traditional farm. It was massively built from logs and lovingly maintained. It had about 10 outbuildings and each had its specific purpose; like smithy, washhouse, stabbur, bakery, milk house, and a barn built from stone and timber. The farm and its summer farm were protected and were run as something of a working museum in the summer time. Soon after this gorgeous old farm was Kvelia shop. Unfortunately, being Sunday, it was closed. Otherwise I would have gone in to sign the 'Norge på langs' book the owners keep. The shop also traditionally donates a pair of hand-made woollen inner soles to all these walkers in the summer, and the occasional skier in the winter. It was another nice touch from Nord Trøndelag.

Day 67. On the descent to Harrbekkvollen farm I could look over the valley to Oppgården farm on the centre left and Kvelia in the middle

From Kvelia there was a 16-kilometre road which went up a valley over a forested pass and then down to Tunnsjø senter. I was not looking forward to it, and started off on foot with my skis on my rucksack, as I suspected it would be a snow and gravel mix like the walk into Nordli. To my surprise the road was very quiet indeed and it was pretty much covered in snow. I put my skis on and started to make good time. As I reached the top of the valley I crossed into Sweden, then on the fast hard descent on the other side I crossed back into Norway, skiing right through the empty border control post. During the 8 kilometre ski through Sweden the entire forest seemed to be in the middle of a logging massacre. Normally the loggers leave a good percentage of the trees standing, especially in Norway, but here there was just the odd one. Even these odd ones looked like they had been left by mistake in this forest slaughter. I reached Tunnsjø senter very quickly and passed straight through it. It had a school, but the shop/petrol station had been closed down, and it seemed unlikely to reopen. It was only another 2 kilometres up the Røyrvik road to where the lady in the petrol station in Nordli had arranged some accommodation for me with her son; so I pushed on. I got to Nynes before 1500. There were two young boys emptying a large trailer of wood through a low window into the cellar of the house. They were working hard and with good cheer, despite their age. This was indeed the house I was looking for, and soon their father, Leif Reitan, came out. The two young boys were pleased when we remarked how much wood they had thrown through the cellar window. Leif took me round to an extremely comfortable annexe attached to the main house. I had a shower, cooked a large meal with some nice mandel potatoes Leif gave me from his cellar store, and later went through to the main house, as they had invited me. It was a nice evening with the Reitan family. The two boys spent a day a week going to school in Sweden and many of the Swedish pupils came to Tunnsjø senter a day a week in a cross-border exchange. The cultural differences between the Norwegians and the Swedes are negligible, compared to their similarities in most places, but here there were no differences at all. The boys were keen to practice their English with me and were remarkably fluent for 10-year-olds. I was fascinated with a device Leif had recently installed on the stove pipe. It was essentially a bathroom vent in reverse, which drew cold air from the outside, and blew it through a heat exchanger attached to the hot pipe from the stove and then into the room. It kept the house at a positive pressure, thereby preventing the draughts normally caused by both stoves and fires dragging cold air in to fuel the fire. It was simple, but very effective.

After a comfortable stay with the Reitan family, where even the kids made me feel at home, I was ready to finish this Nord Trøndelag section with a ski to Røyrvik. Leif's brother owned Fjellvang farm on the very southern part of Limingen lake. Between the two farms the brothers owned a fair amount of forested land and they used scooters to transport the wood. Leif showed me where the 8 kilometre scooter trail they used went through the woods and over the hill before descending through the spruce forest to his brother's farm and Limingen lake. I found the tracks easily enough and followed them through the tall dark spruce and then up the hillside to the birch forest. It was quite steep in places and my skis were not waxed well, making them slippery and hard to ski on. It was a nice ski, however, and I got a brief view down the enormous Tunnsjø lake to the west. Then at the top of the hill the weather changed and a blizzard arrived from the east. It was a strong wind with driving snow and poor visibility. Luckily like most quick changes in the weather it did not last long and by the time I had descended into the spruce on the Limingen lake side it had blown over. The descent to Limingen was steep. Too steep to ski directly, so I left the tracks and made large traverses in the forest using the deep snow to slow me up. Eventually the forest released me on to the fields of Fjellvang farm. Leif's brother had a number of cabins to rent, some of them were already taken by three Swedish men who were spending a week ice fishing on Limingen lake. They were already fishing in the middle of the bay so I skied along their tracks towards them. They were fishing for Røye or Arctic char which is a very red trout-type fish in the salmon family. The fishermen bore holes in the ice with a large auger and then fish through this hole. Sometimes they sit on stools in the open, while others put up large tents on the ice with stoves and beds. These three fishermen had made about 20 holes all together. After a brief chat, where I tried to glean some of the secrets of this winter's pastime, I continued across the bay to reach the small hamlet of Limingen on the other side.

Day 68. Looking down the frozen surface of Limingen lake from the hamlet of Dervika towards the north end and the small town of Røyrvik

It was just too difficult on the ice to contemplate skiing along the shoreline of the lake. There was a crust on top of the snow which collapsed at each step and I would sink down to my shins. It would have been very slow hard work so I opted to follow the road. It was 26 kilometres north-west to Røyrvik. The road was well covered in snow and the wind had deposited spindrift on to its surface. As such it was fast, but my skis were still slippery as I kept the ski skins off. The uphill sections were testing and my arms were working hard to stop me slipping back even with a lot of wax. The downhill sections were fast and generally OK, but there was the occasional area with gravel on the surface. I made fast progress passing old farms and hamlets, like Dervika which had a very wobbly looking old farm surrounded by a collection of simple leisure cabins. Below me was the vast white expanse which was the frozen surface of Limingen lake. It looked difficult to ski across, even from up here. The weather, however, had improved a lot and the sun broke through in many places. The final 10 kilometres to Røyrvik were tedious. The road surface was covered in ice and packed snow. It offered my skis very little grip and it was tiring to ski along, except for the downhill sections. On these I went like a rocket, along the largely deserted road with virtually no cars. At last I reached Røyrvik. It was not before time, as my feet and ankles were sore after the 50-odd kilometres on frozen icy roads over the last two days. Røyrvik seemed a friendly town with about 500 houses and a large school, shop, petrol station and a simple hotel. The shop was still open so I bought some snacks. I ate these in the shop at the table most rural shops have in Norway. As I was eating there was a bit of a commotion outside which heralded the arrival of Andre Spica. He had just turned up in a van with a couple of friends after a few days rest with them in Sweden well to the south of Gjevsjøen. I was half expecting to see him, so we decided to share a room in the cheap hotel. Inevitably we also decided to travel together for a couple of days through Børgefjell. I did not want to ski too much with Andre as I was faster with just the rucksack, and I did not like the style of his trip, where he jumped in and out the whole time. There were also a couple of hydropower technicians at the hotel. They were measuring the snow depth in the forests and mountains around here, to calculate how much water they would have in the reservoirs later in the season. I was pleased to have finished the messy end of this Nord Trøndelag section with its tedious ski journeys along the road. However, the memories of the remote hill farms of Gaundal, Holden and Gjevsjøen set in their clearings in the extensive pine forests are memories I will cherish for a long time.

SECTION 9. Nord Trøndelag.
11 days. 269 km. 71.5 hours. 5070m ascent. 5270m descent.

THE SKI: SECTION 10. BØRGEFJELL AND HATTFJELLDAL

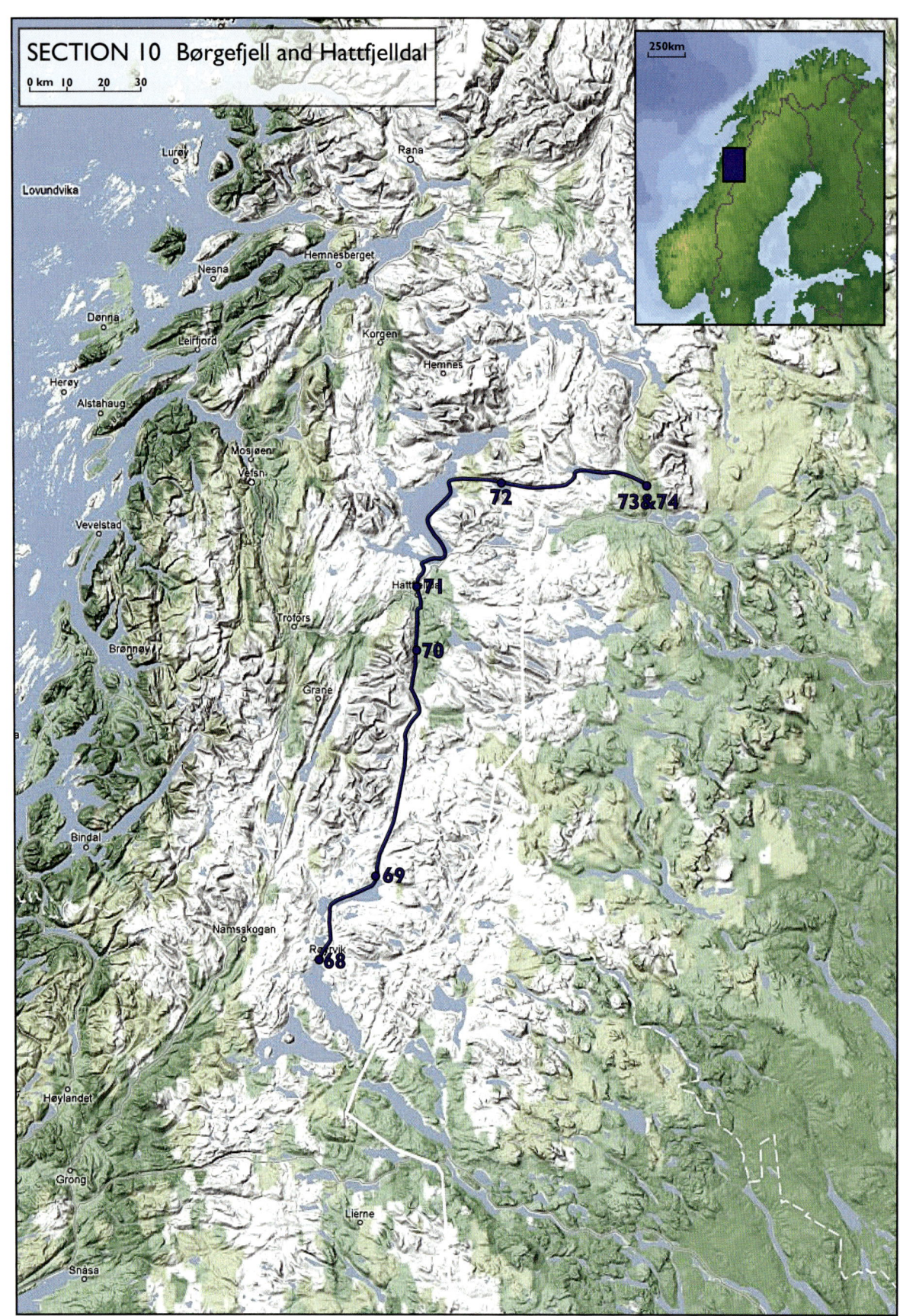

THE SKI: SECTION 10. BØRGEFJELL AND HATTFJELLDAL

It was just below zero on the mild, overcast, morning and there must have been just enough heat coming through the roofs of some buildings to melt the underside of the snow which lay on them. The result was it no longer adhered on to the roof's surface and all round Røyrvik it was sliding off in metre-thick avalanches. A car or human would be damaged by these heavy cascades, but Norwegians are alert to this and stay well clear while the thaw is on. We set off quite early, up a snow-covered road for a couple of kilometres to the north and then took a smaller road for the 14 kilometres to Namsvatnet. The ski up the road was fast on the hard-packed snow and I had very little wax on. On the few uphill sections my skis wanted to slide back, and I had to work hard with my arms, but on the largely flat road I could double pole very quickly, and on the barely perceptible downhill sections, I flew along. Andre had to keep his ski skins on as he had his sledge, and lost most of his potential glide. He was soon far behind. I passed a few farms en route. Some were very well kept, while others looked like the parents had passed them on to their children, who didn't really want to farm, so they were mothballed and looked unloved and unpainted. The forest along this road stretch was mostly spruce with some birch. Frozen tarns dotted the forest. I passed one traditional, ancient homestead, where there was an old couple cutting wood with a combined saw and splitting device attached to the back of a tractor. They had cut a vast pile and were obviously going to sell it. At Namsvatnet parking place there was a small information room and a cabin to rent which was owned and run by Røyrvik Fjellstyre. This committee looked after the mountainous region in the area, issued hunting and fishing licences, made sure no one infringed regulations, and policed the area. The committee also rented out some cabins, one of which was this cabin at Namsvatnet, and another was the one at Viermahytta. I chatted with the Fjelloppsyn man who was responsible for the day-to-day running of Røyrvik Fjellstyre and its activities. While I was chatting, a Sami arrived and unloaded a snow scooter from a van. Sami people are also known as Lapps, a term the Sami find somewhat derogatory. He was going to a Sami hamlet in the vicinity of Viermahytta to clear the snow off his cabin roof. This hamlet would largely be used when the Sami have to look after the reindeer which migrated here for the summer. His reindeer were now down on the coast near Steinkjer for the winter, but would return here in the spring. The Sami are exempt from many of the rules governing snow scooter use in Norway, and have special rights due to their indigenous peoples status. Some Norwegians, mostly the more conservative redneck contingent, say the Sami occasionally misuse these rights, drive snow scooters where they want, and also hunt illegally. Generally, the Sami are responsible, as they go about their millennia-old reindeer herding lifestyle.

Andre arrived after an hour with his sledge scraping and bouncing down the icy road. When he had rested and chatted with the Fjelloppsyn man and the Sami we set off. The route we decided to follow was across the lake to the north side of Namsvatnet. It was marked and well used by various scooters to access some cabins at Sandvika on the other side. The route then followed the north shore of Namsvatnet lake and occasionally veered into the fringes of the spruce forest along the shore. The scooter tracks stopped a few kilometres from Viermahytta by the cabins at Bustadslåtten. There were some ski tracks which we followed for a kilometre along the shore which led to a lonely ice fisher. He had spent the last nine days staying in a cabin at Bustadslåtten and came down to the lake every day to sit on his stool and hoist the occasional small Arctic

Day 69. On Namsvatnet lake we passed a single ice fisherman who had spent a week fishing for small Arctic char in the peace and quiet

char out of the hole he had drilled. He liked the peace and quiet to unwind from his job as a psychologist. Andre spoke enthusiastically with him, while I pondered why anyone would do this. When we left him and continued along the lake we soon saw the flash of snow scooter lights coming towards us. It was the Sami we spoke to earlier, returning from clearing his roof. He claimed March was the most snow-rich month and that it was better to clear it now, because if it got too deep and then rained, the snow would act as a sponge and the weight would be enormous and possibly damage or break the roof timbers. We chatted with him for a good half hour. He also told us there was a small mountain church just above the shore here in a Sami summer hamlet called Reiret. The church was called 'Kristi Krybbe' and it was a small octagonal log building with Sami architecture. There were

Day 69. Viermahytta cabin was a cosy compact and warm building just on the edge of Børgefjell National Park

still services held every week in the summer. We said our goodbyes and followed his tracks. He had gone out of his way to make a track for us to follow all the way to Viermahytta cabin, which saved us floundering about in the deep snow of the woods for an extra hour or so. We were there in half an hour. It had a stove, gas, six bunk beds and would be easy to heat up. I got the stove going while Andre collected snow. It was only 1600 and we could look forward to a warm cosy hut for the evening. Andre had some cognac and we polished that off in the evening as we chatted in front of the fire.

We got up at 0500, almost entirely due to Andre's greater morning discipline. It still took some two hours to have breakfast, pack my rucksack and his sledge, wash up and tidy the cabin, so we didn't leave until 0700. It was a calm, overcast, day with mist obscuring everything but the valleys. I set off with the mission to ski right over Børgefjell to Susendalen on the north side of the park where there were some overnight possibilities. Andre thought he would overnight in a shelter before the descent to Susendalen. Luckily the snow was at last consolidating in the forest. The recent mild weather, which was sometimes even a few degrees plus, had changed the structure of the snow crystals and they had bonded together. When this refroze it provided a hard surface which supported my weight. It had frozen well last night so the 6-kilometre ski up through the forest was quite easy. The spruce quickly past and we were straight into the mountain birch without a band of pine trees. As I skied past one birch, there was a white and black flash at my feet as a ptarmigan which had been partly buried under the snow took off, clucking loudly to alert others. At the upper edge of the birch woods I stopped and waited for Andre, who was slower with his heavy sledge. We then climbed up into the higher, treeless and snow-filled, flat valley east of Gaukarvatnet lake. Here there were undulating moraine piles to ski through and many small tarns to ski across. We made quick time in this easy skiing terrain. The weather seemed to be improving and the sun was trying to

Day 70. Looking back down Viermadalen where the cabin was with the large Namsvatnet lake in the background.

break through. There was a bright luminous quality to the snow against the grey mist higher up. We crossed Store Kjukkelvatnet and reached a locked cabin on the north side. It was probably owned by a Sami who used it for reindeer herding in the summer. We had lunch in its lee and then continued north across a couple of smaller lakes and climbed a small rise to the east of Gammalkallfjellet to reach a high Arctic plateau.

The weather which had been improving all day finally cleared. There was blue sky to the north while to the west the distinguished queen of Børgefjell, Kvigtind, 1699 metres, pierced through the mist as it rose up steeply into the sky. Some of the slopes were still covered in stubborn mist but the general shape of the mountains and glaciers were obvious. It was a beautiful sight seeing

Day 70. Me skiing across the high Arctic plateau to the east of Kvigtind while half way across Børgefjell

Day 70. Andre Spica hauling his sledge under the gaze of Kvigtind on the high Børgefjell plateau

this grandeur partially veiled like a bride. For the next four hours we had a euphoric ski over this wonderful high Arctic plateau with its thick cover of smooth snow. For the entire 15 kilometres the sun beat down on us as we gently climbed and descended easy slopes under the stately, protective gaze of Kvigtind. As we skied north across the plateau, taking many photographs and marvelling at the mountain scenery, Kvigtind slowly receded and Golvertind, 1682 metres, approached. If Kvigtind is the queen of Børgefjell, then Golvertind is definitely the princess and she dominates the northern half of this plateau. After an inspiring ski we eventually crossed the frozen Guevtelsjaevrie lake and reached the shelter at the north end. My map indicated this shelter was a rustic cabin which was probably open. However, it was quite a substantial private cabin, which was locked. I had already decided to carry on down for another 10 kilometres into Susendalen and try and find accommodation there. When Andre arrived at Guevtelsjaevrie cabin he decided to follow me down rather than camp there. It was mostly downhill to Susendalen, and I veered north-west to try and descend the wide ridge. I desperately wanted to avoid the awkward, knolly terrain at the edge of this broad ridge, as it started to drop off steeply into the forested side valleys on each side. It was tempting to traverse down the side of the ridge, and the lie of the land tried to lure me into these side valleys, but I knew it would lead me into trouble. Andre with his sledge was not so manoeuvrable and he had to take it off and walk for a couple of tricky sections. Soon I was far ahead, and hoped Andre would climb back on to the ridge, as when he disappeared from my view I saw him heading into a gnarly area. Rather than wait, I decided to ski on in the daylight and try and get a cabin for us. The ski down the ridge was initially enchanting. It was not too steep and the snow amongst the birch woods was firm. I weaved in and out of these twisted trees for a good 3 kilometres. I crossed a few frozen marshes on the crest of this broad ridge. It was a great descent until I reached the first spruce trees. As I entered the spruce forest I also came across some scooter tracks. I tried to follow them but they were too steep so I zig-zagged through the spruce forest, falling in the deep soft snow a couple of times.

Day 70. The vast empty high Arctic plateau in Børgefjell to the east of Kvigtind and Golvertind is quite featureless

Eventually the forest terrain became too difficult and the scooter track was too steep for my tired legs, so I took the skis off and started to walk. Just as I was putting the skis on my rucksack, Andre arrived. I was astonished to see him as I feared he might have veered into the difficult area but somehow he managed to escape. We walked down together and soon reached the snow-covered lane on the west side of Susendalen. Putting our skis back on we skied down to the farm my map said had accommodation. It was about 2 kilometres away but the lane was icy and fast and we were there in 10 minutes. It was a beautiful old log farm called Sørgård. The trouble was it was completely closed and there was no one there. What a disappointment! We went to the next farm, Nordmo, and asked the farmer there what he knew. Andre and this farmer made some quick arrangements with another farmer 4 kilometres back up the valley at Furuheim. The dialect was so strong I only just understood the drift of what was happening before it was too late. There were cabins at Furuheim and they also could serve food, so the owner of the cabins was coming down to pick us up in a van. It was my intention to ski the whole of Norway and I wanted to avoid vehicles, snow scooters, buses, taxis etc. So I had to turn down the offer of the van. In addition, I was not going to walk 4 kilometres back up the valley to return the same way again tomorrow. So I also declined the accommodation at Furuheim. There was some accommodation another 11 kilometres

Day 71. The wonderful comfortable house at Kvalpskardmo which our host insisted we stay in for free.

to the north down the valley at Kvalpskardmo. We made a phone call and it was arranged. It was 1900 and already dark so I would not get there until after 2100. Still, it was a very quiet lane and a nice evening, so I prepared to set off on foot with the skis back on my rucksack. Andre had had enough and was not keen to walk for another two hours. He asked the van driver from Furuheim, who had already driven 4 kilometres to find his business evaporating, to drive him and his sledge the 11 kilometres to Kvalpskardmo! It was a very nice walk for me. There was not enough light for me to ski and my head torch didn't really show the road's surface and potential gravel, so I walked the whole way. Some stars were out, but it was too overcast to see the northern lights. I still have not seen them on this trip. It was a long walk through the dark night for my tired feet, but eventually just after 2100, I reached Kvalpskardmo. The cabin turned out to be a very comfortable three-bedroom house with two bathrooms and a great stove which was radiating heat throughout. Andre welcomed me with a meal he had cooked. When it was finished I sat in front of the fire. Glowing in the after supper slumber I just stayed awake long enough to feel smug with today's 53 kilometres and then to unpack my sleeping bag and wriggle into it. Børgefjell was now behind us and it was a mere 18 kilometres down this lane to the town of Hattfjelldal.

Day 71. The forestry track between Kvalpskardmo and Vefsnmoen was occasionally used by snow scooter which made for an easy forest ski

I was tired when I dragged myself out of bed at 0730. My ankles and the soles of my feet felt sore. The lady who owned the house came over in the morning to chat with us. Andre and she were laughing a lot and talking about her dogs. She rented out a few cabins at this pretty rural hamlet of Kvalpskardmo tucked away in the forest at the end of the road. The season had not really started for her yet, and she said we were unique visitors so we could stay for free in her lovely comfortable, well-equipped house. I felt embarrassed by her kind generosity. As I wandered exhausted through the dark forest last night I would have given an arm for this wonderful house, yet it was free. We set off at 0900 under a cold blue sky. The snow-covered lane I had walked down yesterday stopped at her cabins but there was an uncleared forestry track which continued down the west side of Susendalen valley for 9 kilometres until a lane reappeared again. There was the occasional snow scooter which used this uncleared track so it was perfect to ski down. I shot off as my skis were well waxed and enjoyed the fast undulating ski through the spruce forest. I nearly took my jacket off as it was warm but the long downhill sections were cold. After nine lovely kilometres through an avenue in the spruce I reached the lane on the north side of the forest. This lane was cleared as it served the single picturesque farm at Vefsnmo. There was a herd of sheep in the snow-covered fields. Usually sheep are kept in the barns all winter in comfortable conditions before they go up to

Day 71. The farm at Vefsnmo was quite isolated at the end of a lane in the forest on the very quiet western side of Susendalen valley

Day 71. The sheep at Vefsnmoen were of a much hardier variety than the usual sheep and could spend much of the winter outdoors

the summer pastures. I suspect these sheep were bred for their fleece which was used as specialist wool. From this lovely farm we followed the lane for 5 kilometres until we had to cross the Susna river to the busier east side. I was getting rather bored of skiing along roads, even deserted ones like this. The snow is packed like ice and the skis are very slippery, despite copious waxing, which is hard work on my arms. In addition, on the downhill sections, which are very fast, there is a lot of gravel embedded in the snow which damages the skis and strips off wax. I had skied or walked down the very quiet west side of Susendalen for about 26 kilometres since coming down from Børgefjell last night. It was an interesting cultural landscape, dominated by homesteads and small scale forest harvesting.

After we crossed the bridge, the snow on the road was just too sparse to ski along, so I packed away my skis for the final 3 kilometres. Andre had to ski with gravel, and occasionally tarmac, scraping the base of his sledge for some sections. We passed a few chatty pedestrians walking their dogs before we reached Hattfjelldal. It was a town with a sawmill and perhaps 500 houses. It had a shop with a sports department, a bank, a post office, a café, and a cheap hotel with poor barrack-style rooms. We checked into a barrack room and then went out to explore the limited highlights of Hattfjelldal. We both had things to repair and food to buy before we met up in the café later for a fry up. Tomorrow we would split up again. I would head on to Røssvatnet and then go halfway up it before leaving it to cross into Sweden to pick up the very southern end of the Kungsleden track by Hemavan. Andre will continue to the north of Røssvatnet and then go through Okstind and Saltfjellet where he had arranged to meet another friend. Kungsleden is a long hiking and ski route from Hemavan to Abisko. It is about 500 kilometres altogether. After a bit of to and fro at the southern end, where the Kungsleden heads quite far east, it then turns north for what I hoped would be an expressway to Arctic Norway. On the southern section there are a few stretches where the cabins are 60 kilometres apart, but I feel confident I could do these in a day now given the longer daylight hours and my fitness. Halfway along the Kungsleden track is the village of Kvikkjokk. Just to the north of Kvikkjokk is Sarek, probably the finest mountain wilderness in Europe. I was looking forward to the Kungsleden, it would mean 500 kilometres or two weeks without having to think about route choices, without roads to ski along, without deep forests to flounder in, and with a few cabins where I could meet other skiers to socialize with in the evenings.

We managed to get an early breakfast at the hotel. Andre and I were going different routes now and I had a long day to Sivertgården. While he was faffing with packing his sledge, I decided to go as there was little point in me waiting. Apparently there were some prepared ski tracks and also some snow scooter tracks through the forest between Hattfjelldal and Røssvatnet. It was just a question of finding them and navigating along them without a good map. I was advised to take the road to Krutvatn for a kilometre where I should find the prepared tracks. I did this, but must have taken a wrong turning somewhere and ended up in a snowy garden in a suburban street. After asking a resident I finally found the ski tracks and followed them north. They were a bit confusing to follow as there were so many, but by good luck I managed to thread through the maze until I seemed to be on one heading north. The ski tracks went up through the forest passing old farms, abandoned in winter, and crossing the occasional snowy forest glade until I climbed on top of an open ridge. From the ridge

Day 72. There were some lovely old farms which were wrapped up for the winter in the forest between Hattfjelldal and Røssvatnet

Day 72. From the top of the ridge above Hattfjelldal I got a great view east to the curious mountain of Hatten which is probably a nunatak

I got a great view over to Hatten, a curious block of a mountain which was probably a nunatak, and gave the region its name. From here there was a fast and exciting run down through the spruce forest to Røssvatnet lake. This lake is the second biggest in Norway. It is dammed and the level fluctuates some ten metres. The question now was do I go round the east or west side of the large island of Røssvassholmen at the south end of the lake. The dubious advice in Hattfjelldal, which had already led me into a suburban garden, said west was best, but there was a wooden signpost at the lake's edge which said east. I chose east. There were some magnificent mountains on the west side of the lake, with one very prominent mountain called Kjerringtind jutting into the sky. The day was getting better and better and I was warming up under a blue sky.

The scooter tracks followed the shoreline rather than cut across to the eastern tip of the island. I followed them, as to leave them and start across the sometimes loose snow would have been madness. Soon I reached Grubben and could see cars on the road from Hattfjelldal to Krutvatn. The tracks continued to follow the shoreline all the way to the hamlet of Krutå rather than cut across the bay. This was a large detour round a semi circle but they were much faster to ski along than the loose snow on the lake's ice. At Krutå I met a local family who were ice fishing. They had caught about 20 Arctic char and while I was chatting with them they caught the biggest, a half kilo specimen. They told me the snow scooter tracks went all the way to Varntresk some 20 kilometres further up the lake, which was where I would leave Røssvatnet lake and start to ski through the woods to Sivertgården. They also told me

Day 72. There was an exhilarating ski from the top of the ridge down through the spruce forests to Røssvatnet lake

they thought the tracks followed the convoluted shoreline rather than cut across the bays. I left them and continued round the shore. The route now became difficult as there must have been strong winds here. Much of the snow had been blown off the ice, leaving it bare, and the remaining snow had been sculptured into ridges and shapes like a blacksmith's anvil. This hard wind-shaped snow is called sastrugi and its larger versions in the poles are the nightmare of polar explorers. It slowed me up considerably and I had to be careful not to break a ski. Luckily this bare ice and sastrugi mix was small scale but it lasted a good 10 kilometres until I reached the halfway point at Brustad. After here I must have left this windy area as the conditions improved. The snow became much more uniform and the scooter tracks reappeared. It was late in the afternoon when I reached Sørdalen and its collection of farms looking pretty in the low sun. Unfortunately, I still had yet another peninsular to go round to get to Varntresk, 5 kilometres away. As I rounded this final peninsular the view to the north became very clear and the whole of the Okstind massif appeared. These mountains are 1900 metres and quite

Day 72. To the west of Røssvatnet lake the impressive Kjerringtind mountain rose steeply from the shoreline to a pointed crest

Day 72. I passed a family who were fishing for Arctic char and as I was chatting with them they caught this half kilo specimen

alpine in character. The evening light did them justice against the blue sky. The scooter tracks at last reached Varntresk bay where there was a collection of some 20 houses. It was now 1730 and I still had 10 kilometres to go, guaranteeing a finish in the dark.

As I started skiing through the spruce forest the weather changed abruptly as a snow shower arrived from the east. It was blowing into in my face and got so heavy at one stage, I considered camping. The scooter tracks now started to climb up a valley out of the spruce and into the birch forest. Luckily the blizzard passed and the wind died as there was no protection from the bare birch trees. On and on it climbed, most of it very gently for a good hour and a half, crossing open frozen marshes and sneaking up rivulet beds. I disturbed plenty of ptarmigan. Just as I thought about putting my head torch on I reached the top of the climb. I could just make out Famnvatnet lake below me and could see a twinkling of lights on its north shore. One of these was Sivertgården farm. I was dreading the ski down in the dark, but the snow scooter track provided a very gentle run down. I enjoyed it, despite my tiredness, once I was confident it was not going to plunge down beyond the limited range of my head torch. It wove down through a wide shallow path in the birch trees for 2 kilometres until it reached the snow-covered lane. Once on the snowy lane I only had an easy 2 kilometres to go. I skied along the road as it was well covered in snow and passed a couple of houses before I finally reached Sivertgården farm at 1930. The farmer, a young man, was in the barn with the 40 sheep he had. Despite it being arranged, he was surprised to see me, and amazed I had come from Hattfjelldal, as it was 55 kilometres. He was very kind and even carried my skis to the small cabin he rented out. He showed me his house for the toilet and shower. He offered me bread his wife had just baked and some spreads. It was exactly what I wanted, as I could not be bothered cooking the dried food in my pack. The farmer and his wife were not from here, but had bought the farm at the turn of the century. It was dilapidated so they got it cheaply. Since then they had restored the two houses and various cabins, built a barn, raised four children and held down jobs as a teacher at Varntresk school and as a nurse. Their farm was one of about five on the north side of Famnvatnet lake. Behind them rose the birch forest which then petered out up the mountain. He lost a few sheep every year. Mostly to wolverine but occasionally a bear also took one. Like most Norwegian farmers who hand-fed their sheep through the winter months this upset him and the children especially. He had seen wolf prints around the farm but never seen one. When I returned to the cabin, half buried in the winter snow, the huge stove was shimmering with heat and the room was like a sauna. I ate the bread and a large jar of marmalade and then fell asleep in the chair with the heat burning my face.

Day 72. The farms along the shore at Brustad were not only basking in the sun but also in tradition

Day 72 The difficult skiing conditions on the lake with hard bare ice and small scale sastrugi were compensated by a great view of Okstind

Day 73. The farm at Sivertgården was in an idyllic setting on the slopes overlooking Famnvatnet lake

I did not sleep that well, despite being tired. Each time I moved a leg in my sleep an inner thigh would contract into a painful cramp and wake me up. While I was grimacing with one leg in a painful tight knot the other one would suddenly start as well. It must have happened at least 10 times during the night. When I did get up in the morning, I went down to the farm house and was invited in for coffee and given more bread and marmalade for breakfast. I was initially undecided as to what I should do. My body wanted a day off, and the overcast sky and the light snow encouraged this, but I was also eager to get to Hemavan and the start of the Kungsleden. By the time I decided to go and had faffed around with the packing it was already 0930 and it was now snowing heavily. I skied down the steep field as some young children in the other cabin also went the same way. While I carefully traversed with the occasional turn, these children just blasted down the slope as if they were immortal and put me to shame. Once on Famnvatnet lake I found the line of twigs marking the scooter track which went east up the lake, over the Swedish border and continued to Tangvattnet and eventually Hemavan. Since I started to follow this scooter track just after Hattfjelldal yesterday barely a scooter has passed me and the tracks were covered with 10 centimetres of new snow.

I quickly reached the end of Famnvatnet lake and then started through the undulating birch forest. My skis were very slippery and the wax was not providing enough grip so I decided to put on the short skins. It is extremely tiring skiing without any grip, especially on one's arms on uphill sections, as you use the poles to stop you sliding back. The snow showers died away as I went through the forest before Raudvatnet lake but it remained grey. This section of birch wood seemed thick with ptarmigan, perhaps because it was near the border. Raudvatnet lake seemed very peaceful. It was a long narrow lake surrounded by birch forest. Despite being on a marked scooter trail to Sweden there were still no scooters. I almost wished for one to consolidate the new snow. Towards the east end of the lake was a wooden post embedded in the ice. On it was a curious sign customs had put up about contraband goods. It seemed very incongruous here at this arbitrary border.

From Raudvatnet lake the scooter trail was now unmarked as Sweden has much softer laws on snow scooters, and they can pretty much go where they want. There are general thoroughfares from which hunters, fishermen and joy riders can come and go as they please. I climbed the gentle slope up to the two Raurejaure lakes and skied across them for a couple of kilometres to a serene cabin. I did not know where to go now as my map ran out, but I knew I had to head over the ridge to Tangvattnet lake. The scooter thoroughfare seemed to traverse up the south side of Ruffie hill so I followed it hoping for the best. On the way up I met another skier and she explained I was on the best route and told me to continue down to Tangvattnet lake and then head east and follow the road. I struggled up the south side of Ruffie feeling hot

Day 73. The weather slowly improved as I skied down Raudvatnet lake and over the border which was marked by a single post on the ice

and unwell. My legs were tired, I was thirsty and I had not had the opportunity to recover after yesterday. At the top of the slope I crossed a saddle and then saw Tangvattnet lake below me. On the far side was a string of farms. The farm buildings were all clustered round a farmyard in the middle of white sunny fields. It looked good farming country but I am sure most of it was sheep and dairy. Behind the farms were the inevitable birch woods leading up to the bare white mountains beyond. The descent from the saddle to the lake was quite steep. Luckily I still had the skins on and this slowed me down a lot but I still had to traverse through the woods occasionally. It was great snow here with a firm base under a couple of centimetres of loose snow on top. The snow conditions in the forests were at last consolidating. I reached the lake just to the west of a peninsular. Once I skied round the shoreline of this wooded peninsula I could look down the long Tangvattnet lake. Way beyond the end of it I could just make out the downhill ski slopes cut into the forest on the hill above Hemavan. My heart sank as it looked a good 20 kilometres away, and it was. The time was already 1500 so a head torch finish was on the agenda.

Day 73. From Ruffie hill there was a great run down the slopes to the south shore of Tangvattnet lake with its farms on the sunny north side

I followed the scooter thoroughfare down the lake. There seemed to be a lot of leisure cabins on the north shore. Eventually I reached the lake's outlet after some 8 kilometres near a small community called Stabbfors. Here the scooter thoroughfare entered the forest. The route was extremely bumpy as scooters tend to make divots in the snow in the forest. After a difficult 2 kilometres of this awkward track it recrossed the road at Stabbfors village. I decided to abandon the bumpy track and walk down the road so some other muscles could work while my skiing muscles rested. The walk down the road was a relief from the scooter track. Very few cars passed me and I met a lady on a large Icelandic pony. Before I knew it I had reached the bridge over the fledgling Umeälven river, which would eventually become one of the largest rivers in Sweden. It was 1900 now and time for the head torch. I managed to find a snow scooter thoroughfare just to the east of the bridge which according to the horse rider went down the east side of the river to the northern end of the town. I put the skis back on and in half an hour I had reached Hemavan. It was a large town, perhaps the biggest I had seen this year, with a considerable downhill ski centre. It was also a long town. I walked down a pavement for 2 kilometres in the dark with some teenagers wondering what I was doing with skis on my rucksack. When I got to the centre there was still a shop open. I went in and bought some treats. I had drunk a litre of a fizzy drink and scoffed a large bar of chocolate before I even got to the checkout. I was famished. I had done nearly 100 kilometres over the last two days on a loaf of bread and a large jar of marmalade. I seldom carry anything for lunch now, and If I have anything I don't stop, but eat the snack, like chocolate, on the move. At the shop they told me the youth hostel was just 500 metres down the road, and luckily it was. The youth hostel was a large collection of some 15 big wooden huts. It reminded me of an army camp. In the central hut they were clearing away a buffet. They allowed me to take a serving before it disappeared, so I made a huge pile on my plate. After eating I returned to my hut, had a glorious powerful shower which ripped the grime off my back, and then went to sleep at once, as I was quite exhausted.

I slept very well and woke up early. However, I rolled over and fell asleep again for another three hours. When I woke the sun was high in the blue sky. I went through for breakfast to find they had cleared it up long ago. My legs felt very tired and I knew I had to rest. I also had a lot of writing to catch up on. The writing was done by mid afternoon, but my legs were still not up to the three-hour ski to the first cabin on the Kungsleden, so I went to the reception and paid for another night. The lady there said that this youth hostel had indeed been a military base but it was now affiliated with the Svenska Turistförening. She let me use the internet to investigate some of the Kungsleden sections ahead. The section I really wanted to find out about was from Jäkkvik to Kvikkjokk. There seemed to be a dearth of information on these 100 kilometres. I did not go and explore Hemavan. It was a downhill ski resort and did not arouse my curiosity at all. I am sure there are some cultural gems here, but I think it would be difficult to find them in an afternoon.

SECTION 10. Børgefjell and Hattfjelldal
6 days. 193 km. 46.5 hours. 2230m ascent. 2260m descent.

THE SKI: SECTION 11. SOUTH KUNGSLEDEN

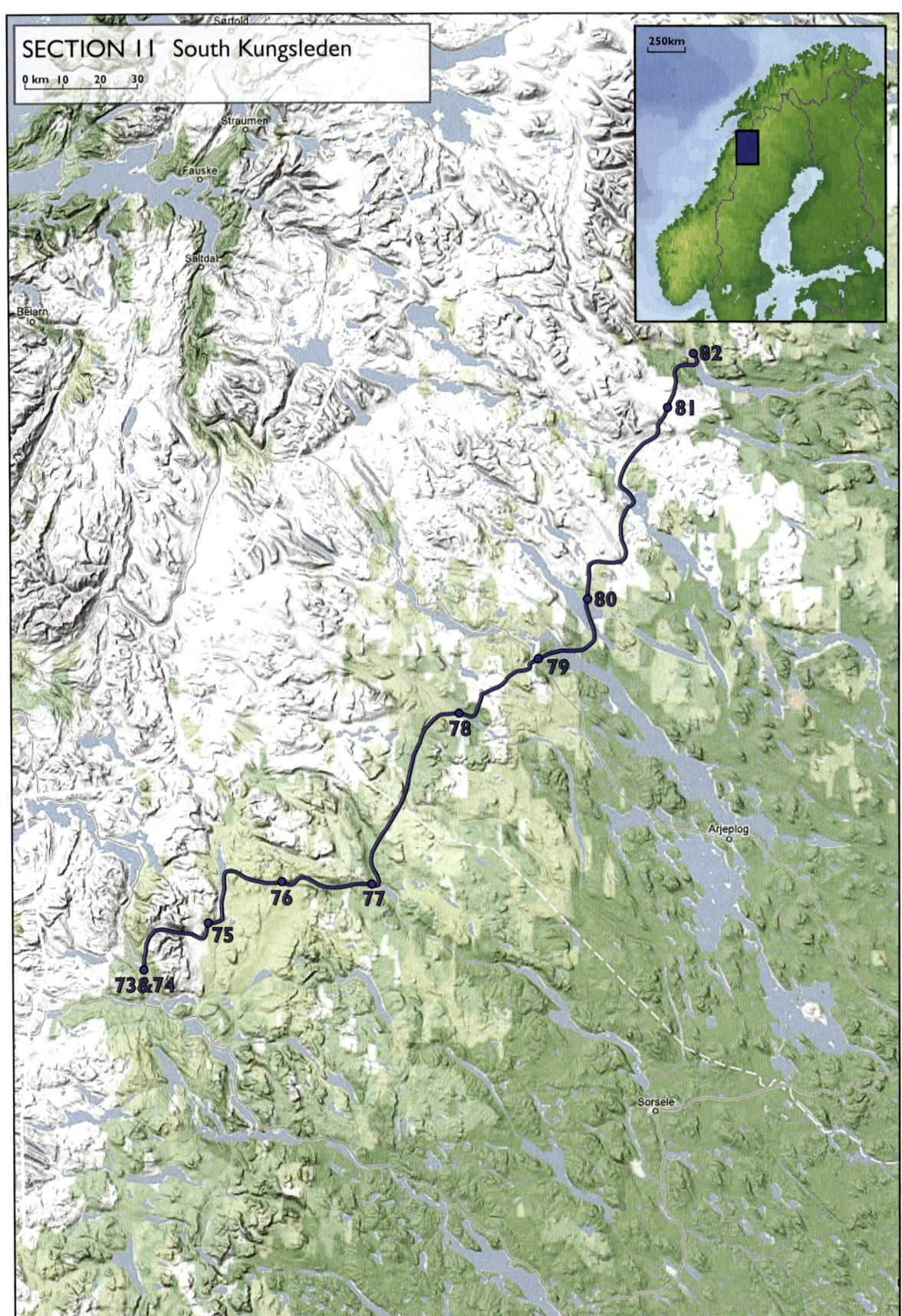

THE SKI: SECTION 11. SOUTH KUNGSLEDEN

Day 75. The south end of the 475 kilometre Kungsleden which went through forests and the Caledonian Mountains in Sweden to Abisko

I started to walk up Kungsvägen road past numerous rental chalets to the massive Hemavan Högfjällshotellet which squatted on a prow above the town like an ugly Rhineland castle. After 2 kilometres and just before the hotel which catered for the downhill ski clientele who overran this town, there was a wooden arch. This arch marked the start of the Kungsleden and was my escape route from the resort. The Kungsleden is a 475 kilometre walking and skiing track which goes from here to the north of Sweden. The northern half and the very south of Kungsleden are well served by cabins, but in the middle section there are just a few simple shelters often without stoves. I thought the Kungsleden would be the quickest way north instead of the more usual way through Okstind, Saltfjellet and Sulitjelma on the Norwegian side. I calculated the Atlantic low pressures, which might be at their worst now during the spring equinox, would affect these three mentioned Norwegian mountain areas first. By the time these weather systems had passed over the mountains I hoped they would be a spent force. March is traditionally the month with the most snow and I thought most of it would fall in Norway, leaving Kungsleden in something of a snow shadow with just the strongest weather fronts having any force beyond the mountain barriers. If any bad weather did break through the mountains then I would still be able to follow the Kungsleden with ease through the many forests, rather than have to stumble around in mountain white outs on the Norwegian side. These mountains here were still the remnants of the Caledonian Mountains as they have been since Hardangerjøkulen. These vast nappes of rock were thrust eastwards over the older bedrock without regard to today's arbitrary borders and extended far into Sweden up here. The mountain areas of Vindelfjällen, Arjeplogsfjällen, Sarek and Kebnekaise in northern Sweden, like Helags, Sylan and Skäckerfjällen in southern Sweden, are all the remnants of these once mighty 10,000 metre high Caledonian Mountains. More recently, Scandinavia was subject to geological forces which caused the west fringe to rise, heaving the eroded stubs of the original mountains into the air. It is these eroded stubs, which have been further eroded by the recent ice ages into a chain of peaks and valleys which form the present Caledonian Mountains of almost the entire length of Norway and north Sweden. This tilting of the landmass is the reason why all the rivers of Sweden flow north-west to south-east into the Baltic. The Kungsleden I was about to embark on weaved through the Caledonian Mountains in north Sweden occasionally going near, but not beyond, the eastern limit of the thrust fronts where they slide over the pre-Caledonian bedrock basement.

I walked over to the symbolic wooden arch and put my skis on and set off up the prepared trail through the birch forest. High above the forest I could see an eagle being harassed by two acrobatic ravens who were trying to drive it away. They were diving down on to it and then just twisted and contorted at the last second to avoid the collision. The sun was out and the forest was glistening with new snow. It was a very peaceful quiet ski through the rest of the hushed forest until I climbed up to the tree line. I soon crossed the deserted ski pistes and the empty chairs of the ski lifts which connected this mountain to the town, now far below. Once past the downhill ski development I contoured round the side of the bare white mountain. There was a heavy snow shower charging out of Norway to the west, obliterating the calm blue skies I had enjoyed so far this morning. I just had time to admire the delta formations in the Umeälven river I crossed two days ago as it flowed into a lake, before my view was obscured by the grey clouds charging towards me. Soon this

Day 75. The birch forest above the busy town of Hemavan was hushed and peaceful under the blue sky and the glistening sun

Day 75. The Umeälven river forms levees which are fertile and colonized by birch trees forming wooded patterns in the delta

snow shower enveloped me and the wind started to whip up the spindrift. It was still another 8 kilometres to Viterskalsstugan cabin up a side valley which almost had the characteristics of a hanging valley. A team of snow scooters went past, had a discussion about the weather amongst themselves and then decided to turn back. The wind was increasing by the minute but luckily it was behind me. Soon it was almost blowing me along the line of marker stakes which showed the lie of the land in this near blizzard. The route was quite flat but climbed gently for at least an hour until the dark shape of the cabin started to loom out of the white landscape above the two or three marker stakes I could see. I went into the cabin for shelter and to see what would happen with the weather. It was very comfortable with a resident warden. It sold some provisions, so I bought a chocolate and drink, and relaxed in front of a warm stove. The weather was deteriorating and it was now a proper blizzard with heavy snow and gale force winds. The spindrift was lashing the cabin and the wind was howling in the stove's pipe. I waited another two hours and finally the wind dropped and the visibility improved enough to contemplate leaving to ski the next 13 kilometres to the Syterstugan cabin.

I dressed up well and ventured out getting a face full of spindrift as it flowed round the cabin. I skied east up Syterskalet, a classic U-shaped glacial valley. On each side of the valley were the high craggy mountains of Norra Sytertoppen and Södra Sytertoppen. These two steep mountains rose very steeply above me for nearly 800 metres to around 1700 metres but the steep craggy ramparts defending the alpine summits were lost in the clouds. There was a large area of avalanche debris on the south side which I kept away from. About half way up the valley the wind and snow returned. The wind in particular got quite violent and was up to a force 9 or even 10. It was buffeting me around and almost blew me over a couple of times. I reached an emergency shelter and I had to heave hard to open the door against the wind. The shelter was firmly fastened

Day 75. The blizzard at Syterskalet was short lived but was probably storm force for an hour or so while I sheltered in this small hut

down with many guy wires and I am sure it must have seen some biblical gusts of wind during its history in this natural wind tunnel. I managed to struggle out and get a photo of the violent maelstrom. At this unheated cold shelter I studied the map again and saw there was just a short climb to a saddle and then an easy descent to Syterstugan cabin. I guessed that although the wind was ferocious here it would be better after the saddle and on the descent, so I decided to venture out and make for Syterstugan. The climb up to the saddle was not as windy as I had feared and was only about force 8 and the route I wanted was marked with stakes which gave me confidence I would not get lost in this white out. After passing the shallow saddle the weather improved still further and the visibility was now many hundreds of metres. The 3 kilometre descent down the

Day 75. Looking back to the U-shaped valley where the emergency shelter was between the Sytertoppen mountains

far side of the saddle took me all the way down to Syterstugan cabin. It was a wonderful shallow descent which was generally covered in consistent snow. However, I still fell a couple of times when the snow surface changed abruptly from icy to soft and deep and I could not read it. The cabin lay in the upper birch trees above the woods on the west side of Tärnasjön lake. Syterstugan cabin also had a resident warden, called Morgan, who was here for the spring season, and one other guest. Morgan was a biologist and volunteered to do the spring shift at this cabin for a couple of months each year. He had seen me coming and had already lit the small stove in the room I was to sleep in. I bought some food from the warden's shop and then cooked a large meal. The three of us chatted while I ate, but although I speak fluent Norwegian I find Swedish difficult to converse in. My brain was working overtime trying to keep up and I soon gave up and started to write under the paraffin lamps.

I had a very slow start as the weather outside was quite changeable with frequent snow showers between clear spells. The wind was slight but increased in the snow showers. I eventually set off at 0930 for the short 14-kilometre ski to Tärnasjöstugan cabin, by which time the weather was much better and the snow showers had almost ceased, leaving longer clear spells. I skied down into the added shelter afforded by the birch woods. The descent to Tärnasjön lake was magical, it was so gentle I really just stood as I glided down across the glistening snow, sparkling like crystals in the sun. I wove in and out of the birch trees for the 3 kilometres down to the lake. I was well below the tree line here and the shore of the lake and the islands were covered in the slow growing, twisted, stocky mountain birch. As I have come further north the altitude of the tree line has dropped considerably. In southern Norway it was about 1000 to 1050 metres. Here in north Sweden the highest birch grows at just 750 to 800 metres. The

Day 76. Looking north across the birch to the delta and marshes at the north end of Tärnasjön lake which were partially obscured by showers

southern end of the lake here has an archipelago of small islands. These islands were formed by moraine mounds which were laid down by the retreating glacier some 10,000 years ago. In the summer, the walking track goes over them with numerous small bridges connecting each island. It must be quite idyllic here in August and a bit like wandering through a Japanese garden. It is supposed to be so pretty, the previous king had a summer cottage near here called Forsavan. The fishing between these islands is said to be excellent and is restricted. The winter route went to the west and then north of this archipelago but I still could appreciate its pure beauty under the bright winter sun which made the snow a brilliant white. Once past the archipelago, the ski trail then cut across frozen lake for 7 kilometres to reach Tärnasjöstugan cabin. I was lucky because for these entire 7 kilometres there was a heavy snow shower which remained static over the northern half of the lake and stayed there until

Day 76. The vibrant Nordic light highlights even the smallest details on the brilliant luminous snow and in the vivid woods and forests

I reached the cabin. I bought some snacks here and chatted with the lady warden. She seemed amazed I was contemplating skiing for another 14 kilometres to the next cabin having already done 14 this morning, but the truth was they were very easy stages and the first 14 kilometres had only taken two and a half hours.

I left at 1300 and continued up the frozen lake for another 2 kilometres before following the scooter tracks into the forest on the east shore. From here there was a very gentle climb up through the birch trees and across bare frozen marshes to the tree line. The sun was out again and the wind was behind me. The marked scooter route climbed on to the bare snow-covered hillside and I got a great view looking back down to the forested tarns and delta at the north

Day 76. Atmospheric light on the plateau between the cabins of Tärnasjöstugorna and Servestugan

end of Tärnasjön lake. It was bad weather at the north end of the lake and it seemed I was just on the edge of the weather divide. I felt justified I had chosen this route and was not stuck in a cabin in Norway peering at a blizzard out of the window. The scooter route continued up across the snowy slopes over a saddle before descending to a small lake. The snow on this plateau was deep but firm and it was not necessary to follow the scooter tracks. I skirted round the north of the frozen lake before climbing up on to the plateau again and over a second saddle to reach the bigger lake called Servvejavrrie. There were a couple of small cabins here which were probably owned by Sami and used for reindeer herding and fishing. After the second lake there was a nice gentle run down the valley back into the birch woods again. The whole ski across this undulating plateau was very enjoyable and I really felt the benefits of my fitness and my lightweight rucksack. The Nordic light across the plateau highlighted every dimple and ridge in the snow and when I reached the woods the trees were vibrant against the vivid snowfields. It is difficult to describe this intense, glowing, bright, light which highlights every detail. It is very much a feature of northern climates, as opposed to southern climates, where everything merges together more. After an easy kilometre through the birch trees I reached the sheltered Servestugan cabin. It was nestled in a small valley among the birch. The sun was just setting through these trees on the surrounding mountains in a crimson glow.

The cabin was very tidy and well kept as all had been so far on Kungsleden. I was the only guest. The warden, Sigvard, was a retired army officer. He had the leg-pulling, jokey antics which years of army banter had developed. I bought some food, got settled in and then Sigvard appeared with coffee and a dram of Jägermeister. Sigvard was extremely knowledgeable and his English was better than most of the English. We spent the next three hours chatting about Sweden, The Svenska Turistförening, which owned these cabins, and numerous other topics. He was anxious about the current decline of outdoor enthusiasm and the growing apathy about nature in Sweden. I had seen the same thing in my visits here, and Norway especially, over the last 30 years. He told me an amusing story to illustrate this, which had happened twice recently. A young guest at the cabin here came rushing out to him when he was cutting wood in the wood shed. The guest said the kitchen and living room area where the large wood-burning range was positioned, was now thick with smoke and something must be wrong with the chimney. Sigvard went in assuming the vent on the stove's flue pipe had been knocked shut, thereby blocking the chimney. The room was indeed thick with smoke, but when Sigvard looked in the stove's fire box he saw there was no fire at all on the bare grate. With disbelief he saw the guest had made the fire in the cooking oven beside it, which is usually used to cook food and bake bread!

I was up early to see the promise of a good day glowing in the sky where the sun would soon be rising. I was ready to go at 0800 but paying the bill, fetching wood and saying goodbye to Sigvard took a good half hour. The first part of today's ski was a near continuous 5-kilometre descent down the valley to the Tjulträsket lakes. It was an exciting and cold start to the day as I flew down through the icy birch woods. Most of the time I was barely in control as the ski and scooter track was so bumpy. I had to snowplough continually to keep my speed down, and as the compressed slot I was skiing in was so narrow, this was not that effective. Once or twice I had to veer into the deep snow of the woods to slow down. The skis I was using were designed for

Day 77. Looking down the sometimes exciting 5-kilometre descent from Servestugan to the Tjulträsket lakes in the valley in the distance

speed rather than manoeuvrability with very little 'waist' so they were difficult to turn in the deep, inconsistent forest snow. I fell once in deep soft snow and must have been virtually buried. I had to remove my rucksack to get up as the deep snow offered no support when I pushed up on it. With legs burning with effort I eventually reached the first of the lakes.

Since Hemavan I had been passing through the Vindelfjällen Naturreservat. I would continue to ski through it for a couple of days yet. The Nature Reserve is a 5600 square kilometre area which is quarter the size of Wales and makes it one of the largest areas of protected nature in Europe. The rules in the Vindelfjällen Naturreservat are not as strict as they would be if it was a national park but there are restrictions. For example, snow scooters can only go on dedicated routes, and fishing and hunting are restricted. Vindelfjällen Naturreservat is best known for its Arctic foxes. There are over 100 multi-chambered lairs in the reserve, each with many entrances. These lairs have been used by many generations of Arctic foxes for hundreds of years. Key to how the Arctic foxes flourish and breed is how the small rodents, like lemmings and voles breed. Every 3-5 years there is a population explosion or lemming year. It is thought that after such a year, the plants, mostly grasses and sedges, which have nourished the small rodents and been severely gnawed, produce unpalatable chemicals which hinder the rodents' digestion. The plants only produce these chemicals for a few years and then start to 'forget' to do so. With their defences weakened, the rodents can feast again and the population explodes over the course of a few months. A lemming gestates for about three weeks and can have 10 young per litter, and the females reach sexual maturity after just two weeks. In the course of a summer an adult can produce six litters. In theory, a pair of lemmings in April can produce a dynasty of many thousands by late September. In the lemming years, Arctic foxes and many birds of prey maximize their breeding. Indeed, some can only breed successfully in such years. During a good year 10 of the 100 Arctic fox lairs in Vindelfjällen can be occupied, and between 50 and 100 fox cubs can be raised. The resulting abundance of predators in the year following a lemming year and the newly unpalatable grass and sedges hinders any growth in the small rodent population and it wanes again for a few years.

Day 77. At the end of the smaller Tjulträsket lake there was a beautifully restored Sami mountain farm with a cluster of buildings

Once on the lakes it was a very pleasant and easy ski down the first and smaller lake. To the south, two buttresses rose steeply from the lake. While to the north, the birch forest rose up the gentler hillside. At the end of the first lake was a very traditional homestead called Geunja. It was originally a Sami mountain farm which had recently been restored to its former glory. It had a collection of about eight small houses. The larder, or stabbur, was a much smaller simpler version of the grand stabburs I had seen earlier in Norway. This small stabbur was raised up on four log stilts. Obviously there was not as much food to store here due to different farming methods. For the Sami, food was on the hoof rather than in the granary. The second and larger lake was 6 kilometres long and took about an hour to cross. The weather was very pleasant but there was one short snow shower just to remind me what it could be like. At the end of this lake the quiet scooter track undulated quietly through the conifer forest. Three scooters went past, towing little mini caravans about a metre and a half high and two metres long. They were obviously serious ice fishermen and their mini caravans probably contained a sleeping platform and a hole in the floor, so they could fish in bed. The

Day 77. After a week of bare mountain or birch woods the return to the sheltering comfort of the pines was always reassuring

Day 77. Just before Ammarnäs the frozen river was woken by gentle rapids where the water found it hard to freeze and ducks gathered

last 5 kilometres down to Ammarnäs were quite idyllic; partly because I was back in the conifer forest and partly because the sun was out. The trail was also very easy to ski along. There were a number of glades in the forest and most had old grass-drying sheds dotted around them. They were well ventilated, so the grass could just be heaped in and would dry through the autumn and be used as winter fodder for animals. The nearer I got to Ammarnäs, the more glades and sheds appeared. Certainly, the practice of gathering grass and storing it in these sheds had now ceased, but there were still plenty of old horse-drawn, hay-gathering implements around the sheds. The trail passed close to the river, where there was a long stretch of small rapids. As I approached the river bank, three mallard ducks took off. There was very little water in the river as most of it was frozen in the mountains waiting for the spring thaw before it rushed down transforming this quiet river. After the rapids, the scooter track descended to the river and followed its frozen surface for the final 2 kilometres to Ammarnäs. Indeed, the river surface had become something of a scooter road here, with signs for scooter tracks to other destinations up to 70 kilometres away. I reached the road bridge over the river and headed up to the shop and hostel which lay nearby.

It was just after midday and glorious weather. The hostel was pragmatic but not that nice. It was full of children on a school tour. However, it had a kitchen, washing machine and showers. The shop had fruit, vegetables, meat and chocolate, so I could cook a good meal. It also had all the maps I needed to Kvikkjokk. I then went to the small nature centre which had a very good compact display of the flora and fauna of Vindelfjällen Naturreservat. It was run by a very enthusiastic biologist who went out of her way to explain some of the area's natural features to me. I returned to the hostel and noticed again Ammarnäs had a very nice vibe to it. Every person I passed nodded or waved and seemed eager to enquire what I was up to. The town had something of a frontier feel to it, with friendly pioneers and Sami reindeer herders greeting me and wishing me a good day. There were 120 people who spent the winter here, but there was no secondary school so the children had to make the 180-kilometre round trip to the school at Sorsele every day. I returned to the hostel and had a hearty supper, as tomorrow I had a long ski to Bäverholm. It was about 40 kilometres, with most of it above the tree line.

I managed to get up at 0530. It was already light and there was a strong glow in the south east heralding the arrival of the sun. It was quite fantastic how quickly the daylight hours were increasing now. At the start of my journey at Lindesnes it was getting light around 0900 and dark by 1600, which was a mere seven hours. These figures hardly changed throughout January because what little daylight there was to be gained by the earth starting to tilt back relative to the sun, was cancelled out by me moving further north. However, now approaching the spring equinox, the earth was no longer just starting to tilt relative to the sun, but was tilting at its maximum speed. As a consequence, each day was considerably longer than the previous one, and here at Ammarnäs that was about seven minutes a day. So now it was daylight from 0530 until 1900 and this would rapidly increase as I went further north. I followed the scooter tracks back to the Tjulan river near the shop and skied downstream on the frozen surface for a short distance. When the Tjulan river and the scooter tracks reached a more residential area at the town centre, the scooters were not allowed in, to prevent disturbance. The tracks

Day 78. The centre of Ammarnäs, with Potato Hill in the background, was an area the snow scooter routes had to bypass round

had to bypass this centre by leaving the river and detouring in a wide circle through the fields to the south, which were peppered with well-ventilated log hay sheds. In these fields there was a major scooter track junction, with routes radiating out in many directions, like spokes from a hub going to towns and villages 70 kilometres away. I took the one to Adolfström which was signposted as 55 kilometres. This route went north east across fields in a wide detour around the town until it got to the frozen Vindelälven river. The route then dropped down the bank on to the river and followed its frozen surface north to a bridge. It left the river here and started to follow a lovely lane covered in deep snow on the east side of the river. Only one scooter passed me between the town and this snowy lane. Because the rider carried skis with him, I assumed he was a Sami rather than a joyriding Swede or Norwegian, who would seldom carry skis.

Day 78. The Sami stabbur at Talludden homestead beside the Vindelälven river was on a pole to keep it above the snow and vermin

It was a very pleasant ski beside the Vindelälven river for 8 kilometres. The river dropped down the occasional rapid and small waterfall, and at these places the ice had frozen into vast globular formations looking like giant candle wax. The sun was out, making the landscape and birch and pine trees vivid in the sparkling bright snow, but it was still cold at around minus 15. I passed many more old, log-built hay sheds and a very quaint restored homestead. This homestead had a very traditional Sami stabbur which stood on one pole. The reason the Sami stabburs are higher than their larger counterparts further south was to keep the building high over the snow, to hinder wolverine gnawing into it, which they could do if it was lower. Soon after this homestead the lane left the valley and headed up the pine-clad slopes to the east for 4 kilometres, until it reached a maze of fences and corrals. This was an area where the reindeer were collected in the summer and marked, and then re-collected in the autumn, when some selected ones were killed and butchered. All this happened in the open, with very little transport stress, so reindeer meat is about as organic as one can find. The route now climbed up through the remainder of the birch woods and on to the bare mountain side. The white rolling hills were covered in snow so hardly a rock showed. I passed two small lakes and a reindeer herder's cabin where Sami would spend part of the summer, especially during the marking and ear clipping in July. The sun had started to disappear now behind a veil of mist and the wind began to pick up. By the time I was up on Björkfjället it was strong enough to create spindrift. I had hoped it would diminish as I descended the north side but it got worse. When I reached a steep mountain called Laddiebakte it was a gale. The snow cover here was very thin and there were large areas of bare ice where rivulets had welled to the surface and had frozen, and other areas where gravel and heather outnumbered the snowfields. To the east of Laddiebakte there was the wide open Dellikälven valley which was covered in birch trees. It was typical of the valleys here which were like shallow slots in the mountain plateau. These valleys drained the mountains and channelled the water down into the great forests around the Baltic Sea. After I passed the steep east face of Laddiebakte mountain the wind started to diminish and the snow cover started to return again. I was doing quite well so when I reached the emergency shed at Sjnulttjie I went in for a break. This shed was built because the Svenska Turistförening cabin here had burnt down a few years previously. This replacement would make a nice alternative to camping. Just as I was leaving the cabin, three families with infants arrived on scooters. They had been fishing. The infants were very well wrapped in papooses for their travels on the sledges which the snow scooters pulled.

Day 78. The view eastwards from the foot of Laddiebakte down the Dellikälven valley which drained this mountain plateau to the Baltic

Day 78. The descent down the bare mountainside and through the birch forest to the homestead at Bäverholm was one of the best yet

The last 15 kilometres to Bäverholm was pretty easy. Initially, there was a 4-kilometre ski across the very top of the tree line until the tracks crossed a frozen river. Then they climbed over a spur to the bare mountainside again. The wind was back for this stretch, whipping up spindrift. Finally I began a wonderful descent. It was perhaps the best descent of the entire trip so far. Firstly, it went down the gentle bare mountain and then into the birch forest. It was not too steep, so I could enjoy it, even in my tired state. Below me was the lake I was heading for, called Iraft. Like many mountain lakes in northern Sweden it contained a delta where silt was deposited by the river flowing in. Eventually this delta will consume the lake. As I descended, the weather became more benign. Soon the first pine trees appeared and then I was back in the comfort zone of the protective pine forest, after a day of being buffeted by the wind on the bare mountains. After a couple of enchanting kilometres through the pines I reached Bäverholm. It was a pioneer's homestead, which had been turned into a café-come-restaurant, and had a few rooms to rent. It was rustic, cheap and friendly, and had a nice vibe. I had not expected such a nice place in this remote frontier hamlet. I took a room and then went to the café. It was not even 1800. The café was covered in stuffed animals and birds. Moose antlers lined the old wood-panelled walls. Pictures of fishermen with prize trout were posted everywhere. There was just me and two Norwegian ice fishermen staying. Both Norwegians were drunk and one was a know-all, so I ignored them until they got the message. After a supper of reindeer I tried to write but it was very difficult to concentrate and keep my eyes open after another 50-kilometre day.

When I woke at 0500 I was shocked to hear the roof dripping. When I looked outside I was even more astounded. It was drizzling and there was a strong warm wind. A warm front must have been passing by and was causing havoc with this winter wonderland. I returned to bed full of angst. Surely spring had not come so early. If there was some freak of weather and this was the start of spring, then my ski trip was over! I had another look again at 0700 and was relieved to see the drizzle had stopped and the temperature was just hovering above zero, but the wind was still strong. I eventually left quite late at 0900 and skied into the channels in the delta. I was partially blown and partially skied down the delta until I reached Iraft lake itself, and I could see Adolfström 4 kilometres across the lake. There was still a good force 6 wind directly behind me and this helped my ski glide tremendously. Then I realized it was not necessary to ski at all and just stood there, hardly moving a muscle for those 4 kilometres, as the wind blew me along the entire lake in about 20 minutes. It is very seldom one has such good luck. I stopped at the shop in Adolfström for chocolate and some advice. The interior of the shop was like a stage set for a 1920s period drama. Old scales and a hand-operated cash register were on the thick wooden counters. Ornaments adorned the roof and everything was on wooden shelves or in pigeon holes. The couple who ran the shop explained the best way for me to ski to Jäkkvik, which was through Pieljekaise National Park and then over Pieljekaise mountain.

Initially my route took me up through the pine forest to the north of the village. After a while the pine vanished and I was in birch woods until I reached Lutaure lake. There were a few friendly scooters which passed me. I occasionally ventured off the scooter track into the forest snow. It was impossibly deep and loose, well above my knees. I hoped that when this short thaw refreezes it will support a skier's weight. There was a route marked with branches across the lake for skiers only. Snow scooters were not permitted here as it led into the Pieljekaise National Park. It seemed no other skiers had been here for a while. The route then went through the birch forest for 6 kilometres over a small ridge. My heart sank at the top of this ridge when I saw I had to cross a shallow valley with deep snow before climbing up to Pieljekaisestugan cabin. After slogging over this valley, I stopped at the cabin for a break. It was simply furnished with a kitchen, stove and four beds. It would have been comfortable to stay here, but I had to continue up through the birch woods towards Jäkkvik. The birch woods in this area are the reason this small, somewhat unglamorous, national park was created in 1909, together with a few other

Day 79. Having skied through the birch woods of the national park the open firm slopes of Pieljekaise were firm and easy

Swedish national parks, the first in Europe. This area of mountain birch was completely undisturbed and natural 100 years ago so it was decided to preserve it. As I passed it today it was dormant in its winter hibernation. In midsummer, however, this would be a transformed environment. The birch trees would host a huge amount of insects, and millions of migratory birds would arrive from warmer climes to take advantage of this feast. The forest floor would be completely covered in wild flowers and grasses, hosting further insects. It is another world from today's frozen winter wilderness. One species of insect which inhabits these birch woods is a moth. Sometimes the larvae of these moths reach epidemic proportions, as last happened in 1957, when the larvae devastate the trees, sometimes irreparably. In addition to a rich bird life, there are other mammals here too, like hare, fox and occasionally, even wolverine and bear.

I was lucky there were some old scooter tracks to follow through the rest of the woods, and it was a short trip through the remainder of the birch forest and on to the bare mountainside. Once I was above the tree line the snow got firmer and I easily skirted round the west side of the modest Pieljekaise mountain. In an increasing wind I reached the highest point and started the lonely descent. As I skied down the rounded ridge, the valley into which I was heading, slowly revealed itself. Firstly, I saw the dark birch woods on the far side of the valley, then the flat frozen west end of the vast Hornavan lake unfolded, and then finally, the village of Jäkkvik in a forest clearing was laid out a long way below me. The descent was absolutely fantastic. It was not that steep, but steep enough to keep moving. I covered the 5 kilometres in an exciting 15 minutes. First through the birch woods and then the comforting and maternal pine forests again to arrive at the disappointing Jäkkvik. This was no quaint frontier village on the edge of a wilderness, but a culturally bankrupt resort with a strong snow scooter culture. There were many spoilt Norwegians who had more money than wisdom showing off their expensive snow scooters at the shop. They seemed to have flocked here for the weekend, to take advantage of the cheap alcohol and liberal snow scooter regulations, for a couple of days joyriding. As the youth hostel was booked by a single group of school children and was full, the shop phoned a cabin owner who had just one free. It was expensive but sounded very comfortable. I had no choice other than camping. I bought food in the shop and went to the cabin. It was very comfortable indeed, and I could spoil myself with an inside shower and full kitchen. I cooked and ate a good meal, wrote and pored over the maps for the route to Kvikkjokk, during which a camp seemed inevitable in a couple of days time.

Day 79. As I descended Pieljekaise, views to the north slowly unfolded over the huge Hornavan lake and Jäkkvik, in the bay in the middle

Given I had a relatively easy day I did not hurry in the morning at all, and enjoyed a lie in, had a shower, a leisurely breakfast, and pottered around the comfortable cabin until 1000. It was a stunning day, with a clear dark blue sky and a bright warm sun. I headed down to Hornavan lake, which is the deepest in Sweden at 221 metres, and at once I was on the scooter track heading east up a wide inlet towards the main lake. The slight wind was behind me and I was skiing fast. There were quite a few scooters about and nearly 20 must have passed me. By the way they were driving, they all seemed to be joy riders, but they were all polite enough, giving me plenty of space, and many waved as they went past. When I reached the main lake, I looked down it towards the town of Arjeplog which I knew was at the east end. I could not see the end of it for the curvature of the earth, and reckoned it

Day 80. Looking south across Hornavan lake to Pieljekaise mountain which rises to the south of Jäkkvik village lying hidden in the forest

must be at least 50 kilometres long. I crossed the lake to the north side by the small islet of Nammatsholmen. Here the scooter track left the bright lake and headed up through the forest. I could feel my slippery skis needed re-waxed for the imminent climb so stopped in a warm forest glade. With the new wax gripping the snow I ambled through the pine trees to a small tarn. Here a reindeer herder had put out a large circular bale of hay for his herds, to supplement their food which was at its scarcest at this time of year. I was surprised to see about 30 reindeer feeding at it. I assumed all the domesticated reindeer were still down in the forests to the east. These reindeer fled as soon as they saw me. The scooter tracks now veered south east across a couple of lakes which was disconcerting, as I should have been going north. Having just seen the difficulty the reindeer had running through the deep forest snow, I was reluctant to leave the scooter track and try my luck wading through it. Eventually, as I was beginning to despair that the scooter track was going completely in the wrong direction, it doubled back and started to head north, gently climbing through the pines, some of which were very old and venerable. It was a delightful ski through this forest as I climbed gently for some 200 metres. There were many reindeer tracks among the pines so there must have been more in the forest here. Eventually the pine trees petered out and the birch took over and remained the only tree until I reached and crossed the ridge. From there I had a gentle descent through the birch for some 15 minutes until I reached Riebnes lake.

Although it was sunny on Riebnes lake there was a bitterly cold wind which cut through my clothing. I had to stop and put on my windproof trousers and warmer mittens. Quite a few snow scooters passed me. It was Saturday and the weather was good, so people were out. As a skier, I felt quite unique. I had not seen another skier for days. The mountain of Riebneskaise dominated the south side of the lake as I skied along it for 8 kilometres until I reached the roadless hamlet of Vuonatjviken on the north shore. It was not as quaint as I had hoped. There were many private cabins and the Johansson's homestead. Jan Johansson had grown up here, and now with his wife, Eva, lived here all year. They had a small enterprise, renting out cabins to hunters, fishermen and outdoor enthusiasts in the summer, and scooter riders and skiers in the winter. They also arranged outdoor trips and catered for their guests, if

Day 80. As I skied toward Vuonatjviken along Riebnes lake the mountain of Riebneskaise dominated the south west (left) shore

necessary. I was given a pragmatic but charmless cabin which was relatively expensive. Still, I had a roof between me and the cold night, which I was sure would come. Eva Johansson cooked a meal for me and a party of eight guests who arrived on snow scooters and were staying a few days. It was served in a very nice log cabin which did have charm. The meal was smoked reindeer stew which was astonishingly tasty, and she gave me a bag of sweets for tomorrow. There was a painting in the dining room which depicted someone being held under the ice by uniformed men. I asked Jan about it. He told me it was a true scene from a few hundred years ago. When silver was discovered in the mountains of Swedish Lapland the Swedish entrepreneurs and authorities needed the ore to be transported from the deposits to the smelters. The Sami, with their reindeer sledges seemed the obvious choice, but the Swedes tended to exploit them and they soon refused. On some occasions the Swedish authorities sent a few troops up to subdue the ring leaders. One of their methods was to smash a hole in the ice and hold the belligerent Sami under the freezing water, by his hair, until he agreed to transport the silver ore again.

Day 80. The small cabin at Vuonatjviken was quite basic, but the Johansson's more than made up for it with their cooking and advice

Jan, who knew everything about the region, said it was more like 80 kilometres to Kvikkjokk, rather than the 60 I thought it was. However, he said there was an emergency shelter at Tsielekjåkkstugan in about 60 kilometres which might be more feasible. I went down to my no-nonsense cabin after the meal to write and recalculate the distances. It was indeed 75 kilometres to Kvikkjokk, and 57 to Tsielekjåkkstugan. Still, today had been the spring equinox, and it is remarkable how long the days are now, so I had plenty of time, if I made an early start. The spring equinox is when the sun crosses the equator on its way north again. It is when the day becomes longer than the night in the northern hemisphere and shorter in the southern hemisphere. It is when the sun rises in the North Pole and stays up for the next six months, and when it sets at the South Pole for a six-month night. They call it the first day of spring here in Sweden but it will be well below minus 20 here tonight! Tomorrow, I would also pass the Arctic Circle which is just a few kilometres to the north of Vuonatjviken. The Arctic Circle is the most southerly latitude at which you get the midnight sun on the summer equinox, which is the longest day on the 21st of June, give or take a day. At the Arctic Circle the sun does not set on this day but just dips to touch the horizon and heads back into the sky again. In the very north of Norway the sun will not actually set for about a month each side of this summer equinox and just revolves around the sky.

I got up at 0330 as I knew it would be a long day. It was still completely dark outside on this very crisp, clear and bitterly cold night of minus 29. The stars were bright and the constellations were sparkling like the frost on the ground when my head torch passed over them. I eventually set off at 0500 when the light was just appearing. It was cold and my skis gripped firmly on

Day 81. The dawn glow in the south east has all the promise of a superb day to come

the snow with yesterday's wax still on. I climbed very gently up through the pine forests, crossing the occasional lake, for an hour, bellowing great clouds of steam each time I exhaled. Just before the sun appeared, its glow cast a rose hue over the hill tops. At 0600 exactly, the rich glow in the south east eventually yielded the sun, which appeared through the twisted dark branches of the birch trees. Not long after sunrise I crossed the Arctic Circle. This was a hugely significant moment for me and had been a goal for weeks now. It was too cold to have much of a celebration, despite the slowly rising sun. My route now turned east with the snow scooter track and followed the Arctic Circle for 7 kilometres before it veered north again to climb out of the forest and into a saddle between two hills plastered in snow. As I passed through the saddle I got a view to the north. It stopped me in my tracks and filled me with awe. There was mountain range after mountain range stretching away to the north. All were brilliant white under the pure blue sky, and as they went north they got higher

Day 81. Before the sun crept over the horizon and up through the birch woods it cast an alpenglow over the mountains like Keitsekaise here

Day 81. Even with the rising sun it was a bitterly cold in the early morning when I crossed the Arctic Circle

and higher, culminating in the awesome massifs of Sarek. I paused here to take some photographs and delight in this rare view, which was almost equal to anything I had seen approaching Jotunheimen two months previously. The alpine massifs of Sarek with their tremendous 2000-metre mountains were still some 70 kilometres to the north as the crow flies so they were indistinct. It was difficult to pick out many individual peaks from the serrated jumble on the skyline but I could recognize some favourites which I had previously climbed.

From the saddle there was a very gentle descent to two lakes strewn with a mass of small islets. I skied back into the birch woods as I approached the lakes. When I reached them it was an enchanting place. I skied across the warm surface, sneaking in and out of various islets. Occasionally, when I passed an opulent drift of snow, I could feel the heat from the sun reflecting back off its concave surfaces. This was a fairytale setting and I felt quite euphoric as I passed through the islets.

I skied up a small rise at the end of the second lake and then started the long descent through the birch forest towards Tjieggelvas lake. As I neared the lake, the terrain got steeper, and I walked for a section as my legs were already burning from constantly braking. The spruce, and then the pines returned as I skied down the last slopes and spilled on to the lake's surface. On the lake the sun was working up a heat in the absolutely still day. I had to stop to strip down to my vest and ditch my hat and gloves; something which was unthinkable a few hours earlier in the dawn. A snow scooter, the first of the day, slowly approached me with a friendly bear of a Swede riding it. He stopped and chatted. He had been ice fishing, but with no luck so far. It was a short hour's ski along the northern tip of the lake, past mountains submerged under thick smooth drifts of brilliant white snow, to reach the village of Västerfjäll. This village really had a pioneer feel to it. There were some 10 to 20 homesteads here. I could not see any sign of life but there was the smell of smoke. This village has no road and was probably just used in the summer, with the odd cabin rented out in the winter to scooter drivers doing some ice fishing. The village had a very quaint, simple church and tower, which was built in 1957, reflecting its Lutheran origins. I had lunch here at 1330 and realized that at just under halfway I would not reach Kvikkjokk today. The next leg was the 11 kilometres to the Sami village of Parka. My route took me along the bumpy scooter track through the pine forest initially. This pine forest especially had the divine Nordic light through it and today it almost looked celestial in the radiant and calm glow. The simple colours of the pine trees against the white snow were really quite mystical.

Day 81. As I reached the first saddle a stunning view appeared with range after range until they merged into the serrated horizon of Sarek

Day 81. I skied north up Tjieggelvas lake to Västerfjäll village with high mountains rising out of the forests, lining the shoreline on both sides

The scooter tracks skirted round to the south of the scattered cabins of the Sami village of Parka. Nobody was here at the moment and the Sami would probably

Day 81. The pioneer village of Västerfjäll had no roads or electricity, but had a quaint Lutheran church built in the 1950s

only use it in connection with reindeer herding and hunting in the summer and autumn. Beyond Parka the last hurdle of the day loomed in front of me, as I was now resigned to stay at Tsielekjåkkstugan. This barrier was a long high ridge well above the tree line. It was a big climb for my tired legs. Due to the steepness of it I put my skins on and set off. It was not as bad as it looked and I got a second wind, probably caused by an urgency to get to the shelter now the sun was low in the sky, and it promised to be a very cold night. The descent down the north side of the ridge was steep. Too steep for my tired legs to keep control, so I walked a short steep half kilometre section to save me picking myself up after a foreseeable fall. At the bottom of this steeper gully I put my skis back on and had a superb glide down a gentle hillside for 2 kilometres until I reached the first birch trees and the small shed. I reached it as the setting sun dipped west below the Tarrekaise massif, illuminating it in a yellow glow. The temperature was plummeting.

The shed was tiny with just enough room for two sleeping platforms and a tiny stove. However, there was at least an evening's supply of wood scattered about outside. Much of it was buried in snow or embedded in ice around the shed. I found an axe and started to smash the ice and soon had a small pile. I chipped all the ice off it and peeled off as much of the flammable bark as possible to light a fire. With a lot of care and blowing it eventually got going. I then collected snow in the four battered, blackened pans which were not really clean and closed the door. By now my extremities were clumsy and painful with cold. The small thermometer I carried said it was minus 36 outside and still falling. However, within an hour it was very cosy in the shed, and I could take off my duvet jacket and saw my socks were steaming dry in the torchlight. I had a dehydrated meal, two litres of hot cocoa and started to feel lethargic. With the hot stove shimmering and radiating heat into the small shed, I felt very content in the nest of down feathers which was my sleeping bag. It had been a long and momentous day. I could not really fault any aspect of it. The scenery was wonderful, the weather was magnificent, there was a rich cultural landscape, and to top it all I was warm and comfortable in Tsielekjåkkstugan shed after 57 kilometres.

Day 81. The mountains to the north of Västerfjäll provided a wonderful backdrop as I skied beside them to reach the Sami village of Parka

I slept remarkably well in the small cabin. It insulated me well against the dangerous cold of the night, which I thought must have been below minus 40. In the shed, my damp clothes seemed to have dried off and I was ready for a new day. Well from the waist up anyway, my legs seemed to be a bit reluctant to jump into action so soon. When I ventured outside it felt much warmer and was now just minus 16. There was even a freak snow shower passing. Above this light shower and all around there was not a cloud in the perfectly blue sky, so I

Day 81. As I skied down the final slope to Tsielekjåkkstugan shed in the dusk the Tarrekaise massif stood out against the cold sunset

Day 82. Tsielekjåkkstugan shed was small but once I got the fire going it was soon cosy and protected me against the minus 40 of the night

could not see where it came from. I got ready in the sun of the morning and eventually set off at 0900 in perfect weather again. After crossing the frozen Tsielekjåkka river I started up a gentle slope to the north. The Tarrekaise massif dominated everything to the west. The valley beneath, Tarradalen, is teaming with wildlife. Unfortunately the Swedish Environmental Protection Agency (Naturvårdsverket) feels it is necessary to manage this wildlife. Last year they issued a licence to hunt and kill three bears which were thriving in Tarradalen. There are also a few lynx in the valley. When I skied down it last year two helicopters flew over me. Later in the day I learnt the Naturvårdsverket had chartered the helicopters. They were en route to shoot a newly identified lynx with a tranquilizer, measure it, and put a radio transmitter collar on it. I was horrified when I saw this and thought there were too many biologists, with too many resources who were chasing too few animals. I soon reached a very shallow birch-covered ridge by the Lastak tarns. As I crested it the Pårte Massif suddenly unfolded across the entire northern horizon. Pårte is one of the 13 or so large mountain massifs in and around Sareks National Park. This massif alone contains two mountains over 2000 metres, namely Pårte and Palkatt. They are not particularly difficult, but Palkatt has some glacier crossings and steep ridges. However, they are extremely remote indeed, and I spent just under a week climbing these two mountains in unsettled weather in September 2004.

From the Lastak tarns there was a wonderful descent down the scooter track through the birch woods, then through the spruce trees and finally into the reassuring pine forests again. I ended up in a small valley to the south of a nunatak called Nammasj. A nunatak is a block of rock which partially protruded from the inland ice sheets during the glacial periods. Nammasj sometimes protruded above the ice and sometimes was covered by the vast glacier which flowed down the very deep Tarradalen valley. When the ice flowed over the hard knoll it rose up the ramp on the upstream side and then ripped blocks of rock off the downstream side, so it is very steep there. This is usual for all nunataks, especially in north Sweden. I passed to the south and then east of this nunatak and then skated out of the thick forest on to the blindingly bright surface of Saggat lake. It was just a 3 kilometre ski north through the delta of two large rivers which met here, to the charming village of Kvikkjokk with Pårte as a backdrop. This delta is laid down by the glacial silt from the glaciers of south west Sarek. The delta grows by at least a metre a year as silt is deposited at its drop off zone which is slowly extending into the deep Saggat lake.

Day 82. From the Lastak tarns I looked over the nunatak of Nammasj and beyond to the massif of Pårte which is one of 13 massifs in Sarek

Kvikkjokk is a Swedish settler village. In the 1660s the government was giving incentives for Swedes to come and settle at remote outposts in Lapland. People were encouraged to set up homesteads. Soon after the first Swedish pioneers settled here silver was discovered nearby, and also at Alka to the west of Sarek. This forged its present identity somewhat and made it more significant than other settler villages. Today, Kvikkjokk has a church, shop, many cabins to rent and a hostel run by the Svenska Turistförening. There are 18 people who spend the winter here. The school children take the bus at 0530 every morning for the two and half hour, 130-kilometre trip to school in Jokkmokk every day then return the 130 kilometres in the evening. In the spring and summer the village lives off tourists. Snow scooter drivers, fishermen, some hunters, many outdoor enthusiasts and scientists all arrive

Day 82. As I skied across Saggat lake to Kvikkjokk the mountains of Pårte and behind it Palkatt dominated some 25 kilometres to the north

here. It is the southern gateway to Sareks National Park and lies at the end of some popular walking and skiing tracks. Even Carl von Linne (Linnaeus) stayed here on his Lapland travels when formulating his theories on taxonomy. I checked into the trekking hostel and they kindly did my washing. The wardens at the hostel were getting to know me quite well as I had visited them about five times in the last decade and it was nice to be welcomed so enthusiastically. After supper I went to see my friend Bjørn. He is tenth generation Kvikkjokk, his ancestors being one of the original settlers. Bjørn ferries walkers across Saggat lake and shows them the hidden gems of the delta land in the summer while his partner, Helena, is an artist with a gallery in the village. Bjørn is an accomplished amateur naturalist and is a library of information on the area. He knows where the eagle owls nest and when and where the elg will come and feed on aquatic weeds in the delta. He made me an elg stew, and despite the fact I had already eaten, it was so good I had to have a second dinner.

SECTION 11. South Kungsleden
8 days. 255 km. 60 hours. 4200m ascent. 4260m descent.

THE SKI: SECTION 12. NORTH KUNGSLEDEN

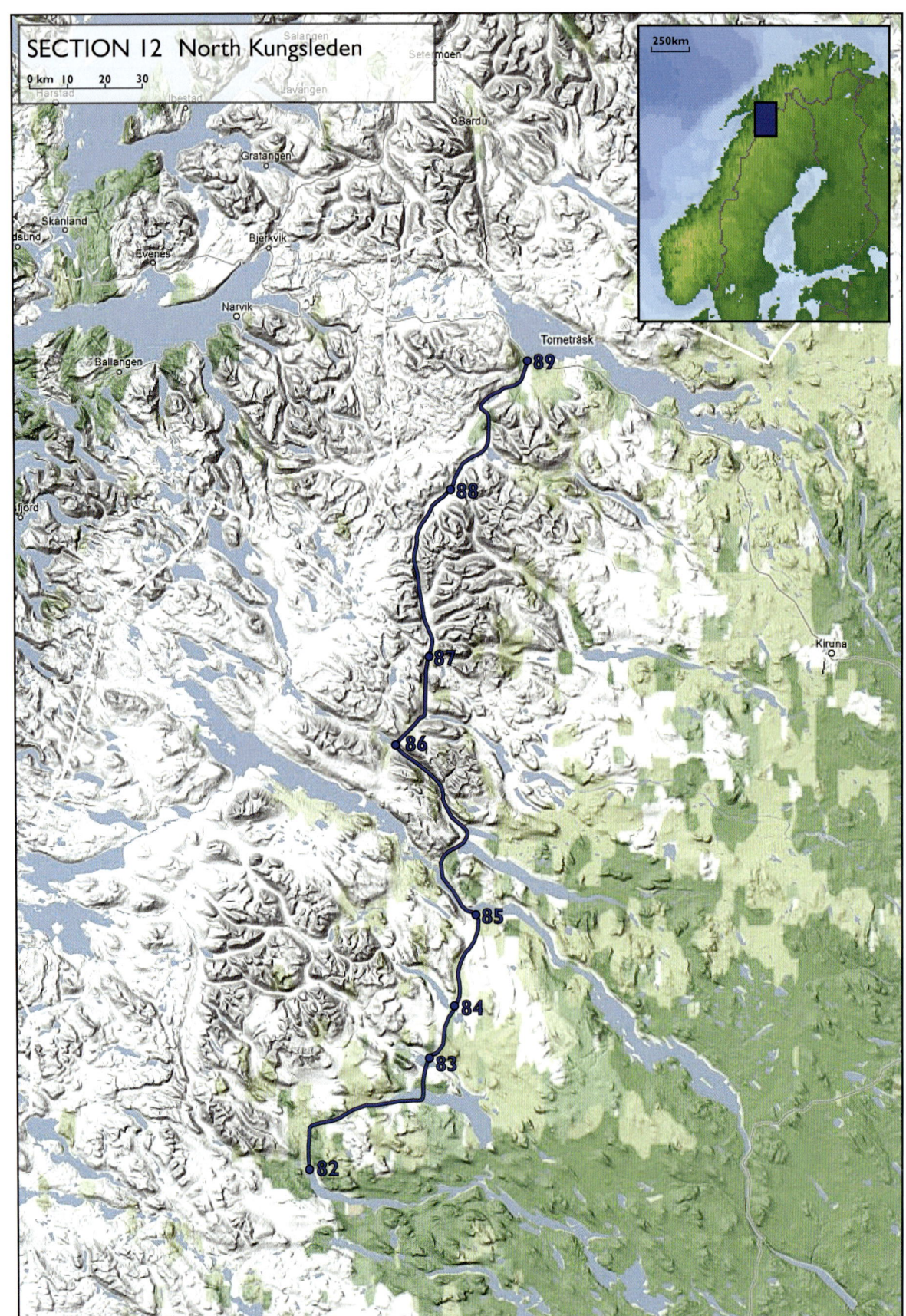

THE SKI: SECTION 12. NORTH KUNGSLEDEN

I wanted to ski 40 kilometres today to Aktse cabin, as I was conscious that I still had a long way to go and the spring thaw was only a month away at the most. Indeed, when I looked at the maps I felt some unease at the distance still left and the time I probably still had to complete the ski section. It was very much becoming a race between me and the seasonal cycle. This cycle would not wait for me, but it might be benevolent and delay the pending spring thaw. However, I also had my writing duties to attend to and could not really leave Kvikkjokk with a settled conscience, unless I had caught up. So, after breakfast I tried to write, but I kept getting involved in conversations, as my erratic concentration wavered. By 1030 I still had not done much and had to go and sit on my own. Just after midday I had caught up, and was ready to start the next section of North Kungsleden, which would see me to Abisko.

It was another beautiful sunny day. The wax on my skis was perfect for the cold snow and it gripped well. I made fast time through the forest and up the hill, hardly noticing the incline. The forest on each side was sumptuous mature spruce and pine trees. Before I knew it I was at the Dahta lakes. There is a summer route which goes off here to the Sami summer settlement of Pårek and the Pårte Massif beyond, but there was no sign of that now. The mountains were looking splendid, covered in deep drifts of snow. Half way across the Dahta lakes I turned east and started heading along the very beautiful Rittak valley. It was sandwiched between the Pårte massif to the north and the crags of Kabla to the south. The valley was gentle, calm, sunny and peaceful and a delight to ski along. When I reached another lake, called Sjabttjakjavrre, I came across a herd

Day 83. The easy ski from Kvikkjokk up through the rich conifer forests to Pårte cabin was quiet and enchanting

of some 20 reindeer lying on the ice. They got up and ambled into the forest while I was still a few hundred metres away. In another couple of weeks, whooper swans will arrive at this lake. Landing on the ice they will wait for the first melted patches of water, then breed here and at other similar lakes in the area. At the end of this small lake was Pårte cabin. It was just after 1500 and I had already done 17 kilometres in a little more than two and a half hours. It would be ridiculous to stop so soon, especially as the snow conditions were very fast. I decided to skip Pårte cabin and blast along the next 24 kilometres to Aktse cabin. I would probably reach there just after dark. The next 6 kilometres down Rittak valley were utterly idyllic. The easy ski track followed the frozen river, crossing it regularly from glade to pine forest and back to glade again. The late sun was starting to give the pines an orange hue in the warm evening colours. A century ago the Rittak valley was once thick with bears and its beauty was fabled.

All this came to an abrupt end after a forested rise to the east end of Rittak lake. The next lake was Tjaktjajaure and it was dammed. The water level fluctuated some 30 metres. This reservoir filled up in the summer months. Then in the late autumn it froze over to a depth of about half a metre. In the winter the reservoir was emptied to produce electricity. As the water level fell, the ice fell with it. However, where the ice rested on submerged knolls and slopes it stopped falling and broke into large angular slabs. The result was a barren wasteland of ice slabs lying across the floor of the empty reservoir. Before Tjaktjajaure lake was dammed, to enlarge it so it extended up the previously renowned Rittak valley, this was a beautiful pine forest with tarns and a gentle river. Luckily there was a scooter route over these jumbled ice slabs which had also been covered in a metre of winter snow to smooth off the edges. The scooter route went along the southern shore for 6 kilometres before cutting across the lake to the north side. As I descended one of these huge slabs of frozen ice to reach the original valley floor I was caught out by an unseen bump. My skis and feet flew forwards and upwards and my bum came crashing down on a sharp ridge of bare ice. Fortunately it was my left buttock which bore the brunt and this was now quite well muscled and padded. Had it been a bony hip, or even worse my coccyx, I might have had a broken bone. None the less it was very sore and I writhed on the ice for a few minutes feeling nauseous and staving off the reflex to be sick. After a few minutes the pain eased and I realized the damage was not as bad as it could have been, but I knew I would have a large long-lasting bruise.

With light just starting to fade I reached the north shore. I left the surreal ice slab world and entered the forest again, just to the east of the steep block of a mountain called Tjakkeli. There was a kind of peninsular here between two lakes which were separated by a gentle and shallow saddle which was just 4 kilometres through the forest. I scarcely had enough light to see the undulations of the scooter track as it weaved through the trees across this saddle. It was dark in the denser patches of forest and just before I considered my head torch at 1900 I reached Laitaure lake. This lake was undammed and happily unaffected by any water level fluctuations. Laitaure lake is home to perhaps the biggest and well-known deltas in Lapland. The huge silt-laden Rapaätno river, which is fed by some 40 glaciers and is the artery which drains half of Sareks National Park, flows into this lake. The sediments in the river settle as it enters the lake, laying down a magnificent delta of lagoons, channels, embankments and marshes. The delta is already about 10 square kilometres and has filled half the lake. The delta has a dramatic location squeezed between the mountain of Tjakkeli and the sheer walls of Skierffe. The Rapaätno river has probably already filled-in at least three lakes in the 40 kilometres of Rapadalen valley which lies above Laitaure lake. The delta lands of these in-filled lakes contain meanders, ox bow lakes and lagoons where aquatic weeds thrive during the summer. This has allowed the evolution of the renowned very large Sarek elg who feed on the vegetation in these lagoons. At the same time, the forests beside these deltas are a lush paradise of fertile birch woods which are busy with flourishing wild flowers and bristling with wildlife.

After a short ski across Laitaure lake and a climb through the woods on scooter tracks in the near dark I eventually approached Aktse cabin at 2000. Aktse cabin has an unrivalled setting under the sheer face of Skierffe, but I could not appreciate it in the dark. I was guided up the last half kilometre by the flickering candles in the cabin's windows and the smell of birch smoke from the stove chimneys. I found a room in one of the cabins here. There were seven of us all together in this large cabin, including two friendly Germans, who had just emerged out of the wilds of Sarek where they had spent the last week. I gravitated towards them to hear their opinions of this magnificent wilderness, which is arguably Europe's finest. By now the cabins were in the middle of the spring season and I was virtually guaranteed to find companionship in each one. Things had got a lot busier since the short lonely days of January, when nobody ventured out into the harsh mountains. I reheated some reindeer meat Bjørn had given me in Kvikkjokk, and chatted with the others before stretching out on the soft mattress on my wide, comfortable bunk, with a small wood stove in the room keeping it warm.

Day 84. Climbing the slopes north of Aktse cabin with the dark 600-metre face of Skierffe overlooking the large silty delta in Laitaure lake

I slept well in the comfortable cabin and I was reluctant to get up at 0730. My legs were quite stiff, but the knock I took on my bum when I fell on the icy surface last night was sore. I almost had to limp around the cabin. I had breakfast, resigned to the fact that Saltoluokta was not on the cards today, and it would just be the 14 kilometres to Sitojaure cabin, due to my injury. I chatted with two Swedish ice fishers and the two young Germans. When they had gone, I pottered round the cabin, having a very lazy morning and I eventually set off at 1200. Initially it was a steep climb through the spruce forest, so I decided to walk rather than put my skins on the skis and use them, and luckily the ski track was firm enough to do so. Behind me Laitaure lake was slowly appearing through the trees. Its delta land was quite visible to the west. On the other side of the valley was the steep block of a mountain called Tjakkeli. In the middle of the delta land was another nunatak, which was also called Nammasj. This one was a more classic shape and better known than its namesake at Kvikkjokk. To the north of the delta land was the celebrated and often photographed landmark of Skierffe. This peak overlooked the valley with the face rising vertically up from the delta for 600 metres in a great dark wall. I have been up Skierffe in the winter and looked down on this delta. Everything was white except for the gentle curves of the levees beside the river channels and lagoons which are covered in a thin dark line of birch trees like a giant monochrome paisley pattern. Unfortunately I did not have the time or energy to climb it again, as the view from here into the remote wilderness of Sarek's angular hidden massifs would have been magnificent on this

Day 84. Looking above the delta in Laitaure lake to the northern half of Pårte massif beyond with the 2000-metre peak of Palkatt in the middle

clear day. After some photos I continued to climb the ridge separating Laitaure lake from Sitojaure lake and after a laboured two hours made the crest. My bruised buttock causing me to limp, if one can limp with skis on.

The top of the ridge was 1000 metres high and well above the tree line. On my west was the white rounded curves of Njunjes, which obscured much of the view into Sarek, while to the east was the vast forest and lake tracts which stretched many hundreds of kilometres to the Baltic. I was on the very eastern part of the mountains and the very eastern extent to which the colossal geological blocks and sheets of rock had been thrust over the top of the more ancient geological basement some 400 million years ago in the Caledonian Mountain building continental collision. The sun remained warm and bright for the long gentle descent to Sitojaure lake. At one steep section I took my skis off and walked as I could not contemplate landing on my bum again. Down and down I went until I was in the birch forest which surrounded this 600-metre high lake which was too high for conifers. It was a short ski across the lake to reach the cabin. I felt very lazy skiing along it. There was none of last night's vigour and I eventually got there at 1600. The cabin warden was also a characterful retired army officer. He kindly gave me some dried bread, butter and cheese to supplement my dehydrated meals. The cabin itself was quite new, warm and comfortable. I was here once in 1984 and again in 1986 but the cabin I stayed in then had burnt down and this was the replacement, still owned by the Svenska Turistföreningen (STF). The two friendly Germans who were at Aktse were also staying here, together with an Austrian couple, who despite being 70 years old, were still very sporty. In the dusk we also had a visit from a red fox who appeared outside the cabin.

It was imperative for me to move northwards as quickly as possible, but it was also bordering on criminal to take the tame option of the Kungsleden rather than go through Sarek National Park when the weather was like this. I have been through Sarek six times in the winter, usually on my own, and apart from the occasional stunning day I have never enjoyed the stable weather which I was enjoying at the moment. However, with my injured buttock and shortage of time it would have been foolhardy. Looking north-west up Sitojaure lake I could see some of the eastern massifs of Sarek, most notably Skårki and Apar. Between them is the deep Pastavagge valley where avalanches in winter sometimes fan across the valley floor and even continue up the lower slopes on the opposite side.

Day 84. The cabin at Sitojaure is owned by the STF and lies in the birch woods at the edge of Sitojaure lake on the easy Kungsleden path

Sarek National Park will always be associated with Axel Hamberg, a scientist and geography professor at Uppsala university. He thoroughly explored these 14 alpine mountain massifs in the late 19th Century, set up some research stations, and wrote a comprehensive book on the region in 1922. He was also responsible for ensuring the wilderness of Sarek was preserved and was instrumental in setting up Sarek National Park, Europe's first, in 1909. Its 2000 square kilometres make it one of the largest national parks in Sweden, and certainly the jewel in the crown and the finest wilderness in Europe. It is one of the few national parks which are still pristine, and there are no facilities in Sarek for those who want to explore it. The only concessions are to the Sami reindeer cooperatives, whose reindeer have come here for the summer months, long before the national park was established. The most widespread of these herding cooperatives is the Sirges Sameby which is found in the north and central Sarek, and the Jåhkågasska Sameby in the south of Sarek.

Day 84. Looking north west up Sitojaure lake towards the base of the Apar and Skårki massifs on the eastern edge of Sarek

The two happy, chatty Germans were already breakfasting with the admirable 70-year-old Austrian couple. I soon joined them, and afterwards I had a final banter with the good natured warden before I left at 0900. It was now just minus 18 and rising fast. The route north followed the barely used scooter track north up the gentle valley. My skis gripped too firmly to the cold snow as I skied up through the birch trees, and they were balling up as the icy crystals accumulated in a compact layer underneath, so I had to stop and scrape them. There had been a lot of snow here recently and the hills on either side of the valley were smothered in a thick cover of snow. The bruising on my bum after the heavy fall two days ago, was not such a hindrance any more, but I could still not put much power through that leg without feeling some pain. I saw some fresh wolverine tracks here. They only weigh about 15 kilos but have large paws up to 10 centimetres across. With these large paws they can travel well across soft snow and can sometimes catch reindeer, which is their main prey. I continued up the valley for a good two hours until it flattened off completely, not that it was ever steep. Here there was an emergency shelter which was about half way to Saltoluokta. I could see from the two sledges outside that the young Germans were lunching here. However, I did not feel like a break so continued. The very gentle valley I was following now veered to the north-west towards Pietsaure lake, sandwiched between the craggy mountains of Rasek and Gierkav. I was not going down on to this lake but over a gentle spur to the north. I climbed the very shallow incline to the top of the saddle separating this valley from the larger, deeper valley to the north, where Langas lake was. The descent from the ridge to Saltoluokta lodge was wonderful. It was becoming a familiar pattern. First the descent down the open hillside to the birch forest, then through this to the comfort of the pine forest where the lodge lay. Just before I reached the charming lodge, tucked away in the pines, I saw an unmistakable waxwing (*Bombycilla garrulus*) with its distinctive pink crested head.

Day 85. The view from the saddle down to Saltoluokta lodge which is hidden in the pines on the south shore of Langas lake

Day 85. The view from the saddle up Langas lake to the north west where the magnificent Stora Sjöfallet waterfall once cascaded

From this saddle above the lodge I got a great view up Langas lake to the north-west end. There was once a great waterfall here, called Stora Sjöfallet. It was so breathtaking and large the whole area was made into a large national park in 1909 with the waterfall as its pride and joy. The waterfall was sometimes called 'Europe's Niagara', which was an exaggeration, but it was, none the less, one of the most spectacular and voluminous waterfalls in Europe, and well worth preserving as the centrepiece of the large Stora Sjöfallet National Park. Tragically, as soon as this natural wonder was preserved by Swedish law for posterity, the government in its wisdom decided to overrule its previous edict. The law was changed to allow the removal of much prime area from the young national park. This included the pristine valley of pine forests and lakes through which the large river which later cascaded over Stora Sjöfallet flowed. This was so the river could be exploited for hydro-electricity. A brutal dam was built just above the falls, which created a huge reservoir, drowning the pristine valley of pines and lakes. If that was not enough, the entire contents of the river was put in pipes and diverted through turbines, completely bypassing and ruining the jewel in the crown of Stora Sjöfallet National Park which had just had its heart torn out. This means the ice on Langas lake is dubious. Not only is Langas lake itself dammed, so the water level fluctuates due to the outtake, it also has two hydro-electric inflows at Vietas which alter currents in the upper section of the lake. As a consequence the hydro-electric company is forced to build an ice route between Saltoluokta lodge and the north shore by Kebnats. They do this by spreading water on the ice at the beginning of the season. If they fail to maintain a route over the ice until a certain date in the spring they are obliged by law to ferry tourists across the lake by helicopter. Luckily for me the ice route across the lake to Kebnats was firm, as I could not take a helicopter, and the alternative was a long detour.

Saltoluokta was a bit of a disappointment. It was built in 1916, just before this beautiful valley was flooded, and it retains much of its charm, with old log walls and rustic furniture. However, the Svenska Turistförening seemed to be losing the plot, and I felt I was staying at a boutique hotel rather than a mountain lodge. The pretentious ice sculptures of love hearts outside the main entrance seemed quite inane. The staff were very nice but did not seem to know much about the vicinity at all. The manager was adamant I had no alternative other than to take the scooter across the lake and thereafter the bus to Vakkotavare from where I could ski to Teusajaure cabin. He followed the party line with such dogma I was suspicious he would try and prevent me skiing across the lake and following its northern shore to Vietas. I felt I knew this area better than he did, having skied north and south along these lakes over the last 25 years. It seemed most of the guests had arrived by snow scooter to enjoy the good food, for which Saltoluokta had built a reputation, and to do short timid day trips. At dinner I was seated at a table with some rugged Swedish men, while the majority of the more refined, chic guests were seated at other tables for the meal which had much promise. The friendly Germans had left to return home. One of my dinner companions was a 67-year-old Swede who was doing the whole of the Kungsleden with eight dogs pulling him and his large sledge. Before the meal, the manager suggested various wines as an accompaniment to the different courses. However, when the courses arrived they were a complete anti-climax; a mixture of nouvelle cuisine and cremated elg. Overcooking elg is a cardinal culinary sin and gives it the texture of dry liver and the tenderness of a suede boot. It was so overcooked, none of the Swedes at my table ate it. I was hungry though so chewed until my jaw muscles ached. Rather than the fine Merlot to accompany the dinner which the urban manager suggested, my own recommendation to compliment the elg would have been a mug of diesel! My dinner companions were all outdoor types who fished or hunted frequently, promised to cook me elg properly should I visit them later. After the meal we went through and sat in front of the lovely old fireplace for a short chat before I retired to write.

I managed to get a packed breakfast at 0630 and set off at 0700 as I had a long and unpredictable day. I followed the marked route for a kilometre west from the lodge then straight across the lake. On the north side, instead of continuing to follow the stakes east for the 2 kilometres to Kebnats as requested, I went north-west along the shoreline for 11 kilometres towards Vietas. The urban manager at Saltoluokta insisted nobody could go this way, but contrary to his assumption there were many snow scooter, dogsled and ski tracks which went along the shoreline here. It was a very pleasant ski in the morning sun. The craggy mountains each side of the lake were catching the sun and the pines on the north shore were a bright green in the light. Just before Vietas I reached the small bay where there is a scattering of simple cabins and a base where tiny helicopters operate from in the summer. The track now headed into the forest here and went beside the main road for a short distance to the leisure hamlet of cabins, café,

Day 86. Skiing up the north west end of Kakerjaure towards the deep valley which cuts through the mountains to Teusajaure lake

pub, shop and petrol station at Vietas. I didn't stop here as it was just 1000, but I had done 14 kilometres already. In hindsight, I would have been better continuing to Vietas yesterday for a shorter day and less pretentious food. From Vietas there is a small road which goes north beside the river to Satihaure lake. This road is not cleared, but a few scooters had been along it, flattening it down, so it was easy to ski along. No scooters passed me, and I was lost in thoughts as I skied through the pines in the hot sun. Craggy mountains towered over this valley on each side. Just before the lake there was a large collection of fences and corrals for reindeer herding. As I was passing it the 67-year-old Swede who was sitting at my table yesterday, came zooming up to me. He had stayed for late breakfast and had not left until 0900. He had eight huskies pulling the sledge on which he rode. He stopped the sledge and stamped in the snow anchor. We chatted for about five minutes and admired the day. After a few minutes the dogs became impatient. Initially there was the occasional bark, but this soon rose to a crescendo of yelping. The dogs then started to strain and leap against the harness as they quivered with excitement to get going. I noticed the large snow anchor which was deep in the snow, was slipping forwards as the dogs strained. He could do about 70-80 kilometres a day at about 10 kilometres per hour, taking only a week to do the entire Kungsleden from Hemavan to Abisko as opposed to my two weeks.

Day 86. Looking back east from Teusajaure lake towards the wild valley between this lake and Kakerjaure lake

The ski along the side of Satihaure lake was extraordinary in that there was hardly any snow. It must have been in a severe rain shadow. Luckily it was only a couple of kilometres but I had to walk half of it. Without a sledge this was no problem. Perhaps it was the effect of the wind on this open expanse. I passed this open area and then went into the birch woods again where the snow had settled. There was a short ski now beside a frozen channel between Satihaure lake and Kakerjaure lake. When I reached the latter the tracks descended on to its frozen surface and turned north-west again. It was a very easy ski along the lake in the sunny windstill day. To the north was a long line of sheer cliff, rising some 500 vertical metres. Small cascades of water had frozen into huge buttresses of ice, like giant dripping candle wax. It was an ice climber's dream. Even on the south side there were steep crags, but not cliffs. There had obviously been a powerful and abrasive river of ice scraping down here in the glacial periods. At the west end of Kakerjaure lake there was a marked route through the birch forest for 7 kilometres to Teusajaure lake. This valley was something of a hidden world. I think very few people came here. The snow was covered in elg tracks and there was evidence of them eating birch buds everywhere. There were also hare, fox, weasel and ptarmigan tracks around. There were also a few fresh wolverine tracks. The steep craggy mountains on each side of the valley were a good 1000 metres higher than the deep valley floor and these would offer superb places for the wolverine to find a lair. It would be impossible for Sami to drive their snow scooters up from the valley floor in pursuit of these cunning animals. They are not allowed to hunt wolverine, but occasionally do, discreetly hiding them once done. The wolverine is the number one enemy of reindeer herders and has been for thousands of years. It is in the Sami's cultural DNA to eradicate these animals. By the time I got to Teusajaure lake I was tiring. Luckily the weather was benign and I had an easy ski up some 10 kilometres of lake to reach the cabin. Had I had the wind against me I would have struggled. Teusajaure lake is in a deep valley with craggy mountains on each side of it. The sun was going down ahead of me producing a warm glow, but unmemorable

Day 86. Heading west up the long narrow Teusajaure lake which lay at the bottom of a deep slot between high craggy mountains

sunset. However, behind me the snow slopes on the high mountains were turning bright yellow in the evening sun above the dark shaded valleys. I reached the cabin at 1800 and was the only guest. The very nice warden, Marianne, came down to explain things. I lit the fire, unpacked and settled down for supper. Later, Marianne came down for a chat. She had been in these mountains for some 40 years as a walker, skier and now warden. She knew the Swedish mountains and its people and villages well. It was fascinating talking to her. Some people consider the northern Kungsleden between Abisko and Kvikkjokk to be among the world's great treks. However, the 'missing link' between the unsightly Vakkotavare cabin, where one takes the bus to Kebnats past the industrial hydro-electric complexes at Suorva and Stora Sjöfallet rather ruins it. Perhaps the wilder route I took today could be a better alternative, certainly in the winter, if a break is made at Vietas.

It had been a cold night, down to minus 26, but the day looked like it would be yet another dazzling one. My original plan was to go the 36 kilometres to Sälka cabin, however, I was tired. My body told my mind to dither and dawdle, and besides I had some writing to do. I soon gave up on Sälka cabin and settled for Singi cabin which was only 23 kilometres. So I lit the stove and settled down to a warm leisurely morning writing in front of it. Marianne came down from her small cabin for a chat and to tell me she was off for a ski. I finished at 1100, then tidied up and fetched more wood from the wood shed. Just as I was about to leave, a group of Swiss arrived. I recognised the guide, who I had met up here last year. His group had just come from Kaitumjaure cabin. They all had randonnée equipment; wide short skis, huge uncompromising double boots and binding

Day 87. Teusajaure cabin occupied an idyllic site in on a sunny alluvial fan on the north side of the lake

on a hinge which could be locked down. For all but the downhill section they used full-length ski skins. I have seen loads of Germans, Swiss and Austrians on this equipment here. It is very suitable for the steeper Alps, but far too cumbersome and heavy to use here, and this group all seemed to have the inevitable blisters. There must be frequent magazine articles in these countries which propagate the myth that it is sensible to go along the valley floors in Kebnekaise with randonnée equipment. I eventually left just after midday and the weather was still glorious. Initially I had a short steep hill to climb and as the snow was frozen hard I walked it. It only took half an hour and then I was up to the tree line and the terrain eased off enough for me to put my skis on again. There was now a gentle climb to the top of the saddle between two mountains before I could start my descent again. At the top I met Marianne, the hut warden, returning from a picnic in the sun. She must have been nearly 60 but was gliding quickly and effortlessly on her Nordic skis, while her Teutonic counterparts were still comparing blisters in Teusajaure cabin. There was a lot of snow on the mountains here and all the imperfections were smoothed off under large drifts. Kaitumjaure valley and cabin soon came into view as I crested the ridge. It was a lovely short run down into this wide open valley. Once in the valley I pretty much followed frozen river through the birch woods until the track climbed slightly to reach the cabin. It was sited on a knoll overlooking the birch woods and had a fantastic view down the Kaitumjaure lake which was a brilliant white in the sun.

Day 87. The sunny saddle between Teusajaure and Kaitumjaure lakes afforded me my first view north to some of the Kebnekaise massifs

There was no one staying here and the warden was cutting wood. She had a small shop where I bought some food for this evening and some snacks for immediate consumption. As I ate, we chatted. She was a keen paddler and was interested to hear about my trip. She had been at the cabin since it opened in mid February, and it was often minus 40 then. She

Day 87. The stunning view from Kaitumjaure cabin down Kaitumjaure lake and over the birch forests which surround the lake

had heard a lynx just two days ago. After spending an hour here I continued to Singi. It was just a two and a half hour blast up the large Tjäktjavagge valley for 14 kilometres. The route took me north across two large frozen marshes which lay on the valley floor, trapped by steep crags on each side. There were now ski tracks to follow, rather than scooter tracks, so it was a fast ski. As I went further north the valley got deeper as it cut through the middle of the whole Kebnekaise area. To the east of this valley were the highest and most alpine of the mountains, including Kebnekaise itself, and many other sharp angular mountains at or around 2000 metres. I could not see their summits from here but could see the bases of the ridges extending down from them. To the west of the valley were slightly lower mountains which were still a respectable 1800 metres and harboured a few glaciers. Singi cabin lay on the floor of this vast valley at the bottom of the ridges which came down from Kebnekaise. It was something of a luxury to be skiing so late in the evening in full daylight, and the lengthening evenings reduced the anxiety I usually felt about the approaching darkness. If the weather was benign, as it was this evening, there was also peace and tranquillity in the dusk, as birds were starting to roost and a few animals took the opportunity to move silently. The only time I have seen a wolverine was on one such evening just north of here. This evening I just saw a couple of foxes. When I reached the cabin it was surprisingly busy with about 15 people. I knew four were Germanic because of the wide randonnée skis at the door and the rest were Swedes. I chatted briefly with everybody while I prepared and ate my dehydrated dinner. The warden came for payment in the early evening and we recognized each other from previous visits I made here; she even remembered my name. In the evening everybody suddenly went to bed very early, at 2000, which was great as I could then write undisturbed for an hour and I eventually went to bed at 2200.

Day 87. Singi cabin is on the floor of the Tjäktjavagge valley at the foot of ridges which lead up to the peaks in the Kebnekaise massif

It was windy all night and I listened to it howling in the chimneys as I lay in my warm bunk. It was much warmer outside in the morning at only minus 10. There was quite a bit of activity in the cabin when I got up at 0700. Most people were eating breakfast and some were already packing. I eventually got going at around 0930 after chatting with most people. It was overcast but the wind had died off. The first part of the route was the 13-kilometre ski up to Sälka cabin. It was a shame it was overcast as there would have been some great views up Rabots glacier to the west face of Kebnekaise. The further north I went, the clearer it got, and by the time I got to Kaskasavagge valley I could look up it to see the impressive western peak, 1914 metres, in the very alpine Kaskasatjåkka massif. There were also some good views up Stuor Reaiddavagge valley towards Nallo

Day 88. Looking up Kaskasavagge to the alpine peak at 1914 metres which lies to the north west of the Kaskasatjåkka massif

Day 88. Sälka cabin lies in the middle of the deep Tjäktjavagge valley, it is at the hub of a network of walking and skiing routes

cabin. The mountains up that valley were some of the most impressive in the whole of the Kebnekaise region. Just before I reached Sälka, a convoy of dog teams came towards me. There was the very large lead sledge with a lot of equipment which was being pulled by 10 dogs. This lead sledge was manned by the guide. Behind him came eight clients, each with their own sledge, pulled by four dogs. These commercial dog sledge tours tend to overnight at Sälka, which is a collection of three cabins. It is one of the Svenska Turistförening's busiest and best located cabins, as a few skiing and walking routes meet here and it is also a good base for day tours. As I skied to Sälka I passed at least 10 people skiing south in addition to the dog sledge tour, and when I got there it was empty. The warden was there and she sold me a few snacks. I ate them in the very familiar cabin which I had visited some 10 times now in the last 25 years. After I had rested for an hour it was time to move on.

The next leg was up to Tjäktja cabin, a 13-kilometre ski up the valley and over the Tjäktja pass at about 1140 metres. The weather was improving significantly, yet everybody who was skiing towards me and had come over the pass, told tales of near storm conditions. One man had a beard full of ice, so I was starting to believe them. It was a long gradual climb to the pass. The incline was really quite gentle for most of it, so it was not too taxing. Just at the last bit it did get slightly steeper, so I had to herring bone up the slope. Just before the top I entered the mist and had one last look at the white valley to the south I had just come up. There was no wind at all now, which shows just how quickly the weather can change. There was a small emergency shelter at the top which was there long before the Svenska Turistförening built the new cabin at Tjäktja in the mid 1980s. It was now redundant really as this new cabin was just another 4 kilometres down the north side. My skis had been waxed perfectly for the climb up but on the descent to Tjäktja cabin they refused to glide, which was a shame as it would have been a nice ski. Even when I scraped them they did not run well as the temperature was falling quickly and I could not completely remove all the wax which was suited to the previous warmer conditions. Tjäktja cabin had about 10 people staying, and a friendly warden looking after them. I was tempted to stay but there was still another four hours of daylight left and a very easy 13-kilometre ski down to Alesjaure cabin. The conditions were perfect, so it would have been stupid to postpone it, and if the wind was against me tomorrow it would have been difficult to forgive myself.

It was a fast descent down the 4 kilometre slope into the main valley called Alesvagge. Here there was an unmarked route from Hukejaure cabin which joined the trail I was on. Someone had come this way pulling a sledge in the last hour or two. I saw he was using the same short skins as me. It had to be Andre, who had followed a different route for the last two and a half weeks, but had to go through the bottleneck of Alesjaure to continue north. When I saw this skier had been skating on his skis with the sledge behind him on the odd flat section, I knew it must be Andre, as one needs to be competent and fit to do this. It was a very pleasant ski down to Alesjaure. The wax had worn off and I was gliding well. The weather was back to its perfect state and the sun was starting to set as I arrived. The mountains around Alesjaure were turning yellow under the blue sky. Particularly impressive was the view up to Påssustjåkka where I had previously gone a few times over a glacier as an alternative and spectacular route to Nallo cabin. I soon reached the steep slope up

Day 88. Looking up towards the glaciers in the high convoluted mountains of the Påssustjåkka massif where there are some ski routes

Day 88. I got to Alesjaure in the atmospheric blue hour in the evening after the sun had gone down

to Alesjaure cabin. I took my skis off for the short climb. At the top I was greeted by the warm beaming smile of Andre who came out to meet me. He had seen me coming in the evening light and said my gait was quite distinctive. He greeted me with a beer and a small shot of moonshine. It was good to see him. After settling down I went through to the joint kitchen and living room. There were about 12 people in there, all men. There were Swedes, Finns, a Norwegian and a Dane, in addition to Andre, who was holding court. I joined the conversation. Andre had done some long days but had been hampered by the weather and a broken sledge. He had to take a lift through some of Saltfjellet to reach a new sledge on one occasion. If he had not I would have been well impressed at his speed.

The sun was shining into the room when I opened my eyes at 0700. It is amazing how quickly the sunrise and sunset changes at the moment up here. Each week the day length increases by well over an hour. In another eight weeks the sun won't set here at all, but will just revolve around the sky for six whole weeks. As I go further north the period of midnight sun will get longer. I got up and had breakfast and chatted with the two hut wardens, who were also here last year when I passed through. One said the route to Nallo cabin over West Påssus Glacier had become difficult over the last few years and now recommended East Påssus glacier to Påssustjåkka before the demanding descent to Nallo cabin. Andre, me and a Norwegian guy with a dog, set off eventually at 0930. They both had sledges, so were slower, and I went ahead. After a half hour the Norwegian with the dog overtook me. He had attached the dog to a harness and it speeded up his skiing immeasurably. It was warming up greatly, and by the time I reached the emergency shelter after a couple of hours skiing, I had to strip down to my vest. It didn't

Day 89. Looking northwards from Alesjaure down the string of frozen lakes to the mountains above Abiskojaure lake and cabin

last long, as although it was hot in the sun there was a bitter chill in the breeze. So the jacket went back on as Andre caught up. There was now a nice easy climb for a good hour up a gentle incline to a shallow saddle. From here there was a great view over to some spectacular mountains in Norway called Storsteinsfjellet. I have noticed them each time I passed here. As we went up this incline we passed some 30 skiers coming towards us. They seemed to be in at least three commercial guided trips from Belgium, France and Germany. The French had tiny rucksacks and the Germans were each pulling a massive sledge. The French had got it right, as the cabins they would be using had everything they needed, except a change of clothes. From the top of the saddle there was a lovely run down to the edge of the birch forest. Here, Abiskojaure lake appeared, with the cabin at the west end of it. At the tree line the ski track became a lot steeper and I had to snowplough a good proportion of the way down. I had come up here some 10 times on my own, with friends or with groups

Day 89. The Norwegian man attached the dog to his harness and then easily caught me up and overtook me

Day 89. Looking out over Abiskojaure lake and the birch woods around it from the south under Giron mountain

I was taking, and I never noticed how steep it was until this first descent. From the bottom of the slope it was a short pleasant ski through the birch forest and then along the frozen Kamajåkka river to the wonderfully positioned cabin. The cabin was sited at the edge of Abiskojaure lake in the birch woods. I have regularly seen the northern lights, or Aurora Borealis, from here. We stopped for lunch and despite the temperature we sat outside in the sun on a bench and watched a selection of birds, including many waxwings, feeding on the food the hut wardens had put out.

After lunch all three of us continued down to Abisko. Initially, this took us across the lovely Abiskojaure lake for 4 kilometres. Thereafter there was a stunningly beautiful 11-kilometre ski down beside the Abiskojåkka river through birch woods until we were finally back in the soft, green, maternal pine trees again. To the south, the mountains were a brilliant white in the sun. There was a deep valley between two of the mountains which was known as Lapporten or 'Lapland's gateway'. Before I knew it I was going under an arch which signified the northern end of the Kungsleden. I was rather sorry to be finishing it and the last 15 days and 475 kilometres had been a really inspiring time, which left me feeling quite elated. I was also rather jubilant I had made such good progress northwards and was looking forward to heading back into Norway and unknown tracts of mountain areas again. Abisko Fjällstation is an ugly but practical building. It looks like an old factory. However, it had cheapish rooms and Andre and I decided to share one. There was also a shop with the American brand of dry food I was trying to avoid, a restaurant and a washing machine. Once we were relatively clean we went to the restaurant where there was a buffet.

Day 89. Skiing along the idyllic Abiskojåkka river looking back up over the first of the pine trees to Giron mountain in the middle distance

With little etiquette we heaped enormous portions on to our plates, drawing some disapproving stares from the staff and other guests, who thought we were being gluttons. The maps for the next section had been posted from Oslo by Hartmut and had already arrived. I studied them in the evening. My only concern was my replacement skis and bindings had still not been sent from Oslo yet. I was supposed to collect them in just two days from the village of Innset in Norway which was quite a detour from my planned route. After that I would ski through the Øvre Dividal National Park, about which I had only heard good things and looked forward to. Andre would take the quicker five-day route along scooter tracks to Kilpisjärvi in Finland, which I would have been tempted to do had it not been for the skis to collect at Innset.

Day 89. Looking south east from near Abisko Fjällstation through the birch woods to the valley known as Lapporten or Lapland's gateway

SECTION 12. North Kungsleden
7 days. 219 kilometres. 49.5 hours. 2750m ascent. 2680m descent.

THE SKI: SECTION 13. TROMS AND DIVIDALEN

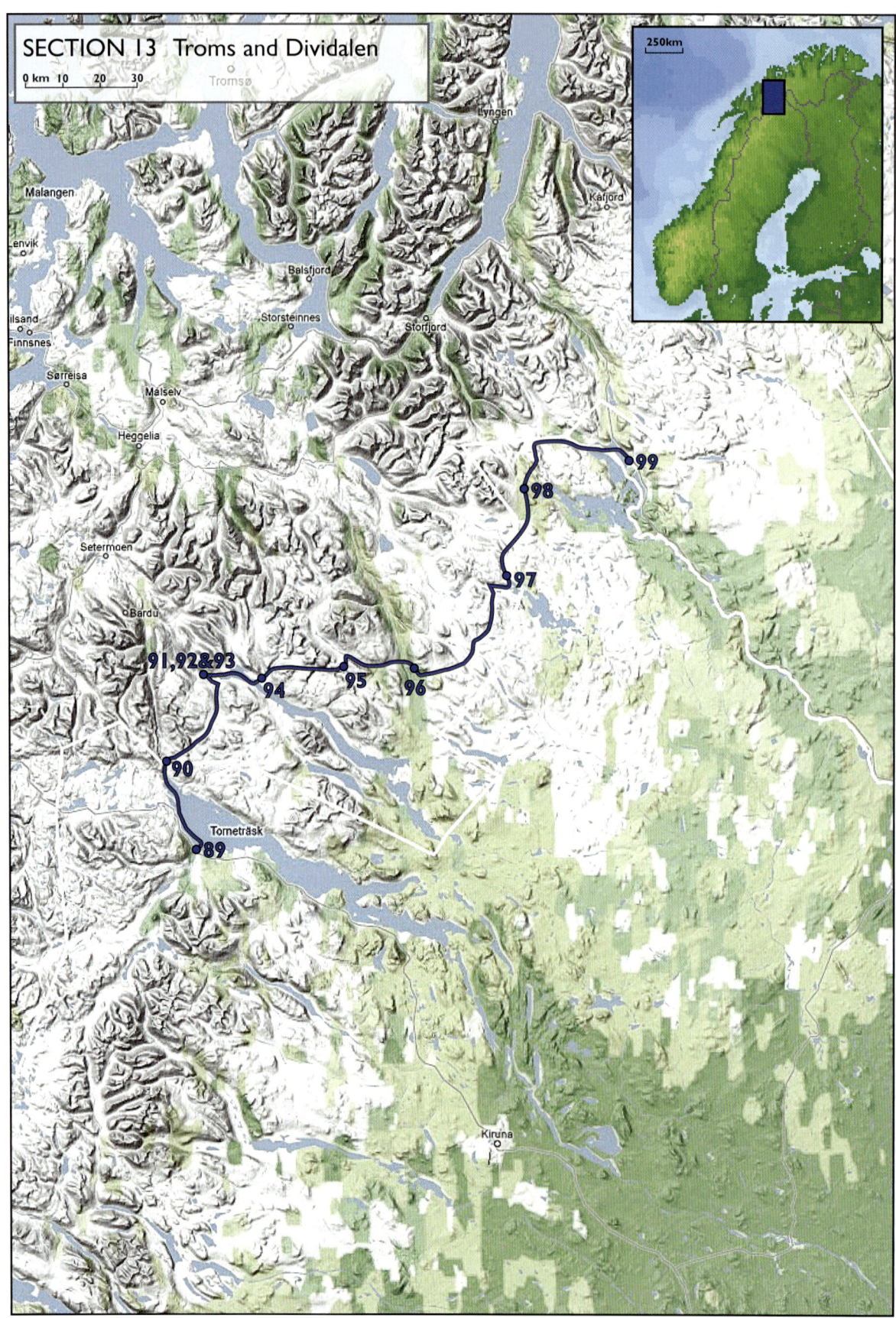

THE SKI: SECTION 13. TROMS AND DIVIDALEN

After breakfast I had to sort out food for the next week. I made sure there was no shop in Innset before buying food at the hostel's shop. Muesli and milk for breakfast, a bar of chocolate for lunch and a dehydrated meal with mash potato for supper. I would definitely lose weight over the next week. However, my rucksack went from 17 to 23 kilos which was nearing my limit. I phoned again about my skis and heard that they had been dispatched from Oslo that morning, so they should be in Innset when I arrive. I said goodbye to Andre, who was bound to stay here another day, as his food package and supplies had not arrived here yet. I left just before midday, on yet another beautiful day, and headed down the slippery slope to Torneträsk lake. En route to the lake I took the wrong turn as I did not register the sign to Bjørkliden until long after I had gone whizzing past it. I ended up a half kilometre to the east of the hostel, which meant I then had to double back. Once on the lake I could appreciate its vast size – 10 kilometres wide and 70 kilometres long. I had to ski over the estuary of the Abiskojåkka river which entered the lake here. It extended a surprisingly long way out into the lake. I thought I was skiing over ice, but kept seeing stones poking through the snow. Eventually I found some fresh scooter tracks heading to Bjørkliden and followed them. It was a fast surface to ski on, and I made good time, covering the 8 kilometres to Bjørkliden in just an hour and a half. There was a train line beside the lake, perhaps the most northerly in the world. It is used to transport huge amounts of iron ore mined in Kiruna and Gällivare to Narvik in Norway. This mining sustains the entire economy of Swedish Lapland, if not northern Scandinavia. Once it reaches Narvik the ore is loaded on to ships and exported to mills around Europe. It felt odd to be skiing over a lake with an ore train of 100 wagons trundling past in the snow. After Bjørkliden the train and road veered away from the lake and descended westwards to the coast.

I also veered from the shore and headed north across a bay. It was very warm and I had to strip down to my vest to avoid soaking my newly-washed jacket with sweat. There were just some old tracks here to follow and the going was much slower. There was a mist coming across the lake behind me, but I was still in brilliant sunshine. I slowly neared the STF cabin of Pålnostugan. I was quite curious to see what it was like and how many visitors the warden met in the course of a winter. There was a deep gorge beyond this cabin where I would aim for tomorrow, passing a cabin on the Norwegian side en route to Innset. When the old ski tracks I was following reached the vicinity of Pålnostugan cabin I looked round for it, but could not find it. All I could see was a small shed. I approached the shed, and as it was unlocked, went in. I then realized that this shed was in fact the cabin.

Day 90. The very simple cabin at Pålnostugan was an STF cabin but it did not have any firewood or gas and was very rustic and cold inside

This was not what I had expected and there would definitely not be any other visitors, nor warden. There was no gas, and no wood either. I could easily have spent a cold night here, but the Norwegian cabin at Lappjord was just another 3 kilometres away, but through potentially difficult birch woods and then across the border. I decided to continue to it, quite confident it would be better. The route up to it was difficult. I skied to the end of the lake and found a fence. There had been a party of some 10 skiers coming down this way. I followed their tracks but could not climb the steeper sections without zig-zagging through birch forest. It was slow, hot work. A couple of months ago it would have been dreadful, but I was quite fit now. Just before the route really started to climb, there was a reindeer carcass, which was half buried in the snow beside the fence. I wondered if a wolverine had killed it in the autumn and stored it here. It was now being picked clean by foxes and ravens by the look of things. The next one and a half kilometres were hard. The small skins were no match for the slope and I had to zig-zag up the steeper sections wrestling with birch branches. Luckily the snow was getting firmer but I was still sinking in up to my shins. I had been spoilt over the last three weeks with snow scooter tracks; this was a reality check again. It would have been very, very hard with a sledge. Before I saw Lappjordhytta cabin, I smelt wood smoke so knew there were people there. I soon saw it, a good way above me, on a spur overlooking the valley. It was a slow, long slog up to it, but eventually I arrived. It was a very nice cabin.

Day 91. The cabin at Lappjordhytta overlooked the canyon-like valley of Sørdalen which was the outflow to Torneträsk lake previously

There were eight people there already; seven Germans and a Swedish guide. They were very welcoming and invited me to join them for their dinner of pasta and bacon, which they were just about to eat and they also gave me wine and coffee. They were a very nice bunch, from the Stuttgart area, and had made a Swedish ski tour every year for the last decade with the same guide, Peter, who worked at Abisko Fjällstation and was also a renowned photographer. There was a lot of banter and laughter in the evening. As always, when there is a good gathering of outdoor men, there are lots of stories and in the interests of one-upmanship I am sure a few were embellished. It was a very good natured evening and I was thankful I had persisted up the steep slope with my inadequate ski-skins and had not called it a day at the very rustic and freezing cold Pålnostugan cabin in Sweden. The Germans were up quite early. They all polished off a huge pot of porridge for breakfast and even early in the morning there was a lot of banter. After breakfast, all the cabin chores were done, like preparing kindling for the next users. I could see why they chose Peter as their guide. He was knowledgeable, diplomatic and very amusing. He told me that the gorge I had noticed yesterday, which turned into a 25-kilometre long canyon-like valley, called Sørdalen, as it headed down into Norway was in fact the old river bed which drained Torneträsk lake. The river used this drain to the west because the current outflow to the east was blocked by the huge mass of glacial ice which covered much of inland Sweden for long periods.

I set off about 0900 just before the Germans. The weather was overcast and the ground was covered in a sprinkling of new snow. My first task was to climb the hill above the cabin. With my short skins and in the deep snow I made bit of a hash of it and I was floundering about like a baby elg. I could see the Germans looking at me and muttering. After 10 minutes the snow at last got firmer and the gradient easier. I cleared the rest of the birch trees and started heading up the slope towards the mist while I weaved between rounded knolls. It was a sustained climb and after a long hour I had only reached the Gurttejavri lakes. Due to the mist I could barely see them and had to confirm my position with my GPS. I had been well and truly spoilt in Sweden with marked scooter trails, fast conditions and good clear weather. I was now back to the reality of wilder mountains again. Indeed, it felt like I was back in the struggle of Setesdalsheiane. I could see very little in front of me when the frequent snow showers came through. Occasionally, to the north and west, I caught glimpses of the base of the very craggy Ruovdoaivvit mountain or the smooth slope of some of its glaciers, mostly, however, I was peering a few metres ahead to see if the terrain went up or down. I saw a couple of cornices here and there as I went along my route in the valley which made me wary. Between snow showers I could see a bit further. On one such occasion I climbed up the long slope to the saddle in Lairevaggi valley. At the far, or north, end of this saddle were a collection of at least 20 Sami cabins and a series of corrals and fences. This would be an area where the reindeer were marked and had their ears clipped in the summer. Curiously none of the cabins were marked on the map, yet they were old and weathered.

Day 91. During a lull in the snowstorm I came across the Sami summer village in Lairevaggi where reindeer husbandry tasks were carried out

After these cabins, the weather deteriorated further, and the snow showers became one. The wind was blowing the snow directly into my face and eyes and it was difficult to see. As I descended the gentle slope to Salvvasvaggi valley it was impossible to see if the terrain rose or plummeted just three metres in front of me. I moved

Day 91. Just before I got to Innset I stupidly wandered into a trap of tangled birch wood which was covered in deep, loose snow

forwards very slowly, carefully heading from rock to rock when I could see them, and occasionally throwing snowballs again so I could get a reference from their landing divot. As I came down a bit further, the visibility slowly improved. The slope was gentle, but I still had to move with care as there were a few side ravines coming into the main valley, and all of these had large drifts and high cornices to negotiate. At last, the birch forest appeared, and I was able to judge the lie of the land much better. I was a bit quick off the mark with my descent to the dam, and did not traverse round the high shoulder of the hill far enough. When I eventually saw the dam I was way below it. Rather than climb back up to it, and then ski round across its top, I set a direct course for Innset, some 3 kilometres down the valley. There was a river to cross, but I guessed most of it would be in pipes to a power station. The descent to Innset turned into a winter's hell. The nice slope I had been lured to ski down, turned into a nightmare of thick snow in a tangled birch forest. It was the type of terrain that would have made Jack London consider an office job. In two hours I forced myself through the thick snow in the dense forest. I had only travelled a couple of kilometres through this horrendous terrain in the two hours. If I took my skis off, I disappeared up to my waist in snow and tangled branches. If I kept the skis on, they were continually getting caught in these same buried branches, with the ski-skins virtually useless in helping me get any purchase. At last I made it to the road and knew it was just a short walk to the husky farm run by Bjørn and Regina Klauer. It was already 1800. As I walked down the road I heard the 60 huskies yelping excitedly; I found out later it was feeding time. When I reached the farm the excitement was over and the dogs seemed satisfied.

I met Bjørn, who was up to his elbows in offal and was preparing to produce five tonnes of dog food tomorrow. After he scrubbed his arms he showed me to a room in his fantastic guest house. Bjørn ran quite hard core and uncompromising dog sled tours. He would not use snow scooters to resupply en route, so would go off with everything he needed for a week and completely avoid civilization. He was just back from a 1000-kilometre trip from Kirkenes to his base here. He would have nine dogs on his sledge and each client would have about six. He used and bred Greenland huskies. Their forte was their strength rather than speed, which Alaskan huskies have or endurance which Siberian huskies have. Greenland huskies were much hardier; when thirsty they would just eat snow, while Alaskan huskies had to have their food as a soup to

Day 91. Bjørn Klauer's 60 dogs were all Greenland huskies which are much tougher than the faster, Alaskan husky

help keep them hydrated. I once heard someone compare Greenlanders to diesel lorries! Most of Bjørn's clients seemed to be Germans, and there were still a couple of clients from the last trip in the guest house. It was interesting chatting with them about their lengthy 1000-kilometre trip which took three weeks. They held Bjørn in the highest regard. I had just seen his operation for an hour, and it was very evident it was extremely well run and managed. Bjørn had also walked and skied the length of Norway, some 25 years ago, just before he moved here. He still cherished the experience, and must have felt I was a kindred spirit and that we belonged to a loose brotherhood, as he insisted I stay for free at his guest house until my skis arrived. The skis were the reason I made the detour to Innset. It was because the metal edge had come off one of my skis and on the other one the binding heel plate had cracked and fallen off, leaving just a screw head. It was a bit of a detour and had cost me a day or two plus the rest days waiting for the skis to arrive. I could have bought skis at Abisko Fjällstation, but the guarantee on the ones I had was still valid so I had invoked it. If I had bought skis at Abisko I could have

Day 92. The Greenlanders had small kennels but they never used them and preferred to sleep directly on the snow

headed straight over Torneträsk lake to a restored Sami turf hut, or gamme, at Snurijåkkåtan, and then could have continued the next day to Gaskashytta cabin. Alternatively I could have taken the tempting scooter tracks to Kilpisjärvi, as Andre intended to do. After the comfort of the Kungsleden I felt I needed more of a challenge again and the first day back in Norway certainly provided that.

I had skied over 500 kilometres without a day off, so with no sign of the skis I did not get up until 0900. Regina Klauer took one of the dog sledging clients to Bardufoss airport. While down the valley in civilization she kindly investigated the whereabouts of my new skis and found out they would probably get to Tromsø tomorrow and Setermoen the day after, when they would be delivered here. So it seemed I would have a couple of rest days before they came. I had a lot of writing to do, so it was a good opportunity to catch up. After a few hours I went down to see what Bjørn was up to. He and a neighbouring musher were making dog food. Bjørn had purchased a second-hand industrial mincing machine, it could do about a wheelbarrow full of potential food in one go. Into it went pig's organs, cow's intestines, fish and fish organs, nutritional pellets and oily supplements. The raw materials came from a fish processing plant and slaughter house. It all got churned together in a large vat and was then minced together in the large steel grinder. What came out of the mincer was mixed further and then emptied into large plastic 25 kilo trays which looked like fish boxes. They managed to mince and mix enough food to fill 200 trays. That is five tonnes of minced dog food. The trays were then stacked in a large freezer until they were needed. This was only enough food for about two months as the dogs each ate a bit more than a kilo of this meaty, fatty, nutritional mix a day. The whole operation was carried out with industrial efficiency and the premises were designed and built to ensure it was a smooth operation. None the less, it looked back breaking work, as there were such huge quantities of everything. Finally, when all the offal and fish was minced and stacked in the trays in the freezer, the whole place and all the machinery was power washed. It would remain dormant for two months until the next five-tonne batch had to be made. I wrote more in the afternoon and then went to help Bjørn in the early evening. The dogs had spent most of the day sleeping on the snow, as they were still tired after the recent three week trip pulling sledges from Kirkenes, were starting to perk up. As the time neared 1800 all the dogs were on their feet and alert with their ears erect. All 60 of them were looking at the door of the food plant and freezer, anticipating a food sledge coming out with a large bucket of thawed food on it. When we pushed it out of the building, there was a frenzy of enthusiasm and noise. Every dog was leaping on its chain and quivering with excitement. The sledge was slowly taken down each line of dogs and they were each served a large scoop of the meaty gruel. It was just placed on the snow. They gulped it down in seconds then licked the snow where it lay. After half an hour all 60 dogs were served and the noise was abating.

On my second rest day at Innset I did not get up until I was hungry at 0900. It was a beautiful day outside and it was a shame to waste it, but I had to. I made a phone call in the early morning to try and track down my skis. Apparently they had just arrived in Tromsø and would be sent to Setermoen very early tomorrow morning and should be delivered here to the husky farm soon after that. It confirmed exactly what Regina had said yesterday and made me feel more assured. I needed something to do, so I asked Bjørn if he needed any help. He was just about to feed the dogs an extra morning's feed. This was because the dogs had lost a bit of weight

Day 93. Each of the Greenlanders ate a bit more than a kilo of the meaty gruel at their single meal at 1800 each evening

Day 92. Some of the Greenland huskies looked very refined and might have had some Siberian husky genes in them such as the blue eyes

after the recent 1000-kilometre trip and needed some extra meals to bulk them up again. Despite the feverish, quivering, excitement of the dogs at feeding time, they were all made to sit before the food was given to them, and nearly all of them did. Later on in the morning we collected all the dog dirt. Most of it was frozen and it was easy to scoop up into a bucket, but some had to be dug out of the ice surrounding it. The buckets were then emptied into a growing pile which would melt into the pre-dug pit come spring and then be covered up. This job was done twice a day. Bjørn and Regina would also spend quite a lot of time inspecting and pampering the dogs and were generally very good to them. Later in the afternoon I pored over my maps, as I had to try and work out a route to Máze. Just before 1800 the barking and howling of 60 excited dogs started again, soon working up into a crescendo. It was feeding time again, and their Pavlovian juices were starting to flow. I went down to help Bjørn with the feeding by pulling the sledge with the large tub of meaty mush. Soon after feeding there was the second round of collecting the dog dirt. Later that evening, another nine clients arrived at the guest house. They were here for a week's dog sledding tour Bjørn had arranged. It seemed he was barely back from the previous trip and was off again already, but this must be the busiest time of year for his business. I spent the evening chatting with most of these eager guests, who were as excited as the dogs would soon be about their forthcoming trip.

I had yet another lie-in, this time to 0830, when it was time to phone the post office in Setermoen. "Yes, the skis had arrived from Tromsø that morning, and yes, they were already in the small postal van for delivery later today at around 1300". That was great to hear and everything seemed to be going to plan now. I went through to Bjørn's restored farmhouse, we chatted for a good hour about many outdoor things. Our conversation was interrupted by the arrival of the postal van. They had my skis and they were exactly as I wanted. No mistakes, which was a relief. I finished my chat with Bjørn and then picked up my packed rucksack. After saying goodbye to a few of Bjørn's new clients, I set off. It was a beautiful day, but it was already 1400 and I had to make the 14 kilometres to Gaskashytta cabin. The first 4 kilometres were up the gravel road to Altevatnet dam. It looked much nicer in the sun than when I walked down it in the snow a couple of days previously. Indeed, the valley I came through from Lappjordhytta, called Salvvasvaggi, looked absolutely wonderful and sparkling in the sunlight. Below its entrance were the inviting and benign birch woods which gave me such a hard time three days ago. I soon reached the dam after passing a massive parking place full of snow scooter trailers and another unsightly area full of static caravans. There are many such caravan parks in rural locations in Norway and one must question the planning regulations on seeing them. There were also a lot of leisure cabins in the area, but with their unobtrusive log walls and turf roofs they are not an eyesore compared to the white caravans with their gaudy extensions. At the dam there was an official marked scooter track which went over the lake to many cabins on the south shoreline. Snow scooter drivers were obliged to keep to the official route.

I christened my new skis by waxing them and then set off down the scooter track descending some 20 metres to the water level. This reservoir was now emptied and the ice which had formed earlier in the winter was lying in metre thick sheets around the side of it. The ski over the lake was busy as it was the first day of the Easter holidays. There were people of every age skiing

Day 94. Looking east over Altevatnet lake from the north side of the dam where the official scooter track goes down through the birch trees

Day 94. Skiing across Altevatnet lake with the bulk of Rohkunborri rising from the lakes and forests of the tundra

and quite a few being pulled by dogs. There were also a lot of scooters, far more than I had seen at any time in Sweden. Most of them seemed to be going backwards and forwards to the cabins beside the lake, but a few were picnickers and ice fishermen. It was a relatively easy ski for a good 6 kilometres along the south side of the lake past many cabins. I then saw someone crossing the lake about a kilometre ahead of me in the direction I wanted to go. So I made for his tracks and followed them over to a large flat delta on the north side where two large streams flowed into the lake. The man went into a gorgeous old rustic timber log cabin. He came out as I passed, and we chatted a bit. He looked quite a character, with his modest and rural vadmel clothing, and a large white beard. Vadmel is a fabric manufactured from boiled and kneaded wool, and is quite like a thin, flexible, high quality felt. It is very warm, even when wet, and shares a lot of the same properties as tweed. The cabin I was going to was just another 2 kilometres up the alluvial delta. It was a very easy ski across firm snow through an open birch forest interspersed with frozen marshes. The cabin was very nice indeed, with a sofa, two solid tables and 10 beds in two small rooms. There were two ladies already there, both from Sørreisa, a small coastal town a short distance further north. They were heading off for a short evening ski just as I arrived. It gave me plenty of time to write and melt more snow. Before Inger and Mona returned, I heard them laughing. They then burst into the cabin and cooked a delicious mince dish and invited me to join them for dinner. Then out came some Cinzano and red wine, which perked up their good humour even more. It was a very easy, fun evening, with plenty of jokes and laughter, and we chatted until midnight. This cosy Gaskashytta cabin was the perfect antidote to the static caravans and smell of two-stroke exhaust fumes at Altevatnet, which was another world away at less than 10 kilometres. I was jubilant at being back in the mountains again and back on track with my new skis, and I also had a small reason to celebrate because as I reached this cabin, I also clocked up the 2000 kilometre mark.

Day 94. The cosy Gaskashytta cabin was only 10 kilometres from busy Altevatnet dam yet was in a much calmer environment

Day 94. Mona and Inger brought plenty of good humour and spirit to the cosy, comfortable Gaskashytta cabin

I slept well and woke at 0700. The stove was out, so I relit it and cooked breakfast. It was a glorious day again, with the temperature around minus 8. The girls were soon up for their breakfast, which was good humoured. During it, Mona explained much of the intricacies and excitement of ice fishing. After breakfast there was a photo session and goodbyes, before I set off at 0930. My route was initially up through the sparse birch woods and then on to the bare hillside in Gaskkasvaggi valley. It looked quite rugged up the valley. The birch trees stood out sharply against the brilliant white background of this bright Arctic light. The route went up the valley for a good 3 kilometres into the mountains until it veered east and continued to climb. There were a few older ski tracks but it was not necessary to follow them as

Day 95. Outside Gaskashytta cabin in the sunny birch woods with my skis and the short orange kicker skins attached to the base of them

the snow was hard. There were some firm sastrugi formations, caused by the wind, which made the skiing more difficult. It was warm enough to pack my hat, gloves and jacket and just go in a vest. The impressive mountains around me were not high at around 1500 metres, but they were very craggy. A few of the glaciers which had shaped this landscape remained in the higher reaches of the mountains. The majority had gone, leaving steep corries with small lakes. As I climbed up the valley the gradient eased, but a bitter breeze forced me to put my jacket and gloves back on. The next 10 kilometres to Vuomahytta cabin were quite unexpected and very scenic. I had assumed the landscape here was quite ordinary, but it was quite the opposite. The mountains on each side, especially to the north, were very impressive indeed. They were as exciting as the mountains in Rondane in southern Norway. As I passed through this wild rugged landscape the valley started to descend slightly. I had to ski most of the way down, but the gentle descent allowed me a long glide on each step. Occasionally it got a tad steeper and I could freewheel down the odd slopes in a silent glide. The weather was still marvellous but there were some altocumulus clouds appearing in a mackerel pattern in the blue sky. These cloud formations are often the first signs that a weather front is encroaching into a region of high pressure and is a precursor to deteriorating weather. I soon saw the cabins on the edge of the Vuomajavri lake.

This lake and a few others in the immediate vicinity, notably Anjavatnet, were famed for the size of the Arctic char which lived in their mosquito larvae rich waters. There were many smaller fish here but also a few giants. Every year somebody fishing through a hole in the ice here caught a colossal Arctic char around five kilos. As a result, the cabin here had its fair share of fishermen. Unlike Sweden, however, these fishermen

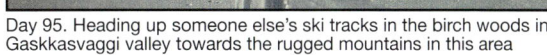

Day 95. Heading up someone else's ski tracks in the birch woods in Gaskkasvaggi valley towards the rugged mountains in this area

had to ski to the cabin as snow scooters are not allowed. Most came with sledges. In the cabin I was in there were three middle-aged fishermen and in the other cabin were three younger teenagers, who arrived at the same time as me. The teenagers each had a sledge and had just arrived from fishing in the neighbouring Anjavatnet lake, where they spent a few days camping. There were also a few groups camped on the lake itself. They were well ensconced with large walls of snow blocks built around the tents and fishing holes to keep the wind off. While I was dithering about going on or not, two of the fishermen returned from the lake and we started chatting. They were very knowledgeable and interesting, and were keen to show me how to ice fish. It was only 1430, but rather than ski the remaining 5-6 hours to the next cabin at Havga, I decided to stay here and write. During the course of the afternoon, the cabin filled up with skiers arriving from other cabins. Firstly, two lady skiers who were responsible for the maintenance and running of Dividalshytta cabin arrived.

Day 95. Looking north from Gaskkasvaggi up to the rough mountains of Inner Troms with Mattagaisi in the distance

Day 95. Looking west back down Gaskkasvaggi towards the mountains around the west end of Altevatnet and the village of Innset

They knew a lot about the area and I picked their brains. Then a very easy going, friendly couple arrived from Dividalshytta cabin. Then the two ice fishermen I spoke to earlier plus a third one returned from the lake with the day's catch of a few half kilo Arctic char each. They prepared some for dinner and let the others freeze outside. I tried to keep up with the conversation in the evening, but the soft melodic north Norwegian dialect was difficult for me. I felt myself getting more and more tired and eventually crashed quite early at 2130, falling asleep immediately.

I woke when the three ice fishermen, who were the first people up, came through to the living room where I was sleeping. It was another fine morning and my prediction on seeing the altocumulus clouds yesterday was thankfully wrong. I had now enjoyed something like three weeks of great weather with only the very occasional day where it was poor. It was cold outside, however, and the temperature was minus 15. After listening to the other guests I decided to go to Dividalshytta cabin, rather the tiny cabin at Havga, which only has two beds as I had originally planned. I had wanted to avoid the forest with its potentially deep loose snow and therefore chose to go to Havga to avoid the worst of it. However, it seemed the forest had a firm trail through it and I should not encounter any problems. It would mean a relatively short day. I therefore decided to take up the outgoing and amusing ice fisherman's offer to come down and fish for a couple of hours. I was curious to find out why so many tough outdoor men were obsessed with sitting beside a hole with a small fishing rod. The fisherman was delighted to explain everything, and lent me a hole in the ice, a reindeer skin to lie on, and a fishing rod with the tackle on which he baited with about five maggots. The maggots would hopefully

Day 95. The slope down the sunny valley towards the shallow lakes around Vuomahytta cabin where Arctic char grew to a colossal size

entice the Arctic char, who are spoilt by the high density of mosquito larvae which the rich nutrients in these shallow lakes support. It was these larvae the fish lived off and grew large and fat.

Day 95. Vuomahytta consists of two cabins which are quite a Mecca in the spring for ice fishermen hoping to catch a prize specimen

The method to fish for them was in theory quite simple. Firstly, find a spot where you knew or guessed the water depth was about two or three metres. Then bore a hole with a 20 centimetre auger through the metre thick ice. This could take a good quarter of an hour. Then build a sheltering snow block wall round the hole to keep the wind off. Next, cover the bottom of the sheltered area with foam mats and reindeer skins to lie on. Then bait a hook with five maggots and a shiny reflecting device. Many people threw egg shells into the hole and these lay on the bottom so you could see the fish swimming over them. Finally, lower the shiny weight and maggots into the hole so the maggots were suspended just off the bottom. I did just this and then put my head over the hole to peer down to the bottom of the lake. I blocked any light with my head so there

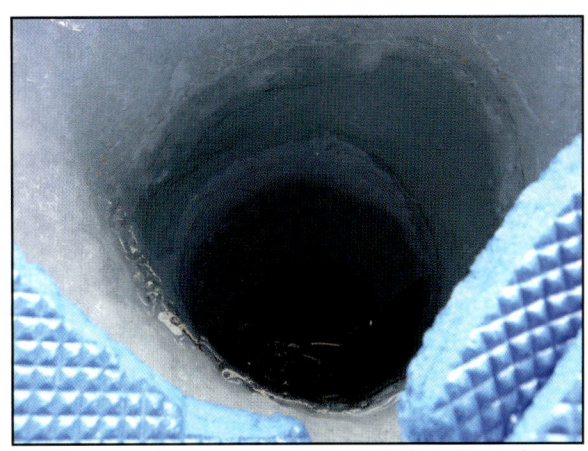

Day 96. I lay on a foam mat and some warm reindeer skins on the metre thick ice and dropped the line down the hole into the lake

was no reflection and my breath stopped the water in the hole freezing over. I saw a couple of 20-centimetre fish come over and sniff the bait and then head off. Suddenly, a 50-centimetre fish appeared. I had been told the really big ones have white edges to the fins. This one certainly did. It swam off without showing much interest but then reappeared a few minutes later. I was getting excited hoping it would bite. It just sniffed again and swam off. However, it showed up after another couple of minutes and gracefully swam over to the baited hook. I stopped moving it, hoping it would bite. Alas it again merely sniffed the bait and headed off. Obviously they were just not feeding. I waited another half hour but despite the sun and the reindeer skin, it was getting cold. I never saw the white-tipped monster again, but a few small ones came by. I can see some of the excitement in it now, having seen the big one with the white edges to its fins. I returned the fishing equipment to the exceptionally friendly and amusing fisherman and returned to the cabin empty handed.

The weather was still glorious as I set off on the 18 kilometres to Dividalshytta cabin. Just after I left the cabin I started a wonderful downhill run to Anjavassdalen. I went bombing down it on firm snow which was covered in a dusting of new frost. I must have been going at least 25 kilometres per hour, and the wind was humming in my ears. I suddenly got a premonition that I might sink in if the snow surface softened. Two seconds later I suddenly broke through the crust and my skis and shins disappeared into the sugary loose snow beneath this firm skin. The result was spectacular. From the waist up I kept moving at 25 kilometres per hour, while from the waist down I stopped almost immediately. This resulted in me pivoting up on my ski tips and being airborne for what seemed like a couple of seconds, before crashing back to earth with my head and chest ploughing a divot into the snow. When I finally came to rest, there was snow everywhere. There was snow behind my sunglasses, up my nostrils, in my ears and down the opening in my jacket. I was lucky I had a soft landing. On looking back at my tracks I saw I was airborne for almost three metres before I landed again. It was a classic head plant, and probably my most spectacular crash on the whole tour. After dusting myself down, I continued much more carefully down the slope to the floor of Anjavassdalen valley. To the west of me, further up this valley, were further spectacular mountains and corries.

Day 96. Having left Vuomahytta cabin I skied east down the lovely open Anjavassdalen valley towards Dividalshytta cabin in the distance

Despite the sun being out there was a bitterly cold wind coming up the valley against me. I had to stop to put on my mitts, as the gloves alone were too cold. The route was a metre wide trail of ski tracks which were quite firm now. These tracks traversed down through the birch trees on to the floor of the valley, where the frozen river meandered down in static curves in the shadow of the steep cliffs of Blåfjellet. Once on this shallow frozen river the ski route followed it for a magical 10 kilometres of great skiing. Very occasionally the river was open and I could look into the holes in the snowdrifts and see crystal clear water flowing across stones. The sun was beating down again, warming me, and the wind had abated now as the birch trees were taller and growing more densely. A dipper, Norway's national bird, flew from river opening to river opening in search of larvae. I stopped for an unnecessary bar of chocolate in one such place to look at this tough bird surviving the Arctic winter. After this wonderful run the ski track split. The one to the left and north descended to Frihetsli and the parking area down the valley. The tracks to the right headed across easy birch forest initially

Day 96. On the lip of Dividalen valley I looked down to the green valley floor covered in pine trees

to the lip of the valley and then descended steeply down the side into the depths of Dividalen. From the lip there was a fine view into and down this beautiful forested valley which was green with pine trees on the valley floor. The whole of the upper section of this pine-covered valley, much of the tundra plateau on the east side of the valley and the area I had skied through today, comprised the Øvre Dividal National Park. It was all a very pleasant surprise for me, as the ruggedness and beauty of the area far exceeded my expectations.

After a difficult steep descent in deep snow with plenty of zig-zagging, I at last reached the frozen Divielva river on the valley floor. The snow was too deep, unpredictable and difficult to ski down in a series of smooth turns, so I had to traverse backwards and forwards through the trees until I was on this river. I skied up the river for a kilometre until I reached the ski tracks which went up the west side of the valley to Dividalshytta cabin. Luckily, as promised by some of the guests last night, they were good tracks. These tracks had been made by skiers over the last month. They were largely firm, quite visible and followed a gentle gradient up through the magnificent grand old pine trees. An eagle perched in a tree took off as I approached quite closely. Rather than fumble for my camera and lose the moment I just watched it. I occasionally deviated off this irregular ski track into the loose snow of the forest and got a taste of what a nightmare the half metre of un-compacted sugar snow could have been. In other places where the snow was not so deep I did see the odd blueberry bush poking its head through the snow which I took as a worrying sign of impending spring. It took a pleasant hour to climb up the vague tracks to the cabin in the evening sun. Soon the pines petered out and I was in the birch woods again with a clear view west across the pines below me and up Anjavassdalen valley which I had had

Day 96. The pine trees in Dividalen valley were big mature specimens which could now enjoy the protection of the nation parks regulations

the pleasure of skiing down just a few hours previously. There were already two other people here at the cabin. A father and son team who had been fishing in a lake to the east. They had got quite a few trout and were now on their way home to Tromsø after a few days camping on Beassetjavri lake. We chatted a lot and I got some good tips from these two knowledgeable people. We had a great evening until we went to bed at 2130. With some astonishment, I noticed it was still light enough to ski. Every day now is 10 minutes longer than the previous one.

I got up as I planned at 0700 as did the father and son fishing team. Breakfast was a slow, social affair and I did not get packed and away until 0900. They had been good company and I enjoyed my stay in the cabin with them. I set off from the cabin on yet another beautiful day. I followed their advice and skied along the tracks they had left yesterday as they descended from Beassetjavri lake. These tracks meandered through the birch woods

Day 96. Sunset at Dividalshytta cabin looking west across Dividalen valley and up Anjavassdalen valley which I had just skied down

Day 97. Having skied out of the woods I got another great view across Dividalen valley and straight up Anjavassdalen valley

for a couple of kilometres then headed east up into Julosvaggi valley. I followed them and soon was above the tree line heading into a bright rolling landscape of shallow hills. As I climbed, the benign sunny weather clouded over with a very bitter chill to the breeze forcing me to stop and wrap up more. A good hour and a half after leaving the cabin I reached the open exposed Beassetjavri lake which lay in a dip in the undulating Arctic tundra. This is where the father and son had been camped fishing. There were a couple of tents on the ice a short distance away so I detoured over to them for a chat. They were occupied by two young men from south Norway. They had managed to get quite a few fish over the last days. This lake only contained trout and they fished with baited lines which they left. Each line was on a small rod with a bell on it to alert them to a bite if they were lying in their nearby tents. I left them and skied across the lake, over the south east ridge of Jerta and then headed down to a wide and open valley. The valley was covered in small lakes which were interconnected. In the winter snow, however, it was difficult to make out the lakes. There was a hill opposite called Mielggat which I was aiming to skirt round the south and then east of, but it was so insignificant I had difficulty finding it on the undulating tundra. It looked much more on the map. I skied down into this very wide and flat valley full of tarns and frozen marshes, crossed it and then headed up into the streambed to the east of Mielggat. It was an easy but sustained climb for almost 3 kilometres as I headed north. En route, the weather misted over and I could virtually see nothing. I tried to use my GPS to pinpoint my location, but it was still set up for Norwegian maps, and I was now using a Swedish map, with a different grid system. It was too complicated to reprogram the GPS in this weather. I continued assuming I was where I thought I was.

Day 97. Having fumbled my way up Vanasvarri in the white out I was given a reprieve at the saddle when the mist cleared

As I was climbing up the valley to the south of the Vanasvarri massif, I got the occasional glimpses of the surrounding landscape, which confirmed I was on the right course. When I neared the top of this windy saddle the weather opened up a bit more and I could get my bearings from some crags. I then fumbled on for another couple of kilometres, on the level across a wide windy saddle, hoping I was going the right way and using my compass occasionally. When I reached the descent on the north side of the saddle the mist cleared and I could not only see the entire descent down into the Deartavaggi valley, but also the sunshine on the mountains across the valley. It is always a huge respite when visibility returns. In poor visibility one is almost helpless. The descent was initially superb, until it reached a small lake. From here there were some terrible sastrugi formations which were very tedious to ski across. I had to be careful not to break a ski in this terrain. Once over the lake I followed the stream bed down to the main valley. I was wary of three contour

Day 97. As I skied down Vanasvarri into Deartavaggi valley I had to cross a lake covered in small sastrugi formations

Day 97. Looking west from Rostojavri up Deartavaggi valley towards Dærtahytta cabin with the foot of Vanasvarri massif on the left

lines on the map, which seemed to indicate there was a steep rampart across the whole descent, and the stream bed was the only weak point. This was not the case and once I was below it I realised I could have descended anywhere. The stream was quite exciting, however, with good snow on the huge drifts on the west side. These drifts overhung a deep ravine some 10 metres deep. In a few places the craggy sides of this ravine were exposed and the bare angular rock sat beneath the overhanging cornice. To ski off something like this in the blindness of a white out could easily be fatal. As I reached the valley floor I saw some cabins about 4 kilometres to the west. I looked on the map and saw they were the Dærtahytta cabins. I could easily have gone via them and saved myself the problems of the climb over the saddle in the poor visibility. It would have been a few kilometres longer, but it would have certainly been quicker.

Once in the valley, the snow conditions were superb again, with a firm base topped with a couple of centimetres of loose powder snow on top. The Norwegians would call it 'silke føre' or silky conditions. I skied east for 3 kilometres until I reached Rostojavri lake. Just before it, I came across some very new scooter tracks. I followed the scooter tracks over a small spur as they veered to the north and then saw the cabin just 2 kilometres ahead. The scooter tracks I followed led right to Stor Rostahytta cabin and belonged to one of the State Forestry wardens who looked after this new cabin. He had also just arrived on his snow scooter towing a large sledge of birch logs. There were three 60-year-old skiers here, and just one free bed in a room with four bunks. The three other skiers were Paula, Oscar and their friend Ivar. Paula and Oscar seemed very nice, but Ivar was clearly drunk. He was bordering on unintelligible and Paula and Oscar were telling him to behave. I wanted some peace and quiet and was wary of someone who was so drunk in the late afternoon. I had no option, other than camping, and did not want to do that if there was a warm comfortable room and bed here, despite drunken Ivar. As it transpired, Ivar was not actually as drunk as he was leading me to believe, and I managed to have some sort of conversation with him when I sat down inside. I have noticed over the years that acting more inebriated than you actually are, is something of a Norwegian trait. I soon found out that Ivar was not a hopeless drunk who managed to stagger upon this place by accident while riding a snow scooter, but was a supreme outdoor enthusiast. He was 62 years old and had spent much of his early life in the Norwegian military as a 'marinejeger', which is Norway's much respected elite forces unit. He did not tell me this but I found out later. He had climbed the Troll Wall some 30 years ago, been storm bound on the Eiger, kayaked round Spitsbergen and spent many months each year camping and fishing in remote spots. He had kayaked much of the north Norwegian coast which I was planning on doing soon. Remarkably, he had retrained as a dentist and practised when he was not in the outdoors. He did nothing by half measures, and almost immediately, poured me a powerful but delicious cocktail, which was half a tumbler of cognac topped up with half a tumbler of Bailey's Irish Cream. The second drink he poured me an hour later, was 96% alcohol by volume, homemade moonshine and Bailey's mixed together. In the meantime, Paula and Oscar served me a meal of elg meat balls, which were delicious. There was no chance of writing, so I enjoyed the evening and listened to Ivar's stories, none of which I thought were tall or embellished. He was pouring himself large helpings of 96% moonshine, and was drinking with abandon. It seemed if he didn't have adrenaline coursing through his veins on some madcap adventure, then he would have alcohol pumping through them. He was going to live life to the full, even if it killed him. Despite Ivar being drunk, he was good company, and Paula and Oscar kept him in check and humoured him. In the end, the moonshine got the better of him, and he stumbled to bed in the middle of an incomprehensible rant about the evils of cannabis. I should imagine there would never be a dull moment if Ivar was about.

We all got up at 0700 and Paula made some large haddock fish cakes for breakfast which were eaten with homemade cranberry jam. It was a fantastic change to the usual porridge. Ivar joked with us all despite his hangover. The three of them were heading down the valley towards Dærtahytta but would be stopping just before it in a small Sami cabin which was probably used for reindeer herding and fishing. All three had some Sami blood, as did many Norwegians whose families had lived in north Norway for a couple of generations. This meant they had to ski into the fresh southerly wind in a temperature of minus 9 in very poor visibility. I would be heading north with the wind behind me which was a far more comfortable scenario. They had packed most of their belongings on to their sledges and I had my rucksack ready at 1030 so started off. The visibility was quite poor when I set off and it soon got a lot worse, and I could just see for about 30 metres. The wind also increased from a force 4 to a 6 at least. After about 3 kilometres I decided I needed to put my windproof salopettes on as my legs were getting cold. This was a tricky operation in the wind and I had to be careful nothing blew away. Once I was more sensibly dressed, I continued north up the valley in a sphere of visibility which was only some 20 metres. Luckily it was pretty flat and I was going up the valley in the same direction as the wind. At times I was almost blown along. The skiing conditions were very good, but not quite the silky conditions of yesterday. There was the odd old ski or scooter track which appeared momentarily, but they were barely visible and not worth following as the snow was firm.

Day 98. Ivar packs his sledge outside the small new cabin at Stor Rosta which is managed by Statskog

Day 98. Skiing through poor weather en route from Stor Rostahytta to Pältsastugorna cabins as the mist rises revealing a featureless tundra

I had adjusted the settings on my GPS so I could find my position, as I needed it on this flat valley. There were some lakes, but it was impossible to tell what was lake and what was frozen marsh. I could also not see any features to the side of the valley, due to the mist, so was reliant on the GPS to pinpoint my position. After what seemed like a couple of hours, I got to the area where I had to bear more north east and follow a different valley. I went on a compass bearing for a good half hour, until there was a clearer spell and I could at last see some dark crags and then the shape of the hills on each side, and consequently I started to feel slightly less bewildered. The visibility got better and better, until the whole open smooth rolling tundra landscape appeared below a mist which obscured all the raised ground. It was a bleak and featureless landscape which I could now gaze across. My route now crossed into Sweden and then climbed up the gentle spur of one of the shallow ridges which descended from one of the mist-covered and concealed peaks of Moskangaisi mountain. It was a great shame this mountain and the neighbouring Pältsan were hidden, as I had heard much about them and on the map it looked a spectacular massif with many high angular peaks. At the top of this wide rounded ridge was a wonderful descent all the way down to the valley where the Kummaeno river flowed. Just where the river flowed from the bare tundra and into the sparse upper birch woods was a collection of some cabins, which I assumed were Pältsastugorna. I enjoyed this easy gentle descent across open snowfields and then across the sides of moraine piles to reach the cabin. There was a flock of snow buntings hanging around when I arrived and they stayed a while. I had just got into the cabin and unpacked when the next blizzard came sweeping in from the south and everything outside was obscured again. I was the first to arrive. A few groups of Finnish skiers and two young Norwegian girls burst in out of the blizzard during the course of the afternoon. It was not a very sociable group, however, and everybody pretty much kept to themselves. They were a far cry from the extroverted Ivar Olsen. It suited me well, as I had a lot of writing to do.

Day 99. A break in the weather on the Duoibal plateau around the area of the lakes revealed a desolate tundra environment

I woke at 0600 and looked outside. There was a blizzard with heavy snow and a strong wind which was almost gale force. The visibility was only about 50 metres. So I went back to bed and got up at 0730 when it had improved marginally. I had breakfast with the six Finns which was a sombre affair with no-one seeming very jolly at all. There was a choice of two ways to Kilpisjärvi; either through the woods down the Kummaeno river to Kummavuopio and then up Alajärvi lake to Kilpisjärvi which was 40 kilometres, or the 25 kilometres over Duoibal mountain. The latter was what I had planned, but I needed good visibility to go this way. As I ate my breakfast of dehydrated monkfish and mashed potatoes I pondered the possibilities. Given the weather was improving the whole time I eventually made the decision to go the shorter, more demanding way, over the mountain. I set off at 0930 with the remnants of a snow show still blowing around. The route over Duoibal was very up and down. I climbed the initial steep slope to gain the top of the plateau and hoped I would remain up at this altitude, however, I was on a roller coaster of a route. The route dropped down to a lake in a deep bowl and crossed it. This descent was not that steep at all but the poor visibility made it difficult. I could not make out the windblown ridges and dips in the snow and at least one caught me out and sent me tumbling. After I had climbed back on to the barren plateau, where the visibility was poor, I had another difficult descent to a second lake. This yo-yoing up and down from the plateau to lakes in this very barren landscape with dull rolling hills and a grey light was very uninspiring.

Once I was back on the plateau again after the second lake the visibility started to improve slightly. There was a distant view, largely obscured by clouds, of some spectacular mountains to the west in Norway. I could look down into Stordalen in Norway where there was a small tourist cabin called Goldahytta. Beside this cabin and beneath a crag was Treriksroset. This was the meeting point of Norway, Sweden and Finland and it was quite a popular destination. The ski route I was on forked on

Day 99. Looking north from the Duoibal plateau down into the misty Stordalen valley and the vicinity of Goldahytta and Treriksroset

this plateau, with one route going down to Treriksroset, and the other going down to the west end of Kilpisjärvi lake, which is where I wanted to go. The descent to the lake was quite exciting in places. Firstly, it descended open hillside and I could make long traverses. After that, however, it followed a scooter track down through the forest. This track offered a consistent surface but it was narrow and steep. The forest beside this track would be mostly firm with a sudden trap of knee deep sugar snow. I chose the scooter track, snow ploughing firmly as I could not see what was round any corner. With burning leg muscles I arrived at the lake. It was only 1300, and I thought I just had 7 kilometres to Kilpisjärvi town. There was a slight wind against me on the lake, but it was mostly a side wind. I soon came across a dedicated ski track. I put my skis into the prepared slots

Day 99. The final descent down Duoibal towards Kilpisjärvi lake which I had to ski down to the town under Saana mountain in the middle

and started to ski vigorously. I was flying along and getting a good glide with each step. Before long I was reaching the built-up town of Kilpisjärvi.

Or so I thought, and it is what the map said. However, there are two built-up areas at Kilpisjärvi and they were separated by 5 kilometres. I was at the one with the youth hostel, but not the shop. The youth hostel was fully booked with Norwegian families on snow scooter holidays, and it did not seem the type of place I was hoping for anyway. The owner kindly phoned and arranged a reasonably expensive hotel room for me at the other Kilpisjärvi. After having a huge buffet meal here I set off. The 5 kilometres were very easy and fast. Again there was a nice ski track and the busy buzz of scooters on the lake had to avoid the track. I soon reached the hotel. It was part of a chain called Lapland hotels. My room was in a dilapidated barrack-style building. It was exceptionally bad value for money. I tried to find somewhere else, but it was Easter, and the whole town was full of Norwegian holidaymakers, so I took the room. I then went shopping and bought six days worth of food for the next leg to Máze. I was surprised the shop was open, as everybody said it would be closed. Back at the barracks nothing really worked. The water was tepid, the sink was almost off the wall in the shared bathroom and the shower curtains were barely attached. I washed all my clothes in the sink and shower and treated the whole place with the disrespect it deserved. It was not a great end to an otherwise superb section. The friendliness I had enjoyed in north Norway and Sweden seemed to be lacking here. Indeed, it seemed Kilpisjärvi's primary purpose is to extract money from Norwegian holidaymakers and shoppers, and I was merely a cog in this wheel.

SECTION 13. Dividalen and Troms
10 days. 177 kilometres. 52 hours. 3390m ascent. 3340m descent.

THE SKI: SECTION 14. NORTH FINLAND

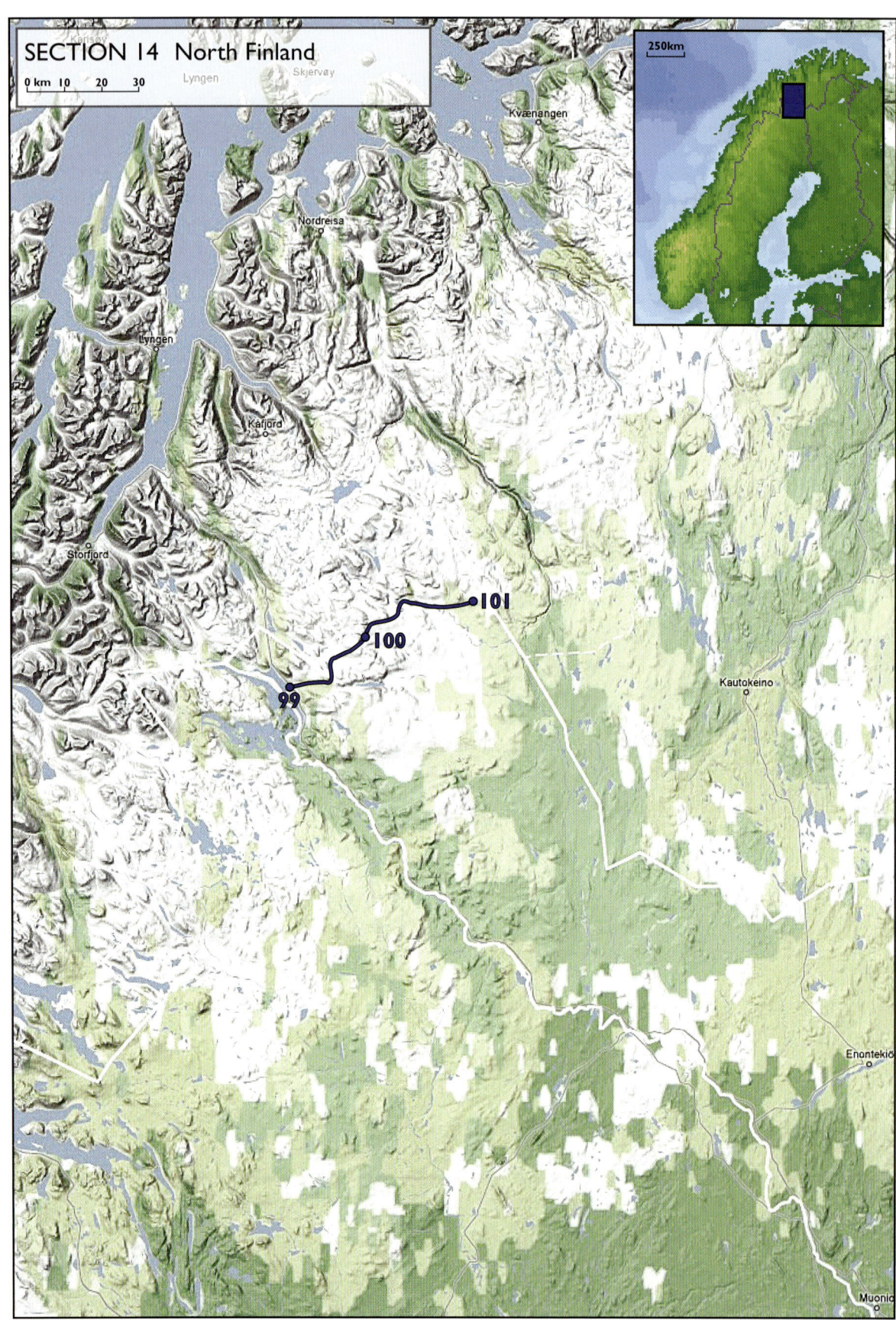

THE SKI: SECTION 14. NORTH FINLAND

The hotel redeemed itself with a generous breakfast. As I left I reconsidered my food supplies and doubted I had enough for the estimated six days until Máze. I returned to the shop and topped up a few items. I also bought a red ski wax as the temperature was now plus 2, and the blue extra wax I normally used would just be too hard to stick to the wet round crystals which the snow was rapidly becoming. I eventually left Kilpisjärvi mid-morning, and it was not a moment too soon. I put the red wax on my skis; its sticky texture gripped the snow well and prevented my skis sliding back. The ski and scooter trail left from just behind the shop. Luckily there were not that many scooters on it, as it was a 'pay as you go' scooter track. The route quickly left the buzz of Kilpisjärvi behind as it headed up through birch forest for a kilometre to a small lake called Cahkaljävri. As I crossed this lake I passed a lot of skiers returning to Kilpisjärvi. A few had large sledges and obviously were returning after a longer expedition, possibly from Halti which is Finland's highest mountain at a mere 1324 metres. At the far end of the lake I missed the turning to Saarijärvi cabin. It must have been much earlier than my map indicated. So I carried on along the scooter track for another 3 kilometres, having seen a valley on the map I could ski through to regain the route I missed, and then continue to Saarijärvi cabin. About an hour after I left Cahkaljävri lake I was just considering leaving the scooter route to head up the small Muvravaggi valley to cut over to Saarijärvi cabin when I saw some skiers coming towards me.

Day 100. The enthusiastic Jan Kopka is an adventure bike racer who also arranged eccentric bike tours through Finland's winter tundra

However, for skiers they seemed to be moving quite fast so I assumed the level bit they were on was actually downhill, due to some sort of optical illusion in the mist. As they approached I saw a familiar movement which was not skiing, but cycling. I could hardly believe it but there was a group of seven cyclists. They were on a weeks' tour around the snow scooter tracks of North Finland. They were led by Jan Kopka, who I later found out was a very accomplished Czech road racing cyclist, who had to retire from this sport as he got too old for it in his 30s. He then took up adventure racing, taking it to extreme limits, like racing in the Alaskan winter or down the Great Divide in the Rockies. His infectious enthusiasm for extreme cycling encouraged this group of Czechs to sign up on this tour he was running. Jan Kopka designed and built his own bikes for this with very wide tyres and specially-designed front and rear forks to accommodate them. Each bike cost around 5000 euros. They were struggling a bit today in this soft wet snow, but apparently when it was harder or frozen they could easily do 50 kilometres in a day. I was fascinated. I must say the Czechs are right up there with the French when it comes to innovative sports. However, they both lie behind the New Zealanders, who are at the cutting edge of crazy with bungee jumping and surfing down large rapids. I am not sure if this snow cycling will catch on, but Jan Kopka deserves success for originality alone.

After chatting with the Czechs for a good half hour, I started north up Muvravaggi valley. I was delighted to see that there was actually a marked trail going up here, as off the route the snow was difficult. I was using a 1:50,000 map for this area as opposed to the 1:100,000 I had used for the last month and was pleasantly surprised how fast I was moving across the paper. In no time I was at the top of the saddle and on my way down the other side. When I thought Saarijärvi cabin should be about 2 kilometres away I rounded a corner to see it was just 300 metres ahead, which was a rare treat. The Finnish cabins in this area are either free and quite rustic, but with wood and gas, or you can choose to have a bit more luxury and pay to hire a more opulent adjacent cabin or room in the free cabin. It seems a very good system. In this cabin there were two rooms; the free room and the salubrious room, where a group of older Finns were staying and who were just returning from a trip up Halti. In the free part of the cabin were a few groups of Norwegian skiers on a day tour from Kilpisjärvi. They were having lunch here before returning. I started chatting with them. They were enthralled with my journey and were able to offer me some good tips. They left after an hour and I continued north east to do the remaining 10 kilometres to Kuonjarjoki cabin. These 10 kilometres were fast. The red wax was gripping the snow well as I pushed up a gentle rise. The landscape was rounded and quite featureless. Indeed, in the mist it was really

Day 100. The featureless winter tundra in north Finland was relatively dull after the high mountains of Norway and Sweden

quite drab and nothing like the spectacular mountains of Norway and northern Sweden. At the top of this shallow incline was a gentle descent to the cabin with its two tier status. The free part had a Dutch couple who were living in Norway and another group of six Finnish girls who were students. All were nice but I gravitated towards the Dutch as their English was fluent, and the Finns were struggling a bit as their language strengths are Swedish and Russian. It was a sociable evening and I had to wait until everybody else had gone to bed at a surprisingly early hour before I could write. I didn't slide into my sleeping bag until 2300.

Everybody started to stir around 0630 and I got up at 0700. Outside there was a west wind and it was just below zero with spindrift blowing about. I set off at 0900 and headed east with the wind at my back. It was quite sunny despite the wind. A group of dog sleds soon came quickly towards me. There were five sleds each being pulled by the smaller, faster Alaskan type of husky. The dogs were working hard, pulling the sleds up the shallow hill, and their long tongues were hanging out, bouncing with every step. As I dropped down into the very shallow side valleys the wind dropped off, and after a couple of hours it was even absent from the ridges. It was turning into a nice day. I stopped and chatted with a couple of Germans on snow shoes plodding up the hill. It was the wrong mode of travel entirely and they would have been much better off even with a couple of Jan Kopka's bicycles. While I was chatting with them one of the young Finnish girls, Saija, from Kuonjarjoki cabin caught up. We continued together for an hour to Meekonjärvi cabin, she on her enormous wooden ex-military skis and Nokia gumboots and me on my fast mountain skis. Her skis were really designed for the forest. Most Finns had huge skis which were about

Day 100. Kuonjarjoki cabin is a typical two tier cabin in North Finland with a free rustic room and a comfortable room available for a fee

two and a half metres long and quite wide. They must have been double the surface area of mine. The cabin at Meekonjärvi was nicely positioned on the valley floor beside frozen lakes and under outcrops of steep black crags. They looked like basalt or gabbro. The cabin here was a free cabin and had a sleeping platform where about eight people could lie. There was also a stove and a gas cooker. Outside was a wood shed and toilet. I chatted here with Saija over lunch, when another two Finns showed up. They had come from Taapmajärvi cabin and said there were firm tracks there. This was good, as it was where I was aiming for today.

I said my goodbyes and started off west down a chain of beautiful lakes. These lakes were gorgeous now, but must be even more stunning in the summer time when the birch trees around them are full of insects and birds, and the forest floor is covered in lush flowers. The crags soon faded behind me, and in front to the east, was an undulating landscape. The change in the landscape felt significant. In front of me was the old ancient basement of the Baltica tectonic plate, the

Day 101. Five dog sleds passed me on the way to Meekonjärvi cabin, each being pulled by six Alaskan huskies

Day 101. Looking back westwards from the climb up to Taapmajärvi cabin where one can see the east margin of the Caledonian Mountains

oldest rock in Europe, while behind was the edge of the Caledonian Mountain thrusts and nappes which had been forced eastwards from the edge of this continental plate. I had been skiing through the eroded stumps of these geological sheets and blocks of rocks for the last three months, but now I was leaving them behind for the naked, undulating ancient basement. As I skied down these lakes I passed a whole family of seven, all spaced out evenly in a line, fishing through holes in the ice near the small free cabin at Jogasjärvi. I didn't stop here as I was making for Porojärvi cabin, just another 3 kilometres away, where I was intending to have another break. When I got there I found that Porojärvi cabin was another beautiful lumber cottage. It had no gas, but a wood stove which one could cook on and a large supply of wood. There was room for six to sleep here on a wooden platform. It was very quaint and it was an excellent service by the Finnish state forestry department to make such accommodation available to skiers and hikers.

I left here at 1600. It was getting warmer and I was down to my vest. I had to put extra red wax on for the climb. The problem with this is that when such unseasonably warm spells end and the temperatures go back to minus 10, the snow will stick to the ski, until this sticky wax is removed, and removal can be a problem without spirits. I was hoping it would wear off. It was a very gentle, easy 9-kilometre climb to Taapmajärvi cabin. The mountains were now fading far behind me. There were many reindeer tracks as these domesticated animals were now migrating from the forests where they had been wintering to their calving grounds and summer pastures, which were around here. It seemed a herd of reindeer had also been around the tiny cabin at Taapmajärvi, as the ground was trampled and covered in droppings. Soon after I arrived a young Sami on a scooter with a huge trailer showed up. He had sacks of food pellets for the reindeer in the trailer. He spotted his herd with binoculars and headed off to them. I lit the fire to cook on, but it turned the little cabin into a sauna, making me too sleepy to write or even cook, so I had to sleep for an hour until the place cooled down with the door open. After supper I managed to write then crashed out at 2230, just as it was getting dark. The temperature outside was still plus 2, which worried me as I had the potentially difficult upper Reisadalen valley to cross tomorrow and needed firm conditions for this.

Day 101. The lovely cosy cabin at Taapmajärvi on the plateau near the Norwegian border was surrounded by many reindeer tracks

SECTION 14. North Finland
2 days. 51 kilometres. 16 hours. 640m ascent. 500m descent.

THE SKI: SECTION 15. REISADALEN TO MÁZE

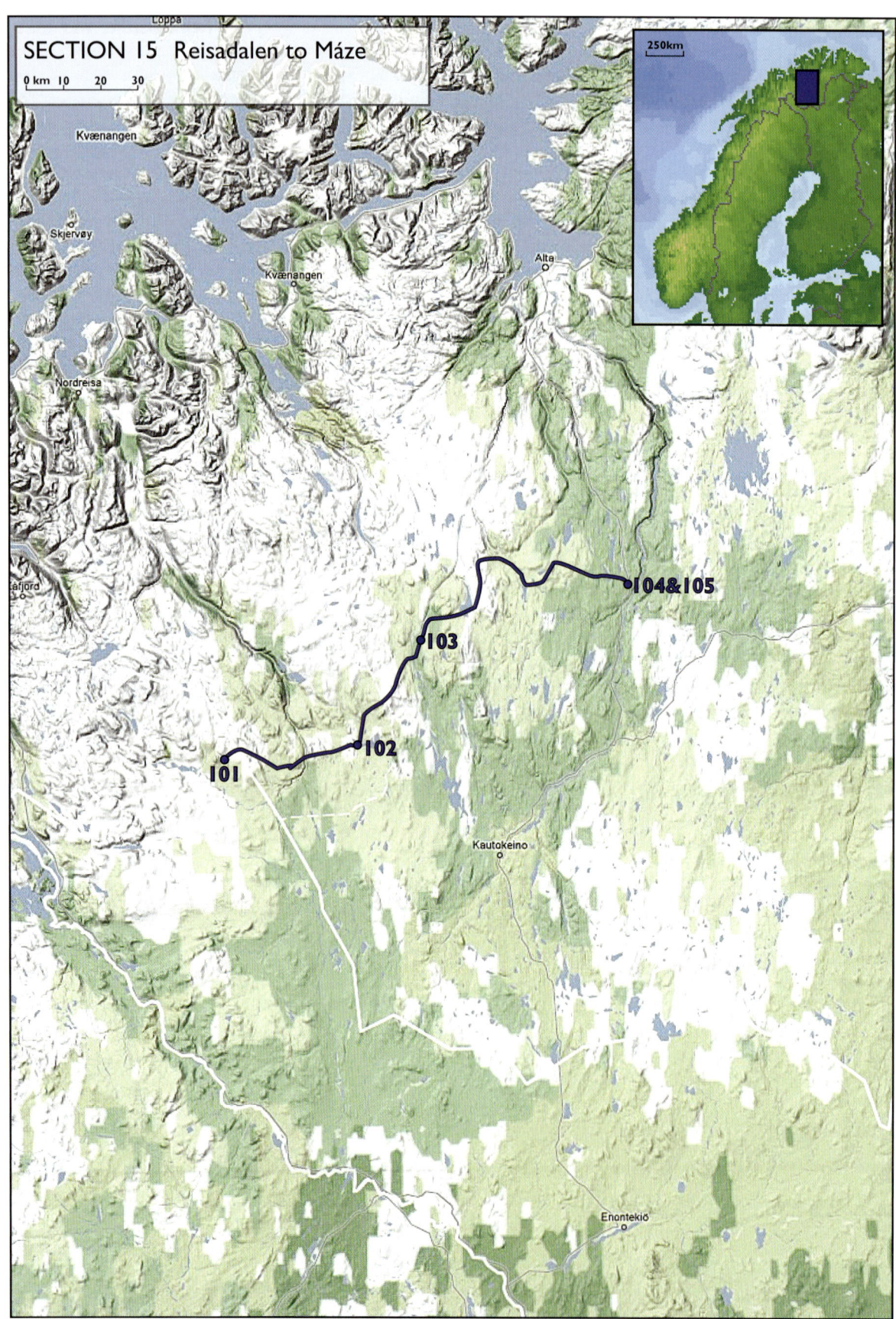

THE SKI: SECTION 15. REISADALEN TO MÁZE

I was up early and was both excited and apprehensive about crossing upper Reisadalen. It was misty weather and almost windstill, but the temperature was plus 2 and this was worrying as I knew the snow might be deep and I needed it frozen firm. As I had breakfast and packed, the mist started to burn off but then returned. I set off and skied round the north side of Jorba Cierte, a rounded mountain on the Finnish and Norwegian border. After a couple of kilometres there was a reindeer fence which pretty much ran along the border. This would have separated the grazing of one Sami herding cooperative from another. They did not always follow international borders between Norway and Sweden, but perhaps it was stricter with Finland, due to its Soviet history. Once round the north of Jorba Cierte I continued east over the gentle south ridge of Sagge Cierte where it was very misty again. Once I descended down the east side of this ridge the visibility improved again and I had a great ski across the plateau, called Njallalahku, which was its Sami name. The visibility was clear, the snow was firm and there was a slight descent for most of the 8 kilometres which made it a very pleasant ski. The only negative point was I could see the top end of the 50-kilometre long ribbon of a deep canyon which cut a gaping slot into this ancient geological basement. Much further to the north, and downstream, this canyon was called Reisadalen, but as its deep slot meandered south across the ancient basement it was called Njallaavzi. Somehow I had to cross this canyon, as a detour would be very costly and quite likely take an extra day at least. I had heard much about it, nearly all of it bad. I had been warned that the snow in Reisadalen was very loose and very deep. The winds which sweep this largely treeless plateau blow the snow and spindrift across its surface. When it reaches the deep slot of Reisadalen it drops into the canyon and builds up into deep deposits in the calm canyon floor and sides. Because this snow is loose, uncompacted and full of air it can be metres deep. It is impossible to ski through this type of snow as one's skis just end up vertical in front of you. You have to take them off and wade through the snow. By 1130 I had reached the edge of the plateau and could look down into the canyon.

Day 102. After skiing across the Njallalahku plateau I reached the lip of the daunting Njallaavzi canyon

It was a good 100 metres deep and I peered into it with anxiety. The craggy canyon sides were covered in rocky outcrops and birch woods. Getting down would be difficult, as I had to thread a route between the crags, many of which I could not see, but getting up the other side would be a very difficult challenge, if not a complete nightmare. At the worst I would be able to descend into the canyon but would not be able to get out again. In this case I could be stuck in the bottom for a night at least. I stood at the top, procrastinating and dithering about the various outcomes which might befall me, before I summoned the courage to take the step down into it. The descent was not as difficult as I feared, but it was very steep. I kept my skis on and traversed down between birch trees and rocky outcrops. I was sinking in up to my knees at least as I negotiated a safe descent, wary of the avalanche danger, in addition to the outcrops all around me. Luckily I did not descend into any dead-ends surrounded by crags and have to retrace my steps, as I wondered just how I would do it. I thought it would be near impossible to return the way I had descended. Occasionally I glanced at the other side and the task which would soon be a massive problem, but tried to ignore it. I had reached the point of no return now anyway. After half an hour I gingerly finished my precarious descent through the outcrops and trees and reached the thick tangled woods at the bottom of the canyon on each side of the river. It was very deep snow here and I had to struggle hard to get to the river. To compound the difficulties, the river was largely open and at least knee deep. I had to push and flounder through the birch woods for at least half an hour until I found an icy bridge which I deemed to be a safe enough place to cross. This was conveniently at the bottom of the steep slope on the east side, which I had previously thought should be possible to escape from the canyon.

The ascent was horrible. It was only 100 metres of ascent over 250 metres but it seemed so steep. I tried to traverse up the slope, but despite my efforts to go up, I just went sideways and after half an hour I had nothing to show for my efforts, other than a deep trench at the bottom of the slope. My ski tips were in

Day 102. Wading up through the waist deep snow towards the top of the Njallaavzi canyon after having spent five hours crossing it

front of my chest as they stood almost upright in front of me. I took them off and started to wade through the snow. It was possible, but very slow, and I could only progress by digging a slot above me and heaving all the snow down below me, in a kind of swimming motion. At one stage I had to get my shovel out and dig a trench up the steep slope. Frequently I hauled myself up on the trunks of the birch trees and then once past them I could get my breath back by resting on them. One of the trees was rotten and suddenly gave way and I tumbled and slid some 15 metres back down the slope again until I got wedged between the slope and another tree. The snow was continually up to my waist at least, and sometimes it was chest deep, with the consistency of dry, loose sugar. As I climbed up the steep side I released a lot of small avalanches of this loose sugar snow. They started off as a small V by my buried leg and then fanned out until they were three or four metres wide, when the whole mass seemed to implode into a hole which its own weight created. I fought and clawed my way up this wooded slope, displacing and dislodging huge amounts of snow past me for the best part of four hours. I struggled to keep the snow out of my mittens and clothes, but despite my best efforts it crept into my pockets and through my zips. In addition it was extremely hard, hot work and I was sweating a lot as I inched upwards. I was getting wetter and wetter, but was using huge amounts of energy, so kept warm. After the best part of four hours the gradient at last started to ease slightly, and the snow became only thigh deep. It was still impossible to ski for another hour, when with huge elation I approached the top of the canyon. Here the snow became firmer as the birch trees thinned out and had allowed the winds which sweep across this plateau to compact the snow. I was free again, but wet and exhausted.

Day 102. Looking south up the deep slot of the Njallaavzi canyon from the lip of the plateau on the east side

Once on the open plateau again I was jubilant and in a happy mood. I still had to cross the Raiseatnu river in another 10 kilometres, but as long as it was still covered in ice I should have no more obstacles until Máze in about 80 kilometres. I skied well across the open mountain heading north east across undulating mountains. The snow cover here was quite sparse and it was melting, so there was a lot of willow scrub poking up above the snow. I tried to avoid it as I broke through the crust when I skied over it. At last I crossed a final mound and then started the descent to the Askkasjohka river meandering across the wide, open section of the Reisadalen valley, just above the point where it entered the canyon. This river was a tributary of the Raiseatnu river but still quite large. I was apprehensive when I approached the river. If it was open and the ice was suspect it would mean a very long detour. As I arrived I saw there was water and slush on the river in most places, but luckily for me it seemed to be above ice. Under this water and slush the winter's ice still seemed

Day 102. Crossing the Askkasjohka river was tense as there was water and slush on top of the winter's ice which was now starting to melt

Day 102. I found a campsite amongst the birch on the north shore of Raisajärvi lake and buried the tent's storm flaps in snow for stability

to be intact. None the less I took my skis off and put them on my pack, undid the hip and chest buckles and held my ski sticks at the bottom so I could jab the blunt tips of them into the ice if I went through. The river here was about 10 metres wide and for the first few metres I was very slow and cautious, while the last three metres I covered with huge strides in a nervous sprint. Once I was across I realized I was probably over cautious and that the foxes who had gone before me were much more experienced. This was the second, and hopefully last, hurdle between me and Máze which was now only 70 kilometres away. It was only 1700. The sun was still quite high and despite the rigours of the canyon I still had some energy left. I skied for about another 5 kilometres until I got to the west tip of Raisjävri lake. I skied across the firm ice of the lake here to avoid crossing the Raiseatnu river which flowed out of the lake near here. Just across the other side, on the north shoreline was a good camp spot, so I dug a hole in the snow and put my tent up in it. From the camp I could see a clear route through some remaining woods in Reisadalen valley, to the bare mountainside to the north which I could take tomorrow. With me in my sleeping bag in the tent, I cooked dinner with the fly open. It was still just above zero with a breeze and it did not feel like winter at all. I kept my damp clothes on in the hope they would dry off and not cause too much condensation in the bag or tent with its open flysheet. Once the domestic chores were done I started to write and reflect on the day. If hell ever did freeze over, I suspect it would be something like Njallaavzi canyon.

Day 103. Skiing out of the woods of Reisadalen valley and on to the frozen Cieknaljohka stream to make my way into the mountains again

It had been a warm night, with the temperature hovering around zero. By the time I had eaten breakfast, packed down the tent it was already 0800. I should have been leaving much earlier to catch the best of the frozen snow and firmer conditions before they thawed. I was still off the maps I had, so just had to go by sight for about 5 kilometres. I could see the bare, white mountains to the north in the middle distance which were on the edge of my next map and where I wanted to be, so I just pointed towards them. Generally my skis stayed above the surface and I rarely broke through as I weaved across the frozen marshes and through the birch woods. I got to the base of the mountains just where the vast ice meander of the frozen Cieknaljohka stream oozed down the valley beneath the white slopes. The stream seemed to be flowing underneath the ice and then seeping on to the surface where its route was blocked. Once on the surface it freezes. Many streams do this, with the result that the whole stream bed is a mass of thick ice. After climbing over a few reindeer fences I started up the snowy slopes of Albbasoaivi. It was a relief to be on firm snow at last. I would endeavour to keep above the tree line today at all costs. The climb was nice and I had great views down to the wooded lowlands which surrounded Raisjävri lake. After an

Day 103. Skiing up the slopes of Albbasoaivi with the wide Reisadalen valley below me with its mosaic of frozen lakes and marshes laid out

easy hour of climbing, in glorious hot sunny weather, I came upon a scooter track going north in the direction of the derelict Bidjovagge mine. In Finnmark there are many official snow scooter tracks which radiate over Finnmarksvidda plateau in a web, and connect many of the remote towns to each other. There are virtually no restrictions about using these tracks, and people may use scooters on these official tracks in preference to a car on a road for many journeys. One might encounter a scooter an hour along them, and they were marked by branches stuck into the snow. My problem was these tracks were not marked on the topographic maps I had, and I didn't have a clue where they went when I came across one. There was so little traffic on them you could not rely on asking anybody. There were maps available, published by the council, and most people using these tracks had local knowledge. I just had to make a reasoned guess as I had neither.

When I came across this one, I optimistically and naïvely hoped it was going to Máze and started to follow it north. After an hour it reached the derelict mine at Bidjovagge which is where I wanted to be. It continued northwards from the mine but then unfortunately the scooter tracks veered north-west up the prominent ridgeline, while I wanted to go north east. With reluctance, I had to leave the tracks on which there were no scooters for the two hours I followed them. I now decided to head north east across the open mountainside into the Njivlojohka river valley. On my map this valley had little forest, but in reality it was covered in patches of birch forest and in between there was willow scrub. I had a great ski down the very shallow side of this valley for a few kilometres, making for the southern end of a prominent mountain called Sieiddas and made great time. When I reached the valley, my worst fears came true. The sun had softened the already loose snow in the birch forest and scrub willow thickets. These woods and thickets were full of ptarmigan, which having survived the winter, were just a few weeks away from the spring buds. There were also elg droppings everywhere as they passed backwards and forwards through the area, nibbling small branches and even bark. The trouble is, on a warm day like this I did not want to be in elg country, I wanted to be higher up in reindeer country! I forced myself through the willow scrub and the birch trees which covered the southern ridge of Sieiddas and skied into an area in the valley called Njivlovuopmi. It was probably once a lake which was then filled in by a silt delta, and now was a flood plain through which the river meandered. Crossing Njivlovuopmi was very hard. The soft sugar snow seemed to have no bottom. The tangle of willow scrub constantly snagged my skis. I fell a few times because branches under me collapsed and it was a laborious job to stand up again. Sometimes I had to remove my rucksack and use it as a firm base on which to push from, otherwise my arms disappeared up to my armpits. It took nearly two hard hours to go 2 kilometres. In the end I reached the Njivlojohka river, and decided the slim chance of falling through the ice on it was a better alternative to fighting through the willow scrub.

I was aiming for two huts marked on my map by the small tarn at the north end of the three Cuovzajavrrit tarns. I would make for them, and if they were open, I would sleep in them. It was still early in the day but because the snow on top of the vegetation was so soft, and collapsed into the bushes when I skied over them, it was really a waste of effort to continue. I got to the northernmost lake, where the huts should have been, but they had vanished. After double checking coordinates, I put the tent up. As soon as I had finished the tent the weather turned and a sleet shower came in. This would just melt things further and I was getting quite worried. The temperature then dropped and the sleet froze on to the tent as blizzards started to sweep in and the snow piled up. It seemed, by accident, I had decided to put the tent up at the right time as while I cooked in the warmth of my sleeping bag winter returned with a fury. This was what I needed and I hoped it would get worse.

Day 104. My camp at Njivlovuopmi at 0300 in the morning after I managed to get up for a very early start following a stormy night

When I woke it was still dark; but not pitch dark. I felt dawn was approaching. I felt refreshed and decided to get up without looking at my watch. I thought that if I looked at it I would have been provided with an excuse

Day 104. Skiing up the frozen Sallejohka stream towards Carajävri lake just after the early sunrise, but before the blizzard suddenly arrived

to lie a few more hours until a more conventional time. By extrapolating back later it must have been 0300. The sleet shower of yesterday evening had frozen on to the tent as the temperatures dropped to well below freezing. Then as the sleet turned to snow it covered the tent. I had trouble getting all the snow off the tent. Eventually packed, I set off at 0445. It had already been light for at least 45 minutes. It was overcast and there was always the threat of further showers. I set off into the forest and scrub in the direction of Carajävri lake. I quickly realized it was not the best route. I looked at my map again and saw that it would not be much longer if I followed the Coalbrejohka river for an hour until the side stream, called Sallejohka, joined it. I could follow this side stream to the open hillside. I thrashed a route through the scrub to Coalbrejohka river and started to follow its smooth meanders of snow-covered ice. It was much easier and quicker. When I reached Sallejohka I left the river and skied up its frozen alluvial channels. Just to the south, on a mound, were a collection of five small Sami huts with their characteristic pyramid roofs. They were obviously used for reindeer herding, as there were fences nearby. The climb up the hillside on the south side of the Sallejohka stream was a relief. I was no longer imprisoned in the tangle of willow scrub and deep snow of the birch woods. With confident strides I could power up the 7 kilometres to Carajävri lake. The only problem seemed to be the worsening state of the weather. It went from overcast to dark and atmospheric and then the first flakes of a blizzard hit. It was a short, sharp blizzard which lasted for about an hour. I made it to Carajävri lake in the midst of it with poor visibility. Almost as quickly as the blizzard came, it then dissipated, and by the far side of the lake it was absolutely stunning weather with not a cloud in the sky. There were still some large residual snowflakes falling, but they were gently floating down out of a light blue sunny sky!

Day 104. After the blizzard on Carajävri lake the weather became so calm I could melt snow on the gas stove without using a windshield

Day 104. At the Jeardnejohka stream valley I came across a Sami tent which was very comfortable inside and covered in warm reindeer skins

At the far side of the lake I came across two lines of branches marking two scooter tracks and a junction. I knew they were here from seeing them on a map at the husky farm in Innset. The track I wanted climbed up from the east side of the lake to a saddle, before it veered north. By the time I got to the top of the saddle I was parched, which despite drinking too little and seldom carrying water, hardly ever happened to me now. I could easily have continued but the weather was now absolutely perfect. Just an hour after the blizzard had blown away, I sat in the blazing sun and melted some snow on my gas stove without having to use a windshield. It was colder now at perhaps minus 10, and this was also perfect. From the saddle there was a 9 kilometre descent down the Doaresjohka stream valley. The conditions were near perfect; a firm base with a dusting of new snow on top. I just had to watch for occasional sastrugi formations. Within two hours I had made it all the way to the edge of the map and a bit beyond, where the Doaresjohka meets the Jeardnejohka stream. At the junction here was a Sami tent. There were fresh scooter tracks around it, but nobody was in, so I had a peek. It was extremely tidy inside. Twigs and straw lined the snow floor and were then completely covered in reindeer skins. A paraffin stove, hearth and flue made up the centrepiece. Around the perimeter were four camp beds. It looked very comfortable, and the dark green walls of the tent were absorbing the sun's heat. I followed their fresh scooter tracks, assuming they would go to Máze. After a short distance branches appeared beside the scooter trail. This was great; perhaps it was an official track to Máze. The tracks went over some small ridges and crossed some small ravines, but I was unworried as they continued to head east towards Máze. Then the tracks seemed to veer south east on to Soagnojavri lake where they veered south. I looked at my map and now feared they might be going to Kautokeino. My heart sank and I started to worry. If they went to Kautokeino I would soon have a major headache, as I would have to leave them and head across country through potentially difficult terrain for 20 kilometres to reach Máze. Just as the reality was sinking in two scooters appeared from behind a ridge and came towards me. I didn't need to flag them down as they stopped anyway, amazed to see a skier. They were like modern car drivers, stopping to admire a vintage classic or even a horse and cart. They had just the news I wanted to hear. Just round the ridge the scooter track separated, with one branch going to Máze. They had just come from Máze and checked their odometers which read 25.3 kilometres. They were two very chatty Sami who ran tours in the wilderness for clients, and were just en route to stock up their tent for a group who would arrive shortly. I didn't tell them I had just had a nosy round it an hour ago. I got them to show me where the scooter track went on my map. It was an obvious route and I felt reassured. It was just 1600 so I felt confident I would make it to Máze. For good measure they pointed to a lake on my map and said there was an open hut, but probably without wood, I could use which was about half way.

I set off with vigour, fuelled by my fourth 100 gram bar of chocolate of the day. The route did exactly as they said. It turned east behind the ridge and then crossed two smaller lakes to reach the sunny Roggejavri lake. From here there was a short cut up a steep valley to the top of Suonjeroaivi hill. There was a scooter trail junction here with one route going west and the other going east to Máze. It was a rollercoaster of a ski from rounded hilltop to rounded hilltop for some 8 kilometres as I followed the trail east. I suppose snow scooters have to follow routes where the snow lingers longest and the ups and downs are not of the same consequence as to a tired skier with a backpack. But long below lurked the deep snow traps in the forest and willow scrub as a reminder to why I must follow the scooter tracks up here. Eventually the tracks and I came down from the hilltops and into the forest by Havgajavri lake. The hut they told me about was on the east side of this lake in the birch trees but I felt strong enough to continue to Máze.

Day 104. On the final descent to Máze after a 60 kilometre day I was treated to a lovely sunset over the rolling Finnmarksvidda plateau

There was one last climb up and over Stuoroaivi hill. From here there was a wonderful view over the endless Finnmarksvidda plateau. It was mostly very gentle rolling hills which gently sloped down to wide open wooded valleys before rising gently up to the next group of rolling hills. This is the oldest landscape in Europe, some three billion years old. On the other side of the hill was another junction with a signpost for scooter routes, even to Karesuando which was some 150 kilometres away on the Finnish/Swedish border. There was also a sign to Máze, which was just 7 kilometres away, along a snow-covered track through birch woods. Despite the abundance of scooter tracks I had only seen three scooters since coming back into Norway, three long, hard days ago. It was a far cry from Kilpisjärvi in Finland where the air smelt of two-stroke exhaust. These 7 kilometres were exactly what my tired legs wanted. It was easy for the first half and then the second half was a gentle downhill slope. I just had to stand to glide down through the birch woods at 10 kilometres an hour. I was elated and belted out loud verses from various Bob Dylan songs as the trees whizzed past. The sun was setting behind the framework of black branches and twigs of the birch. It was a good end to a great day. I reached the road, crossed it and went to Máze Turistsenter. It was closed but there was a telephone number to ring. Within 10 minutes I was in a cabin. It was around 2100. I just had a lot to drink to quench my thirst and crashed out. I could not be bothered to eat. It had been a long, hard day of nearly 60 kilometres and 16 hours without a meaningful stop! I knew when I went to bed I could look forward to a rest day tomorrow.

When I woke in the morning I realized with great joy that I was just waking up to a lie-in in a warm cabin. I didn't bother looking out at the weather as it had no bearing on the day. Instead, I rolled over with all the contentment of a squirrel in a warm, safe hole filled with acorns. It was a rare luxury. Eventually I got up at 1000. The hut I was in was not a proper cabin, and it was very poorly equipped. There was a one-ring cooker, a small noisy fridge, two beds which looked like they had been nailed together by prisoners using old pallets, a table and two chairs and a wall heater. However, the hut did provide somewhere for me to write, rest my body and dry my clothes. The last section was hard. Each of the three days had been difficult and there was little respite. The struggle across Njallaavzi canyon and then the fight through the birch woods and willow thickets of Njivlovuopmi were probably the most difficult terrain I had encountered on the whole trip. In retrospect, my choice of route here was not the best. It was eye-opening to fight these challenges, but I would not want to do it again. The next time I would not venture blindly across Finnmarksvidda, but would take more care to plan my route and try and avoid these desperate sections by following snow scooter tracks more religiously.

I spent the rest of the morning in my hut, looking at maps and writing. I finished this by early afternoon when the Sami lady who owned and ran the café, the simple cabins and the campsite arrived to open the café. I had already had a small breakfast, but I was still very hungry, so I went over to the café and ordered two lunches. The portions were small and the prices were quite steep. Later in the afternoon I showered, washed my clothes and then had a well deserved siesta. I went back to the café in the evening for dinner. I was getting used to the poor value for money in this part of Norway, and the small portions, so ordered two meals again. There were a couple of Sami customers in the café slowly drinking beer and speaking Sami. I got chatting to them but they insisted on speaking English, rather than Norwegian. Their English was terrible and I quickly got frustrated with it. They both owned reindeer but paid somebody else to look after them. They said reindeer were not that valuable and it took five reindeer to equal the value of one cow. Returning to the hut I planned to get up early and ski the 35 kilometres along scooter tracks to Nedre Mollisjok Fjellstue.

SECTION 15. Reisadalen to Máze
4 days. 115 kilometres. 36 hours. 1580m ascent. 2000m descent.

THE SKI: SECTION 16. MÁZE TO LAKSELV

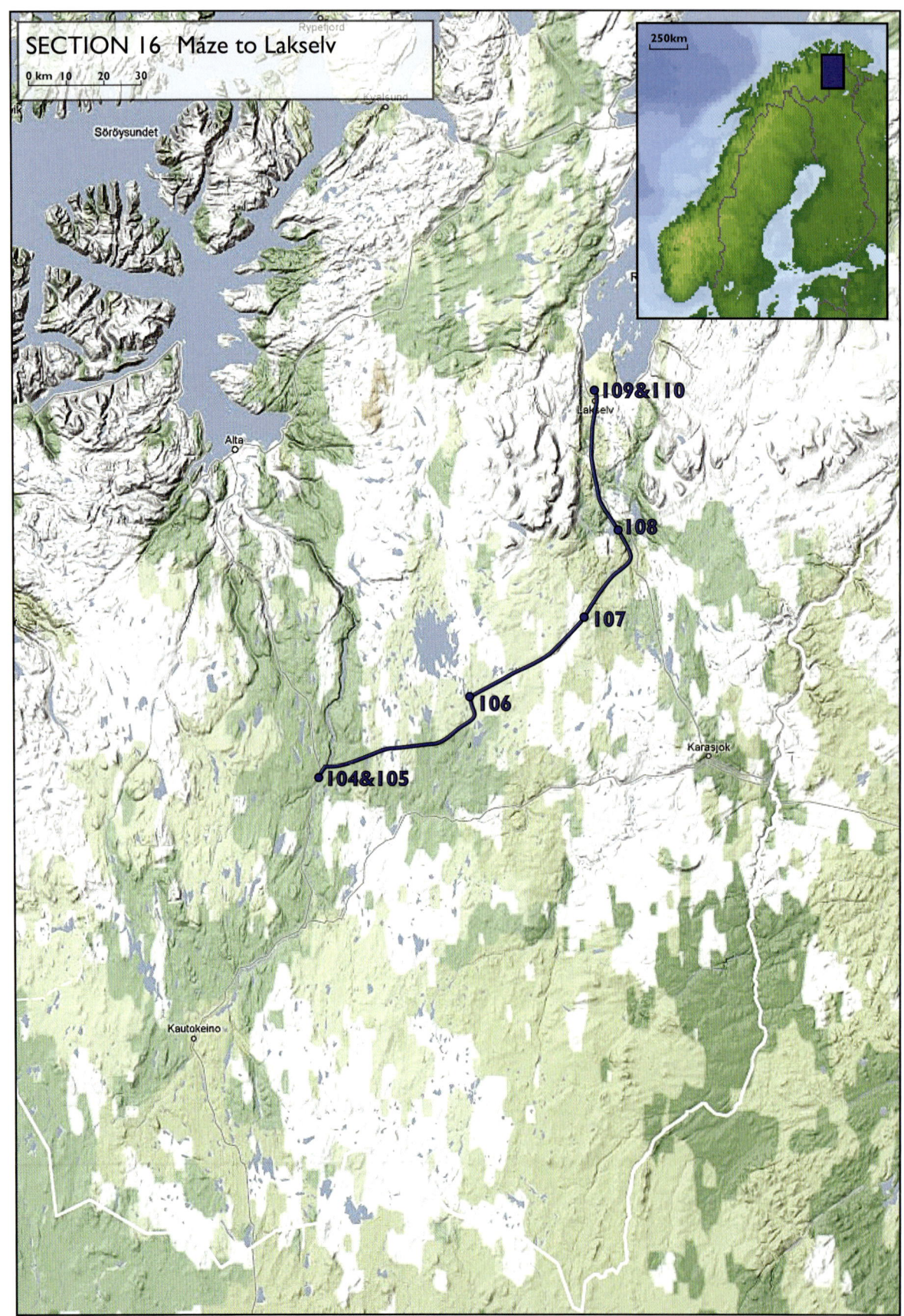

THE SKI: SECTION 16. MÁZE TO LAKSELV

It was a clear, cold, crisp morning with the temperature around minus 5. It was just what I wanted. I left the camping ground with its small huts and headed up to the main road. Here on the west verge was a scooter track which went all the way to the other part of Máze some 3 kilometres to the north. The scooter track was beside the road for most of this, before it descended steeply down a narrow chute to northern Máze. I took my skis off for this descent and walked down to the bigger of the two parts in this extended hamlet. It had 200 houses, a shop, primary school, but no accommodation, while the southern part only had about 100 houses in addition to the cabins and café. The shop was still closed, so I continued down to the bridge over the Alta river. I was told the ice was no longer safe on the river, and I could see this when I walked over the bridge as there were many open areas. On the east side of the bridge there was a gravel track down to some picturesque farms. After 2 kilometres the gravel road ended and a scooter track began. This track climbed steeply up the side of the deep Altadalen valley through four hairpin bends to reach the lip of the vast Finnmarksvidda plateau again. Once on the plateau I put my skis on again and set off. It was great conditions, with a very firm base covered with a sprinkling of new snow. I made very quick time, gliding over these undulating rolling hills as the track rose over gentle ridges where the snow was sometimes sparse and then descended the eastern slopes where the snow had accumulated. Between the ridges were frozen lakes, which were ringed in willow scrub. It was a very gentle and easy landscape to ski through. I soon crossed a ridge which was the watershed between the Alta and Ragesjohka valleys. From here I glided down across further lakes until I entered the birch forest again. A few kilometres through this brought me to the Ragesjohka river. Just on the other side was a homestead called Rageslouppal. This homestead was remote, rustic and run down. Old ramshackle sheds were full of defunct rusting machines. The homestead looked more like it belonged to west coast Scotland or Ireland and not very Norwegian at all. Apparently an older single man lived here, who was supposed to be quite a character. There was a scooter outside so I knocked, but there was no answer.

Day 106. Having climbed out of the birch woods of Altadalen on to Finnmarksvidda plateau I could look into the valley's deep slot

Day 106. Finnmarksvidda plateau is the old basement of the ancient continent of Baltica on which the distant mountains have been thrust

I was a bit confused as to the best route from here to Nedre Mollisjok Fjellstue as the unused scooter track I had been following seemed to peter out in the debris of Rageslouppal. There was a very faint unmarked track heading east into the birch woods and I hoped it would guide me through the 8 kilometres of bare hillside, marsh and woods to the Iesjohka river where I knew there were scooter tracks up the river to the lodge. I set off rather apprehensively along the scooter track, wary it would just vanish into difficult terrain of willow scrub and birch woods. True to form it just vanished, and I had to pick a route myself. However, contrary to the nightmare I had earlier in the week with deep loose melting snow, I could now go where I wanted. The snow mass had refrozen again and was now completely firm. In addition, the few centimetres of new snow made for great conditions. Despite the fact I was making my own way in the woods, I was thoroughly enjoying it. I was not quite confident enough in the overall firmness of the snow to taunt it, but I never broke through once, even when going over juniper bushes and willow scrub. With relief I reached the Iesjohka river just to the south of a wider stretch called Gorzelattu, which was almost a thin lake. There were scooter tracks here and they seemed well used, as it was an official track. The tracks headed up to the west of the river, rolling through the forest for a while. There were large patches with very little snow as this winter had been very windy in Finnmark and much of the loose snow had blown on to the lee slopes, which this winter were the north slopes. Where the track reached the Iesjohka river again it crossed the ice to reach Nedre Mollisjok Fjellstue and the general hamlet around it. There was no road to this hamlet and in winter time the official snow scooter track was the main artery.

Day 106. Nedre Mollisjok Fjellstue is in a Sami hamlet where reindeer play a crucial role as shown by the raw meet drying in the cold wind

There are two lodges; this private one and a self-service cabin called Mollesjohka Fjellstue, some 4 kilometres to the north, administered by the Den Norske Turistforening. A few guests said this was the better of the two, but initially, I was sceptical. This scepticism didn't last long. I got a reasonable room, there was a great shower, the dinning/sitting room was comfortable and sociable, and the food was excellent. The whole place had a very nice, happy, relaxed, atmosphere, which emanated from the owners, Per and his wife, Randi, who were both Sami and had grown up here. Most of the guests were doing the classic five-day ski trip from Alta to Karasjok. I was going perpendicular to this route. There were 20 other guests at the lodge and half of them were a group of lively ladies, many of whom had skied in Spitsbergen. Due to them, the delicious evening meal of reindeer was a very social and happy affair. In the evening, the host, Per, and a local guest told me about an open cabin at Stiippanavzi, halfway to Skoganvarre, which was priceless advice. It was owned and run by the military.

Breakfast was a very social affair with the group of 10 lively ladies and the three other groups all telling stories and jokes, yet being very polite and considerate. Outside, the weather was trying to put a damper on things. It was snowing heavily and blowing a force 6. It was a blizzard really. At 0930 Per appeared in his embroidered reindeer hide trousers and fur hat. He looked the Sami he was. He was going to Ravnastua lodge with some supplies and would also make a trail for the 10 lively ladies to follow until they intersected the marked official scooter trail, which they could then follow. They all set off around 1000. I was a bit more undecided as my route was across open moorland with no shelter and very few features to navigate with. If the weather turned really nasty, normally I would dig a snow hole and wait in it until it improved, but here on

Day 107. Per, who ran and owned the superb Nedre Mollisjok Fjellstue is a Sami, and is dressed here in his warm reindeer skin trousers

Finnmarksvidda one did not always have the luxury of digging, as there could be few snow drifts to find if the visibility disappeared. Instead I might have to put up my tent and this would be difficult in a gale and probably impossible in a storm. I did not want to put myself in the situation where I had to find out, so procrastinated a while to see what the weather would do. Eventually at 1100 I decided to go. It was as late as I could comfortably leave if I wanted to get to Stiippanavzi cabin at a safe hour.

The weather was still windy when I left, but the forecast intimated it would improve throughout the day. Initially I followed the tracks of the 10 lively ladies, who in turn were following Per's snow scooter tracks. The snow was compact but must have been less than a metre deep as willow scrub was poking through. After 6 kilometres of this undulating route across moorland and frozen tarns with frequent blizzards passing through, I eventually reached the official scooter track to Ravnastua lodge. I was just going to cross it and continue north east when I met Per returning on his scooter. He said there was an emergency shelter just down this official scooter track. It was called Annesjohka ødestue and was apparently very rustic. I thought I would head for it

Day 107. There was a very rustic cabin at Annesjohka ødestue which was cold and dirty and just suitable for emergencies

and put my windproof salopettes on. It was a fast ski to this shelter as the wind was now partially behind me. I crossed the three lakes as directed and the shelter was in a bay on the third lake. It was old, simple and somewhat dirty inside with grime and coffee residue. There was just one filthy mattress on one of the four sleeping platforms. It was cold inside but I put more clothes on then ate some chocolate. While I was there a couple of scooters turned up. I chatted with a large Norwegian who was driving barrels of fuel to a Sami village where reindeer herders had cabins. The other scooter was driven by a wizened old Sami of at least 75 years, who had lost his teeth a while ago and looked like he was gurning all the time. He spoke no Norwegian. The younger man said the weather would get worse in the afternoon. I believed him and started to hurry with a sense of urgency which the forthcoming doom prompted. It was still 20 kilometres to Stiippanavzi cabin. The wind was still strong outside, indeed I think it had increased to a force 6 and it was coming out of the north which was directly against me. After a kilometre I thought I should turn back. It was bitterly cold and my extremities and face were getting chilled. I put more gloves on and pulled my hood right down and continued. The thought of being weather bound in that shelter, where I could not even put my elbows on the table without them getting sticky and blackened with layers of grime and coffee, was too much. A night in a snow hole or tent would have been preferable to that filthy floor or rotting mattress, so I persevered.

The journey was quite a struggle. The only thing that changed was the amount of bad weather. The wind continued as a northerly force 6 for the whole distance and I had to fight into it. There were frequent snow showers, each one lasting for about half an hour. The flat landscape, strewn with boulders and large glacial erratics, disappeared into the snow during these showers. I frequently had to use my GPS to find out where I was, as there were no features to orientate myself with. During the snow showers I had to remove my glasses

Day 107. The featureless expanse of the Finnmarksvidda plateau offered little navigational clues or shelter when the weather was poor

as they got so covered in snow I could see nothing. Then I really had to pull my hood down and look to the ground to avoid my face getting plastered in snow. Between the showers, however, the sun tried to return. In the sunny periods the light showed up every detail and contrast in the landscape and snow where even the most minute ridges and imperfections were highlighted. It was an exceptionally crisp and clear Arctic light. It took a good five hours before I was just a few kilometres from Stiippanavzi cabin. I could see the dark canyon of Stiippanavzi to the west which was filled with birch trees. The stream in the canyon drained a large area and had cut deeply into the flat undulating ancient basement of Finnmarksvidda plateau. Still fresh from the wintery hell of crossing the similar Njallaavzi just six days previously I was very worried that the cabin

Day 107. The Arctic light was sometimes so brilliant that every subtle feature of the snow and landscape would be illuminated

Day 107. Stiippanavzi cabin was owned by the military but open to all and was sited in a crucial location for me on the edge of a canyon

might be in it. My worries soon dissipated when I saw it perched on a knoll on a broad shelf just down from the lip of the plateau. It was a nice ski down to the shelf and across the firm snow in the birch woods to the cabin. I was nicely surprised at how good condition it was in. Inside it was comfortable with four beds and a wood stove. There was the usual table covered in coffee slops, ashtrays and a collection of empty vodka bottles which I was becoming used to since arriving in Finnmark province, but at least the sleeping area was clean. The problem in Finnmark was that most of the rustic simple cabins owned by various organizations had either legal or illegal snow scooter access and people sometimes used them as a drinking den which took the charm off them. Initially I did not see any wood and then found a whole sack of it. Finding the wood was enough for me to forgive the coffee-spilling scooter drivers who must have brought it here. Within an hour I had the cabin quite cosy. I did not get to bed until midnight and even then there was a glow in the northern sky where the sun was resting just below the horizon before it rose in a few hours time.

I slept well in the cabin and woke with the sun streaming through the large windows at 0630. I got up soon after and put on the dehydrated chicken curry for breakfast. The fire still had some embers so I put on a couple more logs and within five minutes it was roaring. There was no great hurry today, which was just as well, because by the time I had finished writing, had breakfast, packed my stuff and tidied the cabin, it was already mid morning. It was a short ascent back up to the plateau from the cabin. The weather was fair but there was a chilly north wind. After crossing a small lake I climbed slightly and then started a glorious easy descent to another lake. The new snow lay on the firm base to give great conditions. My skis quietly slid over the snow with all the stealth of cream flowing over silk. When I got to the second lake the sun was warm and the wind had disappeared. I was now in the birch forest

Day 108. Inside Stiippanavzi cabin there was some grime but with enough wood to fire up the stove it soon became very warm and cosy

again where it was bright, calm, warm and reassuring after yesterday's hard wind. I followed the stream bed down through the birch trees and across some marshes across the firm snow. The stream was open in a few places and it was easy to get to the clear water for an invigorating drink. A little further on this small stream met the river emerging out of the Stiippanavzi canyon called Stiippanjohka river. Per had warned me this river was dangerous and as I looked across to the other side of it I could see a few holes in the ice. To go through the ice here could be fatal. If the current was strong enough it would sweep me down under the ice with no hope of getting back to the hole I fell through. However, I doubted the river would be more that knee deep at this time of year. None the less I was very cautious and went down the river until the ice was solid for a good

Day 108. I had a fantastic run down the north edge of Finnmarksvidda plateau into the birch woods to the south of Savnjajavri lake

few hundred metres above and below me. I loosened off my rucksack and even the ski bindings before gingerly skiing over. It was a long 20 metres but I reached the other side without any incident.

Once on the west side of the Stiippanjohka river I followed it down along a reindeer fence and soon came across some old scooter tracks. These went all the way through the quiet sunny friendly forest to reach Savnjajavri lake. The lake was about 3 kilometres long. There was a cold wind blowing down the lake into me and I had to wrap up again. I was off the map I bought from Per at Nedre Mollisjok Fjellstue. He told me just to go to the north end of the lake where I would meet an official scooter track which would take me to Skoganvarre. When I reached the northern end I was

Day 108. Looking across the birch woods on the edge of the plateau to Savnjajavri lake in the middle of the photo 8 km to the north

surprised to see a hamlet appear. I assumed the hamlet was called Savnjajavri. It was a Sami community. There seemed to be about 15 houses and cabins. Quite a few had smoke coming out of their chimneys. Most were in an unkempt state with collapsing sheds and a rickety lean-to or three on the house. Surrounding the houses were large scooter sleds, old machinery, old upturned boats, piles of raw fence posts and other rural detritus, like rolls of rusting wire. Half the cabins looked like they were occupied with busy reindeer herding Sami while the other half looked quite desperate with squalid neglected houses. It reminded me of a North American Native Reservation and it looked like the occupiers of these houses spent most of the winter dulling their boredom with vodka. While I dithered about which way to go a heavy snow shower swept over the area. I sheltered on the balcony of an unoccupied house while it endured. After 15 minutes it had passed and I skied over to another part of the hamlet where I could see a house which was occupied. They saw me coming and shuffled out to meet me. I was a little shocked at the family who met me. They were heavily overweight and had the bloated jowls of heavy drinkers. I got some garbled advice for the best way to Skoganvarre, which was 10 kilometres away. The best way apparently was just to follow the scooter track which followed the gravel road which was only open in the summer. This was the only transport facility to this very isolated hamlet. As I skied up the track I reflected on the hamlet and felt a bit disturbed by what I'd found at Savnjajavri. I felt I had stumbled upon an indigenous community which was in cultural meltdown.

The road was for the most part entirely covered in snow and I could make good time along it. Occasionally, however, there were bare patches and I had to walk for a few tens of metres. The road climbed slightly for the best part of 4 kilometres through birch woods. There was a great view to the west towards Beiggavakgaisa, which was the highest in a steep group of mountains rising up from the flat plateau. They looked like sedimentary mountains and I was surprised to see them here. They must have been thrust up on to the ancient basement of Baltica in the Caledonian orogeny 420 million years ago from their original location. This huge block of sediments, called the Gaissa nappe, were the first layer of displaced rock to be thrust on to Baltica's basement as the Lower Allochthon. To the east of these high mountains the plateau descended into a

Day 108. After the sad hamlet of Savnjajavri I went east of the Gaissa nappe sedimentary mountains which had been thrust on the basement

gnarly terrain of small deep valleys and craggy knolls, which is where I was now heading. From this high point in the road I now had a long descent down to the gnarly valley floor. I could see from here they were covered in the luxuriant greenness of pine trees. I had just seen birch trees since Dividalen about two weeks ago so was looking forward to ski down to them. I sped off down the road which was quite steep in places. It didn't

Day 108. I skied along the gravel track from Savnjajavri hamlet down to the maternal pine forests in the Lakselv valley around Skoganvarre

take long to reach the maternal comfort of the pines. I was now in the main Lakselvdalen valley and it was an easy ski along the final stretch of this gravel road until I reached a bridge over the Lakselv river to the main road. The Skoganvarre campsite was a half kilometre down the road.

Skoganvarre campsite was a depressing place. It was a collection of some 50 static caravans and numerous small cabins. The owner was a heavy drinker but seemed to perform his essential duties and was even helpful. His wife, however, was a shaky drunk and walked as if her legs were made of wood, like a puppet. They were both Finnish. Most of their clients were also Finnish who came here to ice fish in the winter and river fish in the summer. I am sure the fishing was just a justification for the clients of the campsite whose main aim seemed to be to totter quietly around the café and their cabins and drink vodka to the limit of physical control. By mid evening everybody was stumbling about in gentle and polite stupor. This campsite seemed the heartland of the 'Vodka Belt'. There was a Norwegian man who came to pick up the now permanent cook. She was employed to churn out fast food for the undiscerning palate, because the owners' wife was no longer capable. He had a good knowledge of the route I wanted to take from Lakselv to Ifjord. He said it would be winter up on that remote part of Finnmarksvidda plateau for another month at least. He said there was a very rustic 'gamme' or traditional Sami turf shelter in Luostejohka where I could spend the first night but that I must camp for the next two. Ideally I should have gone straight from Skoganvarre to Luostejohka but I needed to go to Lakselv to restock my food, buy maps, and repair some equipment. I had a rule not to use any transport on my tour, otherwise I could have nipped down to Lakselv on the bus and bought what I needed, returning in the evening. Instead, I had to ski to Lakselv.

It was a slow start and I eventually got going around 1030. The weather was not what I expected, and it was snowing quite heavily. I thought I would take the scooter track down to Lakselv. It was longer but probably more scenic than the 26 kilometre road. The scooter track crossed over to a series of lakes, the most southerly of which was Gaggajavri. It then followed these lakes northwards and went down Brennelvdalen valley to Lakselv town, but as is so often the case, I was missing the topographic map for this area. I walked down the road to the start of the scooter track where there was a signpost which said 'Lakselv 38 km'. It was now only 22 kilometres along the road, so I opted for the shorter, but more tedious way. The road was not very busy, with a car every 10 minutes, however, I had to walk rather than ski which was slower. The road followed the famed Lakselv river down through a series of small lakes. The river was open in many places as it flowed down from one small lake to the next. This river was renowned for its salmon, Indeed Lakselv means Salmon River. Of the largest 10 salmon caught here last year the smallest was 17 kg and the largest 24 kg. The weather improved considerably as I approached Porsangmoen and I got a great view across the large valley to the high mountains I noticed yesterday on the west side. I also saw how gnarly the landscape had now become. Just before Porsangmoen another snow shower arrived. Porsangmoen was not a village but a military camp. Fences surrounded the place. It was home to the elite Finnmark Jegerkompaniet, and the Royal Marines also trained here for winter exercises. The snow showers quickly increased to a blizzard. It grew in intensity quite quickly so I had to find shelter among some trees and put on windproof clothes and gloves. I also had to lower the skis on my rucksack as they were catching the wind. It was just in time really as the blizzard soon increased in intensity with gale force winds. Two different military personnel took pity on me as I walked down the road and offered me a lift in their jeeps. I had to decline.

For the next three hours and all the way to Lakselv the blizzard varied in intensity, but by and large it was at least a gale. I was walking directly into it and had to look down the whole time. My front half was plastered in snow and my eyebrows were covered in ice. The birch trees at the side of the road were hissing and twisting in the gale and I was also being buffeted about. Even though I was walking it was an effort to make headway wading through this river of a snowstorm. Up on Finnmarksvidda this would have been a full storm. If I had

Day 109. The walk down the road from Skoganvarre to Lakselv was enlivened by a strong blizzard which left me plastered in snow and ice

got caught out in this visibility and conditions it would have been so bad I would have had to have stopped and dug a snow-hole to escape its wrath, as a tent would have been too difficult to set up. It seemed winter had returned with an impressive vengeance. A few more kind people stopped to offer a lift which I also had to decline. I was glad I did not opt to take the longer scooter tracks as these would be very exposed across the lakes. As I approached Lakselv there was a lull in the snow but not the wind. The visibility improved and I could see beyond the verge and down to the valley. It was a large deep valley with the now mature Lakselv river meandering through lazy bends on its floor. What really struck me were the huge terraces of sand, gravel and small boulders on each side of the valley. These were some 100 metres high and many hundreds of metres wide in some places. The river had worn through these deposits. Occasionally a meander would erode the base of the terrace and a whole section of birch-clad terrace would landslide down into the river and slowly be carried downstream to extend the alluvial delta at the fjord. I was tired when I reached Lakselv. Road walking is much harder, and with this strong headwind I felt quite sapped. It seemed quite a suburban town with a small centre and many houses in larger gardens. However, through all this ripped the blizzard, which would have clouded anyone's opinions. There was just one place to stay, a cold hotel called the Porsanger Vertshus. Like most places I have encountered so far in Finnmark it was poor value for money. But outside the blizzard had returned and the gale was blowing at full thrust so I took a room. I had a meal at the hotel and then hand-washed all my clothes. There was a television in the bar restaurant and on the news the main topic was that the north of Norway, especially the coast, was being battered by a 'Storm', which had closed many roads. It was still rattling the windows when I fell asleep.

Remnants of yesterday's weather still lingered when I got up, the wind was still strong but not quite the gale of yesterday. I had planned to have a day off today to buy food, maps, gas, repair some equipment and a do a few other errands. The first of these was a haircut. I had not had one since Christmas and I did not look pretty. There was a hairdresser beside the hotel and she gave me a number one. Even my eyebrows got a hard trim to stop so much ice accumulating on them. Then I managed to buy all the maps I needed to Ifjord, but none for the final section to Kinnarodden itself. Finally I had to buy some food. It was the usual staples of chocolate, milk powder, nuts, drinking chocolate and the expensive but very easy and tasty 'Real Turmat' dehydrated meals. I went for a pizza in the afternoon. I ordered a large one. When it arrived I was astonished. Having got used to poor value for money in Finnmark, I was expecting something which would just taunt my appetite. What I got must have been a good 60 centimetres across and heaped with ingredients. Despite my greediest effort I only managed three quarters of it. I borrowed an old laptop in the evening to check more of the route to Ifjord and beyond. There was little information about this wilder part of Finnmarksvidda. I had the luxury of good 1:50,000 topographic maps so I would just have to make up the route as I went. All I knew was that tomorrow I would initially have to walk 11 kilometres along the road to the farm at Caskilbekk. Here there was a gravel track I could ski up passing through the hazards of the steep birch forest until I gained the open expanse of Finnmarksvidda plateau again and eventually the very simple rustic cabin at Luostejohka. The weather forecast did not make good reading though. It seemed north Norway was going to receive a few low pressures over the next week.

SECTION 16. Máze to Lakselv
5 days. 124 kilometres. 31 hours. 1330m ascent. 1600m descent.

THE SKI: SECTION 17. LAKSELV TO IFJORD

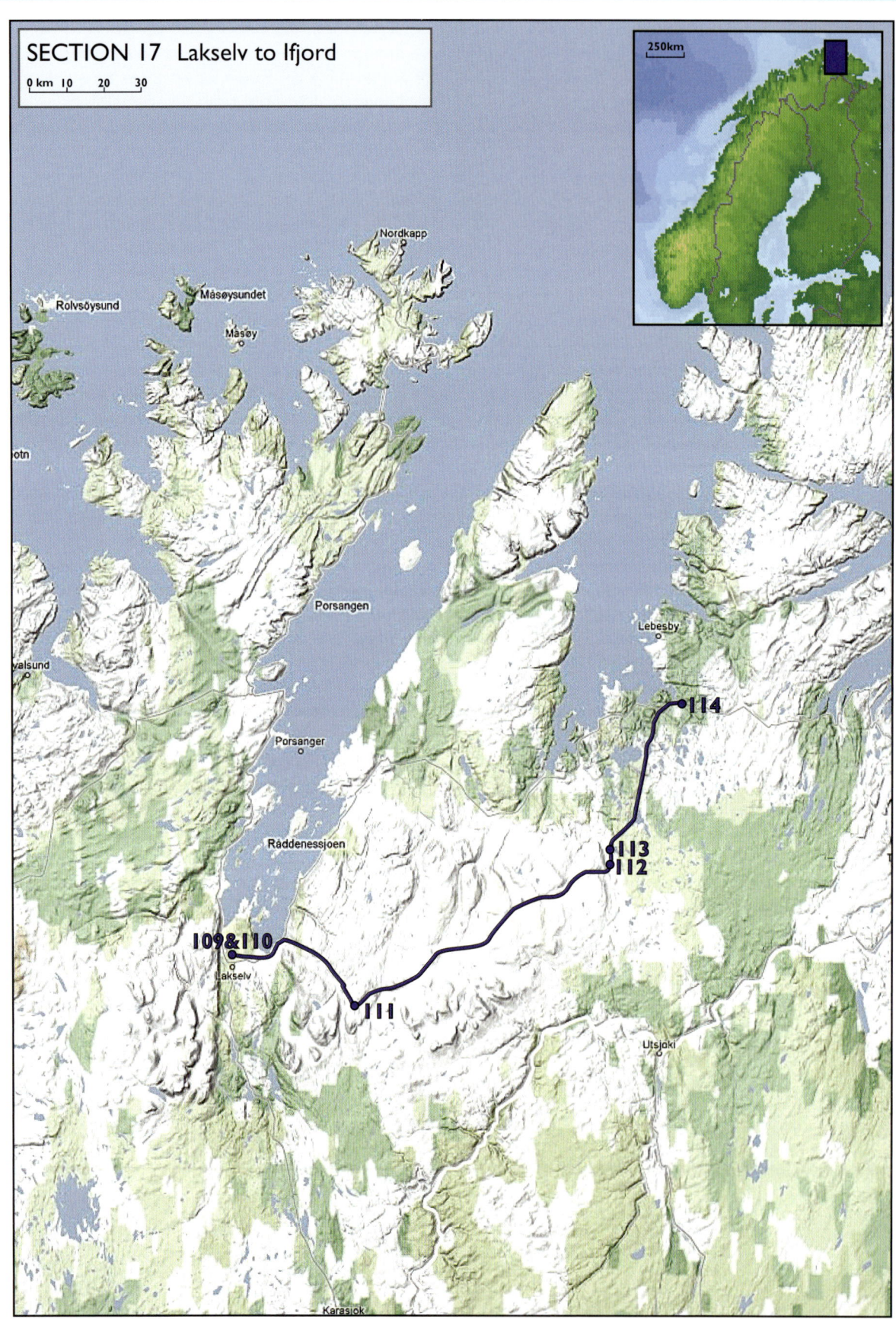

THE SKI: SECTION 17. LAKSELV TO IFJORD

I left Lakselv very early in the morning to walk along the road for 11 kilometres towards Ifjord. I went from the outlying houses of Lakselv straight into the country quite quickly. Once in the country things became more ramshackle again. Every household or farm was surrounded by old machinery, fencing materials, trailers and numerous sheds in various states of disrepair. This rural turmoil was not very Norwegian at all, but seemed quite common in Finnmark. As I went along beside this saltwater fjord I saw it was frozen. It surprised me that the ice around the edge was quite intact, despite the tidal movements, as I expected it to be in fragments. It was quite a long 11 kilometres, much of it being along the rocky hinterland, just inland from the shore. My feet, especially my right foot, were getting a pounding under the ball of my toes. I thought it was the shoe falling apart. I took it off and inspected it and was surprised to see it was in good condition. I had noticed this discomfort before when walking, but after today's 11 kilometres it was quite painful and made me limp. From

Day 111. The 11-kilometre walk along the rocky hinterland beside the inner bays of the vast Porsangerfjord, was along the quiet coastal road

experience I knew that when my skis went on the pain would diminish to a tolerable level. After nearly three hours pounding the hard tarmac I got to the farms at Caskilbekk where the Caskiljohka stream descended from the plateau into a steep gorge. Beside this gorge was a gravel track which went up the shoulder of the gorge, climbing through the birch woods for 5 kilometres. There was a very sparse covering of snow on this gravel track and it was easier to walk up most of it rather than try and ski up until it reached the tree line on the edge of the plateau where there was a cluster of 10 cabins by a reindeer corral. The cabins were owned by Sami and were used for reindeer herding rather than as leisure cabins. Beside most of these pragmatic looking cabins was an industrial container. I stopped near one of these for lunch and the owner came out from his cabin, unlocked the

Day 111. As I climbed up the track on the shoulder beside Caskiljohka stream I could look down the virtually bare slopes to Porsangerfjord

container and opened it so I could get a good view of the cluttered interior. Inside were various tools, reindeer medicine and fencing materials. He took a chain saw out. I tried to initiate a conversation but he was not reciprocating. He was not unfriendly, just indifferent and busy. After 10 minutes he disappeared on his snow scooter, heading off up the hillside into the birch woods.

After the collection of Sami cabins and the reindeer corral there was enough snow to ski again. So I waxed my skis and set off. It was a very gentle climb for about 7 kilometres to a watershed. The higher I ascended the more winter like it became again. Eventually at 300 metres altitude it was pretty much full cover with snow again. Here I could look back and for the first time since the very start at Lindesnes all those kilometres ago, I could look down on to Porsangerfjord, and there in the middle of the fjord it was ice-free and I could see the blue grey sea again. At the watershed around 500 metres I left Caskiljohka and entered Luostejohka which was a very wide and shallow bowl full of deep

Day 111. Once I had climbed above the Sami cabins in Caskiljohka the snow returned and I could see the open sea in Porsangerfjord

Day 111. After I reached the saddle, the wide open Luostejohka valley lay before me on the snow-covered Finnmarksvidda plateau

snow on the Finnmarksvidda plateau. There were two herds of reindeer in Luostejohka valley, both with about 50 beasts in each herd. When they saw me they ran off. Perhaps they associate humans with scooters now and I was a strange thing that could have been a predator moving quite slowly. For the final 6 kilometres down Luostejohka I had a wonderful ski. The wind was behind me and it was marginally downhill. I still had to ski but I was getting long glides with each stride on the firm snow. The weather in the valley was overcast with a bit of sun on some of the surrounding hills. As I skied along the open valley floor I could soon make out the dark spot which was the cabin. It approached fast.

The cabin was private. It was owned by three couples who bought it for nearly nothing a few years ago. One half of one of the couples cut my hair yesterday. However, the cabin was open and it seemed everybody used it and knew about it. Perhaps they were obliged to keep it open. The hairdresser and her husband were visiting next weekend. It seemed he had already prepared the place by bringing up a few scooter sledges of wood. Inside the cabin it was a bit of a mess. Half eaten meals lay mouldy on the table, while the floor was covered in twigs and bark. Overflowing tins used as ashtrays were on the table, surrounded by empty vodka bottles. It seemed scooter folk had been using the place as a party venue. The nice hairdresser was about to get a shock. I got the stove going and burnt huge amounts of plastic and food remains. I then covered the table in newspapers which were only four days old. Once this was done and the place started to warm up, I cleaned two pans and started to melt snow on the wood stove. The cabin slowly started to get cosier, but there was a limit beyond which it would not go due to the grime. I then had a meal and looked at my maps again. From here to Ifjord was about 100 kilometres of winter wilderness. It was quite exposed and if bad weather reappeared there was virtually nowhere to hide. There were a couple of small squares on the map indicating simple cabins. These may or may not exist, and could be locked, so it would be naïvely optimistic to bank on them. However, the first one was about 50 kilometres from here in the direction I wanted to go so I will try and reach it as it might be a more spacious and warmer alternative to camping, as this cabin also was.

Day 111. It was an atmospheric afternoon with the sun breaking through some of the dark clouds to illuminate some hills

Day 111. The cabin at Luostejohka was small and untidy but there was enough wood to warm the single room up and burn some rubbish

Despite the dankness in the cabin I slept well and woke early. I got up soon afterwards and had a double portion of dehydrated chicken curry for breakfast. It was going to be a long day and cereals would not sustain me. It was slightly overcast, quite warm at around zero, and there was a slight south-west wind blowing. I set off at 0700 and thought I would have problems with slippery skis and would have to apply more red wax, but surprisingly they were perfect. It was a 'knall føre' as the Norwegians would say. My skis were gliding well over the top of it.

Day 112. It was a calm morning when I set off across the undulating plateau passing to the north of Vapma mountain to Bissojohka river

It did not take long to get into a good rhythm. I went into an open shallow valley on the north side of Vapma mountain. Indeed, everything as far as the eye could see was smooth and gentle. The sun was out and I was wary about getting my lips more sunburnt. I was for once skiing towards the sun. It was very quiet and remote up here. It was also very isolated. Perhaps a bit smaller than Hardangervidda in southern Norway but far more desolate, and I am sure with equally vicious weather. I crossed the Bissojohka river as high as possible, having been warned to stay up high and avoid the canyon it descended into as it made its way down the edge of the plateau. After Bissojohka river there was a gentle climb between featureless rounded hills to an extensive plain. The map showed this plain was covered in hundreds of small tarns, but I could not see this due to the snow cover. After skiing across this plain for nearly 15 kilometres I came to a large boulder. I stopped here for lunch, huddling in the lee of this single rock, which was obviously a glacial erratic. That is a large boulder which was transported over here in a glacier. The glacier then stopped flowing and melted, depositing the boulder on the surface where it remains. The wind was increasing and must have been a good force 5 now but it was directly behind me. To the south east of the boulder was Rastigaisa, which at 1066 metres was the highest hill on this plateau, and the only feature I could see on the rolling plateau. Even Rastigaisa was quite rounded except for its summit.

Day 112. I stopped for lunch in the lee of a huge boulder on the flat plateau with only the distant mountain of Rastigaisa protruding above

After lunch I continued north east across another wide open and shallow valley with the frozen Stuorrajohka river on its floor. It was difficult to make out where the river was, so gentle were the slopes. The climb up the rounded mountains on the east side of the valley was also very gentle. The wind was starting to increase and it was now a good force 6. Spindrift was flowing over the surface, racing towards a cornice or some other lee where it would come to rest. In this terrain that would be many kilometres. The wind and spindrift was flowing in the same direction I was. I had to ski the uphill sections now but on the gentle declines and flat sections I was virtually being blown along. In one hour I went nearly 8 kilometres until I was just south of the Vuonjaljavri lake. With the increasing wind came a slight worsening of the weather. Behind me and to the north the skies were slowly but surely darkening. The blue sky of the morning had long since disappeared and this worried me. There was nowhere up here to hide from a storm except in a deep snow drift and there were few of them. From the Vuonjaljavri lake I half skied and was half blown up another shallow incline. Reindeer herds fled when they saw me coming. After crossing the watershed of this shallow incline I entered another drainage area, that of the Vazzejohka stream. Some 2 kilometres down this valley the map showed there was a gamme, or traditional Sami turf shelter. There was no

Day 112. Skiing across the featureless Finnmarksvidda plateau north of Rastigaisa was fast with great conditions and a good following wind

Day 112. After lunch I crossed the valley where the Stuorrajohka river flowed and climbed the gentle snow-covered slopes on the east side

sign of it at all so I continued down the south side of this valley to the shed marked on the map. There was no sign of that either. I would have to camp after all, as I had expected. The problem was it was too exposed to camp here. Despite having already done some 50 kilometres I would still have to do another 10 and cross yet another gentle saddle, my fifth of the day. The wind was still directly behind me and would give me a fair bit of assistance.

I set off north east up a line of tarns slowly climbing up to Fasttesjavri lake. There were a few drifts at the start of this valley if I had needed to dig a hole. However, that was not necessary, as within one and a half hours I was on the lake and almost being blown along it. From the map I could see that at the east end of the lake there was a gentle escarpment and the plateau dropped off from about 500 metres down to 250 metres. It should be sheltered down there I thought. When I reached the east end of the lake I got quite a surprise. The lower plateau was indeed down there and it was quite accessible. However, it hardly had any snow on it. It was predominantly a black landscape with some snow patches. I don't think the snow here had melted, I think it never arrived this winter. This would affect my plans to reach Ifjord. There were many small herds of reindeer here taking advantage of the exposed lichen they thrive on. I could see a small birch wood below me and a route of snow down to it. It was quite a steep descent but within half an hour I was down in the trees. Being in the lee of the hill and also being in the birch wood meant I had great protection. The force 6 winds I had experienced all afternoon were probably still raging up there, but here in the forest there was a gentle breeze. I found a quiet place to pitch my tent and levelled off the snow, making a small depression for me to lie in, before putting up the tent. The tent was solid here. I used trees as anchors for the guy ropes in addition to skis for the main anchors. Then I heaped snow on to the storm flaps and crawled inside. If a storm came I would be very snug. I melted snow and by 2100 had eaten and drunk enough. There was still enough light to gloat over a large scale map of northern Norway and see I had done the lion's share of this section to Ifjord today. I had done 63 kilometres in all. I was now supremely fit with legs of steel. I fell asleep listening to the ptarmigan chuckling in the woods nearby.

The wind did indeed get up a bit in the night, and I heard it slicing through the tops of the trees I was camped amongst. I was well camped, however, and felt warm and secure. As was usual after a big day, I was troubled by cramps in my inner thigh muscles. As I moved in the night, the cramp would set in and wake me up, and I would have to writhe on the tent floor until the spasm passed. I also had time to sleep on a new route, and after looking at my map, decided I would ski north for about 4 kilometres to a gravel road. I would follow, or ski adjacent to, this gravel road some 30 kilometres until I came to the main road. I could then follow the asphalt for a mere 4 kilometres to Ifjord. I did not want to walk across bare, snowless, stony moorland, for fear of damaging the metal rod at the front of either ski boot, which is essential to attach it to the ski. Despite knowing I had 40 kilometres to reach Ifjord I could just not bring myself to get up. With the sound of snow on the tent getting heavier, and the wind remaining blustery, I remained in my bag lying snug on the snow. 0800 came and went. 0900 came and went. Eventually, just after 1000, I managed to emerge. It was not a great day. Wet snow was falling, being driven by a northerly breeze. It would be coming directly into my face. With reluctance and a bit of procrastinating I at last had everything in my rucksack and set off at 1130. As I skied through

Day 112. After a long day I descended into the Gaissavuolesjohka valley and made a snug camp in the sheltered birch woods

Day 113. I had only skied 2 kilometres when I unexpectedly came across this cabin by the Gaissavuolesjohka river and decided to stay

the forest, which was firm under ski, I flushed a herd of some 20 reindeer sheltering in the woods. There was also a few ptarmigan here. I had to thread a path through the trees to avoid the odd bare patch, but by and large there was plenty of good snow. I had barely skied 2 kilometres when I crossed the main river in this valley called the Gaissavuolesjohka and then came face to face with a totally unexpected cabin. I went to investigate. It was open, it was tidy and it was clean. It had a stove but no wood, but there was sufficient wood in the vicinity which I could collect with the surprisingly sharp saw and axe which I found hanging in the cabin. The weather was still miserable, I had 40-odd kilometres to go, and it was already midday. It did not take me long to decide to stay. Within an hour I had found and gathered enough wood to last until the next morning. I cut it up on the cabins steps, then using handfuls of tar-rich and flammable birch bark soon got the damp, frozen logs alight in the stove. It was a small cabin and it heated up quite quickly. Before long I had snow melting in the big pots on the stove and my damp items were hanging up to dry. I soon felt very much at home. It was still snowing heavily outside and all afternoon I never once regretted stopping. There were no clues as to who owned the cabin, but it was probably owned by the local government and used as a hunting cabin, there are many such cabins in Norway. People could buy a licence to hunt small game in most mountain areas of Norway and then use these cabins as a base. In the warmth of the stove I wrote, as the snow continued to fall outside. I had a wonderful relaxed evening, looking into the embers of the stove and realizing that I was now going to make it to the very north of Norway.

It was so much easier to get up in a warm cabin as opposed to a cramped tent, and I sprung out of bed at 0500. It had already been light for a couple of hours. By the time I had breakfast, tidied the cabin, packed away my tent and other previously damp, but now dry items, it was 0700 and I was off. As fortune would have it, the strong wind had swung round to the south again and would be behind me, and it was below zero so the snow was firm. There was no blue sky, but it was still bright. Initially I skied down an almost unnoticeable decline through the remainder of the birch forest. I saw a red fox here. It was keeping a good 100 metres in front of me, turning round frequently to make sure I was not gaining on it. It kept this up for a kilometre obviously unaware of the danger a human could potentially have. I followed the river for 2 kilometres until it suddenly emerged from under the ice and vanished into a dark hydro tunnel. Just beyond the tunnel was the gravel track I was aiming for. It was bare in a few places but generally covered in snow. Initially I followed it diligently but realized there was no point, especially as it undulated so much. Instead I decided to follow a line of frozen lakes. The first of these was the long and narrow Mohkkejavri lake. Although it was dammed and the water level would have varied, the ice looked safe. The surface was firm and hard and I started to fly along with the wind behind me. I passed a dam and kept well to the east of it and three islands near it, as this is probably where the water was removed and there was more likely to be currents affecting the ice quality here. I soon reached the north end where the lake tapered into a narrow bay and then river. I could see parts of the river were open so I hugged the slopes on the side as I went past. Although I was at 200 metres altitude there were few trees with just the odd birch copse in sheltered side valleys. It must be too hard here even for the rugged birch.

Day 113. It did not take long to warm up the cabin and make myself at home, while the snow and sleet continued outside all afternoon

Day 114. Looking south back up Mohkkejavri lake over the ice I just skied over on an overcast and snowy day

The open river widened out into two more narrow lakes, which were smaller than Mohkkejavri lake but connected to them by the river. They were covered in thick secure ice so I skied along their length. With the wind helping me I made good progress towards the dark crags of Vadasbakti hill. Just after these crags there was a short cut which would take me over a gentle spur and cut out the longer detour on to Store Måsvatn lake. I didn't think it was a risk to take the short cut and was surprised how gentle the climb to the saddle was. The descent down the other side was long and easy and I made good time here. At the saddle I got some phone reception. In the wind and light snow shower I managed to send an email with a mail shot I had prepared to 600 people who had signed up to receive them off my website. It seemed odd to be able to initiate this technology from such a remote place where I had not seen anyone for three days now. After the long and easy descent I arrived at Loavddajavri lake. It was only 3 kilometres long but difficult to ski. Previously a lot of the snow on top of the ice had melted, forming wet slush. This had now frozen over with a 2 centimetre layer of ice. Occasionally I broke through which gave me a fright as it was still wet underneath for 15 centimetres until the original surface of the thick ice. The weather now was deteriorating with more frequent and wetter snow showers. After this lake the terrain suddenly becoming very gnarly and steep with small cliffs and deep ravines scattered throughout. Just before yet another lake called Tredjevannet I had real problems negotiating a continuous 10 metre high band of cliff which stretched across the whole hillside. After a good half hour's searching I at last found a route down through the crags to reach the lake. However, my problems were not over yet, as I had to get to the east side of it and the ice looked dangerous. I opted to try and cross the stream before it went into the lake. This stream had huge open ice-free areas but was only shin deep and five metres wide. I was not in danger if I went through but would probably get wet feet. Luckily I found a snow bridge and sped across it with fingers crossed. It held.

Day 114. The bleak empty landscape between Mohkkejavri and Store Måsvatn lakes was typical of today's route in frequent snow showers

On the other side of this stream was a forest track covered in deep snow which was mercifully quite firm. It did provide an easy route up through a final birch forest to a saddle. I was surprised to see other ski tracks here and fresh ones at that. I had a Man Friday moment. I followed his tracks through the wet snow of the forest and up to the saddle. It was sleeting heavily as I reached the saddle but everything lying on the ground in the forest remained firm. At the saddle I left Man Fridays' ski tracks and lost the route of the gravel track so just cut across down across the moorland and through the birch forest to reach a small lake. On the other side of this lake was the main road to Ifjord. The hamlet lay in the valley just 3 kilometres down this road. I had made it. It was only 100 metres altitude here and below this there was a severe lack of snow again. I had not noticed it all day as there had been enough. The bare area I encountered at the end of my long day a couple of days ago must have been due to a meteorological quirk, rather than altitude. I walked down the road for an hour to reach Ifjord, where I could smell the sea. Here beside the tiny hamlet was a bay with seaweed. I reached the junction and the utilitarian café, motel and cabins. As it was sleeting a lot now I took a room rather than a cabin which meant easier access to showers and café food. The room was not up to much and the whole place was quite tired. The owner, Halvdan Hansen, was extremely helpful, interested and pleased to see me. He made sure I was comfortable and made me an enormous hamburger. He didn't know too much about the route north from here but phoned a friend of his who did, namely, Vidar Karlstad, the self-styled 'Vidar the Viking' who lived in Mehamn.

Vidar knew the area well and explained the route to Mehamn. It seemed I could ski the whole way with a night in a heated shelter and a night in a tent. I just had enough food left to be able to eke out the three days it should take. Hopefully the weather will be kind to me.

SECTION 17. Lakselv to Ifjord
4 days. 131 kilometres. 31 hours. 2030m ascent. 1930m descent.

THE SKI: SECTION 18. IFJORD TO KINNARODDEN

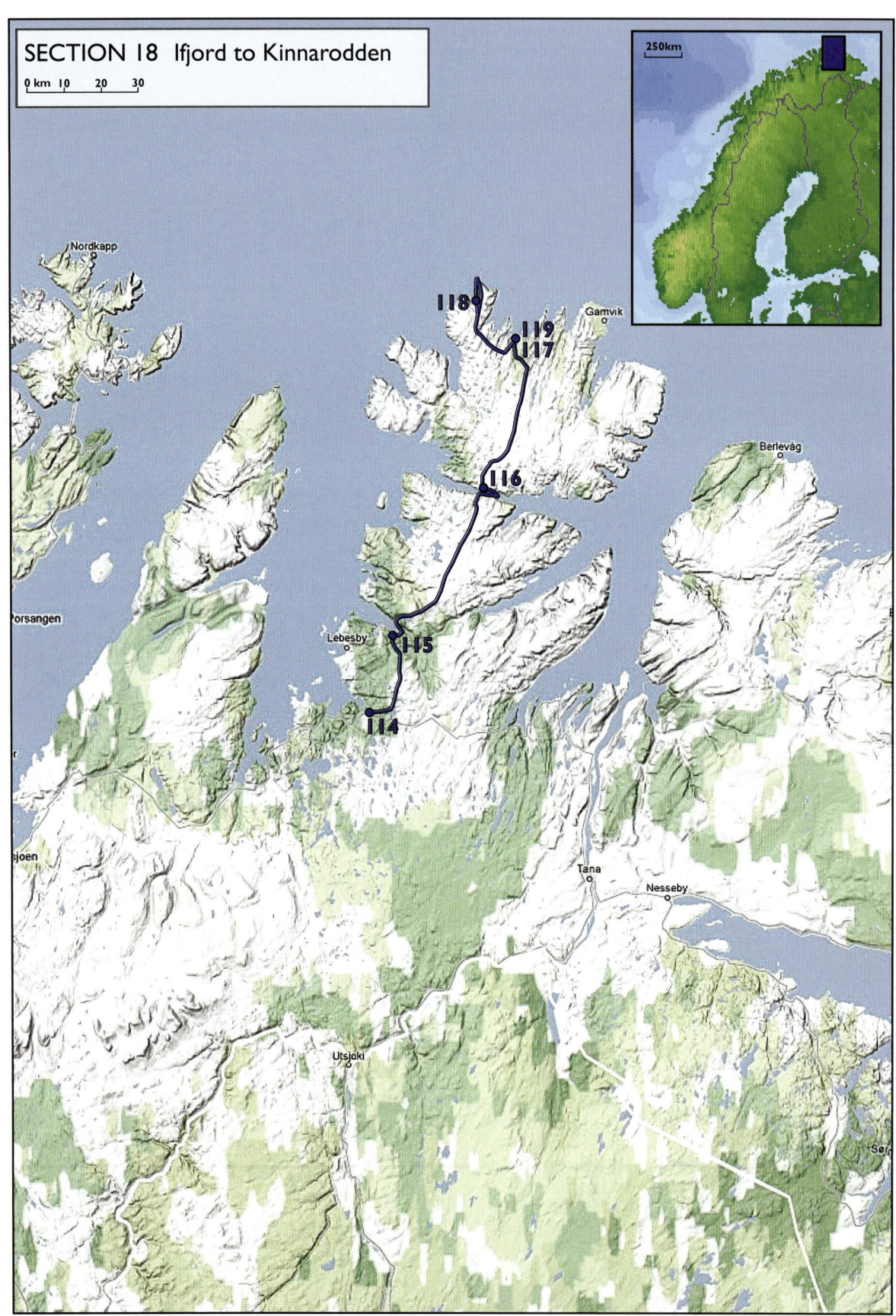

THE SKI: SECTION 18. IFJORD TO KINNARODDEN

I did not sleep well in the stuffy basement room and struggled to get up at 0730 for the great breakfast Halvdan had laid out for me. As I ate, we chatted, mostly about Finnmark politics. I had heard so much about it over the last month. Indeed, everybody seemed to be talking about it and telling me stories to reiterate their point. A lot of these stories were sensationalist, tabloid, even redneck, and helped to propagate myths, but others had some considered thoughts and interesting reflections on the rapid political evolution which Finnmark was undergoing. Halvdan fell into the latter camp and he helped me formulate an opinion. The political and social change seemed to have been initiated by the Finnmark Act of 2006. This Act, which took about 25 years to develop, emerged from the confusion and resentment created by the Norwegian Government when it rode roughshod over Sami presumptions in the building of the Alta hydro-electric dam in the early 1980s. As a result of this conflict the Sami were left deeply unhappy about the imposition of the Norwegian Government edicts over lands they had used for centuries, and many Norwegians, especially southerners, sympathized with them. There was a feeling among the Sami and these southern Norwegian politicians that the rights of each group needed to be clarified on many topics. The most notable topics were land ownership, rights over natural resources, hunting, fishing and berry picking, and most importantly, the seasonal grazing areas and migration paths for the Sami reindeer husbandry. After 25 years of debating, negotiating, some constitutional amendments like the Sami Act of 1987, the setting up of a Sami Parliament (Samediggi), and the ratification of the Sami as indigenous peoples, the Finnmark Act was finally produced.

The jist of this Act removed the Norwegian State and its land department, Statskog, as owner of the vast majority of land in Finnmark (96%) and made The Finnmark Estate the new owner of this land which amounted to 45,000 square kilometres, which is well over twice the size of Wales. The Finnmark Estate is governed by a board of six members, with three being appointed by the Samediggi in Karasjok, and three by the Finnmark County Council in Vadsø. Along with the board to run the estate, two other bodies were set up; The Finnmark Commission and the Uncultivated Land Tribunal for Finnmark. The Finnmark Commission tries to establish acquired rights or ownership which individuals or groups living in Finnmark have on lands newly taken over by the Finnmark Estate from the original Statskog. While the Uncultivated Land Tribunal for Finnmark is a court set up to decide disputed cases, about who has rights of use or ownership of areas and resources, on the lands of the Finnmark Estate. All three of these bodies created by the Finnmark Act are supposed to be ethnically neutral. Every person living in Finnmark, be they Norwegian, Sami or Kven, who were originally Finnish peasants who migrated to Finnmark in the 18th and 19th Centuries, are supposed to have equal rights.

However, wherever there is a new status quo, people and groups tend to jostle for position. Wherever there are new opportunities, people and groups try to take them. Given the opportunity to establish in tablets of stone, verbal and traditional agreements, people will seize the chance. The Finnmark Act has given the Sami confidence to question the current political and social landscape. After nearly two centuries of Norwegianization, where there was an active policy to assimilate minorities into Norwegian culture, law, economy, society and religion there is now a resurgence in Sami culture. With the tool of the Finnmark Act the Sami are flexing their newly found muscles, and the Norwegians don't like it. Many of them are suspicious and have misgivings as the Sami try and establish rights and ownership. These claims all have long historical roots which go back a couple of centuries, since Norwegians migrated along the coast of Finnmark to establish fishing communities along the Arctic Ocean, causing conflict. Mining companies extracted minerals on traditional reindeer grazing lands without regard to the Sami herders, and as I saw in Sweden, the Sami were even press-ganged into transporting the ore on their sledges in winter. In most aspects of life, Norwegians held the upper hand, and the law encouraged this, throughout the last two centuries. Now, with the introduction of the Finnmark Act and a redressing of the legal status quo, some Sami are digging into history to address their previous suppression. There are many compensation cases going through the courts for historical grievances which the average Norwegian living in Finnmark considers greedy, and they feel threatened by them. The common theme most Norwegians seem to dwell on, was how the Finnmark Act seemed to disproportionately favour the small number of reindeer-owning Sami at the expense of the other Sami, like the Sjøsami (or Sea Sami), ethnic Norwegians and the descendants of the Kven. It was fascinating to listen to Halvdan and we spent hours discussing the topic, with me asking questions like a reporter.

By the time we had finished talking it was approaching midday. I still had to pack and get going. While I packed, Vidar phoned Halvdan to say he had sent some maps down by bus to the heated shelter in Bekkarfjord which

Day 115. As I skied over the plateau towards Martadalen the skies became quite overcast making the light very very atmospheric

I could use to reach Mehamn. He had also marked the line of old telegraph poles which I was to follow on this map. This was hugely useful and I was very grateful for Vidar's effort, considering I had not met him yet. At midday I was ready to go. It was disturbingly hot at around 12 degrees and the snow was wet and granular. The only wax which could cope with these conditions was klister, an extremely sticky chemical paste which is applied to the bottom of the ski. It is so sticky that it even sticks to wet snow. However, without spirits it is impossible to get off. So if the temperature drops, then the colder snow will adhere to it so well that it just balls up on the underside of one's ski and it is impossible to ski. I have found through experience it is dreadful stuff and now never use it. Today I could avoid the need for it by using my short ski-skins, while many others use cloth sports tape under the skis. Initially I followed the scooter track up through the birch forest. It started just opposite the café. I had to stop after just a few hundred metres to remove my hat, gloves and jacket and even then I was sweating going up the hot incline. It was a very nice ascent in pleasant surroundings in the birch woods with a gentle enough climb so my short skins could find enough grip. After an hour I had climbed above the birch and was on the edge of a higher plateau. I left the scooter track here as the snow was firm and headed north across the plateau. Beneath the snow were rocks and short heather and numerous ground-hugging bushes which produced berries. If I walked where the snow was thin, these berries burst, staining the snow crimson. I made my own route north keeping as high as possible. It was completely calm but it was becoming quite overcast. I crossed numerous small lakes and the west end of Giksjavri lake. A bit further to the west and I would have been in very gnarly terrain. The snow was pretty good here but there were numerous bare patches. From Giksjavri lake I climbed a steep hill to cross a watershed near Suolojavri lake. This was located at the top of the plateau and I got some good views from here. It was still warm and without wind so I found a bare patch and had lunch sitting on some tundra-hugging bushes. The descent from the saddle to Suolojavri lake was short and easy. After crossing the lake I reached the top of Martadalen valley. This valley was plastered in snow and was open and smooth. It was difficult to believe I was only 250 metres above sea level. It felt more like 1500 metres again. The ski down Martadalen was fantastic. I had removed my short skins and there was just enough descent so I had a long glide with each step.

As I went down the shallow valley, a scooter came up towards me with a man and a boy on the back. It slowed down and the driver took off his helmet for a chat. The man was Peder Jenssen and it was his son on the back. I think he knew I was going to Kinnarodden before he stopped as it was his first question. He commended me for choosing Kinnarodden over Nordkapp as my final destination. They were going up to do some fishing on their modest 20-year-old scooter. He lived at Elvebakken farm in Bekkarfjord, just down the valley and kindly asked if I wanted to stay there in a cabin instead of the council's waiting room for weather-bound drivers. I said yes, so he rang his daughter to tell her to warm the cabin up. We then parted and I carried on down the lovely Martadalen. The incline was not quite enough so I could freewheel but I could ski quickly. Soon Peder's scooter tracks which I was following reached the birch trees and veered west round the small Martadalsvatnet tarn. Then there was a steeper descent, where I had to snowplough strongly to stop myself running off out of control through the remainder of the birch woods. Down in the valley was

Day 115. The ski down Martadalen towards Bekkarfjord was very easy as I just had to follow the scooter tracks left by Peder Jenssen

Day 115. The tiny dairy farming hamlet of Bekkarfjord was beside a small fjord which branched off from the bigger Laksefjord

black water without any snow on it. It was the salty sea water of Bekkarfjord. Surrounding it were fields, many already ploughed, with their furrows appearing from under the melting snow. Peder's scooter tracks naturally went right to his house. He had five children and the eldest daughter showed me to the cabin. It was already warm, having been heated by the large electric panel. I dumped my rucksack in the cabin and set off on foot for the kilometre walk along the road to the waiting room. Here I hoped I would find the envelope with the maps and route to Mehamn which Vidar had left for me. The walk took me along the agricultural fringe of the fjord. It was great to be near the sea again. The familiar noise of two squabbling herring gulls and the excited crescendo of plovers were soon to be very common place on my forthcoming kayak trip, but it was nice to hear them after four months of winter-clad mountains. Bekkarfjord seemed quite an idyllic place with five farms spread out beside the placid inlet. The odd piece of ice floated on the surface, but otherwise it was calm and black.

The maps were at the waiting room as promised. They were perfect, and I could use them to go the final 70 kilometres to Mehamn. I was surprised at Vidar's efficiency, it was out of the ordinary. Back at the farm cabin I wrote my blog before being invited in for a supper of the fish which Peder and his son had just caught. It was mostly Arctic char, fried in butter from his own dairy cows. His cows, and those from the two others farms in this hamlet, account for the most northerly dairy herd in the world. After supper, when the youngest two children had been put to bed, Peder and his eldest son went out to try and catch some king crabs. These crabs are invading the Norwegian coast, having migrated from Russia. King crabs were initially imported to northern Russia from Kamchatka but they had now spread and were crawling down the Norwegian coast. Environmentalists fear they might devastate the cod spawning grounds in Vestfjorden by Lofoten when they get there, but locals in Finnmark were enthusiastic about them. They were the source of a blossoming fishing industry here and they were fast becoming an important component in the tourist industry. There were also many families, like the Jenssens, who fished them for the pot, as they were easy to catch and so abundant.

I slept well in the Jenssen's cabin and got up reasonably early at 0700. It was overcast, but very warm. The temperature was plus 6. The bare patches in the yard, and in the fields near the house, were growing quickly and were saturated with water. Outside the house there was a large box with about 30 of the red king crabs which Peder and his son had caught last night. After breakfast I tried some of the king crab legs. The legs were boiled and cut open with scissors. Inside, the meat was the same colour, taste and consistency as crabsticks. I got into conversation with Peder, as the weather deteriorated into showers, and didn't leave until 1030. It was an interesting visit for me to stay with this friendly and active family and get some insight into life on this peninsula on the Arctic Ocean.

I initially followed the road for 10 kilometres to gain height up on to the plateau again. It was the easiest way if I was to avoid the melting snow in the birch woods and lower slopes. There were some tremendous views down Bekkarfjord inlet to the main Laksefjord, and then across this large wide fjord to the remote Sværholt peninsula. This wild peninsula was very steep sided and rose precipitously from the Arctic Ocean

Day 116. As I walked along the road by Bekkarfjord I could look down the inlet and across Laksefjord to the wild Sværholt peninsula beyond

Day 116. Looking down across Bekkarfjord to Elvebakken farm whose soggy fields were emerging from under the winter snow

straight up to a snow-covered plateau at about 400 metres altitude. After the 10 kilometres I reached the cluster of Ørretvatna tarns. By now I had climbed back up to about 200 metres altitude and the whole hillside was covered in deep snow again. Vidar had advised me to leave the road here and ski down into Nikolasdalen, cross it and then climb up the south and east side of Gavdnjavarri mountain. I did this quite easily and as I climbed up I got a great view to the east down the forested Langfjorddalen valley. At the end of the valley, where the birch woods meet the sea of the deep fjord, were a couple of roadless hamlets on the east side of the peninsula I was skiing up. These hamlets were once thriving communities of Sjøsami or Sea Sami. They were Sami folk who did not have reindeer and lived almost exclusively from the sea. The reindeer-herding Sami considered the Sjøsami to be a lower status as they did not have any animals, but eked out a life from the sea. I had heard a story, now a few times, which people told me to emphasize their point when trying to convince me of the Finnmark Act's inspired greed of the reindeer-owning Sami. The Sjøsami populations of these two hamlets and Gamvik council wanted to build a road to them and fulfilled all the permissions. The construction started and people rejoiced. However, the reindeer-herding Sami who had the right to graze their beasts here objected and forced a halt to the construction. Their argument was that some of the grazing would be lost and they wanted an eye watering amount of compensation. The legal dispute was still lingering when I went by in 2009 but will inevitably be resolved once the compensation is agreed.

Once I was round the east side of Gavdnjavarri hill and had climbed to a pass, the whole of the plateau opened before me. It was at about 400 metres altitude and everything was plastered in snow. This was a return to winter proper and in contrast to the soggy morning at Bekkarfjord I now felt I was crossing Hardangervidda in February. Below me on the north side of the pass was a line of telegraph posts. Vidar recommended I follow these posts for some 20 kilometres across the plateau. They were the remnants of an old telephone line from at least 50 years ago and the wire had long gone. His route was perfect and the next 20 kilometres were a very good and quite fast ski. The weather was very changeable but on the whole it was overcast but there were a couple of very heavy snow showers where all visibility disappeared except for the telephone posts. The ski route went on and on undulating over gentle

Day 116. Looking back down the line of old bleached and defunct telegraph poles which I followed across the open plateau

ridges and then descending into shallow valleys. I had to work most of the time as I opted to keep my skins on and this cut down on any glide I could get. Eventually after some four hours the route started to reach the northern end of this block of land where it dropped off steeply to fjords. There was only one way down the northern edge of this plateau, and that was down Smielvdalen valley, which was also the route the road took. I had been skiing parallel to the road, but a few kilometres to the east of it. It was easy to head west across the plateau to reach the exposed windswept road which must see some wild weather. Smielvdalen valley was about 4 kilometres long and it dropped quite steeply down to Eidsfjorden. There were masses of reindeer tracks and droppings here, the reindeer must have just migrated from the interior of Finnmark and come down this road to cross the isthmus on to Nordkinn peninsula. This is contrary to the reindeer migration patterns elsewhere. Reindeer are severely bothered by flies; one type lays eggs in the reindeer's nasal passages and throat, then maggots hatch which eat these regions. There are few flies in the very high mountains of central Scandinavia, and very few on these windswept peninsulas, which is why they are preferred by reindeer, and Sami alike. The reindeer are herded out to this peninsula; a tricky operation as the reindeer are uncomfortable about being herded down to the sea, via the narrow Smielvdalen valley. Recently, a herd bolted up the steep slopes and got into trouble, many lost their grip and slid on the steep snow and were killed.

Once at the sea by Eidsfjorden the road then heads east along the fjord and beneath the cliffs the reindeer came to grief on, until it gets to a narrow isthmus some 500 metres wide and long at the hamlet of Hopseidet. This narrow, boulder-strewn neck is all that connects the Nordkinn peninsula to the north to the mainland; otherwise it would be an island. It was my goal for the day, and as I walked along the south shore of Eidsfjorden I noticed an abandoned workers hut on the north shore, and decided to investigate. I doubled back for a kilometre to reach the hut. It was unlocked, however, it was bare and uncomfortable inside, but it saved me from pitching the tent. I got there just in time, as a sleet storm and high winds came blasting down the fjord from the west. After I unpacked and spread my belongings on the floor, I looked out of the window and saw it was miserable outside, with a sleet blizzard. The small steep waves were crashing on to the boulders along the shore, with spray being whipped off the foam. There were some tystie, or black guillemot, bobbing about in the waves braving the elements. I managed to cook and then stretched out on the floor to write, but soon fell asleep.

In the morning, the weather was still unpleasant, with frequent snow squalls coming up the fjord. A lot of fresh snow had fallen in the night, turning the landscape white. The weather forecast said it would brighten up at midday, so given the long evenings now I decided to wait in my sleeping bag on the floor of the hut. The weather forecast was spot on, and just before midday some blue sky appeared, so I got ready to go. Right outside the hut were very fresh otter tracks left in the snow in the previous hour. From the hut I pretty much headed straight up the hill hoping to intercept the road above me. On the way up I came across a herd of about 50 reindeer. Despite the fact these reindeer are domesticated they are still very wary. This herd was no exception, and ran off when they saw me. Once on the road I followed it as it climbed northwards for about 3 kilometres. During this distance it climbed to over 200 metres altitude and the difference was huge. Up here it was full winter again, with vast deep snow fields smothering any boulders or frozen tarns in an ocean of white. I eagerly put my skis on again and kicked away from the road. The conditions were superb, with the base layer of snow frozen firm and a light covering over the top. Even with the skins on, I was gliding very well. By now the sky had cleared up completely and there were just a few lingering clouds. I headed off to the north east of the road across some tarns and then up a hill. While crossing one tarn, I crashed through the new icy crust on top of the slushy snow, which was accumulating on top of the submerged thick ice. I went in up to my knee, but luckily my gaiters kept the icy water out of my boots, however, my heart was momentarily in my mouth. I soon found the old weather-bleached telephone poles again, they headed over to Mehamn, and I just had to follow them. To the south and east I could see how the flat plateau rolled out to the rim of this table-like platform, before it dropped steeply for 300 metres into the sea, but I could not see the sea. As I skied further north along the line of poles I was astonished to see just how much snow there was. It almost felt like I was skiing across a glacier, as the landscape was very smooth and there were no rocks or bare patches. It would be a while before all this melted, revealing the sparse vegetation and boulders underneath. I decided to take my skins off, as the gradients were so small. If I could have skated with my mountain skis and rucksack, I would have been really flying. But it was too exhausting to keep it up for more than 30 seconds.

After a few hours of this exceptionally nice skiing I came to a small rustic hut. It must have gone up when the telephone line was built, and it looked over 50 years old. It was called Futelvstua. There was an outer store room full of snow and wood, then there was an inner room with a very efficient stove, and a third room with four bare beds without mattresses. I got the stove going using wood from the well-stocked store room. There was a visitor's book, and it seemed the hut was well visited by local skiers on day trips from Mehamn. I had a late lunch, using the last of my dehydrated meals. After lunch I continued north, following the old telegraph poles, and the skiing got even better as there was now a slight downhill bias. Within an hour I had reached a point on the plateau where it looked like it would get a bit gnarly if I carried on north, so I veered west and made a long diagonal descent to the road. It was a superb descent and the icy surface was firm and fast. In the space of 15 minutes I had gone about 4 kilometres. I passed two herds of reindeer and as I was going so fast they did not have time to decide to run before I was gone. I reached the road at Ostebakken where there were some Sami

Day 117. After Futelvstua cabin I had a wonderful ski down off the plateau past herds of reindeer to the Sami cabins at Ostebakken

cabins. I skied along the snow-covered verge for a few minutes until I rounded a corner, and the fishing town of Mehamn came into view. Beyond it was the Arctic Ocean. It was a quick hour down to the outskirts of Mehamn. The snow petered out on the edge of the town, so I took my skis off and walked the last 2 kilometres to the youth hostel owned by Vidar, who had sent me the maps.

Vidar was a lively and jovial character. It was easy to see he was a hard-working adventure entrepreneur, and was quite well known in the area. His youth hostel was very comfortable, and beside it he had five new rorbuer, or traditional fisherman's houses, which he rented out. The only problem with the youth hostel was it lay across the bay from the centre of Mehamn and was a kilometre and a half from the café or shops. I checked in and he gave me a beer as a welcome, he said I had earned it. He was extremely knowledgeable about the area and had even built a number of stone cairns along the route to Kinnarodden, which I would follow tomorrow. He lent me a map to Kinnarodden and explained the route to me. It was rare to get such unequivocal advice, and I felt I had landed in good hands. It would take two days to make the trip to Kinnarodden, and I would have to camp on a remote Arctic beach, famed for its white sand, in Sandfjorden bay which was just to the west of Kinnarodden. Once Vidar had gone, I walked into Mehamn past racks and racks of cod drying in the cold wind, and bought some food in the kiosk which I could cook in the hostel. I went to bed full of excitement about tomorrow.

It was a nice day when I woke late in the morning. I had to go into to Mehamn again and buy some food for the next two days. I bought a few bulky and luxurious treats to reward myself with a nice meal tonight and breakfast

Day 117. As I arrived in Mehamn, I came across rack after rack of cod, drying in the cold winds to produce stockfish which is a major export

tomorrow. I did not set off until midday, but it didn't really matter any more, because although the sun sets around 2200 now, it remains just below the horizon for a few hours, and it is light throughout the night. After passing the tiny Mehamn Airport I put my skis on and started up the slopes of Rundhaugen, a hill to the south west of the town. It was covered in snow, but there were many branches from the smothered willow scrub poking through. At the top of Rundhaugen I was once more on the plateau and overlooking the town. Just then my phone rang. It was a friend who was a newsreader for Radio Scotland. We did a telephone interview and it was apparently broadcast later that afternoon. It seemed very unusual to be talking to him when skiing up a snowfield above the Arctic town of Mehamn, while he was recording the conversation in a BBC studio in Glasgow. The plateau here was still covered in snow. The interior to my south was absolutely plastered in snow, while the headlands sticking out to the Barents Sea to the north were generally bare of snow. There

Day 118. Heading up the small claustrophobic valley between Sørfjorddalen and Bjørnviktuva on my way to Kinnarodden

Day 118. Once I was out of the claustrophobic valley and back on to the plateau I could see Magkeilhetta headland rising out of the ocean

were many herds of reindeer here. Curiously, these herds seemed to be quite small with 10 to 15 beasts in each, as opposed to the herds of 50 or so I had seen earlier. The females were heavy with calf, so it was important not to surprise them and make them bolt. I crossed the small Sørfjorddalen valley and started to ski up an even smaller side valley, with a line of lakes on its deep floor. It was cold in the valley, well below zero, and the snow was firm. After a couple of smaller ridges between the lakes I started to climb up the end of this slightly claustrophobic valley and on to the plateau. Here the views opened up again and I could look out to some of the very craggy headlands jutting out into the Arctic Ocean. Magkeilhetta looked especially menacing as it burst out of the sea. Vidar had warned me to keep south here, as the terrain to the north was very gnarly, and I could see what he meant, as it was a warren of crags and holes. The cairns which Vidar had built continued up Bjørnviktuva which was one of the biggest hills on the plateau.

As I crested the summit of Bjørnviktuva, the eminent headland I had been skiing towards for the last four months came into view, just some 10 kilometres to the north. It was an exciting moment to be so close. I could see a lot of snow in front of me, but this vanished as I cast my eye toward Kinnarodden itself. With impatience I set off down the north side of Bjørnviktuva and had a wonderful ski down into Sandfjorddalen which was full of ptarmigan and reindeer. The valley had a deep cover of snow which covered the lakes and made it look like a bit of a winter's Shangri-La. Where this lovely valley veered west down to the sandy beach where I would spend the night, I had to leave it and climb up the stone-covered side to reach the final section of plateau which went out to the headland. There was so little snow I had to walk across these stones, but once I reached

Day 118. From Reipnakktinden I followed the cornice which hung over the ocean as I made my way towards Kinnarodden in the distance

the plateau again, it was covered in snow, so the skis went back on. Even out here there were many small herds of reindeer, finding good grazing on the exposed vegetation. I skied to the high point of the plateau, called Reipnakktinden, and there, just 2 kilometres away, was Kinnarodden, with its massive cairn in the overcast evening. The trouble was there was a deep valley whose sides were covered in boulders between me and my ultimate goal. The descent into this valley was covered in loose boulders and looked difficult. Vidar had told me it was best to descend on the sharp ridge above the sea cliffs to the north east edge, where the boulders were firmer. It was by far the best route, and I went a little further and just walked along the inner edge of the large cornice which hung over these sea cliffs. The sea was quite calm with little swell and just a slight chop where the current was flowing past Kinnarodden headland. I had expected it to be worse, given the weather just 36 hours ago. I would have kayaked round the headland in these conditions, with the only hesitation being, it was

Day 118. Looking east from Reipnakktinden along the craggy north face to Magkeilhetta headland with Kinnarodden to the back of me

199

so cold. There was the odd snow flake in the overcast sky and it was a bit breezy as I started to climb up the boulders on the north side of the valley. I took great strides up the steep slope with adrenaline completely overpowering any lack of breath I might have felt as I surged up.

As I approached the top, the momentous cairn revealed itself on the flat surface of the final headland. It was not the very end though, as I had previously seen that the headland continued for another few hundred metres, until the cliffs started. I passed the cairn and continued across the boulders. Above me were spirals of seabirds soaring in the updrafts created by the headland. Occasionally I passed the top of a gully on the west side where the steep basalt columns had weathered more and allowed me to peer down to the gentle swell washing over the rocks far below. Suddenly the headland started to narrow, as the cliffs on the west and east side started to come together, squeezing the flat surface into a narrowing point. I kept going until there was nowhere else to go. Beyond were cliffs on three sides. At the bottom of this cliff was a large rounded rocky islet separated by a narrow channel. I stood staring at the rock for a good minute, transfixed by it and almost frozen in the position I was in. I was quite mesmerized by the sight I had spent the last 118 days striving towards, and it took a while to dawn on me that I had made it. There was no outpouring of emotion or excitement, but I felt a calm euphoria. I spent the next hour on this very wild and remote platform above the sea, reflecting on my journey. It had been a remarkable adventure, almost a pilgrimage through unblemished nature, and this pristine citadel was a shrine which filled me with wonder and awe. I must say Kinnarodden is quite a spot.

Day 118. I suddenly came to the edge of the plateau and stood for a minute transfixed by the rock below at the very north of Europe

Day 118. After four months skiing north I suddenly reach the northern point of the continent at Kinnarodden and could go no further

After basking in quiet contentment and looking out over the ocean sunset I realized I was getting cold. I took a few more photos and started to retrace my steps back to the boulder-filled valley which was called Nordavindskardet, which translated means 'Pass of the north wind'. At the south end of this valley I dug my heels in down a steep snowfield to reach the rocky shoreline. The walk along the shoreline was much harder than I had anticipated as it was covered in enormous amounts of driftwood and snow which covered the underlying boulders and rock formations. Those 3 kilometres took well over an hour as I slowly stumbled and slipped towards the sandy beach. As I walked along here the sun went down in a blaze of orange, so bright, it also turned the paler boulders and logs along the shoreline orange. Mercifully, I did not damage the bars on my ski boots during this walk, which is testament to how strong they are. Curiously there were a lot of small fish washed up and dead among the driftwood all the way down this rugged shore. I never found out what type they were, but they were about 10 centimetres long. The beach at Sandfjorden was an absolute pearl.

Day 118. The walk along the snow-covered boulders and driftwood to Sandfjord beach in the distance was harder than expected but worth it

It was a kilometre of very light coloured sand between two dark imposing cliffs. Above this flat wide beach was a kilometre of sandy heather and moorland. I was too tired really to explore it now so just found a dry, sandy, snow-free place to camp and put the tent up. After fetching water from the stream at the west end of the beach I contemplated making a huge pyre with some of the driftwood lying about. Once I was in the tent though, I decided to stay there and fell asleep with a contented smile.

Day 118. I reached Sandfjord beach after the sun had set out beyond Kinnarodden peninsula with the remnants of a snow show still falling

I was glad I had chosen Kinnarodden as the end of my ski journey. It is not like its rival, Nordkapp, which I could just make out earlier in the overcast evening, some 50 kilometres to the west. Nordkapp has a road, a massive parking lot full of camper vans, a visitor centre and much other fanfare. I also chose Kinnarodden because it is part of the mainland, while Nordkapp is on an island. This also meant that Nordkapp would have been difficult to reach as I wanted to do the journey under my own steam. I would have had an unlawful and ghastly 8-kilometre walk through a dark road tunnel under the fjord with frequent cars passing me. It was certainly not easier to finish at Kinnarodden. Quite the opposite, in fact, as it probably added 200 kilometres and an extra week on to my tour. The extra was worth it, though, as it was a virtuous and undisturbed headland; one for the connoisseur.

Day 119. When I woke on Sandfjord beach the sun was blasting down on to the tent and it felt like a different season

When I woke at 0700 the tent was hot, as the sun had been beating down on it and heating it up like a greenhouse. I drowsily opened the zips and looked outside and could have been forgiven for thinking summer had arrived. The sky was completely cloudless and uniformly dark blue. There was not a breath of wind and the sun was blasting down. Even the seagulls on the beach were lazily walking up and down in front of the tiny waves. The only thing which was busy was a small stoat, completely white in its winter coat, except for the black tip of its tail. It was frantically bobbing in and out of the driftwood searching for food. In a month it would be spoilt for choice with bird's eggs, but now it was obviously looking for small rodents which had survived the winter. It was so relaxing and pleasant in the sun I ambled about in a vest looking for fish boxes and driftwood to build a table and stool. I then set out a celebratory breakfast spread. Fresh bread, butter, smoked salmon, slices of cured lamb thigh, prawn salad and blackcurrant syrup. I had a wonderful breakfast with the sun burning my back while I sampled the treats with the small waves lapping at the white sand. After breakfast I pulled my mattress out of the tent and lay on the grass and had a morning siesta while I digested the sumptuous meal. It was quite remarkable how different the weather was from yesterday. It felt like a different season. After a sleep in the sun I thought I had better get going. Everything was in my

Day 119. Looking across the warm peaceful beach to Kinnarodden at the end of the headland, to the left of Nordavindskardet saddle

Day 119. I had brought all the ingredients for a celebratory breakfast to Sandfjord beach as porridge would just not do

rucksack by midday and as I left there was just the odd wisp of mackerel cloud formations in the sky.

I climbed up the steep dunes and moraine to the extensive raised beach, which extended up the valley for a good kilometre above the current beach. This flat dry moorland was covered in heather and grass and would be the breeding grounds of many birds in a month or two. The birds would nest on the ground and hope their camouflaged eggs and chicks were sufficiently protected from the many predators. I had to walk over this moorland before I reached the snow and thought about putting my skis on again to climb up into Sandfjorddalen valley. Initially I had to weave up the valley floor trying to join up the patches of snow, but as I climbed the vegetation soon became smothered by the snowpack. The stream which flowed down the valley had carved a slice through this snowpack. Under the snowpack hundreds of smaller rivulets would be flowing to feed this larger stream, each melting the ice which it once was. The stream's flow was being swollen by the arriving spring and it was simply bursting through the snow carrying blocks of snow and ice before it. This was the 'vårløsning', or spring loosening, where the solid ice and snow of the winter melts and breaks up. Soon every stream would be in spate. The climb back up the valley was wonderful. The mackerel clouds had disappeared and the sky was blue again. Ptarmigan flew from outcrop to outcrop as I chased them up the valley, while the reindeer ran with their unusual gait up the sides. I had a real spring in my step and felt elated as I surged up Bjørnviktuva hill again. At the top I turned and had a last look at Kinnarodden and the blue ocean around it, while I took off my ski-skins for the last time. From this hill I had a wonderful descent back along the lakes in the deep claustrophobic valley to Sørfjorddalen. This area was teeming with reindeer that were making the most of the reindeer moss, a type of lichen, which was becoming exposed on the rocky outcrops. I skied across the small plateau to the gentle slopes of Rundhaugen hill, where I could see the fishing port of Mehamn

Day 119. A last photo of Sandfjord beach with Kinnarodden in the background and my faithful X-Pod rucksack fully packed and ready

spread out below me. Naturally it was with a feeling of sadness that I skied down the last slope through the willow bushes to the final narrow strip of snow beside the airport until there was nothing but heather and I had to take my skis off for the final time. It was a short walk back to Vidar's hostel, past row upon row of cod drying in the breeze, on huge racks to produce hundreds of tons of stockfish. Stockfish is unsalted and retains all the original nutrients of the original cod, but without the water, so it can be preserved. It has been a vital export for Norway for centuries, principally to the Catholic Mediterranean countries and also West Africa.

At Vidar's, I taped up the skis ready for posting to Oslo, as it would not be possible to ski to Kirkenes, as my original plan. I walked into Mehamn to buy some

Day 119. The streams were now bursting through the snowpack as the 'spring loosening' was starting to throw off the icy yoke of winter

rewarding food and returned to the quiet hostel, where I was the only guest. After supper I had a shower and felt the joy of brushing my teeth with a full-sized toothbrush, after months of using a fiddly stump. From tomorrow, I would allow myself to use a bicycle, as after 119 days the ski tour was finally over. It had been a total of 2684 kilometres with 46,160 metres of ascent and descent. In total, this had taken 754 hours of skiing. So my average was about 3.5 kilometres an hour. I cannot begin to summarize the tour, but in a nutshell it had everything a ski tourer is looking for; variety, challenge, superb nature and interesting people. It also nurtured my nomadic DNA, which was just buried under 50 generations of a relatively sedentary condition.

Day 119. From Rundhaugen hill I could enjoy my last descent down patchy slopes towards the fishing town of Mehamn spread out below

I had a very long lie until 1000 when there was a knock on the door. It was a journalist from the Finnmarken newspaper. He wanted a photo and interview, but I was still in bed. We agreed he would return in an hour. I got up, had a breakfast of bacon and eggs, and just managed to finish it before the journalist returned. We went outside and he took some photos and explained that another journalist would phone later and interview me for the text part of the article. An hour later, I had just started to write, when the phone rang, which was a very rare occurrence really. I expected it was the journalist. It was a journalist, but a different one. She was from *Fjell og Vidde*, the prestigious magazine of Den Norske Turistforeningen. It had some 200,000 members who received the magazine. We arranged an interview later in the summer. Then the journalist from the Finnmarken newspaper rang, and I gave a telephone interview and directed him to my website for more information. All this excitement was eating into my writing time and I still had not finished by mid-afternoon when I had to go into Mehamn and post my skis to Oslo, but I kept my boots to cycle the next leg.

I then went to pick up the bicycle from Vidar. He had a few which he rented out in the summer. It was nearly new, and looked the part, with 24 gears, but I could see underneath the shiny chrome and paint that it was a Chinese bicycle, and there were a few bits on it which were already wobbly. It would do the distance, but I wouldn't be speeding down any hills, in case the front forks sheared off. The seat looked so uncomfortable, and sinister, I wondered how long it would be before I was saddle sore. I reckoned the cycle to Kirkenes would take about six days, as it was 400 kilometres. However, the roads I would be going over were still very wintery and would go through some mountainous regions. I took the bicycle back to the hostel in the sleety weather which kept sweeping in throughout the day. It was the perfect day to hide indoors and finish my writing and chat with Vidar and his friends when they came by the hostel.

SECTION 18. Ifjord to Kinnarodden and Mehamn
6 days. 150 kilometres. 41 hours. 3060m ascent. 3100m descent.

THE CYCLE: SECTION 19. MEHAMN TO GRENSE JAKOBSELV

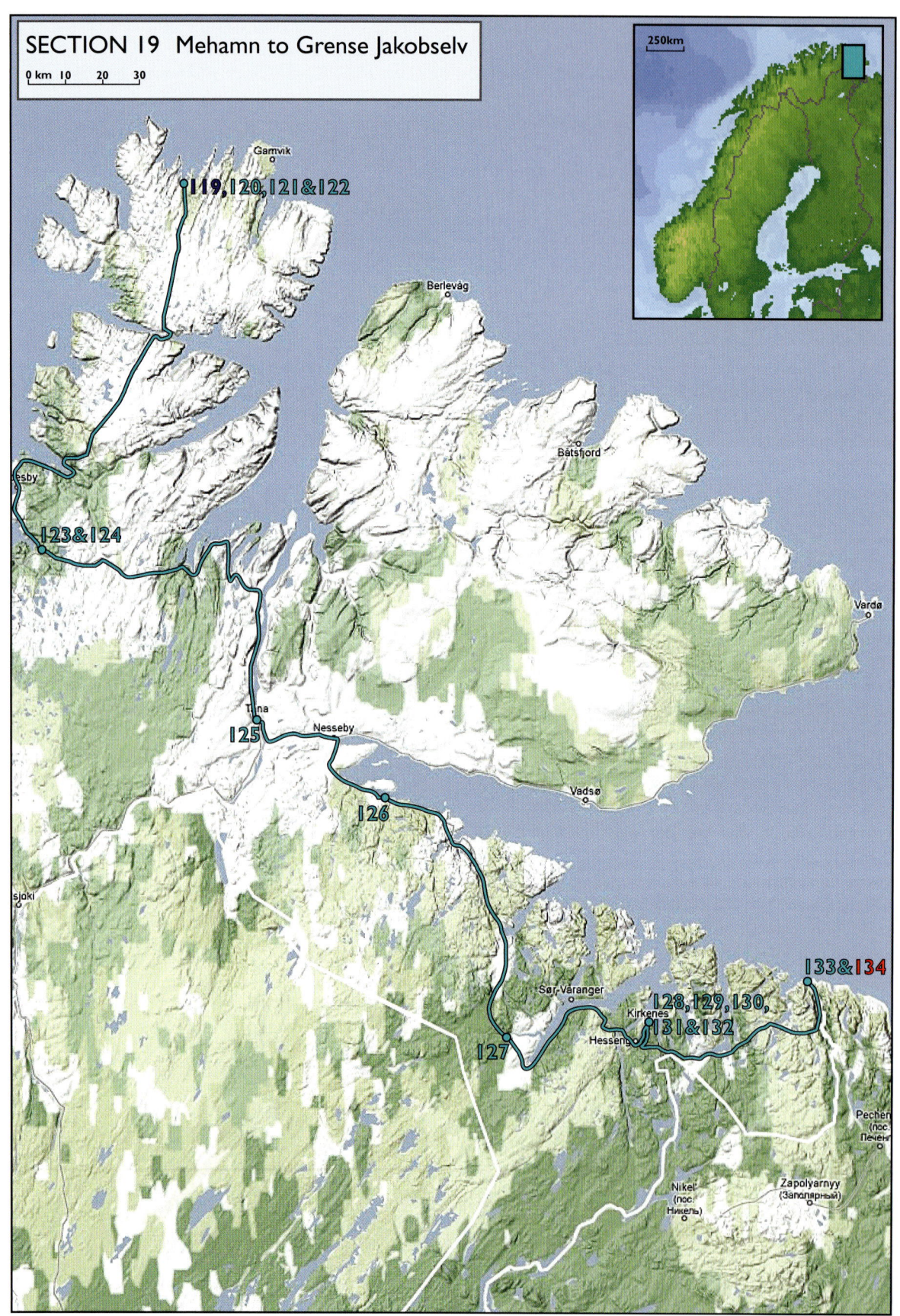

THE CYCLE: SECTION 19. MEHAMN TO GRENSE JAKOBSELV

Day 120. The hostel at Mehamn was across the bay from the town centre and included some new rorbuer style houses

It was with a touch of sadness that I took my skis round the bay to the town centre, to post them back to Oslo. I passed the rows of hanging cod drying in the bitterly cold breeze as I sauntered along the fishing port's wharfs. When I got to the post office it was closed, indeed, the whole town seemed remarkably quiet for a Friday. I asked someone why and he looked at me as if I was ignorant! He explained it was the 1st of May. Having been on the very fringes of society for the last four months, it had not occurred to me, so I returned to the hostel with my skis. I made up another package to post. As I had to resort to Vidar's simple bicycle (which did not have panniers) to reach Grense Jakobselv on the Russian border, I would have to take what I needed on my back in my rucksack. I would have to be very ruthless to keep the weight down to around 10 kilos. I decided to ditch the tent and rely on erratic cabins or very sparse roadside motels. I would take my sleeping bag, an emergency bivouac sack and a foam mat in case I got caught in a storm. The foam mat I thought might also come in handy to cushion the evil-looking seat. It was fast approaching 24 hours daylight, so darkness would not hinder me, and there was nothing alarming in the long-term forecast. Despite these long days, winter still had a firm grip on some of the route I had to cycle. That evening more guests arrived at the hostel. They were three middle-aged Finnish men who had come up for a few days to fish through holes in the ice on lakes and tarns across the peninsula. True to form they had had a belly full of vodka. It seemed to be a national trait and it was not endearing.

It was pouring rain the next morning and it would not be a great day for cycling over the two exposed 350-metre plateaus between here and Bekkarfjord. I wandered back into the centre of town and posted the skis and the other package of superfluous equipment. Vidar helped me find a hotel where I could stay in Kirkenes, and where Øivind could send a few gadgets to, as I could now afford to carry the tiny laptop and a larger GPS. It was the Barents Frokosthotell, the cheapest place in town, and an infamous haunt of Russian trawlermen. After lunch I went for a wander around the town. It was essentially a fishing town with a population of about 1000. Indeed, if it were not for cod it would not exist, as there was no other resources to sustain it. The fortunes of the town were dependant of this king of fish and getting it to the European markets.

Day 121. Mehamn is a fishing port and the sheltered bay is lined with wharfs to land and process fish, mostly cod

There were plenty of trawlers and fishing boats. The smaller boats would go out for a day or two and fish the coastal waters, while the larger boats would go out for a week or two. The boats would land their catch at one of the fish processing plants which surrounded the reasonably sheltered bay. At this time of year, all the cod was being hung to make stockfish or dried cod. This is the oldest way to preserve any food and was very important in Norway before preservation by salting became economically feasible in the 1600s. During May it is windy enough for the cod to dry out without freezing, but still cold enough to deter flies. Later, when spring starts to unfold and the temperatures rise, cod could no longer be hung to dry as flies would swarm over the fish and lay eggs on it. The landed cod, and a small amount of other whitefish like haddock, which was destined for stockfish, would have the head and digestive system removed, then the tails of two fish are tied together and they are hung up over a round log, some 20 brace along one log. There are 300 of these logs in a row and 10 rows to one drying rack. Mehamn had two of these huge areas laid out in drying racks with about a quarter of a million fish drying. These fish would dry under nets to protect them from seagulls. After a month or two

Day 122. During the spring most of the cod landed was gutted and hung over drying poles in pairs to dry into stockfish

of drying, the cod were completely dehydrated but retained the protein and nutrition. As long as they were kept dry they were hard, and no bacteria or insect could penetrate them indefinitely. They would then be collected into dry airy warehouses where they were further dried and matured and made ready for export. Much of it was exported to the Mediterranean, with some of the lower quality fish going to West Africa.

The next day I got up early for the long cycle over to Bekkarfjord, or even Ifjord. It was a fine day, overcast, dry, and wind still. I made good time out of town, but Ifjord was a long way off, with two large hills to climb. The good progress didn't last long. After just 4 kilometres, and not even half way up the first hill, I had to stop. The saddle was desperately uncomfortable. I had suspected it might have been, so I had taken some tape. I cut a section off my foam mattress and taped it on. Then I cut another section and placed it between my underpants and trousers. It was instantly better and I climbed up the hill to around 300 metres in one go, and then started across the plateau to the south of Mehamn. After having the freedom to go where I wanted on skis, I felt very confined by the road. I did not like having to stick to a thin strip of tarmac, close to the sterile gravel, on the verge and the occasional crash barrier. There was little of interest along it. There were no plants bursting through the snow or ptarmigan hollows filled with their droppings. Now and again the repetitive cycling was excited by a ridge of spindrift which had blown on to the uniform tarmac, or a very infrequent car. I did see the occasional herd of reindeer. The speed I was going at was fantastic. Having been used to skis all year, I could not judge the distances on a bike well. I would see a landmark and assume I would reach it in half an hour. Yet within ten minutes I was long past it. The plateau itself was misty, and after a good three hours I was descending the south side of the Nordkinn plateau. Wary of the bicycle's quality, I cautiously descended to the narrow isthmus which connects the Nordkinn peninsula to the mainland at Hopseidet. The isthmus was only 500 metres wide and seemed to be mostly composed of boulders and gravel. I was very surprised that in the tragic seafaring history of north Norway, nobody had dug a channel here to avoid taking boats round the treacherous northern coast of Nordkinn. I would have to paddle this same hazardous coast in a month, and would be disappointed if impatience gets the better of valour, and I am forced to portage here rather than go round Kinnarodden, due to prolonged bad weather.

After Hopseidet, I had to repeat the morning exactly, with a steep and sustained climb up to around 350 metres and then 20 kilometres across the plateau. There were hardly any reindeer, or their tracks, here at all. Obviously they had been herded across the isthmus a few weeks previously, to their calving and summer grazing lands on the Kinnarodden peninsula. It was a fast cycle across this second plateau, which was again misty. Very infrequently a snowplough would pass, clearing a rare drift. Towards the southern end of the plateau the sun started to break through the mist occasionally, and there was a great view down to Torskefjorden. It was once inhabited, but the farms along the fjord are now abandoned and used as leisure houses. It was the first time I had seen trees for a week, and even if they were small, twisted birch, it was pleasant. Then came a lovely descent down the south side of this plateau to the rather idyllic hamlet of Bekkarfjord. I noticed just how much the snow here had gone in the week since I stayed. The streams were all open now and flowing in spate. Water dripped from every overhang. I dropped in to see the Jenssens, but the whole family, bar the quiet

Day 123. Half way across the second plateau there was a great view down into the valley where Torskefjorden cut into the peninsula

old dog were away. It was still early at 1430, and I had already done 72 kilometres with two big climbs. It was just another 34 kilometres to Ifjord, so I set off with gusto. The gusto soon ran out. The road was initially easy to Lebesby. It followed the rough coast of jagged outcrops with some gentle looking islands just offshore. After Lebesby, however, my energy ran out and I was getting very saddle sore. Although it was only 17 kilometres it took well over two hours. It was quite hilly and I opted to walk the uphill sections and freewheel down. I reached Ifjord motel just at the same time as the forecasted rain. It was not a luxurious place at all, but I was made to feel very welcome by Halvdan, the owner, and the Swedish couple who ran the motel. They seemed genuinely interested in my skiing adventures of the last week, since I left here heading north. I got the same room and after a double hamburger wrote. It was now pouring sleet outside and would have been thoroughly miserable to endure. It had been a good day, but my legs were tired and I was saddle sore. Tomorrow was another long day of 88 kilometres to Tana Bru, and I was worried my bum would not tolerate another long day in the saddle. Halvdan gave me more tape to further cushion the saddle with more foam, and that would hopefully postpone the inevitable torture.

Supremely fit as I was, I was just not used to cycling, and did not sleep well at all. Each time I moved in my sleep, my whole thigh started a massive cramp and this woke me up instantly. I then had to wait at least 30 seconds, sometimes a minute, before the painful spasm subsided. Occasionally, while I writhed on the bed, my movements would set the other thigh off, and I would have to endure a double helping of pain. When I got up at 0700 I felt tired and unrested. Not only were my legs stiff, but I was quite saddle sore. Yesterday's 10-hour cycle was well beyond my comfort zone on this painful bicycle. As I ate breakfast I gawped through the window at the pouring rain and sleet. It was 88 kilometres to Tana Bru with many ups and downs. The forecast said rain all day and then dry for the next week. I decided to stay put long before I finished breakfast. Later in the morning my phone rang. It was Kimek shipyard in Kirkenes. My kayak had just arrived and they had put it in an unused store where it would not get damaged. It was a huge relief as there was plenty of scope for a muddle here. It poured with cold rain all day and it seemed the death of winter and the birth of spring. I watched the river below the café swell through the day with large chunks of ice getting dislodged and carried down by the black oily current. All the small becks I skied over two weeks ago, when they were frozen solid under drifts, would now be swollen torrents fed by melting drifts. The decision to post the skis and cycle to Kirkenes was definitely the right one. There were four groups of people trying to ski the length of Norway behind me. They all started in mid January and were at least a month behind me. They had already endured this soggy end of winter, and the beginning of the 'spring loosening' in the last week as they were 1000 kilometres further south, and all of them had thrown in the towel. To do this ski trip comfortably one has to start in late December and be quite single minded about it. I had just made it by a few days and I had been relatively lucky with the weather throughout most of the winter.

I got up at 0600, and already the sun had been up for hours. It was an overcast day with a slight east breeze when I set off a couple of hours later. The east breeze was cold. I had to wear gloves and balaclava and most of the drips from overhangs had developed into small icicles. The road climbed up with purpose and within a few kilometres I was already at 200 metres and it was considerably colder in the bitter headwind. All yesterday's sleet was drifting around as snow up here, the road, however, was generally clear. In many places beside the road, there were some very impressive snow drifts which had built up all winter, with some of them well over five metres high. After passing a couple of cabin areas, probably owned by Sami, as they were beside lakes, the road continued to climb up on to the high and exposed plateau. It would have been miserable up here yesterday. As there was no other traffic, some of the drifts were far too deep to punch through on the bicycle, so I had to wade through them and haul the bicycle after me. It was still very wintery up here and I could easily have skied across this plateau; and it might have been quicker! At last came the long-awaited

Day 125. After leaving Ifjord I cycled up into the Ifjordfjellet mountains where there were still some impressive snowdrifts beside the road

Day 125. After crossing the bleak Ifjordfjellet mountains there was a nice run down through snowfields to Vestertanafjord

descent from the plateau down to Vestertana Fjord and the hamlet of Suorsjohka. I assumed this hamlet was Sjøsami, or Sea Lapp. These Sami did not participate in reindeer herding but lived beside, and eked a living from the sea. As I cycled round the bay I saw a white hare on the road. It was huge and bounded off with great leaps when it noticed me. There were also a couple of sea eagles in the bay. They are bigger than golden eagles and live largely from carrion and some fish they manage to catch, as opposed to the golden eagle which catches prey and only resorts to carrion in rare circumstances. This reflects a bit in their personality. The sea eagles look like scruffy vagrants compared to their cousins, with none of the pride and panache a golden eagle has.

The next 20 kilometres were along the coast and cutting over various headlands with quite a few steep ascents and descents. It was a cultural landscape with small homesteads beside the fjords where there was some flat land for grazing. There were occasional harbours with a few small fishing boats and the large high traditional A-frame shaped drying racks for the cod. I stopped at a small shop in the village of Ruostefielbma where some people recognized me from the article in that day's 'Finnmarken' newspaper, which I had not realized was published yet. The final 25 kilometres to Tana Bru was just what I needed. The road was flat as it headed south along an old moraine terrace above the largely frozen Tana river. The birch forest on this terrace was throwing off winter's imprisonment, and around each birch tree the warmer air had penetrated and melted a wide ring, which exposed the ground plants beneath. The whole hillside looked like a bundle of Dalmatian dogs; mostly white with masses of black spots. The Tana river is one of the great rivers of the north. It drains a huge area of north Norway and Finland. By the time it gets to Tana Bru it is ageing, but still virile enough not to meander across its flood plain. It carries down vast amounts of sand and gravel from the interior and deposits it as it reaches the fjord. The river was still largely frozen, but through gaps in the birch woods I could see there

Day 125. I had to pad the seat out well with some foam underlay to keep me from getting too saddle sore due to the rucksack

were some bare patches of open water and the ice of this slow section of river was starting to break up. It would be impossible to cross this river at this time of year without a bridge. That is what Tana Bru has, and it is why it is a reasonably important town. The Tana is also a very rich fishing river and has sustained populations of Sami along its banks for generations. These Sami were called Elvesami, or River Sami, and made up the third socio-economic group of the Sami. Like the Sjøsami, the Elvesami were more sedentary, with a home base and a number of satellite camps used for seasonal hunting and fishing. Along the Tana river the Elvesami could exploit the very rich salmon migrations and they also once hunted fur mammals, which they traded with Sjøsami and the previous Pomor Russian traders along the coast. There was just one hotel here, and

Day 125. The cycle round Vestertanafjord passed a few Sjøsami hamlets which were just starting to throw off the winter

Day 125. The mighty Tana river flowed in the broad valley from the centre to the left where it entered Tanafjord and discharged its flood

the manager gave me a very reasonable rate when he saw the two-page article about my journey, in the very paper he was reading.

I had already arranged a cabin to stay in at Grasbakken, some 40 kilometres to the east. The new padding on the seat helped to keep the saddle soreness to a bearable level, but after yesterday's 90 kilometres I was looking forward to a shorter day. Initially I cycled over the bridge which spanned the Tana river. It was flowing quite fast here and must have been 50 metres wide. Huge slabs of ice, nearly a metre thick and the size of half a tennis court, went drifting by under the bridge. They slammed into an ice jam further downstream with much crunching as they hit the jumbled build up. It seemed some of these vast slabs, weighing many hundreds of tonnes, were forced on to the bank where they had scythed down large birch trees and sometimes bulldozed great mounds of river bank in front of them before coming to a halt. It was a spectacular sight to see the awesome power of this melting river. After the bridge there was an easy 4 kilometres beside the river which flowed through narrow lakes and lagoons, and these were still covered in ice. However, some great chunks of it were breaking away to flow down to the ice jam below the bridge. From here the road now climbed up for a long gentle ascent which seemed to go for ever. There was an increasing easterly wind along this section and this slowed me considerably. Even on the gentle descent down the other side I could rarely freewheel because of the wind. After a good hour I reached the small town of Varangerbotn, which was at the head of a massive but quite open fjord. The head of this fjord was still covered in ice for a couple of kilometres, as it was now so far east the effects of the Gulf Stream were diminishing. I stopped here for a snack in a petrol station, and partly to rest and warm up before the next 20 kilometres along the south side of this massive fjord against the bitterly cold wind. Varangerbotn had a large collection of substantial and traditional wooden buildings which were very Sami in design. It was the regional offices of the Sami Parliament, or Samediggi, which had its headquarters in the Sami capital, Karasjok, in the interior of Finnmark.

The journey along the south side of the fjord was slow. The wind was a good force 4 and it was due east and directly against me. I frequently walked the uphill sections rather than pedal in the lowest gear. There was remarkably little snow here now. I think this whole region had received little this winter. Huge areas of the surrounding moorland were bare. The birch trees showed no signs of spring yet, but there were catkins bursting open on some of the willow bushes. There are at least 20 species of willow bush in Scandinavia, and some are so similar that the only way to tell them apart is when their catkins are showing, as they contain the differentiating features. There were a few ravens flying in the wind. They are remarkably acrobatic birds and seemed to be relishing the wind and the opportunities it gave them to show off their skills. They were constantly diving and twisting. There were many small homesteads along the road here. I assumed many were Sjøsami hamlets judging by some of the traditional outbuildings. None of the houses here are more than 65 years old, as the Germans laid waste to northern Norway when they retreated at the end of the Second World War. Only a few places were not completely burnt and destroyed. They did this so the advancing Russians would find no livestock, food or shelter. After passing through some of these small hamlets I came to Grasbakken. There were two log cabins here which had been transported whole from Pasvik in Finnmark's interior. They even had small birch trees growing out of their turf roofs. One was open for me, as arranged. It was already warm and cosy inside and I felt relieved to be out of the bitter wind. The father of the owner soon arrived for a chat and to collect payment. He was extremely friendly, and curious about my journey. Because of his size and stature, I assumed he was a Sjøsami, but then culture and ethnicity along the Finnmark coast is a bit of a melting pot, and it is impossible to generalize. Alarmingly, he said I had come at the wrong time. In May, he said, it was a constant strong east wind. I should have waited for June! After he left I melted into the luxurious chair and enjoyed the soporific warmth. I am not taking to cycling like a duck to water, and it is hard work on both legs and rump in the headwind. I know my rucksack is partly to blame for my rump, but panniers are hard to come by in Finnmark, at short notice.

Day 127. The Sjøsami museum at Byluft had a wealth of old fishing artefacts such as longlines, glass buoys, Nordland boats and nets

I peered mournfully out of the window in the morning and saw it was still a good easterly wind with the occasional snow shower. The first 10 kilometres were cold and miserable with the wind directly against me and occasionally blowing the passing sleet shower down my neck. There were plenty of white horses in the fjord and the wind must have been a good force 4. It took a good hour to reach Byluft village with the wind sapping my strength and the sleet showers sapping my spirits. At Byluft there was a sign for a Sjøsami museum. Usually I would just cycle past in a determined way, but the thought of getting out of the weather was very appealing. As it turned out, it was quite fascinating. The museum was owned and run by Helmer Losoa. He was a Sjøsami and had grown up and lived at this homestead for some 70 years. During this time he had amassed, collected and beach-combed a large shed full of artefacts from coastal life in Finnmark. He explained this was a Sjøsami stronghold and many of the hamlets I had been through, and also on the north side of Varangerfjord, were entirely composed of them. Helmer was rightly proud of his heritage and also his collection. There were the traditional Nordlandsk boats which the Sjøsami would fish from, old fishing nets with pieces of wood and bags of sand as floats and weights respectively. There were longlines with a hundred hooks and glass buoys filling the boats. There was a wall with Sjøsami costumes, including his mother's dresses, many old skis and the traditional Sami shoe, with the curled pointed toe, to fit under a strap on the ski binding. There were many farm instruments and also a Sjøsami gamme, or turf shelter. I could go on, such was the richness of his collection, which were all genuine articles. After looking through this collection we went out. It was nearly a blizzard now, so he invited me in for a coffee. We chatted about the plight of the Sjøsami. He intimated that the Sjøsami and Elvesami are the poorer, lower status Sami, while the Fjellsami (Mountain Sami) are the richer, higher status Sami due to their large reindeer herds. The Fjellsami, Helmer insinuated, consider themselves a cut above their more sedentary cousins. But such is the disdain which pastoralists and nomads throughout the world's history have felt over their agricultural neighbours whom they consider to be feeble and torpid.

Day 127. Typical Sjøsami dresses in the museum at Byluft. Many of the dresses belonged to the museum owner's mother

The blizzard soon passed and I reluctantly left and continued past Gandvik, battling against the wind for another 10 kilometres or so, until I got the turn off to Bugøynes some 20 kilometres out on a peninsula to the east. I did not know it, but within a week I would be staying at this charming fishing village. Just beyond was Brannsletta, a protected area, which was a geographical feature rather than a place. It was a glacial delta some 12,000 years ago. As the glaciers flowed into the sea here, channels under the ice deposited large amounts of sand and gravel in ridges called eskers. When the ice withdrew, these eskers became exposed and were

Day 127. A traditional Sami shoe made from reindeer skin showing how the front hook fits on to the simple binding on a wooden ski

further transformed by glacial lakes upstream bursting, and also by the erosion of sea waves as this landscape was 100 metres lower due to the thick ice sheets pressing the land's surface down. Huge stranded ice blocks were also once found here, as icebergs and stationary glacial remnants became isolated and stranded on the eskers. When these vast ice remnants eventually melted, they left depressions in the valley floors which are seen today and are often filled with water. Once the ice sheets had melted, and their weight flowed away, the land has slowly risen some 100 metres so the old beaches are now exposed well above sea level. It was a fascinating delta and valley for glacier enthusiasts. From here it was still some 40 kilometres to Neiden, but thankfully the route was much easier and the wind rapidly diminished as I went inland. The first 20 kilometres were up this glacial valley and then over a pass before the descent to Burgøyfjord. This verdant dairy hamlet had about 10 farms and 20 houses, and was located at the end of a very steep-sided fjord, more reminiscent of south west Norway. From Burgøyfjord the road followed a huge open valley. It was sleeting heavily again, but between showers I could see two vast marshes on my west. The first was Sakrismyra, and the second was Ferdesmyra. Both seemed to be at least five kilometres across or twenty square kilometres. These would be very important breeding grounds for the numerous marsh-loving bird species in a month or so. The more southerly Ferdesmyra marsh was protected as a nature reserve. From this second marsh I enjoyed an easy descent to Neiden, past a spectacular set of rapids crashing over rocky shelves and ice buttresses as the large Neidenelv river plunged towards the sea. The only place to stay was a very scruffy hotel, which had just been unlocked after being boarded up for a couple of years. It was irritatingly expensive, but it was now late in the evening and I was exhausted, so I threw in the towel and stayed.

I left the hotel at 1030 the next morning on a beautiful warm day with the sun out and no wind. The first challenge was the hill out of Neiden. The descent down the other side took me into Munkelvdalen, at the head of Munkfjorden. The head of this fjord, where the Munkelv river flowed into it, was a very shallow delta. A bit further north the Neidenelv river also flowed into this fjord, creating another vast shallow delta which just about stretched across the fjord. These two areas are shallow enough to be covered and uncovered by the tides so the whole area is brackish. This, together with the nutrient rich deposits carried down into the deltas by the rivers, meant the area is excellent for silt-dwelling organisms. These organisms provide a rich feeding ground for waders, ducks, geese, and many other different species observed here. Some

Day 128. The deltas of the Munkelv and Neidenelv rivers formed big fertile deltas in Munkfjorden which were a magnet for wading birds

species are able to spend the entire winter here without migrating. Of particular interest are the 400 or so black throated divers and the 100 red throated divers which gather here in the spring. Once the road passed the deltas it continued north up the fjord. There was remarkably little snow now and it really felt like spring, but I could not see any buds on the birch trees yet. There was a nice view out to the large Skogerøya island, which split the fjord into two. Along the coast, here were huge rafts of eider ducks enjoying the sun. The scene made me eager to get to Kirkenes, get rid of the bicycle and get into my kayak. I had to leave the coast again and follow the road through the dull brown landscape, which was still bland after recently emerging from winter's snow cover. I cycled past the small Kirkenes Airport before the descent to Langfjorden. This fjord was topped up by the sea at high tide and emptied over some considerable rapids at low tide. It

Day 128. Looking across Neidenfjord, teeming with eider ducks to Skogerøya island on the right and the mainland in the distance

was low tide when I passed and there was quite a flow of water gushing out into the bay. After another climb I was soon on the descent to Kirkenes, which was much bigger than I expected, it was perhaps the biggest town I had been in all year. I sped down the hill to the town centre where the hotel and Kimek shipyard was.

I saw the shipyard from a distance, it was difficult to miss it. It was by far the biggest building in Kirkenes and the only landmark needed. The hotel was also easy to find. I had been warned about the Barents Frokosthotell wherever I had been in the last week, and was expecting the worst, as it had a reputation as a dive for hardy, rough Russian sailors. It was by far the cheapest hotel in Kirkenes. However, I was very pleasantly surprised, as the hotel was newly refurbished and most of the guests were sober Norwegians. It would suit my purposes perfectly; to prepare for my kayaking trip, so I locked up the bike and enjoyed a shower. I then went over to Kimek to meet Stein, who has been absolutely invaluable to this whole operation. Kimek is a huge concern, repairing large Russian trawlers, and it was recommended as a delivery address for my kayak by the Kirkenes Tourist Office months ago. Stein was the contact at Kimek and he said he would receive my kayak when it came off the lorry and store it until I arrived, all on a voluntary basis. He had put my kayak in an unused store shed. He gave me a key to the shed, giving me full access to my equipment over the weekend. It could not get better, but it did, as Stein also gave me a very generous donation from some people at Kimek to the cause I was raising money for; to build schools in the Limi Valley in Nepal. Stein showed me round the shipyard and explained many of the operations they did on some of the rusting hulks of Russian trawlers they received for repair. I asked why Russian trawlers would come to get repaired at Kirkenes, with obviously higher costs, and he explained that it was because the shipyards in Russia were so unreliable. When my tour of the shipyard was over, the very helpful Stein headed off for his weekend, and I returned to the store shed and unwrapped my kayak. She looked superb. The finish was tremendous, the extras all looked well fitted and the shape and size were all I had hoped for. The moulds for the kayak were not even made when I ordered it, so I went on what Tiderace promised the finished article would be. At first sight, it was better than promised. All my kayaking equipment and clothing was inside the kayak, having been shipped to Finland, where the boat was made, and then transported up to Kirkenes with it. I unpacked all the equipment and took it back to the hotel. I had the whole weekend to sort out all the pieces I wanted for kayaking and pack the pieces to get shipped to Oslo, like my ski boots, which were the only shoes I had worn all year. It would be wetsuit booties from now on, exclusively. At the hotel, the postman had delivered my small laptop and a new GPS with 1:50,000 maps already loaded on it, both had been sent from friends in the south of Norway. I had hoped to paddle the coast with a 1:400,000 road map for general orientation, and a GPS to give detail when I needed it for landings or camping spots. It had been a great day, I was relieved to be in Kirkenes, united with all the equipment I needed for my kayak trip.

I slept well and had to use the blackout blinds to darken the room from the very long daylight hours. The first thing I wanted to do was to amble around Kirkenes. I also wanted to get some ideas for food which would do me for a two-week stretch. It was a lovely warm day as I headed out. The hotel was pretty much in the centre of Kirkenes, so everything was very easy and convenient. I sauntered around with the relaxed air of someone on holiday, which I suppose I was, for a couple of days. I pretty much located everything I wanted and got some ideas for food by the time the shops started to close for the weekend, around mid afternoon. There were a few other guests at the hotel, including two men from Bodø, who would be staying a couple of days doing a construction job. One of them was a keen sailor and had a share of a very traditional 42-foot Nordlandsbåt. These boats have a large square sail, and this one also had a rare topsail. It is an iconic boat and quite reminiscent of the Viking boats. He showed me a 10-minute film of the boat on his laptop, from a trip to Brest in Brittany last year for a traditional boat gathering. It was a beautiful craft. By the end of the weekend I had worked out what equipment and food I needed to buy, and had gone through all my recently-arrived equipment to make sure everything was as it should be. I then started packing some of the many dry bags and tried to work out what would go where in the kayak. I had arranged for the kayak to be transported the 60 kilometres to Grense Jakobselv, which is Norway's border with Russia, in a couple of days on Wednesday. I would have to walk or cycle to the border on Wednesday. It all seemed to be going according to plan so far, which I viewed with nervous satisfaction.

Over the next two days I went to the sports shop and bought a petrol stove, a couple of fuel bottles and some clean petrol. This stove is heavier than my gas stove, which I will also take, but burns far hotter without giving out condensation. Its heat output is 3000 watts so it should warm the tent in no time and dry clothing quickly.

I now had my bigger Macpac Olympus tent, which is heavier than the Macpac Minaret I used for the ski tour, but gives me much more room. I could not find any flares at all so gave up on them. I then went food shopping and filled a trolley. In the end I only bought food for 10 days, but it was still a considerable pile. At the hotel I packed it into 24 hour packs, so each evening in the tent I would open another pack which would contain dinner, the next day's breakfast and lunch. I packed it into three dry bags; each one weighing about six kilos. I had not been too careful with weight and volume, as I usually keep each day's rations to less than a kilo. I went to the post office to check the maximum weight for a parcel to Oslo. It seemed I could send up to 25 kilos, which was more than I was expecting. This was good news, as I could send everything I did not want back to Oslo in one go. When the package finally reached Øivind he picked it up and took it home. He thought it was very light as he had been expecting more. He opened it to find an acoustic guitar. Somehow the labels had got mixed up, and a bemused musician near Øivind received a rucksack, full of worn out and filthy skiing equipment. After a fair bit of amusement, everything was rectified. On the Tuesday afternoon I managed to track down a ship's supplier who could get some flares, so I ordered them. Unfortunately, they would not arrive for a couple of days, but they would send them to Bugøynes where I could pick them up from a King Crab dealer. After many hours packing, I then had to carry all the bags from the hotel to the shed where my kayak was stored. It was a huge pile. I have got quite used to bigger boats at around 380 litres and the Tiderace Xplore X was in that category. However, I had never had a skeg before, and was surprised at how much room it takes up. After a few hours I had pretty much everything in the boat. The last evening in Kirkenes I decided to have a pizza. I heard the staff at the pizzeria speaking Kurdish, so I threw a few Kurdish words in myself. They were surprised, and wanted to know how I could speak a few words. I told them that some 25 years ago I had spent a couple of summers with some Kurdish pastoralists as they moved around the mountains of south east Turkey with their black tents and herds of sheep and goats. When I came to pay, they said it was free.

When the day came to leave Kirkenes I had done just about done everything I needed to do, except get the flares and some tide tables. The tide tables were not that necessary, as I felt I would soon get an intuitive timing for the flow and ebb. It did not really matter too much about the tide as I was not going to wait for them. If I was in a sound and it was against me, I would just have to find eddies or pause, and if it was with me, I was lucky. The tides here were smaller in amplitude than in the UK, but there were larger amounts of water on the move. The range of the rise and fall of the tides would be biggest just after a new moon and a full moon and smallest at the half moons. The greater the range the greater the flow of currents. I did not even know what phase the moon was at as I had not seen it for ages due to the near 24 hour daylight. I put Vidar's bicycle on the Hurtigruten ferry, where it would return to Mehamn and then went down to Kimek's shed where my kayak was, and waited for my transport to Grense Jakobselv on the Russian border. The previous year I had met a Norwegian skier, Ole, who had skied the length of Norway and had got buried in the avalanche for 10 hours, which I mentioned earlier. We had skied the length of Jostedalsbreen later, before he joined the army and got posted to Kirkenes. He used his contacts here to ask if there was anyone at the border post who would drive my kayak from Kirkenes to the Russian border. One of the officers at the border post volunteered, and even offered to bring a bicycle for me to cycle the road while he drove. It was this officer I was now waiting on and he arrived punctually at midday.

His name was James, an unusual name for a Norwegian I thought. He was an imposing man at 1.95 metres high. We chatted in Norwegian about my trip and his job. I asked about his name and he said he was half Scottish. His mother was from Mallaig and he had spent some school years there. He even had relations on the Isle of Skye who I had met once when I lived there. We switched to English, and his broad West Coast dialect was completely untarnished with any Norwegian accent. It is a small world, I thought. We unpacked the loaded kayak into the van and then put the kayak on the roof. He then set off and I followed on the bike. Immediately, I realized something was seriously wrong with the crankshaft on the bike. I took it to the two sports shops in town. They were not interested and said it would make it the 60 kilometres, without even looking at it. I was not so sure, but had no choice. With the clunking crankshaft I peddled off on the road to Murmansk. Just after the turn off to Grense Jakobselv, and after only 25 kilometres, the whole thing fell to pieces. I cursed. There was still 35 kilometres to go. I could use the bike as a scooter for the flatter sections and freewheel the downhill sections, but it would still take at least six hours. I phoned James, now back at the border post with his team, on duty. He said he would see what he could do.

Day 133. The road between Kirkenes and Grense Jakobselv passed the frozen Jarfjordfjellet mountains with winter still in this tundra

It was a very pleasant walk along the road at the southern end of the Jarfjord. The sun was out and the sea was calm. The tide was also out, exposing silt flats and seaweed beds. Then I started the long climb up to the Jarfjordfjellet mountains. Here, the road climbed to almost 200 metres. It was a different world up here. The lakes were still ice-covered, and the hillsides had considerable snow on them. The drifts at the side of the road were a few metres high. This section of road is blocked in the winter. Just before the top, an army jeep stopped, and a chirpy young soldier hopped out with a bike. It was in perfect working order. He took the knackered bike. It was a nice pleasant cycle across these mountains for another 10 kilometres. There were a few lakes under the steep ramparts of many dark crags. The run down to the border post was quick, but cold. In the valley I was heading down to was the Jakobselv river. The deepest point of the river was the border with Russia, so as the meanders move slowly over the decades, so does the border. On the other side of the river was a birch forest with large snow patches still, and this was Russian territory. James showed me round the border post and the vehicles. One vehicle which was especially robust was a two sectioned troop carrier with four belts for traction. It was amphibious and could go through the soggy spring forest with deep icy pools without any problem. From this border post there were many smaller lookout posts where soldiers monitored the border up the entire valley.

There was still another 10 kilometres to the sea itself, so I set off on the bike. There were a few farms down here, but all agricultural activity was abandoned some 30 years ago, and the farms were mostly leisure houses now. The problem was the blocked winter road. The military had their winter vehicles, but the farmers did not, and it was too difficult to eke out a living here. There were some 10 farms and 40 cabins in the valley. The river ran on my east, often flowing swiftly through piles of ice-chunk debris and trees, as it was in spate. James caught up at the Oscar II Kapell, the much photographed church, built to try and encourage a community and establish Norwegian sovereignty here some 100 years ago. Just beyond this chapel was the beach. It was a kilometre of fine sand with a couple of smaller beaches nearby. It was supposed to be one of Norway's finest beaches, but I had seen many finer ones. I cycled to the west end of the beach where the road, and the rather fraught 400-kilometre bicycle ride from Mehamn came to an end. The cycle ride was really a way of linking the two main courses of this journey without resorting to vehicles. Despite the best efforts of cheap Chinese bicycles to hamper my cycling trip, it had been interesting and enjoyable. Cycle touring is not really for me, though, as I find the confines of the road far too limiting. It had not been a planned, or well-organized section, but if I did it again the only difference

Day 133. Looking down into the valley where the Jakobselv river flowed marking the border with Russia lying on the valley's far side

Day 133. The end of the 400 km cycle ride was the beach at Grense Jakobselv where the Oscar II Kapell was sited to mark Norwegian land

Day 133. The Tiderace Xplore X kayak at Grense Jakobselv with the first few kilometres of the paddle to the headland on the right

I would make was to have a better bicycle which also had panniers. We unpacked the van and unloaded the kayak, we then went for a walk around the area at the end of the beach. The border post, traditionally, has a weekly swim here every week of the year. In January or February the air temperature can be -30 centigrade, so warm vehicles are used to dry off in, after an icy sprint back up the dark beach after the swim – where the soldiers had to get their heads under the water. There was none of that today. It was a warm +6 degrees in the air with a few streaks of snow on the hill. The waves were relatively small and the sun was going to set in a half an hour. It was a very pleasant evening. There was the odd iceberg which had got swept out of the river and was melting on the shore. James told me the water temperature was around +3 throughout the year. After James left, the sun just dipped below the horizon. In a week it would not set at all at these latitudes. I put up my tent, collected some water and cooked supper on my new petrol stove, which warmed the tent up very quickly.

There was another paddler, Tom Amundsen, who was also doing the same trip. He set off from here about a week ago. I found a good luck message he wrote with stones in the sand. It read "LYKKE TIL JAMES – TOM", which was a very nice touch. He was already up in the Båtsfjord area so I would be unlikely to catch him up. As I went to bed on the sandy grass, I had a chance to reflect on the enormity of the journey I was about to take. I did not have the same apprehension as I did at Lindesnes the night before the ski trip, in fact, I was eager to start. However, there can be no doubting that the kayaking section is a more serious undertaking than the skiing section. The mere fact knowing Tom was on the same journey, albeit, some 200 kilometres ahead, made me less apprehensive. I woke early and listened to the rain on the tent. It was not heavy, but it seemed

Day 134. The beach at Grense Jakobselv was right on the Russian border and there were Russian watchtowers on the central knoll

consistent. There was little wind and the tent barely flapped. The skies were dark with clouds which were hardly moving. It looked like the wet weather was here for a while. The forecast said all day. Rain does not really hamper the kayaker at all. It is of little consequence, compared to wind, which is the big factor. However, it makes breaking camp a bit of a nuisance. In addition, I had a lot of writing to do which I had postponed for the last few days. I made a start on this and finished at midday, with the rain still falling. It would have been perfectly possible to start kayaking, but given the good weather forecast for the next few days which would still allow me to cross Varangerfjord I decided to wait a day. I settled into my warm bag for a siesta, with the rain still splashing on to the tent and I did not wake until 1700. After supper I went for a walk along each of the beaches. At the far end of the bigger beach was the Jakobselv river, and beyond that a Russian lookout post on a knoll. The smaller beach was perhaps the nicer of the two, as it was more sheltered and was hemmed in by outcrops.

SECTION 19. Mehamn to Grense Jakobselv by Bike
14 days. 398 kilometres. 43 hours. 4300m ascent. 4260m descent.

THE KAYAK: SECTION 20. VARANGERFJORD

THE KAYAK: SECTION 20. VARANGERFJORD

I woke early in eager anticipation. It was overcast, but dry and there was just a slight breeze from the north. I went back into the tent for breakfast and started to pack everything into drybags. I then got into my new drysuit. This all took much longer than I had anticipated, as I dithered nervously, checking and double checking everything. After about three hours I was finally ready to pack the kayak. I carried it down to the smaller beach and then did two journeys with the drybags threaded along my arms. It took a while to get everything in, but I had more room in the kayak this time than in Kimek's shed when I tried it initially. With everything in, I had final contemplation, dragged the kayak across the wet sand, sat down in the seat with my legs astride, then put each leg in, pushed off and took my first stroke at 0930. It was the first time I had been in this kayak.

Day 135. The small beach at Grense Jakobselv with the kayak packed and ready to launch for its epic voyage

It felt comfortable, stable and reasonably fast. It was all I had hoped for. It kept a good line with the rudder up and turned reasonably well when I leaned it. Before long I was halfway across the bay and starting to relax in the calm conditions. The landscape on the mainland was desolate; almost prehistoric. The hills were dark, bare, barren rock and around 300 metres high. They had been rounded smooth by previous ice ages, and the hollows and crevices were covered in numerous patches of snow. It was a bleak wasteland in today's misty weather.

As I paddled along this wild Arctic coast there were all the usual sea birds I was acquainted with when paddling in Scotland. Their familiarity was comforting in this hostile environment. There were masses of eider duck, the male brilliant white and black and the female a drab speckled brown, around all the islands in the bay. They had mostly collected into rafts on the sheltered south sides of the islands where the water was calm and glassy. There were also many black guillemot, or tystie,

Day 135. Crossing the first small fjord after the launch on a damp but calm day, with snow on the coastal mountains down to the shoreline

out in the more exposed bays. These birds were more solitary. On a few of the headlands, nervous shags plunged into the water while I was still a few hundred metres away. There were all the usual gulls with the blackbacks and herring gulls being the most widespread. Along the shore, small flocks of stints quickly hopped up and down on the washed rocks, following the rise and fall of the swell as they searched frantically for small insects. If I approached too closely the stints rose as one, and the entire flock twisted and turned in the air at speed, like a single bird, before they eventually settled on some rocks further along the shore.

I passed Pasvik, a large lonely bay with steep crags around it, where there was an austere simple cabin on the rocky land behind the shore. This house was obviously a fishing and collecting base of perhaps Sjøsami origin. Just beyond it I started to cross the mouth of Jarfjord which was about 5 kilometres across. It had some skerries at its mouth. I wondered if it was

Day 135. The lonely Pasvik bay where there was a single cabin which is probably used as a base for subsistance fishing and collecting

217

Day 135. At Holmengråfjord there was a satellite Sjøsami hamlet of wooden cabins and some old traditional turf gamme as above

moraine debris the glacier front had deposited or if it was the lip of a basin the glacier had carved. Both are quite common features of fjords. On the west side of Jarfjord was Holmengråfjord. I went into its entrance and spotted some old cabins. There must be a landing nearby I thought, so I headed for them and managed to land at a boulder beach behind a small island. There was a collection of some 10 cabins. Some had the old Sjøsami gamme beside them. There were many empty racks to dry fish on. Around a lot of the cabins there was fishing equipment piled up, some of which looked like it had not been used for a while. Indeed, the cabins were somewhat tired, with peeling paint, rusty hinges and bleached shutters. It was obviously an old Sjøsami fishing base, used for a short period each year as one of many, and had now become partially abandoned.

During the paddle past Pasvik I felt the left footrest fall off as I wriggled back into my seat. I assumed it had just come off the rails. An inspection of the rudder did not bring happy thoughts. It was completely broken. The footrest and pedal had snapped at the neck. It was totally unrepairable. I was fuming. It looked as if the plastic neck had sheared because it was just too brittle. There were some hairline cracks in it, as in a burnt Bakelite saucepan handle. I know the new owner of Smarttrack rudders shifted manufacture from the US to China and there was obviously not the same expertise with the plastic mix or curing process. My blood was boiling but luckily there was no phone reception for me to vent my frustration. I had been wary about the rudder when I ordered it, as it did not fold away and was always exposed. I thought the blade might break off, so I also had a skeg fitted, as a back-up. However, I had not expected to deploy the skeg after just 15 kilometres of easy paddling.

I continued west with improving weather round this peninsula to Bøkfjord fyr lighthouse. It was the last lighthouse in Norway to become automated and was manned right up to 2006. When it became unmanned it ended a 350-year-old culture which started at Lindesnes with the first manned lighthouse in Norway. The lighthouse sat squatly on an outcrop by the shore and beside it was the large white well-kept keeper's house. Down by the shore were a couple of red sheds near a jetty where supplies like diesel, for the generators, were unloaded. This was a very important lighthouse, as it marked the entrance to the fjord up which Kirkenes sheltered, and Kirkenes is probably the most important harbour east of Tromsø, and also the end of the Hurtigruten ferry line. From this lighthouse I could see Kim Island, my goal for the day, only some 15 kilometres away. I had to cross the open mouth of Bøkfjord to reach it. The crossing was broken by Kjelmsøya, a large barren island with many rocky islets and skerries off its north coast. There were a lot of terns in the vicinity and I presumed there must be a colony on one of these islets. I could not be sure they were Arctic terns, as opposed to common terns, as the only obvious difference is the former has a clean red beak, while the latter have a black tip on their red beaks. If they were Arctic terns they would have migrated all the way from the Antarctic to their summer breeding grounds up here in the Arctic, before returning again to the Antarctic. This 75,000 kilometre round trip each year is the longest annual migration of any animal. As I crossed the second half of the fjord the weather cleared, and I had to reach for my sunglasses as the reflection from the late afternoon rays shone directly into my eyes and warmed my face. The dark mood that lingered over my frustration with the shoddy rudder system slowly started to lift as

Day 135. The coastline near Bøkfjord fyr was barren and very little could grow on the sparse soil in this harsh Arctic climate

I approached Kim. I wanted to land here as it was a blackback gull nesting colony. I had heard some locals still came out to such places to collect some of the large eggs at this time of year. A week or two later the eggs would be fertilized and contain embryos, but at this time they just had large yokes. As I approached the island I could see it was covered in nesting gulls, and from just above the shoreline to near the top, gulls squatted on their nests or stood beside them, watching me with suspicion. I had no doubt they would have launched a noisy aerial attack to harry and ward me off if I stepped ashore. I went round the island to try and find a place to land but there was just too much swell to find anywhere without bashing the shiny new gelcoat.

Day 135. The seldom-used Sjøsami hamlet at Skogerøyvær beach comprises five wooden cabins used to fish and collect eggs

I searched for an alternative spot to spend the night, and spotted a beach about 2 kilometres to the south. As I paddled towards the beach I noticed some simple wooden cabins, which were probably once a seasonal Sjøsami hamlet, used for a few weeks a year to fish and collect eggs on Kim. The hamlet was called Skogerøyvær. As I continued towards the beach I thought I saw smoke, or my eyes were playing tricks in the evening light. But soon I could see without any doubt, it was indeed, smoke. I made a beeline for it, and a few hundred metres out I spotted a kayak. This was the only vessel I had seen all day on this remote hostile coast, and it was a bit of a 'Man Friday moment'. When I landed, the other paddler, Jon, came down to meet me. We had a quick chat before I found somewhere to pitch my tent on grass and heather on the large, flat, shelf which was the older raised beach, beyond the sand and boulders. With the tent up, I had to strip down and remove the entire rudder system from the kayak. I now realized how over-designed, over-complicated and over-priced the Smarttrack rudder system is. The rudder systems on my other kayaks, and on other kayaks I have tried, are far more robust, simpler and easier to repair in the field. Once this cancer was removed, I had to fashion some footrests from a fortuitous slab of foam I found lying on the otherwise pristine beach, so my feet could brace against something until the footrests were repaired.

This whole operation took a couple of hours, but I could now return to the beach where Jon was throwing ever increasing amounts of bleached driftwood on to the roaring fire. I learnt he was also intending to paddle Norway's entire coast. He too had started from Grense Jakobselv, but had taken three days to get here at his relaxed tempo. He told me he had just started kayaking a year ago. He had picked quite a voyage to inaugurate his second year as a kayaker. I liked his optimism and ambition. It was admirable, if not a little crazy. With the pair of us throwing unlimited supplies of driftwood on to the fire we had a roaring blaze and had to move our log seats back. The sun headed towards the horizon at a very shallow angle; soon it would not even reach the horizon. Beside this fire in the setting sun it could almost have been Greece or the Caribbean with the calm sea lapping on the sandy shore. When I moved away from the fire, though, I was quickly reminded I was still in the Arctic, and that frost had been forming on the tent some 50 metres away.

Day 135. Kayaker Jon Westgård enjoying the driftwood fire on Skogerøyvær beach at midnight with the sun barely below the horizon

I had stiff shoulders when I woke the next morning. The sun had already been powerful for a few hours and all the dampness which had accrued on my camping equipment over the last couple of days had evaporated, leaving everything crisp. Outside it was a glorious day and it was almost completely windstill. Today I just had to paddle the short distance to Bugøynes to pick up my flares and try and sort out what to do with the rudder system. I had not intended to come so far into the vast funnel, which is Varangerfjord, before crossing to the north shore, but the flares and rudder made it necessary. This also suited Jon, and we decided to try and find a cabin there for the night. He was ready before I was and set off across the smooth glassy bay, creating a small bow wave which was still visible after many hundred metres. When I left there were some porpoises rising in the bay. I paddled past the headland towards the north side of Kjøøya island which was set at the mouth of a dark steep-sided fjord. I passed the island and then headed north west towards Bugøynes itself across 8 kilometres of open water. There was a very gentle swell behind me and a very slight breeze against me, so conditions were perfect. The makeshift footrest I had made seemed to be working and gave me something to push against and stopped me slouching. I noticed how quickly the birdlife diminished as I left the coast. It was a very easy crossing, taking only about an hour and a half until I approached the base of the cliffs and snow-filled gullies on the west side. I then turned north for a kilometre to enter the sheltered Bugøynes harbour which was enveloped by the protective Bugøy island.

Day 136. Entering Bugøynes harbour from the east where the king crab wharfs are and paddling towards the isthmus where the church is

The harbour had a number of jetties and seemed to be a place for the larger boats to land their catches of king crabs. There were at least two wharfs to process them. Otherwise the small town seemed very charming. I landed at the beach where Jon had already arrived. I then went to investigate my flares. The first thing which struck me about Bugøynes was just how helpful and friendly everybody was. At the shop/post office/chemist the owner bent over backwards, contacting everybody who might know the whereabouts of my flares. They had not arrived. I telephoned the firm in Kirkenes and told them to sort it out. They would just have to get some to Vardø. The shop owner offered us coffee. While sitting there, everybody who came into the shop chatted. It seemed Bugøynes had a population of just 220, a secondary school and a couple of king crab businesses. It also had a research station into these recent crustacean arrivals which were becoming big business. It had a quaint church and some nice older houses spread out on the peninsula. I later found out that this charming town was not burnt by the Germans at the end of the war. The commander of the garrison stationed here was considered to be a gentleman. As Bugøynes did not have a road, he was dependant on local fishermen to evacuate his troops when the order came. Contrary to instructions he made a deal to spare the town in return for this evacuation. After he reached Tana he was reprimanded and told to return to raze the town. However, other retreating Germans had destroyed the bridge over the mighty Tana river and he could not re-cross. On his return to Germany he was jailed as a traitor for the last months of the war. I was told he returned as a tourist in the 1960s and was warmly welcomed by the people of Bugøynes. This was not usually the case in Finnmark. Even today, many people, especially the older ones, still harbour resentment about that meticulous destruction of all the farms, homes, boats and even churches.

There were some cabins to rent on the other side of town. It was a half-kilometre walk, or a 2-kilometre paddle round the small hammerhead peninsula, to the west beach on the other side of the isthmus. Naturally the paddle was much easier and we could look across the large Varangerfjord. On the other side was the town of Vadsø under a snow-covered plateau. It was

Day 136. Approaching the beach on the west side of Bugøynes isthmus with the church rising above the cabins

tomorrow's task to cross this vast fjord and I hoped I had not squandered the calm weather on today's pleasant, tame paddle. The beach on the west side was idyllic. It was some 200 metres of very light brown sand overlooked by a few houses and the same church which we saw from the other side. At the south end of this beach were five small log cabins. Jon and I took one for the night from the lady who rented them. Her ancestors had come from Finland and settled on the Norwegian coast some 100 years previously in the Kven migrations. These Kven were impoverished Finns who relocated to Finnmark 100-200 years ago to eke out an existence on Finnmark's coast alongside the Sjøsami, or to find work in the burgeoning fishing industry.

Day 137. Our host, Elsa, in her traditional Nordlandsbunad dress which she donned to celebrate the 17th of May, Norway's National Day

It was a second absolutely stunning morning, with a reasonably calm sea lapping at the golden sands below the cabin, under blue skies and a warm bright sun. It was also the 17th of May, which is Norway's National Day. Norwegians are very patriotic. Not in a disturbing or assertive way, far from it, they are patriotic in a very comfortable and confident manner. I think much of this is because Norwegians still have a strong sense of belonging to rural communities; communities where the same families have been connected for very many generations over centuries. They are justifiably proud of this attachment and it gives them strength in a fast changing world. There was no industrial revolution here to uproot and disenfranchise people from their rural heritage. Throughout Norway a lot of preparation goes into the 17th of May, but one thing above all is a spring clean. Winter has gone, and the gravel on the pavements, the litter uncovered by melting snow, even leaves and twigs in the garden have to be tidied up. The whole country gets a polish in the weeks before, with gangs of schoolchildren helping to collect litter, and the fire departments hosing down the streets. Once the country is clean, the flags come out, the Bunad, or national dress, gets unpacked and the country is ready to celebrate liberation from Sweden in 1905, after centuries of Danish and Swedish domination. Brass bands march, there are various parades, everybody is in a good mood and a fair amount of alcohol consumed. Today, the flag waving will probably be extra vigorous, because Norway won the Eurovision Song Contest last night, and it is still taken somewhat seriously here. Jon was enthused by the celebrations and took a tour into town while I repaired and modified a few things on my kayak. By midday we were both ready to celebrate the 17th of May by paddling across Varangerfjord to Vadsø and beyond. I looked at Jon's packed kayak in disbelief. He had so much stuff he could not cram it all into the hatches. The remainder went into two very sturdy drybags which were attached over the fore and aft hatches. While it might be OK on this calm day, there was no way he could paddle the approaching exposed coasts of Østhavet, Nordishavet and Lopphavet with such a top-heavy load. The wind resistance would be huge and any surf washing over the boat would make it very unstable. To roll this kayak, one would need great technique and the strength of a long-haired Samson, and Jon was as bald as me.

There were a few eider duck when we came through the small collection of islands and started across the Varangerfjord. The town of Vadsø on the other side of the fjord looked much closer than the 13 kilometres it was, and it looked a large town, like Kirkenes. We decided to veer to the east of it and towards the village of Kiby. The view ahead was of the tame, flat, snow-covered Varanger peninsula, while to the south I could look down the dark rugged coast broken by deep fjords. It looked like a dramatic postcard from here, and a lot more impressive than when I paddled along it on

Day 137. Leaving Bugøynes and heading across Varangerfjord to the town of Vadsø 13km across the fjord just to the left of the kayak

Day 137. Jon Westgård crossing Varangerfjord with his kayak decks piled high. In the background is the southern shoreline of Varangerfjord

my first day. After nearly three hours we finally landed on the small sandy beach at Kiby for lunch. As we set off mid afternoon the skies were darkening and the forecast north easterly breeze was beginning to blow. Despite the wind directly against us we made good time. The tide was still going out and it compensated marginally for the headwind. My kayak sliced through the water cleanly with relatively little slap, and I was pleased not to get facefuls of icy spray. I measured the water temperature at only 3.2 degrees and any splashes on my face stung with the cold. Jon, with his decks piled high, struggled a bit in the wind, and I pulled away to look for a campsite. I passed numerous small coastal hamlets, all with brightly coloured wooden houses and surrounded by bleached sheds and small racks for drying fish. Most had a small beach, but no real jetty, so launching days would have been limited for the small-scale fishermen here. As I paddled close to the coast I saw a huge flock of red knot. These birds arrive here from their wintering grounds in Africa and stage here before continuing to their breeding grounds in Iceland and Siberia. When I approached, the whole flock took off as one and circled in the sky before landing again. They moved with the same telepathic ease as a shoal of small fish.

As I approached the island of Ekkerøy I saw the long, sandy, spit which connected it to the mainland and formed a sheltered bay. A breakwater had also been constructed by the small village, forming a harbour. It had a huge old, traditional wooden wharf, built on log stilts which stuck out into the bay. The buildings looked like they had seen better days but were not derelict. I thought it best to wait for Jon, who was only 10 minutes behind me. We both decided to stay, rather than continue for another two hard hours into the cold, windy, evening until we reached the next landing possibility at Krampenes. We pulled the boats up the boulders on the beach and unpacked them on to the wharf. It seemed the buildings were hibernating, waiting for the tourist season to begin in mid June. Then they would open again as a café, restaurant, museum and

Day 138. A small part of the huge red knot flock who stage here after wintering in Africa to build up for the further flight to Siberia or Iceland

what looked like a bunkhouse for the short summer. Nothing was open now, and everything looked very bleak. There were a few cabins around the small village. Jon knocked on the door of a nearby house to ask about accommodation. An old man, who was no more that a metre high answered. He and his dwarf brother both lived here, and they invited us in for a coffee. Later, he took us to a cabin he had and said we could have it for the night, for a ridiculously cheap price. It was very nice, with a shower, and was the perfect alternative to a tent on this cold, windy, evening. While I wrote, Jon went for a walk, and discovered a vast kittiwake colony. There were a few locals surreptitiously collecting kittiwake eggs from the nests on the steep exposed crags above the sea. One had a whole bucket full of eggs.

After breakfast, I went to pay the cabin owner. He was loading chunks of rubble beside his house into a tractor bucket. He said it was a privilege to have us using the cabin and refused to take any money. I volunteered to load up the rubble while he sat in the tractor, driving it off occasionally to empty the bucket before returning to have it filled again. After a few loads, the ton of rubble was gone, and he could mow his lawn again. It only took an hour but as a 78-year-old he would have struggled. The tide was still coming in when we set off and the wind was still against us, but as we went round the south side of Ekkerøy it was more sheltered and we could bob about in the swell and look at the huge bird colony which largely consisted of some 30,000 kittiwakes. They

Day 138. Part of the 30,000 strong kittiwake colony on the steep south side of Ekkerøy peninsula, where they breed on inaccessible ledges

were nesting anywhere it was steep enough to afford some protection from the marauding weasels and mink which would steal eggs and chicks. As the cliffs were striated there was plenty of nesting opportunities. Blackback gulls also used to nest here, but they moved off to the island of Lille Ekkerøy when the weasels and mink, and perhaps humans also, got too numerous. We slowly cruised along under the numerous nests on the cliffs, quietly observing the birds. There was a lot of courting and mating going on and many noisy squabbles. At the east end of the Ekkerøy was a sea eagle which flew off as soon as it saw me. From Ekkerøy we crossed the bay to the fishing hamlet of Krampenes with the stiff breeze against us. After some two and a half hours we pulled up on the beach for lunch and found a sunny spot out of the wind. Krampenes was a typical hamlet of this coastline. It had 10 houses, each painted different colours and each surrounded by an array of sheds. There were some drying racks with a few cod drying on them, but it seemed fishing, as a profession, had pretty much died out here.

I was concerned at the slow progress we had been making. Jon was also reconsidering his intended paddle along the demanding section between Vardø and Tromsø, and was thinking it would be wiser to skip it and take the Hurtigruten ferry instead. In the light of this I decided to push on in my more suitable kayak, and leave Jon to potter along at his own speed, which allowed him plenty of time to photograph and investigate. So we said goodbye on Krampenes beach. I hoped we would catch up in a couple of months, as he was laid back and good company. I set off straight into the wind heading towards Komagvær. It took two hours paddling into the wind to gain the headland at Skallneset which was a mere 7 kilometres. After the headland the wind picked up and it got quite choppy with steep metre-high waves. The kayak performed well, and sliced quietly through most of them. I decided

Day 138. Krampenes was typical of the coastal hamlets, with a few wooden houses surrounded by bleached sheds and fish-drying racks

not to cut across the bay, but to claw my way up the coast to the village of Skallelv first. I went past a couple of eerie-looking derelict houses near the shore. It must have been a hard life fishing from these bleak, exposed hamlets for previous generations. Skallelv village, with its yellow church, slowly got closer as I paddled up this barren shore. As I went up the long sandy beach, which extended nearly all the way to the village, I was side on to the waves. They were still a metre high and quite a few had white crests, but there were no surprises from the kayak, and a kayak with hard chines might have sprung some here.

By the time I got to Skallelv I was tired, cold and ready to call it a day. I paddled up the small river estuary and then beached the kayak in fresh water at the side of the stream, where huge chunks of ice had been recently

Day 138. Paddling up the estuary at Skallelv, to camp on the river bank between some fishing sheds

washed down. I carried everything up in one go and then returned for the kayak and carried that up. My feet were freezing, as they had been wrapped in my wet wetsuit boots all day, and despite two pairs of socks under the drysuit, they were now numb. The temperature was around zero, but it felt much colder in the bitter wind. Within an hour I was in the tent with the petrol stove roaring, like a miniature turbine, thawing out my hands and feet, and within two hours I was well fed and overheating. I had still not managed to get hold of anyone at Tiderace Kayaks to sort out the rudder problem. However, Tom Amundsen, who was a week ahead of me in his kayak and having a hard time on the exposed Østhavet coast phoned and tipped me off about a kayak dealer in Tromsø. His name was Bjørn Eines of Bjornskajakk. I phoned him. A more helpful person one would be unlikely to meet. He said he had a boat for sale with the Smarttrack rudder system on it. He would remove the footrests and rudder pedals from it and send it to Vardø by express post. It might arrive before me. Payment, he said, would be sorted out later with Tiderace in the UK. This was music to my ears and a great relief.

Day 139. The river mouth at Skallelv was covered in blocks of ice which this icy torrent had carried down from the interior

I woke early to the rustle of ripstop nylon and the sound of rain. When I poked my head out of the window I realized it was not rain but a very light hail, like frozen drizzle. It was just below zero and the wind was still from the north east which was exactly the direction I wanted to go. It did not invite me out of the tent, as the wind was bitterly cold. I retreated back into the warmth of my sleeping bag and stayed there all morning. In the afternoon I went for a walk around the village. The estuary which was on the south side of the village was where the Skallelv river discharged the ice cold water it had brought down from the interior. There were large chunks of ice along the bank. Above the ice blocks were lots of old sheds but many were derelict. In the village itself there were perhaps 40 houses, but only 20 seemed to be lived in. The remainder were either holiday homes used for the weekends, and holidays in the summer, or simply abandoned, and a few were already derelict. Passing the church I had a look inside. It was very Spartan, with simple benches as pews and very little other adornments. A vestibule was stacked with a jumble of chairs. It gave the impression that the remainder of the congregation here had come to accept that this community was moving to the larger towns and it was only the old who were left. The village had an air of decline to it. In one garden I spotted a whale skull. I think it was from a minke whale and the blowhole was visible in the top of the skull. It was depressing to remain in this village for the day, but glances to the white caps and snow showers reassured me it was the right choice.

I woke early, and the wind was still strong and from the north east. I could not face another day in the tent at Skallelv and decided to claw my way up the coast into the wind to see how far I could get. I had breakfast, dismantled my tent, packed my kayak, and it was still before 0500 as I took my first stroke of the day. It was a bitterly cold, frigid morning and I had put many layers on under my drysuit to try and maintain my warmth and even then my hands and feet were soon numb. As I set off across the first bay I passed a vast raft of eider duck with about 200 birds. As I approached, the whole raft took off and circled around me a couple of times before landing on the water behind me. It was a slow paddle along the coast as I slowly pulled my way upwind. My speed was just a discouraging 3 kilometres an hour. My face was frequently splashed with icy spray and occasionally blasted with hail, so I had to pull my balaclava right down over my face. After I paddled past Komagnes point I got more of a taste of what I could expect for the rest of the day, with steep metre-high waves, many of which were breaking. I just could not build up any momentum as I hugged the wintery coast north to Komagvær. It was an uninteresting shoreline with very shallow land sloping up from the coast. The waves made it more interesting, but it was becoming a wet ride and it was still zero degrees. I stopped just after Komagvær on one of the beaches east of this hamlet and saw a fox foraging in the seaweed, desperate for a salty morsel after the long winter. There was also a sea eagle here and it was the first of about 10 which I was to see today. Most were perched on an outcrop or pillar of rock observing the world go by and hoping for something to scavenge. Their distinctive stance made them appear more vulture-like in profile.

After the break I continued slowly up the coast towards the point of Langbunes. I saw Jon was camped here and shouted to him. I could not land here as the waves were breaking on boulders and I could damage my kayak, so we shouted to each other, barely understanding what the other was saying over the roar of the surf and the hiss of the wind whistling in our ears. Apparently it was already 1000, and I assumed Jon would stay put and have a day off. I told him I was hoping to get to Vardø and waved him goodbye, before a larger wave could surprise me and carry me sideways towards the large boulders on its surf. Rounding the relatively insignificant Langbunes point was a very wet experience, with the water from the steep waves sweeping up the deck, slamming into my chest and soaking my balaclava. Far ahead to the east, there were some of the sun's rays streaming through unseen gaps in the cloud, but everything I could see was overcast. I crept past another headland and then saw the large Kramvik beach fringed by snowdrifts. The surf here seemed much smaller and I decided to land. The landing was an anticlimax, and the southerly aspect of the bay meant the easterly wind and waves hardly made it to the beach. I noticed there were sea eagles to the west end of the beach, and some reindeer foraging for grass around the snowdrifts to the east of the beach. To complete this Arctic scene there were large slabs of ice washed up at the high tide mark, which must have been carried down by the river, or have drifted here from the icepack at the west end of Varangerfjord. I had lunch and a stretch on this alien, bleak beach without a tree in sight, and then set off for Kiberg before I got too cold again.

As I got to the peninsula which was sheltering the beach, I saw Jon's kayak come crashing through the waves. Somehow he had managed to launch on the bouldery beach with the pounding surf at Langbunes and had paddled the 7 kilometres to catch me up. Even from a distance he looked like he was enjoying ploughing through the waves with spray flying off the baggage strapped to his kayak's deck. We waved to each other but were too far apart to talk. I tried to keep up with him, but he was on a mission and blasted across the next bay to reach the small beach at Indre Kiberg, where he landed. I was tired when I eventually caught up with him, but did not land, and indicated I would carry on to the next bay where there was the small town and harbour of Kiberg. I had now abandoned all thoughts of reaching Vardø, as the wind was still a good force 5.

Day 140. Looking back from Kiberg harbour to Jon Westgård who was still struggling in the waves as he fought into the wind by the island

I paddled out of the gusty, but flat, bay toward the large waves at the headland. They seemed bigger than anything yet. There was an island and I could sneak through the wide channel it formed. The other side of the channel was mayhem. The waves here were two, to two and a half metres, and every second one had a large white crest. I could see there was a tide pushing me through this gap and it was the same current which was making the waves very steep. It was a very wet few minutes as I paddled hard to crash through, with water sweeping into my chest again. After a few hundred metres I was through and I could see Kiberg breakwater a couple of kilometres ahead. The waves on this final stretch were still two metres, but only a few were breaking. The kayak kept turning away from the wind and waves, like a weather vane, despite me having the skeg right up. The resulting paddle was a near continuous set of sweep strokes to keep broadside to the weather as I gained on Kiberg. It was almost impossible to turn into the whitecaps when I saw them coming. I finally pulled into the harbour sheltered by the breakwater. It was calm here. It seemed to be high water. I calculated that to set off now to round Kibergneset with the big easterly swell hitting the ebbing tide would be madness, especially as I had already been paddling for 10 hours. So I beached the kayak. I went up to the only shop in the village of some 100 houses and got a warm coffee as I dripped around the table. A fisherman came over and chatted with me and reinforced what I thought about the sea off Kibergneset. He advised me it was best to wait until tomorrow and tackle it on a flooding tide and the forecasted lighter winds. My confidence with the kayak was increasing all the time, and I felt stable in it even with the big seas of the final section today. However, I just had 29 kilometres to show for a lot of effort and 10 hours of paddling. Having my hands in the protective poggies all day, and the state of the sea, meant I didn't take any photos until I reached Kiberg.

Day 140. The harbour at Kiberg was a welcome respite from the icy waves and wind I had endured for the last three days

I spotted Jon fighting his way down the coast and went to meet him. He was quite exhilarated by the tumultuous slot of wild water between the headland and island, and the final bit up the coast. He said he had never been in such big waves. The adrenaline was still flowing in him and I could see the glint of victory in his eyes. We decided to stay here and found a cheap room. We unpacked the kayaks into a wheelbarrow and took everything 400 metres to the simple lodging. I cooked myself in the shower, until the hot water had burnt red streaks down my chest and finally expelled the cold I had suffered for the last three days. In the evening we went for a walk through the village. There seemed to be an air of decay here also. There were some 20 houses on the road to dereliction, and everything needed a coat of paint. On the wharf one of the large abandoned fish processing sheds roof had collapsed. It seemed the town was in steep decline as everything had now moved to Vardø, 15 kilometres up the coast, including the fish processing plants and the school.

It was sunny as we set off, the wind was now just a force 3 and the temperature had risen to five degrees. It was almost warm after the last few bitterly cold days. The tide turned at 0900 and started to flow into the fjord again, and we intended to be going round Kibergneset at slack water. We paddled out of the harbour and rounded the southern end of the peninsula. The sea had a large swell, which was a bit confused, but otherwise it was benign. As we paddled north to Kibergneset the swell got larger, but it was still benign. We were lucky. This is the most easterly mainland point in Finnmark, and indeed Norway, and it sticks out into the Barents Sea creating some strong tidal currents. Locals said when the weather is bad this can be a fearsome place. At the point itself I spotted a couple of puffins. It was the first time on this trip I had seen these comical, but

Day 141. The last few kilometres to Vardø with Jon briefly appearing out of the swell as he paddles towards this historic Arctic town

tough, little birds. I hoped they were the first of many as they brighten up even a grey day. The huge golf ball listening station in Vardø soon came into view. Vardø was built on an island lying off the east coast of the Varanger peninsula in the Barents Sea, about 10 kilometres from Kibergneset. The whole journey was broadside to the swell, which was at times very big. Only occasionally would one of the crests of a wave break and this would just be a small white cap. By and large it was a bumpy but easy ride. Jon and I would frequently be out of sight of each other due to the swell. As we approached Vardø there must have been a tidal current running west to east across the south of the island. This current ploughed straight into the incoming swell and made the waves much steeper with more frequent and bigger white caps. This only lasted for a kilometre and then we were into the sheltered bay on the south side of the H-shaped island with the houses in the middle.

Vardø is the most easterly point of Norway and is slightly further east than Kibergneset, and even Istanbul for that matter. Despite its remote location, the small island has an excellent harbour. People have exploited this for centuries, and Vardø claims to be one of the oldest towns in Norway, dating to the 13th Century. It was perhaps one of the most easterly Medieval harbours which did not block up with ice during the winter and was therefore at the centre of an Arctic trading network. We went to investigate our errands. Jon to enquire about the Hurtigruten ferry to Tromsø and me to the shop where Bjørn had sent my rudder parts. These parts were still en route, having been held up by the postal holiday on Ascension Day, and would not arrive until tomorrow. I located my flares in the ferry terminal, but they were completely the wrong type and totally impractical, so

Day 142. One of the old fishing wharfs at Vardø is the Pomor museum with displays on these Arctic Russians who traded here for centuries

I sent them back, and discouraged by the disappointment gave up on trying to get more. Jon found out it was cheap and easy to take his kayak on the Hurtigruten ferry to Tromsø and that the daily departure left in a couple of hours at 1600. We carried his kayak through the open streets of Vardø to the terminal and then he used his Norwegian charm to get a good rate for me in a plush hotel near the harbour. It would take about 30 hours for Jon to get to Tromsø from where he would continue south down more sheltered waters. He had been good company and I had enjoyed his laid-back humour over the last week. Hopefully I will catch him up again sometime on the coast south where he would probably be sitting in front of a huge fire on some beach.

There was no hurry the next day as the rudder parts would not come until well after midday. I went for a wander around town. There were lots of shops which had closed down in the recent past. Some even had dated stock behind the dusty windows and peeling paint walls. It looked like someone had just locked up for the evening a few years ago, and never opened it again. Others were completely empty. In the main street there were about 15 shops still functioning and 10 that were closed or bankrupt. This town had obviously fallen on hard times, but people were optimistically hoping the Barents Sea oil pipeline would come ashore here, if oil production ever started. Indeed, a well-known Norwegian businessman had started to buy large tracts of land to develop industrial buildings. Apart from the diminishing fishing industry, the main source

Day 142. Looking across the harbour to the wharfs and shops on the east side of the sheltered inlet

of employment was the early listening radar station, which was now the biggest employer. Not even the recent 3-kilometre tunnel, under the strait to the mainland, could stop the continual drain of the younger population to more glamorous opportunities further south. I got the rudder parts in the afternoon. Not only had Bjørn of Bjornskajakk sent the correct parts, but he had also sent the tools to fit them and some silicone to make sure the screw holes were watertight. This was a tremendous service and I was highly indebted to Bjørn for this, as Tiderace Kayaks in England were just too far away to be effective. It took me two hours to refit the kayak and when I was happy with it I posted the old parts and the tools back to him. But by now it was late afternoon and the tide was half way out. If I set off now I would soon have to paddle against the current up the coast to Hamingberg. I decided to stay another night in Vardø. When I went to bed I could see the tide outside the window slowly starting to come in, enveloping the rocks as it came up the foreshore. I would leave on this same tide as it started to ebb at 0300. This ebb would hopefully carry me a very small part of the way up the very exposed and remote Østhavet coast to the fishing town of Berlevåg, some 100 kilometres to the north west.

SECTION 20. Varangerfjord
8 days. 146 kilometres. 37 hours. 0m ascent. 0m descent.

THE KAYAK: SECTION 21. ØSTHAVET

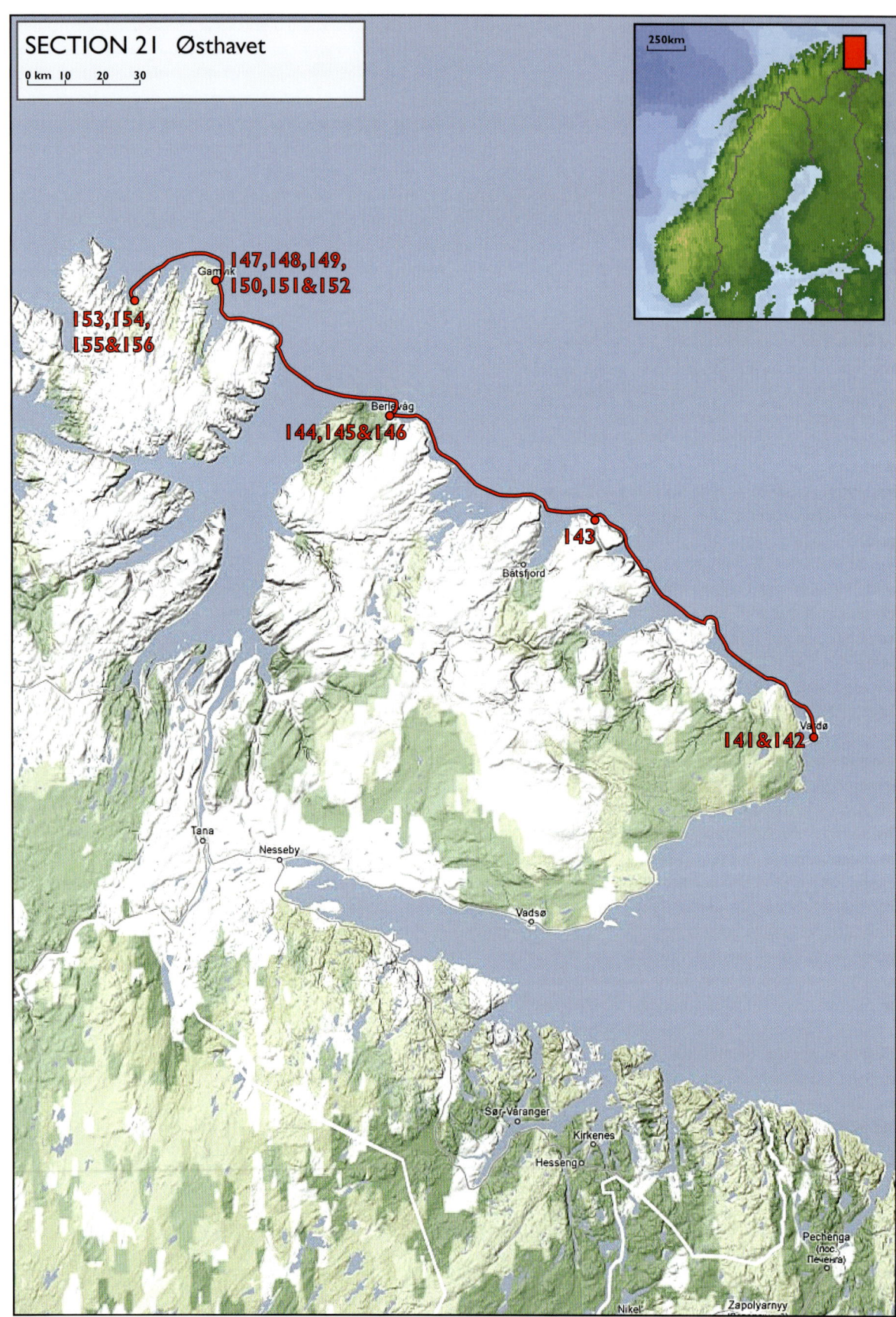

THE KAYAK: SECTION 21. ØSTHAVET

The alarm went at 0300 and I got up at once and started on my pre-packed breakfast. I finished it as the north going Hurtigruten ferry arrived at Vardø quay. By the time I had packed up the boat and pulled on my waterproof spraydeck, the Hurtigruten had already departed and was out of the harbour which was returning to its quiet sleepy norm. As I paddled out of the harbour entrance the south-east breeze started to give me a small push. Initially I went between the main island and Reinøya island. Reinøya is rich in birdlife and attracts many international birdwatchers. The large swell of a couple of days ago had gone from about three metres to a mere metre. It was coming from the stern, as was the breeze. The tide was also ebbing in the direction I was going, so without much effort I was cruising along at 8 kilometres an hour. From the north tip of the main island, I cut across the overcast sound to the jagged grey rocks and small boulder beaches along the coast, to the shattered headland of Blodsyktodden. This serrated coast was wild and rugged and looked like it was often pounded by the huge swells sweeping south from the Barents Sea. On reaching the headland, the view across the open Persfjord unfolded, and I could see right up to the rounded promontory of Hardbaken some 20 kilometres across the fjord to the north west. I started to head across the fjord to a great rock edifice near Seglodden. From the foot of this tower I planned to follow the steep coastal cliffs with their many snow-filled gullies etched along them to the now abandoned village of Hamningberg. However, the conditions were so favourable, I just cut straight over the fjord setting a course for the distinct knoll of Hardbaken jutting into the ocean.

Hamningberg is a village which was abandoned some 40 years ago when Norway was poor and the government withdrew support for services like keeping the road open in winter and schooling. As a result, people left, and the 10 houses here are now summer cabins. It would not be allowed to happen in today's Norway, with its bursting coffers. There was a tiny road, only open in the summer, along the coastal cliffs to the very remote hamlet where the houses still looked like they were maintained by the children, or even grandchildren, of the community's original families. I had been in the kayak for four hours when I reached and rounded Hardbaken. I needed to land and stretch my legs, so I paddled round to Skjåvika beach. For the first time this trip I saw some seals on the skerries here. I was also lucky to see a couple of sea eagles having an aerial fight, with one no doubt chasing the other off its patch or partner. In the sheltered bay I found a spot to land at the bottom of a series of raised beaches, which was typical of much of the coastline here. The land has risen many, many metres since the weight of ice sheet disappeared some 10,000 years ago, and the beaches formed at the various sea levels were simply elevated in increments. The beach I was on merged with the previous beaches into a long shallow slope of bare boulders and cobbles. It was now strewn with driftwood; most of it huge logs and tree trunks. I had no water so went for a walk to find some, however, the whole landscape was so boulder-strewn and porous, even in the gullies which came down from the plateau above, there was no chance of finding any. There was an old sea cave at the base of a cliff now far above the ocean.

Day 143. Approaching the abandoned hamlet at Hamningberg off the fertile isthmus between the mainland and Hardbaken on the right

Skjåvika bay was just at the south entrance of Syltefjord, which is a steep sided inlet some 5 kilometres wide and 10 kilometres deep. There was a very remote hamlet, Nordfjord, at the head of the fjord with a few hardy inhabitants who also spent the winters here, despite the only transport being snow scooter or boat. On the northern side of Syltefjord is a long line of cliffs, buttresses and rock towers. Some of these towers stand proud of the steep terrain here and are a haven for sea birds, as the cliffs prevent any predators preying on chicks and eggs. The main bird colony is on a tower called Store Syltefjordstauren and it is covered in nesting gannets. Even from 5 kilometres I could make out the paler coloured rocks which would be covered in guano or bird droppings. Unfortunately, visiting this colony would have been a considerable detour, so I skipped it. I headed straight over the fjord with the wind behind me and the negligible current against me. On the north side was a bay called Russevik which Tom Amundsen had warned me was an exposed boulder beach with potentially big surf and a poor camping place. To the north of this bay was a headland called Syltefjordklubben which I headed

Day 143. Looking north west across the 5km of Syltefjord the first headland of Syltefjordklubben then the distant Korsnes on the right

for. As I paddled, the grey drab morning was replaced by an advancing curve of perfect weather which was nothing but blue sky and sunshine. But it was still too cold to take my poggies off my hands though. The trip across this fjord was fast and easy. The wind which was a good force 3 gave me an extra couple of kilometres per hour. All sorts of sea birds came to investigate me, especially gannets which circled above me, curiously judging me with their piercing eyes. There were also quite a few puffins, tysties and guillemots.

As I went round Syltefjordklubben the swell and waves hit the flooding tide and this slowed them considerably, making them much steeper. The momentum of the upper part of the wave carried them on while the bottom part slowed, so there were tumbling white caps everywhere. They were smallest near the shore where the current was less, so I could paddle a less bumpy path here, but had to remain vigilant for skerries which could suddenly erupt when a larger swell rose up on them. Once I was passed Syltefjordklubben and into quieter waters I headed along the coast and into Stormollvika bay. I found a sheltered spot to land here and sneaked in. The steep kilometre-long beach was a vast pile of boulders which seemed to loom over me up to a height of 25-30 metres. If I camped here and the wind changed to north I would be stuck, imprisoned by huge waves dumping on to this unforgiving beach. There was not a hint of that now in this quite glorious sunshine. For the first time since Bugøynes a week ago it was almost warm. I lingered a bit on this beach but did not bother looking for water, as despite the map showing a river, I could not see one and assumed it was under the boulders which stretched for a good few ankle-twisting kilometres. It certainly was a wild spot. I also wanted to stretch and wait for a while until the tide slowed, otherwise the next headland, called Korsnes, could be bumpy as it was a bit more exposed than the previous ones. It was just across the small but isolated Makkaur-Sandfjord. After an hour's pause I set off and crossed this small fjord in glorious sun. I reached the headland quickly and the anticipated current and choppy water were almost gone. The tide must be turning and the water slack. I soon saw the lighthouse at Makkaur fyr some 5 kilometres along the coast. With the wind continuing behind me it took less than an hour to reach it.

Day 143. The wild Arctic boulder-strewn beach at Stormollvika allowed a calm landing at the sheltered south which was protected by skerries

By now the sun had veered round and was almost in my face. It was so bright, and with its reflection from the water you would get snow blindness without glasses. On the rocks below the lighthouse was the smashed, rusting bow of a large ship. It was shocking to see just how high above the sea level the waves had carried this massive iron edifice, before wrenching it into smaller pieces. After the wreck I paddled into a bay where the lighthouse was and I managed to get out on the kelp-covered boulders. The Makkaur fyr comprised of the lighthouse itself, two accommodation buildings for previous lighthouse keepers, and numerous sheds. It was all automated and unmanned now. I had a look round and then prepared a meal in the lee shelter of a shed and in the full glare of the warm and comforting sun. My plan was to have a bite and a couple of hour's siesta and then continue through the evening and night to Berlevåg. With a full belly I laid out the foam mattress and sleeping bag on a grassy patch and slept. It was just 1800 but I had been awake since 0300. The sun must have cooked me in my bag, as when I woke at 2200, I was hot and confused. The wind was still in my favour, but the tide was just about to turn against me again. Suddenly the bravado of paddling to Berlevåg disappeared and I decided to stay at Makkaur fyr. I found that one of the sheds was unlocked and open. I went in and there was a table, chair and

Day 143. A large rusting shipwreck had been driven up the rocky coast by huge waves under the very nose of Makkaur fyr lighthouse

space to sleep on the floor. It was rustic and relatively clean, but there was a lingering aroma of salt and diesel. I was sure no one would mind me sleeping in here rather than putting the tent up, so I started to prepare for the evening. I pulled the boat higher and took out a few more possessions from the hatches and carried them up to the shed. Then I made myself comfortable, before I quickly fell asleep again, very contented with the day's progress and grateful for the weather after the near week of misery in Varangerfjord. Yes, it had been a perfect day, in a paddling paradise!

When I woke and looked out of the shed in the morning I got a nasty surprise as the comforting, stable weather of yesterday had been barged out of the way and it was pouring sleet and rain. The shed's gutters were spewing out huge amounts of water on to the concrete yard. It would have been miserable setting off in this, despite the slight breeze. I grabbed another hour's sleep before I had breakfast. The rain and sleet showed no sign of stopping, so I started writing in the hope that perhaps by the afternoon things would get better. The advantage of paddling up here in the Arctic is that one can set off at any time without regard to limited daylight. As I wrote the weather slowly improved with the downpour breaking up into showers and then the showers becoming sporadic. When I finished writing I was optimistic it would return to the reassuring, warm tranquillity of yesterday. I delayed setting off for an hour and went to have a look around the lighthouse itself. It was a very solid stone building with the rotating light in a short tower. By midday the sky was clearing and it was still calm, so I packed up and carried the drybags down to the kayak. There was a sea eagle perched near my kayak which disappeared when it saw me. As soon as it was airborne a raven went out of its way to go and pester it. The huge eagle was no match for the fast and acrobatic raven and retreated out of the bay with the raven still harrying it. At the kayak I adjusted the rudder slightly. Then I slid the half-loaded kayak on wet logs to the thick layer of wet kelp near the water's edge where I could drag it. The tide was just starting to come in as I pushed off at 1400.

Day 144. Looking west from Makkaur fyr lighthouse past the mouth of Båtsfjord then Kongsfjord with the Berlevåg peninsula in the distance

There was a slight breeze and the negligible tide against me but I made good time in the sun. It was not like the north shore of Varangerfjord where I felt I was paddling in treacle. I quickly reached the entrance to Båtsfjord where there was still a lot of snow. I did not go into the fjord but just cut across its mouth to reach the cliffs on the west side of the entrance. After just two hours I reached the dramatic headland of Vesternes with its sawtooth profile looking like the front cover of a Tolkien novel. A dark, wet, smooth, rock towered what seemed like 200 metres almost vertically with the occasional needle and spire which had resisted erosion. I was intending to land here and stretch before the next

Day 144. The dramatic 200-metre-high cliffs at Vesternes marked the entrance to Kongsfjord

Day 144. There was a large smooth swell as I paddled over the 15 kilometre puffin-riddled Kongsfjord, towards the dark Nålnes headland

leg but there was no chance. I would have to wait until I crossed the 15-kilometre-wide Kongsfjord. This fjord was more of an open bay, dotted with a few islands nearer its head, rather than the classic slot-like fjord. It was known for its rich marine life and even coral, and I later found it was a classic scuba diving location. The wind had by now completely disappeared and the sun was out, making it a magnificent day. However, there were clouds quickly forming over the Berlevåg peninsula on the other side of Kongsfjord, some three hours paddling away. This made me a bit nervous as the weather can change very quickly up here with the infamous Polar Low Pressure weather systems, which can develop out of nothing. These short-lived vortices are usually just 1000 kilometres across and can arise quite unpredictably. If one suddenly swept in when I was half way across a wide fjord I would be in serious trouble. I could see the dark Nålnes promontory on the other side of Kongsfjord, and as I could not land here on this jagged coast, I decided to set off at once. The clouds forming gave me a sense of urgency. A large swell was sweeping in from the north which I had not noticed in the morning. The surface of the ocean was glassy though. After a good hour my confidence that I could outrun any incoming bad weather started to grow.

The second half of the journey was much more relaxed and although the skies were becoming very dark the wind did not pick up at all. There were many puffins here and I think they must have been nesting on one of the islands in Kongsfjord which was predator free. They were not forming huge rafts of 1000 birds or so, but many groups of 10. Occasionally, there were single birds. These individual puffins would be the most curious and almost swim towards me to investigate. I appreciated their company and had my lunch here as I drifted through one of these groups. With a few kilometres to go, the effects of the curve of the earth were getting smaller, and at last I could see the white surf along the bottom of the cliffs at Nålnes as the large wallowing swell broke. The ebbing tide was quite strong

Day 144. The clouds which had been threatening all afternoon, finally started to clear, as I paddled towards Kjølnes fyr lighthouse

off this peninsula and carried me north into a bay called Sandfjord, which I could see had a huge sandy beach. I did not go in but crossed the mouth heading for the tower of Kjølnes fyr lighthouse. The tide was with me here and I made good time along the coast. There was a little rain from the dark skies and a couple of squalls of wind, but the tidal current carried me through all this, and soon I was approaching the lighthouse. As I paddled away from the cliffs and mountains around Sandfjord, the clouds vanished again, and I was reaching for my sunglasses. Kjølnes fyr was a more traditional lighthouse. It was a tower built on a rocky spit. There was a road to it and the now disused keeper's houses looked in good order. There was not as much tidal current as I had expected, or hoped, and I had to paddle round the rocky spit.

Day 144. The unmanned Kjølnes fyr lighthouse lay on a barren spit protruding into the Barents Sea near Berlevåg

Once I was round it I could make out Berlevåg quite easily, and beyond that I could see the Nordkinn peninsula. Between the two was Tanafjord, an infamous stretch of water.

The swell had vanished again, and with the numerous coves along the next 6 kilometres of shore, I could have easily landed. However, with the clear windstill evening and a slight current, I thought I would just push on for an hour and get to Berlevåg before it got too late to find accommodation. It was a very pleasant glide along the coast for an hour and I was soon approaching the massive breakwaters. I looked over my shoulder as I made for the gap and saw the Hurtigruten ferry 2 kilometres behind me. I knew I would have enough time to nip through the gap before it arrived. However, the tide was draining out of the harbour inside the protective arms, and I had to paddle hard to overcome it. When I looked round again the ship was only some 500 metres away pushing a large frothing bow wave in front of it. I had to sprint across the harbour to keep out of its way, as it was closing fast. It gave its normal three blasts on the foghorn to announce to the town it had arrived, and then gave me three blasts to tell me to get the hell out of the way. At one stage the ferry, which was called the *MS Nordlys,* was just 100 metres away and there were a few people on the quay pointing at me, but I was too exhausted after the five-minute sprint to be embarrassed. I beached on the sand where the river entered the harbour, by a sandy beach. This luckily was near the camping and pensionat. I had been in the kayak for eight and a half hours nonstop, which is testament to its comfortable seat and the capacity of my bladder. The owners of the pensionat had seen me arrive, just ahead of the *MS Nordlys* ferry, and came over. I secured the kayak and then they even helped carry some of my drybags up to their hostel. Within half an hour I was settled in a very comfortable, well organized, artistically decorated building, with a super kitchen, nice showers and great washing machines. It was owned and run by a Swiss-German pair who had settled in Berlevåg half a decade earlier. I cooked a meal, had a shower, put on a wash and went to bed late. I had always intended to have a day off in Berlevåg and I was told that tomorrow evening was also the weekly choir practice for the well-known Berlevåg Male Choir.

Day 145. Berlevåg harbour is protected by massive breakwaters which allow the fishing fleet to exploit the rich fishing grounds nearby

I spent the morning writing and cleaning when two locals arrived at the pensionat. They were Bjørnar and Arnt Eirik. They both lived in Berlevåg and ran the local online paper called Berlevaagnytt.com. They had both recently started paddling, and were keen to pick my brains. We chatted a while before I went to the Fishermen's café for a late lunch. Unfortunately, I was the only customer there, and it was very quiet. After the meal I went out and explored Berlevåg. The first thing one notices about Berlevåg are the massive breakwaters. Without them, Berlevåg would quite simply not exist, and the Hurtigruten ferry could not dock. Despite the very rich fishing grounds just off the coast here, the fishing fleet is vulnerable. Its harbour is fully exposed to a north-easterly wind. On a few occasions in the late 19th Century, storms pulverized the whole fishing fleet assembled in the bay, and pushed the wrecks on to the land. The people of Berlevåg knew breakwaters were essential for the town's survival and they decided to build them over 100 years ago. However, the water was deep and the breakwaters each had to be about 700 metres long. For the next 75 years the people of Berlevåg built the breakwaters with a pause for the German occupation. After the war the construction project continued in earnest, with even a 5-kilometre railway being built to bring massive rocks from a quarry to the breakwaters. Huge concrete blocks were also cast to line the outer walls. However, a storm in the late 1950s showed the construction to be too lightweight to withstand the huge waves, some over 10 metres high, which flung the 25-ton blocks about and punched holes in the arms. Berlevåg then used a French idea to line the breakwaters. These were tetrapods; a 4-legged, 25-ton block of concrete. The tetrapods not only locked together, but their shape dissipated some of the wave's impact. The concrete foundry now switched to making these, and over the next few years produced some 10,000 of the 25-ton tetrapods. In the 1970s the breakwaters were finally finished. At their base on the sea-bed they are over 125 metres wide and 700 metres long, and only a fraction of this Herculean task is visible above the surface. It really was an impressive project by this small community to ensure its survival. Its legacy has been to encourage a strong community spirit, pride and confidence, which give the town and its people a strong character epitomized in its friendly people, successful choir and well-kept buildings.

Day 145. The wharfs and harbour at Berlevåg were still lively with boats landing fish and taking on ice throughout the day

Berlevåg lives entirely from the sea, and is ideally placed to exploit the very rich fishing waters of the Barents Sea. The mainstay is cod. There are two types of cod; the less-travelled fjord cod which seems to spend much of its time in the fjords like the nearby Kongsfjord, and the migratory cod. This latter type is more numerous and larger. It spawns in and around Vestfjord in Lofoten in the winter months and then travels up the Troms and Finnmark coasts during the spring, arriving around Berlevåg in late spring. In the summer it goes out into the Barents Sea and then returns to the Lofoten area in the winter to spawn again. There is also rich fishing for haddock, and recently, the king crab. There used to be a large lodde, or capelin, fishing industry here, but they have been over-fished to dangerously low levels. The demise of the lodde population has consequences for many other species, as this small salmon-type fish provides nutrition for cod and many other fish, like herring which feed on the sprat. I had a quick wander around the busy harbour and then tried to find out about the choir practice.

I spoke to one person on the street who looked more like a rugby player than a chorister. Luckily he was actually in the choir and he invited me along to their practice that evening in the community hall. The Berlevåg Male Choir is well known in Norway; indeed, two films have been made about them. The choir has also travelled quite widely. I turned up a couple of hours later as 20 or so of the members arrived. They were big men, many with beards and shirt sleeves rolled up. They were undoubtly the lifeblood of the community. They seemed interested in my trip and most chatted with me. They were a very friendly, confident bunch. Before they started, one of them introduced their foreign guest and there was applause. The choir was led by Odd Frantzen. Despite being in a wheelchair he was very dynamic and energetic. Apparently, one day as an

Day 145. The Berlevåg male Choir is renowned and was made up of 30 burly members and led by Odd Frantzen from his wheelchair

adult, he woke to find he could not walk any more. It could be his energy and passion which led to this choir becoming so successful. During practice he was very precise and picked up on the slightest errors. When the choir started it was a magnificent sound. Enough to send shivers of awe down the back of any self respecting Welshman. These were powerful voices. Odd Frantzen, despite being in a wheelchair, had probably the most powerful and finely tuned male voice you could find. It was a privilege to listen to them practice. Their version of Ave Maria was especially potent. After the practice I went to what was almost a pub for pizza and beer with a few of the choir members.

The weather forecast, both short-term and long-term was disturbing. There seemed just the odd window of respite in a week which promised gales, and even a storm. This was an unfortunate coincidence, as that same week I aimed to be paddling round the very exposed northern headlands, including Kinnarodden and Nordkapp, and also crossing wide fjords. First, though, I had to cross Tanafjord, and from many conversations I had had recently, it was clear that Tanafjord was not a fjord to be trifled with. There seemed to be an

Day 146. Newly landed pallets of haddock were quickly taken into the processing plants and filleted and packed on the quayside wharfs

opportunity to cross it tomorrow, and I nervously contemplated it as I went to bed.

When I woke in the morning, the flags were snapping wildly in the wind. I went out to have a closer look and I could see I was not going anywhere in the near future. The harbour was full of small breaking wavelets and if I peered through the gap between the arms of the breakwater I could see some large breaking waves. It was not a morning to cross the difficult Tanafjord in a small trawler, let alone a kayak. I went for another walk about town and down to the fishing wharfs. A boat had recently landed its catch of haddock. There were six large tubs of it with at least a ton in each tub. These fish were caught using longlines. Each longline had perhaps 1000 hooks and quite a few of these static, baited lines were set out with a marker buoy at each end. The lines were left for a few hours and then retrieved. Nets are also used, but apparently many fishermen prefer the longlines as they are not so indiscriminate in their catch, and spare the fish which are not ready to be caught yet. This long-sighted approach must be rare in today's world, where immediate profit is king, and the future is ignored.

After my walk I visited the museum. It had all manner of artefacts, but was perhaps not quite as good as the amateur collection the old Sjøsami, Helmer Losoa, had at Byluft on the south side of Varangerfjord which I visited some three weeks ago. What this museum concentrated on was the building and importance of the breakwaters and Berlevåg's war history. During the German occupation, Berlevåg was a thorn in the occupying forces side, and it seemed a few partisans operated from the mountains around the town. When they retreated the Germans took revenge by burning the whole town flat. Not even the church was spared. The cranes used to build the breakwater were also destroyed during this time.

Day 146. The preferred fishing technique was a longline (black) which had hundreds of baited hooks on individual nylon traces (red)

When I returned to the pensionat, the wind was increasing. A few bins had been blown over and even gravel dust was being whipped into the air. The flags were cracking in the cold northerly wind, and the harbour was quiet, with none of the fishing boats setting out. The weather forecast predicted the weather would calm down around 2200 and then remain passive for about 15 hours before it started to blow again. Then the wind was expected to return with a vengeance for a few days with a minor storm forecast. I had a few hours to kill until 2200 so returned to the library and then went to the pub for a pizza. At 2100 I returned to the pensionat. The wind was indeed decreasing rapidly and the flags were hardly moving, and by 2200 they were completely still. I decided to go for it, otherwise I would be stuck in Berlevåg for days, and started to pack with a knot in my stomach and a feeling of apprehension. I set off at 2300 and paddled back out to the gap in the massive breakwaters.

As soon as I was out of the harbour, I met the northerly swell, which had been building in the strong wind all day. It was massive, with huge rollers coming out of the north. Some must have been a good four metres. With the lack of wind, however, they were smooth and unthreatening. I decided to keep out of the mouth of the infamous Tanafjord and make a bee line for the north edge of the fjord on the west side at a place called Omgang. This way I hoped I could keep out of the worst of any wind or tidal streams for which the fjord was renowned. Omgang, however, was about 25 kilometres or five hours away. The first part of the trip was down the coast

Day 147. Looking across Tanafjord with the cliffs of Kinnarodden on the west side looming up above the gentle swell

along a coastal plain to the base of the steep Tanahorn mountain. By the time I reached it, I was already a good few kilometres offshore to the north of it, and could start to peer into the opening of the vast Tanafjord. On the far side, now some 20 kilometres away, was the Nordkinn peninsula. I had a great vantage point over to its classic plateau shape from here. It was a 300-metre high flat table top still covered in a fair bit of snow. Hanging from the side of this plateau like a curtain was a vast wall of cliffs. The swell continued to come in from the north as I started across the fjord proper. There was a slight wind from the south east, as forecast, and this would help push me along. I was cruising over the fjord at 7 kilometres per hour. It was not until I got to about half way did I start to relax and get a bit less apprehensive about being surprised by weather. The sky was clearing the whole time, and when I was halfway across there was hardly a cloud in the sky. Unfortunately there was just a slither of it in the north so I could not see the midnight sun. I could just see its dramatic glow on the dark clouds.

Around half way across and still with 10 kilometres or two hours to go, I noticed the wind, which was a force 2 previously, was now a 3 and had swung round to the south. I was closing in on Omgang which was at the northern end of the base of the cliffs on the far side. I assumed the tide had turned by now and was flooding into the fjord and against the wind. The more I paddled towards the base of the cliffs the more the wind increased. I still had about 5 kilometres to go now and it was up to a force 4. Worryingly there were numerous large white caps appearing everywhere, especially ahead of me. I think what was happening was the south-east wind was being blocked by the huge line of 300-metre high cliffs which was channelling it northwards. The closer I got to the base of the cliffs the greater the funnelling. The last 3 kilometres were

Day 147. As I paddled across Tanafjord the midnight sun was blocked by low cloud on the northern horizon

hard. It was a southerly force 5 now with the steep waves, well over a metre high, breaking frequently. From the north, the previously gentle three-metre swell still continued to pile in, and this was meeting the steep wind-driven waves coming from the south, further confusing the water. In addition to this, the tide itself was flowing into the fjord now and was causing the waves to become yet steeper. I paddled hard, with a constant eye to my left to see when the larger waves were coming, and frequently had to lurch into the crashing surf to stop myself getting pushed over by breaking waves. The left side of my face was getting showered in cold spray and surf and my poggies were filled with icy water. It was about 0300 in the morning and the tide flowing into the fjord must have been going at full bore.

After nearly an hour of powerful, and strenuous paddling I was at last getting through the worst of it, and only had about 500 metres to go when I started to get some shelter from the southern wind and waves behind a headland, and I was now out of the worst of the tidal flow. The hissing of the breaking waves and the wind slowly diminished until it was almost quiet. I then paddled into the small protected bay at Omgang to relax, as the last hour had been a hard fight. Had the wind strength gone up to a force 6 I would have been at my limit, if not beyond, in these very choppy confused seas. I can now see why Tanafjord is not to be trifled with. There are geographical features which funnel the wind and increase it two or three fold, not least the steep cliffs. I was also told about the high wedge of the Digermulfjell mountain ridge which splits the fjord into two arms further down and this helps to accelerate any southerly winds. In addition, there are the tidal currents which are at times quite considerable, as inner Tanafjord is a large body of water which gets filled and empties every six hours. A few people also told me the enormous amounts of fresh water being discharged by the Tana River in the spring melt can also cause northerly swells to rear up and topple over. On the sea charts it is marked as an area with dangerous waves.

Day 147. Omgang was an abandoned village on the west side of Tanafjord by a tussock grass-covered peninsula

Omgang was a relief. It was almost pastoral with a few small cabins on a tussock grass peninsula. When I arrived, three sea eagles took off and started circling. Sea eagles seem to be very wary and take to flight as soon as they spot humans. There was also a herd of about 20 reindeer near the beach. I wandered about stretching my legs, and walked over to the small lighthouse, before setting off again at 0430. Just to the north of the lighthouse at Omgang there was a strong tidal flow heading east. This was flowing straight into the larger swell coming from the north east. I had to tread a path through here, avoiding the places where the swell was bunching up and breaking. Slowly I fought my way round the point against the current, for what seemed an eternity, until the current started to diminish and I at last started to creep past the rocky coastline of Koifjord with the occasional boulder beach. Beyond the beach were undulating hills covered in fields of barren stones. There were a few valleys twisting down from these hills. Down each valley came a strong southerly wind and I again had to dig deep to claw my way up the coast. I could not go too far into the shore as the northerly swell was breaking all the way along the coast here. There was a continual roar from the surf, and long plumes of spray were being whipped off the crests of the breaking waves by this force 5 southerly wind. Having already felt exposed and apprehensive once this night, I was very reluctant to cut across the open Koifjord directly to Gamvik. I thought it better to hug the relative safety of the surf-pounded coastline for almost two hours until I approached some islands. I then stopped ferrygliding into the south wind and turned north, letting it carry me towards the great white landmark of Gamvik church 6 kilometres away. I made good time, surfing the metre-high waves and within an hour I could finally relax, mentally and physically, as I was blown through the arms of the relatively small breakwater and into Gamvik harbour.

Day 147. Looking into the head of Koifjord during a lull in the wind by the islands before I turned and started heading north towards Gamvik

Gamvik was small, with a population of just 200, spread out along the shore of the bay. It did, however, have a shop and also a guest house in a large old wooden building. I got there at 0800 but Jan Reidar, the owner, was already at work. Luckily, his daughter was there and she phoned him before she went to school. I had arranged accommodation with him last night from Berlevåg. I retrieved the bare minimum from my kayak and retired to the warmth of the room, had a hot shower, drew the curtains and went to sleep. I did not wake until the early evening. When I got up, Jan Reidar was back from his work, and welcomed me. He was knowledgeable about the area and also a good cook, preparing a simple but tasty smoked cod meal. In the evening, I relaxed in the living room and watched the weather forecast on television. It did not make good viewing, with gales for the next two days followed by a storm in three days time. It looked like I would be in Gamvik for a few days yet. Fortuitously there was also the Champions League Football Final between Barcelona and Manchester United, which the Spanish club won. By the time I had watched it and realized I was here for a while, I started to surrender my

Day 147. The village of Gamvik with the landmark of the rebuilt church on the right and the guest house on the left

outdoor mindset and let a more passive attitude creep over me as I went to bed.

I did not even need to get out of bed to see what the weather was doing, as I could hear the wind whistling round the building, and driving against the window. It was a strong south-easterly wind of certainly force 7, maybe even 8. It was also high tide around 0800 and the small breakwater was taking a pounding with every wave crashing into it, sending plumes of spray into the air. I had breakfast and then went to check my kayak. I had pulled it quite high up but a combination of low pressure and this easterly wind could have caused the sea level to rise another metre. When I got there I found the water had not been far off. I hauled it up the grass, gaining another two metres in altitude, and placed it beside some upturned boats. It was still full of my belongings so it was well weighted down for the forecasted storm. I then returned to the guest house and wrote while looking out of the window. Sometimes, if the weather was just on the brink I felt guilty I was not out in it. There were no doubts today. It was a churning cauldron on the skerries outside the harbour. After lunch I went to have a look round Gamvik. It did not take long! However, I discovered there was a museum here, so went over to it on the south side of the bay. It was similar to Byluft or Berlevåg, but had more informative displays. One of the more interesting was some details of settlement in the region since the ice disappeared some 10,000 years ago. There have been archaeological remains found at a number of locations in the area dating back to this time. Even since the war there have been some significant demographic shifts, with some previously important settlements, like the now desolate Omgang, where I was very relieved to have made landfall after Tanafjord, not being repopulated after the war.

Day 148. Looking out of the guest house window towards the harbour wall and the skerries beyond, which were being pounded by the gale

Jan Reidar was going away for the weekend, and as I was the only guest, it did not make sense for him to keep it open. He had a friend, Frank, who rented out a house in the village. I went to have a look at it. It was perfect. It was a traditional house which was probably 50 years old. It had three bedrooms upstairs which felt a bit smaller due to the coombed ceilings caused by the roof. Downstairs there was a good well-equipped kitchen with a dining table and a large fridge. Beyond the kitchen was a living room with a bookshelf full of books and a television. There was also a bathroom with a shower off the downstairs hall. The house had everything I needed and it was also cheap. Frank did not stay here but lived in a cabin near Slettnes fyr lighthouse, so I had the whole place to myself. I could live here permanently, so it would be no problem to wait out the forecasted gales here until the queue of low pressures in the Arctic Ocean had passed. I returned to the guest house in the wet gale and gazed at the huge waves breaking on the skerries in a frothing mayhem. It was too far to judge, but I thought some of the waves were a good five metres. Unfortunately this weather will leave a legacy for days to come with a large swell, even if the weather becomes stable and the wind calms down. During the night I got up occasionally to look at the weather, which seemed to be increasing. It continued to build up all night to a force 10. The whole sea around the skerries was now obliterated by airborne surf whipped off the fury of the crashing waves. The flag outside the guest house was cracking in the wind, and even the flagpole was bending. Occasionally, sleet showers would also sweep in on the storm force winds peppering the window. Even the guest house itself was shaking and creaking when some of the gusts hit it.

The storm had abated by the morning, but it was still a good gale and the sea was still mayhem with huge waves smashing on the skerries in violent explosions. After breakfast I moved across the road to Frank's house and set myself up in there. I was keen to go back to the museum before it closed for the long Whitsunday or Pentecost weekend, which meant two days holiday in Norway, in addition to the weekend itself. At the museum I focused mainly on local archaeological and human history.

There were settlements in some coastal regions in Koifjord, which I crossed two days ago, which go right back to the Mesolithic era (12,000 to 6500 years ago) and stone tools, especially of quartzite, were found near these settlements. These settlements also continued into the Neolithic era (6500 to 4000 years ago) where there are more extensive finds of kitchen middens, stone constructions for reindeer hunting and stone storage chambers. These eras are the Middle and Late Stone Ages respectively.

Day 149. Frank's comfortable three-bedroom house which I rented for four days while the storm and gales passed through Gamvik

In the Bronze Age (4000 to 2500 years ago) and Iron Age (2500 to 1500 years ago) metal, antler and bone tools became more common and some ceramics were used. The houses in these metal eras also became smaller, suggesting people were becoming more mobile, as they moved about exploiting different resources at different seasons. However, there is very little from this era found on the Nordkinn Peninsula, compared to the earlier Stone Ages, and it seemed the earliest people moved elsewhere.

In the Medieval Period (1500 to 500 years ago) most of the settlements in the region seems to be Sami. They combined fishing and farming. There are some Sami labyrinths here from the end of this period around 600 years ago. These labyrinths are close to Sami grave sites, probably used for ritual purposes. There is not much history from this period until the Norwegian and Russian traders and fishermen arrived around 400 years ago.

It seemed that Norwegians moved up the coast from Nordland and Troms in the early 1500s, settling on the coast beside some of the Sjøsami communities. Many of these Norwegians were fishermen who had followed the cod north from Lofoten in the spring season. Sometime later came Russian fishermen who also arrived initially to fish. The Russians realized there were many items they had which they could trade, like timber, flour, salt and wool, in return for fish and furs. This was the beginning of the long Pomor trade which saw many Russians settle on the Finnmark and Nordkinn coasts. This trade continued up to the Bolshevik revolution in 1917.

From the late 19th Century onwards, Gamvik, the now deserted Omgang, and the rest of Nordkinn became important fishing centres. Svend Foyn invented the harpoon and established a whaling station in Mehamn. There were fish traders from all over Norway arriving to buy fish after the Pomor trade ceased. Much of the fish was dried into stockfish making it easier to export. This continued until well after the Second World War when Gamvik started to lose out to the better harbours of Mehamn and Berlevåg.

That night the gale returned with a vengeance and threw rain and more sleet on to the windows. As I lay in bed I could feel the house juddering when some of the stronger blasts hit it. I was not at all worried, as

Day 150. One fishing boat and a couple of tourist boats operated from the small Gamvik harbour which was very quiet during the gales

Day 151. For five days the gales threw waves and surf on to the skerries outside the harbour walls, before the winds finally abated

this house would have seen a lot more than this in its 50 years on this windswept coast, and I am sure it has endured a couple of force 12 winds. In the morning I looked out of the window at the sea. Despite the fact the wind was westerly and going offshore, I could see many white caps as the waves left the shoreline. Frank visited for a chat and to make sure I had everything I needed. He lived up near Slettnes fyr lighthouse and said that the previous day the whole ocean there was white as the huge swell pounded the skerries on this shallow coastline. He thought I would be here for another three days at least, as it would be dangerous to take a fishing boat out in this, and certainly not a kayak. The ocean around the lighthouse was renowned for waves and currents, and it is also marked on the marine charts as an area with dangerous waves. The lighthouse itself was over 100 years old and was rebuilt after the war when the top half of it was blown up by the retreating Germans. Surrounding the lighthouse today is a nature reserve, primarily for wading and coastal birds.

I spent much of the next three days hibernating like a recluse in Frank's house. As it was a holiday weekend the simple shop and cafe was closed, so there was nowhere for people to gather. In addition to that, the weather wavered between a force 5 to 9 the whole time, with frequent showers of a sleet-like rain. I ventured outside for a constitutional walk each day to stave off boredom and see what was going on, which was very little. Indeed, in those three days I did not speak to anyone else after Frank left. As I walked around Gamvik I noticed that it was not as run down as some of the other towns and villages in Finnmark. Generally, the houses were well painted, and there was some pride in the gardens. The fish processing plant looked a mess, though, and it reflected the fact that Mehamn, some 20 kilometres down the road, had all but taken over. There were many houses in the town, at least 50, yet there did not seem to be much employment, apart from the school, museum and the very small fishing operation. Apparently there were a lot of retired people who lived here and quite a few commuted to Mehamn to work.

Day 151. Reindeer wandered around the empty streets of Gamvik, feeding on the unfenced gardens where there was ample grass

On the Sunday I noticed there was a lot of activity around the church. The church itself was rebuilt after it was destroyed in the war. It is something of a landmark on its small knoll, and was the first thing I saw in Gamvik after the hard paddle across the Tanafjord. The reason for the activity was that not only was it Sunday but it was Whitsun or Pentecost Sunday. This commemorates the descent of the Holy Spirit upon the Apostles and other followers of Christ. This is one of the important weeks in Norway for confirmation ceremonies of young teenagers into the church. It seemed there were a few confirmations at Gamvik church today. I also saw some leaves for the first time this year. They were on the only trees which were tough enough to grow here,

Day 152. It was not until 1st June that I saw my first sign of spring flowers which was this hardy primrose

Day 152. A traditional A-frame used to hang brace of cod to wind dry in the cold spring months to make stockfish

which was the scrub willow. Even the hardy mountain birch did not survive this far north. The vegetation at sea level here is the same as about 1400 metres in Jotunheimen. As I wandered around the few empty, windswept streets, I met a herd of reindeer that were doing the same and looking for some fodder in people's unfenced gardens. The gardens were generally just rough lawns and nothing more. In one garden I saw my first wild flower of the year, a yellow primrose which must have blossomed in the last few days. The museum was closed, but they had two outside exhibits, the first was a traditional large A-frame used for hanging cod on to dry when Gamvik was a viable harbour and many boats landed their catch here. The other was the boat, or pramma, which was used to shuttle goods and people from the quay to the Hurtigruten ferry as the quay was too small for the ferry. The pramma was in use up to 1990 when the ferry ceased to stop at Gamvik.

I had been keeping an eye on the forecast, naturally, and there seemed to be a short weather window which would open for about 12 hours before the gales returned. I was eager to take it, otherwise I would start to lose momentum and could be stuck here for another half week. I was apprehensive about the swell on the skerries around Slettnes, given the predominantly northern gales in the last half week. The gales would have created unhindered waves across the large fetch of the Barents from the polar region. Tom had also warned me about Slettnes as he paddled round here 10 days ago. He said there were two navigational stakes in the sea and I should go round both of them, giving the outer one a wide berth. I phoned Frank to settle up for the four nights and he came down for a cup of coffee and a chat. He was rather sceptical of me attempting the paddle tomorrow, despite the forecast. He told me

Day 152. The old Gamvik pramma was used to shuttle goods and people to the anchored Hurtigruten ferry when it previously called here

there was also an inside passage which would not force me out into the exposed ocean to go round the skerries but could not anticipate how it would be tomorrow. I had pretty much made up my mind to go and felt certain I must make the effort at least. Frank threw a final spanner into my confidence by telling me that the coastline was also called 'Dødens Kysten' (The Death Coast) because of the many sailing and fishing boats which had been wrecked here over the last two centuries with the untold loss of mariners' lives.

It was eerily calm when I went to bed at 2300 and when the alarm went at 0400 nothing had changed. The sky was overcast and the weather forecast was now saying the winds would return again at midday. I managed to pack and launch the kayak by 0600, and set off just after the only fishing boat to operate out of Gamvik. Once outside the harbour I turned north and cut inside the skerry which I had seen take such a pounding from the waves over the last days and indeed still was. Although the wind had taken a rest, the swells generated by the storm far to the north in the heart of the Barents Sea, were still sweeping down. As I paddled out I was surprised to see another skerry being pounded by the breaking swell nearing the land, almost blocking my way. There was a narrow passage about 50 metres wide where the swell was not breaking, and I decided to dash between them hoping a rogue wave would not appear when I was at the most vulnerable. Before I went I waited just to make sure none of the bigger surf would topple. Nothing alarmed me, so I started to paddle hard and soon I was in the thick of it, climbing up steep three-metre waves and dropping out of sight between them. It must have been shallow through this passage as the swell was affected by the bottom drag, which made them higher.

Once through the gap I could see that there were skerries all the way up the coast to the now visible Slettnes fyr lighthouse. I could also see massive waves breaking on them as huge green claws of water reared up out of the sea and pounded down on the churning froth sending rebound plumes exploding into the air. It was a frightening sight and I decided to give them a wide berth and kept a good kilometre offshore to the east of these skerries and the coast. As I paddled north the swell seemed to increase in size to about four metres. The crests were far apart and the lack of wind meant they were relatively unruffled, but they were moving at a tremendous speed as they rampaged out of the ocean to the north.

As I drew level with the lighthouse the distant headland of Kinnarodden appeared. It had been my intention to go round this today, but now I was in this massive swell my confidence was waning. If there was any tide off that exposed headland the sea would be very unpredictable. But my immediate concern was just to the north of Slettnes fyr lighthouse where there are two washed skerries, and many underwater skerries and rocks lurking just beneath the surface. These extend for a good few kilometres offshore making Slettnes a volatile and dangerous headland, possibly the most dangerous in northern Norway and it is also marked on the marine chart as an area with dangerous waves. With Tom Amundsen's warning ringing in my ears I prepared to paddle to the north of the marker stakes. I also considered Frank's advice about a sheltered inner passage but from my fluctuating view point on the pinnacle of the massive swells I could not see how this could be possible and the whole coast seemed a boiling mayhem of white surf. There was no alternative but to continue north for a kilometre at least, and certainly well north of the two markers which I could not see, even when I was momentarily perched on the crests of the swells.

As I continued north the waves seemed to increase in size again. There were some five- or six-metre monsters which came out of the heaving sea to the north. Between waves it was like being in a deep green valley. I had only seen waves of this size once before and that was when I poked my nose out of Dusky Fiord into the Southern Ocean and rounded Five Finger Point after a storm, before fear and common sense got the better of me and I turned back into the relative safety of Dusky Fiord. These monstrous waves here went rushing underneath me as I rode them like a small scrap of driftwood. I could occasionally see how they would rear up on to the skerries round which I was detouring, into what looked like an erupting green pyramid some 10 metres high, before crashing down in an incredibly violent explosion of spray. If I strayed over these shoals I would die. It gave me added impetus to paddle even further out offshore to put some distance between me and this terror. When I was about 2 kilometres north of the coast and a kilometre north of the skerries, I still could not see the stakes Tom had told me about, and assumed I had gone round them, so I turned west and started to arch round the very visible danger, giving it a wide berth. I could see the dramatic headland of Bispen easily now which was beyond Slettnes and not as proud a headland. I anticipated the sea would be less frightening there and could not wait to reach it.

The swell was now coming diagonally from behind me, and as the wind had picked up a bit, some of these mountains of water were developing crests which were quite manageable, but given the magnitude of the waves it did little to settle me. I frequently peered nervously behind me and was getting edgy, especially when I heard the swish of even a small white cap behind me. Keeping the huge terrifying toppling 10-metre waves on the shoals a kilometre to the left of me I continued towards Bispen. A particularly big set of waves suddenly emerged from the north and I lurched forward on their faces before sinking back into the deep dark green valley between them. As they hurtled towards the land, a shoal on my right, which I thought had no right to be in what I thought was safe water, awakened. It caused the giant wave passing over it to suddenly erupt into a gigantic light green pyramid which toppled with a huge roar. I was just 100 metres away and it terrified me. My anxiety was becoming acute and I could feel my mouth getting parched as my saliva dried up. If I had been just 100 metres further to the west I would have been pitch poled end over end in a Hokusai wave which would have rolled a small fishing boat. With the tremendous pressures and forces I might easily have been ripped from the kayak, or have been too confused and bewildered in the icy water to be able to roll.

Very much on edge I veered away from this shoal and to the left. I then noticed that the mayhem of toppling waves which I had previously been keeping at a safe distance was now getting alarmingly close and was less than 500 metres away to my left. It suddenly dawned on me that the current was carrying me towards them. I had calculated I would be paddling round Slettnes at slack water, but I later found out that there was always a three kilometre per hour east going current round all these headlands due to the effect of the gulf stream as it flowed out of the Atlantic Ocean and into the Arctic Ocean and Barents Sea. With a current welling up from the deep and accelerating over the shallows and shoals I realized I was being carried quickly towards the giant waves which were rearing up in huge green claws and toppling over on to the visible shoals. If I got carried amongst them there would be no escape, and I would soon be lifted to a great height and dashed on the rocks with hundreds of tons of water obliterating the kayak and me. My mouth now felt very, very dry, as if I was sucking cotton wool.

With extreme urgency I started heading due west again, literally paddling for my life. I was paddling faster than the gulf stream and with a frequent eye to any white crested swells coming broadside out of the north I slowly started to put some distance between me and the terror behind me. After a good quarter of an hour of frantic paddling I at last felt confident I was out of the current and away from this acute danger. I then veered to the south again towards the buttress of a headland called Bispen. The further I paddled out across Sandfjord the smaller the swell became until it was just a mere four-metre ridge of moving water, something that would have concerned me a few hours ago, but now, something for which I was very thankful. Soon I could see into Sandfjord which was a narrow fjord with steep cliffs on each side. Far to the south, at the fjord's head, there was likely to be a large sandy beach, judging by the terrain and name. The beach would be pounded by surf, I thought, ruling out a landing, so there was probably nowhere to land until the day's revised destination of Mehamn. I carried on across the fjord with my mouth rehydrating and a sense of relief.

Bispen, translated as the Bishop, looked like a chess piece of the Gods. It was a vast angular tower of rock at the end of a rugged peninsula. This peninsula was very steep on all sides and with very folded geological strata. There were many puffins bobbing about in the sea here but I could not see anywhere they might have been breeding. There was a grassy covered island, called Kamøy, just 2 kilometres to the west, and I assumed it must be there. However, when I reached it half an hour later, I found the island dotted in brooding blackback gulls with many gulls standing erect on the grass slopes and ledges guarding their nests. I paddled through the strait between the rocky headland and the gulls of Kamøy and it was like walking out of a blizzard into a warm cabin.

Day 155. Sheltering behind the very calm skerry outside Mehamn after rounding Slettnes and looking towards Kinnarodden

The sea started to calm down as the rebounded waves and swell diminished and the confused, unpredictable surface they cause, called clapotis, calmed down. I paddled into the fjord with the wind behind me as I almost cruised down the bare, grey rock-strewn peninsula towards some shallow, grassy islands surrounded by skerries which the swell was gently washing. I went behind the skerries into the quieter water and this was the first time I had felt confident I could take my hands off the paddle all day. There were more gulls nesting on this island and many hundreds of eider duck were bobbing about in the lee in a vast raft. I took some photos here which in no way showed the state of the sea some three hours earlier. My bladder was bursting now and in light of what I had just been through, I was not fussy at all and just unzipped the drysuit fly and peed into the bottom of the boat rather than contorting myself to fire over the side. I would just have to rinse the boat and drysuit in the sea at Mehamn. In less than 20 minutes I was paddling into the sanctuary of Mehamn harbour.

As I approached Vidar's Hostel he must have seen me coming. He had a course running, and he and the delegates all came out to cheer me from the jetty. It was a nice welcome, and I quickly forgave Vidar for the bicycle and the week's saddle-soreness the seat had given me. I did a victory roll for him and was shocked at just how cold the water was on my head. Then I capsized the boat, right by the shore and waded out, rinsing everything. I dragged the boat up, got out of my drysuit and walked straight into Vidar's dining room, where the bacon and eggs were already prepared. It almost felt like a homecoming and it was good to be back in Mehamn. I had finished my ski here, started my cycle here, and now I'm here with my kayak.

After the meal I had a shower and a chat with Vidar. He seemed very keen to join me on the next leg around Kinnarodden headland. This could be an advantage, because he knew the sea here like the back of his hand, but it could also be double trouble, as he was a Sunday paddler and his kayak was a simple one, like Jon's. If we got into a similar situation which I had to fight out of this morning, I don't think I would have the resources to spare to help him. He suggested going at midnight because of the tide. He then left to do one of his many jobs; which this time was to be the air traffic controller at the small airport. I had a siesta, but before I slept I lay on the bed and reflected, with some satisfaction, on the challenges I had endured on the Østhavet coast of the Barents Sea. This section of coast, which stretched between Vardø and Mehamn, was now over, and had tested me. The next section, round the northern peninsulas, is the Nordishavet, and I desperately hoped it would not put me in the same danger, despite its huge potential to do so.

Day 156. While I spent three days in Mehamn there were many snow showers which were coming in on the bitterly cold north winds

The midnight paddle came to nothing, as the wind increased to a force 4 from the north, and this would have done nothing to dampen the huge waves. The next morning it was the same, and the forecast said it would get more windy through the day. I resigned myself to a day in Mehamn. I walked round the bay to the small café and had a breakfast roll and coffee, as a snow shower piled in from the north. This was quite a surprise for June 3rd. After some shopping, I went for a walk down by the fish wharfs. There must have been about 50 boats which landed their catch in Mehamn. Many were local, but some were from Lofoten or Vesterålen and followed the spring cod up here and will be returning soon. Again a lot of the fishing seems to be done with longlines with hundreds of hooks on each line. In the afternoon I went to the library where I could immerse myself in some of the bird books. There were many of the wader type birds which I wanted to identify. As I returned to the youth hostel, in the increasing wind, I saw a red-throated diver and a common merganser swimming about in the harbour. Back at the hostel, I found there were a couple of ornithologists staying. They were on their way to the Nature Reserve at Slettnes fyr lighthouse to look for wading birds. They were both from southern Norway and very informed about the birds up here. They asked me whether I had seen any Brunnich's guillemot which belong to the more Arctic polar regions, but sometimes brood on the northern shore of Finnmark. I confessed I did not know about them and assumed all I saw were the common guillemot. The difference between the two is a narrow white streak behind the mouth. The ornithologists were somewhat jealous of my red knot encounters and said the main aim of their journey up to Slettnes was to see them. That evening I returned to the café in town which was serving stockfish. This is the finished dried cod which was hanging on huge racks in the southern half of town. There must have been the equivalent area of two football pitches which were dedicated to drying the cod the boats landed each day. Locally it is called Boknafisk. It was well cooked, and beautifully presented, but this did not hide the taste. I was hoping for the salted cod I had in Vardø, but instead, I got something with an almost leathery texture and a half rotten taste.

The weather was slightly worse than expected in the morning, with the north wind making the flags snap and bringing in frequent snow showers. The forecast said it would deteriorate for a couple of days, so I was stuck in Mehamn. Having had the mouth-parching fright around Slettnes, I was not eager to repeat the experience, so just had to be patient. I took a walk through the town to the bay on the north side of Mehamn, where it was possible to see the ocean to the north. There were a lot of white horses on top of the large waves in the broad Mehamnfjord, so despite my frustration it was painfully obvious it was not the day to attempt to paddle round Kinnarodden, the most northerly extremity of Mainland Europe. The wind and snow did not deter many fishing

Day 156. The entrance to Mehamn harbour was subdued in the north wind but some hardy fishermen still went out to set or retrieve lines

boats from leaving the harbour to go out with their baited longlines for another shift at sea. As I wandered along the wharfs en route to the library again I saw a pair of long-tailed ducks and red-throated divers swimming in the harbour. There were quite a few species here if one took the time to look. In the library I wanted to look at books on Norway's coast and bird books but met an older family there and started chatting. They were all visiting their childhood homes, having moved to other areas in Norway some 20-40 years ago. They were an interesting and lively bunch, and I arranged to meet some of them tomorrow, if I was still here. They told me the weather would soon change, and summer would unfold overnight, exploding in vibrant shades of new green. There was very little evidence of that now, and I still had not even seen one of the rare birch trees in bud yet. That evening, I neurotically checked the forecast again, and my spirits lifted. There was at least half a week's great weather due to arrive in a couple of days. This would be enough to see me round Nordkapp and on to Havøysund. Hopefully there will also be enough time to visit the renowned bird colonies at Gjesværstappan. I could hardly wait to get started.

On my last day in Mehamn I went along the wharfs past divers and ducks again to meet Hanne at the café. She was one of the family I had met yesterday. After lunch she showed me around the town where she had spent her first seven childhood years before moving south some 40 years ago. It was interesting to get a local view. We walked out to the small peninsula to the north of the town where there were some ruined German fortifications. I got the same view out over Mehamnfjord I had yesterday and could see the swell was at last starting to dwindle. After the walk I returned to the youth hostel via the wharfs again. I spoke with one fisherman who had just landed nearly a ton of black halibut. He had caught them on 12 longlines, each with 300 hooks. He would leave the line out for 24 hours before returning the next day to take them up and set another 12 lines. He said it was normal to catch about 300 fish in this 24 hour period. He was from Lofoten and would be returning there in a little under a month. I would hopefully beat him to Tromsø as the forecast still looked promising when I went to bed. I was now mentally and physically prepared for the paddle round Kinnarodden again and was champing at the bit to get started. I would be going on my own, as Vidar had reconsidered his bravado, after I told him about my escapade at Slettnes.

Day 156. There were many divers and ducks in the basin of Mehamn harbour. Here are a pair of long-tailed duck *Clangula hyemalis*

SECTION 21. Østhavet
14 days. 171 kilometres. 34.5 hours. 0m ascent. 0m descent.

THE KAYAK: SECTION 22.NORDISHAVET

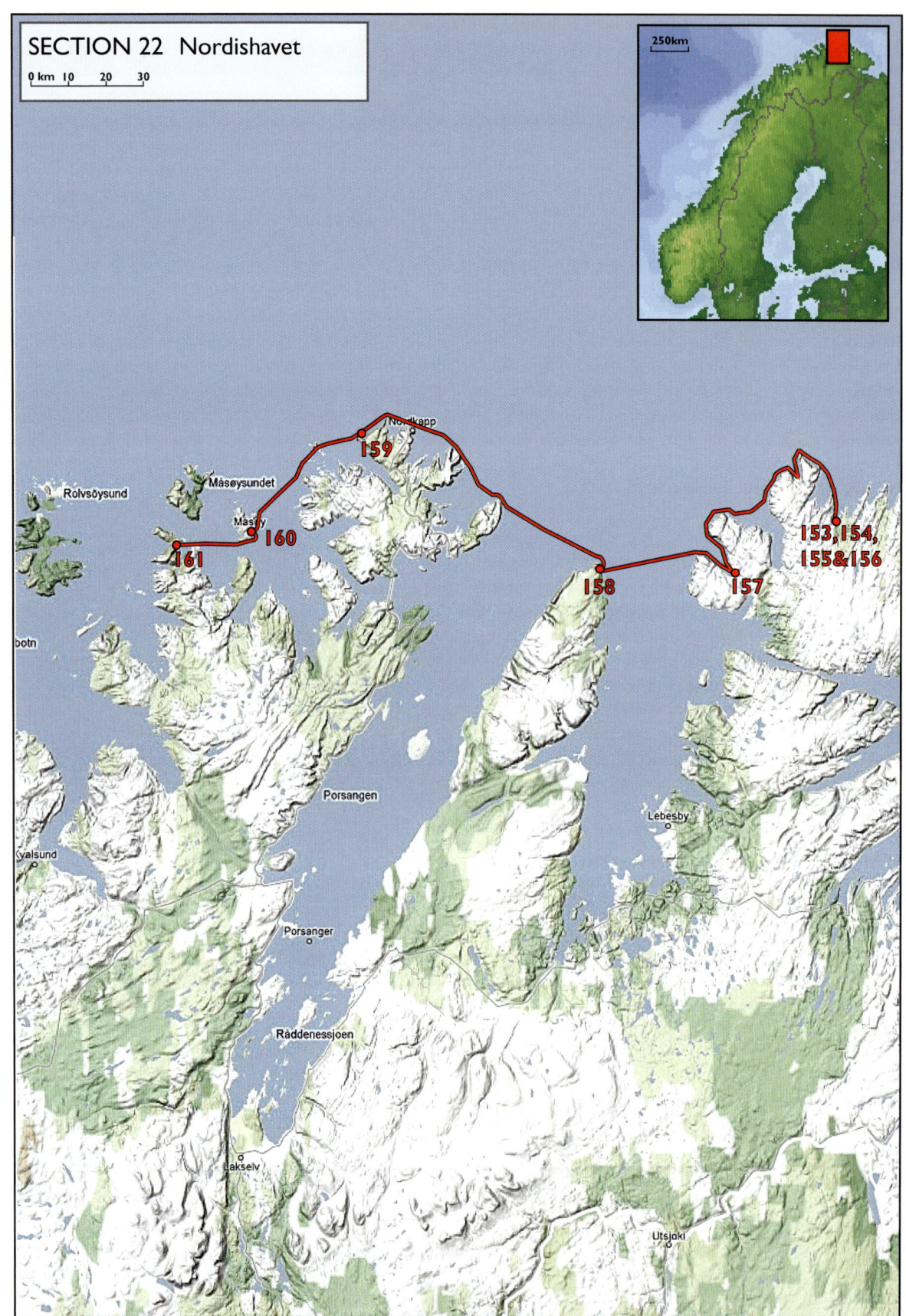

THE KAYAK: SECTION 22.NORDISHAVET

I got up very early to catch the tide before it turned at Kinnarodden, as I did not want a repeat of the difficulties I had experienced at Slettnes. I managed to man-handle the boat down the steep, rocky shore, pack it and then launch by 0530. I paddled out of the harbour and across Mehamnfjord towards the steep Smørbringen headland. The weather was not as good as I had hoped, with the odd sleet shower, but the wind seemed only to be a force 3. Although there was still a considerable swell, there was hardly any white caps on the waves. I felt quite comfortable in these conditions, but there was a nervous knot of anticipation in my stomach. Once past Smørbringen I headed across the more exposed Magkeilfjord to reach the spectacular headland of Magkeilspira, which was the lofty culmination of the steep west side of this fjord. As I paddled across this fjord, the swell got bigger, and there were more and more white caps appearing. Vidar had told me there was a cabin in a sheltered inlet at this dramatic point, and I had intended to stop here and gather myself for the rounding of Kinnarodden itself. However, I could just not see it, and assumed I had passed it, but just as I approached the headland the cabin appeared at the end of a slot-like inlet. Unfortunately, the sea around the narrow entrance to the inlet was very choppy with a lot of clapotis, and the landing beyond this boiling chaos looked very rocky, so I would just have to carry on. Just then I felt something disturb the balaclava I was wearing. It took me a few seconds before I realized what was happening. I looked up and there was a pair of outstretched wings. A seagull had actually landed on my head, and it was now perched there. I thought it was a herring gull so got rid of it with a hand. It flew off, circled round and landed in the water beside me. When it landed I saw it was the much more gentle kittiwake. It glared at me with a perplexed look and tipped its head to one side, as if I had hurt its feelings. Had I known it was a kittiwake before I instinctively reacted, I would not have swept it off, but would have let it travel with me a while perched on my head.

Resigned to the fact the next stop would be after Kinnarodden I continued north round the headland. Here things got unpleasant. The falling tide was being swept round and was ploughing into the swell and waves arriving from the north. The sea became very choppy and confused, with water hitting me in the chest. In addition, a strong sleet squall arrived at the same time and the wind increased to a force 5. The heavy sleet was being driven right into my face and I could not pull my balaclava down. I could not let go of the paddle and I also had poggies on which I would not get on easily again in these conditions. I thought a cold face was better than cold hands. The choppy confused sea only lasted for a few hundred metres but the sleet shower lasted about half an hour. It was almost snow and where I could see grassy ledges on the atmospheric

Day 157. Approaching the exposed headland of Kinnarodden after the sleet squall and in a big northerly swell

cliffs above, I noticed they were turning white. This big swell and the sleet were not the conditions I had hoped for to go round Kinnarodden, the most northerly mainland point in Europe. However, I was almost committed, as to waver now would have meant a two-hour paddle back to Mehamn, as there was no landing possibilities. As I approached Kinnarodden the sleet stopped, and although the swell remained, the sea became less confused. I could see the skerry at the foot of the cliffs. But to the north of that I thought I could see a line of breaking standing waves. I got worried and nervously sat bolt upright. The closer I got, the more I could see they were not an unbroken line of tumbling surf, but that they were just many scattered breaking crests. None the less, I did not want to go through them, as with this swell they were not friendly white horses, but roaring white gauntlets, erupting out of the sea clawing at the dark sky. I paused and watched them for a while.

There was a narrow channel between the foot of the cliffs and an offshore skerry. It was a slot about 4 metres wide and 300 metres long, called Avløysa. But it is not possible to see the channel entrance until you reach it, just before the tip. I was sure that in this swell the entrance and exit would be very difficult, despite Vidar assuring me it was a well-known rabbit run for small boats. The problem was, if I went closer to investigate, the falling tide might sweep me past the entrance, round Kinnarodden point and into the confusion of white claws leaping from the sea. I thought the best option was to paddle back along the coast for a kilometre, and then head out to sea for

Day 157. On the protected Sandfjord beach again (see page 201) after rounding the angular Kinnarodden headland in the background

at least a kilometre, where the current would hopefully not be so strong and I could have more control over my destiny. Once I had paddled back under the cliffs and started to head north out to sea I noticed the current here was not nearly as strong as I had anticipated. I then headed west again to go round Kinnarodden giving it a wide berth. I was a good kilometre north of it and could see the ocean was quieter around me and the large northerly swell was barely disturbed. I then had the confidence to turn southwards.

I assumed I was in the last third of the ebbing tide, so the current should be heading south west. As I approached land again on the west side of the headland, though, I noticed that I was having to paddle hard to make much progress. I then realized that I was paddling with the small tide in my favour, but against the overwhelming background current of the Gulf Stream, which was flowing at 3 kilometres per hour against me. In another five hours, both the flooding tide and the Gulf Stream, would be conspiring together to create a fearsome tide heading north east. When this double current charged into this large northerly swell there would be dangerous conditions. I have heard that even the large Hurtigruten ferry gives Kinnarodden a wide berth in such situations. Soon I was level with Kinnarodden and paddling south against the current along the foot of the cliffs under some very spectacular coastal architecture for 2 kilometres, passing jagged towers and the serrated Reipnakktind, until I burst through a small tidal overfall into the relative sanctuary of Sandfjord. The beach at the end of the fjord was a bit of a detour, but I needed to get out to stretch my legs and eat, so decided to paddle the extra 2 kilometres. I already knew what a nice beach it was, having camped here the night after completing my ski trip. There was just a small swell on this side of Kinnarodden, so the surf should not be too difficult. The large amount of snow which was here over a month ago had now largely gone. There were still reindeer on the slopes surrounding the fjord. I landed on the beach in tiny surf and got out, relieved I had just paddled round Kinnarodden without any incidents. I stopped here for a good hour while another snow shower swept in from the north, and pushed the sun out of the way. The tide was just turning while I was on the beach. I found a sheltered rock and hid behind that with an eye on my kayak for half an hour until the shower was over.

With the sun now back I set off south. The coast between Sandfjord and Oksefjord was as spectacular as anything I had seen on the trip so far. The cliffs came straight out of the Arctic Ocean (Nordishavet) and soared up for 300 metres. The strata were generally vertical, so there were no ledges which the kittiwakes, guillemots and razorbills like to nest on. Surprisingly I did not see any eagles here. The current was still against me and I made slow progress as I went past these spectacular cliffs. There was still a large northerly swell and it was being steepened by the current, and the rebounding waves were forming clapotis. There was the odd cove here, but they were not at all protected. I eventually rounded a point and started to head due south into the wide entrance of Oksefjord. Given the sea condition there was no temptation to cut across the fjord too early, so I continued along the coast, passing many more spectacular cliffs with long stretches of vertical geological strata. There must have been some incomprehensible forces at work here to tilt such huge depths of rock 90 degrees. The snow showers continued to come through and they just about obscured the near coast with its small coves. In just about every cove there was the twisted, rusting remnants of a large trawler

Day 157. The coastline between Sandfjord and Oksefjord was spectacular with 300-metre high cliffs erupting from the ocean

Day 157. Every cove in outer Oksefjord contained a smashed ship but unfortunately the views were obscured by the frequent sleet squalls

or small ship. Eventually when I thought I was deep enough in the fjord to avoid the worst of the ocean current, and with only 6 kilometres to the other side, I started to cross Oksefjord. The fjord itself looked very barren with steep bare rock lining both sides and no vegetation. Slowly, Kjelsvik approached, and the smaller bird colony, which I would miss as it was deeper into the fjord, was just about visible with the white stains of guano. When I reached Kjelsvik I could see it was a nice bay and would have made a good camp spot. Landing would have been tolerable, as the beach was composed of steep pebbles and was slightly protected from this northerly swell.

I decided to push on round the next headland, cross Kjøllefjord and camp near Finnkjerka, a unique rock structure. But the 5-kilometre journey round the outside of this headland was very bumpy. The swell which had never really disappeared all day was back in force and the current here must have been strong. It was very choppy with a lot of clapotis from the rebounding waves. For nearly two hours the kayak was leaping from crest to trough and then surging back to the crest again. I passed many more coves here, but all were very exposed and barren. Most of the coves were surrounded by 300-metre high cliffs. At last the final headland appeared, and as I rounded it Finnkjerka appeared on the other side of the Kjøllefjord. It was much smaller than I expected, as it is a famous landmark. However, the massive cliffs beside it would make most things look insignificant. I could see from across the fjord there was nowhere to camp on the other side for a while, so I followed the north coast. Here there was a steep line of cliff for 2 kilometres until a bay. I nearly landed on the pebble beach in this bay as there was a small stream cascading down the rock, but there was nowhere flat to pitch a tent, except on the large pebbles, so I continued into Kjøllefjord. The whole of Kjøllefjord was incredibly barren. There was just no vegetation on the north side until well into the fjord. It reminded me of the barren arid landscape of Central Asia rather than lush Norway. The land here could not sustain any farming at all and it is only the sea which is productive. I continued to hop from cove to cove looking for a camp spot until I was just 3 kilometres from Kjøllefjord town. There was a good spot here but with the wind behind me I decided to continue to the town and get a bed in the hostel. It had been a long hard day and perhaps I deserved one.

Day 157. Kjelsvik bay would have made a fine camp spot as I could have easily landed on the pebble beach in these conditions

The hostel was an old fisherman's wharf and factory. It was on its own about a kilometre out of town. It was not what I wanted, and it looked deserted. I was sure I would be the only guest. To make matters worse there was no way of landing. It was a high steep quay of large stone and broken concrete. It was not inviting, so I continued to the heart of the town where there was also a beach. I landed on the beach and soon had a very cheap room in the hotel's annex. It was perfect. I paddled to the sheltered inner harbour and got on to a floating jetty. A few people came over to chat. One was the off-duty policewoman, who helped me lift the boat on to the jetty. She was good friends with one of the couples who had done the Norge på langs ski trip this year, just ahead of me. I unloaded the items I needed and carried them up to the nearby annex. After a warming shower I went out. Kjøllefjord seemed a very friendly town. Everybody stopped to chat, especially the large team of schoolchildren on their bikes. The town was about the size of Mehamn with probably around 1000 inhabitants. I went to the hotel to eat. While waiting for the food I felt I was still lurching backwards and forwards, due to the residual effects of the swell earlier today.

Day 158. The north coast of Kjøllefjord was a barren waste of rock and stone, more reminiscent of arid Central Asia than lush Norway

I slept very well, delighted I had at last got past Kinnarodden, but still had a few more difficult challenges in the near future. The first one was today when I had to paddle over the near 20-kilometre wide Laksefjord to the very remote and wild Sværholt peninsula. The weather was well in my favour and it was bright and sunny, the skies were blue and there was a gentle north-west wind coming down the fjord. It would be against me but it was only force 3, and it was forecast to drop. I packed the kayak and chatted with a couple of fishermen before I cast off at midday. Once past the breakwater I could look down the fjord to the rock outcrops at the end, known as Store Finnkjerka. Despite the diminishing headwind I made good time up the fjord. I followed the south side, which was not quite as barren as the north side, but not far off and still covered in bare rock and stones. There was a bay, Mostadvika, half way up with a nice stream, but landing looked difficult and there was no flat land for camping. After Mostadvika bay the south side of the fjord became more and more impressive as it grew in height to 300 metres again. The first massive outcrop was Svartberget, and then the rampart of cliffs continued all the way for the 3 kilometres to Finnkjerka. The cliffs were so high and imposing it was impossible to capture them with a camera. At Finnkjerka there were two rock formations or structures which were unusual, and one of them resembled a church, hence the name. They were both relatively small and only about 35 metres high, if even that much. I had expected them to be much more impressive, as the Hurtigruten ferry and occasional cruise ships, made an effort to point them out. I stopped at their base to take a few photos and prepare myself for the almost 20 kilometre crossing.

Day 158. The coastline on the south side of Kjøllefjord was vertical with great cliffs rising 300 metres, like Svartberget pictured here

Once I had left Finnkjerka and entered Laksefjord I expected the wind to increase to a force 4. However, I had a pleasant surprise as it was completely still with the rolling swell having a smooth glassy appearance. It was so calm I easily spotted the fins of a couple of porpoises which were gently surfacing at the headland. Currents would meet here and encourage smaller fish to gather, which the porpoises would eat. I looked over to the northern tip of the Sværholt peninsula and the whole journey was under blue skies and across a glassy sea. I could not believe my luck, as I needed clement weather, and this was the extreme of it. The wild Sværholt peninsula jutted out into the Arctic Ocean (Nordishavet) on its own between its more famous neighbours of Kinnarodden and Nordkapp. While it was not subject to the same tides, it was still an exposed spot on the northern edge of the continent. At the end of the Sværholt peninsula there was a large promontory, called Sværholtklubben, which was a bird colony. Just to the south of this promontory was a bay, called Sværholtbukta. There were some old houses in the bay apparently and some good camping spots. It was my destination as I took

Day 158. The rock formation at the south entrance to Kjøllefjord looked like a church and was well known as Finnkjerka

Day 158. After Finnkjerka the cliffs continued south down the east side of the enormous Laksefjord which was nearly 100km long

the first strokes into Laksefjord. The weather remained fantastic for the whole crossing. It was so still I could spot puffins from about 500 metres and the occasional lazy roll of porpoises lolling near the surface. After a kilometre I could look south into Laksefjord and see that the impressive rampart of steep cliffs continued down the coast. As always, on long crossings, it took ages for me to see that the destination was starting to draw a bit closer, and the distant shore was a darker shade of haze. Usually, on a long crossing, there is a bit of angst the weather will deteriorate badly half way across, there was no such worry today, but a bank of dark cloud was building to the north and was slowly approaching.

As I approached Sværholtbukta bay I could see the sanctuary of the abandoned houses in the unkempt pasture. As the clouds were almost upon me, I decided to make a small detour to see the bird colony before I landed. It was a massive colony and the cliffs were plastered in kittiwakes. I had also seen some guillemots and razorbills on the crossing, so assumed they would also be here. I had also seen a lot of puffins on the crossing. Puffins do not nest on ledges, but in burrows, or in holes beneath boulders. They also nest in colonies. Puffins are therefore much more vulnerable to predators such as weasel, stoat, mink and even fox. They have to nest in areas inaccessible to these predators, such as islands, or the top of sea stacks. I had seen many puffins for the last fortnight but still not spotted an area where they might be nesting. After my reconnaissance trip to the bird colony I paddled into the bay. I did not take the kayak right up as I was considering paddling the next 20 kilometres to Helnes fyr lighthouse on the next peninsula. It would have been criminal to waste the weather.

Day 158. 20 kilometre crossings are always a worry, in case one is surprised by bad weather, but today, Laksefjord presented no angst

I ate some snacks and then started to explore. It seemed there was once a small community here. The houses could have been pre-war and too remote to have been burnt. There was a barn with living quarters attached to it, numerous small cabins, a house Norman Bates would have felt at home in, and some ruined buildings along the shore. All the cabins, and Norman Bates' house, were locked with very rusty padlocks which would be seized solid. I peered through the windows and could see peeling paint, damp mattresses and browned newspapers from the 1990s on the rustic tables. It seemed that once the community was abandoned around the war the cabins were kept as places to fish and collect eggs in the summer months. However, it now seems even the cabins are abandoned. Behind all this was a small graveyard with eight graves all from before the war, which proved this was once a thriving community. The barn was open and I went in. It still had stalls for animals and a lot of old wooden barrels. The roof had a few holes in it and the doors to the

Day 158. The promontory at the end of the Sværholt peninsula was a large bird colony, with mostly kittiwakes nesting on the strata

Day 158. Sværholt was once a small community but was abandoned a few decades ago and was slowly being reclaimed by nature

hay loft upstairs had blown in. At one end was a room which someone had been trying to turn into a cabin. There were six bunks, a table and chairs, and a rusty stove. Its many windows let a lot of light in and it was a comfortable space. The view from the windows was marvellous. There were binoculars left here and I think this place is sometimes used by keen birdwatchers who visit the colony.

I was dithering over whether to stay or not when it started to sleet and there were some gusts of wind. This was forecast to arrive. I easily abandoned the momentum to continue across Porsangerfjord in favour of the shelter of the barn. I secured the kayak and took all the necessary drybags to the barn. Once I was ensconced, with my down jacket on, it was actually very comfortable and there was water from a brook nearby. Looking out of the window I could survey the bay. A sea eagle was perched on a rock waiting for some carrion. Common and golden plovers flew around the hummocks of grass. There were many thrushes nesting in the vicinity, and on the crags nearby, where I spotted a nest with six eggs. They were even nesting in the roof of the barn and came and went through the missing hayloft door. Reindeer and their newly born calves wandered around the barn, oblivious to me inside, and I could get a good view of them from my lookout. If I went outside they would all bolt. They were eating the grass shoots and leaving the young nettles alone. Sværholt also had an air of sadness to it. There must have been two or three families living here once, and now it was all gone. The grass would claim back the graveyard, the buildings would collapse and be scattered by the winter storms, erasing any trace of those happy summer days some 100 years ago. As I wandered around I wondered what had happened to the descendants of the Kraabøl, Sjøveian, Nilsen and Vaihaaja who were mentioned on the gravestones. Some must still be in Finnmark, while others might have emigrated to North America.

Day 158. The barn at Sværholt had many farming relics but was now just used as a rustic shelter for hardy birdwatchers to camp in

Day 159. From the windows in the gable of the barn I could survey the bay and the pastures outside where reindeer and their calves grazed

After an eerie night in the creaking barn, I woke to see the weather was still poor. The cold north-west wind and the occasional light sleet shower gave me plenty of excuses to stay put and see what happened in the afternoon. I made some hot drinks from the stale remnants left on the shelves by previous visitors, and settled down at the table beside the window to write. Outside the window a herd of reindeer grazed with their new born calves, and above me in the loft the noisy, young thrushes erupted into a frenzy each time a parent returned with morsels. I enjoyed my relaxing morning in the barn and by midday I had finished writing. I noticed the weather had showed some improvement, but I was still a bit uncertain about setting off across another 20 kilometre crossing. I decided to get ready anyway in case the wind eased off. By the time I had everything in drybags near the kayak, the whole of the Nordkinn peninsula across the fjord suddenly transformed from dark dull shades to bright sunlit greys and browns, and I plucked up the confidence to set off at 1400. I paddled back to the bird colony, which I saw was mostly kittiwakes with a few shags and two sea eagles. It was not as extensive as I initially thought, with a low density of birds on the huge rock face. After cruising beneath it for a while in the choppy sea I turned north west. Some 20 kilometres away across Porsangerfjord was the distant Helnes fyr lighthouse at the end of a dark peninsula. I could see the peninsula easily but not the lighthouse.

It is never pleasant crossing large open distances. The far side takes ages to approach, the weather can change and the task seems never-ending. After I had gone about 5 kilometres the weather started to deteriorate again, with the wind increasing from the force 3 up to a good 4 if not 5. White horses started to appear everywhere and I was starting to get the odd faceful of spray. In addition, I suddenly realized I was right in the path of the Hurtigruten ferry when it made the crossing from Honningsvåg to Kjøllefjord. I still had half an hour before it should appear, but it would pass nearby. There is no way it would see me, a small yellow speck in a sea full of white horses, until it was too late. I had no smoke flares I could set off to warn it if it was heading for me, and there was no way I could out paddle it. With the increasing wind, and the thought of the ferry bearing down on me, I started to get anxious and considered turning back. There was still 15 kilometres to go which would be at least three hours in this headwind. With one nervous eye to the weather from the north-west and another on the headland to the west, where the ferry would eventually appear, I carried on. After a good hour the wind started to diminish to a soft force 4 and the number of white horses started to recede. In addition I was probably now well to the north of the route the Hurtigruten ferry would pass. It must have been delayed as it had still not passed. Slowly but surely I pulled my way towards the dark cliffs on the south side of the peninsula. The weather was improving the whole time, and I was thankful that my earlier indecisiveness allowed me to continue. When I was about 5 kilometres from Helnes fyr lighthouse I started to relax. Soon I started to make out the individual buildings in the lighthouse complex and then I was paddling under them as I rounded the headland. I had crossed both Laksefjord and Porsangerfjord in the last couple of days and each was a significant hurdle to have jumped.

Day 159. The crossing of the 20km wide Porsangerfjord from Sværholt in the distance caused concern at the start of the passage

Day 159. The early evening view from Helnes fyr lighthouse across the calm Kamøyfjord where I passed dolphins en route to the far headland

I wanted to land here. There was a small inlet on the south side and a jetty and boulder beach on the north side. I opted for the latter, and as the sea was becoming benign, the landing was quite easy. My map indicated that the lighthouse might contain some self-service accommodation, possibly in the old keeper's cottage. Looking from the jetty I found this surprising, but I know further south in Norway a few of the old lighthouse cottages have been converted. I strode up the path with some optimism to have a look, but on reaching the small complex, I was disappointed. Someone, or some group, 'Destination 71 Nord' had made a misplaced effort to turn the old keeper's cottage into a tourist facility. One of the large sheds had been turned into a wet room and sauna, but it stank of rot, and in places the panelling was torn off and insulation spilled on to the dirty floor. There was a hot tub in the courtyard of the cottages but it was now full of damp debris and a dead hare. The accommodation lodge was locked and when I looked through the window saw it was full of empty

Day 159. As I rounded the final headland the imposing bastion of Nordkapp, Europe's Northern Cape, rose from the Arctic Ocean

bottles and every surface looked sticky. It looked a mad idea and once the original naïve enthusiasm had waned and the money and alcohol run out it seemed the work was abandoned. It was very disappointing and I thought the lighthouse had been partially ruined by the clumsy and tacky improvements by the tourist company. I did not feel like staying, as it was only early evening and the wind had now dropped to a force 2.

I decided to continue to Hornvika bay, just before Nordkapp, where I knew there was a rustic hut. I set off across the desolate Kamøyfjord to the steep headland on the other side. As I approached it a school of six dolphins came towards me, breaking the surface with gusto but not jumping clear of the water. I could not tell if they were white-beaked or white-sided dolphins. They swam under me and then vigorously resurfaced on the other side again. They were large, perhaps three metres, and they could easily have tipped me into the icy water, but they deftly gave me enough space. They were not at all curious, as one would have expected, but swam past as if on a mission. As I continued towards the headland, the wind dropped off almost entirely, and I was again able to see puffins at a quarter of a kilometre as they sat on the calm surface almost looking lost. I was also paddling into the sun which was blasting into my face, warming it. I was in paddling paradise again.

The peninsula I was passing had two large steep-sided corries. On the floor of each semi-circular corrie was a lush green meadow. The meadows were virtually isolated, being bound by the steep craggy mountains on three sides, and the Arctic Ocean on the lower lip, where there were boulder beaches. The sun was giving a wonderful golden hue to the meadows and the southern corrie sides. Soon I was approaching the shaded headland which formed the last ridge or sidewall of the second corrie as it plunged steeply into the ocean. I passed a few more puffin and passed close to the rocks as I went past the point, and there standing before me across the next fjord was a massive headland, a

Day 159. The convoluted fortress of Nordkapp rose 300 metres from the depths and withstood everything Arctic storms threw at it

cape of continental proportions. Rising proud, some 300 metres straight out of the sea, was the solid and robust Nordkapp, standing defiant against all the Arctic Ocean could throw at it. Just to the south of it I could see Hornvika bay. Given the proximity of the two I decided to skip the bay and head straight across the fjord to the headland. I could not envisage better conditions to go round this infamous and notorious headland. The tide should be turning about the time I would reach it in an hour, leaving just the background gulf stream current of some 3 kilometres an hour. I paddled across the glassy sea towards the foot of the cliffs. I had been told to stay well out from the base of the cliffs, but there seemed to be no reason in today's gentle sea. As I approached the foot of the cliffs I could see the small waves, which were just knee high, gently lapping

Day 159. I was lucky I could go round Nordkapp in these very calm conditions, and at midnight, due to 24 hours of daylight

Day 159. Just to the west of Nordkapp is the modest peninsula of Knivskjelodden which is slightly further north of its famous neighbour

at the slabs of rock. I was lucky and very thankful I had not turned back earlier today. I paddled right up to the base and followed it round. The cliffs were enormous and very, very imposing. Huge ridges jutted out and vast overhangs enclosed dark mysterious caverns. This was coastal architecture of immense proportions. As I paddled round, the cliffs became yet more and more impressive. I was just a miniscule and irrelevant spectator in this humbling nature.

The sea began to become turbulent and choppy in places as currents welled up from the depths below. It was almost sinister the way a boil would suddenly appear. This, combined with the green rock base of the cliffs, and the daunting slopes rising far above, made this a very eerie place. The ghosts of many sailors were on these rocks here. Even in these ideal conditions, it was slightly alarming to be here, and I can imagine in rough weather it would be spine chilling. Just three years ago, in 2006, a Norwegian who was rowing the length of Norway in a small boat was swept into these rocks in fair weather and died, as the boat was dashed against the foot of the cliffs. Nordkapp was definitely not a cape to be trifled with. It was exactly midnight as I passed Nordkapp and although the sun was up and well above the horizon, the midnight sun was not shining, as there was a bank of dark cloud to the north. I passed along the foot of the cliffs for a good 2 kilometres with an increasing tidal current against me, until I paddled into the exposed bay to the west of it, called Knivskjelbukta. The waters here were quieter, and I could turn round and reflect on the enormity of what I had achieved so easily, with a huge helping hand from the weather. I took some photos and was jubilant with victory. However, I still had to go further north, as on the west of this bay was another headland, almost insignificant beside its massive neighbour, called Knivskjelodden. It is this modest headland which is the most northerly point of Europe, as it lies slightly to the north of Nordkapp. Both the dramatic Nordkapp and the modest Knivskjelodden are on the island of Magerøy.

Day 159. After I rounded Knivskjelodden, distant islands appeared and I headed for two shoreline snowdrifts to the left of the kayak's bow

Day 159. As I reached the snowdrifts, I realized with delight, that they were two beautiful white sandy beaches at the ruined hamlet of Tones

I crossed the open bay and paddled round the curved tip of Knivskjelodden, hugging the coast to keep out of the flooding tide and gulf stream current, which was now starting to run at 5 or 6 kilometres per hour. The sea was getting choppier as the increasing swell bounced back from the rock but I was round smoothly. From here it was all south to Lindesnes again which was some 2000 kilometres down the coast. As I paddled round Knivskjelodden a different landscape unfolded with every paddle stroke. There were islands appearing ahead. This was the first time I had really seen islands on this trip, except Vardø. I could also see a bay some 5 kilometres down the rugged coast beyond Knivskjelodden. It looked like there were still some snowdrifts lingering in this bay beneath green

Day 159. I rammed the kayak up the beach and went to explore the pasture to find a good campsite after a momentous day

pastures and I hoped I would be able to land here. I made for the snowdrifts along the edge of the bay, as the grass beyond them looked lush and a great spot to camp. It took about an hour to reach them. When I was half a kilometre from them I suddenly realized, with delight, that they were not snowdrifts, but beautiful white sandy beaches. What a stroke of luck this was, finding this idyllic and easy location. The beaches were protected by some seaweed-covered skerries which I had to thread through, and then I could aim for the white sand, which was now basking in sunlight. Two hours after midnight I had the luxury of ramming the kayak up the sunny beach, rather than carefully negotiating a boulder-strewn shoreline.

I hopped out of the kayak and explored the lush meadow above the beach. There were the remains of old houses here and there were many good campsites. I took one just above the beach. Far above, in the boulder field on the hillside, was a large grassy pasture which was covered in large blackback gulls standing sentry over their nests and eggs. Just as the tent was up an isolated rain shower arrived but I was already in the tent. I skipped supper and wriggled into my sleeping bag. Both shoulders were sore, particularly at the joint where the collarbone joins the upper arm bone or humerus. I hoped I had not done any long-term damage to the tendons or cartilage in the rotator cuff area. It felt a possibility. This concern did not prevent me falling asleep as soon as I was in my salty sleeping bag as another shower peppered the tent. What a lucky day I had enjoyed after the indecision in Porsangerfjord, when I nearly returned to Sværholt in the force 5 headwind.

When I woke the sun was beating down on to the tent and warming it so much I was cooking in my sleeping bag. I had to open and tie back both ends of the tent so there was a through draught to cool it. As I gazed across the small bay, with its turquoise sands basking in the sun, I noticed an otter or mink swimming across it. This must be a plentiful time of year for either

Day 160. In the morning I sauntered round barefoot on the soft pasture while basking in the warmth of what felt like the first of day of summer

of these animals with plenty of birds eggs around, in addition to the usual crustaceans. Leaving the ends of the tent open, I basked in the warmth, luxuriating in the tranquillity of this idyllic spot, very content that I had almost completed the most exposed coastline of the whole journey. After the last three days' efforts, there was little hurry, and I snoozed for another four hours until midday. I did not have a plan for today, other than to visit the bird colony at Gjesværstappen, which was reputed to be the richest along the Norwegian coast, and was just two hours paddling away. When I got up I sauntered around the campsite barefoot in shorts and a thin fleece. It was perhaps the first time this year I experienced anything like a proper summer's day, which as it was approaching mid June, I thought I was due. Although there were ruined houses here it seemed

Day 160. From Tones I paddled across the ocean to the archipelago of Gjesværstappen, with the largest island, Storstappen, above the bow

Day 160. As I approached Storstappen more and more puffins joined a whirlwind until there were thousands of birds circling around me

that this place was abandoned long before the war, as just the stone foundations remained, and even they were quickly being buried by sand and grass. On a day like this I could again imagine the idyllic hamlet which once stood here at Tones and could imagine the joy of the summer in the simple lives of the families. Looking at the ruins of these bygone times almost brought a lump to my throat. This really was an idyllic spot. It was difficult to make the decision to leave but the weather was perfect. I carried everything down the beautiful white sand, packed the kayak and pushed off at mid afternoon, gliding over the crystal clear water with its turquoise and green hues.

There was a light following wind as I paddled lazily without any strength or vigour across the open water to the largest and most northerly of the island group of Gjesværstappen. The sun was still shinning and the light was strong and bright, twinkling off the scatter of ripples. As I approached the archipelago there were more and more puffins, some guillemots, tysties, and even some razorbills, milling about on the water. As I neared Storstappen island these birds got denser and denser until there were many groups or rafts of 100 birds or more. As I approached these groups they took off and joined the throng already circling around me and the kayak. The closer I got, more and more birds, predominantly puffins, took off and joined this whirlwind of curiosity. Occasionally, one would come very close, trailing its splayed feet behind it, and turn at the last minute before hitting me. Soon I could see a vast raft of puffins on the north-east side of the island. When I was 100 metres away, the whole raft of some 10,000 birds took off and joined the throng of birds circling around me. I was amazed there were no collisions. During the final kilometre I noticed more and more vast rafts on each side of me. A lot of these rafts also contained razorbills and guillemots who seemed a lot more confident and less reluctant to take to the wing. Indeed, I was quite surprised and a little disappointed the puffins were so wary of me. A year previously I visited the Shiant Islands in the Outer Hebrides which is home to about a quarter of a million puffins. Here I could paddle right into the midst of the rafts and they would lazily shuffle out of the way at the last minute so I was cleaving a bow wave of birds. The puffins here at Gjesværstappen were a far more distrustful bunch.

Day 160. The common guillemot was plentiful along the ledges on the shoreline of Storstappen. Here is a bridled type with white spectacles

When I reached the north-east tip of Storstappen I paused and started to slowly cruise south down the east side. There were kittiwakes, razorbills, guillemots and shags lining the guano-covered outcrops and crags above the shore. Above this were steep grassy slopes which went up some 300 metres to the craggy ridges on top of the island. In these grassy slopes were many tens of thousands, if not hundreds of thousands, of puffin burrows. The sky was teeming with puffins flying

Day 160. Also plentiful along the shoreline of Storstappen was the razorbill, which like the guillemots, nested on ledges on the rock strata

Day 160. Puffins were the most numerous of the Auk type birds and nested in burrows in the grass or between boulders on higher slopes

to and fro from these burrows. As I surveyed the slopes a white flash would suddenly appear. This was a puffin with its white chest emerging from its burrow into the light of day. It would survey the surroundings for a minute or two before launching off the slope and with a quick wing beat of tiny wings make for the sea. Above this frantic puffin activity were at least five sea eagles circling. There were no gulls or ravens harrying them here although they must have been around. The sea eagles would have been looking for carrion, fish and dead birds. They would not have the speed or agility to catch the fast puffins. After a good hour watching this birdlife I reached the southern end of Storstappen and the strait to the nearby neighbouring island of Kjerkestappen. There did not seem to be as much bird life on Kjerkestappen despite it being quite similar. I paddled between the islands and continued round Storstappen. The vast slope on the south side also seemed to be riddled with puffin burrows. I don't know how many puffins were here but the colony seemed on a comparable scale to the Shiant Islands and there were 250,000 there. I did not see any gannets at all around this archipelago. I had heard there was a large colony of them here, but must have missed it. As I came round the south side of Storstappen I saw there was a steep outcrop on the north west of the island which I did not investigate. I assumed that this was the gannets' fortress and they were breeding here.

I now turned south west. With the wind behind me I decided to go to Måsøy island. There seemed to be a bay on the south side of this island with a few cabins on it. It was a good 10 kilometres across the ocean to the north-eastern tip of the island. It took a couple of hours before this craggy tip was within touching distance. On the journey over I could look straight into the deep sound, called Magerøysund, which separated

Day 160. Razorbills, guillemots (here the non-bridled variety) and puffins mingled together to form vast rafts of 10,000 strong

Magerøy from the mainland. There seemed to be a current coming out of it on the ebbing tide, and this was even disturbing the waters I was paddling across, so it must have been strong in the sound. Previously the Sami used to force their reindeer to swim across this kilometre-wide sound to their summer grounds. I hope it was at slack water otherwise a few would have got swept out to sea. Today the Sami use boats to ferry the reindeer over. Once I reached the northern tip of Måsøy I paddled in the shade down the east coast. In the waters here were many tysties. These birds are usually quite solitary birds compared to their gregarious cousins the common guillemot, yet they were gathered here in groups of 20. They tend to nest in crevices and cracks near the waterline and their nests are harder to see. Towards the south of Måsøy were two bays on the east side separated by a narrow peninsula. From the map I assumed they were just some cabins, but as I approached the first bay I saw they were proper houses. I crossed the bay and rounded the peninsula to reach the second

Day 160. To the north-west of Storstappen was a steep outcrop which I missed and assumed it was the fortress where the gannets breed

Day 160. As I paddled into the south bay on Måsøy I was surprised to see a small village complete with a church

of the bays where I had not expected to find very much either. However, I was soon looking into the deep sheltered bay at the end of which was an idyllic sight. A large beach of light sand was spread across the entire head of the bay. Above this was a village, complete with a white church and some 20 houses across a large pasture. As I gazed into this tranquil sight, bathed in the evening sun, I noticed people walking and even a car. I had not expected anyone here at all. I paddled in and rammed the kayak up the simply stunning sandy beach. I walked up the beach to the grass along where there was a crescent of houses and I assumed a track. Just then a tractor came ambling along. I waved to it, hoping it would stop so I could ask the driver a question. It was going to stop anyway, as it's not every day someone comes paddling into this bay in a yellow kayak. I asked the driver, a 70-year-old man called Astor, if there was anywhere to stay. "Not officially." He said "But I am sure I can find a corner for you to sleep in". He pointed to a small homestead and told me to wander over when I had the boat up and was organized, then drove off slowly.

After I secured the boat and unpacked what I needed I went over. Astor welcomed me in and sat me down at the table and started to quiz me. I could see he was a character. He asked me if I was hungry. "Yes I am" I said, and with that he started to prepare supper. There was one dish I had wanted to try since I started paddling in Finnmark, and that was exactly what Astor was boiling; 7 large herring gull eggs to be precise. The eggs were huge; about three times the size of a hen's egg. The shell was very thin, dark green and speckled with dark spots. Inside the white was opaque and not as firm as a hen's egg and the yolk was a bit drier, almost powdery, and more yellow than orange. I ate five and was completely full. I was curious about the eggs and how they compared to the other sea birds. Astor told me the best eggs were tysties, which had very strong orange yolks, but they were difficult to find and collect. He also said puffin eggs

Day 160. Astor invited me to spend the night at his house and fed me herring gull eggs and plied me with Glenfiddich

were very good. The eggs I had just eaten were not that good for eating, but apparently they were very good when used for baking. To me they still tasted delicious. We then retired to his living room where he specially opened a bottle of Glenfiddich he had been given. He poured a very large dram for each of us and started to tell me all about the island. There were 24 people living here, two of whom were teachers for the two pupils. One of the pupils was Astor's 16-year-old grandson who soon joined us. There was a ferry five days a week and a shop which was owned by the community of Måsøy. A couple of fishing boats landed fish here which were processed by the island's very small processing plant. The processed fish was then sent to the mainland at Havøysund on the five times a week ferry. There was also some small scale farming here. Many of the houses on Måsøy were now holiday homes for people who

Day 161. A traditional rorbuer in the sheltered bay at Måsøy. Previously the fisherman and his family would have lived and worked here

Day 161. The simply stunning south bay on the idyllic Måsøy was very much cherished by the locals who were proud of their island

had some family connection to the island and visited every summer. Others were rented out to tourists who had discovered this charming, idyllic community on the edge of the Arctic Ocean.

Astor told me that Sværholt, like many places in Finnmark, was evacuated by the Germans towards the end of the war and the inhabitants shipped south. Then at the end of the war these places were burnt flat. Once the war was over, many of the original inhabitants of these remote coastal hamlets never returned from mid or south Norway. In many cases too few inhabitants returned to make a viable community again and after struggling for a few years to rebuild things the community was then finally abandoned in the 1950s. This is what happened to Sværholt, but in the case of Måsøy enough people returned to make it a viable community again. Astor had recently lost his wife of some 50 years. I did not touch on the subject as it was clearly still painful. However, this was a very close community and he had a daughter and grandchild here. We chatted late into the evening as the midnight sun appeared through a saddle in the hills across the bay. We eventually went to bed in the small hours after a great evening. I thoroughly enjoyed his hospitality and hoped I had not taken it too much for granted. I also enjoyed his company as he was an outspoken man who was too old to be bothered being politically correct or diplomatic. I hope I filled his evening with interesting conservation and my accent was not too demanding.

Breakfast was another two herring gull eggs on toast. I then slowly started to gather my things and pack them. Måsøy was not the place to hurry. There was a beautiful 'rorbuer' or fisherman's cottage on the south of the bay still with its jetty, where the boat would moor and unload. On the jetty was lots of fishing equipment and

Day 161. Some of the men of Måsøy island came down to the beach to see me off. Astor is on the right and his grandson on the left

many brace of cod hanging on racks drying. There was also the shed where the cod was filleted and processed, longlines were baited and equipment was repaired. All the offal and waste from filleting the fish would drop into the sea beneath. Long ago the fisherman and his family would also live in these quarters. It was home, workplace and jetty in one. This particular rorbuer was really more of a working museum than modern house. As I packed the kayak the men of Måsøy gathered to see me off. There was Astor, his son-in-law, his grandson, and three others. It was a nice gesture. I shook hands with all of them then dragged my kayak across the sand into the clear waters. I launched and paddled into the bay heading east to the headland. Before I disappeared I turned and waved my paddle and could see them waving back. Måsøy was a special place, and to find it left me feeling elated. In this sunny weather it was quite idyllic and the warm friendly welcome and hospitality can only really be found in such rural communities untarnished by the stresses of fast living.

Day 161. The south shore of Måsøy was lush with the succulent rock rose growing on many of the ledges along the crags

Day 161. A typical longline fishing boat with the characteristic sail deployed to help propulsion and also giving stability while fishing

There was a small kittiwake colony on the cliffs at the entrance to the harbour as I turned south and then west along the south coast of the island. The south coast itself was really quite lush, with huge bunches of the succulent rock rose growing on all the ledges along the crags. There was a bit of a current along the south shore in my favour and I was paddling at a fair speed. A fishing boat from Havøysund passed me and waved as he went by. He had the slight breeze behind him and had deployed a small sail to help him along. This characteristic sail not only helps marginally with propulsion but also aids to stabilize the boat while fishing. I rounded the southern tip of the lovely Måsøy, and Havøysund came into view some 10 kilometres to the west across the open fjord. It was a larger town of over 1000 inhabitants built on the south shore of the small island of Havøy. Between Havøy and the mainland was a narrow sound, 300 hundred metres wide and a couple of kilometres long. It offered a good harbour and the town developed as a fishing centre. The town was now connected to the mainland by a bridge. On Havøy itself, apart from the town, were 12 large wind turbines. There were a couple more, but during a storm the brake mechanism failed and they spun themselves to destruction, one flying apart in a centrifugal frenzy. I made good time across the open crossing, despite the wind being against me. At one stage it was nearly a force 4. There must have been a considerable tidal flow as I was still doing nearly 8 kilometres per hour despite the headwind. On my right hand side was something new and welcome. It was a large island called Hjelmsøya. There were even a couple of islands beyond that, one with the world's most northerly lighthouse on the inhabited and remote Ingøya. Since the Russian border I have largely had the open Barents Sea and Arctic Ocean on my right and been very much at their mercy. It was reassuring to see this huge barrier now appear between the unpredictable and wild Arctic Ocean and me in my small kayak. It was also reassuring to know this barrier would remain there for most of the remaining 2500 kilometres of my journey, except for a handful of infamous exposed coastlines and peninsulas, so I would be able to risk paddling in poorer weather and would not be pinned down as I was at Gamvik and Mehamn.

Day 161. Havøysund was sited on the small island to the right on the shores of a narrow sound which was spanned by a modern bridge

I arrived in Havøysund rather quickly. It was almost industrial compared to what I was used to. The fish processing operations and boatyards here were on a larger scale than Kjøllefjord and Mehamn. There was a small marina in the sound just in front of the hotel. I pulled into that and levered the kayak on to the floating jetty. There were a lot of sea angling boats here which Germans and Swedes were chartering to fish cod and halibut. Near the hotel was a quiet pensionat with cheap rooms which Astor had told me about. I found it quite easily and got a lovely room at a great price. It even had a washing machine. I showered, put on a wash and then settled down to write and process the photos I had taken so far. Some eight hours later, after a marathon office session, I had finished all my digital duties, and both me and my clothes were clean and pristine. I then treated myself to a celebratory steak at the hotel. Tom Amundsen had reached Havøysund some two weeks earlier and had pampered himself with some rewarding luxuries after his hard kayak from Vardø. I remember being envious of him at the time, but was now enjoying it myself.

SECTION 22. Nordishavet
5 days. 180 kilometres. 39.5 hours. 0m ascent. 0m descent.

THE KAYAK: SECTION 23. HAVØYSUND TO STJERNSUND

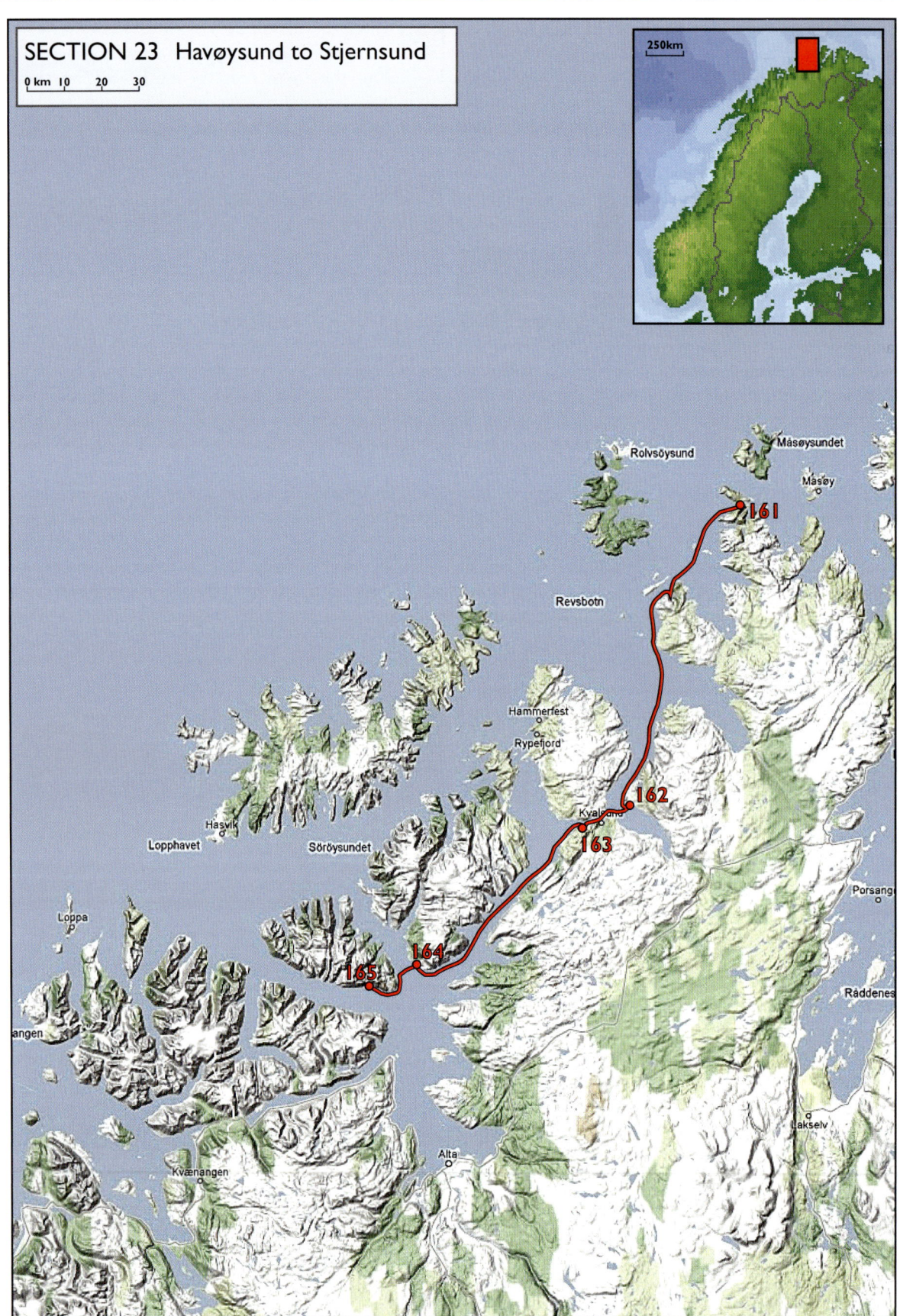

THE KAYAK: SECTION 23. HAVØYSUND TO STJERNSUND

I had the last of the two herring gulls eggs Astor had given me for breakfast and then finally managed to get going around midday. It was a beautiful day again. I had missed the tide through the sound and it was now just turning to flow against me, but I did have the wind behind me. I would generally choose a following wind over a following tide. I cruised down the west side of Havøysund until the open seascape to the south opened up. Out to sea on my north-west were the islands of Ingøya and Rolvsøya. Both were situated in a very rich fishing area and still had viable communities on them. Despite their remoteness, I heard tourism, especially rod fishing, was rejuvenating these islands, and Ingøya was also enjoying a cultural boost with a well-known pottery workshop thriving on the island. Paddling south in the lee of these outer islands, I

Day 162. The island of Ingøya was far out to sea in the north-west. This island and neighbouring Rolvsøya sheltered this coast a little bit

could see the smaller islands of Store and Lille Latøya some 5 kilometres across the sea. I aimed to pass between them. They were low and grassy and I hoped they would be a haven for birds. However, when I arrived an hour later I saw very few here. There was a flooding current between the islands which made the small waves I was riding on topple over, creating a tongue of surf. I hugged the rocky shore of Store Latøya to keep out of this tidal stream until I reached the narrows where I had a short furious paddle to break through the current. From Latøya the wind was still in my favour for the hour's crossing over to Burstadnes, and I made good time cleaving across Snefjord and down past the mainland towards the flat, shallow island of Reinøya. This island was lush and green as if it was grazed upon by farm animals.

Day 162. Looking across the narrows between the two Latøya islands where there was a tongue of tidal current and some surf

Astor on Måsøy told me there was a nice harbour near here at Burstad, and I planned to stop for something to eat. I found the entrance quite easily, where some narrows lead off the head of a bay. Once I was past the narrows, the whole landscape opened up again and there was a small fjord completely protected from the sea. Around the fjord were a few old houses, half of them now derelict. There were also the stumps of a ruined jetty beside two of the more habitable houses. I pulled ashore in front of the houses and went to explore. Both houses were open and I had a look inside. They were cabins now, which a few groups used, judging by the entries in the guest book. A stoat had ripped a lot of the food packaging open. In one house was a photo from about the 1960s. It showed both these houses in pristine condition, with gardens and a large well-kept white wharf and processing plant with some larger boats beside it. It seemed hard to imagine and also surprising a place could be abandoned and fall into disrepair so quickly. One of the houses even had a piano in it with an old carpet on top of it to keep off the occasional drip. When I visited the ruined wharf, I saw the stumps were all charred and the place must have been destroyed by fire some 20-30 years ago. I thought about staying in the

Day 162. An abandoned house deep in the small sheltered Pollen inlet near the once thriving hamlet at Burstad

red house, but I had only done 20 kilometres so far, and the weather was in my favour. Although it was drizzling I decided to cross the open 10 kilometres of Revsbotn fjord while the going was good. Once I was over this fjord I would be in sheltered sounds for the next 100 kilometres, where only gales could hinder me.

Day 162. Paddling down from the Burstad peninsula towards the fjord-like slot of Sammelsund with Kvalsund town 30 kilometres ahead

I followed the rugged and wild, but unspectacular, coast for 10 kilometres past craggy slopes, rather than the impressive cliffs I was starting to take for granted. I also passed a few of the ubiquitous sea eagles, which I was also starting to take for granted, and after the first cursory glance, now largely ignored them, unless the acrobatic ravens were around to harry them. After two hours I reached the southern corner of the peninsula and could look across the next 10 kilometres of open fjord. The wind had died away completely now, but the gentle drizzle continued for the entire crossing. It was late in the gloomy evening when I reached the other side, where there was a small roadless hamlet with about 10 houses. I could not tell if there were lights on in a few of the houses, or whether it was the reflections of the golden, late evening sun as it broke through the cloud behind me. I got the impression that Bekkarbukt hamlet was only used infrequently in the summer. I paddled past the hamlet, keeping a few kilometres offshore, and entered the fjord-like slot of Sammelsund, which was sandwiched between the mainland and the large island of Kvaløya, or whale island. I had calculated that the tide would help me down this 20-kilometre sound and was looking forward to the free ride. I was to be disappointed, however, as the tide seemed to be flowing north and I was only doing a sluggish 4 kilometres an hour. It felt like I was paddling in treacle again. I could not understand why, but I assumed that there were so many basins and fjords emptying and filling, and these would influence the direction of tidal currents, which might be at loggerheads to my intuition. It seemed that predicting the tides in these sounds would be an art, rather than a science, which only local knowledge could unravel.

As I paddled down the sound I initially noticed a few scrubby birch trees. Soon these became larger and their copses were becoming bigger. By the time I approached Brennsvik there were extensive copses of five metre birch and many of them seemed to be turning green. This was very exciting for me, as I had been looking for signs that I was leaving the harsh Arctic winter and entering the lush temperate spring for a while, and this was the first confirmation. This was a much softer landscape than the incredibly rugged and weather-harsh Nordkinn coasts a week ago. It was a sign that things were going to get warmer and more comfortable, especially while camping. I paddled past the farming hamlet of Brennsvik, where I had hoped to stop, but the boulder-strewn beaches were exposed, and if I landed here I might get stuck should the northerly wind increase during the night. As I paddled past the beaches I saw a couple of very small farms and fishermen's sheds. I was also excited by the fact that I could see a few sheep and cows grazing in the tiny fields surrounding the farms. They were the first livestock I had seen grazing this year, and it was more proof that I was entering a gentler, calmer environment. Of course, this livestock would not be able to survive here during the snow-filled winters, if they were not brought into the relatively luxurious barns and fed on imported fodder. I decided not to stop here but to carry on despite the fact it was now after midnight. At the end of this shoreline was a promontory, called Klubben. Beyond Klubben there seemed to be a very sheltered inlet, and as it was just an hour away I made for it. After the Brennsvik farms the coastline reverted to rugged remoteness again, with a couple of abandoned grey derelict houses testament to a lifestyle too hard to continue in these easier times. In front of one roofless wreck I saw a fox foraging along the shore, perhaps looking for eggs or even a chick now, or some fish or mollusc carrion. I reached the bulbous headland, rounded it and paddled into the sheltered inlet of Klubbukta. I was delighted to see a very quaint hamlet, sheltering along the protected pebble beach, and a small harbour. There seemed to be five permanent houses where people lived all year and twenty cabins and fishing sheds. There was even a very small fish processing plant. I put up my tent beside a shoreline shed on lush grass. Once I was in my sleeping bag I realized I was tired after the 65 kilometres and could not be bothered cooking supper.

Day 163. A typical view of the sheltered inlet and harbour at Klubbukta where there were some small scale fishing enterprises

I did not wake until midday, which was low tide. There was apparently a very strong tide at the narrows by Kvalsund for a few kilometres. A few people told me "it is like a river". I would therefore wait until the tide turned again in the early evening and drift down this river, rather than fighting it now. This gave me a good few hours to write and to wander around the hamlet, exploring its fishing sheds and the harbour. The hamlet was remarkably well kept for Finnmark and around each shed the grass was neat. It was more like the orderly and tidy Norway I was used to rather than the scrap-ridden Finnmark. In front of many of the sheds were small jetties and near them frames with cod hanging in the wind to dry them. This was not on the large scale as Mehamn, but looked more of an economic sideline to supplement other occupations. Under some nets there were maybe 1000 cod drying. The locals had also built nesting trays on the posts of the cod drying racks and on the sides of many sheds, and most of these were in use with brooding kittiwake pairs. Underneath the sheds it seemed eider duck were being encouraged to nest. The sheds were full of fishing equipment and parts of old diesel engines were stored in them. Along the crescent of sheds there was also the occasional diesel engine bolted to a concrete plinth with a winch on it. These simple engines would be started occasionally, and the winch wire would be threaded through large pulleys on sturdy posts and then down to a cradle or trolley. When the engine was going it would haul the cradle up the shingle shore. By putting the wire through different pulleys, a winch engine could serve three or four trolleys along the shore. I spoke to one man about the tides through the narrows of the sound, but he rattled off instructions so complicated, my eyes glazed over and the instructions went in one ear and out the other. He did say that the currents and tides here tended to wash things into this fjord. Judging by the number of whale ribs and backbones around the village, I assumed old and sick whales ended up on the beaches here quite often. I packed up my tent, tinkered with some equipment and eventually set off in the early evening, just as the tide started to recede down the shore. There were a lot of red-billed terns in the bay to see me off.

Day 163. Paddling across Repparfjord with the current against me and heading for the bridge spanning the Kvalsund narrows over to Kvaløya

The wind was behind me and I made good speed into the fjord. I was hoping to meet the current soon which would carry me through the sound. I met the current soon enough, but it was going the wrong way! It was flowing towards me and piling into the small waves I was riding and making them break. I could not believe it. My speed halved and I had to paddle hard to reach the town of Kvalsund on the other side of the Repparfjord. I thought I was in a large eddy, or maybe the basin on the south side of Kvalsund drained to the north, in addition to draining southwards. This basin did contain the large Altafjord and maybe this was partly emptying north through the sound and against me. It did not match what the old man had told me, or my intuition. I felt cheated, as I had expected an easy ride after yesterday's effort. After well over an hour of paddling against a current I reached the other side and the town of Kvalsund. My reward was that Kvalsund was a green and lush place with fields basking in the sun and tidy red barns along the road. This was more the cultural Norway I was familiar with from my many journeys to the south.

Kvalsund is the centre of a dispute concerning a Norwegian mining company called Nussir and the Sami reindeer herders. Nussir want to develop a vast quarry to extract copper in the hills above Kvalsund. They have the

Day 163. Arriving at the hamlet of Beretsjord where there was a small pebble beach and strip of grass where I camped

backing of the local population and the local authority, as it would create well over 100 jobs. However, the land they want to dig up is land the Sami have used for centuries, and it is an important area for the reindeer to recuperate after calving. Given the new legislation of the Finnmark Act, the quarry cannot go ahead without the approval of the Sámediggi or Sami Parliament. Currently they are reluctant to give it, as they know the land will be destroyed. Some Norwegian politicians have claimed that the Sami are looking for unrealistic compensation for the loss of these reindeer pastures, and have branded them greedy. The Sami say that they are not interested in the compensation, but do not want this land destroyed and their rights ignored. On their side there is a centuries long history of mining enterprises in both Sweden and Norway riding rough shod over the Sami and breaking promises. It will doubtless go ahead in the future, once a deal is brokered, as the value of the copper which can be extracted is immense.

After passing Kvalsund town I paddled towards the large suspension bridge over the narrows. By now I had no clue as to which way the current might be flowing. When I reached the bridge I saw it was flowing north against me, but not with any resolve, and I could easily paddle against it. I again felt disappointed to be denied a speedy ride. I think my plan in the future, calculating for tides, is to ignore them and go when it suits me. If the tide is against me it will eventually turn within three or four hours, and if it is with me then I am lucky. I was feeling quite tired and without the anticipated current to help me decided to have a short day, get an early night and try and curb my burgeoning nocturnal habit. Shortly after the bridge I spotted a pebble beach with a grassy strip and some fields above that. It was the tiny hamlet of Beretsjord. I had the tent up soon afterwards and managed to get to bed in the early evening with a cuckoo celebrating its arrival from warmer climes by singing in the birch trees nearby.

Day 164. Paddling down Kvalsund after Beretsjord towards Seiland island which was mountainous and contained two small icecaps

Day 164. Paddling down Vargsund with the wind and tidal current behind me. Seiland island is on the right and the mainland on the left

I woke early and it was a stunning morning with clear blue skies and a slight northerly breeze in my favour. As I breakfasted in the tent, a herd of reindeer sauntered by, one put his nose in the tent and was surprised to see me sitting there motionless. It bolted off pulling the front tent pegs out in its panic. Once I got going with a sun hat on my head and the poggies off my hands I went shooting down the sound with both the wind and current carrying me along. Ahead of me was the island of Seiland, Norway's seventh biggest island. The mountains of Seiland went up to 1000 metres and there were two large glaciers, or even small ice-caps, on the island and I could just make one of them out. Seiland also seemed remarkably green. I found out later it had a very broad range of minerals in its rocks and

Day 164. The small verdant sunlit hamlet at Saraby showed me that summer was bursting open and unfolding around me

these provided good nutrition for the birch forests. Indeed, the island up to 300 metres, was covered in the vibrant, invigorating green of fresh spring leaves. There was the odd scattered homestead along the coast, which were probably now abandoned. It was a wonderful, fast and sunny paddle down the sound on the south side of Seiland island, called Vargsund. I kept to the mainland side of the sound and cruised past a number of small hamlets with green luxuriant fields and bright green birch forests. The wealth of minerals must have extended over the sound to this side also. It was so refreshing after the harsh moonscape of the Nordkinn and Varanger peninsulas. In less than three hours paddling I had done almost 20 kilometres and reached a pebble bay with a hamlet of 10 houses round it. They were all sitting in green pastures, bright with the sun shining on them. Along the shore were fishermen's sheds and large bunches of bright yellow marsh marigolds where trickles of water came down. The hamlet was called Saraby and it looked calm and tidy.

I pulled up on the beach where a father and son were launching a boat. The father had recently been fishing in the fjord and had filled up his cod drying rack with about 100 fish to see him through the year. He explained it was now too late to properly dry fish to become stockfish, as the fish would not dehydrate and harden in time to stop the flies laying eggs in it. So he had treated them in some solution and was hanging them for a few weeks to become Boknafisk. I had recently tried Boknafisk in Mehamn and was not taken by it as I thought it tasted somewhat rotten. I chatted with them as they waited for the tide to lift their boat from the cradle. It was a very relaxed rural scene in the warm weather. I have gone almost straight from the Nordkinn spring, which would be winter anywhere else, to summer in a week. Summer was exploding around me in a green flash.

Day 164. Along the shore at Saraby were hundreds of clumps of marsh marigold which looked very vivid after the last weeks

However, although the birch trees here were getting thicker, lusher and delighting me, it was only similar to the vegetation in Jotunheimen or Southern Norway one would expect to find at 800 metres. However, during the previous week at Nordkinn, it was more like the vegetation at 1500 metres in Jotunheimen!

I left this calm hamlet and carried down along Vargsund, with Seiland island on my right. As I paddled, I slowly crossed over to a deep craggy inlet on the island, called Store Bekkarfjord. Most of the interior of the island of Seiland was a National Park. The park also took in some coastal areas and Store Bekkarfjord was one. It was an electric verdant green with wild craggy slopes behind it, going up to steep snowfields and the ice-cap beyond them. After a few more rocky headlands, some of which had some strong tidal rips, I paddled round a buttress to reach the very small hamlet of Hakkstabben, where I had thought to spend the night. I beached on the pebbles and then went up to explore the jetty area.

Day 164. The birch woods along the shore slopes of Seiland were especially vibrant due to the mineral rich soil of the island

Day 164. The post office, shop and jetty at Hakkstabben are on the left of the bow while the hospitable Bergly's house is above the bow

There was a large building on the jetty, which was the post office and an old fashioned and quaint shop which was closed. Beside it was a grassy patch were I decided to camp. While I was eating some biscuits before setting my tent up, two girls came over. They were the Bergly sisters and they were running the shop while their parents were away. They lived in the large house beside the lovely old barn I had noticed from the sea. They had seen me arrive. They opened the shop and asked if I wanted to stay. They said I could use their brother's room, as he was away. It was an offer I could not refuse, and it led to a great evening with easy conversation in front of a fire and a great homemade pizza. This was the second time I had been invited for dinner and had been given a comfortable bed. The friendly hospitality I am finding along the Finnmark coast is truly remarkable. I did not find it in the interior of Finnmark when I skied up at all. Perhaps coastal peoples all over the world are more outward looking, trusting and friendly than those who live in deep, isolated valleys and are more suspicious of visitors who previously might have stolen their livestock. Coastal Finnmark was like the small places on the west coast of Scotland or Ireland, where people are both hungry for outside contact, and are also genuinely warm, friendly, and curious.

In the morning the girls made a wonderful breakfast and we spent a lazy morning chatting and drinking coffee. Outside, the wonderful sunny weather of yesterday was replaced with a grey mist and frequent showers of a light drizzle; and there was no wind at all to blow it away. The elder sister then got a phone call to do an emergency driving errand. Hakkstabben is at the southern end of an isolated 8 kilometre stretch of road connecting the two or three small hamlets along the south-east corner of this large island. The few cars outside the occasional houses along the road are marooned here, and no other cars can join them unless a car ferry is arranged to call at Hakkstabben. As the Bergly's have the post office and shop, and stay beside the jetty which is the lifeline to these hamlets, they also have the contract to drive medical personnel about in emergencies. Today there was one such emergency; a child at the other end of the road had broken his arm after a bicycle crash. The doctor was en route in a fast boat from the town of Alta, and the sisters had to be ready to drive him when he arrived at the jetty in 15 minutes. While they ferried the doctor up the road, and then returned with him and the injured child back in their car to the waiting medical boat, I waited in the house. I found some books on the coast of Norway and immersed myself in them while the drizzle continued. Later, I went down to my kayak to try and readjust the rudder again. The rudder pedals are just so stiff it is a real effort to use the rudder. I loosened the wire and taped some foam mat on to the rudder pedals to bring them forward a bit. The rudder is a never-ending problem, and the pedals just do not work smoothly. I was starting to curse the day the Smarttrack brochure landed on Tiderace's doorstep. Once the sisters returned, I was half way through packing up the boat in the drizzle, which looked like it was set to last the rest of the day. I was very grateful for their cheerful company, tasty food, comfortable sheets and hot water, and gave each a big hug before I pushed off.

The drizzle continued all the way over the 5-kilometre wide Rognsund to a small islet just off the shoreline of the angular and serrated Stjernøya, whose steep mountain slopes quickly disappeared into the mist. Stjernøya was about 30 kilometres long and also had mountains which went up to 1000 metres. Being close to Seiland it must have shared much of the geological and mineral features, as it too was green and fertile. When I reached the islet beside Stjernøya I could see it was a gull colony, with many lesser blackback and herring gulls nesting on its rocky surface on grassy tufts. Despite the fact I cruised by the shore quite closely, none of the birds left their nests as I paddled past. I assumed that if a herring gull left its nest a blackback would be straight into it and eat the incubating egg. There was a small current flowing south, down the island, and this helped carry me along to the southern tip, where it flowed into another current coming east, producing some turbulence. I stayed out of it by hugging the coast. Just after the headland was Halvorvik bay with an old house. The house was still maintained, but only used in the summer as a cabin, probably by the sentimental children of the parents who

Day 165. As I paddled along the steep south shore of the mountainous Stjernøya island towards Davatluft inlet it poured with heavy rain

once lived here on this rich meadow. I stopped for a stretch and squelched around the soggy grass, as the drizzle now turned to heavy rain. With my drysuit on everything but my head and hands stayed dry, but it still sapped the spirits. Beads of water ran out of my fleece balaclava and down my face and neck before being diverted down the outside of my drysuit by the latex neck seal. I continued west along the south coast of this rugged island, passing a steep coastline which rose up to the birch- and juniper-clad hillsides and on to the bare rock and snowfields of craggy peaks lost in the mist. Like Seiland, Stjernøya does not have any mammal predators. This lack of fox means there is a rich population of hares. I could see many of them in each of the grassy meadows along the shore. They were easy to see, as the white remnants of their winter coats showed up when they moved. Apparently there are plenty of eagles on the islands due to the number of hares. After an hour of torrential rain, with the rain drops bouncing off the water, scattering globules of water across the capillary surface, I passed another meadow at the head of a shallow estuarine inlet. I decided to call it a day here, despite the fact I had only paddled some 15 kilometres from Hakkstabben to this abandoned hamlet at Davatluft.

I paddled into the inlet which was shallow, and brackish, due to the swollen stream emptying into it. There were plenty of long-tailed duck bobbing about. I paddled up the river a little, until the bank was firm, and then pulled the kayak up on to the soggy grass. From here I dragged it across the meadow until it was above the high water mark. I left everything in the kayak, in the drybags, while I put the tent up. Then I transferred everything I needed, still in the bags, into the nylon porch and did the zip up. Before I went into the inner tent, I extricated myself from the drysuit, and half naked and steaming, wriggled into the inner sanctuary. I got the petrol stove going at once and soon the place was like a steamy sauna. Supper was very simple; mashed potato with a tin of spam chopped into it, which left me enough time to write. The rain drops continued to splatter off the tent all night. When I finally did the zip up for the last time, I saw an otter wandering past just 10 metres from the tent.

SECTION 23. Havøysund to Stjernsund
4 days. 127 kilometres. 25.5 hours. 0m ascent. 0m descent.

THE KAYAK: SECTION 24. LOPPHAVET

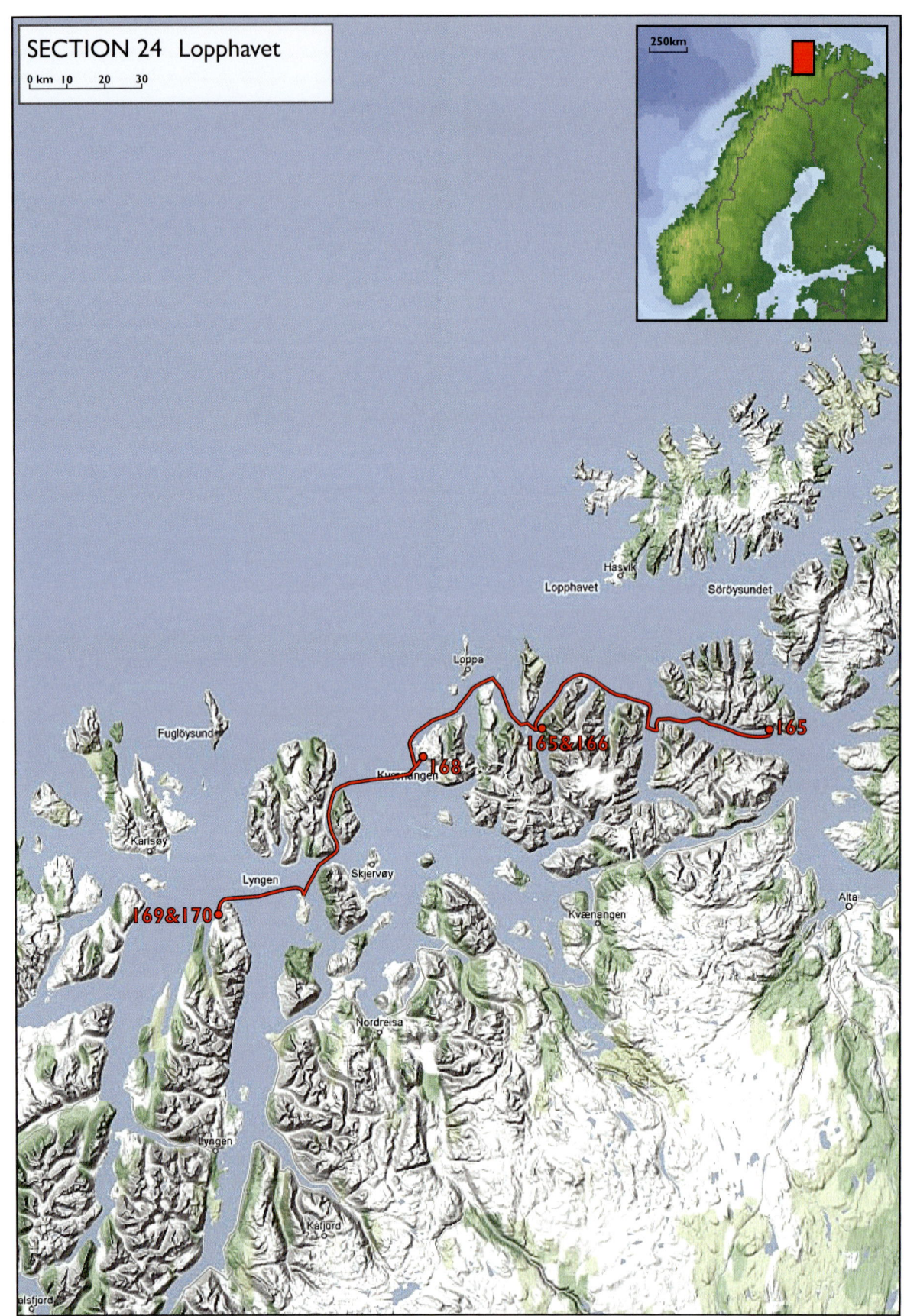

THE KAYAK: SECTION 24. LOPPHAVET

It was still raining heavily when I woke early. With a great effort I managed to get up, have breakfast and start putting everything back into drybags. I wriggled into my drysuit and packed the kayak, leaving the tent up. When it was all done I shoved the dripping tent into a large drybag, forced it into the kayak and shoved off into the calm estuary. The long-tailed ducks were now replaced by a group of goosander which swam in the tidal estuary. Many had their tails in the air as they scoured the silty bottom for small crustaceans and fish. Five kilometres on the other side of Stjernsund the mainland was lost in the mist and rain, as were the high mountains above me. I could just see the lower slopes which were very lush. Thick bunches of the succulent rockrose were now in yellow flower, and a purple flower, either purple saxifrage or moss campion, grew on the frequent rocky shelves. Despite the rain I could hear a lot of birdsong in the birch woods. As I paddled, I heard some shrieking, and turned to see two otters playing. They were just 30 metres downwind, so I stopped paddling and drifted towards them. They were either playing or courting, and were emitting loud squeaks as they writhed on the surface. I got to within about five metres, and when they saw the yellow kayak, both dived at once. I paddled past the deep bay of Simavik, with an old farm in the green pastures on the valley floor. This valley floor was cut in two by the swollen river which was a raging torrent at the moment. This farm was probably again abandoned in the 1960s, but maintained by the descendants. The next bay had a large industrial concern in it. It

Day 166. The lonely abandoned farm in Simavik bay still seemed to be maintained as a summer leisure house with a small cultural sideline

Day 166. On the west side of Oksfjord was Klubbnesvika, a small hamlet now just comprising of four summer houses and small holdings

was an underground mine, extracting nepheline syenite, a low silica feldspar type mineral, which is used in glass and ceramic manufacture. It was quite a surprise to see the large wharf, with huge storage facilities to store this mineral, on this otherwise empty and unspoilt island. After the mine, I decided to cross the sound while I could see across it and the moderate headwind allowed. It was a slow but sure crossing. The advantage of the poor weather was that it made the other side seem much further than it was, and I arrived quicker than expected. I paused on reaching the far side and a redshank appeared on the rocks near me. Above were a couple of sea eagles. By the end of the day I would have seen at least 50 of these huge birds. One can only get an idea of the scale of them when you see a raven or large blackback gull harrying them.

The wind and tide were against me while I made the final journey up the coast to Øksfjord. Unfortunately the weather was obscuring the mountains here, because this was now classic fjord country with narrow fjords cutting deep into high mountains. My map indicated that just on the other side of the peninsula from Øksfjord was a glacier which descended from these high craggy peaks all the way to the sea, calving icebergs. I reached the fjord, but the town itself was a 3-kilometre detour up the east side. I knew if I stopped here I might get stuck, seduced by hamburgers and the thought of a hot shower, so pre-empting my weakness I went straight over to the simple life on the other side where there was the tiny hamlet of Klubbnesvika. There was a rough boulder beach here, so I stopped for lunch. There was someone on the beach and he came over for a chat. He owned one of the four houses. They were all in excellent condition and their barns and outhouses were well maintained. However, these were also just summer houses now and nobody lived here through the year. The barns had not seen animals for 50 years. The owners had moved across the fjord to Øksfjord for more modern occupations. Small holding and subsistence fishing at Klubbnesvika had been abandoned in the 1960s in the days of their parents, who had moved away from this hard life. He thought there was some accommodation in Bergsfjord.

Day 166. Looking east from Klubbnesvika across Stjernsund to the wild island of Stjernøya just clearing after 24 hours of heavy rain

If the weather in the exposed Lopphavet, just round the corner was reasonable, I would try and reach it. Bergsfjord was about 30 kilometres and the blatant wind and more negligible current would be against me, so I bade an early goodbye and set off into it.

There were three main headlands to go round after Øksfjord to reach Bergsfjord. These took me out of the shelter of the sounds into the open ocean again. This ocean is called Lopphavet. I noticed how much bare rock there was before the vegetation started. As I paddled into the Lopphavet it quickly rose to 10 metres above sea level. In the sounds it had only been a metre or two above the high tide mark. Lopphavet was not on the same scale as Østhavet and Nordishavet where it was a good 30 metres, but it was enough to show the weather here could be rough. Other than that I did not notice any difference in the sea state. I went round the first peninsula and then crossed Nuvsfjord to Sommarnes, a lonely and abandoned farm which was now derelict. In the bay in front of the farm was a salmon net trap. I could see a large dead salmon in the net just below the surface. The salmon traps are constructed from a visible and large mesh net which the salmon can both see and swim through. This net is placed perpendicular to the shore for about 300 metres, jutting out into the fjord. The salmon which are returning to their river to spawn, swim along the shore with their senses tuned to the river they themselves were spawned, hatched and fledged in. As they swim along the shore, homing into their estuary, they will come across such nets. Although the salmon can see the net they will not swim through it and veer away from the shore to detour round it. At the end of this 300-metre large mesh and visible net is a V-shaped trap of small mesh monofilament net which they cannot see. The salmon swim into it and become ensnared in it, eventually drowning as oxygen cannot pass over their gills. Every day or two the fisherman will come along and empty the nets. I saw six such salmon trap set-ups today along this coast. However, because these traps can be so effective, their use is heavily regulated and they can only be used for a couple of weeks a year.

Day 166. The roadless hamlet of Rokkenes was on an alluvial fan in the remote Ullsfjord in dramatic but obscured scenery

I continued round the headland and came to the next fjord, called Ullsfjord. There was a roadless hamlet here, called Rokkenes, on an extensive alluvial fan which was green and fertile from the shore to the foot of the mountains. This hamlet, which was only accessible from the sea, would also have consisted of summer houses and was probably also abandoned as a permanent settlement some 50 years ago. I paddled across the fjord and round the last peninsula. There was a steep outcrop rising out of the sea here, called Stauren, which seemed inundated with sea eagles. At one stage there were six in the air around me. I could see one return to its eerie in the crags on the mountain. These birds

Day 166. Heading down Bergsfjord to the town of the same name, with the dark mysterious Silda island on the right

Day 166. The charming village of Bergsfjord was only accessible by sea, as it was surrounded by impressive mountains

were massive, bigger than a golden eagle, but without the same pride and nobility. I had hoped the wind would be behind me for the final 12 kilometres down Bergsfjord to the village, but it was still against me. The light was dark and dramatic, obscuring the 1000-metre mountains and bringing in the odd rain shower. Across the fjord was the gloomy, lonely and mysterious island of Silda, which I am sure, had no permanent settlement.

I eventually rounded a point and entered the bay where Bergsfjord village lay. I asked a fisherman about accommodation and he pointed me to a nearby house. I knocked on the door and the owner appeared. His name was Cort Buck Rustad and I could see by his manner he was a refined and interesting man. He had just returned from a trout fishing trip in Scotland and also knew the Bergly family, with whom I stayed at Hakkstabben a couple of days ago. Across the small road was a shop which he also owned, and attached to it was a lovely apartment. He gave me a very cheap rate and then opened the shop so I could buy something nice for supper. Afterwards he left me to get on with unpacking the minimum I needed from my kayak on the nearby beach and securing it well above the high water mark. Given the windy forecast, I had already decided to spend the next day exploring this charming village in a bay of sandy islands surrounded by steep snow-capped mountains. I returned to the gorgeous apartment and rinsed the salt away in the hot shower before laying on the soft cotton sheets.

Day 167. Around Bergsfjord bay and on the islets in the bay were a number of white sandy beaches under the dramatic mountains

When I woke I was pleased to see the forecast wind was indeed blowing, and my day off would not be guilt-ridden. I spent a few hours writing and then went for a walk in the village. A few things struck me immediately about the village. Firstly, everybody was extremely friendly and chatty. I suspected Cort had told them about me when they came to his shop, which was the nerve centre of the village chat. Secondly, the gardens here were tended with real pride and many were already blossoming. A lot of old barrels and containers were used as flower pots around the old wharf area. The village seemed to be quite self sufficient. There was a hydro-electric plant which easily supplied the whole village. There was a very tidy boat yard to repair and maintain the 10-12 fishing boats based here. The old wharf area was well preserved and part of it was now a quaint restaurant. There was an isolated road here, its ends truncated by wilderness. It was a 3-kilometre lane really, between the 20 houses, and the only way to get on to it initially, was by an infrequent car ferry. What Bergsfjord lacked in asphalt it certainly made up for in charm. It was right up there beside Bugøynes and Måsøy as a contender for the best place I had visited on the kayak trip so far. In the bay in front of Bergsfjord were a number of small islands. It looked like either mackerel or red-billed terns were breeding on the lush

Day 167. The wharf at Bergsfjord was still used to land fish and maintain equipment while part had also been turned into a restaurant

grass on one of them. There were a few sandy beaches in the inlets and on the islands in the main bay. This all made a very idyllic scene compared to the drama of the surrounding landscape. Spectacular ridges and serrated mountains, which were still covered in large snowfields, surrounded the village in every direction, apart from the fjord, and island of Silda beyond the bay.

Day 168. A tern egg at the colony on the islet to the south of Silda. The tightly packed nests contained just one or two eggs

After a calm, content day's pause in Bergsfjord it was eventually time to leave. I said goodbye to Cort and thanked him for his hospitality, then launched. Initially it was an easy paddle, threading through the islands of the bay, then across Bergsfjord itself to the southern tip of the wild and dramatic Silda island. There was a small rocky islet here with a lot of terns nesting on it. I went to take a photo, but realized the memory card was still in the laptop. I had to stop, get out, unpack the laptop and remove the card if I was to have any photos today. I found a sheltered slot on the rocky shore where I could land on the islet, and pulled the kayak up on to a slab. While ashore I went up to look at the nests of the tern colony. The nests were close together and were just a simple scratch in the grass. There were either one or two small speckled dark green eggs per nest. As yet nothing had hatched. I left before I caused the birds to be away too long and the eggs cooled down. There should have been an ebbing tide helping me round the south tip of Silda and north up Sandlandfjord, but there was none. Just a headwind to slow me down. It was a slow pull through the sea of treacle across this fjord to reach the shore hamlet of Bogen. In nearly three hours I had only done 10 kilometres. On my east, the steep wild west side of Silda slowly unfolded. It was a rugged island without any trace of human life on it. North from Bogen to the mouth of the fjord took another hour and I paddled over a few more salmon traps, but could not see any fish in them. At the mouth of the fjord was a shallow islet called Marholmen, and after that there was an open 20-kilometre stretch along the open, exposed Lopphavet ocean again. I rode the current between the mainland and Marholmen and went crashing through some roller coaster waves into this ocean. Once in the ocean again the kayak started jumping about on the large clapotis, caused by the rebounding waves and the current. As I looked down the coast here, I could see there was little shelter and the next four hours were going to be bumpy. There was nowhere to land, so I hoped the wind stayed at the northerly force 4 which it now was. I could not really take my hands off the paddle to photograph or even put my sun glasses on for a while.

Across an open strait to the north was the island of Loppa. It had about 15 houses on it but I am not sure if it is inhabited all year. The north of the island looked wild and remote, yet the south where the village was situated was green grass which looked grazed. In front of this green grass was an absolutely stunning and large beach which extended for at least half of the south side of the island. Keeping it to the north I slowly pulled myself down the bouncy coast until I got to Frakkfjord. If I needed it, there was the possibility to paddle into this fjord and seek shelter behind a small headland. But with the wind easing a bit I got the confidence I needed to carry on for another three hours. Crossing Frakkfjord only took an hour, but much of it was in a big four metre swell inherited from the stronger wind of yesterday. However, now I was away from the coast I did not have the unpredictable and bouncy clapotis to contend with until I reached the other side when it returned. Once there I still had another 10 kilometres until I reached some sort of sanctuary. For two hours I paddled along

Day 168. The south side of Loppa island which lies in the exposed Lopphavet ocean. The beach and village are just visible

this bouncy coast, passing the aptly-named Trollvika bay, with its towers of rock at the entrance. This part of the coast was very dramatic. It was also very wet, with plenty of spray being blown off the clapotis and the kayak's bow. I could not really take my hands off the paddle to get my camera out, except on one occasion, where I dared lose the non-waterproof camera for a dramatic shot. As I approached the western end of this exposed coast, the swell started to diminish, and soon I was approaching a small island, called Brynnilen. There was just a small gap, which I surged through on a wave, and suddenly I was in a calm bay on the other side, and the worst of Lopphavet was behind me.

Day 168. Some of the dramatic coastal architecture at Trollvika bay on the open Lopphavet shoreline

From the bay I got an obscured view of the magnificent mountains across the next fjord, which was the 15-kilometre wide Kvænangen. Despite the overcast skies, and the lingering mist on these mountains, I got a taste of their alpine nature, as the steep snow-covered peaks rose 1200 metres straight out of the sea. Had it been a clear day, I might have been able to see the next peninsula beyond them, which was home to the 1800-metre Lyngen Alps; one of the most renowned mountain ranges of Scandinavia. In calmer waters I paddled round this headland until the hamlet of Segelvik appeared. Just before arriving there I left the challenging Finnmark province and entered into the spectacular province of Troms. Segelvik is a small community of some 20 houses and 8 fishing boats, and a short section of isolated road. There was a nice beach and a small harbour behind the breakwater. I paddled to the harbour, where there was a characterful fisherman repairing his salmon trap nets. I levered the kayak on to a floating jetty and went up to the fisherman on the jetty. He asked me where I had come from and seem surprised when I said the Russian border. He asked me if I wanted somewhere to stay. I was always looking for somewhere less cramped than the tent to write and stretch out, so I said yes. He pointed to the small wharf and said there was a loft above the fish processing works. Apparently it was owned by the council, it was open

Day 168. There was a gap to surge through between the mainland on the left, and Brynnilen island on the right, to reach calmer waters

and he gave me permission to use it. I went to have a look and it was perfect, with a pragmatic bathroom and even a simple, but rusting, washing machine. Returning to thank him I unloaded the boat and carried my stuff up. Soon I was showered and had a clothes wash on. I had been very lucky with the kind hospitality of coastal Norwegians in Finnmark. I wrote that evening, but I was still lurching in my seat at the table, as the cochlea in my ears were still trying to compensate for the surging swell and bumpy clapotis earlier in the day. By the time I got to bed the predicted good weather was arriving.

I slept well in my sleeping bag on the bed, which smelt slightly of fish, and woke to a fantastic day which filled me with joy and excitement. I went down and had a chat with three fishermen on the jetty. They were all in their

Day 169. The morning showed off the tranquil Segelvik and the well-protected harbour to its fullest glory

Day 169. The cheerful salmon fisherman who let me sleep in the wharf at Segelvik, sold his catch to the public at Tromsø market

50s and seemed to be good friends. They were content in their small-scale fishing enterprises, and too old and wise to be overly ambitious. They joked they did it to keep active and out of trouble. At this time of year they fished primarily for salmon, using the nets. At other times they fished for cod or halibut. They told me it was a great year for salmon and they were catching plenty. Instead of selling the salmon to a middleman, they sold it directly to the public. When they had enough they would take one of their boats down to Tromsø and sell their weekly catch at the fish market. They certainly had the good humour and banter which come from being a market trader. They explained to me there was a problem with the cod market at the moment. The price of cod is set by a Norwegian government department rather than the market. However, the price set was too high, and cheaper Russian and Icelandic fish have flooded the traditional markets. Nobody is buying the more expensive Norwegian cod at the moment. The Norwegian fish buyers cannot sell the cod they buy from the fishing boats, so they are not buying from the fishermen. The fishermen must hang cod to make dried stockfish which does not fetch the same price. However, stockfish can be stored for a long time, until the international market prices improve or the government department lowers its selling price to compete with Russia and Iceland. Indeed, I have seen cod drying everywhere, both on a large scale, like in Mehamn, and on a small scale where individual fishermen dry their own cod and then sell it on, keeping some for themselves.

I set off at 0900 and paddled round the protective headland. The full vista of the two very spectacular and alpine islands of Arnøya and Kågen appeared in their full glory. It was a magnificent sight; the most impressive of the kayak tour so far. As I paddled across the 15-kilometre wide basin, called Kvænangen, I decided to aim for the middle of the northern island of Arnøya. The wind was twisting me that way and felt a more natural direction. I was now also in cruise ship country and two went past. I thought it best to cross this shipping lane perpendicular to it, rather than paddle along it, as these large ships would probably not see me. The crossing was easier than I thought and it took just three hours until I reached Arnøya. It was hugely spectacular, with cliffs which went up 500 metres and an array of jagged snow-covered peaks above them. To the east of Arnøya was another island, called Laukøya, which was no less magnificent. Between the two was a sound called Lauksund, a fjord with two ends to the sea in a deep and impressive slot. I paddled into Lauksund and began to paddle south. It seemed the current and winds were now on my side and I was doing nearly 9 kilometres an hour. I paddled past two hamlets on Laukøya at Hellnes and Storelv. The houses here were typical homesteads with a small barn for a score or dozen sheep, a few cows and a horse. In addition, each house had a boat

Day 169. Paddling across Kvænangen fjord towards the islands of Arnøya, Laukøya and Kågen was a kayaker's paradise

Day 169. Paddling down the sound of Lauksund towards the fertile fringe of farms along the shore at Lauksletta on Arnøya island

Day 169. There was a marvellous beach at Lauksletta between the sound and the green fields of the line of farms beneath the mountains

shed by the shore, for all the fishing-related activities. Previously the boats were smaller and could be hauled up the beach. These two hamlets would have been essentially self sufficient, living off the land and the waters in the sound. However, this idyllic but hard life had been largely abandoned in the 1960s and 1970s. As I paddled down I could see that the houses and barns were well maintained and there were still around 100 sheep grazing. I imagine the sheep are left to fend for themselves for the summer on this predator-free island and collected in the autumn.

I crossed the sound and stopped at a small beach at Lauksletta, on the opposing island of Arnøya. It was a tremendous setting to stretch my legs and revel in the sumptuous scenery. There were many more houses on this island, along a fertile fringe under the lofty snowfields and sharp peaks. Many waterfalls tumbled down from the high mountains above, to the populated fertile strip. It felt people lived here permanently, and not just in the summer. After lunch I continued south down Lauksund, past a couple of salmon farms to Kågsund, which was a T-junction of fjords. Kågsund separated the two alpine islands of Arnøya and Kågen. On this latter island, standing before me was the massively impressive Kågtind, 1228 metres. It rose steeply from the glistening sea and went straight up to the lofty crags and snowfields, making an overwhelming and serrated skyline against the light blue heavens. In Kågsund I turned west and was rewarded with a yet more immense view, namely that of the Lyngen Alps. I was being terribly spoilt by the weather and scenery which was certainly the most impressive of the kayak trip so far. Indeed, I felt that nothing else would really be able to match this again. These huge mountains form the jagged backbone to the 90-kilometre long Lyngen peninsula. The mountains rise to an impressive 1800 metres and come straight out of the fjord, in a wall of immense proportions. The camera could not do them justice. Many people consider the Lyngen Alps to be the best mountains in Scandinavia. They are without doubt one of the top five ranges.

Day 169. At the south of Lauksund I paddled into Kågsund with the magnificent 1200-metre Kågtind on the other side

Day 169. The mountainside of Kågtind descended into Lyngenfjord where there was an idyllic farm in a clearing in the birch forest

I did not want to cross the whole of 15-kilometre Lyngenfjord in one go, and decided to detour over to the small island of Vorterøy. It soon appeared, behind a ridge descending from Kågtind mountain, lying low and green in the fjord, surrounded by its much more impressive neighbours. About half way across this short passage the northern wind increased from a gentle force 2 up to a force 5. The sea quickly got up and there were white horses everywhere. The kayak was lurching and bucking as I approached the beach, where the metre waves were breaking. I considered capsizing and swimming in to receive the kayak and protect it from the cobble-sized stones on the beach, but decided to surf in with my legs out and jump up as I approached the stones. As I landed a man approached.

Day 169. A vibrant buttercup-filled meadow on Vorterøy with the hobby fisherman's cod drying under nets, and Kågtind in the distance

We chatted and he showed me around his small fishing operation and sheds. He was in the middle of dinner but told me to come up to his house once I was sorted out. I found some lee behind a shed, ate some biscuits and rested for a while in the meadow, thick with yellow globe flowers. I fell asleep in the sun and woke after two hours. By then the wind had diminished to a force 3 again. The man reappeared and we chatted for a good half hour before I decided to continue. He gave me some dried halibut he had prepared. His tidy interesting sheds were full of fishing tackle and bundles of dried cod. It was an idyllic setting, but he only stayed here for the summer. His parents stayed here all year and his children visited in the holidays. It was the typical demographic shift from countryside to urban which Norway has undergone in the last 50 years.

The paddle over Lyngenfjord was slightly more bumpy than I had hoped, and occasionally the wind increased to a force 4 again. I could hear the breaking crests catching me up from behind. Slowly I gained on the tip of the peninsula. At one stage I could look straight down the mountain wall as it plunged into the fjord, each peak separated by a large glacier. At midnight I rounded the tip, called Lyngstuva. Already the wind was dropping again but there were numerous shipwrecks along the rocks here. Even a Hurtigruten ferry, SS Kong Halfdan, lies wrecked here, since it was driven on to a reef in 1918. It was crystal clear to the north and it was the first time I had seen the midnight sun on the northern horizon, unadulterated by mountains or cloud. I paddled round the tip and a few kilometres down the west side to a beach by the hamlet of Russelv.

Day 169. The hobby fisherman's tackle shed on Vorterøy with longlines hanging up and bundles of dried cod stockfish waiting to go to market

I beached here near some houses and found a grassy area, and started to put the tent up. When it was half way up, Mrs Næss came down with a wheelbarrow full of weeds, forked from her strawberries. One can weed strawberries at one o'clock in the morning in the Arctic in June. She was surprised to see me and came over for a chat. "Forget the tent, I can make up a bed", she said. "I will just send the 'gaffer' down to give you a hand to carry your stuff up". She returned to the house and a few minutes later her husband came down to help me up with the full boat. I took the minimum and followed him to the house. Within 20 minutes I was having coffee in a very comfortable house, while a massive omelette was being cooked for me. Soon after, it was a shower and wonderful cotton sheets. I was totally bowled over by their generosity and kindness. Everything that was good about humanity had been shown to me since Måsøy, and it left me feeling euphoric. The Næss's were a large family. My hosts, Frank and Ida, were in their 60s. You could tell quite easily that they were both extremely hard workers who had grafted all hours on their farm and various other businesses for 40 odd years, to raise a large family of seven children. Most of the children

Day 169. As I paddled over Lyngenfjord towards the tip of the peninsula I passed the 90km chain of the 1800-metre Lyngen Alps

Day 169. Passing round Lyngstuva at midnight with the sun clear in the northern sky to the left of the Nature Reserve of Fugløy island

had grown up and left, but one son Cato, still stayed here; if he was not away working on trawlers. A few of the other children and their families lived locally in this kommune, but a few had moved to Oslo.

As we had breakfast I was intrigued to hear all about their history. On this small farm they had made a handsome living by raising pigs for a quarter of a century. Frank had built a large, modern two-storey barn himself to raise them in. Every year they raised 400. It seemed hard work and they had to get up at 0500 to start the day. In addition to this, Frank had also been a fisherman, with a share in a longline boat which he still had. If 400 pigs, 7 children and a fishing boat was not enough to keep them busy, they also kept some cows and sheep on the farm in earlier times. Even now, when they were supposed to be retired, Frank was still fishing and Ida had some large vegetable beds. You could not help but admire them. As we ate and drank coffee the fjord outside the window was getting more and more white horses on it. The forecast said it would increase to a force 6 later, and it was well on its way. I had to cross the 10-kilometre wide Ullsfjord if I wanted to proceed and Frank told me it would be dangerous. At the crossing point, the mountains on either side of the fjord would cause the wind to accelerate further. Frank insisted I stay until tomorrow and said it was no problem, but they had to go out for a while. I would just have to fend for myself in their comfortable house! I wrote, sometimes gazing out of the window at the large waves breaking in the fjord. As I finished, Linda arrived. She was the local ambulance driver and Cato's girlfriend. Cato arrived soon afterwards. He had a couple of boats in the barn, which was now empty of animals, and he was repairing them. I went through with them to have a look. I expected to see a rowing boat,

Day 169. Approaching the hamlet of Russelv on the Lyngen peninsula after perhaps the best day's paddling so far, in stunning surroundings

but Cato had two 10-ton cruising boats in there, and a smaller speed boat. The workshops were huge, clean and well organized, with all the tools neatly hung on shelves and brackets. Even with these boats, there was still only a fraction of the large barn used. Frank and Ida returned in the early evening and the five of us sat down to a lovely meal of Norwegian meatloaf. It was a sociable evening, but I was struggling to keep up with the conversation, as I was not used to the strong dialect. We went to bed with the wind still strong, but the forecast said it was to drop to a force 4 again. I pulled down the blackout blinds and settled back into the soft cotton sheets. I could get used to this again!

SECTION 24. Lopphavet
5 days. 150 kilometres. 36.5 hours. 0m ascent. 0m descent.

THE KAYAK: SECTION 25. LYNGEN TO TROMSØ

THE KAYAK: SECTION 25. LYNGEN TO TROMSØ

Day 171. The view towards the Lyngen Alps was completely obscured by the poor weather and just the bases of the mountains were visible

Ida made the most wonderful breakfast of bacon and eggs while Frank and I chatted. I felt a bit guilty about how much they were spoiling me. When I told them what I thought of their remarkable hospitality they said "That's the way it should be". By the time breakfast was over the wind had dropped to a force 3. After a couple of coffees and more chat I got ready. Frank helped me carry the kayak to the water and after saying goodbye I launched at midday and started south with the breeze behind me. Almost immediately I crossed the mouth of the small and narrow inlet called Nord-Lenangen, a short 2-kilometre trip. The waves were small and hardly breaking as I paddled over. I reached the far side and then started down the outside of the finger of wooded land which enclosed Nord-Lenangen. I was en route to Tromsø, a major goal just round the corner. The sky was grey and overcast and there were showers everywhere. The view to the Lyngen Alps was shrouded in mist. I could only see the stumps of the mountains and the large green valleys between them. Along the coast here was a fertile fringe of agricultural hamlets. In one of the fields, cows were grazing lush, verdant, grass. Just before the hamlet of Hesjebukta I had to cross the mouth of another, almost identical inlet, called Sør-Lenangen. Again, the 2-kilometre crossing to the finger of land on the other side enclosing the inlet was easy, but, I could see the occasional larger white cap developing in the main Ullsfjord to the west, which was my last main hurdle before Tromsø. I paddled down the outside of this second peninsula for a few kilometres to the farming hamlet of Ravik. The wind in Ullsfjord was still around force 4. It was just 10 kilometres, or a two hour crossing, and there was nothing worrying in the forecast, so I decided to go at once rather than eat and dither. On the far, west side of Ullsfjord was the steep mountain of Ullstind. I could make out the birch forest around the base and then the heather slopes up to the rock fields which disappeared into the mist. I set my sights on it and veered away from land.

The crossing wasn't too bad. There was the occasional period where the wind threatened to increase to force 5, but they were short lived, and generally it stayed at a force 4 and sometimes even a 3. Surprisingly, I encountered an unusual amount of puffins. At one stage the air was thick with them, as hundreds circled round my kayak in a large radius. There seemed to be small rafts of them. I cannot imagine where they were nesting, but assumed it was Fugløya some 30 or 40 kilometres to the north. In fact, I have heard puffins will travel up to 70 kilometres from their breeding burrows to collect food. Generally, as I approach puffins they swim towards the kayak for a few seconds, then they turn and swim away, casting nervous glimpses over their shoulder until I am 10-15 metres away. They then dip their heads, perhaps in preparation to dive. Soon after, they either dive or flap across the wave tops in a half-flight/half-swim motion, belly flopping across the waves until they bounce up and are airborne. After a good hour I could start to make out bunches of trees and copses on Ullstind, and after another hour I could see the individual trees. As I entered Grøtsund there were some confused waves, but the further I paddled up the sound towards the hamlet of Snarby the more benign it got. Just before Snarby I pulled in for a stretch on the shore. I noticed there was a campsite marked on the map, a good hour's paddling further up the sound at a hamlet called Skittenelv. I had visions of a quaint cabin and hot shower, so I optimistically phoned them. I was indeed getting soft. They had both cabin and shower and they assured me there was a beach nearby to pull up on. I said I would be there soon. I paddled in the rain, down the sound, passing very quiet hamlets along the shore. I noticed the barns here were getting bigger, indicating more animals and more prosperous farmers. There were numerous beaches, especially where small streams entered the sound from the high mountains to the south, carrying eroded sands.

I reached Skittenelv late evening and was appalled. The campsite was on a grassless field which had been created by bulldozing rubble into the sound. There was about 50 campervans, a hundred huts, garish waterslides and the beach was large stones. I went to have a look. The owners were a breed unto themselves. They had the manner of punch-drunk, bare knuckle fighters who lived off burgers, chips and beer. Less dapper people you will not find

Day 171. Halfway across Ullsfjord with the entrance to Grøtsund straight ahead. Tromsø city was about 40 kilometres down this sound

in Norway, and I was sure they were not Norwegian. The cabin they said they had was damp, expensive and filthy. It was a culture shock and I decided to flee and camp on some tranquil grassy beach. After half an hour's paddling, the bitter taste of Skittenelv had receded. I paddled past a quiet beach and went into the bay to investigate. The tide was coming in, and as I approached the grassy reeds along the shore, a group of eider duck mothers took their newly-hatched brood of ducklings out in a miniature flotilla. I paddled through the reeds, cleaving a path with the bow for 10 metres, until I reached the small pebbles of the beach. Beyond them was a narrow grassy strip before the scrub willow and woods started. I found a good place to camp in a damp area filled with wild chives and the twin flowers of the drooping water avens. The tent was up and I was in the warm sanctuary of my sleeping bag by midnight. Skipping supper for a packet of biscuits, I fell asleep quickly, listening to the rain patter off the tight flysheet.

I woke early after a superb sleep on the soft mossy ground, and after a quick breakfast I was in the kayak and paddling. I was eager to get to Tromsø to indulge myself with a comfortable cabin, food and some culture. I also wanted to see two people, Bjørn and Kåre, whom I had never met, but seemed like friends already with the help they had given me. I was planning to stay in Tromsø for two days and spend at least one of them investigating the city. The best place for me to stay seemed to be Tromsø Camping and I had already arranged a cabin with them. It was not in the city but on the outskirts, and apparently the cabin was quite near the high tide mark and this made everything much easier than a city centre hostel far from the water. Bjørn had kindly offered to lend me a bicycle so I could get around. Tromsø Camping was up a river estuary and

Day 172. Vågnes hamlet lay on a fertile point which jutted out into the Grøtsund and had a typical navigational beacon on it

small section of river. I was informed it was OK to paddle right up the estuary at high tide and then drag the kayak up the river for a few hundred metres. High tide was around 1300, and it was going to wait for no-one. If I missed it I had visions of wading through silt, so I was keen to get an early start. The small hamlets continued along the south side of Grøtsund, first Vågnes and then Tønsvika. Not long after I rounded a point, Tønsnes, and there was the city of Tromsø spread out across an island in the middle of Grøtsund.

It was still well over 5 kilometres away but I could tell it was large. A massive bridge spanned the straits on each side of the island where the heart of Tromsø lay. The city had grown bigger than the island and had expanded on to each of the opposing shores. There were frequent planes taking off from the airport on the island. I passed massive tanks for storing oil and diesel along the mainland shore. Huge warehouses for shipping and oil companies stretched out along the shore. Tromsø was quite spread out, with many single-storey houses on the undulating hillsides, and many five-storey blocks of flats built along the shore and on these same hillsides. After having passed through some very spectacular nature in the last five months I could not say Tromsø was attractive, but I have seen a lot worse. I dare say had I been in a more urban environment for the last five months I would have thought Tromsø was attractive and the natural setting superb. It is the main city of Northern Norway. It is becoming the northern centre for the workings of the oil and gas industry and this ensures a good income. However, it also has a large tourist industry, and is the hub of the cruise ship business in the north, with many cruise passengers starting and finishing trips here. Tromsø also has a large and vibrant university. This university

Day 172. Paddling between the mainland and Tromsøya island where Tromsø centre lay. To the left of the bridge is the iconic Ishavskatedral

has grown considerably since it was established just a few decades ago. This is partly because many students choose Tromsø over the handful of other universities in Norway because of the outdoor opportunities. Off piste skiing, climbing and kayaking on and around the islands around here, especially Senja, has become very popular and is a huge draw for adventurous students.

For me, however, it was still a shock to see such a huge urban sprawl. I was starting to feel at home in the deserted ocean, following a wild and empty coastline. It felt out of place paddling along the built-up shores on this still morning. I imagined people looking at me with binoculars while having a late breakfast on their balconies. One person who I knew was looking out for me was Kåre Kullerud. He taught geology at Tromsø university, and I had emailed him frequently with geological questions. He knew I was coming and said he would look out for me and come and meet me on the shore. I saw someone on the shore at our pre-arranged small beach on a spit and went over. It was indeed Kåre, who was busy taking photos of me. I paddled over and we chatted as I drifted along the beach in the kayak, and he walked. He gave me instructions on getting to a marina where the river estuary and campsite were, and headed off there himself. I paddled past some expensive looking waterside flats for half an hour, nearing one of Tromsø's most famous landmarks, the Ishavskatedral. A huge cathedral, built in a modern style, it was completed in 1965. The cathedral, although modern, is a beautiful building, and the architecture works well. Just before this iconic building I reached the marina and the estuary where the Tromsdalen river enters the sound.

I paddled into the estuary and under two small bridges. The tide was just turning and I easily made it to the start of the river where I could drag the boat. The river, however, had second ideas about me sauntering up it. The recent rains had made for a good flow and I had to wade some 200 metres up a torrent, sometimes above my knees. I nearly lost my footing once. I must have looked ridiculous to any passer by. Just before

Day 172. Paddling into Tromsø after 6 weeks and about 1000km since the Russian border. It was still cold enough for poggies on my hands

the campsite were some more determined rapids and there was no way I could get up those. I hauled the full kayak to the bank and then up through the thick birch forest to the road. Luckily it was over wet, slippery vegetation, but it was still a struggle. Once on the road it was just a few hundred metres to the cabin. Kåre carried two armfuls of drybags and I shouldered the half-loaded kayak, not wanting to do two trips. With everything in the cabin I chatted with Kåre over a coffee. He had skied over Greenland some 25 years ago and said he wanted to do the same Norge på langs ski trip which I had just done. I was encouraging him. He was enthusiastic about helping me with a synopsis of the geology of Scandinavia which had bogged down the publication of my second book on Jotunheimen.

Day 172. Wading up the icy torrent with the kayak for 200 metres to the campsite until the rapids became too big and I had to stop

Kåre left after an hour and I sorted out some gear before Bjørn of Bjornskajakk arrived. Bjørn had helped me out a month earlier by sending me a new rudder when the original one broke. I was very indebted to him for his helpfulness. The rudder still needed some modifications which Bjørn offered to do in his workshop along with another couple of minor problems. Always helpful, he arrived with his car to take the kayak away, and at the same time left me his superior bicycle for me to use during my stay in Tromsø, as I did not want to use public transport or cars. Bjørn only intended a quick visit but we got chatting and he stayed for a few hours. He is a well-known kayak instructor in Norway and holds the highest grades in the Norwegian kayak coaching system. After Bjørn left I tidied up the cups and prepared myself to be a tourist in the city. I may never return here so I felt duty bound to go and explore the city with its rich history of Arctic exploration and fishing. I would of course also have to visit some cafés and coffee shops to stock up on calories! If I did suffer from a culture shock or urban angst I could console myself knowing I would soon be in the quiet, peaceful sounds and fjords again where the ducklings would be starting to hatch.

Day 173. Looking from Tromsøya island across to the mainland where the iconic Ishavskatedral and the campsite was situated

After breakfast in the campsite café I had to attend to all my digital duties of writing, processing photos, updating my blog and clearing a list of emails. I did not want to squander the day doing it, but felt I had to, otherwise it would hang over me like a black cloud. It meant I had to sit in the cabin for half a day in front of my tiny laptop using my mobile phone as a modem. I broke up the tedium of this by washing everything which could be washed in the coin-operated washing machines and hanging them to dry in the sun outside the cabin. By mid-afternoon I was free from chores and could get on the bicycle and go and explore Tromsø for a couple of hours. Tromsø is a very old town dating back many centuries. It was initially built as a seafaring town on a large island in the middle of the sound. Now large bridges connect it to each side of the sound and it has spread off its island to the adjacent shores. As a seafaring town there was no reason for it to be built on the mainland as the harbour on the island was sheltered. It was south of the regions which the Germans had razed as they retreated at the end of the Second World War, so there are still many old houses, wharfs, churches and streets which retain their nostalgic charm. But like many Norwegian towns, much of it was built of wood, making them susceptible to fire. This was never more so than 100 years ago, when these small towns expanded as the population grew, and the centres became more congested as commerce and trade blossomed. A large part of old Tromsø was indeed destroyed by fire 100 years ago, but not on the same scale as Ålesund, a city further south which had to be rebuilt entirely after a fire. I cycled about the quiet streets for a couple of hours on a reconnaissance tour for tomorrow. The sun was blazing down and everybody was in light clothes and shorts. It was quite a contrast to a fortnight ago in Gamvik and Mehamn.

In the early evening I cycled back to the cabin and then out to Kåre's house a few kilometres north of the bridge and campsite on the mainland. He had invited me to a barbecue at his house, which I eventually found in a new development. He and his family had prepared masses of food in anticipation of my appetite and I did not disappoint them. Even I was surprised how much I ate. We sat on his balcony until late in the windless evening, under the hot sun. As the sun passed over the horizon at midnight it lost much of its warmth and we had to go inside. I was delighted to see a small painting on their living room wall drawn by my friend Øivind in Asker, whom Kåre's wife knew. It never ceases to amaze me how there is always some sort of connection in Norway between people. Kåre had crossed Greenland on skis some 25 years ago with a small group of friends and was a keen enthusiast of polar exploration and the Scandinavian outdoors in general. He had a vast bookshelf dedicated to it and I could have spent a week going through it. I had asked him a year previously whether I should ski over Greenland or ski the length of Norway, and without hesitation he said Norway. Greenland was interesting as you climb up to the ice-cap and as you descend it again, but the intervening weeks are boring, he stressed. While Norway was as spectacular and had interest round every corner, be it mountain, wildlife or nature. Having skied over the Jostedalsbreen ice-cap with Ole Bjøråsen a year ago, I could see where he was coming from as the dome is quite featureless. We chatted until 0300 in the morning when I cycled home. It is difficult to feel tired with the sun still shining and the shadows relatively short. Kåre said it was quite normal for people to survive on little sleep in the summer – but they made up for it in the winter!

Bjørn phoned in the morning. He had spent much of the previous evening modifying the rudder pedals and checking the kayak out and was now phoning to say everything was sorted. I am continually impressed by Bjørn's helpfulness and competence. I also spent some time getting another package together to post to Øivind in Asker. They were items I thought I might need but hadn't used them yet, but I still had to carry them up and down the shore each day. Øivind joked he had now set aside a room for me with all the skis, rucksacks and other equipment returning from the north. I then headed over the bridge again into the quaint centre of Tromsø. I went to the post office, barber and a café, then explored more of the wharfs and the heart of the old town before going to the Polar Museum. The Polar Museum had extensive displays from the early days of

Day 173. A street of old wooden houses in the heart of the smaller 19th Century Tromsø with a population of just a few thousand then

the pioneers to the age of the great Norwegian explorers. It was quite well laid out and there was a lot of reading, but with very little in English. The first display was on the early Arctic pioneers, when the Dutchman Barents 'discovered' Spitsbergen in 1596. After that Spitsbergen saw some Dutch and English whale and walrus hunters, followed by Russian fur trappers. There were exhibits on this and then the subsequent Norwegian seal and polar bear hunters who arrived and started to overwinter on the islands in rustic cabins in the 19th Century. The second display concentrated on the golden age of Norwegian polar exploration with the two main heroes being Fridtjof Nansen and Roald Amundsen, but also the often overlooked Hjalmar Johansen. He was Nansen's compatriot, but the authoritarian Amundsen considered him a threat, and treated him poorly. There is no doubt that Nansen was the most remarkable of all. Not only was he an exceptional polar explorer and at least on a par with Amundsen, but he was also a great diplomat and humanitarian and also won the Nobel peace prize for his work with the resettlement of millions of Russian, Greek and Armenian refugees, displaced during the First World War. There were also interesting displays on the ships, particularly Fram which Nansen, Amundsen and Johansen all used. The original Fram ship is in Oslo.

After the museum I had another meal, as the good weather broke and the skies, which had been clouding over all day, finally opened in a downpour. None the less, the sunny weather of yesterday and earlier today, left a good impression of Tromsø. I cycled back over the bridge to the campsite and my cabin. There was a British caravan there now. I went over and knocked on the flimsy door and within a minute the kettle was on. I chatted with the pair for a good two hours before returning to my cabin. I had to prepare to depart tomorrow morning when Bjørn planned to arrive with my kayak. I had enjoyed my sojourn in Tromsø, but was now looking forward to starting to paddle again. Tomorrow I would have to make my way towards the large island of Senja. I had to pass Rystraumen en route which is one of the strongest tidal currents in Norway. It would certainly make for a few exciting kilometres. Given the tide times, I thought I would unfortunately be paddling against the flow – if I could!

SECTION 25. Lyngen to Tromsø
4 days. 67 kilometres. 14.5 hours. 0m ascent. 0m descent.

THE KAYAK: SECTION 26. THE SOUNDS OF TROMS

THE KAYAK: SECTION 26. THE SOUNDS OF TROMS

Bjørn arrived early with my kayak on the roof of his car. He had spent some of his weekend modifying the rudder pedals. He had built up each pedal with 20 millimetres of hard foam and secured it with tie wraps. This allowed for the tension in the system to be released, which in turn meant the wires could move more freely without jamming. With the tension gone, the rudder operated much more smoothly. After chatting with Bjørn for a good hour I finally cast off at 1000 and headed south under Tromsø's high bridge. It was a stunning day again. The tide was starting to flood and there was a considerable current under the bridge against me, perhaps 6 kilometres per hour. I paddled through the current and down the wharfs and jetties on the east side until I was out of town. My dilemma now was whether to cross straight over to the island of Ryøya in the Straumsfjord, or whether to follow the longer east shore and then cut over Balsfjord to the island of Ryøya. At that point, three cruise ships appeared from behind the island of Ryøya, and keen to avoid them I decided to follow the east shore of Balsfjord. After a good hour I crossed to Balsnesodden, a peninsula where two fjords met. Along the shores, summer was continuing to burst out, and most of the meadows around the farms were yellow with millions of buttercups. Although it was just 6 kilometres across the fjord it took nearly two hours, as I had to battle into current flooding out of Straumsfjord. Once at the peninsula I stopped for a pause to both eat and regain my strength. I could see strong currents ahead emerging from Straumsfjord where the island of Ryøya lay in the middle of this sound and split the narrowing waterway into two narrow channels. The currents here can flow at 12 kilometres per hour and it seemed I was just arriving at the end of the middle third, or the strongest, flow against me. I would have to fight to make progress or wait for three hours. I decided to fight it.

Day 175. Paddling towards Balsnesodden with the island of Ryøya in the middle of the fjord surrounded by strong currents on each side

Day 175. The fields of the small holdings along the fjord shores were yellow as millions of buttercups burst into flower

I paddled furiously round a few small headlands, with the river of water accelerating past each spur of rock. I could see the difference in water height of 25 centimetres as it surged past each spur. While I was getting my breath back in an eddy, waiting to sprint around the next spur, I noticed that the current seemed to be turbulent with occasional boils in the middle of the sound. I thought this could be caused by the back eddy, downstream of the island, and the water here might be flowing with less force. I decided to give it a try. I sped towards the edge of the eddy I was in and broke into the green water, cleaving a bow wave as I broke in. Then leaning downstream with the rudder hard upstream I fought to keep my nose pointing into the current as I ferry glided over this river for some 200 metres. I lost a lot of ground, relative to the shore I had been following, but I was now in the disturbed, turbulent, but

Day 175. There were some 20 wild Muskox wandering about on Ryøya and there were plenty of signs warning about setting foot on the island

Day 175. On each side of Ryøya island were channels with strong currents and beyond these channels the mountains rose steeply

less forceful water in the lee of Ryøya island. Paddling hard, I fought upstream for a kilometre as the kayak got buffeted from side to side with rising boils. Slowly, I gained on the east end of the island glancing across to the south shore to monitor that I was in fact moving. With bursting biceps and aching sinews it got easier and easier the closer I got, until at last I was at the calm tranquil beach on Ryøya's east shore.

I wanted to come to Ryøya not only to paddle up its south shore, which I hoped would be out of the main current, but also to see if I could spot any Muskox. Tromsø University Biology Department had put some 20 beasts on this island in the middle of strong currents in the sound. The island was 2 kilometres long and a kilometre wide. It was covered in birch, spruce and some pine, and there were many grassy areas. Much of the east and south was also fringed with small white beaches and seagrass-filled bays. Off the north and south shores were the swirling currents in the narrow channels which changed direction every six hours. These turbulent channels added to the island's mystique and isolation. With the backdrop of the high snow-covered mountains, which rose from the shores beyond the main sound, the island seemed quite idyllic. However, the signs along the shore said there was danger lurking on this green paradise, in the shape of Muskox. These animals are volatile beasts, and despite their considerable weight, are fast and nimble creatures with short tempers. Old males which are expelled from the group by the new alpha male are particularly grumpy and may charge without warning. I paddled up the south shore hoping to see some but only saw the warning signs. I did see many eider ducklings here. They became very stressed if I got too close and started running across the water in all directions. Some dived to elude me but came up after just 10 seconds. The mothers were more calm and relaxed and swam away slowly while the frenzy of chicks scattered. I kept my distance to avoid traumatizing them.

Day 175. Klemmartind guards the east side of the entrance to Malangen which slices deep into the mountain interior on the right

I paddled down the entire 15 kilometres of Straumsfjord before resting. I had the wind and the diminishing current against me, which kept me pinned to a slow speed and it took some four hours to get to Malangen. This wide fjord wove into the interior, twisting through the rugged mountains and splitting into a number of smaller dead-end fjords far inland, where the ice ages had carved deep slots. Before I crossed the mouth of Malangen fjord, I rested in the sun in the calming air of the bright evening. The ripples on the water were quickly vanishing and the sea was becoming a grey mirror. There was some great mountain scenery reflected in it, but not on the same scale as the Lyngen Alps. As I sat in the kayak and ate some biscuits I saw fins and ripples coming towards me. It was a pod of white-beaked or white-sided dolphins, what Norwegians called

Day 175. Some families were fishing for cod on the still evening at the mouth of Malangen under the backdrop of Senja in the distance

'Springer', coming towards me. The last time I had seen them was just before Nordkapp. They passed nearby, exhaling so vigorously they created small plumes. They seemed on a mission to get somewhere, like the others I had seen, and made no effort to investigate me. It was probably just as well as they were three metres long and swimming fast. There were a few families on the fjord fishing for cod in small boats on this now idyllic evening.

On the west side of Malangen was a peninsula covered in thick forest. There was a hamlet by the shore here called Aglapsvik. I could see it had a large and beautiful snow white beach in front of it. It looked gorgeous and very inviting, but was unfortunately exposed to the north west and if I camped here and a strong wind blew from this common direction I would be pinned on the beach, so had to paddle by with a tinge of regret. I wanted to paddle past one last headland before entering the more sheltered Gisund. I could see it just ahead of me and it was remarkable. It was composed of gnarly rock which seemed very red. I had to take my sunglasses off just to confirm how red it was. It must have been made even more so by the evening sun. I don't think it could have been a pink granite as it was just too red, and I suspect it must have been a mineral with a strong iron content which was rusting. The vegetation on this headland was sparse and the terrain looked quite arid. I rounded this rosy headland and then entered Gisund, a narrow 30-kilometre sound between the mainland and the island of Senja, Norway's second largest island. Senja was to be my companion for a few days as I paddled along its inner shore. Kåre was doing some geological fieldwork on Senja and told me the west side is very dramatic with very steep high mountains and deep convoluted fingers of fjord slicing into them. Unfortunately it would have been too much of a detour and too exposed to go round this north-west coast which faced the ocean. Just after I passed the red headland I paddled into a quiet bay with a large beach curved round it. Beyond the beach was a fringe of lush meadow and then a crescent of small holdings and houses. It looked perfect and I rammed the kayak on to the fine light brown sand. There was a great place to camp in the tall grasses and weeds of the meadow. I quickly got my tent up as the air suddenly became thick with mosquitoes. This was the first time I had encountered them. They soon got so thick and bothersome I had to retreat into the tent and stay there. The tent itself though was warm in the evening sun and I lounged about, pleased with the long and spectacular day.

Day 175. The beach at Rødberghamn offered a great campsite in front of the hamlet where only one permanent inhabitant now stayed

I slept well, despite heavy rain during the night. When I unzipped the tent the rain had stopped, but the day was overcast, grey and misty with the threat of new rain imminent. I packed and loaded the kayak and then went to find water. I was now travelling with four litres of water, so when I spotted a great campsite in the evening I was not dependant on finding a stream there. There was a house here with a car outside, so I went over to ask if I could fill up the two bottles. An older man, well into his seventies, answered the door. He had seen me come in last night and set up my tent from his kitchen window. We got chatting and I immediately felt pity for him. He was the only inhabitant in the hamlet now, as everybody else had left for the towns. Despite his fastidious garden and house, he seemed very lonely, and this was brought home to me when he said his wife of many decades was in a care centre having had both her legs amputated. I then noticed the overflowing ashtray beside him and a hue of beige on the walls and ceilings. He kept insisting he was happy, and life was OK, to the extent I thought he was in denial. With the bottles full from his kitchen sink he accompanied me to the garden, shook my hand and watched me return to the kayak. I waved in sympathy as I set off at midday into the mist and drizzle and started to paddle down the long Gisund sound which became quite pinched, like an hour glass, in a couple of places.

It was the type of drizzle a kayaker hardly notices, and I was warm and dry under my drysuit. My head and hands were soon dripping wet though. There was also a headwind and it seemed I was paddling in syrup again. I always seemed to be a bit stiff for the first hour until I have warmed up and lubricated my shoulders to reach my cruising speed of 5 kilometres per hour. I pretty much followed the coastline, as it was much more interesting than cutting over bays. Here I could absorb myself the coastal detail, like many newly hatched ducklings and

Day 176. The Hurtigruten ferry, *MS Richard With*, is one of the newer 11 boats making the daily run up and down the coast from Bergen

characterful old boat sheds. It was a pleasant paddle despite the drizzle and headwind. I also hugged the shore to keep out of the way of occasional ships and the daily Hurtigruten ferry, which unexpectedly appeared from behind a misty headland. After a couple of hours I approached some narrows on the west side, which was by a village called Gibostad. I crossed over to it and landed between some old and barely maintained fish wharfs. One of them was in disrepair and it would have taken a dedicated carpenter to rescue it. There was a shop nearby and I went up to it to treat myself to some simple snacks, to make up for the poor weather. As I wandered around the village in the mist I noticed just how quickly things were growing now. The grass and flowers were knee high and the umbels of wild angelica were already waist height. The birch trees here were no longer the twisted gnarled mountain variety, but tall elegant trees with drooping branches dripping in bright green leaves.

Rejuvenated I recrossed the sound at the narrows and paddled towards the white Lutheran landmark in the village of Lenvik. This church was quite grand, relative to the size of the village. This was because Lenvik was once the main centre in the kommune or community called Lenvik. The kommune is both a municipal unit and a parish. While the demographics have meant the administration and much of the population of Lenvik kommune has now concentrated in Finnsnes, the parish church has remained here. I continued down the coast from the church until a quiet grassy headland gently pushed me out into the sound again and round a point, called Leiknes. On each side of Leiknes were wonderful empty sandy beaches which extended well out into the sea. Paddling past them I could look down and see the sand five metres below me in the crystal clear sea water.

Day 176. Klauva Bay was covered in yellow seaweed making it easy to drag the loaded kayak up the boulders to the high tide zone

As I rounded the pastoral and tranquil Leiknes point, the town of Finnsnes came into view further down Gisund. It seemed a good hour's paddling away, but the wind had swung round behind me and the current might have also given me a small push as I made quick time past the small holdings along the shore with their typical red barns. At Finnsnes town there was a large bridge spanning the sound at the narrows, which connected the large island of Senja to the mainland. It was the only solid link, although there were a few ferry connections. I did not want to stop here, as it was a town.

Instead, I set my sights on a small peninsula on the very south east of Senja island which was just across a large basin. I hoped to find a quiet bay here to camp for the night. I went under the bridge to Senja and into the basin beyond, and immediately found myself in the middle of a sailing regatta. It seemed all the sailing fraternity of Finnsnes were out this Thursday night and there must have been 40 yachts. I managed to keep on

Day 176. There were good campsites and a small stream at Klauva Bay in the shelter of the aspen trees

Day 176. The ruined house at Klauva and other older foundations showed this bay once hosted a small hamlet of homesteads

the fringe of the course through luck and avoided any embarrassment or frantic sprint paddling. After an hour, with the yachts now well behind me, I reached the quiet forested shores of the peninsula which were covered in birch, aspen, and spruce. There were a few rocky beaches along this shore, but the map promised a nice bay just round the corner on the south side. I paddled over the dark deep waters and around the tip to reach Klauva Bay. It was everything the map had promised and I hoped for. The tide was at least half way out and it was easy to land on the yellow brown seaweed covering the rocks. I easily dragged the loaded kayak up this slippery cushion to the bare pebbles of the high tide zone and just below the wet grass in the meadow. I found a nice place to camp on a stone terrace beside the shore and under some aspen trees. It was so still that not even the aspen leaves were fluttering. Now and again the sun came out as I put up my tent. I expected to be overrun by mosquitoes, but remarkably none appeared out of the long grass on this warm, still, damp evening. Across the bay was a derelict house which would not last much longer, and in the copse where I was camped there seemed to be the foundations of a long vanished small holding or even hamlet.

I woke early feeling refreshed in a warm dry tent. The small bay was basking in the sunlight and even the ruined house looked warm. There was not a ripple on the water as I set forth on to the large Solbergfjord. Each shore of the fjord was a pleasing vibrant green in the sun. I needed to cross the fjord, so paddled diagonally over to the south side aiming for the hamlet of Haug. I got over there well before Haug and followed the lovely pastoral shore past a few homesteads. At one I saw people riding horse drawn carriages on the farm lanes. It was very much summer now, and had been an unbelievably quick transformation from a month ago, when I was storm bound in Gamvik with the barren spring landscape still ravaged by sleet and gales. Just passing these rural summer scenes in this soft green heaven filled me with joy. I was in a euphoric mood.

Day 177. Paddling diagonally across Solbergfjord towards the rural hamlet of Haug on the southern shore

Day 177. Looking west down Solbergfjord with the Hurtigruten ferry, MS Nordstjernen, steaming up with the mountains of Senja behind

Not only was the land changing but the water too. I noticed there were many jellyfish in the water now. I stopped to measure the temperature, it was 14 degrees, a full 11 degrees warmer than when I started at Grense Jakobselv just six weeks previously. When I was splashed on the hands or face it no longer stung, but on a day like today, it now felt refreshing as I sweated under the drysuit. Not to be outdone by the horses and carriages on the land the sea provided its own bit of nostalgia when the daily Hurtigruten ferry went past heading north. It was the MS Nordstjernen, the oldest and most traditional of the 11 ships which ply the Norwegian coast from Bergen to Kirkenes on the 11 day round trip. The MS Nordstjernen was built in 1956 and it was exactly what you expected a

Hurtigruten ferry to look like. It was an elegant and graceful ship from a bygone era of simplicity. Slowly the 11 ferries are being replaced with more modern charmless ferries resembling cruise ships, like the MS Nordlys, the one which nearly ran me down in Berlevåg harbour. It made its way up the fjord pushing a bow wave of surf in front of it as it cleaved through the mirror waters with the mountains of Senja reflected on them.

After the pastoral hamlet of Haug was a sheltered sound, Dyrøysund, which headed south between the mainland and Dyrøya island. I was going to take it, but first needed to stretch. I passed under a massively extravagant bridge from the mainland to this small, sparsely-populated island, with I should imagine a population of less than 100. I found some bare rock slabs where I could get out and stretch under this engineering extravagance. It was almost hot in the sun and I could feel the warmth in the rock when I sat on it. Norway is investing massively in its infrastructure. It can afford to do so as it is the third biggest gas exporter and the sixth biggest oil exporter in the world, producing half of what Russia exports. In short, Norway is awash with money. However, the Norwegian Government has been wise and invested the profits from these vast resources in a huge wealth fund. This fund is the second largest in the world, with assets of half a trillion (500 billion) dollars. It is invested in world markets with strict rules on what is considered ethical or not. What is not invested for the future is used for the road infrastructure and there is a vast programme of road tunnelling and bridge building going on throughout the country. It seems there is a policy to build expensive links to remote communities in the hope that they will remain viable and not become depopulated. The bridge to Dyrøya is just one example. The theory is that there will be enough money in the wealth fund to maintain this infrastructure when the oil and gas has run out in a few decades.

Day 177. Paddling down the pastoral Dyrøysund towards the serrated skyline of the Andørja island mountains

After lunch I left the bridge behind me and paddled down Dyrøysund. There were many larger farms in this sheltered piece of water, especially on the mainland. Any doubt about the arrival of summer was soon quelled when I saw a few farmers had started to cut the first batch of grass with their modest tractors in the meadows around the farm buildings. I considered this official that summer was here. I had put up with a lot of hard weather so far this year and I hoped I was about to be rewarded. As I paddled down the sound with the sun twinkling off the wavelets, a truly magnificent wall of mountains, glaciers and snowfields grew in front of me. It was Andørja island. It was not a big island, about 20 kilometres by 20 kilometres, but it seemed crammed full of 1000-metre peaks and most had a very serrated alpine nature. There was a fringe of farming on the fertile skirt round the perimeter of the island before the land erupted skywards like the front cover of a Tolkien novel. I opted to follow the sound on the inside of Andørja rather than paddle round the outside. The only reason I would have had to paddle down its outer north side was if I was heading off to pass through the spectacular Lofoten Islands. If this was the case I would also have needed to paddle round the north and west side of Hinnøya, Norway's largest island, before heading down through the magnificent scenery of Raftsund. I had already paddled round all the Lofoten Islands a couple of years earlier and they were absolutely breathtaking, but I now wanted to see new territory, so was opting to go down the east side of the massive Hinnøya. I hoped it would be as scenic as the Lofotens had been and it also looked a couple of days shorter. If I had not already paddled around Lofoten, I would have had a dilemma about which way to go.

The mountains of Andørja were soon looming above me as I entered the steep sound which separated this mountainous island from the equally rugged mainland. The mainland, not wanting to be outdone, unfolded the dramatic Løksetind peak from behind a ridge and this was equal to anything Andørja had to offer. As the sound, called Mjøsund, narrowed there was a remarkable hamlet on Andørja island. Jektevika with its four houses lay on a crescent of undulating land completely surrounded by high cliffs which encircled it and continued

Day 177. Løksetind, 1237m, was on the mainland side of the narrow Mjøsund strait which separated Andørja island from the mainland

along the shore. The hamlet was completely cut off from any surrounding land and the only access was via the sea. When times were hard in Norway, 250 to 100 years ago, people had to eke out a living in the most inhospitable and remote places. Jektevika was one such place. As I approached yet another extravagant bridge over the sound from the mainland to Andørja, a sailing yacht I had been racing for the last three hours and had pulled ahead off, took down its sails and started its engine. Now I could not keep up as it disappeared up the deep water-filled slot, under the bridge and round the corner, leaving a growing V wake in the still water. The bridge to Andørja was its only connection to the mainland. Beyond this island was another mountainous island of the same size called Rollo. These two islands made up the kommune of Ibestad, with a population of merely 1000, whose administrative centre was on the island of Rollo. A kommune is a political and social community and is akin to a hybrid of a municipality and a parish. The two islands were connected by a tunnel, so the inhabitants of Rollo had to pass under a fjord, and then over this bridge, just to reach the mainland. This kommune must have had a breath of life blown into it with these new connections. Indeed, as I passed under the bridge two large refrigerated lorries left the islands with cargoes of fish. This must have been the mainstay of the islanders, as farming itself would not be enough to sustain a modern way of life here.

The evening was upon me now and the sun was losing its heat. I needed to find somewhere to camp. Along the south shore of Andørja everything was in shade as the high mountains on the island completely blocked out the evening sun to the north. Across this new fjord I had entered, Astafjord, which was just a few kilometres wide, but 50 kilometres long, I could see some hamlets and meadows basking in the sun on the north facing

Day 177. Langlitind, 1276m, rose up from the isolated Jektevika hamlet on the left and was just one of many mountains on Andørja

slopes. I decided to cross and find a glade or meadow along this forested shore. It took a good hour to reach Lavangnes, a hamlet relaxing in the sun on a point where the Astafjord and Lavangen fjords met, but camping seemed limited to a small fjordside field. I was just weighing up tent spots from the kayak when someone came out of a shoreline boat shed. I asked him if it was OK to camp in the tall grass here. "Of course" he said, so I landed and stiffly stepped out of the kayak. We got chatting and he introduced himself as Arve Johansen. Within a few minutes I was invited to supper which would be ready in half and hour. North Norwegians living along the coast are the yardstick of hospitality. I was again overwhelmed by the generosity and friendliness of them. I put up my tent, cleaned myself up a bit and went up to the large old wooden house he had pointed to. As soon as I went in I was offered a shower and given a towel. Not because I smelt, but out of consideration. Feeling clean I went down to the wonderful moose stew his wife, Dagmar, had made. This surely made up for the ruined moose stew I had had at the rather pretentious Saltoluokta Fjällstation in Sweden, while skiing in March, which was overcooked and dry. Dagmar's was rich, gamey and tasted like smooth venison. There was quite a crowd at the table with Arve and Dagmar, their enthusiastic, bright children and some of their children's friends and also Arve's mother. Three generations of easy banter and good humour. It was a happy end to a memorable day which was certainly one of the top five kayaking days so far.

When I woke the sun was beating down on to the tent, overheating me and making me feel groggy. I opened up the ends and let the crystal clear breeze through the tent while I slept for another hour in a slumber.

Day 178. Looking back to the hamlet of Lavangnes and the impressive wall of 1000-metre mountains down the north side of Lavangen fjord

I had been invited to a late breakfast, so went up to the house mid morning. The Johansens were just sitting down to breakfast themselves. It was a happy family affair with all the kids tucking into boiled eggs. I had two strong coffees and it helped with the banter as I was still feeling lethargic. We lingered at the breakfast table chatting for a good two hours until it was midday. After I had packed, Arve and Dagmar came down to see me off and tried to give me some food for the journey, but I was already so indebted to them for their welcome and friendliness I did not take it. It had been a very nice stay and I realized that I thrived on some company occasionally after a few days isolated camping. The weather had lots of promise and for the first time I decided to paddle without my drysuit on. It was great to be liberated from its confines, but I soon noticed how badly my spraydeck leaked. I have yet to find a neoprene spraydeck which does not leak or wick water. Almost immediately I passed the entrance to Lavangen fjord. Looking into it I noticed a very spectacular array of jagged peaks down the north side, rising in a high wall straight out of the fjord up to 1200 metres. I photographed it and then paddled over this small fjord. I only paddled for an hour before I stopped for lunch, by a small sandy beach with a number of boat sheds. The one I stopped at had an oyster catcher chick nearby sheltering in the grass. The parents buzzed around me noisily and then one of them feigned a broken wing. I observed them for a while and then the agile chick made a bolt for it across boulders to another patch of grass. There were also numerous ducklings in rafts, watched over by a few mothers along the shore, and a nearby island where gulls were nesting along the shoreline. The gulls' chicks had also hatched and a few of them ventured out of the protective grass on to bare rock but retreated again when I paddled past.

Day 178. Paddling west down the 50km long Astafjord, with Andørja and Rollo islands on the right and Svellen, 734m, on the left

I kept to the south side of the large Astafjord which was the large arterial waterway from which all the other fjords and sounds emanated from. In total it was about 50 kilometres long but I was only following it for just over half that. All the way to Myrlandshaug were small holdings. I could see many of the farmers had already cut their first batch of grass and it was lying in rows in the field, drying under the sun. In a few days it would be turned with a mechanical rake so it could dry further. When I looked across the fjord from this pastoral scene, the breathtaking compact alpine island of Andørja continued to inspire me. From every angle, this island continued to marvel me with its jagged skyline. When it reached the end of Andørja the course of Astafjord had a small twist and it made sense to paddle over it to the island of Rollo. It was not as alpine or large as its sibling, Andørja, but it was impressive none the less. I reached Rollo at Ibestad and was surprised to see just how developed this small town was with its municipal offices and school. The whole south coast of Rollo was

Day 178. Myrlandshaug was a typical rural hamlet on the south shore of Astafjord with boat sheds, small-holdings and birch forest all around

a scatter of small hamlets, but there was little farming here now on the steep terrain. Despite the high mountains and wild coasts I had not seen a sea eagle for a few days now; the last was north of Tromsø by Lyngen. Obviously they need more open ocean and do not seem to thrive in the fjords and sounds.

Half way along the south coast of Rollo, I crossed Astafjord for the third time, over to the hamlet of Fornes. Behind Fornes the mountains rose very steeply out of the fjord for 700 metres to culminate in the spires of Svellen, a precipitous mountain with a near sheer east face. The whole of the peninsula around Fornes was a dark green and dense birch forest, with the lush trees packed tightly together to give a velvety impression from a distance. In a few clearings in this forest were the red barns and meadows of small holdings. I noticed the wind was picking up a bit and as evening was approaching I thought it was time to look for a campsite. About 10 kilometres further west there was a village marked on the map. It was called Sandstrand, which meant Sandy Beach, so I pinned my hopes on it and imagined a green meadow above white sands where I would be spoilt for a campsite. The two hour paddle down the forested shore was lovely, with the extensive velvet forest continuing all the way, and just occasionally peppered with bright colourful barns and green fields. It was quite idyllic and nourished my soul. I had reached the end of Astafjord by now, with the end of Rollo island, and the huge basin, called Vågsfjord, opened up to the north. Far to the north across it was the distant grey steep-sided shapes of some of the Vesterålen islands, yet another of Norway's spectacular archipelagos.

Day 178. The precipitous Svellen 734m, towered over a small side fjord on the south side of Astafjord near the hamlet of Fornes

While I was paddling along, soaking up the rural splendour and birch forests, I hardly noticed that the wind had now increased to a force 4. Suddenly my meditation was broken by white caps splashing on to the kayak and over the spraydeck. I could feel water trickling down my waist. The spraydeck was slightly porous and was leaking. Neoprene seems an odd material to construct one from. In my drysuit it did not bother me, but now my trousers were getting soaked. It was not far until I rounded a sandy headland with a farm on it, and the village of Sandstrand came into view. It was as I had imagined, with a large sandy beach, a row of fields and then a crescent of houses on the far side of the fields. Along the top of the beach were a row of sheds where each small holder would have kept his boat and fishing equipment. I aimed for what seemed a good camp spot, as the sky darkened over. I found a tent site at once, but the grasses, flowers and especially angelica were so high now I had to stamp it down, but still the groundsheet billowed up. Once the tent was up it was barely visible in the grass from a distance. The high vegetation also helped to shelter it, and despite the fact it was now a force 5, the tent was hardly disturbed. Soon I was out of wet clothes and had the petrol stove roaring away like a little turbine, pumping heat into the tent. I settled down to write, especially when some rain showers started to pelt the tent.

I had calculated that the tide through the northern half of Tjeldsund would start to flood, or flow north, at midday. I really wanted to be there well before that as it was a narrow, 5-kilometre long sound, and there would be a considerable amount of water flowing through it. Tjeldsund was the sound which separated the two massive archipelagos of Lofoten and Vesterålen from the mainland, and I heard the difference in the tidal levels could be as much as three metres between the south entrance in Vestfjord and the north entrance in the Vågsfjord basin. However, despite my calculations and concerns, I seemed to be in denial. I got up late, was slow and lethargic about the packing and I did not cast off until midday, when the tide should have been turning. I had to carry the kayak and bags right down the beach to what seemed like its lowest ebb. This was not good as I still had two hours paddling to get to the northern entrance of Tjeldsund, so I should have the maximum flow against me. The denial was over and reality was sinking in as I took my first strokes in the drizzle under dark overcast skies. It was a pleasant coast down to Tjeldsund with occasional coral or sand beaches, colourful hamlets and the ever-present soft green forests, but the overdose of spectacular scenery and hot sun over the last two days had spoilt me. I made good time and reckoned at even in this late ebbing tide I was getting a helping hand.

When I reached the northern entrance to Tjeldsund I prepared myself for the ensuing struggle against the current. It was even marked on the map as 'Steinlandsstraumen'. But something seemed wrong here. The GPS I had in my pocket said I was doing 7, then 8 and then 10 kilometres per hour. I was flying along, and the shore with its frequent white coral beaches was whizzing past. As I approached the bridge I was up to 12 kilometres per hour. Fishermen at the narrows, by the huge bridge over the entire sound, waved as I sped past them on a river of luck. It went completely against my intuition and calculations that the current was flowing south rather than north, but I was delighted by the quirk. Once on the south side of the bridge the sound became much broader and opened into a basin. I kept to the west side where the currents continued to carry me along. There were a few coral beaches here of bleached white pulverized shell. There were a lot of puffins in the basin. I had not seen any since I entered the sounds at Tromsø and was surprised to see so many here. There were a few low grassy islands in this large basin with brilliant white beaches but I don't think they were suitable for puffins to nest on, so they must have come in from the steeper Vesterålen islands to the north. Across the grey basin on its eastern shore was the small town of Evenskjer, which like so many Norwegian towns, boasted a large white Lutheran church.

Day 179. Sandtorg was an old trading post and inn dating back many centuries and was now a quaint hotel and restaurant

My initial plan was to paddle to Lødingen where I knew there was a cheap pension with a washing machine, and more importantly, I could buy some food for the next week which should take me to Bodø. I only had a day's ration left. However, the wind which had been absent all day was now picking up out of the west, and I could see the current was now flooding north up Tjeldsund. It would be an eight hour slog up the remaining 30 kilometres of the sound to Lødingen, and I did not feel up for it. I pulled in at Sandtorg beach, beside a very quaint looking and historic hotel and restaurant which dated back many centuries. I went to have a look, but the prices were extortionate and I felt self conscious in my dripping drysuit and faded life jacket, so ate my biscuits on one of the benches overlooking the coral beach. I had another look at the map and it seemed obvious I should abandon Lødingen and head down Ramsund instead. Leaving a wet mark on the bench I relaunched and crossed Tjeldsund heading towards a group of flat grassy islands ringed by coral beaches. These islands guarded the northern entrance to Ramsund. I could, and should, have gone round all of them but decided to cut through them instead. But with the tide out, my way was barred by large flats of coral. I got out to survey a route and saw that if I just waited for 10 minutes the incoming tide would soon flood these flats and I would be able to walk the kayak some 200 metres to the other side. It was quite remarkable to be standing on this coral beach, with spruce trees and typically Norwegian boat sheds nearby, and high mountains still covered in snowfields above all that. It seemed a picture from the Caribbean had been collaged on to an Arctic background. The incoming water soon flooded over the beach, carrying upturned limpet shells before it like little boats. Streams of bubbles rose from the newly flooded areas, as molluscs hiding in the sand adjusted to a watery world for the next six hours. When the water was deep enough I walked the kayak over the firm sand and pulverized shell to the south side and cast off down Ramsund.

Ramsund was much easier than I anticipated. There was a new bridge from the mainland to the mountainous island of Tjeldøya. The mountains were lost in the mist.

Day 179. The white coral beach on the sand flats around the small islands by the north entrance to Ramsund were in the intertidal zone

The island would now probably have a population of less than 200 in the winter, but there would be many leisure houses belonging to people who had old family connections to the island. At this bridge there was a bit of a current for 100 metres where I had to paddle hard, but otherwise it was an easy ride up to the town of Ramsund. Along the shore there were many fields, with cows and horses grazing in them. The horses were the fjordhest or fjording variety which are very pale with a dark mane. Fjordings are also renowned for their easy temperament and are supposed to be easy to train. They are strong and hardy, and were previously used as work horses pulling ploughs on small holdings before tractors took over, and were used for carrying loads of up to 100 kilos.

The town of Ramsund was much bigger than I expected. It seemed to be some sort of naval base, and there was a large grey battleship moored in the middle of the sound, a little way to the south. There was also a smaller, more antiquated and rusting boat, which looked like it was used for training cadets, moored at the large jetty. Ramsund did not look like the nerve centre of the Norwegian navy by any means, and it seemed more of a place to store decommissioned ships before they were scrapped. I spoke to a fisherman as I approached, and he told me there was a shop and a guest house at the quay, but there was no guest house. The navy had taken it over and had closed it to all, except visiting defence personnel. It was empty now and looked abandoned. In revenge, and because it was sheltered, I put my tent up on its lawn under some trees. There was a simple café nearby and the shop looked big enough for my needs, but it did not open until tomorrow morning. The café was open and I went there for a greasy meal while I wrote at the comfort of the table. Ramsund seemed very quiet and somewhat deflated. The few teenagers who ventured out seemed bored. I suppose the naval base here sustained the town once, but now it seemed to be going into mothballs and this was eroding the community spirit.

SECTION 26. Sounds of Troms
5 days. 193 kilometres. 41.5 hours. 0m ascent. 0m descent.

THE KAYAK: SECTION 27. VESTFJORDEN

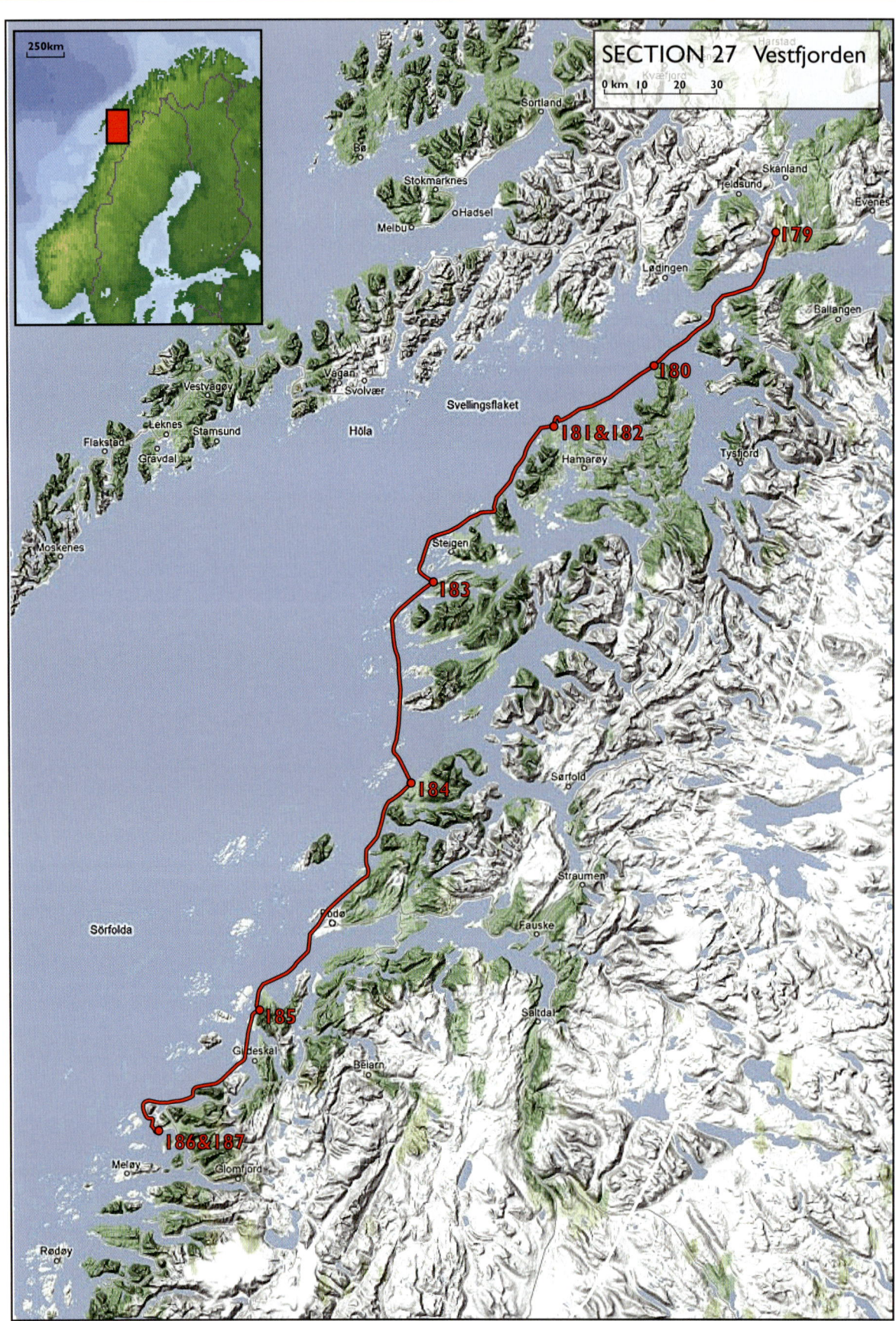

THE KAYAK: SECTION 27. VESTFJORDEN

When the shop opened mid morning, I bought enough food for five days. This would give me six days to reach Bodø. I split it up into day portions, packed it into small compression sacks and then put these in drybags. Once I had packed the kayak, down by the pontoon behind the breakwater, I levered it into the water and set off at midday. There was a slight headwind as I crossed over to the west side of the sound and the shore of Tjeldøya island. Here the sound opened up into a basin which was very shallow on its western side. As I paddled across it, I could look down into the crystal clear water and see the bottom a few metres below me, as if I was looking through glass. There were many old shells and the corals seemed to be growing on many of these, especially old sea anemone shells. I continued south across the basin then between the protective peninsulas which enveloped the other side, through the narrows between them, and out of Ramsund and into Vestfjord. Vestfjord is a vast body of water. It is really more of a 'Sea' than a fjord, as it is 200 kilometres long and up to 75 kilometres wide. This body of water was bounded by the magnificent Lofoten Islands on the north-west side and the mainland on the south-east side. These two boundaries slowly came together in a funnel and merged at the town of Narvik, which was at the head of the fjord in a sea-filled slot, deep in the mountains near the Swedish border. The Atlantic mouth of this funnel extends to the wild islands of Værøy and Røst far out into the Norwegian Sea at the end of the 200-kilometre long Lofoten Wall. This Lofoten Wall is an absolutely jaw-dropping crescent of serrated jagged mountains which envelops Vestfjord and protects it from the worst of the ocean. The mainland side of the funnel extends to the peninsula of Kunna near Bodø city and is riven with famous fjords and peppered with well-known islands. The sides of Vestfjord are very convoluted, dramatic, extremely beautiful and are the epitome of the Norwegian coast.

Vestfjord is vitally important to the Norwegian economy as it is the main breeding ground of the North East Arctic cod stocks. These migratory cod arrive in their millions in the early months of the year to spawn billions of eggs on the sea bed of Vestfjord. The eggs thrive here due to the relatively warm water, compared to the cod's feeding grounds in the Barents Sea. Once the cod have spawned, and the eggs are left to hatch, the adult cod then mill around Vestfjord before slowly making their way north again up the Norwegian coast to the Barents Sea and beyond into the North East Arctic Ocean, Novaya Zemlya and Spitsbergen and their summer feeding grounds. During the spring there is a fishing bonanza in Lofoten and Vestfjord, catching all the cod which have spawned, and this is the mainstay of the economy here. Another fish which comes here

Day 180. Crossing the upper part of Vestfjord and looking north to the quiet homesteads on the south side of the rugged Tjeldøya island

in its billions to spawn is the North Atlantic herring which also come from the Barents Sea in early winter. Historically some of the fjords leading off Vestfjord became very congested with herring in previous decades, which resulted in many millions of herring simply suffocating in the middle of biblical shoals. The winter herring fishing was once very important, but depleted stocks have led to much needed regulation. However, herring is still very important, as it has led to the bourgeoning industry of whale watching. Hundreds of killer whales, or orcas, arrive here each winter to gorge themselves on the herring, and tourists flock here in their thousands to see them, especially in Tysfjord.

Initially, I paddled across the narrow eastern part of Vestfjord, to the hamlet of Finnvika, which was little more than a collection of leisure cabins. I pulled in at this sandy bay for lunch. While I was there the wind died off completely, and the remaining cloud burnt off to leave a perfect day. I had a great view up the upper section of Vestfjord all the way up to Narvik and the steep snowy mountains around it. As I ate, I was buzzed by a pair of redshanks which tried to distract me. They must have had a nest of young nearby. They never feigned injury or a broken wing, like the oyster catchers did, but made a lot of noise instead. After lunch I continued up the fjord, past a shoreline of ice-scoured rock, quite bereft of trees or other vegetation. It was not as barren as the Ishavet coast in Finnmark, but certainly not lush like the Sounds of Troms just recently. But to the north, the Island of Tjeldøya boasted a couple of farms on its more fertile fringe beneath bare mountains of rock and snow. When

Day 180. From the sandy bay at Finnvika looking east up the upper part of Vestfjord to the mountainous interior near Narvik and Sweden

I reached Skarstad at the end of the peninsula and the entrance to the long Efjord, the landscape changed dramatically and I was quite simply awestruck.

As I rounded the peninsula I saw that there was a huddle of small low islands at the mouth of Efjord, and the larger island of Barøya further out, protecting them. These islands looked very inviting, as although they were still a few kilometres away, I could see many were fringed with white sandy beaches. To my left on the mainland was the absolutely enchanting hamlet of Skarstad. It was spread out over a series of white sandy bays, and in each bay there was a homestead. In one there was a particularly fine old wooden villa with its typical 'Swiss style' balconies. Any of these homesteads would have been a magical place to live, with the white coral sand beaches and the cluster of idyllic sandy islands in the sheltered bay. If this was not enough, there was granite Tysfjord mountains and spires as a backdrop. Superlatives fail to quite describe the total splendour of this scene. I had been spoilt by many beautiful scenes this year so far, but this enchanting scene stood out from the rest. I sat in the kayak quite over-whelmed with the turquoise water, the white beach, the green fertile fields, the white homestead, and then perhaps the most spectacular mountain in Norway, Stetind, 1391 metres, rising behind all the steep granite domes. The scene made me quite euphoric, and as I paddled the few kilometres to the cluster of islands between Efjord and Barøya, I kept looking over my left shoulder, savouring the majesty.

Many eons ago (about 1800 million years) the continental crust under Tysfjord had some great domes of molten rock accumulate under it. These immense domes, 10s of kilometres in diameter, rose up from deep in the earth like gigantic globules in a lava lamp.

Day 180. The gorgeous homestead at Skarstad around a white coral beach under the magnificent backdrop of the Tysfjord mountains

As they rose, they melted the rock above them, until eventually they cooled down so much they ceased to rise, and started to solidify. Cooling from the outside over millions of years, they solidified in layers like the rings of an onion. These solidified granite globules, or plutons, were later squashed and distorted in the Caledonian Mountain collision, when Baltica crashed into Laurentia some 420 million years ago. At this time they were covered in layers of younger overlying rock, like a crumpled tablecloth will cover a table in multiple folds. Then, over the next 400 million years, the overlying rock has been eroded to expose the resistant granite plutons. Ice ages have further sculptured these granite plutons into spectacular angular shapes, like Stetind, and the huge domes of exfoliating slabs which fracture along the cooling planes of the original granite rock, just like the peeling onion.

Day 180. Looking across the shallow bay from near Barøya towards the Tysfjord mountains with the sharp Stetind, 1391m, above the bow

The journey over to this cluster of islands between Efjord and Barøya was remarkable. The water was

Day 180. On a sand shoal in the gorgeous sheltered waters by Barøya island with the serene hamlet of Valle across the bay above the stern

Day 180. On a disappearing sand shoal by Barøya with Sandvær Islet on the right and the mountains of Hamarøy in the distance on the left

Day 180. Seen from half way across Tysfjord mouth is the granite spire of Stetind, 1391m, which is Norway's national mountain

not that deep and it was as clear as a sapphire, and as blue. I think I could have seen a coin on the sandy sea bed some five metres below me. Occasionally the undulating ocean floor rose up and broke the surface in a scatter of sandy skerries. I passed between the islands of Revelsøya and Straumsøya which were rocky ice-scoured mounds, covered in a scattering of birch trees with a few turquoise bays and white beaches around their fringe. Beyond them was a paradise of small skerries and sand banks through which I had to weave a path. A roadless hamlet called Valle, with its few homesteads, looked over this divine beauty. It was too good to rush, so I stopped on one large bank of crushed white coral, which was bright in the hot sun. All around me were other sand banks which the incoming tide was slowly washing over, and the odd small islet with white beaches, small soft meadows and a scattering of vibrant green birches. It really was a scene from paradise. The contrast of the Caribbean beach with Baffin Island type mountains, in the hot sun under blue skies, made for one of the most memorable moments of my life. I lingered on the coral shoal until the incoming tide herded me to the last remaining dome of sand, before it too was swamped. I could see across this paradise archipelago of submerging skerries to an idyllic islet called Sandvær, just a kilometre away. It had a large beach, a meadow and a few sheltering spruce trees and would have made a wonderful campsite, but it was too early and I reluctantly decided to paddle on.

I got back into the now floating kayak and headed south, past the lovely Sandvær island and many more islets and skerries which were being isolated or submerged by the tide, and into the mouth of Tysfjord. It was only a short two-hour paddle across this fjord with absolutely stunning views of the granite mountains of Tysfjord to the south and east. The view to the north and west was not going to be outdone by these spires, and produced perhaps the most jagged skyline I have ever seen. It was a Tolkienesque jumble of serrated spires and canine tooth ridges which made up the silhouette of Austvågøya, the most easterly and the most impressive of the five main Lofoten Islands. There were hundreds of jagged peaks which rose above everything else. Unseen among them were deep fjords, like the famous Trollfjord. I had paddled round these five islands and into these fjords a couple of years previously, and it was this ten day trip which fired my imagination to paddle Norway's coast. I reached the other side of Tysfjord in the early evening as the sun was heading round to the north and dipping towards this sawtooth skyline.

There were a couple of islands marked on the map at the end of the peninsula by a hamlet called Tysnes. I thought it would be interesting to explore the channels between them and hopefully find a campsite. When I was far into the labyrinth of channels, I realized

Day 180. I could look west across 30 km of Vestfjord to the jagged 1000m skyline of Austvågøya island in the Lofoten Islands

that they were only islands at high tide, and that my route was blocked by seaweed-covered boulders and silty mudflats. There was a small coral beach, fringed by tall grass up one shallow channel, and I decided to camp here. I had to drag the kayak for the last 10 metres across sandy silt up to the grass. This grass was a metre high and I spent ages trampling it to flatten an area to put the tent up. Only after the tent was up did I notice that during this half hour the water in the channels had completely vanished, and the sea was now some 500 metres away. It meant I would have to leave here at high tide tomorrow, around 0800, unless I wanted to carry everything across sand and silt. The sun warmed the tent late into the evening while I wrote and cooked, but although the sun was shining at midnight there was no warmth in it and it got quite cold outside the tent. I was absolutely delighted as I zipped up my bag, and still felt very elated and lucky to have seen today's stunning scenery and grandeur under hot blue skies. It was much, much more than the brochure promised.

I woke early and looked out of the tent to see the tide was high and the water near the tent, but it had already peaked. I had an hour to pack and get into the kayak, or I would be stranded here hundreds of metres from the water. I set off at 0900 with just enough water to paddle out between the islands at Tysnes before they dried out completely, leaving silty channels which would have been very messy to wade through. It was another incredible weather day and I opted to paddle in shorts and my old paddling jacket. I initially started straight across the large open bay to Tranøy lighthouse, but then decided to head over to Hornnes peninsula instead, to break the 15-kilometre crossing into two halves. This peninsula was just a slight detour and it took me to the base of an unbelievably steep spire of rock, called Tilthorn, which pierced the blue sky at 700 metres. I had only seen such mountains in books before. It must have had two glaciers carving away at each side, sharpening it into a wafer-thin granite ridge.

Day 181. The spectacular Tilthorn, with its very sharp angular peak, rose steeply from the sea at Hornnes peninsula

Day 181. The sea was so calm I could spot puffins from nearly a kilometre away as I paddled over to Tranøy lighthouse

It was incredibly calm as I crossed the remainder of the bay from this awesome spire to Tranøy lighthouse. It was so calm I could now spot puffins nearly a kilometre away as they bobbed on the glassy surface. Only occasionally could I get within 20 metres of them, before they laboriously took off, running across the water until airborne. This bay was studded with islets and skerries across the mouth and there were a few shags on some of the tidal islets. It was the first time I had seen shags since the open sea by the Lyngen Alps. In evolutionary terms, shags have pretty much stayed as they are for the last 60 million years without developing too much, so they obviously occupy their niche very successfully. Part of their success must be due to their wariness and caution, and I can seldom get within quarter of a kilometre of them before they take off. Usually one in the group goes, and then the whole flock who are perched on the skerry follow soon after. I saw only one sea eagle today. The last week had really been the domain of the heron, rather than the sea eagle. I am sure that as the coast becomes less sheltered again the herons will disappear and the sea eagles will return.

As I approached Tranøy peninsula I decided to skip the village and head directly round the shore to the lighthouse. It is a large and graceful concrete building, standing sentry on a rocky perch in a mass of islets. I landed amongst these islets and walked up to the lighthouse to have lunch and a stretch. The lighthouse has a dormant small café with a gallery, but is only open for a few weeks a year in the height of the holiday season. It looked better cared for than the misguided tourist facilities at Helnes fyr lighthouse near Nordkapp had done a month ago. Just as I left the lighthouse and started to cross the next bay to the island of Hamarøy with its impressive mountains, the wind increased. It was initially a force 3 but was soon gusting to a force 5. It was directly against me and my speed at times was down to a mere 3 kilometres per hour. It was a slow crossing, but the kayak cleaved through the oncoming waves, splashing me with just about every one. I could feel the water soaking through my faded cagoule and neoprene spraydeck on to my shorts.

Day 181. Tranøy lighthouse stood like a sentry on the northern edge of a flatter peninsula with the mountains of Hamarøy in the background

Day 181. Inside the bay at Selsøya a magical sanctuary of white beaches, rocky skerries, refreshing shallows and meadows opened up

I was making for a beach on the far side of the bay, on the small island of Selsøya. The map showed there was a broad channel between this island and the large rugged wild island of Hamarøy, which I should easily be able to paddle through. As I approached, I could see this gorgeous white beach on Selsøya. It formed part of the bay where the channel started and I paddled into it. As I paddled into this bay, which must have been a kilometre across, I entered a magical world. The whole bay was quite shallow and the sea floor was almost completely covered with brilliant white sand. Only occasionally did a smooth rocky skerry break through this white veil. Where the sand was covered by the water it was a green or turquoise colour. The bay was the most beautiful I had seen so far on this trip, and this even included yesterday's archipelago at Barøya, which I thought was perfect. I slowly paddled over the greens and turquoises covering the white sands as I threaded my way through the smooth shallow skerries, making for the mouth of the channel. But the channel was high and dry and covered with drifts and small dunes of the brilliant white sand. Where the grass had managed to stabilize them there were yellow explosions of vetch colonies. I think the map was wrong, and the 500-metre channel never got covered, even in the very highest tides. Selsøya island was not really an island, but a peninsula. I left the kayak and explored the beaches. The 500-metre dune-covered isthmus was too far to portage, so I was resigned to paddle round. It was a small price to pay for having paddled into this perfection. The whole bay was deserted, save for a couple of small homesteads nearby, which looked like they were just holiday homes now. Any children who stayed here in the summer weeks would have revelled in the 'Swallows and Amazons' style adventures the bay and its islets bestowed.

After soaking up the beauty of the bay I reluctantly left it and paddled round Selsøya and a few more rocky islands on the north side of Hamarøy before turning south-west towards the craggy Hamnesfjell, 878m high,

Day 181. The entrance to Buvåg inlet was marked with a typical beacon on a skerry, while the steep Hamnesfjell rose steeply beyond

and the other jagged mountains which make up the interior of the wild Hamarøy island, which also is not strictly an island, as it is connected to the mainland by a shallow, kilometre-wide isthmus. To the north, far across the ever widening Vestfjord, was the same very jagged skyline of Austvågøya I had seen yesterday. I only paddled for another hour, as the increasing wind was still against me and progress was hard fought. After just a few kilometres I reached the entrance to a larger inlet which sheltered the small harbour of Buvåg and decided to call it a day. Buvåg was a picture postcard hamlet, with a small wharf and some 20 houses, behind sandy beaches and a grass foreshore. Much of the grassy foreshore looked like it had been grazed by geese. The whole area was covered in wild flowers, especially yellow vetches and sea pinks. There were also large clusters of ragged robin. I found a nice place to pitch my tent on this grass and then spread things out to dry. It was still early evening so I went for a wander to the deserted harbour and found an old picnic table and seat, sheltered from the wind between two small wharfs. I sat here and wrote, casting my gaze across the harbour and vast Vestfjord itself, to the jagged Lofoten skyline in the blue haze to the north west.

I woke early and heard the tent flapping and rain pelting off the flysheet. I looked outside, just to see what it was like, and it was unpleasant, with a south-westerly force 5 wind, heavy rain and a low mist. I would be very lucky to make much headway into it and every kilometre would be a wet struggle. It was not in the forecast, so I was surprised. I zipped up the fly again and retreated back into my warm cocoon. I had not had a day off since Tromsø and my body would welcome a rest. With a sigh of relief I rolled over on to my side for a well received lie in. I managed to snooze, on and off, in my cosy sleeping bag, for four hours while the wind lashed rain against the tent. I was confident I had made the right decision to stay put. By late morning I could sleep no more, no matter how hard I tried, but it was still too wet to venture out. I cooked a simple lunch of mashed potatoes with a can of potted meat chopped into it. This set me up for an afternoon siesta, while I digested it. When I woke in the mid-afternoon though I simply had to move. I had been lying down for some 20 hours now. My ribs felt like that of a beached whale, distorting with an enormous weight and about to crush as they were no longer supported and buoyed up by water. I had to get up, explore and get some exercise and fresh air. I went for a short walk in the hamlet of Buvåg for 3 kilometres, along the road past some well-kept gardens of permanent residents, of which there were about 10 houses, and 10 leisure cabins. It was a nice community, but lacked a heart like Måsøy or Bergsfjord. As I walked, the weather improved, and Hamnesfjell was slowly unveiled from a shroud of mist. There were even some blue patches in the sky and the wind dropped to a

Day 181. Sitting on the harbour wall I was able to write while gazing across the inlet and the vast Vestfjord to the blue hazy Lofoten Islands

Day 182. The fertile meadow I camped in at Buvåg was full of many types of flowers, including ragged robins as pictured here

Day 182. The campsite at Buvåg was a tidal meadow which looked like it was grazed by the geese which migrate through this area

force 3. When I returned to the tent I had a text message on my phone from the two Swedish girls who were also paddling the Norwegian coast. They had left three weeks after me and had portaged across the isthmus at Nordkinn and then gone inside Magerøy, thereby missing Kinnarodden and Nordkapp. None the less they were storming down the coast and were now just half a day behind me at the village of Tranøy. They had also been pinned down by the weather today. I texted back to say we could meet tomorrow and I would wait at Buvåg. I was looking forward to meeting them and sharing stories of the hardships and reflections of the beauty and places we had paddled through.

I woke very early and was packed and ready to go by 0700. I had arranged to meet the two Swedish girls as they paddled past the entrance to Buvåg inlet at this time. It was an overcast and calm morning, with mist lingering on all the peaks along this wild, west side of Hamarøy. Here and there a mountain ridge would break free of the mist and cut a dark serrated line though the white. Hamarøy is where one of Norway's best-known writers, Knut Hamsun, grew up and the wild landscape here must have influenced his psyche. After half an hour's wait the girls had still not appeared, so I sent them a text message. They had gone past an hour earlier, and as they had not seen me they continued on. They had already paddled 12 kilometres so they must have had an extreme start. We arranged to meet for lunch some 30 kilometres down the coast at Grådusan. I was a bit disappointed they had not got in touch to tell me they would be early, or made the slight diversion into the inlet at Buvåg to say hello. I had heard they were on a mission to paddle 50 kilometres each day. Obviously with only 12 kilometres under their belt so far today they felt they had to press on unswervingly. I set off at a more leisurely pace.

Day 183. The wild, west side of Hamarøy was very rugged and composed of many steep mountains covered in a jungle of birch trees

It was an easy paddle on the still sea, with much of the scenery still obscured by the low cloud, but it was slowly lifting and the sun was breaking through in places. This was a rocky rugged shore with very few beaches but some dramatic scenery. The mountains here were high and steep and were covered in a thick birch forest which made them look like a tropical jungle. There were no houses down the entire west side after the hamlet of Buvåg, as it looked too rough and inhospitable for farming and too exposed to shelter a small harbour. Towards the south of Hamarøy was a large bay, called Sandvika peppered with islands and skerries. I peered into it and it looked gorgeous with a rim of white beaches and turquoise water. Around the entire bay was a precipitous horseshoe of mountains nearly 1000 metres high. I am sure it would have been another paradise like Selsøya at the northern end of Hamarøy, which had enthralled me so much a couple of days ago. However, I had a lunch appointment and I knew I did not have time to detour into the bay and savour it.

Day 183. A self portrait after some six months on tour, with the mountains of Hamarøy behind me

Day 183. Fjetterstad bay on the west side of Lundøy island was an almost tropical sight, with a stunning beach and jungle-clad mountains

Reluctantly I paddled across its mouth, weaving through the scatter of islands which protected the white, sandy beaches inside the bay. Then I sped across Økssund to reach the green and forested island of Lundøy. There were many puffins in this sound and as it was becoming calm again I could spot them from half a kilometre's distance.

Lundøy carried on in the same theme as Hamarøy with very steep mountains covered in the jungle of birch. There were a few beaches here but it was the steep dramatic mountains which really grabbed my attention until I got to a bay called Fjetterstad, half way down the west side. It was absolutely stunning. The bay was fringed with the beautiful white crushed coral sands which seemed to be so common here. Around the bay rose steep sharp ridges which climbed straight up to the 900-metre peaks and fluted crags in the interior of this relatively small island. The lower reaches of the mountains were covered in a carpet of thick birch woods, which looked like a rain forest. In the grass above the sand, many hundreds of terns were noisily circling around their nests in this large breeding colony. As I gazed at this from my kayak, along the warm sun-drenched shore, I thought I was looking at a jungle-clad tropical island, like Mauritius. I needed a stretch, and this was the perfect place. I rammed the kayak on to the beach and got out sinking up to my ankles in the soft, white sand. In the mouth of this bay was a lush green island, with an abandoned farmstead nestled down on the vibrant green meadow, above a white beach. Between me on this Mauritius like beach and the island, called Fjetterstadholm, was half a kilometre of shallow, refreshing turquoise water, broken by the occasional shallow skerry, covered in orange seaweed. This farm now looked derelict, but I could not help but wonder just how idyllic it must have been to live in such beauty on a day like this. Isolated here in a winter's storm must have been very different though.

Day 183. The beach at Fjetterstad was also home to a large tern colony who nested in the grassland just beyond the white sands

Feeling jubilant I left this heavenly beach and headed west to a scatter of islands off the northern tip of the next large mountainous island of Engeløy. I could see more white flashes and turquoise hues across the 2-kilometre sound, and knew I would soon be in for another treat. When I got there I paddled through yet another paradise archipelago of small rocky islands with large meadows on them. Many of the islands had white sandy coves enveloped by protective arms of smooth light grey rock. There were also large shoals of white sand under shallow green and turquoise waters in the sheltered basins between the islands. It seemed some of these were so shallow one would be able to walk from one island to another. I spotted a few sheep and goats which a farmer from Engeløy had probably put on the island to fatten up on the lush grasses here over the

Day 183. Out in the bay at Fjetterstad was a small holm with an idyllic old homestead, sitting in the middle of a lush vibrant green meadow

summer. Right on the very northern tip of Engeløy, at a place called Hamnvika, was a wonderful old fisherman's 'rorbuer' or cabin which looked out on to this picture postcard setting. What an absolutely stunning coastline this was. Islands, white beaches, blue skies, warm turquoise waters, idyllic lush homesteads, and all under the tremendous backdrop of awesome mountains; and it was all unexpected. Since leaving Ramsund I had been paddling through perfection which had lifted my already high spirits to an ecstatic level.

After threading through these wonderful islands, I crossed an open bay for a few kilometres to reach the next headland called Grådusan. There was a smaller island here, separated by a white beach which dried at low tide. A line of 10 sheep were now wandering over this exposed beach to reach the rich grass on the island. Under a rowan tree on the island I also spotted the Swedish girls who were waving enthusiastically. I pulled ashore and got a warm hug from each of them. My slight annoyance because they had not waited this morning quickly melted. The girls, Evelynn and Klara, where both in their mid twenties. They had both kayaked along Sweden's coast four years ago and were now doing Norway's coast. They started some three weeks behind me, and although they had taken a slightly different route, saving about a week, they had managed to catch up by putting in many huge days. They were the epitome of Swedish ladies; blonde, beautiful, bold, and bursting with enthusiasm. They had already prepared lunch, and I joined them under the rowan tree, sitting on the foundation wall of a long gone homestead. We chatted excitedly for a good two hours, about the trip so far, without ever stopping for a pause. It would not have been possible to slide a cigarette paper into the conversation. They had met some of the same people I had, and had even stayed with the kind Næss family on Lyngen. They described Ida Næss as an angel without wings. They had also paddled much of the same waters and round many of the same daunting headlands, but had skipped the worst, by portaging 600 metres across the Nordkinn isthmus. They aimed to do 50 kilometres each day and had already done 40 that morning. So they were still looking to do another 10. We carried their very heavy boats right down the beach, as the tide had retreated so much since they arrived, and set off, the chat and banter continuing in the kayaks.

We went round the island and paddled into yet another fantastic archipelago of a few hundred small islands. This was called the Steigen archipelago. There were sandy beaches, turquoise shallows, grassy islets, and tern colonies everywhere. A few of the islands had old summer small holdings on them; many of these were still maintained in good condition by the children or grandchildren of the last farmer or fisherman who had lived in them. One of the bigger islands, Lauvøya, was an old trading post on the historic maritime highway along the Norwegian coast. A century ago it would have been the local centre in a network of small scale commerce and trade. This trading post would export fish, especially dried cod, and import flour, kerosene, metal tools and building materials, like nails. There was a prosperous looking farm there now, surrounded by mature deciduous trees, and a very large warehouse on the jetty. The farm was set in lush green fields, and a short distance away was a sandy spit to an islet surrounded by a white beach. It was a serene setting. As I was still chatting with the girls I could not really soak up the splendour of these last 10 kilometres through this whole scatter of islands, but it was equal to anything I had seen in the previous 100 kilometres since leaving Ramsund.

It was now late afternoon and we decided to find somewhere to camp. As we emerged from one of the many channels between the islands, we spotted a large white beach about 2 kilometres away to the south-east by the village of Holkestad. There was immediate consensus to make for it and camp there. Within half an hour of landing, our tents were up between the usual red boat sheds and we were chatting on the grass for another few hours. I cooked outside in the sun for a change in the still evening. The odd mosquito was a pest. The girls prepared for bed very early and by 2030 they were heading to their tent; and this was a late night for them! They were getting up as usual at 0330 to be on the water for 0500. I retired to my tent to write. I inserted the last of my four laptop batteries to find it was dead. I only had a few minutes of power left. I downloaded the pictures, in case I dropped the camera into the sea, and looked at the map for somewhere suitable to charge all the batteries tomorrow. Kjerringøy, some 50 kilometres to the south looked good. I went to sleep early and prepared myself for a Swedish start.

I woke very early. So early, not even the girls were stirring. As I was packing my kayak there was a remarkable skyscape to the north. I was now approaching the Arctic Circle again. The sun was almost on the horizon around midnight and the adjacent hours, as it was now. The whole sky was dark with cloud except for a strong orange

Day 184. A very early morning scene at Holkestad, looking north to the serrated silhouette of the Lofoten Islands against the midnight sun

glow on the horizon. In front of this glow was the dark serrated silhouette of Austvågøya. It looked like there was a volcano erupting somewhere to the north. The girls emerged at 0400, broke camp and packed with well-practised organization. It was now a dull overcast morning with just a slight northerly wind and the glow to the north over the Lofoten Islands had gone out. We pushed off from the sandy beach at 0500. They set the pace in their narrower more streamlined kayaks and I had to paddle hard in my stable load-lugging barge to keep up. Headland after headland zoomed by with ruthless efficiency. I stopped to take a photo and was suddenly 100 metres behind and had to paddle furiously to catch up. During a rare pause, we spotted a moose on one of the islands in the pretty Måløyvær archipelago to the west of Skotstind. This mountain was at the west end of the typically steep and dramatic peninsula, which ended in this troll-like peak, before plunging into the still sea and patchwork of islands and sandy channels. Moose out here really surprised me, although they are good swimmers. With the wind behind us we made incredible time and by 0700 had already done nearly 15 kilometres. Next, we raced across Leinesfjord, with me often lagging behind. Even in this open fjord was a scatter of islands and holms. It would have been quite sheltered in most seas as the ocean swell would not really be able to penetrate in here. We chicaned through a pretty cluster of sandy islands off the Leines peninsula and then crossed the wide Brennvika bay to reach another mountainous and dramatic headland. Where these mountains plunged into the sea, off the tip of this steep headland, was the small island of Vettøy, with a sheltered turquoise bay and white sands on its northern side. We pulled up on to the beach and enjoyed the sun as the clouds vanished into the blue sky. It was barely 0900 and we had already done 30 kilometres. However, I felt I had blasted past much of this astonishing beauty without having the chance to really savour it.

Day 184. Leaving Vettøy and heading into the strait between this island and Brenntind, 754m, to enter the island-strewn Folda fjord

The next part of the journey was crossing Folda, which was a 16-kilometre wide fjord. However, unlike the exposed fjord crossings of Østhavet and Ishavet, Folda had numerous islands and skerries in a line across its mouth. We hopped from island to island at a more relaxed pace now with the sun getting higher and warmer. I at last got time to take some photos, with the girls waiting for me. Now that they had the lion's share of their daily quota of 50 kilometres under their belts, they took their feet of the accelerator. The main archipelago was Karlsøyvær. It was a cluster of a few hundred small islands and islets, all separated by shallow light blue waters and extensive brilliant white beaches. I later discovered that this archipelago is a renowned nature reserve, created for its prime bird habitat and its importance in the spring and autumn, when many

Day 184. Low tide at one of the Karlsøyvær islands with the kelp showing and the bulbous Eidetind and sharp Strandåtind mountains

migratory birds stage here. We paddled into the cluster of islands and over some of the white sands in crystal clear waters with our mouths open in surprise at the untarnished beauty. This was yet another paddling paradise along this wonderful coast. Again the mainland was not going to be outdone by the idyllic coast, and showed off more of its steep granite mountains with the claw-like Strandåtind, 862m, being the most impressive, with its 500 metre vertical south face.

At Karlsøya, the main island in this serene archipelago, we said our goodbyes. I was heading over to Kjerringøy, hopefully to find a room to wash clothes and myself, charge batteries and eat some vegetables, while Evelynn and Klara were continuing south for another 10 kilometres to camp. As we parted, I could not help

Day 184. The brave, bold Swedish girls were a joy to paddle with for a day through this spectacular Steigen region

but admire their discipline and determination. Their policy of a very early start meant a very early finish and they would probably be camped and relaxing in the early afternoon with 50 kilometres in the bag. Once the first 30-40 kilometres were under their belts in the morning, the single mindedness melted away and there was plenty of time for banter and fun. I could not manage these early starts on a regular basis, as my writing often takes so much time I seldom get to bed before midnight, and then I tend to relax in the mornings before I start. It was sad to see the girls head off as they were great fun and good company. However, I could not hope to keep up with them on their mission, without sacrificing the exploratory enjoyment and sense of wonder my spiritual pilgrimage was bringing me. I crossed the remaining 5 kilometres to Kjerringøy and rounded the harbour breakwater to find a marina full of expensive yachts. It seemed Kjerringøy was a haven for the sailing fraternity to come and relax. There was a guest house but it looked expensive. I tried my usual line of saying I was kayaking Norway's coast, and as usual it seemed to get me a massive reduction. The place was perfect, and the room was great, with power sockets everywhere, and a balcony over the marina where I could hang clothes to dry. They let me use their washing machine for free and went out of their way to be helpful and interested. By 2300 my clothes were dry, all my writing was up to date, all my batteries were recharged, I was clean and ready for a 0900 start the following morning, by which time the girls would already be past Bodø, far to the south.

I had a tremendous sleep in a comfortable bed in the complete dark. It was the first time in 10 days I had not camped. When I woke though, and looked out of the balcony, the sea was full of white horses and a northerly force 5 was even whipping up some spray. By the time I had breakfast I had convinced myself it would be possible to paddle. Although the waves were breaking, they were only a metre or so high due to the small fetch, and the wind would be directly behind me. I also hoped to follow the coast for much of the way. I paddled out of the harbour breakwaters and turned south. I quickly accelerated down the coast, surfing on the occasional steep wave. Out to the west was the steep island of Landegode. It was very craggy. One of Scotland's most craggy islands, Rum, is about three times the size, but Rum would have looked flat beside it. And Landegode was just one of hundreds of such islands in Norway! I draw this comparison, because it was from Landegode that the sea eagles which were reintroduced into Scotland and placed on Rum some 30 years ago, originally came from. As I came down the coast there were a string of islands just off shore. I threaded down through them and eventually found a route through to a sheltered channel on the inside of this string of islands. In retrospect I realized I could have gone on the inside of Kerringsøya island which formed the outer

Day 185. After Kjerringøy I paddled south through a string of islets towards the rugged Landegode island near Bodø

309

half of the harbour and straight into this channel. When I reached Mistfjord I was able to cut across the mouth of the fjord as it was largely protected from the infant swell by the group of small islands and islets which almost formed a peninsula near Fjære. Looking east up Mistfjord showed some classic fjord scenery with a U-shaped valley beyond. Above the valley, steep forested sides and then crags of bare rock and alpine peaks up to 1000 metres, which were still obscured by the vanishing cloud.

On the south side of Mistfjord mouth I entered the sound of Landegodefjord between Landegode island and the mainland. It was a bit of a wind funnel and the force 5 increased up to a force 6. It was still behind me and I was sometimes getting blown along at a tremendous rate. If I caught a good surf wave I was doing 12 kilometres an hour for a burst. Generally the waves were going much faster than I could paddle and passed under me. This resulted in a wallowing motion of stopping and starting which actually tended to slow me down, because although I could surf down the occasional wave, I was also sliding down the back of this wave when it passed under me and I wallowed in the trough and lost momentum. I came to one peninsula at Mjelle with a rocky islet at the end, separated from the rest by a sandy spit. I stopped on the spit and stretched,

Day 185. The small spit at Mjelle between peninsula and outcrop offered some respite from the strong wind until the tide swamped it

before the incoming tide swamped the spit, forcing me to continue. With a good force 6 now howling behind me, I was fortunate to find shelter south of this peninsula by entering a scatter of islands and channels clustered around Vågøya island. I was blown down these channels, as bemused cows watched me as they looked up from grazing the verdant grass. Once I had left the protection of the Vågøya islands I was at the mercy of the northerly near gale again, and it was a bumpy ride all the way down to Skivika on the outskirts of Bodø. Here there was a steep knoll here, called Bratten, and it thrust its rocky bulbous base into the ocean. As I went round it the sea became very choppy indeed. I lurched from crest to trough on the clapotis which was caused by the two-metre waves rebounding off Bratten and confusing the sea, making it very erratic. In addition to this there was a small tidal current adding to the confusion, and the force 6 wind was blowing spray off the crests and explosions of clapotis. It was a wild sea with masses of drama and there was no protection from it. I was now thankful for my load-lugging barge, as it was extremely stable in such seas and looked after me well without too many support strokes. It was the Volvo Estate of kayaks. I thought of the Swedish girls in their fast, but unpredictable, streamlined, sports cars who probably passed here earlier today and would undoubtedly have been uncomfortable in this mayhem.

After this chaos I paddled into a channel and the sea quickly diminished and became more orderly and predictable. I had the two Hjartøya islands to the west and the unfolding urban scenery of Bodø to the east. The trouble with larger towns is that it is difficult to find places to land which is near somewhere to stay. You arrive with 100 kilos of kayak and contents to deal with and secure, and then an inevitable walk to some accommodation or a campsite. It had been quite a palaver in Tromsø and I had Kåre and Bjørn to advise me, while here in Bodø I was ignorant and I was likely to waste a lot of time and energy in finding something. Usually I had the relatively stress-free option of simply ramming the kayak up on a sandy beach, put up my tent and camping gear, then carry the empty kayak up above the high tide near the tent. It usually took less than half an hour. Bodø was second only to Tromsø as the largest town in north Norway, and was a fast growing town with some 40,000 inhabitants. As I paddled along I could see into the harbour area occasionally. It seemed to have a grand waterfront with a number of expensive hotels like Rica and Radisson. Much of old Bodø was destroyed in the war and has been rebuilt with this shiny replacement. I am sure old Bodø was much more characterful than these concrete and glass vanity projects. I was about to cross the harbour mouth when the Hurtigruten ferry steamed out. It was one of 11 boats which take 11 days to do the Bergen-Kirkenes-Bergen trip. It was the *MS Nordlys* on her way north. I felt a familiarity with the *MS Nordlys,* after my near encounter with her at Berlevåg some five weeks previously. I waited nearby until it had finished manoeuvring out of the harbour and steamed north, before I crossed the harbour, wondering if any of the crew on board remembered me.

I paddled right past the whole of Bodø, as I did not see anywhere to land and ended up at the tip of the peninsula it was on. I thought about rounding the peninsula and paddling into Saltfjord a bit. It was more in the lee of the weather and I considered it a bit too risky to cross the open 10-kilometre Saltfjord in this force 6 wind. However, as I came to the tip of the peninsula I noticed that the wind had dropped off to a force 5. I stopped among some islets, ate a late lunch, watched the wind and considered my options. The wind was dropping and I decided to cross while the going was good, as the forecast predicted strong northerly winds for the next few days, and I did not want to get stuck here. As I was about to go a large 'Nordlandsbåt' went sailing past. The Nordlandsbåt is a traditional wooden boat from this area and they come in many sizes from about 15 feet to a whopping 52 feet. They are powered by either oar or sail. The smaller 15 feet boats, called 'Færingen', only have two pairs of oars while the large 'Fembøringen' have six pairs of large oars. The larger boats also have an enormous square sail which is taken down in the evenings to provide shelter over the front of the boat, while it is anchored or in harbour. This one was either a Fembøringen or the slightly smaller Åttringen, and was about 40 feet. It had its burgundy-coloured square canvas sail up as it smoothly glided over the water and up Saltfjord looking like something out of the Viking era. It was perhaps the most graceful boat I had ever seen and I watched mesmerized as it seemed to fly over the water.

Day 185. Resting at the islets south of Bodø, waiting for the wind to diminish sufficiently, so I could paddle across Saltfjord

Just some 20 kilometres up Saltfjord, the fjord narrowed into a channel 3 kilometres long and just 150 metres wide. On the far side of this was a huge body of water, called Skjerstadfjord, which is about 250 square kilometres. Every six hours the whole of Skjerstadfjord must lose or gain up to four metres of water and it must all flow through this channel. Up to a billion cubic metres of water flow through this channel in six hours. The resulting tidal flow is the strongest in the world, and I have heard people say it reaches 40 kilometres per hour. There are many eddies and whirlpools as the tide rushes through and empties or fills the fjord, and a short period of calm water as the currents change direction every six hours. Because the currents here are so strong they carry many organisms and small fish which are swept along by the torrent. Larger predatory fish, like wolf-fish, cod, saithe and pollack, lie in wait and ambush this food as it rushes past. In turn, it has become a very popular place for anglers who hope to catch one of these larger fish which are so abundant.

Day 185. Most of the way across Saltfjord and veering west to go round the flat Mårnes peninsula and lighthouse with Fugløy behind

The crossing over Saltfjord was easy. With the wind behind me, I made very good time, and the waves never really built up. It took just over an hour before I was approaching the other side. I did not land here, but veered off to the west, passing to the north of some flat islands and over the open sea to the lighthouse on the tip of the Mårnes peninsula. Once round it I hoped I would have the protection of some larger islands, should the predicted north wind arrive tomorrow. After the lighthouse I was blown down the coast while I kept my eyes scoured for a place to camp. I didn't really pass any beaches on this rocky coast until I had done some 5 kilometres and reached the village of Våg. There was a harbour, beach, closed shop and campsite here. It was perfect, and as it was early evening I pulled up on to the beach and found a grassy area on the

Day 186. Looking back to the neighbouring hamlets of Våg and Lekanger beneath the near 1000 metre Sandhorn mountain

edge of an official campsite. Despite the distance I had covered today, I did not feel tired, and put it down to the following northerly wind.

I put up my tent when a man approached from a large group of around 30 people. As usual in north Norway it was a friendly, chatty and hospitable visit. He was the winchman on a rescue helicopter based in Spitsbergen. After a few minutes he insisted I come over to the rest of the group for dinner. I zipped up my tent and followed him over to the others, who were all members of the Fauske Small Boat Club. They had come from Fauske in a varied flotilla of boats, and collected here for an evening's gathering. They had a huge barbecue on the go, and generously heaped food on to my plate and opened bottles of beer for me. I tried to join the conservation, but it was too fast and I was too tired to concentrate on the dialect. After a great dinner we all went down to one of the boats a few of them collectively owned. It was a Fembøringen, exactly the same type as the graceful Nordlandsbåt which had enthralled me earlier in the day. The square sail was down over the front of the boat in a tent-type arrangement, and some 20 people had gathered underneath, with guitars and healthy voices. It was a nice evening, almost rowdy by Norwegian standards, with plenty of leg-pulling, jokes and banter. I chatted a lot with the guardian of this communally-owned boat who was eager to explain its history and various uses. I was particularly fascinated by the cabin where the six sailors would have slept. It was tiny, with three bunks on each side of the stern with less than a foot's height separating the interlocking six bunks at the apex of the stern. I did not get to bed until the sun had kissed the horizon and was on its way up again.

I slept well and woke to a glorious calm day. The forecast said it should be a good force 5 which would build up to a force 7 later in the day. There was no sign of that at the moment and I felt no urgency as I settled down to write at a nearby table. At midday when I was finished, the café and shop opened, and I visited both. In fact, I did not get going until mid afternoon, by which time everybody from the previous night's gathering had long disappeared in their various crafts. Luckily the weather remained sunny and calm all day so I did not feel guilty about squandering it. When I did get going, I initially paddled past the neighbouring village of Lekanger, which had the typical fjord landscape of colourful pretty villages, surrounded by green fields and then the steep birch-clad craggy mountains rising high above them. From this charming village I headed off over to the island of Femris. I was going to go down the east side, but the force 3 wind and choppy wavelets kept slewing the kayak to the north of Femris, so in the end I resigned and paddled where the weather wanted me to go. I was then forced to go down the west side of Femris which was delightful. I first had to glide down a channel between Femris and a small island off its north-west shore. This channel opened out into a sheltered basin where there were a couple of lush farms above a quiet beach. The tide was low and there was large lazy leaves of shiny brown kelp glimmering in the sun. It looked a good area for duck but I did not see any. The basin then narrowed again into a channel and I paddled through it to the lee side of Femris island.

Day 186. The gorgeous homesteads in the sheltered basin on north Femris island still seemed to be in use as working small holdings

To my west was another larger craggy island with mountains over 700 metres. It was called Fugløya (Bird Island) and was uninhabited. It almost certainly contained bird colonies as they were marked on the map and the sea was full of puffins, not in rafts but clusters of 10 or so. Puffins spend all year in the ocean, only

Day 186. Kunna, on the very right, was a bulbous headland at the end of a spectacular peninsula and was joined to it with a flat isthmus

returning to land to nest, and rear their single chicks in burrows on islands without mammal predators. They are excellent underwater swimmers and only need to fly in the summer months while nesting and bringing up their young. The rest of the year they are bobbing about on the Atlantic. Their wings and overall shape are therefore more suited to swimming and diving, but they are adequate fliers. On land, and whilst taking off and landing they are, however, somewhat clumsy. When I approach in the kayak they sometimes dive and sometimes fly. Those that fly beat their wings and splash across the waves with their feet splayed. They do not become airborne at once and crash from wave crest to wave crest until they finally bounce off one and are airborne. Their red feet stay splayed like a skydiver until they have enough speed, and then they tuck them away and accelerate. Once they are in the air they are fast, but not really acrobatic.

I continued down the west side of Femris towards some very spectacular mountains along the edge of the coast here. Some of them rose steeply for 1000 metres and there were many immense buttresses which almost gave an escarpment appearance. I paddled along their base, having to lift my head back to see their tops. The slopes at the base of these cliffs were covered in birch forest, before the rock rose up vertically. Unusually, much of the geological strata was horizontal. This was not because it was undisturbed, as this coast has seen violent geological forces at work twisting huge areas, but because of coincidence that these forces left them horizontal after twisting, crushing, stretching and bending them. I paddled along the base to Finnes at the end of these cliffs. I was going to land here for a stretch, but there was a bit of a swell coming in from

Day 186. The 500-metre buttresses on the north side of the peninsula rose straight out of the sea, with horizontal strata like an escarpment

the west now and the shore was rocky. I saw a seal here. I have seen remarkably few seals and otters so far on this trip; perhaps a hundredth of what I would see in Scotland on a comparable trip. This surprises me, as the seas here are full of fish. With the wind increasing slightly to a force 4 I paddled over the bay towards Grimstad and then veered towards the north side of Kunna. Kunna is a large clump of rock; a 600-metre mountain on its own, connected to the mainland by a sandy isthmus 2 kilometres long and 500 metres wide. I could easily have portaged over the isthmus, but I would have needed two trips with my gear, and one with my kayak. About 3 kilometres, or an hour of walking. Round the coastline it was perhaps about 6 kilometres which was also an hour. In addition, I did not want to portage on this trip, it was not 'sportif' as the French would say, so paddle round it was.

I expected it to be quite choppy round the north of the Kunna peninsula. I was now at the very edge of Vestfjord and the shelter granted by the string of Lofoten islands was negligible. Indeed, the other extremity of this fjord, the remote island of Røst, almost lost in the Atlantic at the end of the Lofoten Islands, was perhaps 100 kilometres away. I was now essentially in open ocean and the swell was close to three metres here. However, I did not expect it to be so choppy. As I approached the north-west corner there was a skerry to go round. The swell here was meeting the final stages of the incoming tidal flow, and was also being influenced by underwater skerries. The wind was now a force 5 with spray flying everywhere. Claws of white sea were snapping at my kayak from all directions, and occasionally one would break on it. It was like the rounding of Slettnes fyr some four weeks ago, but in miniature. The tide was against me and I paddled hard for a good half hour, making only

Day 186. After rounding turbulent Kunna at midnight, I got a glimpse of the renowned 250km long Helgelandskysten with its 20,000 islands

a few hundred metres, before I was through the worst of the unpredictable mayhem. Sometimes the waves were four metres and very steep, but luckily none of them caught me out. I was expecting to be capsized at any second and was bracing myself to roll. When I eventually started to get into quieter waters, my mouth was not dry with fear as it had been at Slettnes fyr, but my jaw was clamped tight in concentration.

Approaching midnight I paddled into the bay on the south side of Kunna isthmus, where there should have been a sandy beach. However, it was a wind funnel with gusts of force 7 roaring through and lifting small whirlwinds of spray. It was difficult to paddle into this wind to reach the beach, so I went broadside to it across the bay and followed the rocky coast down for 3 kilometres, hoping to go round a small peninsula to reach the sheltered waters of Hornvika. It did not take long, with the strong wind pushing me and the waves diminishing as the waters became more protected with clusters of islands. Soon, I was in the bay and found a small beach with a flat grassy birch forest above it. It was a great camp spot in a lush meadow, full of orchids and enough leafy birch trees to give me all the protection I wanted. I put my tent up and enjoyed the view southwards towards the northern parts of Helgelandskysten which was a warm crimson in the glow of the midnight sun. Helgelandskysten was the next stage and it is reputed to be the best bit of the Norwegian coast for kayakers, and one of the top five kayaking destinations in the world. It is a 250-kilometre long and 30-kilometre wide collection of some 20,000 islands which form various clusters down a spectacular coast. There was everything on offer here, from sandy skerries to spectacular mountains with large ice-caps spread across the top of them. I had been looking forward to it for ages, and now I was overjoyed I was here, about to embark down it.

Day 186. At Hornneset I found a wonderful place to camp in flower-filled meadows sheltered from the near gale by fully clothed birch trees

Day 187. Looking back to Kunna headland across the windy bay gave me an excuse to have a day off before starting down Helgelandskysten

When I woke, the sun was blazing down on to the tent heating up the inside, but I could hear that there was a good wind blowing. I looked outside and could see it was a force 7. It was the wind on the eastern edge of a large high pressure and if this moved west, as it should, I was about to enjoy many days of good weather. It was the same high pressure which had just allowed Patrick Winterton and Mike Berwick to paddle for an unbroken 74 hours to cross from Scotland to the Faroe Islands a couple of days ago. There was plenty of shelter around the birch woods to lie in the sun and relax. I had not had the time or the weather to do this on the trip yet, and this was a great opportunity. The grasses were now getting high, and in this wind you could see swaths of them rippling as the gusts hit them. Where I was, in a glade between the trees, it was almost still and the

Day 187. From the camp spot I walked the 5km to Reipa along a shore line lane past sandy bays with the Svartisen ice-cap in the far distance

sun was warm. It was easy to snooze. Blackbirds and thrushes flew around the birch and warblers darted from willow to willow. These birds were now spoilt with the annual explosion of insects. There was a feast of them on the underside of many of the new leaves, easily enough to rear a family of chicks. This is why so many of the passerine birds migrate to the northern climes for the summer months.

After a few hours I got bored and went for a walk. Firstly, a few hundred metres to the west to the headland, to see Kunna in the north-west and what the sea looked like in that direction. It was now a force 6 and although the waves were small there were plenty of them breaking. I then went eastwards. There were a couple of nice beaches and a few leisure cabins lost in the woods. The sea here was more sheltered, and it would easily have been possible to paddle south if I kept to the inside of the larger islands of Meløya and Amøya, but I had now promised myself a day off, and was looking forward to a walk in the summer woods and fields. I kept on walking east and passed more nice cabins and boat sheds until I came to a leafy lane. The fjord here was very beautiful with small beaches and meadows filled with flowers. Across the fjord, 30 kilometres to the south, was the smooth white dome of Svartisen ice-cap which covered an area the size of the Isle of Arran. As I wandered the lane, enjoying the warm summer air and woods teeming with birdsong, I passed many small farms. I could smell and see all the fields were recently cut, and the hay was lying to dry in the sun.

I met a man who told me there was a shop an hour down the lane. I set off and soon the lane opened up into a shoreline road through larger farms in the hamlet of Fore. When I reached the village of Reipa, with its large white Lutheran church and shop, I bought some food and took it outside to eat at the table by the shop. The assistant came out and sat opposite me for a chat. Most shops in rural Norway have a couple of tables with coffee and cake for customers to purchase and chat over. These tables are one of the informal meeting places of the community, as most villages will not have pubs. After the meal I walked the 5 kilometres back along the road and then birch-covered lane to my tent. Just four months previously I had skied along lanes similar to this, with bare birch trees on either side, and it was astonishing to see how they had changed into their leafy summer glory with a carpet of wild flowers on the forest floor.

Day 187. Beside the lane all the fields of the small holdings had been cut for hay and these were now drying in the warm summer sun

SECTION 27. Vestfjord
8 days. 261 kilometres. 52.5 hours. 0m ascent. 0m descent.

THE KAYAK: SECTION 28. HELGELANDSKYSTEN

THE KAYAK: SECTION 28. HELGELANDSKYSTEN

I got up very early and packed the kayak in the still morning. I had never noticed midges, or 'knot', before in Norway, but they were out in force this morning, rising from the warm, still grasses. They were nothing in comparison to the numbers found on the west coast of Scotland, but irritating none the less. As I packed the kayak an otter shuffled along the beach just in front of me. Its gait seemed awkward on land, compared to the gracefulness otters have in the water. I pushed off and had only taken a few strokes, when I noticed a sea eagle just 100 yards away. It had seen me but remained unusually confident; as they normally fly off at once. I remained still and after a few minutes this one did indeed fly off. Surprisingly it just flapped its enormous wings, crossed in front of me and then landed 100 metres away on the other side. I watched it, and it watched me, for a good 10 minutes before I set forth across the fjord towards the west end of Meløya. This fjord was not the classic strip of water between steep-sided mountains, but rather an open basin studded with many flat rocky islands and islets. One of the clusters of islands was called Gåsvær. It was a collection of some 10 rocky islets, with sandy shallows between them, covered in clear azure water. White beaches were at the head of many of the coves. On the main island there was a grassy field which had been won by generations of the same family of homesteaders who lived and fished from here. There was still a house on the edge of this field which was no doubt a leisure cabin now. In the bays and channels of this island cluster there were some rafts of eider duck with a few mothers looking after a batch of small ducklings. It was paradise for them in the warm and sheltered waters.

Day 188. An often-wary sea eagle keeping its sharp eyes on me, while basking in the morning sun and hoping to spot some carrion

Day 188. Looking south to the larger islands of Meløya, Skjærpa and Mesøya and mainland mountains south of Glomfjord

I passed through more islands which lay scattered in a dense maze off the west end of the larger Meløya island. These islands were rockier and more ice scraped than I had imagined. There were again numerous bays with white beaches and tall green grass growing in the sandy loam above the high tide mark. I then paddled over sheltered waters to the west end of the next larger island which was Amøya. To the west of me were hundreds of small flat islands, which on the map seemed to be arranged in various clusters. Occasionally, a larger steep island would rise up from these low level islands, like a 500-metre boulder on a table top. To the east of these flattish archipelagos was the dramatic mainland, with its steep 1000-metre mountains, deep fjords and glaciers. I crossed the mouth of one such fjord to reach the next headland of Sleipnesodden, and pulled up on one of the numerous beaches to have lunch. I sat in the grass above the sand and ate as the tide came in and a curlew circled above, sounding a wide variety of calls with its long curved beak. After this idyllic lunch I did not really know where to go next. I should have headed south, but I had been told Rødøya was worth

Day 188. I stopped for lunch on a beach at Sleipnesodden where a curlew circled above making many calls to distract me

Day 188. The Svartisen ice-cap at the head of the fjord is the size of the Isle of Arran and is one of the largest ice-caps in Norway

a visit, and it lay just 5 kilometres across the sound to the west. I had done well in the last fortnight so could afford to explore a bit. I set off towards the near 500-metre bastion of red rock which gave the island its name. After a short distance I had the sense to look behind me and I could now see up another deep fjord to the vast, smooth, white dome of the Svartisen ice-cap, one of the largest in Norway. Crevassed glaciers descended steeply from its gentle rounded surface and carved their way down the flanks of the eroded mountains, almost reaching the sea. 250 years ago, in the mini ice age of the 18th Century some of these glaciers would have easily reached the sea and calved icebergs. It was a surreal sight to see above the stern of the kayak. The view was there, over my shoulder, the whole way across the fjord until I reached Rødøya. Once at the island I paddled down the rocky east shoreline until I got to the village at the south end, where there was a large beach in Rødøyvika bay. Above the beach was a field of cut grass and some large mature deciduous trees, which looked a great camp spot, and I saw there was another tent already there. Just above this small leafy field was a large, traditional, old white house which I later found out was once the priest's house.

As I approached the beach, a young man with a guitar pulled away from chatting to the two lady campers in the tent, and came down to serenade my arrival. He was here to play at the pub that night and told me to come along. He and his group were heading out to one of the most dramatic and offshore islands in this chain, called Træna, for an annual music festival in a few days time, and this was a warm up. I later discovered he was Erlend Øye, a well-known Norwegian indie musician, and frontman for the Bergen band 'Kings of Convenience' and the Berlin band 'Whitest Boy Alive'. We chatted a bit and then he left me to unpack and set up my tent. I went for a walk around the village on the south of the island where most of the 180 population stay. There was a shop, a small café/pub and a fabulous large white Lutheran church, with 500 seats and two of

Day 188. Rødøya church is the spiritual centre of the whole scattered parish, and not just the island of Rødøya with its small population

the biggest wood-burning stoves I had ever seen. The church had many more seats than the population of the island, because it was the centre of the kommune (the council and parish hybrid), which included many more islands. It would be used for baptisms, confirmations, marriages and funerals for the whole of the kommune. The area around the village was very fertile and there were plenty of large trees and lively hedgerows beside the steep lanes. I ate at the café and then walked the 2 kilometres north to Klokkergården, a beautiful old farm building which had been converted into a very good guest house, renowned restaurant and pub. I bought a beer and settled on the lawn to listen to the 'Whitest Boy Alive' with the other two campers and a yachting couple I had met a week ago in Kjerringøy, who had just sailed what I had just paddled. It was a very nice

Day 188. The indie band 'Whitest Boy Alive' perform in front of the Klokkergården guest house in preparation for a concert on Træna

Day 189. About to launch from Rødøyvika beach with the mountains, glaciers and fjords of the mainland across the sound

afternoon and evening on this lush, relaxed, quirky island with its artistic rural vibe. A great welcome to Helgelandskysten.

I woke up in the shade of the huge elm tree under which I was camped, at the edge of the beach on another sunny day. I had to open up the tent before it started to cook me, despite being partly in the shade. After I got up I lazed around on the grass while having breakfast. The ladies from the other tent came over and we chatted for a good hour while I packed and got ready to launch on the sun-kissed beach. I had no plan as to where I was heading when I left the bay near midday. Rødøya was such a lovely island with such a pleasant atmosphere, I wanted to visit other islands which were hopefully the same. A few people had mentioned Hestmona as being a comparable island, so I decided to paddle over to it and have a look. It was less than 10 kilometres to the west and the route looked like I would have to weave through attractive island clusters.

It was a beautiful paddle between the islands of Flatøya, Gjerdøya and over to Sundøya. The latter had a few old homesteads and beaches down its east side. There was a man on one sandy beach at the bottom of his small holding, so I paddled over to chat with him. He said there was little on Hestmona, but the best scenery was on the west side. I took his advice and set off over the crystal clear water in the channel. It was so clear that at times it looked like I was levitating over my kayak's shadow in the white sand a metre below. At the bottom of this enchanting sandy stretch I veered west and paddled across 2 kilometres of open island-less fjord to the north side of Hestmona. When I looked behind me, the precipitous and red-coloured 443-metre high Rødøyløva mountain dominated the horizon. It was the highest point on Rødøya. I was half thinking about

Day 189. Weaving through the lower islands of Flatøya, Gjerdøya and Sundøya towards the great lump of Hestmona with its sharp peak

paddling over to Lovund, another steep 600-metre lump of rock rising high above the flat island clusters, so it would suit my plans if I did go down the west side of Hestmona. Everybody spoke very highly of Lovund. It had a village with a shop, café and guest house, and apparently an artistic atmosphere too. However, the real trump in Lovund's hand is its puffin colony. It is one of the most important in Norway, with quarter of a million of these comical little birds breeding on its rocky north slopes in the scree.

There were nice beaches and sandy islets on the north side of Hestmona where the main hamlet was, but the west side was mountainous and dramatic with no soft edges. As I started down the west side I crossed the Arctic Circle again. I was now below the latitudes where it would be possible to see the midnight sun at the summer equinox, around the 20th of June. While I cruised down the west side, waiting for something beautiful to unfold behind one of the gnarly ridges, the

Day 189. Looking back to Rødøyløva mountain, which at 443 metres was the highest point on Rødøya

Day 189. The homestead at Sjyvika between the hamlets of Hagen and Lurøy on Lurøya island was a typically well-kept small holding

wind quickly increased to a northerly force 5. I put this down to the fact that the wind was being accelerated here round the huge cliffs and would diminish when I got to the south. However, it did not and it was much too strong to consider paddling the partially sheltered 25 kilometres to Lovund. Indeed, I was being blown along at over 5 kilometres per hour just sitting still, so I decided to head south, passing to the west of the cluster of the Kvarøy islands and make for Lurøya island. It was a fast crossing with the wind behind me and I was approaching the island before I knew it. I carried on down channels on the west of the island and shot past the hamlet of Hagen, and then the village of Lurøy itself under the steep mountains in the centre of the island. I had intended to stop here but had so much momentum I was past it almost before I had time to make any decisions. I was blown along for another 2 kilometres to reach the large forested island of Onøya.

I hoped there was a shop at the village on the north side of Onøya, and possibly even a guest house, as I had little food left and only two litres of camping water. I paddled into the convoluted bay and made for the quay area where I landed. There were a few kids about and I asked them for directions. There was a shop here, but it had closed a few hours ago, and there was no accommodation. That was apparently at Lurøy village where I had been blown past half an hour ago, but I was not going back. They said there was a café a few kilometres to the west, near the end of Onøya. They thought there might be rooms here but said they would probably be full. I set off towards the café down a beautiful narrow sound with quaint leisure cabins and quirky boat sheds on each side, until I arrived at a slightly built-up area with a couple of large warehouses full of building materials, some new breakwaters, a fishing boat repair yard, a concrete quay and the grass-roofed café hiding amongst it all. The kids were right about the rooms, and they were all taken. I decided to eat and then head off in search of an island campsite. I sat at a small table, surrounded by groups of the yachting fraternity. I was rugged and unkempt, with salt stains on my clothes, while they were unnecessarily refined and well groomed. The café was not so friendly, but the food was fantastic. The day's dish was a kind of whale meat stroganoff.

After supper, I filled the water bottles and set off to find a place to camp. By now the near gale earlier in the day had completely vanished and it was a calm and clear evening. There was nothing on Onøya so I rounded the western end of it and turned south towards the twin peaks of the larger Tomma island and the flat island cluster of Sandvær before them. I thought with a name like this there must be a beach on it. It was about an hour's paddle south and I brushed past the flat island cluster of Kvitvær, which looked very nice with a few beaches and grassy meadows on it. As I approached Sandvær I could see there were beaches in all directions. I landed at one on the north-west side, after weaving through some sandy skerries and islets to get to it. It was a perfect beach and just above it was a grassy meadow which had been grazed short by sheep. I landed and explored the camp spot. It was absolutely perfect. Perhaps the most beautiful single place I had been to so far on the entire trip. On this evening it was bathed in the low sun which warmed it and lent a rosy hue to the white sands. Once my tent was up I went for a walk to explore my new home. Sandvær was the main island of perhaps a square kilometre which was surrounded by a hundred or so smaller islets and skerries. There were beaches and even small dunes everywhere. Many of the shallows between the islets were also submerged beaches with

Day 189. After the western point of Onøya I turned south to the twin peaks of Tomma island and the flat Sandvær islands before them

Day 189. Looking east from the idyllic north beach on Sandvær, towards the mainland across the fjord on this warm calm evening

every hue from turquoise to pale green. It would have been possible to wade between most of the skerries, and many would be connected at low tide. The beach I was on was one of the biggest in this island cluster and was composed of white sand from smashed coral and pulverized shells. It extended through to the south side of the island, over a white sandy saddle which separated my meadow camp from the main island.

I stood and surveyed the view from this secret paradise. All around, beyond the immediate beaches, was sea. Here and there were other clusters of flat islands, lying dark and low as they undulated just above the sea's surface. The nearest were just a few kilometres away. But rising above them in the distance were the steep larger islands which had withstood the erosion which had reduced everything else to a peneplain. Lovund, Træna, Hestmona and Lurøy islands were isolated clumps to the north and west, while the larger islands of Dønna and Tomma dominated the southern horizon. As I was gazing, enthralled by the view, I heard a sound, and turned to see a flock of 20 sheep and lambs approaching tentatively. They had obviously been placed here by a farmer, so they could roam free from predators and enjoy the fresh summer grass, before they were rounded up in September and taken back to the farm. During the winter months, the sheep will tend to stay indoors while the snow lies deep. During this period they are fed hay as they wander about the spacious barns. They are often hand fed salt by the farmer and his children, so each sheep is individually known by the farmer, who on average owns 20 to 50 sheep. While they don't have the same status as pets, they are still cherished. So these sheep, while a bit tentative to approach too closely, were curious to see whether I had any treats for them. It was a gentle pastoral end to a lovely day, and it was exactly what I had hoped Helgelandskysten would show me.

Day 189. Looking north from the same north beach on Sandvær, towards the sharp Hestmona, rising above all the flat island clusters

I slept well and woke early on a wonderful sunny, still morning. My island companions, the sheep, were lazing in the shade by a small ridge of heavily folded rocks on the edge of a beach. There were a few small trees on the island, but it was mostly grass which either grew on the rocky surface on a layer of thin soil or on the sand dunes. Sandvær was a wonderfully peaceful place on this still, sunny morning. It was difficult to make the decision to start to take down my tent and pack, and I lingered all morning, eventually leaving at midday. Again, I did not have any destination in mind other than southwards, but I did want to go round the west side of the larger mountainous island of Dønna. After I left the beach I paddled out of the white sandy bay through numerous islets and skerries. The water was glassy, and it was easy to spot an otter as it swam from one skerry to another. It rather surprised me to see one here, as I had always

Day 190. Looking west from Sandvær, past the curious healthy sheep, to the puffin fortress of Lovund island some 20km away

Day 190. The north beach on Sandvær in the morning, with the near islets shimmering in the turquoise sea and Hestmona in the distance

thought otters needed fresh water to rinse their coats, and there seemed to be none out here. Perhaps I was mistaken and it was a mink. Soon afterwards I passed a skerry with a lot of terns flying around it. It must be a breeding colony, and I was hoping the otter or mink I saw would not find it. I was curious to see how big the chicks were now, so I went ashore. To my surprise, most were still in their eggs, as they had been in Bergsfjord some three weeks ago. There were a couple of chicks looking very vulnerable in their rudimentary nests. Suddenly, a female eider duck flew off from a tall clump of rockrose almost beneath my feet. I had a look and there were seven green eggs in a down-filled nest hidden in the bush. Conscious I was perhaps disturbing the birds I left the island quite quickly.

Far to the west and well beyond the skerries, and even 20 kilometres beyond the frontier island of Lovund, I could see the island outpost of Træna. It was the most classic of these steep Helgelandskysten islands, with two massive very steep bastions of rock rising up 300 metres from the mantle of the flat island they sat on. Beside it, but hidden by the immediate skerries, were two other flat islands and it was on these three islands that the entire 450 inhabitants of this distant parish or council lived, mostly from fishing, and now tourism. Surrounding this remote community on the edge of the Atlantic were a scattering of some 1000 islets and skerries which protected Træna from the worst of the ocean weather. Træna was a typical 'vær', or a place where through the centuries fishermen have gathered in small communities to fish. Many of the island clusters here on Helgelandskysten end in 'vær', like Sandvær,

Day 190. A newly-hatched and well camouflaged tern chick in the simple scratch of a nest in the tern colony on a south islet in Sandvær

where I just spent a wonderful evening. The fishermen who lived in these small island communities either just came to their seasonal houses in the fishing season, or if they could farm on any land on their island cluster, lived here permanently. It was necessary for them to stay out here in the sea, near the bountiful harvests, because until recently the fishermen could only row or sail their boats to the fishing grounds. These boats also had to be small enough to be man handled out of the sea during bad weather. Large, motorized boats and breakwaters are recent inventions which meant fishermen no longer had to stay in these more exposed and lonely 'vær'. They could now move to larger villages and motor out each day. Today, many of the old fishermen's houses and homesteads on these 'vær' are now leisure cabins. Archaeological diggings around many of these old 'vær' show many have been used since the stone age and some of them are the oldest settlements in Scandinavia dating back some 10,000 years!

Day 190. An eider duck nest hidden in a clump of rockrose with plenty of down to keep the eggs warm

As I paddled south from Sandvær I crossed a stretch of open water before I reached the northern tip of Dønna island. The wind was starting to increase the whole time on the crossing and it was at least a force 4 when I reached Dønna. On the crossing I had seen many puffins bobbing about in the waves who were probably all on a fishing trip from Lovund island. It was the first time I had passed by puffins with beaks full of small fish which they were obviously collecting for the young chicks in their burrows. On reaching Dønna I did not really know what to do. I had virtually no food and I had lingered too long on Sandvær to find an open shop further south, as the next would be near Herøy, nearly 30 kilometres away. It looked like it would be mashed potato and hot chocolate for my eventual supper, as this was all I had. As I headed south down the west side of Dønna the wind was a force 6 and I was being blown along at a tremendous rate. While sitting still I was doing 6 kilometres per hour, and if I paddled this increased to around 9. In this wind, one would normally expect big seas, but due to all the skerries and islets the maximum fetch was only about 5 kilometres so there was no chance for the waves to develop. It is this which makes Helgelandskysten such a safe kayaking destination. After a couple of hours I was half way down the west coast of Dønna and I needed to stop for a stretch. I found a rocky seaweed-covered bay full of herons to land. I was quite wet and getting cold, due to the wind and leaking spraydeck. I did not fancy camping. I had an idea to go all the way to Husvær, where I was planning to go tomorrow. It was still about 25 kilometres away. I phoned them to ask if it was OK to arrive around midnight. The lady who owned the place, Inge, said it would be no problem at all.

I set off for their kayak centre and hostel mid-evening. With the strong wind behind me, the tide with me, and extra vigour in my arms, I made exceptional time. I was doing about 9 kilometre per hour as I blasted down across the Skagafjord to quickly reach Seløya. This small island seemed to be a busy little area and there were plenty of houses, cabins and a marina here. There was a café at the bridge to the island and I could see it was for the yachting fraternity. I went under the bridge and into an open basin between knobbly ice-scoured islands to the west of Herøy. There were quite a few houses around this basin and many rorbuer, or old fishermen's houses, many of which had a well-used larger wooden fishing boat moored to the jetty beside them. I paddled under another bridge at the south side of this knobbly basin and was blown down a short sound. I soon reached the more sparsely populated coastline again, with hardly any sign of human life and felt more in my element. I now had a straight run with the near gale behind me to cross some 7 kilometres of open water before I got to the shelter of the next cluster of islands, which was my destination at Husvær. I was worried about the size of the waves I would encounter at the end of this open stretch. As I neared Husvær the waves grew and grew and I could hear them hissing behind me as the metre and a half breakers rushed past. The decks were constantly awash and there was a lot of water dribbling through the porous neoprene spraydeck and on to my legs. There was about five centimetres of water sloshing about in the kayak and I was drenched, as I did not have my drysuit on. Just before the waves became unmanageable I reached the first two islets of the Husvær archipelago and I was soon in the midst of it. The wind was still a good force 6 but I was now being blown down channels with just ripples beside me.

I found the place I was staying quite easily, which was a surprise given the complexity of the islands. Jon, who I paddled with two months ago, had recently paddled past here and stayed at the same place. He was so enthused by it he had sent me a message strongly recommending it. He also said Helgelandskysten was sometimes like a maze, and that only 1:50,000 maps would do, to avoid getting lost and get the most out of exploring the islands. Jon, like me, had a 1:400,000 and a fiddly GPS with a difficult-to-see screen. I arrived at the Havnomadens Kajakksenter just before midnight. It was run by Bent and Inge Skauen who gave me a very warm welcome, cooked a meal for me and served me a beer in the pub, where there were a few other kayakers and some locals chatting. I was spoilt for company. A few beers and many laughs later I was still in my damp clothes. I went up to my extremely comfortable room, where I could see the sunset with the island of Dønna silhouetted against a crimson sky. I had already planned to spend two days here repairing my kayak, writing and

Day 190. The glorious sunset from the balcony of the Havnomadens Kajakksenter in Husvær with Dønna silhouetted against the crimson sky

enjoying the company of other kayakers, and was delighted the Havnomadens Kajakksenter was so pleasant. I had a memorable shower and then fell asleep in new Egyptian cotton linen, on a soft bed, in what felt like home.

Day 191. The Havnomadens Kajakksenter is a great paddling centre and hostel in the spiritual heart of the gorgeous Helgelandskysten

After the best sleep I had had for a long time, I got up to explore the rest of the kayak centre which was to be my sanctuary for the next couple of days. Upstairs all seven bedrooms led off the large communal area, which comprised one huge room with a superbly equipped kitchen at one end and a sitting area at the other. Out of the living room was a large balcony with a stunning view, and from a corner of this balcony were the stairs leading down. Downstairs comprised of a very large kayak storage area with about 20 kayaks in it, a couple of kayak workshops, the restaurant, the pub and a huge decked area over the shallow sea. From a corner of this decked area was a ramp down to the floating jetty and a small sandy beach. The whole place had been nearly rebuilt from scratch on the foundations of an old fish wharf. It was extremely well laid out and Bent had decorated it with many artistic touches and effects.

It was supremely pragmatic, yet it had a quirky feel to it, and the atmosphere was friendly and laid back. In the workshops, Bent made wooden kayaks from strips of wood which were sanded down to a polished finish, and traditional Greenland paddles, which he used and sold. Bent said I could use the spacious kayak store to do the repairs to my kayak, and this dry, tidy and spacious room was perfect for it. I rinsed my kayak and then put it in there to dry out for the next day.

I then went for a wander down the lane to the village where there was a shop. The village seemed to have a slightly bohemian feel to it, and reminded me very much of the relaxed artistic atmosphere which I had found on Rødøya a few days earlier. There were only 55 people who lived permanently on this small island of Husvær. The island was also linked by a small bridge and a series of small causeways to the adjacent island of Brasøya, which was similar in size and population. This new bridge and causeways linked the two islands, so they were almost a single entity now. To get to the mainland, one still had to take the ferry from Brasøya. The shop was small, but stocked everything from nails to milk. Like most rural shops, this one doubled up as a meeting place, with a small café selling cakes and soft drinks. There was a very limited choice of food for me for the next four days until I reached Rørvik, and what I bought was not going to be a gourmet experience, even by my standards.

When I returned after my short wander round the island, Bent Skauen was holding a rolling class with Sigmund, another instructor, and some guests and locals. Everybody was using the Greenland paddles. Bent looked like he knew 20 or 30 different rolling techniques and was practising them all with a relaxed and automatic fluency. I declined to join them, as I had to catch up with my writing, which was a chore on such a fine day and in such a lovely place. That evening the Kajakksenter prepared a wonderful meal of fresh cod, straight off a passing boat. I ate with the three other kayaking guests as the pub slowly filled up with locals from Husvær and Brasøya islands for Friday night. When the meal was over, the cook and Sigmund produced guitars and soon a few people were joining in. By the time a few beers had lubricated the atmosphere,

Day 192. During the evening, many of the locals gather at the kayak centre's pub for the friendly banter and music

around 30 people were singing along to well-known folk songs and other favourites, and the evening became very lively, if not rowdy. Between the songs there was a lot of chat. I spent most of the evening chatting to two of the other kayaking guests, Pål and Guro, a bright, witty, handsome couple from Oslo. Although relatively new to kayaking, they were confident enough to come up here and explore this part of the Helgelandskysten on their own.

I spent the next day repairing some niggling problems with my kayak. Firstly, I had to clean out the holds, as some sand had accumulated in them and was abrading the drybags. Then I had to improve the rudder pedals and try and repair the back toggle, which I had ripped off a week ago. As I looked for tools in the workshop, I met a local, called William, who was building a kayak from strips of wood according to drawings. I got chatting to him and he seemed to be the island handyman who could turn his hand to most practical things. He quickly offered to help me. I needed an extra pair of hands to do some of the jobs as it was just too difficult to hold a bolt inside the kayak and operate a screwdriver on the other side. Plus, with his practical skills he was able to find solutions which I thought were impossible. Firstly we tackled the back toggle which was screwed into the deck with a bolt, but the Tiderace factory had forgotten to fit a washer and nut to secure it on the inside. We found a suitable bolt, washer and nut and assembled them. This was no easy job, as the washer and nut had to be attached to the protruding end of the bolt inside the back hold, nearly a metre beyond arm's reach. William glued the washer and nut on to a thin baton and then extended it down the stern hatch while I screwed until I eventually got a bite of the nut. Now we taped a spanner to the same baton so the nut would rise up the thread and tighten the toggle bolt.

Next were the rudder pedals. I dismantled the good job Bjørn had done in Tromsø. The foam he had used to build up the pedals had perished and needed to be replaced. William found some very firm foam, used to buffer the edges of jetties on fish farms, and we cut it to shape. Then we attached it to the pedals with cable ties using the same holes Bjørn had drilled. I now had 20 millimetres of hard foam on the surface of the rudder control pedals. The whole system worked wonderfully now as I could slacken the tension in the wires. These wires could also bring the pedals' control surfaces forward, but put so much friction in the system it would not operate. Finally William and Bent helped me glue some sleeping mat on the footwell floor to help protect my heels from the hard surface. My heels had been giving me a bit of trouble recently and were painful, despite the fact they were cushioned by the neoprene of my boots which was wearing out fast. With all this done I rinsed off my drysuit which I had not used for a week, but would not dry, as it was encrusted in salt and attracted any dampness. Bent also showed me some hidden gems to visit on my way south to Vega tomorrow. He recommended a camp spot on the south west of this famous island where he and Inge had stayed on their kayaking honeymoon. He very kindly photocopied some charts to help me navigate through the maze of islands around here to the hidden gems he suggested. Bent and William's help had been invaluable, as I just could not have done these jobs on my own on a beach somewhere.

After supper, which I cooked in the kitchen upstairs, I went downstairs where more locals and some guests were gathering again for a warm calm summer's night on the decking and in the pub. I joined Pål and Guro again who were elated by the day's exploring they had had in their kayaks. It was another wonderful evening with great 'craic' as the Irish would say. Havnomadens Kajakksenter was perhaps the closest thing you got to a proper community pub in Norway, and it had all the banter of a village pub in Scotland or Ireland. Even after two days I was content with the familiarity and friendliness of the place and felt at home on the small island having got acquainted with a few of the locals. I would be sorry to leave, but I am quite sure I will be back at a later date to explore more of Helgelandskysten, as so far it had completely enchanted me.

Day 193. The shop and harbour at Husvær were just half a kilometre south of the kayak centre and just north of the bridge to Brasøya

I was up early to carry the boat down to the floating jetty. I had it packed and was ready to go as everybody else started to appear. I said my goodbyes to Bent and Inge Skauen who were excellent hosts, the other two couples working here and Pål and Guro, then levered my boat into the water and set off with a wave. It was a beautiful morning as I went down the channel past the shop in Husvær in the centre of the hamlet and past the adjacent harbour where a couple of wooden fishing boats were moored. I then passed under the bridge connecting Husvær to Brasøya and left the comforting cluster of islands which had been my home for the last two days. My first destination was Skålvær, an island cluster just 5 kilometres to the south, across a basin with a sparse scattering of islets and holms breaking the surface. Bent had recommended I pass through the Skålvær archipelago as it had a fine Lutheran church on it which would have served a few of the scattered island communities around here. I paddled down the west side of Skålvær, and although I saw the grand steeple of the church, I could not get a good view. Keeping close to the main island I followed a network of sandy channels, some just deep enough to kayak over. The white sand was turquoise and bottle green in the sun. I stopped on Måsøya for a stretch and then headed south west into a wonderful archipelago of flat grassy islands called Buøyan.

Day 193. The 100 or so islets and islands which made up the Buøyan cluster were separated by sandy shallows and grazed by hardy sheep

Buøyan is a collection of some 100 islands separated by shallow sandy channels, many of which it would have been possible to wade, and some at low tide would have been dry. There were a lot of curlew nesting around them and they flew around with their distinctive curved beaks making a wide vocal range of calls. There was also a herd of very rustic sheep on the islands. They were not the refined sheep of Sandvær, but their more archaic, almost feral cousins. These type of sheep can be left out all year and need very little looking after. They lamb themselves and hunker down beside outcrops in the winter storms. If the grass is poor, or covered under frozen snow they can even subsist off seaweed for short periods. Once a year the farmer will come and dispense medication, tag their ears and take a few back to the mainland. From the Buøyan islands I paddled past yet another island called Hestøya (Horse Island). In bygone times, horses must have been put out to graze here, when the fishermen and homesteaders who lived in these outposts did not need them to work or till their small fields. After a channel filled with eider duck and their chicks, I reached Skogsholmen island, which was another of Bent's recommendations. I moored up at the jetty at Skogsholmen, on the south-east of the island, amongst a few of the somewhat flashy, private cabin cruisers which had recently arrived on a Sunday cruise, and still smelt of exhaust.

Skogsholmen is a fertile and leafy island which has a well-known guest house and restaurant on it. This guest house was in the restored boarding school which was originally built in 1940. It was built to accommodate and teach the children of the fishermen and homesteaders who lived in the Vesterøyene, which is the local term for the thousands of small islands scattered around here. Apparently children as young as eight used to row through the islands and across the sheltered basins weekly to go to school. With the downturn in the small scale fishing industry in the 1960s, and a migration away from these islands, the school was closed in 1972. The door was locked and it was abandoned to the elements for some 30 years. It was then restored with some 8000 man hours of work to put right three decades of neglect, and was turned into a museum and guest

Day 193. The old school house on the fertile island of Skogsholmen had been restored to a museum and guest house

house. I walked the half kilometre up the track to the school, passing some of the eight old homesteads which still exist on the island. The island was extremely dry and there was a water shortage. You could see areas where the grass was browning due to the lack of water. The woods here were extremely lush and green with an abundance of wild flowers despite the dryness. It almost felt like a Greek island in this temperature.

There were a few guests at this lovingly restored guest house. Two were nice, older ladies, who looked like the type who might have come here for a week's watercolour painting and quiet reading. They seemed to fit and belong to the atmosphere of this peaceful island. Not so, some of the other guests, who seemed to be day visitors off their cabin cruisers. They were a tasteless noisy bunch, who had over indulged their appetites on the spoils of oil, but had not developed the wisdom to temper this excess. In contrast to the watercolour ladies, this rabble of 40-year-olds sat on the balcony drinking beer and smoking roll-ups. They were as unappealing as the British on Costa del Chav, complete with barbed wire tattoos around their bingo wings. If the walk had been more than half a kilometre from their cruisers at the jetty, I doubt they would have bothered coming here. I hoped they did not visit frequently, as their basic gratification did not sit well against the rural charm of the island, and this lovingly restored historic school house.

Day 193. On the north-west of Vega was the small hamlet of Valla, where I spotted this typical Nordlandsbåt in the sheltered inlet

I returned to my kayak after a meal and then continued south. It was now mid afternoon, and as the crow flies I had only done about 10 kilometres so far today. I had really enjoyed the entire morning and early afternoon exploring, but felt I now needed to push through a sparser scattering of islands to get to the north-west of Vega. Vega Island is a UNESCO World Heritage Site. It was the site of one of the earliest Stone Age settlements in Scandinavia, and has virtually been populated for the last 11,000 years since the ice sheets started to withdraw from the area. In the last 1500 years the island inhabitants have developed a subsistence based on fishing, hunting, some agriculture and not least the collection of eggs and down from eider duck. Eider duck nest around these islands in their thousands. The islanders encourage them by building duck houses, which the duck like to nest in, away from predators like seagulls. In return the islanders take some eggs in spring and collect all the down from a nest at the end of the summer which is about 15 grams. It takes about 80 nests to make a good duvet with at least a kilo of pure duck down.

I paddled to the picturesque village of Valla and hoped to see some of Vega's culture, but it was a small village at the end of the road. In the harbour was a typical Nordlandsbåt which I think was a 'hundromsfæringen' as it was around 18 feet and had fittings for two pairs of oars. I then paddled down the west side of Vega between it and the Island of Sola. There was a strong wind against me of about force 5 and my progress was very slow. The west side of Vega was rocky, mountainous and barren with the shoreline largely being boulder beaches. It reminded me of Finnmark, and while it was beautiful in its own right, I wanted something softer. I felt a bit disappointed and was anxious I had missed the cultural landscape of Vega, which I assumed was on the more sheltered north and east sides. The beach on the south-west corner which Bent had recommended did not inspire me, and I paddled on without stopping

Day 193. The west side of Vega was bare, rugged and devoid of any sign of human life and reminded me very much of Finnmark

Day 194. The beach at Juvika bay was very beautiful and the sandy grass I was camped on was covered in purple orchids

until I was now paddling east along the south coast. I saw more otters here than anywhere else on the entire trip and passed four in as many kilometres. The coast remained wild and barren past the first bay at Ervika, but then as I entered Juvika bay it softened dramatically. I landed on the white beach, and found a nice place to camp on the edge of it, in a sandy meadow. It was nearly midnight when I eventually pitched my tent and for the first time in months I had to dig out and use my long redundant head torch, as it was getting dark.

I was up early to a warm, still, bright morning. It was just now that I really appreciated just how beautiful the beach I had landed on last night was. There were purple orchids growing all round the tent on the sandy soil. Above the beach was a small meadow of cut grass and a forest of small pine trees and juniper bushes surrounding it. I went for a short walk across this meadow and through the tinder dry and dusty woods, to a small peninsula to look at the sea beyond. It was absolutely mirror calm with everything reflected perfectly without the slightest distortion. My plan today was to paddle over to Torghatten where I had been told about a good campsite by Tom Amundsen who had passed this way in his kayak a few weeks earlier. He said it was to the south of the unique mountain and one could look up through the hole from the tent. It was only about 30 kilometres and I hoped to arrive early. The weather was so warm today, I decided to paddle with just my lifejacket, sunhat, shorts and spraydeck on.

After I launched on the sandy beach at low tide I paddled out past a couple of skerries and then across the silvery sea where I cleaved a small wake which split in a huge 'V' behind me. It was the type of day where I could spot puffins from a kilometre away. I also saw a few individual porpoises breaking the surface with their small fins in gentle rolling motions. I seldom saw them in groups of more than two or three. After an hour I reached a small cluster of 10 low ice-scoured flat islands called Dypingan.

Day 194. As I paddled over Vegafjord to the Torget peninsula it was so still I could spot puffins from over a kilometre away

There were a lot of tysties, and I was curious to see if they were breeding here, so went ashore. The islands were almost yellow with many clumps of the succulent sedum flowers. There were some grasses, dried brown in this arid spell, and the taller nettles and angelica, which flourished in the wide crevices where some dampness was retained. The whole place was covered in droppings from geese who must have feasted on the grass before migrating further north. I did not see any tystie nests but there were many seagull chicks on the island. Their parents watched from a good distance as I wandered about. These seagull chicks, although only a week or two old, were already quite streetwise and either stayed still, hoping their camouflage would work and then when I got too close and they realized they were spotted they dashed for the taller vegetation of nettle and angelica to hide in.

Day 194. Off the end of the Torget peninsula was a sheltered basin with some old fishermen's houses and sheds around it

Day 194. Looking from my campsite past the 160-year-old farm to the unique Torghatten, which had a hole right through the middle of it

After exploring these islands I carried on across the open 10-kilometre wide Vegafjord to the archipelago of Burøya near the mainland. The weather remained perfect and I had to put my old cagoule on to stop getting sunburnt. I weaved through the Burøya, crossed another basin and reached Torget, a convoluted peninsula on the far side of which was Torghatten. This was the mountain with the hole through it and my destination for the day. As I went round Torget the adjacent islands and skerries enclosed a lovely shallow basin. The largest of these islands, Helløya, was almost attached to Torget by a narrow sandy causeway which was so shallow, tractors could cross to work the small fields on its grassy top. There was just enough water for me to get over in the kayak at this low tide. Once through these narrows, Torghatten appeared, but I could not see the hole yet. To get to the south side of the mountain I had to weave through islets and skerries. I got stuck a few times on the seaweed and had to wait a few minutes for the tide to gain a few centimetres to allow me through. I found the place Tom had recommended, but it was far from the water with the tide as it was. Instead, I camped near the entrance to the inlet, in tall grass and in full view of the hole in the mountain.

Just up the inlet from my campsite was a lovely old farm. I met someone staying there and he said it was 160 years old. It was previously owned by his great grandparents. They had brought seven children up here. These seven children jointly had 26 grandchildren, of whom he was one. These 26 now collectively owned and maintained the farm. They each had allocated weeks to stay here and once a year they all gathered to tackle some larger projects, like re-roofing the barn, and enjoy their cultural heritage. He said there was an easy path up to the hole and pointed the way. I set off through the summer woods, dusty with pollen and carpeted with ripening blueberries. There were many wild roses beside the path and all were in flower. Most were pink but there were also some white flowered bushes.

The mountain, Torghatten, was 258 metres high, but half way up it there was a hole which went right through. I did not appreciate just how big this hole was until I approached it. It was about 20 metres across and at least 40 high. It went right through the mountain from one side to the other for about 300 metres. This hole must have been formed by stormy seas as a sea cave. Eventually, the waves must have punched a hole right through the then island by eroding a weaker vein of rock. In the midst of the ice age some parts of Scandinavia were covered in kilometre thick ice, much like Greenland is today. This depressed the whole landmass like a cork bathmat floating in a bath of syrup with a brick on it. When the ice was removed, the land slowly rose up again as much as 800 metres in some places, like the Gulf of Bothnia, in the same way the bathmat would rise if the brick were removed. So, while

Day 194. Looking south from the hole through Torghatten to the 160-year-old farm, my campsite and the islands, skerries and beaches

this hole was formed at sea level by the action of waves, it has since risen well over 100 metres in the last 10,000 years. There was naturally a great view from the south side of the hole down to the farm, the inlet where I was camped, and the typical Helgelandskysten seascape of islands, holms, skerries and the ever present glorious white sandy beaches. I walked through the hole to the north side where there was another spectacular view over yet more islands, stretching the 15 kilometres to the small mainland town of Brønnøysund. This was a jaw droppingly beautiful coastline.

Day 195. The bay on the north side of Lyngvær, where the water was 28 degrees, had a view north to Torghatten 15km away

I woke early as the sun warmed the tent and lit up Torghatten. It did not take long before I was packed and ready. I had to hurry a bit as the water was withdrawing, even from the entrance to the inlet, and I did not want to carry everything an extra few hundred metres. I made my way through a maze of skerries to the edge of the more open fjord called Torgfjord, in perfect conditions again. I then crossed this 3-kilometre wide fjord quickly, as it was a shipping lane, and I did not want any encounters, although I could not see any ships or ferries. Once over the fjord I paddled south to a cluster of islands covered in heather and small birch trees called Lyngvær. I spotted a sandy bay as I arrived and paddled in over the clear bottom chasing my shadow. There was a great view here northwards to Torghatten and even the Seven Sisters mountains on the mainland at Husvær's latitude. I got out to stretch and when I stepped into the shallow water it was warm. I measured the temperature and it was 28 degrees! On the smooth bare rock across the small bay a few eider duck mothers were trying to herd a throng of small ducklings over a rise and into another bay and out of harm's way. I had an early lunch here of biscuits and tinned pork, as I lay on the hot rocks casting an occasional eye over the calm sea and endless islets without a care in the world. I could even see hot air shimmering, as it was heated by the rock.

When I left I paddled through the rest of Lyngvær's islands and was surprised to see this place once had a smaller fishing concern. Two ruined wharfs, bleached pale by the weather and now windowless, stood on stilts on the foreshore. They were probably abandoned in the 1970s and it would only be a matter of time now before a storm flattened them. Near them were a couple of ruined houses and a row of five low sheds which were purpose-built for eider duck to nest in, so their eggs and down could be harvested. Apart from these derelict buildings, this was a pretty group of islands with some sandy beaches and many convoluted channels between them. It was a haven for duck and there were hundreds of them here. Often the duck would dive as I approached, especially in a narrow channel where it was difficult to escape, as the ducklings could not fly. The mothers could hold their breath for well over a minute before they came up, but the ducklings could only manage 10 or 15 seconds. What often happened is the whole raft would dive as I approached. Then when I was over the spot they had disappeared, all the ducklings would start to pop up on to the surface around me, like fluffy brown tennis balls released from the depths.

Continuing south I went round the outside of the craggy and forested Kvaløya and the smaller Gimlinga and then started across the mouth of Bindalsfjord to the peninsula on the south side. As I crossed the fjord the weather suddenly changed from the warm still day, as the wind picked up, a squall of drizzle passed through and a large bank of fog started to develop to the south west, which was where I was heading. The hills on the south side of Bindalsfjord were glistening silver as the newly wet slabs reflected the sun. With a nervous eye on the bank of fog I watched it charge north, enveloping all before it, until even the large island of Leka was subsumed. I was not too happy about this, as there was a shipping channel nearby, and I would not be able to avoid an eventual ship until the last minute. I needed to stop anyway, so I pulled into a bay tucked away behind a row of skerries near the hamlet at Nord Gutvik. There was a wonderful beach here, fringed with grazed grass, ideal for camping, but it was just mid afternoon and too early to stop. My map said there was a campsite on

Day 195. Paddling south across the glassy sea from Lyngvær to the larger wooded island of Kvaløya to the left of the bow

Day 195. After crossing Bindalsfjord the weather changed and a squall passed soaking the rock slabs above Nord Gutvik bay

Leka island, just 10 kilometres away, so I unwrapped my phone and tracked them down. They said they had a cabin available. It was both cheap and near the sea, only 200 metres apparently, so I said I was on my way.

By now the fog had lifted but there was a force 4 against me. The crossing of the 5 kilometre Lekafjord was quite choppy and I had to paddle vigorously into the waves for a good hour to reach the relative shelter of a fish farm on the Leka side. It took another hard hour to paddle down the east coast of this island to the breakwater where the campsite was located. En route I passed the simple ferry terminal where the small ferry which connected the island of Leka to the rest of the world docked every hour. The 200 metres from the water turned out to be a kilometre walk up a hill, which irritated me. Taking the bare minimum I needed, so a single trip would suffice, I started up the track to the reception. It was located in a nice hamlet, with cows grazing in all the meadows in the surrounding fields. The lady at the campsite was something of an amateur geologist, and she soon dispersed my irritation with the walk, by explaining a lot about the geology of the island.

Geologically, it seems Leka is a very interesting place. Leka is different to the adjacent grey rock on the mainland, which is largely the 1800 million year old gneiss of the basement. The rocks on Leka are much younger and are sitting on top of this gneiss basement. This is in much the same way the Caledonian thrust sheets or nappes are sitting on top of this same basement, often in layers, further inland to the east. The Caledonian nappes are largely comprised of rocks which were formed on top of the oceanic crust and the arc of Aleutian-like volcanic islands, before they were squeezed and shoved on to the continental basement in the tectonic collision; Leka is different. Leka is composed of rocks which were the oceanic crust itself, and even part of the deep mantle below it. This is a very rare occurrence and only seen in a handful of other sites around the world like Oman, Cyprus and California. An oceanic crust which is thrust on to the continental basement like this is called an ophiolite. In the case of Leka a fragment of oceanic crust was thrust on top of the continental crust and then thrust sideways, so the very upper surface of the oceanic crust, the pillow lava, is easternmost followed by the basalt. In the middle of the island there is gabbro, which is in the lower part of the oceanic crust. What is remarkable in the case of Leka, is the very lowest part of the oceanic crust is here also, towards the west of the island, in the form of dunite rock. And then even more remarkably we find some of the upper mantle, which is what the oceanic crust sits on, along the western edge of Leka, in the form of hazburgite. Erosion has now exposed this sequence and it is visible on the surface to a trained eye. The dunite and hazburgite rocks are very dark normally, except where they are exposed to weathering. Here, the iron-rich rock rusts and hence the central and west side of Leka are reddish. The eastern part of Leka is gabbro, basalt, and on the very eastern edge, pillow lavas which are also dark, but lack the concentration of iron to rust significantly. This ophiolite was thrust on to the basement in the Caledonian orogeny 420 million years ago when Baltica and Greenland collided.

The lady at the campsite showed me to a nice cabin, built of the reddish dunite stone, with a grass roof. The campsite owners had constructed a whole row of them from the stone, which they said was iconic of the island. Inside, it was cosy and solid, but very unusual, quirky and a bit hobbit-like. The lady then lent me a barely functioning bicycle which just managed the 2-kilometre round trip to the shop. On my cycle I noticed how well organized and relatively affluent the island was. There were lots of notices about communal events and activities, and lots of information on the natural history of the island. I found one notice that said Leka, like Vega, had been populated for the last 10,000 years, since the Stone Age, as cave paintings on the island testify. The 500 inhabitants of Leka seemed justifiably proud of their unique and homely island. That evening I sat at the table in the solid cabin and cooked on the small electric stove, which is always part of their inventory, and caught up with most of my writing.

Day 196. There were rafts of eider duck mothers with collections of ducklings around every corner for this entire section

The rest of the writing I left until the following morning. By the time I had carried everything a kilometre back down to the jetty again, it was already after midday. There were many Germans at this campsite; they were part of the important sports fishing tourism business which I saw more and more of as the summer progressed. Groups of Germans and other Europeans come here and rent small boats of about 20 feet with an outboard engine. Then three or four people head out to the fjords and fishing grounds with at least two rods per person to fish. The fishermen are usually very dedicated and spend most of their holidays on the boats, hoping for the big one. The seas round Leka often provide some big ones, especially halibut, which makes it a popular destination. A month before my visit, a Dutchman caught a 62 kilo halibut, and a fortnight after a German caught a 120 kilo halibut, both on fishing rods. By the jetty at Leka Camping there were photos of many other huge cod, ling, pollack and wolf-fish.

After I left the jetty I paddled between Leka and the smaller island of Madsøya to the east of it. This sheltered area harboured three large salmon farms in different basins, which seemed to be a very high density to me. I paddled quite close to each of them and the whole operation seemed to be quite automatic. There was a large barge beside each farm with large metal hoppers full of small food pellets. Long black round tubes radiated from the barge, with one going to each of the eight to twelve circular pens in which the salmon were contained. The generators and machinery on the barge would blow pellets down one of the tubes for a minute to distribute food to the salmon in that pen. Then it would blow down another tube, until all the pens had received a scattering of pellets, then it would start at the first pen again. Every week or so, a boat would go up the coast filling the food hoppers with new food pellets and refilling the diesel tanks for the generators. The farms and the barges were not discreet, but did not intrude into the fjordscape as much as they could have done. When the salmon in a pen were ready to be harvested, a different ship would come along, put a wide hose into the pen and simply suck the entire contents of the pen into a holding tank on the ship where they were transported live to the processing plants. While salmon farming is environmentally harmful, and the ethics of it controversial, it is a huge industry, especially in Norway. This industry is being forced to get its house in order by the government and pressure groups.

After Madsøya I sneaked through various islands and some more open stretches to the archipelago at Risvær. This was quite a fascinating cluster of islands, consisting of perhaps 40 smaller islands. Two of the larger islands in the centre had a substantial house built of timber logs and clad in planks. These two islands were also connected by a short stone causeway which only flooded at high tide. I was intrigued by this sight, so went ashore, landing by the sand near the causeway. I went up to the first house which was in ruins, with the door off. Inside, it was completely covered in sheep dung and wool. It was the same with the other house, but you could see they were once rather substantial houses in their day. There was a small mixed wood behind the lower house and I could see the wild, almost feral, sheep, many with their redundant fleeces trailing behind them, peering through the trees at me. I found out later that Risvær had once been an important trading post for at least a century, up to the middle of the last century. It was apparently the most important trading post on this part of the

Day 196. An old mooring post and one of the two once grand houses at the now derelict trading post at Risvær

Day 196. Looking from Risvær to the mainland which is where the fortunes of this once flourishing island group have moved

coast. Ships and boats going up and down with wares along the Norwegian coast would stop here to pick up produce and deliver goods. There was only some of the mooring stakes, the massive stone quays and these two derelict houses left from once prosperous times.

From Risvær I continued to the Island of Gjerdinga. This had a small hamlet connected by ferry to the mainland. It had avoided the fate of Risvær, as it had more sustainable farms. It had now embraced tourism, and many of the old houses were restored as leisure houses, rented out to Norwegian and European tourists. It seemed to sustain the place and the car ferry which passed me was full, with eight cars, which was not bad for an island with perhaps a kilometre of gravel road and 30 houses or cabins. From Gjerdinga I crossed the narrow shipping channel to the mainland and followed it for some 10 kilometres along the shoreline. A few freighters passed me, going slowly as the signs requested, and I barely noticed their wash. The shore and the islands in this sound seemed very lush and the farms were vibrant green with fertility. In a couple of hours I reached the area where the sound opened up into a basin with a scattering of small forested islands. To the west of this basin was the town of Rørvik, which I could not see due to the islands. To the east was the industrial spread of Ottersøya which was a disappointing wasteland of concrete and industrial buildings. There was a bridge connecting the two and as I had previously decided that it was my goal for the day, I did not stop here, but carried on for a kilometre to Sande.

Day 196. The farms along the south shore of the 10km channel from Gjerdinga island to Rørvik enjoyed lush fertile fields and a great view

I had hoped somewhere called Sande would have a beach and I was right. Just south of the industrial wasteland at Ottersøya and the modern bridge I returned to the tranquillity and beauty of rural Norway again. When I landed on the beach I was surprised to see someone already there with a kayak, behind a grassy ridge. Naturally he came over when I landed and we got chatting. He was retired and he and his wife had restored a cabin nearby, he said, pointing to a new building a few hundred metres way. He was extremely helpful and helped me carry my loaded kayak up to a sheltered grassy area where I could camp. He then invited me over for drinks after I was organized. I had a quick supper and then sauntered over the field of cut grass to his house on this warm summer's evening. He and his wife welcomed me warmly. A lot of drinks were offered, but I declined the whisky as I still harboured optimistic thoughts of writing later. So I plumped for coffee. While this was brewing, I was given a towel and told to use as much hot water as I wanted in the lovely bathroom upstairs. We chatted for a good two hours afterwards. It is always a pleasure to chat with intelligent, well-informed, thoughtful Norwegians, and I learnt a lot that evening about some of the history and social changes of the area. Luckily, most Norwegians are like this, and the shallow rabble I met with their cabin cruisers on Skogsholmen a few days earlier were the exception. I returned to my tent around midnight with a tinge of sadness that I had reached Rørvik. It was the southern end of the astoundingly beautiful Helgelandskysten with its small flat island clusters, abundant white beaches occasionally interspersed with a relaxed, almost bohemian culture. Helgelandskysten, like Vestfjorden before it, had been a paradise.

SECTION 28. Helgelandskysten
9 days. 296 kilometres. 66 hours. 0m ascent. 0m descent.

THE KAYAK: SECTION 29. FOLDA AND FROHAVET

THE KAYAK: SECTION 29. FOLDA AND FROHAVET

I woke early to drizzle on an unexpectedly calm morning. These were good conditions to cross Folda, an open 10-kilometre stretch of water which was exposed to the ocean and had something of a reputation. I set off mid morning and immediately passed a beautiful large Lutheran church at Lundring. It must have been of some importance in the area, and I suspected it was the parish church of Nærøy kommune. A few kilometres further south I paddled into Arnøya archipelago. I thought I was finished with idyllic islands, now I had left the Helgelandskysten, but these were as sandy and grassy to rival anything that paradise had. There were numerous channels between them, some very shallow in the low tide, but luckily I did not encounter any waterless stretches. I was nearly two hours exploring and weaving through this enchanting area. I stopped on one sandy island when I saw it hosted a tern colony. I went ashore to have a look at the chicks, which I felt sure must be growing by now. I could not believe that they still had not hatched. I was beginning to suspect that some fertility disaster had affected the terns up here and they were guarding useless eggs. Leaving the terns, I crossed Arnøyfjord and approached another cluster of islands, which sheltered the harbour of Abelvær. As I entered the islands I came across a large raft of eider duck. There were about 5 mothers and at least 20 ducklings. They had grown considerably in the last weeks and were now about half the size of the adults. The chaotic frenzy the smaller ducklings had, just 10 days ago, was now replaced with a cool, adolescent confidence. Through the islands I reached Abelvær which seemed much bigger than it should have been. There were a couple of huge semi-derelict fish processing plants or warehouses from days when the village was thriving. Now the main industry seemed to be a medium-sized boat yard, with a 100-ton fish farm barge being overhauled.

Day 197. After leaving Sande I passed Lundring church which was the parish church for the Nærøy kommune

Day 197. The Arnøya archipelago was a collection of about five sandy islands and a hundred islets between Rørvik and Abelvær

From Abelvær I went straight into Folda. On this calm and overcast day it would not present any problems, so I set a bearing for the northern tip of Otterøy, some 10 kilometres away, across the grey fjord. The grey, almost featureless shore on the far side approached very slowly, and initially I hardly seemed to make any progress towards it. Gradually, the equally grey and unexciting island of Jøa started to pass by on my east side. I could see how it was exposed to the west weather and how the coastal rocks had been washed bare of any vegetation for quite a height. I reached Otterøy with the drizzle becoming more consistent and decided to carry on across Namsenfjord and into a sheltered archipelago. I saw many porpoises, but again they all seemed to be solitary rather than in a large group.

Day 197. Crossing Folda with the distant grey Otterøy some 10 kilometres away across the featureless fjord

Day 197. Paddling towards the light beacon on Feøya with the steep heavily folded rocks of Havsteinen above the bow

This cluster of islands, off the western side to the entrance of Namsenfjord, were a welcome relief from the drab Folda landscape earlier in the day. Firstly, I passed some massive battlements which were 60-year-old German gun emplacements from the Second World War. The town of Namsos, further up the fjord, was strategically important to the German war effort, and they spared no effort to defend this port. They considered it a realistic alternative to Narvik from which to ship iron ore from the Swedish mines at Kiruna to industrial Hamburg and Bremerhaven in Germany. There are the wrecks of many ships lying at the bottom of Namsenfjord, from the Allied campaign to keep the harbour and fjord, and stop it falling into German hands. Once past the battlements I was into a mass of islands and skerries again. I weaved my way between them as it was impossible to go in a straight line. I had an eye out for a campsite as I went past these rocky islands, but nothing grabbed my interest along the damp, grey, rocky shores. I paddled to the north of Feøya island and entered a deep basin beyond it, hemmed in by it and the steep neighbouring island of Havsteinen. The steep red rocks of Havsteinen had great geological features on display, with a very clear folded anticline. As I paddled past it, admiring the great curves of red and black bands, I noticed some of the hardy rustic sheep grazing on some of the very steep slopes with the same sure footedness of a chamois. I paddled past the north tip of Lauvøya and looked down its east side to see the white spire of a large Lutheran church and several farms gathered around it in a hamlet. The church must have once been the centre of this coastal parish.

I soon lost sight of it as I paddled round the north tip of the relatively flat and leafy island and started down the west side. Before long I reached a gentle seascape of flat islets and sandy shallows. In one of the bays was a tranquil meadow of grazed grass, above a small quiet sandy beach. It looked too good to pass, and it was already mid evening, so I paddled through the lazy seaweed choking the bay and rammed the kayak up the sandy beach. As I set up my tent on the grazed meadow, a few sheep appeared, and then about 30 materialized from between the juniper bushes around the meadow. This herd of 30 gathered about 50 metres away and watched me. They were larger, more cared for and quite dapper, compared to the rustic, semi-feral variety I usually saw on the islands. They were probably looked after in barns over the winter, on the farms on the other side of this fertile island. They stood looking at me for a good five minutes, and then suddenly one ran towards me, and then the whole herd charged at me, stopping some five metres away. I jumped up to put myself between them and my tent. They were racing to see if I might have a snack or salt lick for them, and soon dispersed back into the junipers and pines when they realized nothing was on offer. I withdrew into my tent, grateful it was not flattened in the stampede, and soon had the petrol stove roaring away. Before long it was quite cosy, and the continuing drizzle quietly pattering off the tent made it more so.

I was lazy in the morning, and although I woke early I did not set off until nearly midday. Disgraceful really, after an early night! My arms felt heavy, as they often do for the first hour, after I left the lovely Lauvøya and crossed over to Kvernøya and rounded its south-east tip to enter a sound with a scattering of islets. On the west side of this sound was yet another archipelago of small and large islands. On the first of the larger islands, Halmøya, was a very well-kept and large farm with a beautiful old white farmhouse sitting on a bright green field against the grey surroundings. Generations of hard work had gone into wrestling that field from

Day 197. My calm campsite on the west side of the green island of Lauvøya where my tent was nearly flattened by a stampede of sheep

Day 198. The large farm on the south shore of Halmøya was well sited in a large meadow which must have been won from the barren hillside

boulders and slabs to produce this well-manicured pasture. Beyond Halmøya I cruised into an area where it was difficult to navigate with the road map and GPS combination. There were some 20 larger islands surrounded by at least 100 smaller islets and skerries. I just aimed south west and enjoyed exploring. I never knew what was round the next corner. Sometimes it was a sandy channel with beaches on each side, sometimes it was a deep channel with darks waters. Occasionally my route was blocked with weed-covered shallows which had dried in this low tide, and I had to paddle on to the next channel. This was the type of paddling I liked most, rather than having the predictability of watching the distant headland getting imperceptibly closer.

There were many excitable oyster catchers on these islands. I spotted a couple of them with their single chick. These chicks were about half the size of the parents, and the considerable work the parents had put into rearing the chick, feigning injury and warding off predators had almost paid off. The chick was not so vulnerable now, and would be flying in a month, almost ready to fend for itself. After a leisurely couple of hours I eventually reached the west side of this maze, at Kvaløya and stopped for lunch on a small beach. Since Tromsø about a month ago I had been spoilt for beaches and had found I could pretty much stop where I wanted to. The grey overcast weather of the morning was quickly burning away under the hot sun, and the day was turning into a stunner. I lazed on the beach, feeling the heat as my black clothing absorbed the rays and quickly dried it, leaving powdery salt stains. This was exploratory kayaking at its best again! After lunch I crossed the more exposed, but narrow mouth of Jøssundfjord, which was completely still and unthreatening in today's weather, which almost felt too hot! After just half an hour I reached the other side, rounded a headland and paddled into a large bay, sheltered by a barricade of protective islands. The shoreline of this bay was quite convoluted, and within one of its deeper inlets lay the hamlet of Hasvåg, behind some breakwaters. The

Day 198. The beautiful homestead on the small sandy island of Sandøya in the centre of the sheltered Halmøya archipelago was idyllic

road map indicated it had a campsite but I could not see it as I paddled past. I had learnt not to rely on the facilities this map promised, and assumed it must have closed or never existed. I was not tempted in to see, as I was beginning to shy away from campsites, as the lure of a shower was more than often offset by the banal humdrum of 50 families in camper vans. Instead, I continued along the empty coast for another half hour to the hamlet of Småværet.

Småværet had about 15 houses, a few small jetties, a simple shop with a pub attached to it. I asked the lady who ran the shop and pub if I could camp nearby and write in the pub. "No problem", she said, and took me down to a sheltered, out-of-the-way, grassy patch and said I could put my tent up there. I put the tent up on the crisp ground and left it open, so it did not overheat,

Day 198. The pub and café at the tiny fishing hamlet of Småværet was a characterful place and a great watering hole

and went up to the pub to write. It was full of character but completely empty. It also served food so I ordered 'Bacalao', a Spanish dish from Galicia made from Norwegian fish. The main ingredient is 'Klippfisk', a salted cod which has been dried in the summer sun on rocks. Beside the jetties were five sedentary cabin cruisers which all belonged to a group of friends and their families. They were spending a week of their summer holiday going from sheltered bay to hamlet on their boats. Most of them spent the whole afternoon on deck sunbathing. It is quite remarkable that this same country in which I spent the winter skiing north can now serve up this Mediterranean weather everyone has enjoyed in the last month. I wrote for a few hours in the comfort of the pub, as the lady who ran the pub and shop came and went serving customers and chatting. Every half hour or so her husband would stealthily appear and scurry to the fridge, sneak out a can of beer before disappearing again. Once he was safe in a back room I would hear the tell-tale phhssst as he opened it. He was clearly a heavy drinker, who felt guilty, and had to disguise the fact. I felt sorry for his hardworking wife. As evening unfolded, the pub slowly filled up as the sunbathers came in to eat, and by the time I went back to my tent for an early night there were perhaps 15 people eating dinner.

Day 199. The lighthouse at Buholmråsa which stood sentry over the rocky coast was constructed of many cast iron plates bolted together

It was a beautiful still morning when I woke early. I was eager to make the most of it after the previous slower starts, so after a quick breakfast I was ready. The kayak had spent the night on the floating jetty, so I just had to lever it over the wooden lip and into the water. There was an increasingly strong north-east wind developing as I paddled out of the small harbour and into the ocean. This wind was a good force 3 and it seemed to be on the up. It blew me down the flattish coast to the classic Buholmråsa fyr, a classic Norwegian lighthouse which was constructed from hundreds of pre-formed curved iron plates which were cast in a foundry, transported here and then bolted together. It stood sentry over this rocky headland beside a couple of white keeper's cottages. I was blown past the lighthouse and veered south to go inside the two Raudøya islands. With the wind now increasing to a force 4 and still behind me, I made good time and the waves were still small as there was not the fetch. Suddenly a ship appeared from behind the next headland. I was surprised to see such a big vessel using these channels so near the coast, as the shipping lane was on the other side of the Raudøya islands. I assumed it would continue north from the headland out into the open ocean. But abruptly it changed course and started coming straight for me. Its engines emitting a low rumble above the sound of the wind as it pushed a cascading white wave ahead of the bow. I was bolt upright now deciding which way to paddle. I thought it would pass just to the south of me, so turned right angled to its path and paddled furiously north. It must also have veered slightly to the north, as I could not catch a glimpse of its side until it was a mere 500 metres away, when thankfully more and more of it started to appear. With a surge of adrenaline coursing through my veins I continued north and the throbbing tanker passed some 100 metres to the south of me. I could see men on the ship's bridge looking my way and one of them pointing at me. My heart was thumping as it surged past me, as I turned to meet the wake coming from its bow wave.

I soon reached the same headland where the ship appeared from and paddled into a basin with the town of Sandviksberget at the south end by some narrows. It was a relatively industrious place with a large ship unloading on a wharf beside a couple of concrete foundries. There was also a small shipyard here

Day 199. Being blown towards the slightly industrial Sandviksberget town having just passed the strait where I had to avoid a ship

repairing some trawlers and small coastal ships. I surged through the narrows by this busy village and spilled into another basin with a few islands ringing it. The wind was now a force 5 and the waves were getting larger and whiter. Generally, the waves were moving too fast for the hydrodynamics of the kayak to keep up with them, and I started to wallow down the back of one wave and surge forward on the face of the next. Occasionally, I managed to stay on the face of a couple of the larger waves and surf on them for a while. At one stage the GPS showed I managed 15 kilometres per hour down the front of one. Despite the choppy seas, there were a few German sports fishermen out in small boats with about 40 horse power outboards. I could tell they were German, because there were three or four people standing up per boat with multiple rods, each secured along the gunwales. I am sure that on a day like today the coastguard gets a few calls when the outboards won't start and people drift in the strong winds towards rocky islands or out to sea.

When I reached Børøya island there was another narrow passage between it and the mainland. The wind was really funnelling through here; it was a good force 6 but the waves were small again with spray being whipped off the many crests. I surged through these narrows and was swept into Brandsfjord. I was a bit wary of crossing this short fjord in case the wind increased to a force 8, but it was only 5 kilometres and there was an island half way across, if things started to get out of control. The kayak was extraordinarily stable, but in a large following sea, waves tended to wash over the stern and hit me in the back. As soon as I set across the fjord I was surprised to see about 10 large fishing boats, some over 40 feet, anchored at the relatively sheltered entrance to the fjord. There were rows of people fishing off each one and I could see they were Norwegians, as they were fishing with handlines in the characteristic up and down motion called pilking. I don't know why Brandsfjord was so popular. Perhaps it was a fishing competition.

Day 199. Paddling round the final headland before reaching the relative sanctuary of the sheltered Stokken sound

As I approached the headland on the west side of Brandsfjord my confidence returned. It was still a force 6 wind and tumbling waves hissed and roared up behind me, but I was closing in on the sanctuary of land again. I now had a bit of a dilemma as there were two prominent peninsulas or islands ahead. They were called islands, but the map did not show them as such, and the GPS was too difficult to read in these conditions. If I went round the outside of them it was likely to be very exciting, and if I went round the inside I might find an isthmus or causeway and have to struggle back against the wind to go outside anyway. I decided to go round the outside, and as things turned out, it was not as bad as I had anticipated. I had the mouth of one more fjord to cross after these islands, the 4-kilometre wide Skjørafjord, and then a final headland to bounce round. The wind had now started to diminish, but some of the waves were still large at nearly two metres. My feet were working hard to keep the rudder moving, so I would hold a straight line and not broach on the waves, many of which were breaking. With this last headland out of the way, I now left the more exposed waters and entered a sound between this headland and the island of Stokkøya. I had not paused all day and my stomach was twisting in hunger. At last I could take my hands off the paddle and reach into the rear hatch for some biscuits. As I ate, the wind continued to blow me along and the rudder kept the kayak in line with the wind, which was being channelled down the sound in the same direction I was going. I made nearly 2 kilometres while I rested and polished off a packet of biscuits. At the south end of this sound, called Stokken, the water opened out into a large basin, full of steep rocky islands. I turned west before I reached them to arrive at the town of Stokksund and the bridge over to Stokkøya island.

Stokksund was surprisingly industrial, with a few larger ships tied up unloading, and others in a yard for maintenance. Like Sandviksberget earlier in the day I was very surprised to see such industry along this otherwise empty and wild coast, with many leisure cabins hidden in various bays. I had done well today with around 50 kilometres under my belt, and after passing under the bridge the wind seemed to be against me. I was ready to throw in

Day 199. Paddling down Stokken sound to the narrows at the south end where there was a basin with steep islands and the small town

the towel as I clawed along, but there was nowhere to camp. I continued another kilometre, scanning the coast for somewhere to camp but did not see anything suitable. Suddenly I noticed the wind was back behind me again. It was a fine evening, and with the wind on my side again, I decided to paddle on. I passed a couple of very deep bays hemmed in by ice-scoured smooth grey rock ridges with a thin cover of vegetation. These bays in contrast were lush, green and fertile and had a string of neat farms and red barns on the flat land, typical of any rural hamlet in Norway outside Finnmark. It was too far to detour into the bays so I carried on in the glorious evening with the easy wind. I passed a few islands off the headlands between the deep bays which had a lot of geese on them. I kept an eye out for somewhere to camp all the time, but did not see anywhere really good for well over an hour. The spot I was looking for eventually appeared near the end of this convoluted coastline, just before it disappeared at the end of the peninsula. It was a beautiful sandy beach with a few cabins and a tidy farm around it. The beach was welcome, as not only was I getting tired and cramped, having been in the kayak for 12 hours, but I was also wet with water having previously seeped through the neoprene spraydeck and through the holes in my faithful old paddling cagoule. I charged the kayak on to the sand and went to look for a campsite. There was one just above the sand, in a field of cut grass with tall vegetation as protection. I put my tent up and changed out of my wet fleece clothing. I noticed an old table and chair beside one of the cabins and after supper went over to write there. While I wrote, I felt I was still at sea, lurching backwards and forwards all evening until midnight. By then the wind had almost vanished and there was a glorious sunset to end this splendid day.

Day 199. Paddling along the convoluted coast in the evening sun looking for a sandy cove to camp in, which I later found at Tårnes

I felt I deserved a lie-in after yesterday, and I did not get going until just before midday. It was an overcast day with the threat of rain imminent, but it was virtually still and calm. I made my way down the remaining 3 kilometres of the peninsula passing a couple of lovely beaches. Here, right at the tip of the peninsula among some arable fields, was a very quaint white wooden chapel with the characterful Lutheran dome sitting in a small graveyard. Surrounded by white beaches on all sides, it seemed a tranquil place for the departed to rest. Just beyond the end of the peninsula, across a shallow kilometre-wide strait, was the flat green agricultural island of Lauvøya. It was not a large island, but it looked prosperous, with a lot of arable land and numerous large farmhouses. The warm south-easterly breeze coming off the land carried the smell of fresh silage. Much of Scandinavia had been basking in the sun for weeks now and the landmass was heating the air passing over it. To the south was a dark range of mountains rising above the coastal fringe. These mountains separated this coast from the parallel Stjørnfjord on the other side of them. They were rugged and knobbly.

Day 200. Heading past the chapel at Tårnes towards the low fertile island of Lauvøya ahead, with a warm breeze blowing off the land

As I paddled over to Lysøysund I came across a group of terns feeding. They were diving into the water head first with almost the same commitment as a gannet. The breeze was ruffling the surface of the water and it was overcast, and I could not understand how the terns could still see small five-centimetre fish through the disturbed surface and some half a metre of water. However, I frequently saw them re-emerge with the sprat they aimed for. There were also a number of Arctic skuas around. These larger dark birds do not hunt themselves but obtain their food by attacking and harassing other birds who have just caught food and then bully them until they drop it or disgorge it. Their Latin name of *Stercorarius parasiticus* shows their thieving nature. It is an unpleasant bird, whose only redeeming feature is that they are superb fliers and accomplished acrobats, outwitting the tern or kittiwake they are pursuing. Arctic skua are not as menacing as their larger cousins, the great skua, *Stercorarius skua*, which is a fearless predator and will bully even gannets to surrender their catch. I have heard people say the great skua will just grab a gannet's wing in its beak causing the pair to spiral down out of control. The great skua will only release its grip if the gannet disgorges its catch or just before impact with the ground or sea. Great skuas will also kill numerous puffins and other birds, often just plucking out the tastiest morsel, like the liver, and wasting the rest. Surprisingly, I have seen very few great skua on this trip so far and they don't seem to be established in Norway. A fact the numerous puffins are no doubt grateful for.

Just before I reached Lysøysund I passed a Marine Harvest fish farm. It was by far the biggest operation I had seen yet with about 20 heavily-stocked square cages all abutting each other in 2 rows of 10. The feeding tubes were continually blowing pellets to feed the teeming cages, which were dense with large salmon, writhing and jumping. Just beyond this intensive salmon farm of battery-style aquaculture was a narrow sound with a small town along its sides. The town, Lysøysund, was an eyesore. At the east end of the channel was a semi-derelict herring oil factory. Here, the remains of processed fish and by products were pressed and boiled to extract the remaining oil for animal feed and fertilizer. The factory looked as disgusting as it sounds. Its great hulking, rusting buildings were on the cards for demolition and this would leave just the more pleasant west end of the small town standing.

Day 200. The western half of Lysøysund was much prettier than its eastern counterpart with large salmon farm and rusting fish oil factory

At the west end of the town I saw what looked like a café. I felt weak and tired, and the thought of a meal got my Pavlovian juices flowing, so I pulled the kayak up on to a floating jetty and headed up. Had I seen the chef, or noticed the rest of the clientele before I ordered, I would have moved on. The chef was an ugly brute with rolls of fat on the back of his neck. He was wearing clothes covered in last week's tomato sauce. It was only mid afternoon, but the 15 customers were the town's wasters who seemed to be staving off last night's hangover with beer, roll-ups and subdued small chat. They were all 40 somethings and too fat to work, and when they last did it was probably in the herring oil factory a decade ago. I could easily have been in Britain, and it did not feel like Norway at all. Full of grease, I left the town and continued west down the sound out into the countryside again.

I had to detour round the outside of the large Vallersundhaløya peninsula which was connected to the mainland with a narrow but steep isthmus. This isthmus would force me out into the Frohavet, an exposed and sometimes challenging 10-kilometre stretch of coastline. Today in this calm weather it would be benign. Once I had left the narrows at Lysøysund, I paddled into a great basin, so protected from the ocean

Day 200. The shoreline farm at Vallersund lay at the east end of a narrow 5km sound, with a few fishing hamlets along its south bank

Day 200. The western end of the narrow Vallersund sound was marked by this massive stone warden, probably built over a century ago

by the islands of Skjørøya and Valsøya, that it felt like an inland lake, with dense growths of pine forests along the shores. I paddled past Jøssund with its beautiful farms and white church and then on to the narrow sound at the other end of the basin. At the narrowest point, where reeds lined each side of the sound and ducks hid amongst them, was a beautiful old iron suspension bridge carrying the single track road to Valsøya and its few farms. I could imagine a journey over the bridge was a journey a few decades back in time. As I carried on down the sound I passed a few fishing hamlets sheltering behind breakwaters until I reached the last hamlet at Haldorhamn. Gradually the islets and skerries protecting this end of the sound started to vanish and the coastline became more exposed. The entrance to this sound was marked with a massive stone warden. These navigational sentries are common all along the coastline in Norway, and would have supplemented lighthouses 100 years ago, before they were usurped by modern light beacons. They must have been difficult and taxing to build, as some of these landmarks were perhaps four metres high and made from massive masonry. I heard there used to be itinerant teams who specialized in building these structures who travelled the country, building them for the parishes or kommunes who could pay for them. As I left the protection of the last skerries I could see to the northern horizon, where the low lying archipelago of the Froan islands lay 30 kilometres out in the Atlantic, as the final frontier against the ocean's wrath. Right at the western tip of the peninsula were six huge wind turbines. I paddled very close to them as they were situated on the shoreline. They were enormous at close quarters and must have been well over 100 metres high. They were much quieter than I was led to believe, but still a brutal intrusion into this pristine nature.

It was now mid evening and I needed somewhere to camp. I did not want my peace disturbed by these wind turbines, so continued south across Valsfjord to Nes, but as I paddled south along this rocky coast I did not see any inviting sandy coves to land at. I was starting to get anxious that I might also have to continue across the next fjord, as I approached the end of the peninsula and it was now late evening. Suddenly, right on the tip, there was a small beach and a flat grassy area beside an old house, which looked empty and unloved. I landed and set up my tent, not a moment too soon. The rain which had been threatening all day, finally arrived just as I threw everything into the tent, crawled in and did up the flysheet behind me. The rain was so heavy and made such a racket as it pelted the taut flysheet, I could not write. It kept up all night and despite what the heavens emptied on to the tent, the thin layer of ripstop kept me dry all night. I later heard there was some 50mm of rain that night and many areas of the county of Trøndelag had flooding problems.

When I retrieved the dirty pan I put out to soak last night it was half full of water and it was still raining. There was not a breath of wind to blow this deluge away. It was a good day to cross Trondheimsfjord, but I was reluctant to get up and venture out in this downpour, and everything would get soaked when I packed. I eventually made it out of bed by mid morning. I had arranged to meet friends in three days time and still had about 130 kilometres to go, otherwise I would probably have stayed in my dry sleeping bag on this very wet day. Once I had everything in drybags and threw them out into the rain. I got into my leggings and paddling cagoule and joined them. When I was dismantling the tent, heavy with a film of water, I managed to break the end of a pole section. These sections had already been weakened, and a few hairline cracks had appeared, because the salty atmosphere they had been in for the last two months, was attacking the alloy. I also lost the flame spreader for the stove in the grass. It was another phone call to Colin and Karen Bruce who I was meeting and had known for 25 years. They were avid visitors to Norway and lived here for about three months a year in their cabin in Trollheimen. As they ran outdoor shops in Scotland, they were the perfect people to sort out the tent pole and stove part.

I eventually set off after midday. There was a slight interlude in the rain, but then the mist descended over Bjugnfjord while I was crossing it. Luckily there were a lot of skerries and reefs about in the area I was in and

Day 201. The octagonal 130-year-old Kjeungskjær fyr lighthouse emerged like a fairytale from the mists as I paddled past

I knew no ship would venture in here. As I reached the headland on the other side the mist diffused and the wonderful fairytale Kjeungskjær fyr lighthouse appeared out of the grey gloom. It was perhaps the most spectacular lighthouse I had seen so far on this journey. It was built 130 years ago and before it was automated the lighthouse keeper lived in the octagonal shaped floors below the light. As I was admiring the lighthouse the north-bound Hurtigruten ferry emerged from the grey white mist beyond and glided silently north across the still ocean. The misty interlude soon disappeared as the rain started to fall again with a vengeance. I hugged the coast for a while, straying into areas with a lot of long 'spaghetti' weed about. I had noticed it firstly in the Tromsø area. It grows from the bottom in long strands up to 10 metres long, with a good few metres lying horizontal on the surface. It is buoyant, and occasionally I would see some strands of this weed in deeper waters, having lifted the small stone it was still attached to off the sea floor. It then no doubt drifted to eventually touch down again and establish another colony. I don't know if this weed is becoming a widespread problem as I can't remember it from 20 years ago anywhere.

I soon reached Garten island on the northern side of Trondheimsfjord. This fjord was only 5 kilometres across, but I was worried about the traffic I might encounter. With this poor visibility it was not ideal to cross. I paused then started to blast over at right angles to what I assumed was the shipping lane. There were remarkably few ships and the only vessel which gave me cause for concern was an express passenger catamaran, but even with this I had a kilometre berth. There were some remarkable currents in this crossing. The wind was now a force 3 and some of the areas were calm and others contained metre high breaking waves. The tide was in the latter stages of ebbing and the water emerging from the vast basin of inner Trondheimsfjord was warm to touch. However, the frequent waves washing over the deck, and the heavy rain, meant the cockpit was getting water in it through the neoprene spraydeck and I was getting soaked. By the time I got to Agdenes on the south side I was drenched.

I started paddling west but the wind and the tide were conspiring against me and I could only make 3 kilometres an hour against them. It was hard work for little gain and I decided to find somewhere to camp. Agdenes village was just a kilometre downwind, beyond the headland I had crossed over. I turned and was blown into this side fjord. There was a small marina here behind a breakwater. I paddled in and found a floating jetty I could lever the kayak on to and then went to search for somewhere to camp. The rain continued to bucket down and I soon got cold and miserable, with water pouring off the end of my nose and running down my sodden legging into my squelching wetsuit booties. I found some decking beside the marina, and considering the alternative of the drenched metre-high grass, decided to try and put my tent up here. It was easy to wedge the pegs between the slats in the wood, and soon the tent was up with the broken pole section spliced with a spare sleeve taped in place. I now had to sponge as much water as possible off the groundsheet which had formed a film after the morning's packing. Everything was damp and clammy to touch. It was a miserable end to a miserable day. There was nothing better to do than wriggle into my dank sleeping bag and cook a simple supper of mashed potatoes with chopped corn beef stirred into it. I eventually warmed the sleeping bag up enough to feel comfortable and fell asleep to the sound of large rain drops assaulting the fly-sheet.

SECTION 29. Folda and Frohavet
5 days. 190 kilometres. 42 hours. 0m ascent. 0m descent.

THE KAYAK: SECTION 30. THE NORTH WEST – TRONDHEIM TO STAD

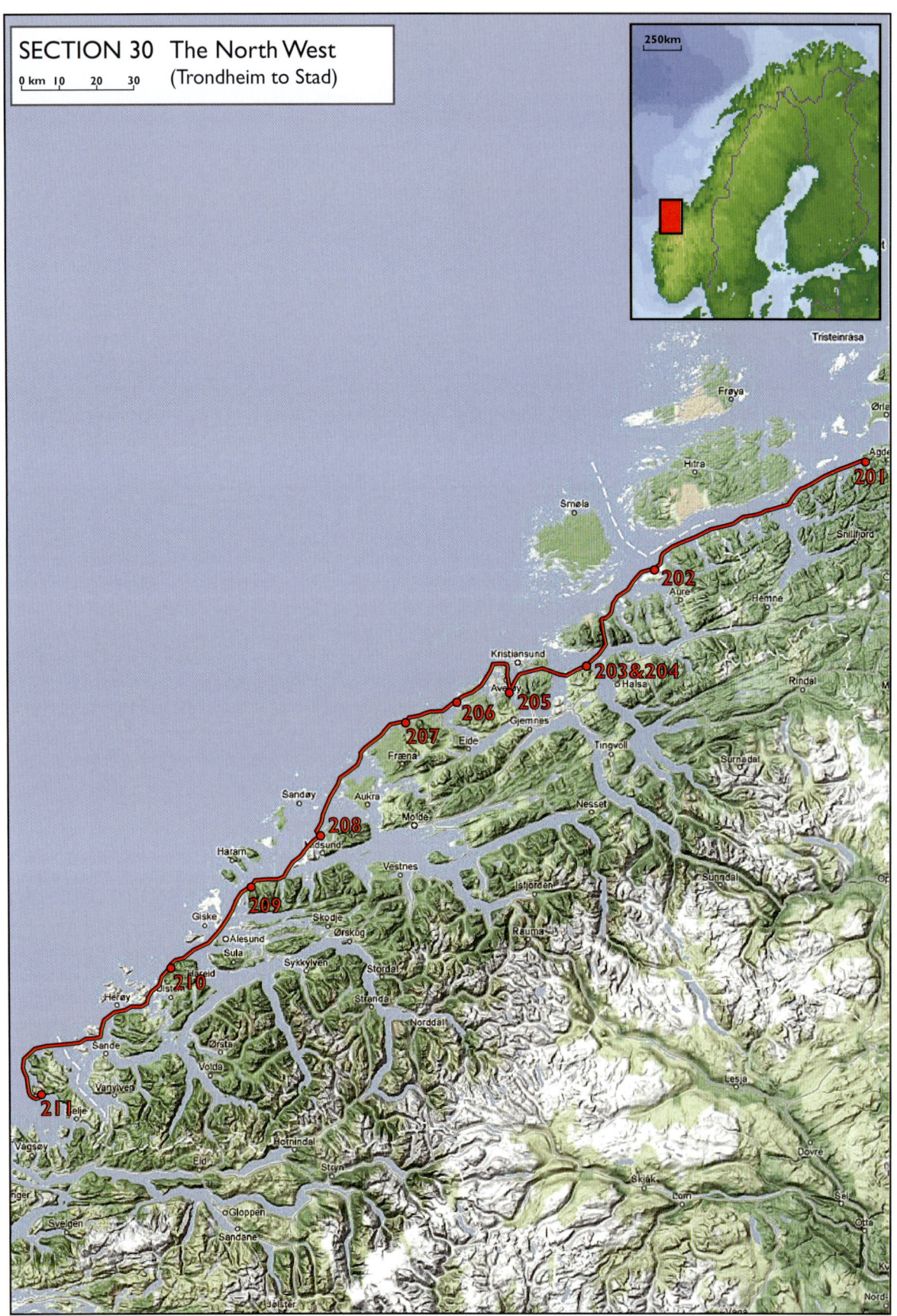

THE KAYAK: SECTION 30. THE NORTH WEST – TRONDHEIM TO STAD

Yesterday's deluge continued through the night and there was another half-filled pan of water outside the tent in the morning, with a further 50mm of water in it. The last 36 hours had been a torrent of a biblical magnitude and it was still pouring. Everything was slowly getting soaked through with condensation and misery. I still had another 100 kilometres to go to meet Colin and Karen in two days, so I could not lie in my steamy, but warm, bag and wait for the rain to stop. I had to get up, find some dry clothes, get into my drysuit and make some headway towards Kristiansund. I eventually got going mid-morning, by which time I hoped the tide had turned slightly in my favour and I could see the westerly headwind was easing. It was nevertheless a miserable slow paddle for the 20 kilometres down the south side of the enormous Trondheimsleia sound.

Day 202. Frothing streams poured out of the sodden forest into the wide misty Trondheimsleia all morning and afternoon

Every small beck was a torrent of beige froth cascading out of the dripping pine forest, across the rocks of the foreshore before it plunged into the sea. I passed the low grey shape of Leksa after a couple of hours as it stood proud against the mist, and in another couple of hours I reached the island of Hemnskjela, with the small village of Sundan sheltered behind. As I arrived at the small jetty I felt drained, and the weather over the last two days had sapped much of my spirit. There was a small shop here with the usual table for locals to have a coffee and chat. I bought a whole roast chicken and a few tomatoes and sat at the empty table, ripping the chicken to pieces with my hands. After 10 minutes I had devoured the whole beast except for a small pile of bones. I then gorged myself on two packets of jaffa cakes and felt like a python which had just swallowed a small deer. I digested this gargantuan lunch over a newspaper, while chatting with the shopkeeper, and an hour after arriving at Sundan I felt great again. Not only that, but I noticed the wind had veered to the north-east and had decreased. It was already 1700 but I felt I could paddle late today. I would have to if I was to meet Colin and Karen Bruce the next day as arranged.

Day 202. Paddling down Trondheimsleia with the tip of Røstøya on the left and the hills on the west end of Hitra in the distance

I continued west down Trondheimsleia. Anywhere else in the world this would have been a national treasure, with its extensive forests and rocky inlets. But the previous coastline from well before Tromsø to Rørvik was a very hard act to follow, and I had been spoilt with spectacular vistas at every headland. So the gently sloping land on the adjacent mainland and on the large island of Hitra, across the sound, seemed ordinary. I skipped across Hemnfjord and reached Stamnesøya and then Røstøya islands. The latter was wild and unkempt and I noticed it was a Nature Reserve. The forest on it was in great condition, with larger pines and thick undergrowth. There were many skerries along its north side, with some protected beaches sheltering behind them. There were plenty of terns nesting on these skerries and at last I managed to see a larger tern chick on a rock slab. Big enough to stand beside the adults, but suddenly very alone when they flew off, and it was left on its own and exposed. There were also many herons along this stretch of coast. It was a pristine pine forest environment, and it had redeemed the whole paddle so far that day. I stopped at the west end off Røstøya where there was a herd of rustic sheep dragging their shaggy dark fleeces along the ground. As I landed they withdrew back into the birch undergrowth.

I paddled past the small pretty hamlet of Taftøysund and made for a collection of tall structures further down the fjord. This was the small oil refinery at Tjeldbergodden which extended down the shore for about a kilometre.

Like most oil refineries it was hideous, but its intrusion into this pristine shoreline was moderated by the fact there was no flare burning or a lingering smell of hydrocarbons. There was a small tanker loading or unloading near a tank farm where all the fluids were stored before and after processing. I did not linger along its quay but blasted past, hoping it would not glaze over my memories of the lush, green, wild Røstøya, with its tern colonies and rustic sheep. I got to the end of the coastline around 2200 as it was getting dark. I now had to cross the 4 kilometre wide Dromnessund sound between the mainland and Skardsøya, which I reached well after sunset, but the improving weather and clear evening let the daylight linger for a while. I felt remarkably good and was paddling strongly. I knew each kilometre I made now was one fewer tomorrow, so decided to go as far as possible. I went past the north coast of the island in the twilight, with the smell of cut grass drifting from the scattered small holdings along the shore until I got to the north-west tip. I saw something quite large in the water in front of me heading towards the island. It was too big to be an otter or even seal head. I thought it was a goose swimming fast but in the twilight could not be sure. Then I thought it was a distant boat on the horizon without any lights on. But when its silhouette reached the small headland, just a few hundred metres in front of me, it did not disappear behind it but continued to the shore so I was confused again as to what it was. Eventually this dark shape reached the rocks and started to emerge so I was sure it was a seal. But then, just some 20-30 metres from it I was flabbergasted to see it was a large red deer. It must have swam over Trondheimsleia from Hitra some 5 kilometres the north. I later found out that this was not that unusual, as red deer are excellent swimmers and Hitra has one of the densest populations in Norway, and the younger males often need to disperse. I could see it was trying to get away from me up a slippery seaweed-covered slab and it kept falling and sliding back into the water. I veered out to sea so as to avoid stressing it more, and allow it to return into the sea and swim along the coast to find an easier place to come ashore.

As I continued to the west side of Skardsøya the swell started to build up. I could hear the surf crashing on to reefs, but apart from white flashes I could not see that well. I tried to keep away from the white as I followed the coastline south. There was no possibility of landing here in the dark with this sea, so I continued south giving the crashing surf a wide berth. Under the dim light of my head torch I could see a bay marked on the map, called Sandvika, on the next island of Lesundøya. It was just a few kilometres away and I hoped it would be a sandy oasis, so decided to make for it. An hour later I was paddling between its protective arms as the eastern sky was beginning to lighten up again. I could now see it was a beautiful bay with a couple of farms and a lovely boat shed which looked like an old stabbur built on piles over the water. It was worth paddling the extra hour to arrive here. The tide was high, so it was a short drag to get the kayak up the narrow sand strip on the edge of a newly cut grass field. I put my wet, clammy tent up and soon fell asleep. I left both ends of the tent open to try and encourage a draft to pass over my sodden belongings on what promised to be a dry day at last.

Day 203. The stabbur like boat shed in the sheltered sandy sanctuary of Sandvika bay on the north side of Lesundøya

I had intended an early start, but I slept like a log and did not wake until mid-morning. The sun was shining, the tent was warm and all my possessions and clothes, which had become so damp over the last two days, were now so dry they were crisp. I finally pushed off at nearly midday and paddled past the beautiful boat shed before turning south west with the gentle breeze at my back. Notwithstanding the last couple of days, I have had remarkable luck with the winds in the last month. I quickly passed the island of Grisvågøya and started across the calm sea towards the three very mountainous islands to my south. Each of these lofty islands was separated by deep sounds, any of which would allow me to reach the long deep Vinjefjord which was once a major river of ice, draining the interior ice fields in the previous ice ages. I opted to paddle down the deep channel between the most westerly of these lofty islands called Stabblandet and Tustna. The trip across the bay to the entrance of this sound was delightful and en route I passed the small Berrøya island, where I was pleased to see someone was restoring the only homestead on it. As I reached Stabblandet, perhaps the most mountainous of the three

Day 203. Paddling west along the north of Grisvågøya with the mountainous islands of Stabblandet and Tustna rising above all

islands, I came across the small island of Solskjelsøya. The east shore of Solskjelsøya looked very idyllic, with old small holdings in green forest clearings along the shore. When I got to the south, however, it looked more dilapidated, with ruined houses and collapsing jetties. There was a sandy beach, near where the cable ferry from the hamlet of Nordheim across the 300-metre sound docked. I landed here. The most obvious thing about the place was the huge piles of clutter. Broken fish farm cages, collapsing sheds, rusting plant, piles of rotting timber, jetties piled high with rotting fishing nets with turfs of grass growing from them. It reminded me of the west coast of Scotland or Ireland, where everything is collected in untidy piles in case it might be useful in the future. Near this junkyard was a notice displaying the island's history. It was long and distinguished.

It was one of the first places to emerge from under the ice sheet when the ice started to retreat some 15,000 years ago, and was ice free 12,000 years ago. The island was smaller then, as the weight of the recently-melted ice sheet pressed the land down. However, the ice sheet was not so thick here, and the later lifting of the land, or 'isostatic rebound', was only about 25 metres and not the 160 metres as in the Oslo area, or the 800 metres in northern Sweden. This island, ice free and partially submerged, relative to today's sea level, was one of the first places the early Stone Age settlers who colonized Scandinavia established themselves some 11,000 years ago. These pioneers were part of the Fosna Culture, the oldest groups of Stone Age settlers found on the Scandinavian Peninsula, who had migrated north from the Germanic Plains following the reindeer

Day 203. Approaching the hamlet of Nordheim on mountainous Stabblandet ahead with the corner of Solskjelsøya on the right

some 12,000 years ago. Here on Solskjelsøya, the first settlers built simple houses on the shore by a place called Vasslia, which was protected from the north and west. They left middens of shells which they collected in the bay. They also left flint weapons and bones from prey they fished for and hunted on the small islands and islets in the region. Especially valuable was the seals they hunted, using the skins for tents, clothes and boats. Today, this 11,000-year-old shoreline Stone Age settlement is 25 metres above sea and nearly 500 metres from the shore due to the rising land. Since then the island seems to have been almost continuously populated, with finds from the Bronze Age through to the start of recorded history and the Viking period. Perhaps in another 10,000 years time, when future archaeologists are digging the south side of this island, they will come across the current junkyard on the south of the island, and call it the culture of a *Homo sapiens* sub species, called *Homo detritus*.

I left Solskjelsøya and paddled down the wooded sound on the north side of Stabblandet. In the interior of the island, a massive steep mountain with craggy ramparts on all sides, rose above the gentle pine fringe. When

Day 203. Paddling down Sålåsund, with the mountains of Stabblandet rising above the small farms perched over the sheltered waters

Day 203. One of the sun-basked islets in the middle of Vinjefjord I passed while crossing to Magnillen campsite on the south side

I reached the deep Sålåsund sound which separated this island from Tustna, I turned south down it with the funnelled wind helping me along. I was surprised to see quite a few large homesteads down each side of the sound, some of them perched on grassy shelves on the steep forested hillsides. At the south end of this 6-kilometre sound it opened up into a basin. Around the shoreline of the basin were some of the greenest fields I had seen yet, and a scattering of larger prosperous farms amongst their lush promise. The enveloping green arms of the basin narrowed on the south side, protecting it from Vinjefjord, and I paddled through this gap into it. Vinjefjord is a long and convoluted slot of water, with many arms stretching nearly 50 kilometres inland, deep into the mountainous interior of Møre and Romsdal. On each side of this steep-sided fjord were heavily forested slopes, and at its mouth was the city of Kristiansund. My goal for the day was Magnillen, just 7 kilometres across the fjord on a peninsula. I made quick time across the fjord, with its small wooded islands basking in the sun, and was approaching the far side when I saw the rhythmic flash of kayak paddles as the wet surface reflected the sun. About 10 minutes later I could make out two paddlers coming towards me. It was Karen and her daughter, Kirsty, in their brand new kayaks. Beside them was Colin in an inflatable doing safety patrol. We soon met and greeted each other on the water and then paddled in a group to land. I last saw them when I stayed with them in their cabin in Trollheimen three years ago, just 100 kilometres from here, but have known them for about 25 years now. Colin had arranged two cabins at the campsite here at Magnillen. We quickly carried the kayaks and all my stuff up to the adjacent cabins and I spilled into mine where I would spend two nights. The ever thoughtful Colin brought a full set of clothes for me to wear during our stay here, and they had also brought the correct spares to fix my tent pole and petrol stove. Karen made a wonderful meal, with masses of vegetables, which I had been craving lately. We then sat around until late in the evening as their kids went to bed and the night enveloped the campsite in a quiet hush. There was a small area for an open fire outside our cabins, and Colin, Karen and I sat around enjoying its flickering flames and some malt whisky they brought.

I slept well, enjoying my first mattress for well over a week. With the recent wet weather of late, and the push to get here, I had fallen far behind with my writing and would have to devote much of the day to it. Outside, Colin and his son, Rory, had just finished making a wonderful cooked breakfast, and we sat outside in the warm morning sun under the fluttering birch trees and ate. The Bruce family were desperate to get into their new kayaks again, and as soon as breakfast was over the boys ran down to the small sheltered harbour. It was easy to keep an eye on them as they practised inside the breakwaters. Once the novelty was more tempered, Kirsty and Karen got into their kayaks, and Colin and the boys into the inflatable, and the family went for a longer tour along the coast for the afternoon. I had to squander the beautiful afternoon doing two machines worth of washing and writing up five days' log. By the time the Bruce's were back, bubbling with enthusiasm about kayaking, and the exploratory afternoon they had enjoyed around the smaller islands along the coast, I was about finished with my chores. That evening we had a barbecue with the overcast evening just stopping short of raining down on us. I dressed for dinner in the clean clothes Colin had lent me, it was luxurious to have cotton fabrics on after half a year of fleece and synthetic fabrics. Colin also lent me a better, larger inflatable mattress for the rest of my trip and a good cagoule, which would save the need to hunt around in Ålesund or Bergen for a paddling jacket, as my old faithful was now perished and rotting. We went to bed around midnight, after a few more beers and banter around the embers of the barbecue. I noticed just how dark it was this night. It was the first time I had seen near total darkness for months.

The whole Bruce family were up and eating breakfast outside when I got up. I had been pampered by their copious food and good cooking. It was not their home, but it felt like hospitality. By mid morning I was packed and ready to set off. Karen and Kirsty were eager to use their new kayaks on a longer trip and decided to follow me down to Årsund some 6 kilometres down the fjord towards Kristiansund. We set off just before midday,

Day 205. Paddling in Vinjefjord en route to Årsund and Kristiansund in my Tiderace Xplore X fibreglass kayak

while Colin and the boys followed in the inflatable. It was virtually calm and there was hardly a ripple on the water as we left. The tide should have been coming in but there was a good current carrying us west due to some local quirk. We followed the coast and then crossed over to the more pristine island of Langøya and followed its south shore. Sometimes it was ice-scoured slabs and sometimes boulders, but above both were the pine forests which dominated the vegetation now. Both Karen and Kirsty were getting confident in their kayaks by now, and one of them would blast off ahead while I chatted with the other. We reached Årsund after an hour and a half and paused here for a snack and to say our goodbyes. They returned to Magnillen with the two younger boys now in the kayaks. They were managing well, despite the fact their shoulders barely rose above the cockpit rim, and the paddles looked huge and unwieldy. It had been a very nice interlude with lots of banter and good company, and it gave me the chance to repair things, rest and catch up. I was sorry to see them go. I now had to paddle just past Kristiansund for my next social appointment which was to visit Sissel and Frederic Johansen, an ex uncle-in-law, who had a cabin some 20 kilometres away, on Averøya. From Årsund I paddled over the quiet Freifjord to the west side where there was a sound, called Omsund, which separated the three islands Kristiansund was built on from the island of Frei. It took less than an hour, and I soon paddled past a headland and saw a number of large ships docked in front of me, and the newer docks at Kristiansund. I avoided this area and headed down a smaller channel, under an older bridge and past some wooden houses along the shore. When I emerged at the other end of it I could look up to the more commercial and residential area of the town. The old Kristiansund was completely destroyed in the war, after a fire bombing campaign by the Germans. After this fire bombing onslaught, only the chimney stacks remained, and they were soon flattened to rebuild the whole town anew. I paddled past Kristiansund, not really getting a flavour of it, as I was a kilometre to the south, across the sound and paddled into Bremsnesfjord. I phoned Frederic to get directions.

Day 205. Heading west from Magnillen towards Årsund, between the mainland and Langøya, with Karen and Kirsty Bruce

Day 205. As I left Kristiansund the old 1956 built Hurtigruten ferry, MS Nordstjernen, overtook me as it headed south to Bergen

He told me to look out for a pile of stones about 5 kilometres away. I doubted I could see it but he reassured me I could. So I scanned the far side until my eyes came to rest on an enormous pile, a hill of stones really, which was very obvious. It was an ugly scar on the otherwise lovely landscape. It seemed it was a super quarry and there was a ship beside the pile which was obviously being loaded from a vast conveyor belt. Frederic said the cabin was right beside this. I was rather surprised, as I was imagining something quaint in an idyllic setting. I paddled over the Bremsnesfjord towards this eyesore, and as I approached the quarry and quay, yet another eyesore appeared behind it. It was a monolith of a factory, belching steam and filling the air with a foul smell. It produced massive amounts of feed for the numerous fish farms up and down the coast. I paddled past the huge bulk carrier into which a river of stone was pouring off the massive conveyor with clouds of dust emerging from its holds. Apparently this bulk carrier would transport these stones out into the Norwegian Sea where they would be used to cover and protect a newly-laid oil pipeline. A few hundred metres after it I could see Frederic and Sissel on a steep weed-covered slipway. We carried my kayak above the high tide mark and then walked up the hill to their cabin with the minimum of my belongings. The cabin had a lot of sentimental value to Sissel, as she grew up beside it. They were remarkably philosophical about the quarry and the salmon farm food production factory, and were optimistic about the future. Apparently once the quarry had removed the entire hill to the north of them, and loaded it on to bulk carriers, which would take another couple of years, the topsoil would be spread out over the bare grey rock and the green and peace would return. One could only hope this would come to pass, but I could not share their optimism, and the fish food factory would remain, whatever the quarry's outcome. In contrast to the surroundings, the cabin was lovely, with a lofty view across the fjord where you could see the currents in the water as the tide ebbed and flowed. I had a shower and then supper was served as we sat out on the terrace amongst pine trees. We were on the south side of the cabin and the opposite side to the quarry, which despite being just a few hundred metres away, was now forgotten. After supper we moved inside and chatted until midnight. It was a warm-hearted evening with some relations I had only met once before, but were very easy to get on with.

Day 206. One of the old derelict fish wharfs along Bremsnesfjord where cod were previously landed to be made into klippfisk

Frederic woke me at 0900 for breakfast. The previous night he had arranged for a journalist he knew from the regional newspaper to come at 1000, and he wanted to get breakfast out of the way first, which suited me. Minute perfect, Roald Sevaldsen from Tidens Krav arrived as arranged, and we chatted for almost two hours over coffee. He wanted to stay longer, but he had another meeting scheduled. Frederic and Sissel walked me back down to my kayak. While we were saying our goodbyes, a juvenile mink came and inspected the kayak. It was completely fearless and even came towards us before disappearing into the stones of the jetty. We said our farewells and then I paddled out of the bay and into Bremsnesfjord again. The massive bulk carrier which was loading yesterday, was now gone; having made a small dent in the huge hill of stones which was still being topped up as I paddled past. I had about a 5-kilometre paddle up Bremsnesfjord again to reach a level with Kristiansund and then continued to the open sea where the Stavnes fyr lighthouse was. I passed a few old fishing wharfs which were falling into disrepair, and some large farms along the shore. A lot of the old shipping wharfs were from half a century ago, when small boats landed their catch locally, and then much of the cod from this catch was salted and then dried on rock slabs beside the sea. This produced klippfisk which is the main ingredient of Bacalao. Processes have now changed, and the traditional labour-intensive way of producing klippfisk has now gone, making these lovely old wharfs redundant. Previously, if rain threatened during the summer months when the klippfisk was drying, the fishwives used to rush on to the rock slabs where the fish was drying and heap them up into piles a little more than a metre high. The piles were then covered with iconic hexagonal umbrellas, which interlinked together to keep the rain off the drying fish. These umbrellas have now become something of a collector's item, and I had noticed Frederic and Sissel had one

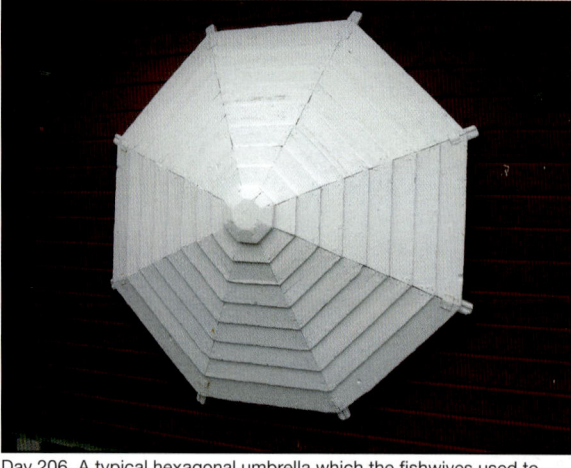

Day 206. A typical hexagonal umbrella which the fishwives used to cover up piles of klippfisk if rain threatened to fall on the drying fish

Day 206. The narrow 50-metre wide Sveggesund had houses on both sides and was busy with cabin cruisers and a restaurant

on the side of their cabin. Once round the Stavnes fyr lighthouse I paddled along the open coast with a small swell breaking along the shoreline and on the rocks. It was quite convoluted with many open inlets. Eider duck seemed to be thriving in these inlets and there were many rafts of them. They were mostly sitting on the weed-covered slabs but took to the water when I approached. The ducklings were now almost the size of the adults and almost black in colour, as opposed to the mother's brown. There was still the odd batch of smaller ducklings that probably were conceived and hatched late.

After a couple of kilometres along the open coast I could leave this more exposed coastline and take an inland shortcut down Sveggesund. It was a narrow sound with houses on each side. It was a colourful thriving place. A bridge spanned this narrow sound, connecting the smaller Sveggøya on the west to the much larger Averøya island. There were a couple of modern fishing boats and a restaurant, but by and large I would say most people who lived here worked in Kristiansund which was just a short ferry trip across Bremsnesfjord. From Sveggesund I entered another charming area of idyllic small islands and islets. It reminded me very much of some of the island clusters on the Helgelandskysten. The only difference being that there were not so many beaches here, and generally the houses and hamlets here were more numerous and more affluent. As I weaved through these islands the mist came in and it started to rain. I pulled up the hood on the jacket Colin had lent me and paddled on for another still wet hour and a half. Eventually I came to the small island of Langøya which boasted a large village. It seemed a busy place with an old white Lutheran church, plenty of large deciduous trees and a lot of quaint restored boathouses and wharfs and some nice wooden villas.

Day 206. Weaving through the misty wet islets between Sveggesund and Langøyasund where there was a shop

I also saw a shop. I made to land on a rocky beach, when someone invited me to use his jetty. He was trying to smoke some newly-caught haddock in a home-made smokery, constructed from an old wooden barrel. I went up to the shop and bought enough to tide me over for the next few days, and a grilled chicken and some tomatoes for this evening. It was then back on to the water again as I paddled through the rest of Langøyasund towards Stor Sandøya. There was no beach on the latter, so I carried on, passing through many small channels and islets ringed in yellow brown seaweed. Despite the traditional cabins, restored wharfs and a few more exclusive leisure homes the whole area still felt quite empty as they were well spread out and there was no small boat traffic. Just after the short bridge connecting the smaller Stor Sandøya island to Averøya there was a large body of water called Hendvågen. It was a nature reserve. The curious thing with Hendvågen is that it is topped up and emptied by about a metre by the tide, which has to flow up a short river to fill and empty

Day 206. The juvenile mink swimming across the sound by the tidal stream in and out of Hendvågen towards Stor Sandøya to find prey

Day 206. The fishing community of Håholmen is at least 300 years old and has been restored to an upmarket guest house and restaurant

this sea lake. As I paddled past, the river was flowing out vigorously. I saw a family of mink near here. There was an adult and two juveniles. They would play havoc with the ducks and would already have eaten many eggs and chicks already this year. One of the juveniles swam across the sound and I pursued it to get a photo. I continued south past more islands, with older buildings still on them, and then came to Håholmen as the rain started to diminish in the misty evening.

Håholmen was an old fishing wharf and trading post which had undergone a more salubrious restoration and conversion to a high class guest house and restaurant. There were a lot of older wooden boats and even a replica Viking ship moored at the jetty. There were also a few larger Bayliner type cruisers from some of the better off guests. It was not for me, but I needed somewhere to camp soon, and was fast running out of options as the evening was getting late and dusk was approaching. Just beyond Håholmen was Lamholmen. It had a beach which extended the whole tidal range and some grassy land to camp on. It was perfect. I pulled ashore and inspected. Just above this grassy camping spot was a small grass-roofed log cabin which almost merged into the hillside. I went up to have a look at it and noticed it was open. I went in and saw a table and a couple of bunks. There was a visitor's book on the table which I read. From the book I gleaned the cabin was also owned by Håholmen guest house and restaurant and it was intended as a place for the staff who worked there to come and escape. Lamholmen was only connected to Håholmen at very low tide and the tide was now coming in, so I assumed nobody would be coming over tonight. It would soon be dark so I decided to take advantage of the cosy cabin. By the time I had secured my kayak and carried my equipment up to the cabin it was dark and I was more relaxed about staying here.

Day 206. Next to Håholmen is the islet of Lamholmen where there is a small hand-crafted log cabin complete with turf roof

Once I was in the cabin I noticed that it was built without any nails. Indeed, the more I looked around, the more I noticed that it was built by a traditional craftsman, with roof joists that had carved joints which locked together and were then further secured with large wooden dowels. As I read through the visitor's book I realized the guest house and restaurant on Håholmen was owned by none other than Ragnar Thorseth and his wife. He had also built this cabin on Lamholmen which explained the craftsmanship used in the joinery. Ragnar Thorseth is a well-known sailor and explorer. His first audacious escapade was to row an open 15 foot færing alone across the North Sea from Måløy near Ålesund to Lerwick. He wanted to get there 500 years after Norway pawned the Shetland Islands to Scotland. He made it in 10 days and just in time to meet the Queen and Prince Philip who were there for the 500 year celebrations. Prince Philip called him "A damn fool" which he took as a compliment. He then spent most of the 1970s and 1980s exploring the Arctic Ocean in small boats he made himself on traditional and ancient Norwegian seafaring designs. In 1975 he sailed a Viking boat across the Atlantic to show the Vikings could easily have discovered America and Vinland long before Columbus did. He also sailed an imitation Viking freight boat, called 'Saga Siglar', round the world in the mid 1980s and overwintered on another boat, called 'Havella', in Kongsfjord in Svalbard in the late 1980s. He was the last of the Vikings, and now I was squatting in his cabin for the night! If he walked in he might be empathetic if I told him about my trip. I could hear the wind was getting up outside and the rain was lashing at the dark window, so I was extremely grateful for the lovely hand-crafted cabin and its comfortable table to write at and bunk to sleep on.

Day 207. The Kvitserk was a replica Viking freight boat on Norway's coast. Ragnar Thorseth sailed round the world in a similar boat

I did not need to get out of bed to hear it was still windy, and looking outside I could see it was around a force 4. I checked the forecast on my phone and it was predicted to continue all day. This was not the forecast I had hoped for to paddle along the next stretch of coast called Hustadvika, which was renowned for its exposure, large swells and difficult conditions. On the other hand it was perhaps easier than getting an earful from Ragnar Thorseth. The tide was right out and I had to go back to Håholmen to get out of this cluster of islands. This gave me another chance to paddle past Håholmen's jetty where a number of Ragnar Thorseth's expedition boats were moored. There was the white 'Havella', and the replica Viking boat 'Kvitserk' was a copy of the circumnavigating 'Saga Siglar', which unfortunately sank in a Mediterranean storm in 1992. I left Håholmen and headed south west. I had wanted to go outside the 'Atlantic Road', but the westerly force 4 would have been directly against me. I opted to seek some lee and go on the inside. It was still slow going as I paddled into the small choppy wavelets towards the nearest of the bridges. With the small waves rushing past me I was under the impression I was going fast. However, when I looked down at my GPS speedometer, I saw I was just doing a few kilometres per hour. The Atlantic Road is a 7-kilometre stretch of road which spans the entire mouth of Kornstadfjord, connecting Averøya island with the mainland. Luckily for the road-building engineers there is a string of islets across the mouth of the fjord here, and the road hops from one island to the next over a series of 16 bridges and causeways, the longest of which is only 500 metres. Many of the bridges are quite graceful and curve as they rise and fall, so the road has become something of a tourist attraction. I shot under the bridge, with the tide surging through the narrows filling up the fjord beyond, which overwhelmed the effects of the wind for an easy minute. Once I was south of the string of bridges the wind was back, but it was only perhaps a force 3. I then headed west along the inside of the islands for an hour to Straumsholmen, where I had to pass under the last bridge and out into the ocean again. Along the inside of these islands were some old fishing wharfs. Some had been lost to the march of time and were abandoned to kittiwakes, which nested on their window frames. Others had been restored, and one was converted to a scuba dive centre.

Day 207. Many of the abandoned fish wharfs on the inside of the Atlantic Road islands where colonized by kittiwakes and their chicks

I had to paddle hard to burst through the tide which was flowing into the fjord under the last bridge, and then I was into more open ocean again. I was expecting a lot worse from this renowned coastline, but found that there were hundreds of small islets and skerries and a few larger islands protecting the inner coast, and that there was no swell at all getting through them. For the next 5 kilometres I had a lovely paddle, despite the drizzle, through an island seascape with plenty of

Day 207. West of the Atlantic Road was a lovely sheltered channel called Smørholmvågen, lined with historic homesteads and eider duck

highlights from the coastal culture. There were a few historic fishing communities, which would have evolved over centuries, with houses, wharfs, salting houses and trading posts, which were probably all abandoned in the 1960s and 1970s, as people gave up this fishing existence in houses on stilts at society's fringe. However, more recently, many of these communities had been restored and had soul and colour blown back into them. As with Håholmen, much of this seemed to be justified and enabled by tourism. One restoration at Teistklubben was exceptionally pleasing, and all the buildings on this flat island community seemed to be restored to their former glory, as if it were a living museum.

Day 207. Teistklubben was a restored fishing community, or fiskevær, built on some islets on the edge of the exposed Hustadvika coastline

A little after Teistklubben the sheltering islets and skerries soon started to vanish and I could see flashes of white exploding surf in the distance. The wind was still a force 4 from the north-west, which was bringing an increasingly large swell in from the Atlantic. I tried to ignore it, but the more I paddled towards them, the more I realised I would soon be in the thick of it. Pretty soon the waves were a metre high, then two, and then three metres. I only saw the land when I was on the upper portions of the swell as it raced under me and piled in towards the shore. There was a small surf-pounded beach in a little bay called Sandvika, and after that it was a rocky coastline with jagged rocks, bereft of any vegetation, as the ocean storms had washed them clean. The swell was a good three metres now and I could hear the constant roar of it as it crashed on to these rocks in white turbulent mayhem, sending plumes of spray high into the air. It unnerved me paddling so close to it, so I veered out to sea until I was a couple of hundred metres out. Here, the swell was more even and I was less likely to be surprised by a rogue wave rearing up and breaking on a hidden skerry. None the less, I felt my jaw clamping and my grip on the paddle tightening, as I realized the consequences of getting driven on to these rocks if anything went wrong. I would be dismembered after a minute or two. This turbulent shoreline continued for a couple of kilometres until it reached a headland with a vast beacon on it. There must have been a nature trail out to the beacon and there were at least 30 people in bright waterproof anoraks heading out to it, or returning from it. I could see many were looking in my direction and pointing as I paddled past. I must have been hidden in the troughs of the swell most of the time. As I approached the headland they all stopped and had their eyes on me. I could feel them thinking "look at that mad bugger", but in reality it looked much worse than it was, as the swell 200 metres off shore was not breaking as it was along the chaos of the shore before them. Once round the headland I doubled back to a beach for lunch. There were some large remnants of the swell heading for the beach and I caught one which was about a metre high and just the right angle for a good 300-metre surf all the way to the beach. The GPS said I reached 15.5 kilometres per hour, which was a record for this kayak so far, and very satisfying. I beached the kayak and went up to a three-sided log shelter with a couple of picnic tables under cover. As I sat down, so did a party of 10 people who had been looking at me rounding the headland 10 minutes earlier. They were fascinated and asked masses of questions for a good half hour, which I answered between mouthfuls of my lunch and some sandwiches which they had donated.

My problem was I was soaked, as I had stupidly not put my drysuit on this morning. The spraydeck, my second one of the trip, was also starting to leak. The wind was still a westerly force 4 which would have been against me, and I still had 20 kilometres of exposed coastline ahead of me down the outside of Hustadvika in this increasing swell. With the cold seeping through my wet clothing, and the prospect of dangerous conditions, I did not feel up to continuing. If I was a dog, I would have had my tail between my legs. One of the crowd said there were rooms just 2 kilometres across the other side of this bay, called Breivika, at a guest house called Hustadvika. I was now beginning to throw in the towel and had fantasies of a bone marrow warming shower, as opposed to fighting for every kilometre as I paddled into the wet force 4 wind. I crossed the bay and saw there were frequent three-metre swells coming into this enclave and erupting on scattered shallow skerries. I now realized it would be foolhardy to continue down the coast, so when I reached the breakwater on the other side of the bay I entered it. Behind its shelter was the large guest house jetty. I levered my kayak on to the floating jetty and got a room. They were not cheap and there were no meals except breakfast. I took the room anyway, and after a wonderful warming shower fired up the petrol stove to cook a meal while being cautious not to scorch any furniture. Warm and well nourished I was at last content with the day.

Day 208. As I left Breivika bay and the guest house I had to thread through skerries and surf to find a route into the open ocean

The next morning was more than I could have hoped for. I was woken by gull chicks nesting on the grass roof nearby, to a still sunny day. After the included guest house breakfast I set off mid morning at low tide. I pushed the nose of the kayak through some shiny brown kelp fronds and weaved my way through a line of skerries where there was some big surf breaking. I found a route which avoided the worst of it and soon I was in the open sea again. The swell was still there from yesterday, but it looked so much more benign in the sun. I could see an exposed headland just a kilometre away and there were no protecting islets or skerries to the north of it. The swell was piling in from the north and crashing on the rocks so I gave it a wide berth. I should imagine it would have been quite fearsome yesterday had I chosen to paddle down here. After the headland was Hustadbukta, with the village of Hustad hidden deep inside it. I was not going to go in but paddled across the bay on the large but gentle swell. As I was half way across I saw an old square sail. It was on a boat which was hardy moving on this calm day. It was just a slight detour, so I went over to investigate. I asked them if it was a Nordlandsbåt and they almost took offence. "No" they said, "it was an Åfjordbåt", which was a traditional boat from the Trøndelag region. However, they still described it as a fembøring, which meant it had room for six sets of oars and was about 42 feet. There was a small shelter on the back of this boat, called 'Braute', where six people could sleep. Like the Nordlandsbåt this shelter was removable if need be. Across the top of the shelter was a series of notches where the tiller could be secured. Like the Nordlandsbåt this boat also had a square topsail above the main square sail. In fact I could see very little difference between the two types of fembøring, other than the Nordlandsbåt would have had a higher prow at the bow and it was perhaps more graceful. There were six people on board this boat, and I chatted with them for a good five minutes before continuing across Hustadbukta. During the entire five minutes I did not take a stroke, so there was absolutely no wind to blow them along.

Day 208. Half way across Hustadbukta bay I saw the traditional 42 foot Åfjordbåt called 'Braute' becalmed on the still day

Once I got to the far side of this bay and reached a the rocky peninsula called Haugneset, I found I was back into a seascape of islets and skerries again and it was easily possible to sneak along the inside of them protected from the ocean swell. Indeed, this would not have been a problem in yesterday's wilder weather either. I paddled down this coast for a good hour with just the occasional swell here and there, but out to sea, perhaps a kilometre offshore, was a line of skerries where the swell was breaking. It was almost like a reef round a tropical atoll. This stretch of the coast did not contain the famous exposure which people had warned me about at all. Larger vessels, and the Hurtigruten ferry, could not venture into these protected waters and would have to stay in the ocean outside the reef, and perhaps this has fuelled the reputation of Hustadvika. I saw a small beach on one of the islets and pulled up on the thick layer of seaweed which had been deposited here. It was quite a brief stop in the warm sun, as the incoming tide soon crept up the beach, and after dragging the kayak a few times I was up to the rocks, so relaunched. Just as I reached the tip of the peninsula, the protective reefs and islets

Day 208. I managed to stop on a sandy outcrop of an islet along Hustadvika which was much more sheltered than I was led to believe

offshore vanished and there was an exposed kilometre to negotiate to reach the final headland. In a few places a submerged shallow would lie quiet while nine swells went over it and then suddenly the tenth swell would rear up in a great wall which toppled over. There was an especially active one right at the end. It lay in the channel I had to go through between the mainland and an islet. I observed for a while, and when I was confident I knew its behaviour, I surged through and spilled into the calmer waters off the small town of Bud. The Hustadvika coast was now behind me. I thought its ferocious reputation was a little exaggerated. The entire coast is perhaps some 30 kilometres and there are just really two exposed headlands, the last one I did yesterday and the first today, in addition to this final headland before Bud. Each of these is a couple of kilometres at the most and there are plenty of landing spots and protection in between. While one might have to pause while going down this coast for better weather, as I did, there is no danger that one is going to get caught out by a sudden deterioration in the weather, as there are plenty of opportunities to seek sanctuary. The same could not be said for the Østhavet coast in Finnmark.

A breeze appeared, and as it was behind me and was pushing me along I decided not to stop at Bud, but continue across the islet-studded fjord to the island of Gossa. I hopped from islet to islet and saw many eider duck high on the rock slabs well out of the water. There were also a few islets covered in geese, but I could not tell if they were breeding here. Far out to my west on the outer fringe of these islets was a larger cluster of small islands on the edge of the Atlantic Ocean. Remarkably there was a small town of about 200 houses draped over their gnarly hummocks, which the map said was Bjørnsund. Probably most of the houses were now leisure homes belonging to the descendants

Day 208. As I reached the end of Hustadvika coastline I passed though a turbulent channel and emerged at the calm waters by Bud

of the fisherfolk who once stayed here, but it looked like there was still a good resident population. It really was a community in the sea. When I reached Gossa I was hoping to land and have a stretch on a beach, but I could not find anything, so in the end landed on a sheltered rocky islet ringed with seaweed. It was easy to land almost anywhere here as the whole fjord mouth or basin was peppered with islets far out into the ocean and well beyond my limited horizon. No ocean swell could penetrate, and any waves which were generated had a very limited fetch. Even in strong winds they would be small. After this break I set my sights on the north west tip of Otrøya. Unlike the flat Gossa I was leaving behind, Otrøya had mountains. Indeed, everything to the south and west was a mass of mountains. Beyond these coastal mountains, which I could see, were some of the most impressive mountains in Europe. These were the mountains of Møre and Romsdal and included the Sunnmørsalpene and the exceptionally spectacular mountains each side of the remarkable Romsdal valley.

Day 208. I passed many rocky islets between Bud and Gossa island and most have eider duck and geese resting on them

Unfortunately I could not see them as they were hidden by range upon range of serrated ridges, each one increasing in height as they went inland. While I was admiring these spectacular mountains in the dark light which precedes wet weather, like the opening bars of a Wagnerian opera, I kept hearing a thump-like cracking sound. I wondered if it was something to do with the kayak. After about 15 such sounds, which I was at a loss to explain, I saw a small school of porpoises overtaking me. They were an energetic bunch and occasionally one would almost leave the surface and crash into the sea again.

As I reached Tangen, on the north tip of Otrøya, the rain started. There were no beaches here, so I continued south to the new causeway out to the island of Magerøya. Luckily there was a bridge in this causeway, so I could paddle beneath it without the need for a long detour, as is sometimes the case. Just beyond this bridge on the south side of this small green rural island was a small marina and about five houses, a farm and a cluster of boat sheds. Despite the umbilical cord of the new 300-metre causeway attaching this hamlet to the larger Otrøya island it still felt a bygone decade. I reached the floating jetty and located a camp spot then levered the 90 kilos of kayak and baggage on to the pontoon. This kayak is a strong boat and one of the few fibreglass boats on the market where I could do this. Most would bend and crack along the hull. In my drysuit I was completely oblivious to the heavy rain and set my tent up beside a bleached boat shed. I managed to get everything inside and sorted out before taking my drysuit off and crawling in. I had just settled in when I realized I was in the wrong spot. There were three seagull chicks on the jetty area outside. They could not fly properly, so scurried about looking suspicious. Their parents were perched on shed tops and posts around them, and me. Each time there was any hint of danger from other seagulls, or me, or even a bush rustling in the gentle wind, the noisy seagull adults would screech to warn the youngsters. In return, the juveniles squawked all night, pestering their parents to regurgitate morsels of fish for them. If one of them did the other two juveniles would create a frenzy of envy and the adults would then start shrieking, assuming their chick was under attack. This continued all night, and by the morning my feelings towards them were not Zen-like and humanitarian at all!

When the noisy gulls woke me in the morning, I could hear that the rain was still pelting down on the tent and the storm flaps where flailing in the wind. I did not even bother to look outside but just rolled over for another couple of hours. When I woke again it was still wet and windy. As I had some writing to do I got the mini laptop out, set up my Thermarest chair and fired up the petrol stove to heat and dry the tent. By the time I finished at midday the rain was sporadic and the wind seemed to have dropped down to a force 4. The forecast was encouraging, so I decided to go for it, but I was sensible enough to put my drysuit on first. By the time I got going in the early afternoon the wind was down to a south-westerly force 3 and I opted to go the shortest way rather than the longer path of least wind resistance.

Day 209. Heading down towards the dark island of Dryna with the blue grey mountains above Hildre in the distance

The paddle towards the first island of Midøya and then along its coast was tedious and slow. I was paddling hard but could only make 4 kilometres an hour into the wind. I also made the mistake of being too far from the shore, so I could not see the shoreline interests and it was only when I got to the far end of the smaller Dryna island that I was within an investigative distance to land again. No sooner had I reached land than I was off again, this time across the 3 kilometre mouth of Romsdalsfjord, a deep fjord which had its roots hidden deep in the mountainous interior. Across on the south side of Romsdalsfjord was a flat fertile mantle which quickly gave rise to steep, craggy mountains covered in birch forest up to about 500 metres and then grass and heather up to the rocky summits around 1000 metres. Along this fertile mantle, squeezed between the foot of the mountains and the fjord were a string of prosperous farms with their bright red barns and white farmhouses. On my west and out to sea were five large islands, they were the northern half of the Nordøyane islands, a string of nine relatively large and hilly islands stretched out in a great 50-kilometre arc along the coast here. All nine of them were inhabited, with 20-30 farms and some fishing industry on each. On the outer north-west side of these islands they must have been weather beaten and exposed, as they

Day 209. Looking back up the extension of Romsdalsfjord to the islands of Dryna, Midøya and lastly Oterøya in the distance

took the brunt of the Atlantic without any protective skerries, but on the more sheltered south-east sides they were green with fields. These Nordøyane islands were the less eroded remnants of the many ice ages, and the once mighty glaciers which drained the interior of Møre and Romsdal would have flowed between them, and over parts of them, as they carved their way to the sea. The four southern islands are connected to each other and the mainland at Ålesund by tunnels and bridges, but the five northern islands are only serviced by ferry. However, there are ambitious plans to link all by road.

I eventually reached the south side of the fjord by the town of Brattvåg, which was at the entrance to a deep side arm of the inlet. It had some small industrial sheds and did not look that inviting in the grey light under clouds pregnant with rain. I would much rather have lived on one of the idyllic Nordøyane islands than in this town hemmed in by dark mountains and warehouses.

Just as I left Brattvåg the skies finally opened and it started to pour down. Luckily I had my drysuit on and it made little difference to me. The shower was short and heavy and after just 15 minutes the sun was out and I was reaching for my sunglasses. I passed a salmon net trap which had been set out for the short period regulations allow and noticed that all the buoys were old wooden barrels, as they all were perhaps 50 years ago. I was still making quite slow time and with the breeze continuing against me it felt like I was paddling in treacle again and my spirit was sapping. I decided to start looking for a campsite, as even if I paddled late into the evening I could only hope to gain another 15 kilometres at this rate. I saw quite a few nice tent sites but realized I had no water, so had to paddle all the way to Hildre where a river tumbled out of the valley into the fjord. I filled up both my two litre water containers,

Day 209. A salmon trap made from nets which where held in place and given buoyancy by the old wooden barrels

and as there was no campsite here continued west. There was plenty of activity on the farms along the edge of the fjord. The farmers were cutting grass with their old well-maintained tractors and wrapping it in plastic where it would partially ferment and produce silage. I am sure this would be the second batch of grass taken off these fields with perhaps another one to come in a month. I approached the headland at Hildre where a quaint white church, or chapel, with a squat square tower stood looking out to the Nordøyane islands where the main church of the kommune stood 4 kilometres across the water. There was no camping at the headland but just round the other side was a bay with a cobble beach where I could easily land. Above the beach was a flat meadow which had just been cut and baled and offered a great vantage over the seascape. By early evening I had my tent up and all my equipment, which was damp from this morning, was laid out drying. It was a glorious evening and the wind had vanished, so I sat outside and wrote, looking out to the Nordøyane islands.

Day 209. The sunset from my campsite looking out to the Nordøyane islands of Haramsøya on the left and Skuløya on the right

Day 210. In the morning I could look across the fjord to the northern half of the 9 Nordøyane islands with Lepsøya and Haramsøya shown

I slept well and woke early. After a quick breakfast I cast off much earlier than usual with the north-east breeze directly behind me. I flew down the coast to the automated lighthouse at Lepsøyrev, a squat solid octagonal tower on the end of a causeway jutting some 250 metres into the sea. It was to mark the passage through the hazardous and shallow sound between the mainland and the island of Lepsøya, which was just a couple of kilometres wide. I soon reached Bjørnøya island and decided to go down the outside of it, riding the favourable wind. I did the same with Kalvøya, but by now the wind had just about died away and the skies were expectant with rain. I was now approaching Ålesund, a major port, and I could see and hear the rumble of larger ferries, and the buzz of smaller boats and the high-speed catamaran passenger ferries. I was in a bit of a dilemma as to what I should do. Ålesund is a very nice city, but staying here for the night was a problem. The campsite was a bit out of town and up a hill, and if I left the kayak elsewhere it would be vulnerable. Even a flying visit for a coffee and a wander round the shops, to look at things I did not need, would be too much palaver. I had already visited Ålesund some five years previously so I was not that curious and decided to give it a miss. It was about the size of Tromsø, and like old Tromsø had suffered the same fate of a major fire. In the case of Ålesund it was much more complete and the whole town was destroyed on a windy night in 1904. It was rebuilt over the next few years with some German help in an Art Nouveau style which was German in origin. It is this which gives the centre its current charm. I dare say the older houses which burnt would have been even more charming. The other big attraction of Ålesund is its location on a peninsula, surrounded by fjords, islands and high snow-capped mountains beyond. I would also be visiting Bergen, arguably Norway's finest city, in about 10 days time and could revel in its richer culture when I get there. So I paddled, past heading for Valderøya, one of the southern-most Nordøyane islands, and connected to Ålesund with a tunnel under the fjord. When I

Day 210. Looking up Grytafjord to the north of Ålesund into the rugged interior of the mountainous Møre and Romsdal

reached there I saw a shop, and as my supplies were running very low I landed between some small boat sheds, and bought enough for five days.

I had a long pause on Valderøya, eating another grilled chicken and making some phone calls. One was to arrange the delivery of a new rubberized Reed spraydeck to replace the porous neoprene one I have. Platou Sports in Bergen kindly agreed to receive it, but I feared I might have problems with import duty, as happened with my rucksack. It was mid afternoon by the time I left and the forecast rain and wind was starting to arrive. I opted to go round the west side of Hareidlandet which is a large island to the south. It would not be so protected but I hoped it would be more scenic. The only problem was I would have

Day 210. The town of Ålesund, which lies on a peninsula surrounded by sheltered fjords, is famous for its Art Nouveau centre

Day 210. Godøya island is the most southerly of the Nordøyane and lies just off Ålesund to which it is connected by an undersea tunnel

to cross another shipping channel. There were a few of the high-speed passenger catamarans in it taking people back to the islands after a day's work in Ålesund. I paddled past the spectacular Godøya island, with some 15 farms along the coastal fringe and a few old and new fishing wharfs, where working boats were tied up. The centre of the island was wild, craggy and steep, rising to around 500 metres. Yet just some 15 minutes by car you could drive through two undersea tunnels and over a bridge and be in the thriving city centre. It was the best of both worlds. It was a long 6 kilometres across the choppy sound to Hareidlandet, an island name which evoked images of bearded Vikings. The wind was against me and it was pouring with rain. I was getting regular facefuls of spray but luckily I had my drysuit on. On the north coast of this empty wild and rugged island there was nothing, except a small lone fishing boat a few hundred metres offshore. It bobbed in the swell, slowly motoring ahead under autopilot. It had a boom out each side with longlines attached to each one. The fisherman was hauling one of the lines in on a small winch and every so often a fish would appear. He would lean over the side and wallop the fish with a 'hyttkrok', a chunky shaft of wood with a spike in it. With this he would haul the fish over the gunwales and dispatch it. We waved to each other as I paddled past. Out to the west ahead of me were the Sørøyane, the southern islands, which were the counterpart of the Nordøyane. The Sørøyane were a cluster of six rugged islands with a population of about 5000. Five of the islands were connected to each other with bridges and also to the mainland by a tunnel. Perhaps the best known of the Sørøyane is the island of Runde, with its famed puffin colony, which I could see rising out of the edge of the ocean.

As I came round to the west side of Hareidlandet the wind really increased. It was coming in strong gusts round the mountain and down some of the valleys. Some of these gusts were very strong and I came to a standstill. The gusts were a good force 8 and lifted spray off the wavelets into my face and tried to wrench the paddle from my hands. After a minute they were gone and I could gain another 500 metres until the next one arrived. After some ten such gusts I finally reached the farming hamlet of Flo. It trumpeted its location with a surprisingly large and very white beach along the mantle of the island, under some very steep 500-metre mountainsides. At the far end was a tremendous breakwater with just the smallest slot in its massive walls. I paddled through it into a Shangri-La. The breakwater walls completely encircled a large beach and turquoise shallows. There was a small campsite

Day 210. The Sørøyane islands south of Ålesund, seen from the north of Hareidlandet. The island on the right is the puffin colony of Runde

along one corner of this beach and I headed for it, ramming the kayak on to the white sands where children played. The campsite did not have any cabins free, but said I could pitch my tent and use their simple kitchen and washrooms. I settled in and then looked at the weather forecast. On this occasion it was not to satisfy my curiosity, but was vital to my survival. I was now within striking distance of Stad, easily the most exposed section of coast since Kinnarodden and Nordkapp. It was not a long section, but it was certainly not a section to be trifled with, and even a couple of Hurtigruten ferries have very nearly come to grief here. I needed good weather to consider it, and good weather was promised the following day, until the evening, when a large low pressure was due to arrive and blow for a couple of days. It had to be tomorrow or much later. I went to bed excited, and with trepidation, but could not sleep due to the foreboding task ahead. However, before I even got to the Stad peninsula tomorrow, I would still have to paddle 40 kilometres.

Day 211. The south side of the puffin colony island of Runde, seen on the calm sunny morning as I paddled towards the Stad peninsula

As soon as I woke I checked the weather forecast. It was ambiguous with possible winds up to a force 6 in the evening. I still had a day's paddling before I got to the start of the Stad peninsula and the exposed section, so felt I had to go for it and hope luck swung my way. I was on the water and paddling out of the breakwaters enclosing the sheltered beach by 0900. As I emerged, the Hurtigruten ferry went past, heading north. Across the fjord to the west were the Sørøyane, with the green island of Runde and its bird colonies basking in the sun, on an otherwise overcast morning. I veered slightly south past the small rocky Vattøya, in the middle of this fjord, and on to rural Torvika which lay in a shallow bay on the east side of Leinøya, one of the largest and most populous of the Sørøyane. Across the fjord back on Hareidlandet, the island I had just paddled from, I could look into a deep bay full of industry. It seemed very incongruous that there should be this industry in such a remote location. It was the town of Ulsteinvik which had two important and innovative shipyards, building large cruise ships and specialist offshore vessels. The shipyards sustained the town's 6000 inhabitants. I paddled past farms in Torvika and then round a gentle headland on the east side of Leinøya until I reached the south end. Here there was a series of bridges and causeways across a string of islets in the sound, which connected the Sørøyane to the larger neighbouring island of Gurksøya, which was in turn connected to the mainland with a tunnel. The ambitious plans of the Norwegian Government to try and create a road link to outlying island communities was epitomized here. To drive to the outpost island of Runde one would have to drive over six other islands and the connecting bridges, causeways and tunnels between them. The expense of creating these links was huge and could only be borne by a major exporter of oil and gas. The principle was to keep these communities viable and to arrest the depopulation of these wonderful and ancient villages and hamlets. I paddled under the bridge and then started heading west through Røyrasund with a scattering of wooded islets. Unfortunately, there was also some industry on each side of the sound as it opened up into the wider Herøyfjord, with a quarry to the north and a large rusting factory at Moltustranda to the south. However, their intrusion was short lived, and in the vastness of this otherwise pristine coastline the scars they left were small. As soon as I rounded the north-west corner of Gurksøya they were long forgotten, as I noticed a gentle swell coming in from the Atlantic. It was only about a metre high and the crests some 50 metres apart. From a higher boat it would have been indiscernible, but from my low position I could see it.

I quickly crossed Sandsfjord to reach the island of Sandsøya, a beautiful island with a few sandy beaches around it. On the south side of the island was a fine Lutheran church, above a beach as white as the church itself. After cruising along the south coast of Sandsøya it was a short paddle over the still fjord with its gentle swell to the islet-studded sound between the large island of Kvamsøya and the smaller Riste island. Kvamsøya had some very nice sandy beaches along its north shore, with quaint old homesteads surrounding each beach. Any of them would have made an ideal campsite if the weather would not have allowed me to continue round Stad. To the north of the sound was Riste, a rugged steep island of grazed Celtic green slopes and a single house. I paused by the beaches of Kvamsøya and ate in the kayak as the easterly breeze calmly blew me, with my toes gently adjusting the rudder to guide me through the islets. As I ate, I passed a dozen seals, the most I had seen gathered on this entire trip so far. There were also many gulls and shags congregating. Most of this year's gull chicks, mottled brown bodies with black beaks, were now able to fly. They could not catch their own food yet and still whined at their parents to regurgitate their catch of small fish to eat. By the time I had drifted through the skerries and finished lunch, I was psyched up to set off round Stad. The first challenge was to cross Vanylvsgap, an 8 kilometre wide stretch of open ocean to the east of the Stad peninsula and Stålet, the first of its four main headlands I had to paddle round.

Stad peninsula has a fearsome and well-deserved reputation. Perhaps the worst on the entire Norwegian coast, and the worst weather in Norway is often found here. Stad is a 30-kilometre peninsula, called Stadlandet,

Day 211. As I rounded the south shore of Sandsøya I got my first glimpse of Stad, between the islands of Kvamsøya and Riste

which sticks out into the Atlantic Ocean. The top of this peninsula is essentially a 500-metre high plateau which drops steeply down to the sea on all sides, except for a few bays. There are no protective islets around this headland and the ocean is about 50 metres deep just off its surf-washed rocks. But there are a few skerries, which rise up quickly out of the depths around its perimeter, namely Kvitnesfluene, Bukketjuvane, Skjerbåane, Gnullane and it is these which make the Atlantic swells rear up in huge crashing waves. Bukketjuvane is perhaps the most fearsome, and in severe storms the waves can rear up to 30 metres on these skerries. The ghosts of many sailors lie around its frothing fringe and even in 2003 the massive Hurtigruten ferry MS *Midnatsol* with all her crew and passengers, was just minutes from joining them. As I paddled past the first of these, Kvitnesfluene, which lay to the east of Stålet, the sea was barely ruffled as the metre swell passed over them. I was perhaps lulled into a false sense of ease as I paddled to the north of them and reached this first headland. The height of the swell was now perhaps a metre and a half and there was a constant roar as it crashed on to the rocks at the foot of the cliff, swept up them and then poured back into the ocean.

Just after Stålet, on the tip of Stadlandet, was a deep bay where two small hamlets called Årvika and Honningsvåg clung on to some flatter land above the ocean. Before the track, and then the small road, was built to these remote hamlets, the only access would have been by sea. The inhabitants would very much have been at the mercy of the ocean, which could have imprisoned them in their sheltered cove for weeks on end, and not allowed them to access the rich fishing grounds on their doorstep. I could look into the cove, and squeezed between rugged grey rocky buttresses and crags were the green fields of Årvika. I could not see the other hamlet which was tucked away deep in the cove behind some breakwaters. Beyond this bay was the next headland, perhaps the main one, called Kjerringa, which translates as 'The Old Hag', perhaps with regard to its craggy, fissured features which rose nearly 500 metres straight out of the Atlantic Ocean. Kjerringa is at the very tip of Stad and the most northerly of the three peninsulas on the west side. Had I looked at the map with less rose-tinted glasses, I would have realized as I paddled towards Kjerringa that I was still in the lee of today's weather and swell. As I approached Kjerringa the south-westerly swell started to build, and build quickly!

Day 211. Approaching the main headland of Kjerringa having already passed Stålet headland and the deep cove with Honningsvåg hamlet

This swell was not local, but was travelling across the Atlantic Ocean from a low pressure centre, where the gale or even storm winds some thousands of kilometres away had generated them. They had travelled at about 20 kilometres per hour pretty much unimpeded from this stormy origin. When I got to the tip of Kjerringa this swell was now a good four metres high, but the crests were 100 metres apart. I climbed for five seconds and then fell back into the trough for five seconds. There was nothing too anxious about this. However, when this swell was approaching the rocky ramparts at the base of the steep slopes, it was flowing into shallower water and this caused the base of the wave to slow down while the top still had momentum. The result was the swell suddenly built to five metre waves which then crashed on to the rocks with great violence and plumes of spray. Then this same wave crashed back into the sea and started rebounding in the direction it came. When the rebounding wave hit the next incoming wave the crest would suddenly leap into the air in a white claw of foam. Of course it is never as

Day 211. Delighted at having paddled round the main headland of Kjerringa, but not yet realizing there is still a long way to go

simple as this and the waves rebound at different angles causing the whole sea to leap wildly, with these white claws developing everywhere. This is called clapotis. I could avoid the worst of this clapotis by keeping far out, and went round Kjerringa a good half kilometre from the base of the cliffs. Here the swell was largely unaffected by the rebounds and was relatively gentle, but I was anxious in case the weather or the sea state deteriorated, as I did not relish challenging conditions in this exposed location. Some 2 kilometres to my west I could see the swell crashing over the Bukketjuvane skerries, the most feared of the hazards round Stad. Even today in this relatively mellow sea they looked like a place to stay well away from, and I could see the occasional explosion of spray as swell crashed on to them. I shuddered to think what they would be like in storms with 30-metre waves rearing up on to them. Many ships have been smashed on them with the loss of their entire crew. Indeed, the seas off Stad are so feared that the Norwegian Government is seriously considering building a 3 kilometre ship tunnel, 23 metres wide and 45 metres high, under the 400-metre high ridge which is the narrow isthmus of the Stad peninsula. This tunnel would allow ships and the Hurtigruten ferry to avoid the potentially dangerous conditions round the exposed Atlantic coastline of Stad.

I paddled for a couple more kilometres round the craggy headland with the sound of pounding surf a continual roar until a bay appeared. This was Ervika bay where there was a large sandy beach at the end of the cove. Beyond the beach were green fields and farms, and I could even see the hamlet's chapel. In an emergency I could have come ashore here but it would not have been elegant in today's swell. The waves were probably big enough to pitch-pole or loop the kayak on its end and I might have been pulled from the cockpit or had trouble holding on to my paddle in the fury of the surf. If I could not roll in the mayhem I would eventually have been washed ashore with my pride and confidence dented. Luckily it was not an emergency and I

Day 211. Looking back to Kjerringa headland at the tip of Stad, with the wind starting to increase to a force 4

was still hoping to get round the remaining two headlands before the forecast wind arrived. I cut across the mouth of Ervika bay to the next headland called Hovden. A kilometre out to sea was another pillar of shoals, Vossa, which rose up from the 50-metre deep sea bed to top out just below the surface. Most of the swells passed over them as they slumbered, but occasionally they awoke when a big set of swells passed over them, and they broke in a loud roar of exploding surf. I was again anxious not to approach too close in case there were other hibernating surprises in the vicinity. On the far side of Ervika was an islet called Buholmen which had a beacon on it. I aimed for it and when I reached the south side of this bay saw there was a large breaking swell on the outside of Buholmen which I would have to detour at least

Day 211. Looking back at Buholmen (right) and Kobbeholmen near the cliff base where there was a narrow slot to run to avoid a longer detour

Day 211. Looking into Hoddevika bay from hear Hovden headland with Furestaven and the lower Furenes headlands on the right

a kilometre offshore to avoid. On the inside of Buholmen, and the smaller Kobbeholmen, there looked to be a narrow disturbed channel which was about 50 metres long and seemed calm enough to consider. I waited and watched this slot-like channel for a couple of minutes and it seemed to be quiet, so I started to set off down it. No sooner had I made a couple of strokes when a three metre-wave suddenly reared up at the far end and surged up much of the channel. I back paddled and sat watching the channel for another couple of minutes, feeling rather unsettled. The wave did not reappear, so rather than taking the sensible option and paddling out for the kilometre detour round the outside of Buholmen, I decided to go for it. When the next set of bigger swells had passed, I dug deep and sprinted the 50 metres through the slot. My heart was in my mouth as the kayak sliced through the foam and emerged some 15 seconds later on the far side. I kept paddling furiously for another 100 metres until I felt I was well clear of any danger. Three headlands down and one to go.

There were now 3 kilometres of very spectacular coastline to paddle down before the next bay at Hoddevika. Huge bulbous buttresses of rock thrust out of the plateau high above and plunged into the ocean. All along the bottom of these cliffs the surf was pounding the rocks and surging up the steep slabs on the lower ramparts. Occasionally there was a sea cave, which was very unusual so far on this trip. It either shows the land here has not risen so much since the ice melted some 10,000 years ago, or that Stad often protruded from the ice sheet which covered the rest of Scandinavia. Between the massive rock buttresses were smooth green slopes and shelves. So green were some of these, one could be forgiven for assuming you were on the west coast of Scotland or Ireland. It was only the much larger scale of the landscape which would make one doubt. This particular section was like a giant version of one of my favourite paddling areas; namely, the west coast of the Isle of Skye. This Celtic coastline continued until I reached another large open bay, Hoddevika. It had a large sandy beach across its far end and a hamlet beyond that, but like Ervika, landing here would have just been in a dire emergency and I was sure the breaking waves would be big enough to cartwheel the kayak end over end. This is a well-known surfer's beach, and not the place to land a quarter of a ton of kayak and contents.

The wind was now a force 5 from the south-east. It blasted out of Hoddevika bay and was starting to slow me up considerably. As the wind was coming from the land it did not create any significant waves over and above the ever present swell. It did mean I had a hard pull across the mouth of the bay to reach the relative shelter of the final headland. This headland started with a huge buttress called Furestaven which was a 300-metre high cliff of strata folded in a magnificent arc. Just beyond it was Furenes, the final headland of Stad, and beyond which I perceived was safety and sanctuary. But as I approached Furenes I noticed more shallows about a kilometre off shore. These were called Gamla and Gnullane and I later found out they were also responsible for many shipwrecks. Dangerous currents often drove hapless ships and boats towards them where the large ocean swells would then rear up and toss them on to the skerries where they would be dashed. To my extreme consternation I noticed that the kilometre between these two renowned monsters and the headland were numerous other skerries and shoals where smaller waves were breaking. This was the area I had to paddle through. As the wind was now a force 6, I was becoming increasingly concerned. I certainly did not want to

Day 211. The 300-metre high cliffs along the coast to the north of Hoddevika bay were impressive and harboured a few surf-filled caves

Day 211. In the lee at Furestaven looking north across the open Hoddevika bay to the rugged coastline up to Hovden headland

paddle outside the frothing monsters as, if the wind increased to a force 8, I might get blown out to sea.

I spent a long time observing the way the larger sets behaved when they passed over these smaller shoals nearer the coast and where they broke. After some 10 minutes treading water, against the increasing wind, I had worked out a route and marked my reference points. With some anxiety I set off and weaved through the skerries. A large set of swells emerged from the ocean when I was half way through, but luckily I was in the right position and away from the white claws which reared up above the shoals, just some 50 metres beside me. Paddling powerfully and anxiously I reached the far side of the danger area and rounded the point. Even when I was well beyond, I kept looking back over my shoulder to see if anything sinister was going to come up silently behind me. At last I had rounded the final headland and now had to find somewhere to land. I had been paddling hard for the last few hours against the wind, and my anxiety had kept my tiredness at bay. Now I was round the final headland my sinews started to whine, but it was a long fight up the coast against the force 6 wind. The waves were choppy and I was constantly getting facefuls of spray. The light was starting to fade as I pulled myself past the empty hamlet of Ytre Fure with two well-kept houses high above the rocks. There was no place to land here, despite the fact the shoals I had just paddled through off the final headland had killed the swell. Looking at my GPS map I could see there was a kind of breakwater some 2 kilometres further east along the coast at a place called Indre Fure. I put all my hopes for a campsite and some respite from the wind and spray into its promise. As I strained up the rocky coast I saw nowhere to land, and when I approached the breakwater was fearful the rocky, rugged coast would continue.

I have occasionally had surprises when figuring out places to stay from the map. Nothing quite matched Indre Fure. Here, on the other side of this small breakwater, was a beautiful white beach. Above the beach was a cluster of very nice buildings and houses in a green landscape. The houses were all surrounded with masses of plants and flowers, especially roses, which were all in full bloom. It was an exceptionally idyllic chocolate-box sight. It was as if I had walked through a wardrobe door into a different world. I landed the kayak on the beach and found a nice camp spot just above it. There was no one around so I put my tent up near a boat shed in the last light of the day. Just as I was about to escape the drizzle and crawl into the tent I noticed a lady appear from the nicest house and go down to the beach. I went over to explain. She had

Day 211. The delightful harbour at Indre Fure was a great surprise and the idyllic hamlet was a rare 'Klyngetun' where the houses were close

seen me arrive and was obviously curious. She and her husband were one of three families who lived here. Like many small places in Norway they had the same surname as the hamlet. They were Kjell and Marit Fure. I chatted with her for 10 minutes until the drizzle and wind drove her back to their house again. I went to my tent, peeled my drysuit off and crawled in with the rain now lashing the tent. I was too tired to cook even a simple supper of mashed potato and ham. I lay there for a few minutes, cosy in my bag, listening to the near gale and heavy rain, very content I had managed Stad and 70 kilometres today. It was not as easy as Nordkapp, but much easier than the Slettnes or Kinnarodden headlands on the Nordkinn peninsula, the first of which was quite fearful.

SECTION 30. The North West – Trondheim to Stad
10 days. 341 kilometres. 79 hours. 0m ascent. 0m descent.

THE KAYAK: SECTION 31. NORTH VESTLANDET – STAD TO BERGEN

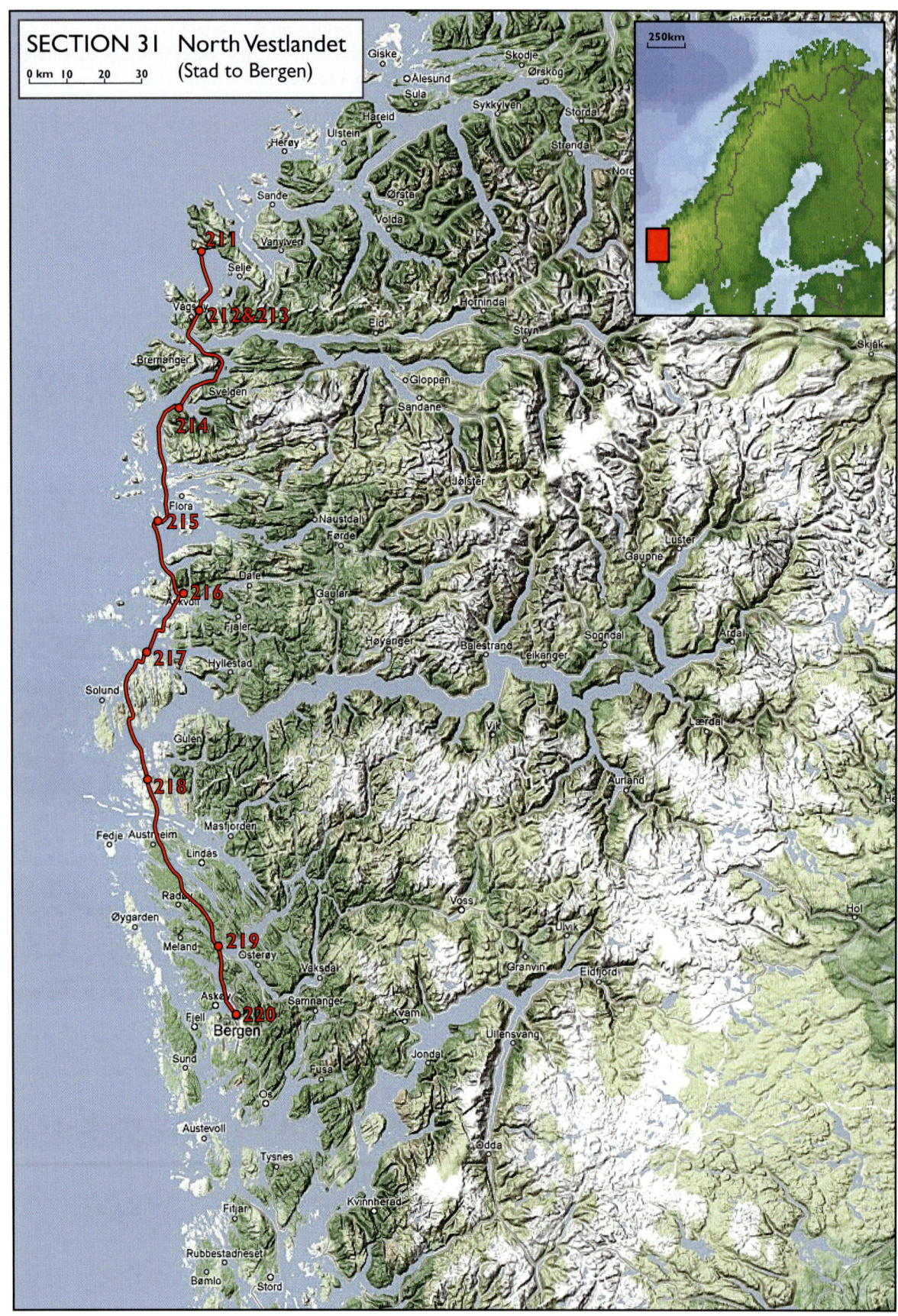

THE KAYAK: SECTION 31. NORTH VESTLANDET – STAD TO BERGEN

I was tired when I woke and my shoulders ached. The rain was still pelting on to the taut tent. I just could not muster the energy to get up and rolled over for a lie-in, feeling I had earned one. When I finally considered getting up it was mid morning and the rain was still lashing the tent. I looked at the forecast and it warned me there would be a lot of rain today 'Sør fra Stad' or 'South of Stad', which is where I was. Stad is often a significant weather system divide and it is frequently used on the national forecast. The forecast also said the wind would remain low until mid afternoon, when it would get up to a force 5. From my sleeping bag I managed to arrange some accommodation at Ulvesund fyr lighthouse. It was almost impossible to have a phone conversation with the rain hammering on the tent. After what I had seen at the Helnes and Tranøy lighthouses I was a bit sceptical about what Ulvesund might offer, but I was keen to find somewhere dry, with this wet forecast. I still had Sildegapet to cross, which was essentially 10 kilometres of open ocean, plus some more sheltered paddling to reach the lighthouse. I managed to pack everything into drybags and get into most of my drysuit before getting out of the tent. With the drysuit on and everything in bags, it did not matter about the rain any more. I carted everything down to the waterline and took down the tent. Just then a small dinghy appeared. Out of the dinghy stepped Kjell Fure, the husband of Marit, to whom I had spoken last night. Kjell was an old sea dog and knew the area intimately. I later read he was involved in a few rescues of helpless fishermen along this coast. He showed me inside his boathouse or 'naust'. It was like a museum with old boats hanging from the roof, huge cognac barrels which had drifted ashore and were used to salt fish. Fishing nets, longlines and glass buoys hung from rafters, and there was a large stack of Walkers wooden fish boxes which had been collected from the shore through the decades. I told him the scenery here reminded me of Scotland and he said everybody says that. He explained Indre Fure was a unique hamlet in that it was a 'Klyngetun'. Usually houses in Norway are spread out, but here the five or six houses and the barns were all clustered together. This is because it was the only safe place to live, as there was a danger from avalanche and falling stones elsewhere.

I did not set off until well after midday. By now the wind was up to a force 3 with the odd force 4 gust. All morning I was rather too blasé and over confident in light of what I had paddled round yesterday, and as I pulled out beyond the breakwater the reality hit. It was now a force 4 and the rain was so heavy it was impossible to see more than a kilometre. I took a bearing and set off. After a kilometre I seriously considered turning back as the swell was a good three metres and many of the tops were breaking. I still had another hour and a half of open ocean to go before I reached relative shelter. However, sitting bolt upright and paddling strongly, I was making good time. The big waves, which were coming from the side, frequently broke, but the white caps were never more than half a metre and the stable boat and odd support brace could easily handle them. Being broadside to the waves I could see the bigger ones coming, but I was nervous the wind might increase to a force 5.

Suddenly the sea in front of me was filled with large breaking waves, many well over two metres with a large frothing white cap on top of a steep green pyramid. I could not hope to remain upright in it. I could not understand what was happening, and thought it was a strong local tidal current or some shoals. I soon realized they must have been shoals, which I found very surprising in the middle of this deep ocean. I later found out there were indeed shoals, called Dragefalla, which rose in a pillar from the seabed and topped out just a few metres below the surface. I could not go through, so decided to veer east and go downwind and round this turbulent area. I was not comfortable going downwind for those few hundred metres, as I could not see the waves coming up behind me. I was happier when I returned to my southern course again, so I could keep an eye on the sea. By now I had abandoned my original plan to cross directly over to Skongsnes fyr lighthouse and decided to head towards Silda island and then head down its east shore in the lee, as I was getting anxious about the sea state. After an hour the dark shape of this small island started to emerge from the grey rain and I felt a sense of relief. Ten minutes later I was keeping a wide berth as I went round the surf-pounded chaotic fringe

Day 212. Paddling towards the lee of Silda island after a hard paddle across the wild 10 kilometres of the open Sildegapet

367

along its northern shore. Then a few minutes later everything suddenly calmed down and I could start to see the rings where the heavy raindrops were smacking into the water. It had been a couple of wild hours and had I known it was going to be these conditions I would have stayed put, cooped up in my damp tent at Indre Fure.

Despite the rain, Silda looked a nice place. It was a small island about 2 kilometres long with a good harbour on the sheltered eastern side. The harbour entrance was guarded by a topless mermaid, who looked out over the marina where many expensive leisure boats were moored up. There was also a sign for a café and a pub, but I was not sure if there was any accommodation here or not. If fact, I did not see a soul as I paddled down past some cabins, detoured into the harbour and continued down past more cabins and a couple of small holdings. There were people here, as I could smell wood smoke but the weather was keeping everybody inside. As I passed the jetty I saw a large pile of aquaculture equipment. It was for rearing the shellfish *Pecten maximus*, better known as king scallops or kamskjell. I recognized the plastic trays, small buoys, blue polypropylene ropes, mesh netting and other equipment immediately, as I once tried to farm them myself on the Isle of Skye for a couple of years, until I realized the hopeless economics of it. I would have been eager to chat with the farmer about his experiences so far, but there was no-one to be seen. As I left the island a great skua came to circle round me, eyeing me up. These birds are fearless brutes and prey on smaller sea birds and disgorged fish which they force gulls, and even gannets, to regurgitate.

Day 213. Looking from the window of Ulvesund fyr lighthouse to the modern light beacon and then across Sildegapet to Furenes on Stad

It was only 2 kilometres across the bay to Ulvesund fyr lighthouse. I could see it clearly. But there was a wind coming up the Ulvesund sound which must have been approaching a force 8. I was barely moving and the 2 kilometres took an hour. I was being covered in salt spray the whole time and my eyes were smarting, but the rain was so heavy they were also getting rinsed. It was late afternoon when I finally reached the lighthouse jetty. There was a small ruined shed where I stored my kayak and then with all the drybags threaded through each arm I plodded up the path to the lighthouse keeper's cottage. In massive contrast to the other lighthouses I had been to, this one was wonderful. It was still owned by the lighthouse board but they leased the building to a calm, thoughtful, artistic lady called Sølvi. She had persuaded the lighthouse board to let her restore the lighthouse keeper's cottage, which was abandoned and falling into disrepair, as the beacon was now automated. They tentatively agreed, and Sølvi and a team of friends and helpers started work. Five years later she had converted the empty shell into a homely café and guest house, breathed life back into the cottage and rescued the fertile berry garden from the encroaching jungle. The interior was very nicely decorated and the whole place had a warm, relaxed, gentle vibe to it. There were a few other guests staying, who were enjoying berry cordials from the garden bushes, home-made cakes and fruit teas. Sølvi gave me a large room, almost a suite, in the basement. The whole place was a lovely surprise, and as soon as I settled in and unwound, I decided I could easily spend an extra day here writing and browsing in the small library. That evening, the five other guests, two of the staff and I sat in the dining room and had a delicate meal of poached cod and fresh vegetables. There were photos and paintings on the walls which Sølvi and previous guests had done. It was a light-hearted evening, but I was still quite tired, so went down to bed early.

I was a bit disorientated when I woke in the morning. There was not the sound of rain pelting on the tent or the rustle of the unused storm flaps. Then it dawned on me, I was in a wonderful comfortable bed with cotton sheets. With delight I also realized I did not need to get up and paddle, as I had given myself a day off as a reward for paddling round Stad. The breakfast of freshly-made bread and many types of home-made jams soon beckoned, and I went up to join the others. It was a social affair, with me chatting to the other guests and those who worked here. I then spent much of the morning and afternoon writing and gleaning some local information from the small library here. I also passed some time in my room downstairs where it was very quiet and tranquil.

Once I had finished I moved upstairs again to the living room where there were a few people coming and going and the day's guests were gathering and getting acquainted with each other. There were about 10 guests today and we all sat down to eat at the same table. Dinner was a fish stew. If you had replaced the cod for smoked haddock it would have been the same as Cullen Skink, a traditional Scottish fish soup. It was a very chatty warm evening with lots of banter between the guests. After supper Sølvi gave all the guests a short presentation on the history of the lighthouse, since it was built in 1870, through to 1985 when the last lighthouse keeper left and the light became automatic. She knew the place well as she was local, having grown up at Osmundsvåg just up the lane. As a child she used to visit the lighthouse keeper's family frequently and remembered it as a vibrant home. When the lighthouse was automated and the keeper's family left, it did not take long for the garden to become overgrown, the paint to peel and the hinges to rust. It felt like she had a nostalgic sense of duty to restore it in keeping with her happy childhood memories, as well as running a successful business to finance the upkeep and pay rent to the lighthouse board. It looked like she was managing both admirably.

Day 214. The island town of Måløy was a busy fishing port and shipping harbour which lay beside the south end of Ulvesund sound

Breakfast was not served until 0900. When it arrived it was worth waiting for. In addition to all the fresh bread and home-made jams, there was also smoked salmon and scrambled egg. I sat with the other guests and we continued the banter where we left off last night. I was delaying my start, but now that Stad was behind me I felt I could relax a bit. It was midday by the time I said my goodbyes to the remaining guests and thanked the staff at Ulvesund fyr lighthouse for their friendly, easy-going hospitality. I set off and headed down the glassy waters of Ulvesund sound with the mainland on my east and the hilly island of Måløy on my west. After just half an hour I reached the large village of Raudeberg. There was a surprisingly large shipyard here with about eight trawlers tied up alongside a quay and another two trawlers in a massive shed. I am always amazed to find such industry in such remote locations and wondered if they are economically viable or whether they are subsidized by the wealthy government. Another half hour down the sound I came to the town of Måløy, which must have had a population of around 5000. Above the wharfs, warehouses and offices along the shore front was a deep crescent of mostly white houses. They were arranged on the lower slopes of the green surrounding hills, which were covered in copses of planted spruce and wild birch trees. Some of the older shipping wharfs were starting to fall into disrepair, but there were also some vibrant areas with some expensive looking new apartments and hotels. Fishing seemed to be the main industry, with all its spin offs, like netting and rope manufacturers. A few shipping lines had wharfs and offices here, like Green Reefers and Norlines, whose ships I had passed occasionally on the trip so far.

Just beyond Måløy town was a graceful bridge over a narrow part of Ulvesund sound which connected the town and island to the mainland. Here the tide swirled in confusing gentle currents as I entered Nordfjord, one of the giants of the Norwegian fjords. Nordfjord is a very long narrow fjord which goes from the coast here and follows a deep slot for some 125 kilometres deep into the heart of Norway. At its head are 2000-metre mountains, many glaciers and the largest ice-cap in Europe. I had to cross this relatively sheltered mouth to the large craggy islands along its southern side. A few tens of thousands of years ago these islands would once have been buried deep in the glacier which flowed over them. Had the ice ages been much longer they

Day 214. Paddling across the mouth of Nordfjord towards the island of Rugsundøya and the high mountain buttress of Hornelen, 860m

would have been worn down by the massive glacier which would then have carried their fragments far out into the Norwegian Sea, where the melting ice would have deposited them. As I paddled across this finger of water the classic fjord views and landscapes unfolded. There were very high steep mountains on each side of the fjord. The lower reaches of the mountains were covered in birch forests and the tree roots must have penetrated every crevice on the rock to find some footing. Higher up the mountains was bare grey rock, over which wispy mare's tails of small waterfalls plummeted as they emerged from the boulder fields and snow packs of the high craggy peaks.

This became even more so when I reached Rugsundøya island. On the south side of the fjord was a mountain called Hornelen, which rose almost vertically from the fjord for 860 metres in one ice-scrapped precipice of bare, light grey rock. I paddled along the foot of the cliffs, keeping far enough out to avoid any pebble or stone which might dislodge from its heights. The current was heading west, giving me an extra couple of kilometres an hour as I headed towards the most impressive of the buttresses which descended straight into the fjord. I was not sure if the tide was rising or falling, as it was gently raining and the tell-tale signs on a dry shore were disguised by the damp. The fact that the water was flowing west was no indication, as there would be so many local quirks to the currents. Hornelen, the lofty precipitous peak I was paddling under, was on a large island called Bremangerland. This convoluted island was separated from the mainland by Nordfjord and a branch of it just round the corner which led to the open sea. This wide branch was called Frøysjøen and when I reached it I headed down it, out of Nordfjord, and back to the open sea again. Frøysjøen soon opened up into one of the most barren landscapes of the trip. It had not been long since the ice sheets and glaciers withdrew from here and virtually no soil or vegetation had accumulated since it retreated. The whole landscape was grey ice-scoured rock, except for a few estuaries where tumbling rivers carried some silt down.

Day 214. The isolated roadless farm at Vingelva beside which is one of the largest Stone Age rock art collections or Helleristninger in Norway

One of these estuaries was Vingelva just 2 kilometres across Frøysjøen sound. Here, hemmed in by the fjord, was a green oasis in the barren grey landscape, where there were two isolated farms with no road access at all. Both farms were surely just summer houses now and it would probably have been a few decades since the last hay was cut here. Although these farms were now isolated, they would not have been any more so than most of the others on the Norwegian coast some 100 years ago, when there were no roads at all and the sheltered sea was the highway. There were some very isolated farms 250 to 100 years ago, some on inaccessible mountain shelves where the children were tethered to stop them falling off. This was when the glaciers grew in the 'little ice age' in the mid 18th Century, swallowing farms, while at the same time Norway's population grew. People were forced to go to the most inhospitable and remote places to clear the land and try and sustain themselves against all odds. The farms across the sound at Vingelva were not in that category at all. Remarkably, beside the farms, in a small side fjord, is one of the largest collections of rock carvings, or 'Helleristninger' in Norway, with about 1500 figures. They were made by Stone Age hunter gatherers some 4000 to 6000 years ago and depict deer, humans and some abstracts. Unfortunately, I could not go over the fjord to see them, as it would have been a few hour's detour.

I paddled down the deep grey sound to the island of Hennøya. There was a hamlet of some five farms here, which like Vingelva just up the coast, were hemmed in by fjord and mountain and inaccessible by land. There was an isolated kilometre of road along the shore connecting the farms but leading nowhere else. I saw an old tractor driving along it which must have been brought over by boat a decade or two ago. All the fields had high grass, ungrazed and uncut, so I suspect that all the farms here are now just used as leisure houses in the summer, by the descendants of the original farmers who lived and raised families here. It was an isolated but idyllic spot. It was too early to stop, so I decided to continue south west down Frøysjøen and hopefully cross a convoluted

Day 214. Looking back up Frøysjøen from the quiet beach at the isolated hamlet of Hennøya with its five dormant farms

side fjord with many arms called Gulen. It did not take long to paddle down the empty rocky coast, as I had a slight back wind. I saw nowhere to camp along this uninviting shore so crossed the mouth of Gulen when I got to it. It was only a few of kilometres across, but the wind rapidly veered round and increased, so I was now paddling into a force 4 and progress was slow. When I reached the far side at Gulestøa, I saw a rare campsite, but it was beside a farm. Fearful about paddling on into the strong wind, and worried there might be no further campsites for a while I decided to ask if I could camp, mindful about encroaching on their privacy.

Johanna Gulestø opened the door before I reached her house. I asked her if I could camp and she said of course I could. But she said she also had a cabin which her three grown-up sons used when they visited. She insisted I use it rather than camp and took me down to it. It was a gorgeous, small, red, chocolate-box wooden cabin with kitchen, shower and a ready-made bed. It was absolutely perfect. Johanna put the heating on and showed me the bed. She said the sheets had only been used once, and that was last week by a couple of kayakers, as it happened. I asked her about them and it turned out it was the Swedish girls, Evelynn and Klara. She said they turned up looking to camp and looking like drowned rats and she gave them the cabin for the night. Once Johanna had made me comfortable and had gone back to her house, I texted them to share the coincidence. They replied, saying Johanna was an 'Angel without wings', and I would have to agree. The cabin was old and traditional. Inside were pictures of the Gulestø family and farm going back at least 100 years. It is not surprising Norwegians are so patriotic when they have such a sense of belonging to a place. After a wonderful shower, I cooked supper in the warm kitchen, and wrote in the cosy living room while the heavy rain poured down outside. As I curled up under the soft feather duvet on cotton sheets I was euphoric with comfort. God bless Johanna Gulestø.

Day 214. The lovely cabin at Gulestøa farm which Johanna Gulestø insisted I spend the wet night in, rather than camp

I slept well in the comfortable bed and did not get up until 0800. The wind was a south-westerly force 3 against me, as was the tide. I was in no hurry, as both were destined to change in my favour later. I went up to Johanna's house and thanked her for the use of the comfortable, dry, quaint cabin, which incidentally was once the homestead's home. I eventually set off mid-morning. The going was very slow for the first two hours as I slowly pulled my way round the peninsula. If I stopped to take a photo I was suddenly 50 metres back to where I had come from, as the tide and wind conspired against me. My average speed was just 3 kilometres per hour. However, apart from the diminishing wind, the weather was perfect with blue skies, and under them a rich seascape of islands was unfolding round the headland on a glittering sea of sunny wavelets. The shoreline was initially rock and grass with a few birch trees, but as I paddled past Pollen bay pines became more and more frequent until the whole shoreline was a thick green pine forest basking in the sun. As I was making slow progress I stopped early for lunch and a stretch at Husefest. There was a small hamlet here beside a shallow inlet. The fields were not cut, and the tall grass was rippling in the wind, but the houses and boat sheds were well maintained. The inlet was full of the very yellow seaweed which contrasted well with the emerald green pine forest.

As I continued south the wind almost ceased. Out to the west was the island of Hovden with its famed bird colony, the most southern on the Norwegian coast. To the south of Hovden were numerous other islands

Day 215. Some of the islands off the coast by Florø with the Stabben fyr lighthouse marking the dangers in the shipping lane on the left

stretching all the way down to the distinctive Alden, with its horse-shaped mountain, Norske hesten, dominating the far horizon. I felt like I was back in Helgelandskyst. I rounded a small headland, and suddenly there was another kayaker. He was Ole Fredriksen, a powerful looking man with arms the size of most people's thighs. We stopped and chatted. He was also on a long trip. He had come from Bergen and was heading up to Lofoten for a month's jaunt. By coincidence, he did the same job on the oilrigs as I had done for a decade, which was Rope Access, or 'Tilkomstteknikk' as he called it. It basically involves a lot of abseiling and climbing up ropes to reach inaccessible work places, where one then has to do a task. We chatted for a good half hour and swapped mobile numbers to give each other tips. He suggested Askrova island as a possible destination for me, as it had plenty of campsites and also some cultural heritage. It was 20 kilometres or four hours away, so that suited me perfectly. The wooded coast then ended at the hamlet of Årebrot which was hidden in the thick pines. After Årebrot I had a small fjord to cross to reach the large town of Florø, which had a population of around 10,000. The fjord was only 3 kilometres wide but there was a bit of boat traffic, both small and large, which meant I had to be on my guard. As it happens I crossed without any boats or ships coming near me. I had no intention of stopping at Florø and skirted round its western side, off the end of the peninsula it sat on. It was a great location on the edge of the sea, surrounded by many small islands, and it looked quite pleasant from the shore with just a few industrial eyesores. There was a huge shipbuilding shed at the east end of town and another factory on the tip of the peninsula in the west. The islands and seascape more than made up for this industry. I left Florø through the maze of islands off the south of the peninsula and then paddled across 3 kilometres to a small cluster of islets called Oddane. I managed to find a sheltered rocky slab to land on and stretch my legs. Oddane were flat and covered in heather and all the islets were ringed with seaweed. Had there been beaches it would have been Helgelandskysten again.

Day 215. Looking towards the pleasant town of Florø on the end of a peninsula among a coastline studded with islets

Day 215. I landed on one of the Oddane islets in the warm afternoon and enjoyed a view out to the steep Reksta and Kinn islands to the west

From here it was another 3 kilometres to the east shore of the beautiful and lush Askrova island. The island was covered in pine forests, especially at the south end where I was hoping to camp. Not seeing anywhere, I paddled on to the sound between Askrova and Tansøya. The two islands were connected by an old narrow wooden cantilever bridge, which could be raised to let sailing boats past. I paddled under the bridge into a charming tranquil basin, surrounded by old fish wharfs and boathouses, a country shop, and many older houses in green fields surrounded by the forest. There were sheep grazing in many of the fields. I could not see a campsite around the edge of this basin, as many of the houses of the hamlet were near the sheltered shoreline, but nearby on Tansøya was a beach with a flat grazed

Day 215. A couple of old fish wharfs on Tansøya just to the south of the small cantilever bridge over to the neighbouring Askrova island

green field. I paddled over to this perfect spot and put the damp tent up to dry in the evening sun. I wrote outside, gazing across the basin until the light started to fade, and the lights of the hamlet started to reflect on the calm water.

I had been through the whole array of camping breakfasts, from porridge to biscuits. Lately, I had settled on a family pack of chilli nuts to start the day. As I wandered about the campsite eating them, a number of sheep who had been grazing in the nearby pine woods came over to investigate. They were hoping I had some salt or biscuits to feed them, but drew the line at chilli nuts, and after sniffing them, left them unlicked in the palm of my hand. This was an exceptionally nice camp spot, with a great view from the green field and pebble beach across the sunny bay to the south side of Askrova where the hamlet was. I set off mid morning and paddled through a narrow gap on the south side of the basin and into the open water of Stavfjord. I was lucky it was a calm sunny day, as Stavfjord was really the open sea. It was the outer mouth of the deep Førdefjord which cuts far inland for some 50 kilometres to its head at the town of Førde. I noticed there was a tide flowing into the fjord, filling it, and I had to ferry glide slightly as I crossed the 7 kilometres to the rocky headland on the south side of it. I was making for the hamlet of Holevika which turned out to be a sheltered green rural oasis on the rocky coast. About half way across the wind suddenly got up and it was soon a force 4. I had to stop and put a jacket on as I was getting soaked in the spray. The last 4 kilometres took well over an hour as I slowly pulled myself towards this hamlet.

Day 216. There were plenty of sheep on Tansøya who came bounding out of the forest when I started my breakfast of chilli nuts

As soon as I was round the tip of the peninsula I started to look for somewhere to land. There were a couple of islands just offshore and barely enough water to paddle the kayak over the very sheltered channels. These were basking in the sun and warm as they were out of the main winds. I landed the kayak in a seaweed-filled inlet and got out to stretch on the rock slabs of the foreshore and heather mounds above that. I took my jacket off again and I lingered on the heather while I had lunch. I could see the tide was dropping now, so could not explain why there was such a flow into Førdefjord, just an hour ago. There are so many local variations with the tides I find it best to ignore them rather than try and predict them. After the warmth of the sheltered lunch I was lulled into a believing the next fjord crossing would be calm, but the wind was back and I had to don the jacket to protect me from the spray again. Despite this it was sunny and I could really enjoy the beauty of Strongfjord with its steep forested sides and a green mantle along the shore where there were busy farms, with their red barns and white farmhouses. The forest here was so lush and thick that the trees which surrounded the glade each farm sat in was ready to envelop it again if the farmer turned his back on it for a few years. On the south side of this spectacular postcard-like fjord with its steep sides was the impressive slot of Granesund. It was a deep channel of water some 5 kilometres long which separated the island of Atløyna from the mainland. It seemed the wind and tide were against me as I slowly pulled my way down its steep wooded sides. When I relaxed, leaned back and paddled less vigorously I was down to about 3 kilometres per hour with the force 4 against me. This jolted me into action and I made better time, but I was soon slouching again. Eventually I got to the bottom of the sound where the small town of Askvoll was tucked away in a sheltered inlet. I needed to stop here and buy some supplies to reach Bergen, so I veered east into the inlet and the warming sun out of the wind. I paddled towards the first jetty, where there were a couple of people watching me coming in. I approached and asked

Day 216. Looking down Granesund with the mainland on the left behind which was Askvoll and the island of Atløyna on the right

them in Norwegian where the shop was. One of them answered in perfect Norwegian and after a few minutes suggested we switch to English, as he was Scottish. We chatted for a good half hour, with me in the boat and him on the jetty, before I landed at a small beach by the jetty in front of the apartment he was renting.

His name was Rich Lennox and he was originally from Scotland where he had worked as an outdoor instructor. He now lived in Bergen, where he stayed for two weeks, alternating it with a two-week stay in Askvoll where he worked. He invited me in to his apartment for a cup of tea. He had paddled much of Norway's coast, and I was as interested in picking his brains as he was about my trip. We chatted for a good hour and he said I could sleep on the balcony he had overlooking the small beach where my kayak was. I still needed to shop, so I took up his offer and got my gear from the boat. It was a glorious afternoon now, and Rich was keen to show me around Askvoll. We headed off down the main street to the centre of the small traditional town. The 150-year-old white wooden Lutheran church was the centrepiece and everything radiated from it. After stocking up at the shops and returning, Rich showed me over the ambulance boat he was on standby to skipper. There were two ambulance boats moored up, one as a spare. Each boat had two 800 horse power engines and could operate in anything but a hurricane, although Rich assured me they could also operate in this if needed, and could manage conditions which a helicopter could not hope to. The range of the boats was the many outlying islands in Askvoll kommune, especially the economically important island clusters of Værland and Buland, where there were large fish farms and some thriving tourism enterprises renting old fishermen's cottages. Some 500 people lived on these islands and Askvoll kommune authorities had to provide emergency medical cover for them, and these two ambulance boats and their skippers were the solution. It did not come cheaply at over five million kroner or half a million pounds per year, but this was a small price to pay to keep the thriving islands viable. Rich cooked supper while I wrote and then we chatted into the early hours. He knew the coast between here and Bergen, and beyond to the large islands of Bømlo and Stord, like the back of his hand and gave me a lot of good tips about the more scenic and interesting ways to go.

Day 216. The typical white Lutheran church in the middle of Askvoll was built in the mid 19th Century

I woke on the sunny balcony with the water lapping gently just a few feet below me, and the sun slowly cooking me in my sleeping bag. I was a bit drowsy after the late night, but Rich made a powerful coffee which soon electrified me. We chatted while I packed and then Rich helped me carry my bags to the kayak. I eventually launched around mid morning by which time the perfect blue skies had started to cloud over a bit and a breeze had arrived. I paddled out into the bay and looked back at Askvoll. It was really more of a large village than a small town. However, its ferry terminal was busy, with the express catamaran passenger ferry having recently arrived from Bergen, and then local ferries radiating out to the islands and smaller coastal villages from this hub. I paddled past a couple of small island nature reserves on the south side of the bay, which sheltered the waters at Askvoll and then entered Vilnesfjord. Vilnesfjord was really the outer portion of the 40-kilometre long Dalsfjord which cut a deep slot inland from Askvoll. I had to paddle across its mouth of reasonably sheltered water to the small hamlet of Eina on the south side 5 kilometres away. The tide was emptying from the fjord and there was a good current carrying me westwards, so it did not take long to reach this hamlet and the west end of its peninsula, despite the increasing wind. Off the end of the peninsula were a couple of medium-sized islands called

Day 217. Leaving Askvoll and looking back to the small town at the entrance to Dalsfjord

Lammetu and Lutelandet with some small islet-studded sounds and channels between them. It was a lost world between them and I enjoyed weaving through the islets, some of which were ice-scoured and bare, yet others were covered in pine and spruce. I saw an otter, a relatively rare beast so far on this trip, before I emerged out of the sheltered waters and into open Buefjord.

The obvious route for me was to the south down Krakhellesund, but Rich had advised against this as it could be a boring slog in a headwind, and it was also the shipping lane. He suggested I head out to the islands of Sula where there were masses of channels and islets to explore and much better nature. He was very knowledgeable so I was going to follow his advice. However, it meant crossing Buefjord, and looking across this exposed 5-kilometre sea was not a pleasant sight. Across on the other side, my destination of Sula was being consumed by dark, ominous clouds which were heading my way on the force 4 wind. However, it did not look any better down to Krakhellesund, although the crossing was slightly shorter. I could easily imagine the headwind in this narrow slot would have been too much today, and with Rich's advice ringing in my ear I set off into the white caps streaming from Sula. After a few kilometres the force 4 increased to a force 5 and then up to a 6. The sea was now covered in breaking white caps and the near metre waves were steep as they piled towards me. The kayak was slicing through some of the waves, but was generally rising up and slapping down into the next. Spray was everywhere and it was lifting off the white caps and forming streaks on the water. It was sometimes difficult to see with my eyes smarting with all the salt water going into them. My progress ground almost to a halt and I was just making 2 kilometres per hour. I could not build up any momentum as the oncoming waves just knocked me back to a halt again.

Day 217. Half way across Vilnesfjord was a small skerry which was marked by a large cairn, and beyond is the steep slot of Dalsfjord

Frequently, a wave would run up the deck and green water hit me in the chest. I had to keep the paddle blades quite low to avoid them taking on a will of their own in the wind. It took almost three hours to complete this otherwise simple crossing, and it was not until I was only a hundred metres from Leknessund that the waves and then the wind eased. I could now get a closer look at Sula and it looked very dramatic and stark. It was not an idyllic landscape of green fertile soils and fjord, but towering buttresses of bare grey rock over a dark fjord. It looked very Wagnerian.

Day 217. Looking from the shelter of Luteland island across Buefjord towards Sula, which was being consumed by dark clouds and wind

Wet with spray, with tired shoulders and stinging sinews, I reached the quiet hamlet of Leknessund with a huge sense of relief. It had been a hard fight across Buefjord and I was a bit shell-shocked. I relaxed in the kayak and slowly drifted past some of the seaweed-covered islets in the sheltered bay I was now thankfully in. About 20 herons took off when I paddled past one islet. They circled round with their ungainly flight and landed again once I had passed. Along the fringe of the bay there were a few modern houses and some traditional ones with old boat sheds lining the water. At the far end of the bay was a narrow channel, spanned by an old bridge connecting the two halves of the hamlet. I paddled under the bridge into another reasonably sheltered bay and parked the kayak on some seaweed-covered rock, so I could eat without drifting. As I ate, a sailing boat entered the bay and dropped anchor nearby. Her sails were well tucked up under the sail cover and she came in under motor. After my late lunch I set off again, paddling past the sailing boat, round the point and into Hersviksund, which I had intended to paddle up. It was hopeless, the wind was roaring up here lifting the spray and twisting plumes into the air. I could not hope to punch into it, and after half an hour I had only gone a kilometre at the most. There was nowhere to camp along the barren, rocky, ice-scoured shore so I decided to turn back. What had taken half an hour to gain was lost in five minutes, and with the wind at my back I was soon back into the sheltered bay with the sailing boat. I paddled past the sailing boat and chatted briefly with them. They said they measured the wind at 21 metres per second, which is a force 9, but I don't think it was as strong as that. I found a place to camp near the bridge in Leknessund, where I had eaten an hour previously, and had my tent up by late afternoon, just as the heavy rain arrived. I crawled in, lay down in my bag and fell asleep at once. I woke mid-evening with the wind and rain pelting the tent. I managed to write and cook a simple supper before total darkness fell much earlier than I expected.

Day 218. The Norske hesten is a distinctive mountain which occupies the entire island of Alden and is a landmark for many tens of kilometres

The poor weather forecast for the morning did not materialize and it was much better than predicted, so I was up quite early and off by mid-morning. As I paddled out of the bay I passed one of the few locals. He was cleaning some old wooden crab pots on his jetty and I stopped for a quick chat. He mentioned I would soon pass 'The Millionaires Road'. I was curious and asked him about it. On the next peninsula was a small fishing hamlet called Avløyp which until recently had no road. Then about 15 years ago one of the few inhabitants there won the lottery. He agreed to lend the council, Solund kommune, about a million kroners to build a 2-kilometre road from the neighbouring hamlet at Stranda, which they did. The lucky winner, Halfdan Avløyp, then had to take his driving test, as despite being in his 50s he had previously no use for a car, as his boat was the only means of access. I bade goodbye and paddled off round the corner into Hersviksund again. It was much easier today and I regained the kilometre I battled with yesterday within 10 minutes. This was a grey and wild landscape with barely any earth. The occasional, hardy bonsai type of birch, eeked out a survival here where it could find enough nourishment in a crevice, but there was scant soil around. Behind me was the island of Alden with its famous Norske hesten (Norwegian horse) mountain sitting on the whole island, making it a distinctive landmark for 50 kilometres along the coast. As I paddled down the sound for a few more kilometres the village of Hersvik appeared. Its few green fields and white church made it look like an oasis in the stark ice-scoured grey rock, with its many smooth bare outcrops. Hersvik would have formerly been a fishing, rather than agricultural, community in previous generations. On the west of the sound were some small chinks in the grey walls, where narrow channels of water cut through to the open basin of Lågøyfjord beyond. I took one of them round the north of the bleak island of Huvøyna. There were many islets in this channel

Day 218. The conglomerate rock was composed of sand, pebbles, cobbles and boulders of an old estuary which was metamorphosed

and there seemed to be a healthy mink population here, which would have devoured many of the nesting chicks earlier in the season.

As I paddled along the side of the islets I noticed all the rock was conglomerate. That is pebbles, cobbles and boulders which have been laid down in a river bed or estuary, and then the spaces in between filled with sand and silt. The whole deposit of boulders, cobbles, pebbles and the silt could have been a kilometre deep and many kilometres wide, much like, and as vast as, the Nile or Amazon deltas today. Indeed, this conglomerate geology today extended all the way for 15 kilometres to Sognesjøen. After this mighty estuary had formed and the river which fed it vanished, by the consequence of continental movement, the sediments would have lain. Then geological forces would have buried them deep in the earth where heat and pressure, or both, would have metamorphosed them into the conglomerate rock I was paddling past. I cut across the open basin which was Lågøyfjord for a few kilometres to reach the headland where the tiny hamlet of Avløyp lay. I could not see it, or its infamous road, as it was sheltered in a deep bay behind a maze of small islands which I paddled into. I wove through channels between the outcrops of conglomerate looking at the constituent pebbles and boulders and marvelling at the barrenness of the archipelago. There were a few pockets of spruce where earth had accumulated, but mostly it was sparse heather and grey rock. You could see it had not been long since the ice retreated from here.

Day 218. Lågøy hamlet was a fresh oasis in an ocean of bare grey rock outcrops which covered most of Sula island

In the midst of this barren, grey, maze where I thought nothing could exist I paddled round a small headland to unexpectedly see the hamlet of Lågøy. Its 10 well-maintained buildings lay neatly on a saddle of green felt beside a solid quay. There were a couple of barns, a white farmhouse and what looked like an old shop and trading station. I later found out that there was a family of boat builders living here for most of the last century. It was a delightful well-preserved hamlet which still did not have a road to it, and probably never would, as it was so remote from land and yet accessible by sea. I paddled past Lågøy almost with a lump in my throat and yearning to know more about it and its history, and started to paddle south down Liasund towards the town of Solund. On the way down the sound I passed many other islands including Litlefærøyna, where a friend of Rich's stayed on a gorgeous homestead, the only one on that island. After an hour the sound narrowed and I reached the pretty, sheltered village of Solund, the main centre on this large island group. Here, in a deep bay on the east side of the already-sheltered sound, was a perfect harbour which was hidden by the further protection of a cluster of islands. I could see a church, modern houses, shops and even some vibrant lawns amongst the mature spruce trees. It was such a lovely sheltered cove I am sure it has been populated by tens of generations of fishermen since the mists of history. Despite the green, refreshingly lush spruce woods and lawns the grey outcrops still managed to burst through frequently. I paddled under the bridge in Solund, which connected two of the main islands of this large group, and drifted down the short Indre Steinsund sound on the tide until it opened up into Sognesjøen.

Sognesjøen was the sea end of Sognefjord, the biggest fjord in Norway and one of the biggest in the world. From where I was now the head of the fjord was over 200 kilometres away, at a village called Skjolden, tucked

Day 218. The sides of Liasund, like the rest of Sula, were bare and barren composed of outcrops of conglomerate

away in a deep valley surrounded by high glaciated mountains. Sognefjord is divided into many arms and there are at least 10 other large fjords which branched off it, many famous in their own right. With these side arms I would conservatively guess the total coastline of Sognefjord was well over 1000 kilometres. Despite its magnanimous proportions it was also a lush and green fjord, and along much of the south-facing slopes were fertile farms whose mineral rich soils were watered by tumbling mountain streams. These farms are so lush and fertile that many of them have small orchards of apple and cherry which produce the famous spring blossoms. It was not always like this. Some 20,000 years ago, at the height of the last ice age, which was called the Weichselian, Sognefjord and the branches feeding it were huge rivers of ice which drained the ice-caps of the interior and surrounding plateaus. This abrasive river of ice, well over 1000 metres deep, scoured a deep trench into the rocks until it reached the sea roughly where I was now. The river of ice then started to spread out across the flatter landscape until it met the sea, where it calved huge icebergs which drifted away. The area I was paddling over was not that deep, at only a few hundred metres, and it was much shallower further out to sea where the icebergs had calved. However, further inland up the fjord, the abrasive river of ice was all consuming and it carved a slot nearly 2000 metres deep in some places. Even though some of it was 1000 metres below sea level, the sea did not flood into it as the vast weight of ice above the sea level kept the ice in the fjord depressed. Then 15,000 years ago when the earth started to warm the ice started to melt over a period of a few thousand years and the sea flooded into this trench and filled its lower half which is today below sea level. The upper half of the trench, now above sea level, is where the farms, waterfalls, cherry blossoms and forests of today lie.

Today there are a few dozen glaciers, the large Jostedalsbreen ice-cap, and thousands of small lakes which feed the many streams and dozen large rivers which flow into Sognefjord. There is a tremendous amount of fresh water flowing into the fjord which generally stays on top of the heavier salt water until it mixes. All the fresh water has to leave the fjord through the 5-kilometre wide Sognesjøen while keeping on top of the salt water and this causes a current. In addition to that the whole fjord has to fill up and empty with about a metre of tidal water twice each day and these create strong currents. If the ebbing tide and the exiting fresh water coincide, and they flow into a strong westerly sea, then the waves can become very difficult and impossible in a kayak, so I was apprehensive about this crossing. However, I could not have hoped for better conditions, and the tide was negligible and the sea was calm apart from a gentle, lulling metre swell. Within an hour I had reached the other side and the island of Hille, with another banana skin behind me.

Day 218. After I crossed Sognesjøen I paddled down a channel to Mjømna with a rare forested island and a local trawler heading north

There was no conglomerate rock here but a return to the old gneiss basement which forms the bedrock of western Norway. The conglomerate on the north side of Sognefjord would probably have been sitting on this far older gneiss which was depressed beneath it. Otherwise the landscape on this side of the fjord was similar to the archipelagos on the north side. There were masses of grey rocky islands, many of which were relatively flat. Between the islands were sheltered channels, often filled with islets. On many of the islets the breeding sea gulls had nearly raised their chicks. Although they were fully grown, and most could fly, they retained their brown plumage and beak. However, they still could not catch their own food and were dependant on their parents. When the parents returned to the islet, or even if they were just resting, the young gulls constantly whined and pestered the adults to regurgitate food. If their demands were not met they would pursue the adults with relentless insistence, jabbing at the red spot on the adult's beak, which must have either served as a trigger for the adults to take pity or surrender to their offspring. As on the north side of Sognesjøen the rocky ice-scoured islands and islets offered hardly any landing spots and even fewer camping sites and there were no beaches at all. I therefore tended to home in on the hamlets scattered through these islands, where there was usually some landing place and a field or two. So I set my sights on the next which was Mjømna, about a further hour's paddling to the south.

Mjømna did indeed have a beach to land at, and a field to camp in. It was bigger than I had anticipated with about 30 houses, a hardware shop which also sold provisions, and a typically white old Lutheran church. I camped in a quiet field near the closed shop and had my tent up by mid-evening as the sky was turning orange. Suddenly there was a burst of activity as a few minibuses turned up at the shop, and then the express passenger catamaran burst around the edge of the bay like a battleship from a futuristic science fiction film. It circled and made for the quay by the shop. Within a few minutes it had disgorged a few passengers, cast off and then blasted off up the sound, with two rooster tails of frothing water emerging from its twin hulls. The minibuses silently departed, and as quickly as it started Mjømna returned to what seemed like deserted. With the weakest of phone signals I managed to ring Tom Amundsen who had just completed his paddle down the Norwegian coast and was now back at his home in Sandnes. He insisted I drop in on my way past in about 10 days, and if that was not possible or convenient, he would paddle out to meet me with some beers. I was looking forward to meeting Tom whom I had been in weekly contact with for three months now. We would have a lot of stories to share.

I managed to get an early start from Mjømna. I had packed the dew-covered tent which was speckled in seeds from the tall grasses into the boat and launched by 0800. It was overcast and calm as I continued down the same channel as yesterday, between the grey rocky islands of gneiss. It was easy paddling and an hour later the widening channel reached the hamlet of Gråvika and the grey 4-kilometre wide Fensfjord which I had to cross. There was an orange glow in the sky where the morning sun had broken through a hole in the sluggish cloud and other specks of orange near the water which had me puzzled. Then I picked up an evil smell and realized these other orange specks were flares from the Mongstad oil refinery. It was some 5 or 6 kilometres further up the fjord and I could see a few ships moored up there unloading their black cargo or loading the refined product. The sight of Mongstad was quite a shock after the relatively pristine 2000 kilometres I had paddled, with just a scattering of industry here and there. Nothing compared to this which looked like it had been transplanted from the Ruhr. Luckily I was not going within 5 kilometres of it, and as I paddled over Fensfjord it soon disappeared from sight round a headland, before it could leave a scar on my memories.

Day 219. Setting off over Fensfjord towards the Lindås peninsula with the air full of the evil stink of hydrocarbons

As I reached the south side of Fensfjord I arrived at the Lindås peninsula. It was virtually an island, save for a small isthmus far inland. In the middle of this peninsula was a large lake, Lurefjord, which was connected to the sea by five relatively shallow and narrow entrances. Lurefjord was virtually landlocked, and looking at the map it promised to be quite fascinating. I planned to paddle through the northern entrance at Kilstraumen and leave 30 kilometres later via the southern entrance at Alverstraumen. I had noticed this unusual feature on the map and had been looking forward to it for days. The other thing one can notice on any map of this area, is the way the valleys and fjords are all arranged in a series of concentric curves. These curves are about 80 kilometres long and 30 wide, and are known as the Bergen Arcs. They are a unique geological feature, and are even visible on a satellite picture of the region. They were initially formed during the Caledonian orogeny, when the tectonic plates of Baltica (Scandinavia) and Laurentia (Greenland and North America) collided,

Day 219. The tidal river at Kilstraumen flowed briskly for 2 kilometres until it entered the almost landlocked Lurefjord which was 25km long

Day 219. The shore along Lurefjord was like an inland lake and it was only the seaweed and jellyfish which reminded me it was still the sea

420 million years ago. In this violent collision, huge mountains were created some 10,000 metres high, which have since been eroded down to their stumps. Along the current Norwegian coast huge terranes of rock, called nappes, were thrust up on to the flatter gneiss platform of Baltica and pushed across it until they came to rest after hundreds of kilometres inland. However, in a few places Baltica was pressed, or subducted, under Laurentia and was heading down into the earth's mantle. The area around Bergen was one such place. But as it was being pressed deep into the earth, part of this tectonic fringe got stuck, but the adjacent areas continued bending around the snagged area. This great chunk of snagged rock, called the Lindås nappe, having been folded into a curve then stopped. Slowly it made its way to the earth's surface again. This happened as the overlying rocks slid off when the continents parted again. The huge geological debris which remained, was later eroded away, effectively exhuming the previously buried and curved Lindås nappe, which is at the surface today. Glacial erosion was most active along the weaker lines of the curved Lindås nappe, and they carved the fjords and valleys into the concentric arcs I was just about to paddle over.

I found the northern channel into Lurefjord, at Kilstraumen, quite easily after crossing Fensfjord. For once the brisk current was going in my direction. It was like a mature river, 100 metres wide, and I rode it for 2 kilometres until it spilled into the long basin of Lurefjord, which it was trying to fill. Once in the Lurefjord basin it lost its momentum and I sat back and relaxed. Lurefjord had the feel of an inland lake. It was only the jellyfish and seaweed which gave it away. There were masses of small islands covered in tall spruce and pine and the undergrowth was thick with willow and

Day 219. In one of the inlets of the sheltered Lurefjord was the small idyllic hamlet of Instebø where some farms were still active

rowan. My pace slowed considerably now, as I weaved in and out of the islets and islands, stopping to take photos and admire the lush surroundings. It was a bit like paddling in the Stockholm archipelago. I deliberately sought the smaller channels, even if it was not the most direct route, just to explore. There were a few cabins

Day 219. Entering the narrow shallow Grunnesund was like paddling through a Nordic fairy-tale

here and there, tucked away in forest glades. There was one channel which looked particularly intriguing, but its name, Grunnesund (shallow channel), and the map, indicated there might be a long portage. Luckily, when I got to the cabins by Vallerneset there was someone on a jetty, and he assured me I could get through. En route to Grunnesund I passed a small hamlet called Instebø. It was the hamlet where a good friend, Arne Instebø, hailed from, so I was pleased to pass it. It was the usual hamlet, with a couple of small active farms and a few others now being used as leisure cottages. Arne's family farm was now just used as a leisure home, as he lived in Bergen. Grunnesund, started near Instebø and it is 3 kilometres of enchanting waterway. It is only 20 metres wide and at times only a metre deep, and it was deserted, except for a couple of small cabins along the

Day 219. Radsund was busy with cabin cruiser traffic and two express catamarans taking people to their weekend retreats up the coast

side, hidden on the edge of the thick spruce forest. It was like paddling through a fairy-tale.

Grunnesund ended all too soon, at the larger Radsund sound, by the village of Festo. This was anything but deserted, and I felt like I was going from a farm track on to a motorway. Radsund was buzzing with cabin cruisers heading northwards. It was Friday afternoon, and everybody was leaving Bergen and heading up to their quiet log cabins on the magical spruce-covered islands on the sheltered Lurefjord. There was a constant wash; sensibly there was a speed limit here of five knots, otherwise collisions would have been inevitable. I started paddling south, towards an island in the middle of the sound with a gorgeous cabin on it, when suddenly not one, but two, of the large high-speed express passenger catamarans appeared from round a corner. Luckily they were subject to the same speed restrictions and I could easily avoid them. Once I had paddled past the gorgeous cabin on the island in the middle, Radsund widened out for the next 10 kilometres. There were some farms on each side and the odd hamlet along the steepening shores. There were quite a few smaller boat sheds along the shoreline, and I assumed they were to house dinghies used for transport, rather than for fishing. The nearer I got to Alverstraumen, the larger the hamlets were, with some houses perched high above the water with steep steps down to boat sheds. At Alverstraumen there were more islands, and these had been fashioned into very nice gardens, with a lavish older house hidden among exotic deciduous trees, like copper beech. There were many other houses along the bank, with all manner of boat sheds from decorative, bohemian, wooden ones to large old dilapidated sheds, whose roofs were covered in thick moss. For the final 2 kilometres I had to fight a strong current which was

Day 219. In the middle of Radsund was a small island with an idyllic cabin and boathouse taking up half the surface

flowing up Radsund to fill up Lurefjord. At times I had to paddle hard just to keep moving forwards on this river. Eventually I passed under the high bridge and paddled into the relatively still waters on the larger Radford.

Day 219. At Alverstraumen I had to paddle hard against the incoming tide past islands with lavish old bohemian houses on them

It was now starting to get late and I needed somewhere to camp. The trouble was, it was getting quite built up, and where it was not, the sides of the fjord were steep. It was difficult to find a place to camp which was not a garden. The road map indicated there was some sort of recreation area on the island of Flatøy, a few kilometres ahead towards Bergen. I decided I had to make for it and hopefully reach it before it was dark. I paddled down the sound and reached the nearside of Flatøy, but could not see the recreation area, so went into the small channel to the west of it. In the twilight I paddled past a very exclusive looking hotel and marina at Litlebergen, on the opposite bank, and then saw a quiet bay on Flatøy. I could see a deserted, grassy, lawned area with a couple of stone jetties and a tiny beach. It was the council-run recreation area on the site of ruined barracks and artillery emplacements. I later found out there had been various defences here for many centuries, as it was protecting one of the three sea routes to Bergen. It was getting late and would be dark soon and this was the perfect camp spot. What a stroke of luck! I put my tent up and started to write at a picnic table with my head torch while I cooked. The midges, however, drove me mad, and I had to abandon it and get into the sanctuary of my tent. It was the first time I had been really plagued by midges (knot) in Norway and they were quite intolerable, but fell well short of the standard one fears on a still August night on Scotland's west coast. I was within striking distance of Bergen now, after the long, varied and largely enchanting day.

It was raining heavily when I woke in the dark, with heavy drops falling on the tent from the large spruce tree above. People from Bergen sometimes complain, and people from Oslo always complain, about the rain in Bergen. However, it only has three metres a year compared to four metres on the west coast of Scotland. By the time I was up, it was light and the rain had stopped. I was eager to get to Bergen by midday, before Platou Sports closed for the weekend. They had kindly agreed to receive my new rubberized Reed spraydeck to replace the second of the porous neoprene ones I had endured. It was only 15 kilometres down Byfjord to Bergen, so I had good time. As I approached Bergen it became more and more populated. Houses were perched on every buttress overlooking the fjord. Many of these house owners seemed to have an obsession to build a boat shed despite the difficult terrain. There were many sheds on waterside shelves and platforms at the foot of crags, and these were almost inaccessible. Those on concrete shelves and platforms had a winch to hoist a small, generally unkempt boat, straight out of the water and on to a damp platform. Access to some of these sheds was down precarious steps, and even ladders bolted on to the cliff face. Amid some showers I paddled down the craggy-sided Byfjord, past the residential suburbs of Salhus, Tertnes and Brevika until I approached the centre. I was still undecided what to do when I entered Bergen.

Day 220. Paddling into to the main port of Bergen where I found a quiet hidden jetty in the middle of town to land and store the kayak

In the end I paddled right into the central harbour in the middle of town. I was lucky to spot an almost hidden floating jetty beside a salubrious hotel, with a couple of modest cabin cruisers moored beside it. It was a quiet private jetty and access to it was via a locked gate; however, I could see it was easy to climb round the gate, so I landed here. I levered the kayak on to the wooden slats of the jetty's surface, secured it with rope at the side, took my valuables and vaulted the gate. Suddenly, I was in the middle of a large city. I felt a bit bewildered. I had not seen anything like this for over half a year. I was still in my wet, salt-stained kayaking clothes and faded rotting jacket, totally unkempt and unshaved, and smelling like a wild goat. I suddenly became very self conscious as I wandered through a sophisticated city of well-groomed beautiful people. Even those who worked at Platou Sports and were used to the outdoors gave me a second look. The spraydeck, as I feared and predicted, had not arrived, although it had apparently cleared customs and was en route. The guy at the desk kindly said he would forward it by post when I had an address confirmed further down the coast.

I have two very good friends in Bergen. Arne, who lived in a suburb some 10 kilometres away, who I could not visit, as it was too far to walk and I was not using any transport other than my own power on this entire trip, and Tone, who lived just a kilometre from the centre. I had known them for nearly 10 years after meeting them in Jotunheimen. While I was climbing all the 2000-metre mountains in Scandinavia, they were my frequent companions for four summers and quite a few spring ski trips. We had shared many fine days, airy ridges, tentative glacier crossings, a few bivouacs and many evenings round a roaring stove in a mountain cabin. However, I could not contact them on their phones, or perhaps they could smell me! So I went to the nearby central youth hostel. They had a room so I returned to my kayak to fetch a few drybags. Within an hour I was clean shaven and distinguished. I now managed to get hold of both Arne and Tone. Arne was just returning from a day trip to the mountains and Tone was in town, babysitting her nephew and niece for the weekend. We soon met up in the Brygge area, near the fishmarket, for a coffee and chat. Unfortunately Tone had to go after an hour and Arne and I went for a meal and a banter. Once Arne went home I was keen to get a lot of writing and other office work out of the way, so returned to the youth hostel in the early evening and managed to do half of my chores. I was disappointed not to have seen more of Tone and Arne, or enjoy some social life in Bergen, but decided I would probably push on tomorrow as the forecast was great.

I very much enjoy Bergen. It is a very old city having existed for about 1000 years. Through the centuries it has often vied with Trondheim to be the most important city in Norway, as Oslo was a relatively minor town until recently. Bergen seemed to dominate commerce while Trondheim was the seat of Christianity and learning. Bergen was built on cod, more specifically dried cod. It managed to establish a monopoly on the dried cod trade from northern Norway to mainland Europe. Mainland Europe was largely Catholic at the time and the whole population needed fish every Friday, so Bergen's importance grew. It became an enclave of the powerful Hansa group, based in Lubeck in northern Germany. These Saxon merchants established a near monopolistic trading network across northern Europe and the Baltic region in the 13th Century, and kept their

Day 220. Looking across the main port from my secluded jetty to the old Brygge quarter in town, which is built along the old quay

position for a couple of hundred years. Bergen remained stable throughout this time with a steady population, but in 1702 nearly the entire city of tar-covered wooden houses burnt down. Much of the present city was built after that, including the famous Brygge. Like all cities, it expanded rapidly in the 19th Century and today has a population of around 250,000. It is situated in a pleasant setting beside fjords and among the seven hills of Bergen. It was European City of Culture in 2000, and this legacy lives on as Bergen punches well above its weight on the cultural scene, with many musical bands and innovative theatre groups emerging from a creative surge called the 'Bergen Wave'. I knew I would return to Bergen soon.

SECTION 31. North Vestlandet – Stad to Bergen
9 days. 235 kilometres. 54.5 hours. 0m ascent. 0m descent.

THE KAYAK: SECTION 32. SOUTH VESTLANDET – BERGEN TO STAVANGER

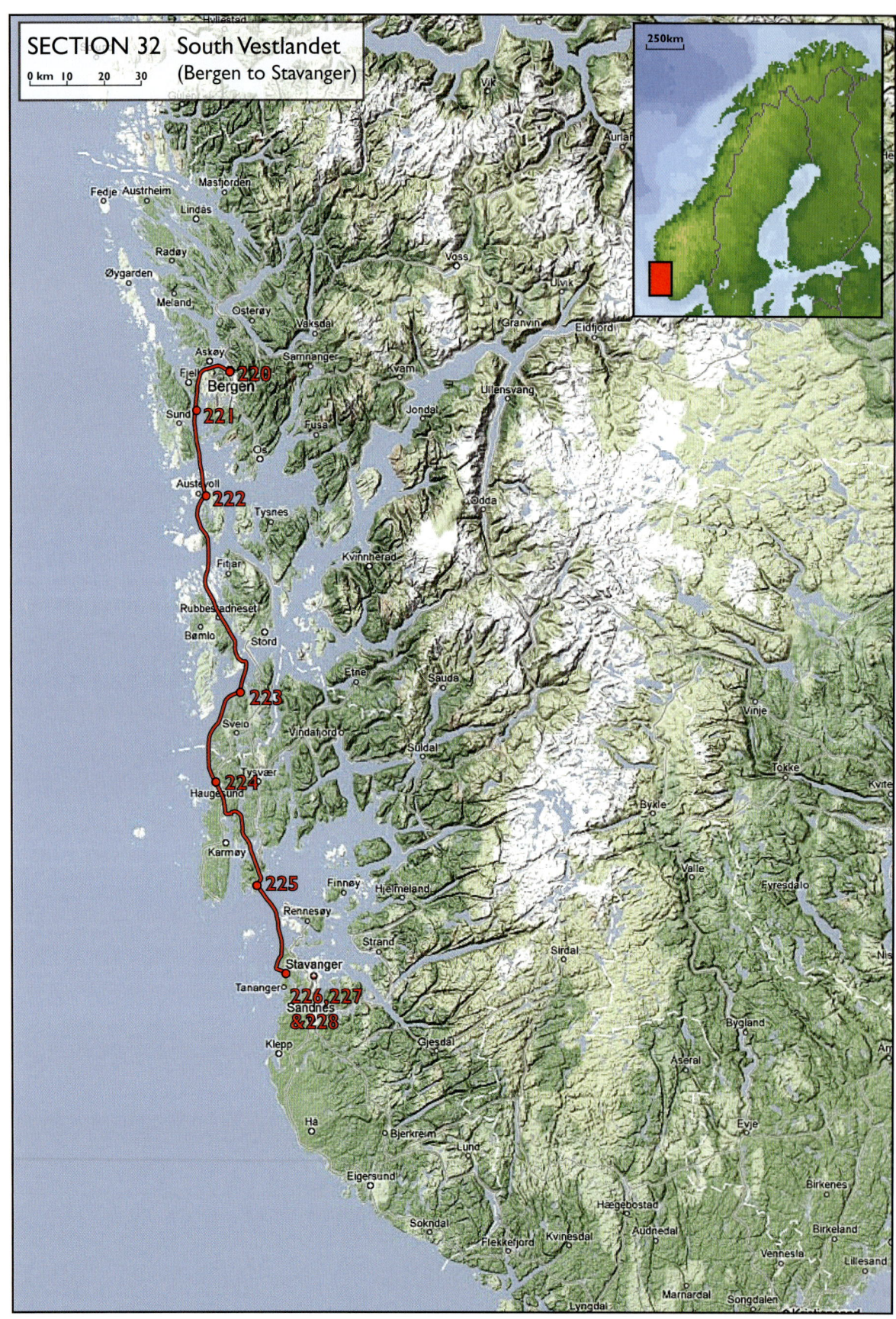

THE KAYAK: SECTION 32. SOUTH VESTLANDET – BERGEN TO STAVANGER

After the productive night in Bergen, most of my writing and paperwork was under my belt, and I was soon up-to-date with everything in the morning. All my clothes were spotless and I was clean-shaven after the comfortable hostel stay. I telephoned Tone to see if she was free yet, but she was still on babysitting duties until late in the evening. The weather was great and the tide was about to ebb, so I decided to pack up and continue down the coast. By the time I had stuffed everything into drybags and carried them to the hidden jetty by the Admiral Hotel where I had left my kayak, it was early afternoon. There was a mass of activity in the harbour with many ships and boats, especially oil-rig supply boats, docking or setting off. Cruise ships were mooring on the outer wall and a Hurtigruten ferry was returning after its 12 day round trip to Kirkenes. There

Day 221. Heading out of the busy Bergen harbour area to Nordnes headland, with the island suburbs of Askøyna in the distance

were also local sightseeing boats setting off and returning, and cabin cruisers weaving through all this. I kept well to the side until I reached Nordnes point and then headed across the next busy bay, called Puddefjord, until I reached the west side. Here there was the large Askøybrua bridge across the entire Byfjord to the large, leafy, island of Askøyna, which was well populated with a couple of Bergen's suburbs. The current was very much on my side, and even with a slight headwind I was doing more than average. It was only when I got to the second large bridge at Knarrvika, after nearly two hours paddling, I lost the current, as the tide started to slow and then turn. By then I was in the wider Kobbaleia sound and it was turning into a stunning evening as I paddled past a few more of Bergen's scattered suburbs, which seemed to be getting more exclusive and rural as I headed south. I decided to go down the west side of Bjorøyna and Tyssøyna islands, as the east side seemed busier with express passenger catamarans and the occasional ship. My choice was soon vindicated, as it was quiet and rural down here, with many older hamlets boasting traditional wharfs and boathouses, interspersed with newer villas. By the time I got to the south end of Tyssøyna it was already early evening. I identified a bay on the map, right on the south of the island and made for it, optimistically hoping I could find a campsite there. When I got there I was delighted, as it was more than I hoped for. In the deep bay was a small beach with some grass around it. It was largely deserted, except for a couple of families who had arrived on small, modest, cabin cruisers. There were some children from these boats swimming in the evening sun. I measured the water temperature, it was 19.9 degrees.

Day 221. One of the quiet hamlets down the mainland side of Kobbaleia sound, just a stone's throw from the centre of Bergen

I saw a picnic table beside a lovely patch of grass on the edge of the birch forest. It would make an ideal campsite, so I put my tent up and sorted myself out. By the time I had finished, the cabin cruisers had retreated back to Bergen's suburbs. Everybody else had left, except for a woman and a young boy who were staying in a large green conical 'lavu' style tent. I went over and chatted to them. The woman was Ann Grete and the young boy was a friend's son, called Gabriel, who she was taking on an eye-opening outdoor treat. They had been here a few days and would leave tomorrow. I chatted with them for a good hour and then returned to cook and write. Just then the skies got a bit darker, the wind stopped and out of the damp grass came billions of midges, or knot. This plague compared to some of the worst Scottish experiences I have endured. Ann Grete gave me some repellent, which made little difference. The only solution was to go into the tent or make a fire. Ann Grete had already collected some green pine and there was a bit of damp drift wood in the seaweed. After persevering for a good half hour, as only a man wanting to prove a point would do, I eventually got a fire going. It kept the midges at bay. We sat around the fire until well after dark, and it was nearly midnight when Ann Grete and Gabriel went to bed. It was Gabriel's first taste of the outdoors, and he was bright and alert to everything which his troubled and urban upbringing had so far denied him.

When I woke, everything smelt of wood smoke, and I even had a sore throat from sitting downwind of the changeable winds around the fire last night. Ann Grete and Gabriel were already up. I went over and we ate breakfast on a rock together. After breakfast I asked Gabriel if he wanted to paddle about the bay in my kayak while I packed everything. He was widely enthusiastic. He was not yet eight, but once I had pushed him off with the most basic lesson, he quickly grasped what he should do. It was an extremely safe bay, so Ann Grete and I just let him get on with it. After half an hour I was ready to pack the kayak and he had to come back to the beach. He was asking Ann Grete if he could get a kayak before he hit the sand. I eventually set off mid-morning into good paddling conditions, with just a slight wind against me under light overcast skies. However, I felt lethargic, despite the two previous short days, and for the first time on this trip I was getting a bit fed up and bored. There was too much paddling in safe water now, the scenery was predictable, putting the tent up and down was getting tedious, and the writing was a constant chore. I was longing for more of a challenge. I could of course get it by heading west for 20 kilometres and weaving down the outer skerries being pounded by the Atlantic swell, but this would slow me down too much. There are some more exposed sections coming up soon at Sletta and Jæren, in a week or so, and I am now looking forward to them. I paddled south over the open basin of water which was Raunefjord and on to the small island of Leröyna, where there was a salmon farm. I seem to be passing about five large salmon farms a day at the moment. I would guess that there are well over 1000 such farms in Norway all together, each with an average of six large round cages. It is an enormous industry along the Norwegian coastline, but relatively unobtrusive, considering the employment and wealth it creates.

Day 222. The magnificent 100-year-old Statsraad Lehmkuhl was a training Tall Ship which passed right beside me

As I reached the narrow strait between the island of Leröyna and the town of Sund on the massive island of Sotra, a fantastic sight came round the corner, and the tedium I had been feeling for the last hour lifted. It was the 'Statsraad Lehmkuhl', a Tall Ship, registered in Bergen. It was a huge three-masted, steel-hulled sailing boat which must have been nearly 100 metres long with its massive bowsprit. I counted rigging for at least 15 massive large canvas sails. In full sail this would have been a formidable and graceful sight. Even with all the sails furled, it was quite breathtaking and special. This was obviously one of the prime examples of a now vanished sailing era, and she epitomized every romantic image one conjures up from this bygone time. I sat in the kayak for a good 20 minutes, quite spellbound as this distinguished, graceful, ship silently motored past like a giant swan. There were a lot of people on board, and I guessed that the ship is now used as a training ship which specializes in taking teenagers and youths on sailing voyages, where everyone is expected to work. After she passed, I carried on through the strait and down to the end of the peninsula on the west, which was the south end of the island of Sotra.

Here, I had an easy 4-kilometre paddle to cross over Korsfjord to the small island of Skorpa, which was the northern-most island in Austevoll kommune, or council. This entire kommune was essentially an archipelago of nearly 1000 islands, centred round the largest one which was Huftarøy, where the small town of Storebø was located. It was renowned as a beautiful location and I was eager to explore its islets and channels. I paddled round Skorpa and then entered a fascinating islandscape. The islets were covered in pines, rowans now red in berry, and aspen. It was so still that not even the aspen leaves were quivering and flickering. I paddled slowly now and weaved and explored as I went. There were a few cabins here and there. There was someone painting the jetty at one of the cabins. He was the typically friendly, capable and modest older Norwegian one cannot help but like and admire. I asked him if there was a shop at Storebø and he confirmed there was. We started chatting. As usual, he asked "are you on a long tour" and I said "quite long". Then, as usual, he said "where did you start" and I said "Kirkenes". This always produces an expression of astonishment. We chatted more and then I left for the shop in Storebø some 6 kilometres away. After I had paddled a couple of kilometres I heard an outboard engine coming up behind me. It was the man from the jetty again. He had obviously told his wife about me, who immediately despatched him to see if I wanted a coffee or beer, or even to stay overnight in a guest cabin they had. He was embarrassed he had not offered earlier. It was a very nice gesture, but it would have meant doubling back some 2 kilometres. I thanked him, but said it was still a long way to Oslo, and I could not really dally. We said our goodbyes again.

I got to Storebø in the late afternoon and found a small marina where I could land the kayak on a floating jetty. Almost at once a couple of people came over. They were from the local kayak club. I chatted with them for a while, but was anxious to get to the shop before it closed, as I needed a week's worth of food. Storebø was a typical small Norwegian town, with lovely old houses and a white Lutheran church, set among pretty leafy lanes with well-manicured lawn verges. However, it also had the usual ugly utilitarian centre of pragmatic concrete, which housed the library, hairdresser, medical centre, a few shops and some administrative offices of the council. This 1970s edifice sat squatly in the centre of the town, defiant about how practical it was, to those who sneered at its lack of beauty. I entered its bowels, found the shop and returned to the kayak with two bags worth of supplies. When I returned to the kayak I abandoned any thoughts to continue, and decided to camp here and use the nearby picnic tables to cook and write. There was enough of a breeze to hold the midges at bay. I soon had the tent up on some wooden decking beside the jetty and was settled at a table writing. More and more people started to turn up at the nearby shed, and I could see by their roof racks they were kayakers. Indeed, it was the local kayak club who were meeting for a midweek evening tour. Naturally we got chatting. They seemed a very enthusiastic and proficient bunch with a range of kayaks. Most were British boats and none had a rudder. Soon there were 20 of them milling around, and all were curious about my journey, boat and how I ended up in Storebø. They showed me around their large council-funded shed. In addition to the 20 kayaks coming off roof racks outside, there were another 20 stored in here. There was also a great workshop area in the shed for building and repairing boats, and well-ordered kit stores. Their club was called the Havstril Padleklubb. Soon everybody had launched and the paddlers set out into the evening for a two hour tour around some of the islands. Once they had disappeared I took the opportunity to write and the rain kindly kept at bay. I had pretty much finished writing when the paddlers returned and could now chat with them again. The club chairman gave me a club T-shirt and a few had a paddle in my boat. Suddenly they seemed to vanish after saying goodbye, and darkness soon fell, so I retired to the tent. When I was half asleep I got a text message from a journalist who wanted to arrange an interview. I made some early arrangements and then fell asleep.

Suddenly the phone was ringing. I could not work out what was happening until I answered it. It was the journalist, and she was outside the tent! It was morning already and I had slept through the appointment. Feeling groggy, I got up and we went to her nearby office where a couple of coffees helped. We chatted for a good hour while she took notes and looked at my webpage. After that we returned to the tent in the drizzle and she took some photos while I started packing, and by mid-morning I was ready to leave. The drizzle was intermittent but there was a good northerly wind, which was what I wanted. I set off round the north of Rostøy island before turning south. The wind was now fully behind me and it was a good force 5. The tide was against me but the wind completely overruled it, and I was doing a good 7 kilometres per hour down the west side of the peninsula towards Bekkjarvik, and the bridge connecting the larger islands of Huftarøy and Selbjørn. By the time I got to the bridge there was quite a swell behind me and I was managing to surf on many of the waves. The price I had to pay for this excitement was a soaked cockpit, as water poured through the inferior neoprene spraydeck. At the bridge itself there was a stronger tide flowing through the narrows and

Day 223. Bekkjarvik village and harbour by the narrow sound was both a local fishing port and an exclusive berth for the yachting fraternity

Day 223. A fine old gaff sailed fishing boat which had been well maintained heading north towards Bekkjarvik harbour

into this northerly swell, causing waves to rise steeply and break, so I kept to the side to avoid the worst. Just after the bridge was the village of Bekkjarvik. It had a small delightful harbour with a mix of old warehouses and a small swish hotel. Traditional boats and exclusive sailing yachts were moored side by side as locals and yachting fraternity mixed. I ate lunch in the kayak, while in the shelter of this small harbour, before venturing out into the northerly wind again. The wind had eased a bit, which was good, as I now set my sights on Fonno island across the open 5-kilometre-wide Selbjørnsfjord.

It was an easy crossing and it was only towards the end that the waves started to break over the back of the kayak slewing it from side to side. Once at Fonno, I paddled towards the west of it, and entered a magnificent archipelago between the massive islands of Stord and Bømlo, both of which one could easily have mistaken for the mainland. On the map, this cluster of islands looked fascinating, and it proved to be just that. I threaded through outcrops of grey rock islets with calm channels in between, slowly exploring. Where soil had accumulated on the shelves and ledges of the rocky islets, heather bushes had grown and they were now in purple flower. There were many juniper bushes growing out of crevices here and there also. There were some old homesteads here with very little green land to cultivate. Long ago fishing must have been the only livelihood in this area. Now, many of these homesteads were leisure homes, and there were also many newer cabins. It was a delightful and idyllic paddle, threading through the channels between the islets and some of the larger islands like Teløyna, Ivarsøy and Åforo. After a few hours though the islets started to vanish, as the islandscape between Bømlo on the west and Stord to the east started to submerge, and soon all that was left was a long narrow sound, called Stokksund.

Day 223. The grey, rocky outcrops made up much of the dense archipelago of islets between the large islands of Stord and Bømlo

It took just three hours to paddle down the remaining 20 kilometres of Stokksund, passing the small towns of Rubbestadneset on Bømlo and Sagvåg on Stord. On my west, Bømlo looked barren and grey, while Stord to my east was both an agricultural and industrial island with a small airport. I went surging past them with the wind behind me and was soon approaching an engineering masterpiece. It was a series of three enormous bridges. Two of them were suspension bridges with a span of at least a kilometre and the third was a long arched bridge with a span of about half of the others. Many millions of barrels of oil must have paid for these bridges. The cost of the bridges is, however, a small price to pay to connect these two important islands to the mainland. This will keep them viable with thriving communities, and prevent more urban drift. When the oil runs out, I hope there is enough money invested in the fund to maintain them and all the others in Norway. Just after the bridges, at the hamlet of Røyksund on Bømlo was a small, narrow, canal which was once too narrow for all

Day 223. Among the islands between Stord and Bømlo was Ringholmen lighthouse marking the narrow channel before it opened into the sound

but the smallest boats. When the fishing industry grew in the mid 1800s and boats necessarily became larger to accommodate the herring catches, the canal was too narrow. These boats had to go round Moster island into Bømlafjord, on a longer and more exposed route, so the canal was widened to three metres. At the same time another five-metre-wide canal was blasted across a narrow isthmus in the middle of Bømlo, at Kuleseid, for 400 metres so these boats could now reach the fishing grounds on the west of the island without having to endure the exposed southern end of it.

I thought about taking the canal to see its history but decided to continue under the middle bridge and round the east side of the small Spyssøya island. From there I could paddle down to the east tip of Moster island and across the 4-kilometre wide Bømlafjord, which was the mouth of the world-famous Hardangerfjord. Along with Sognefjord, it is the most famous of the Norwegian fjords and features in a lot of Norwegian art, literature, music and culture. In summer time it is the epitome of a fjord with green farms along the water's edge, many with the blossom of fruit trees on the plentiful orchards. The head of the fjord was some 150 kilometres inland from me in a narrow slot beneath glaciers. It cut so deeply into the mountainous centre of Norway that I was just 10 kilometres from it when I was skiing north many months ago. As I looked up the fjord I saw two large cruise ships, both dwarfed by the grand mountains in the background. The wind had now ceased and it was turning into a beautiful still evening. I started across the fjord towards the pine forests on the south shore, which were now glowing orange in the late evening sun. Among the forest pines were small farms in their lush vibrant fields which were enjoying the benefits of a temperate summer. When I reached the south side of the fjord I could see it was rocky with very few camping places, and I had to paddle for a few kilometres before this rocky coast withdrew into a sheltered bay with a couple of protective islands across its mouth. I sneaked into the bay in the dusk and paddled past some farms, old boat sheds and some newer exclusive cabins, until I reached the small hamlet of Øklandsnes. In the fading light I spotted a small gravel beach tucked away under a spruce forest with a small field beside it. I stole into the beach and put my tent up in the near dark, filled the water bottles in a small beck, and was in the tent before most of the midges had noticed. After the 60 kilometres today I did not even bother cooking but went straight into my bag and slept at once.

Day 223. The last of the sun's rays turned the pine forests on the south side of Bømlafjord orange but there were no campsites along here

Day 223. Looking out of the sheltered bay from my campsite at Øklandsnes with the sun now disappeared below the horizon

When I woke early, the weather forecast did not make happy listening. It said the calm morning would degenerate into a force 5 by midday and increase further to a force 7 in the afternoon and remain there for a couple of days. There was no time to dally if I wanted to get round Sletta, a 15-kilometre stretch of exposed Atlantic coastline between me and the sheltered port and waters of Haugesund and beyond. I could not afford to be held up before Sletta, so reluctantly got up at once. I took down the tent with one hand while the other smeared midges over my face, packed the kayak and was away by 0700. I ate a packet of biscuits for breakfast as I paddled away from the midges and towards Sletta. It was completely wind still but there was the occasional shower. However, to the north, just 6 kilometres across Bømlafjord, the island of Bømlo was almost invisible under a continual heavy downpour. I made good time past the radio masts at Tjernagelhaug and on to the hamlet of Buavåg, nestled in a deep sheltered bay with a scattering of wooded islets protecting the small harbour. Nervous of the increasing

Day 224. The very protected basin at the sleepy Lyngholmen was the last harbour before the relatively exposed Sletta coastline

wind I paddled with extra vigour and flew down the coast to the very sleepy hamlet of Lyngholmen. This well-painted and cared for hamlet of about 10 houses and a couple of farms was beautifully sheltered by an arc of small islands, which created a very protected basin with just two entrances. I entered one, paddled over the still turquoise sands of the basin in front of the pretty houses and exited the other.

I emerged on the Sletta coastline. Its reputation might have been somewhat exaggerated, as there was still a scattering of islands out to sea and these would have taken some of the force out of the Atlantic swell before it reached the coastline here. It was no Østhavet, Nordkinn or Stad and there seemed plenty of escape routes if one was caught out. Still it was probably not the coastline to attempt in a force 5 upwards, which the forecast had previously said was imminent. It was a force 3 when I started out. It seemed no time at all before I had reached Ryvarden fyr lighthouse, just a few kilometres down the coast. It sat on a rocky spur, washed bare for 100 metres inland by the massive waves which must pound these slabs in storms. The keeper's house was the usual white building with the rounded slates on the roof, and the lighthouse itself was a wood-clad tower. It was an important lighthouse as it marked the entrance to Hardangerfjord and the inner shipping lane to Bergen. The rest of the journey down to Haugesund was surprisingly easy and it only took a couple of hours to paddle along this washed, grey, bare, rocky coastline. All down this coastline were many of the individually marked massive stone cairns on the headlands, to allow ancient mariners to get their bearings when navigating this coast, and showing them where the safe havens were. I was lucky the wind remained at force 3 and the swell was small, but there were many inlets I could have escaped into if the weather turned nasty. As I approached the northern end of Haugesund sound the small swell disappeared completely and I paddled into a bay at the very north of the town.

Day 224. Ryvarden fyr lighthouse was on the Sletta coast and marked the entrance to Hardangerfjord and the sheltered maritime route north

There was a hidden gravel beach here, near two boat sheds, and I landed the kayak there. This was a good tent spot, out of view of the nearby suburban houses. There was an official campsite five minutes' walk through a field, with a large obelisk type monument in it, which I went to investigate. It was the Haraldsstøtta, a monument to Harald Hårfagre. He is recognized as the first king of a united Norway and lived around 1100 years ago during the Viking period. He was a warrior chieftain who fought his competitors, gradually conquering them, according to the saga 'Heimskringla' by Snorre Sturlason. Finally, at the battle of Hafrsfjord near Sandsnes, in 872, he defeated an alliance of west coast chieftains in a sea battle and subjugated Norway under his single rule. I continued to the campsite and spoke to the friendly receptionists. They had no huts available and wanted 300 kroners, or 30 pounds, to pitch a tent, as the absentee owner had raised his prices for the annual Haugesund Jazz Festival, which was currently on. But the very nice receptionists let me use their showers and a small room to write and charge batteries for a nominal fee, so I returned to the kayak to set up my tent by the boat sheds. Despite the fact I was paddling through the pristine nature of Norway, there were always chores to do hanging over me. The spraydeck had finally arrived at Platou Sports in Bergen. They were going out of their way to be helpful, especially Stian, and now said they would forward it free of charge to their shop in Sandnes, where I hoped to be in a couple of days. I also had to estimate a finishing date with my self-styled 'Support Team' of Hartmut and Øivind. They were keen to organize their holidays and a homecoming for me at Hartmut's seaside house in Konglungen by Oslo where

I would finish. I decided I would reach Oslo on Sunday, September 6th, at 1400 hrs. That gives me 25 days to do the remaining 700 kilometres, which I hoped would not be too much. I returned to the campsite in the evening to write, but unfortunately the room they said I could use was the TV room. As coincidence would have it there was a football match on and it was Norway versus Scotland. There was only one other spectator in the room, a Norwegian, and he relished the evening as Scotland were humiliated. After the first Norwegian goal I gave up watching and tried to write, but he was euphoric and cheered and clapped so much I had to ask him to be quiet.

Day 225. Haugesund was a charming maritime city which was built on the herring fishing industry and still retained many old boats and wharfs

It was a windy night down by the shore, with frequent heavy rain showers which continued into the morning. Each time I was about to get up another shower would come through and pelt the tent. I eventually got up mid-morning and it was blowing a good force 5, but straight out of the north, so I would have a strong wind at my back. I set off at midday and was pushed down the north end of Karmsund with waves breaking over the cockpit. Karmsund is the 500-metre-wide sound which separates the mainland maritime town of Haugesund from its more industrial twin on the island of Karmøy across the water. I soon reached more sheltered waters as I entered the old port area with large dilapidated wharfs. I discovered I was to the west of a line of islands and beyond them was the centre. I sneaked through a channel and entered a tidy urban canal which formed an artery through the middle of the old charming city. I almost sat in the kayak as I was gently blown along, past old herring wharfs which had been tastefully converted. Beside them was a large scattering of traditional wooden boats, some well over 50 feet and all well restored and maintained. There was also a metropolitan feel with plenty of glass, metal and concrete buildings. Many ritzy cabin cruisers and sleek modern yachts were moored along this canal between the heavily varnished traditional boats. People drinking Chablis in expensive clothes on their boats waved and made friendly comments as I drifted past. Market stalls lined the main street and there was a real buzz in the air due to the five-day international jazz festival. It was called 'Silda Jazz' or 'Herring Jazz' after the fish on which the economic foundations of the city once sat.

Haugesund ended with more waterside apartments and a high bridge over Karmsund to the large Karmøy island. I was blown under the bridge and then entered another basin fringed with big factories, especially on the industrious Karmøy island side. There were also 11 large ships moored here. Most were container ships, sleeping out the recession and waiting for Europe's hunger for Chinese consumables to reawaken. It was not a pleasant area to paddle through, and was perhaps the ugliest 5 kilometres of the last 2500 kilometres paddling. Yet still there was plenty of greenery and rural landscape between the factories, which anywhere else would have been considered pleasing. I did not have to wait long until I reached an escape route from Karmsund. On the east side was a peninsula with a medium sized island off the end of it called Fosen. Separating Fosen from the peninsula was Røyksund. I turned into it and

Day 225. Røyksund was a hidden Shangri-La of an idyllic 2km channel leading between industrial Karmsund and the wild Førresfjord

entered another world. Between the spruce forests on each side of Røyksund sound was a quiet, sunny, calm, strip of water. It was a sanctuary, a watery Shangri-La, and on each side it was lined with older wooden cabins and boathouses, all set in mature colourful gardens. The sound opened out into a number of basins and then closed again into a narrow channel. There were about 30 swans in one of the basins, calmly paddling along with their powerful feet, while occasionally up ending to graze with their submerged beaks in the shallows. In the midst of the bohemian houses and cabins there were a few businesses. But they were more of the small, artisanal, boatyard type, rather than the huge multi-national concerns along Karmsund. After an easy 2 kilometres, the sound narrowed again, under the small bridge to Fosen and then spilled out into Førresfjord.

The northerly wind was whistling down Førresfjord, and it was a good force 6 but it was at my back. It bundled me down the fjord at a great rate and the waves were so steep and choppy I could not take my hands off the paddle to take photos. I kept close to shore as the waves were smaller here. If the waves get too big the kayak slows considerably, as it cannot catch and surf these fast-moving waves, which pass under it. It therefore tends to wallow a bit, sliding down the back of one wave and accelerating down the face of the next, for a second or two. I made good time down Førresfjord towards the pair of green, pastoral Bokn islands 10 kilometres ahead of me. I went round the east of Høvring island and then south through a cluster of rocky islets, which were very rugged and angular. Just as I was about to cross the strait to Vestre Bokn, four ships and the express ferry suddenly appeared from the south, between the Bokn islands. Not wanting to have to dodge them in choppy seas I veered east towards Austre Bokn and followed its coastline south. The sound between the islands narrowed under the high arching Boknasundbrua bridge, which connected these two islands. With the swell piling down from the north, and the tide racing through the narrow sound from the south, the paddle under the bridge was exciting. The steep choppy waves were two metres high and I had to make many support strokes with the erratic sea bucking and kicking behind me. As soon as I was under the busy bridge the sea calmed down and I could cross the sound and continue down to the south of Vestre Bokn island.

I understood now why the bridge was so busy, as looking at the map it showed this was the main road to Stavanger from the north. All the vehicles were heading over the bridge to the southern tip of Vestre Bokn where two large ferries crossed Boknafjord constantly. As I paddled in the same direction I passed an islet with about 30 herons resting on it. Birds seem very wary of my yellow slow-moving kayak, and the herons especially. They were all airborne while I was still 200 metres away. Yet they won't bat an eyelid when a speedboat goes past. I was blown past a couple of camp spots, but paddled south to the ferry terminal and continued past the breakwater beyond it, where I hoped to camp. I did not want to cross the 10-kilometre Boknafjord in this force 6 wind. While it looked benign here with the spray barely lifting off the wavelets, I knew on the other side the waves would be big. This was a problem in itself, but more importantly the ships and express ferry would just not see me among the breaking waves. But beyond the breakwater there was nowhere to camp at all; it was a bleak wave-ravaged shoreline of bare rock and slabby outcrops. What little vegetation there was, was limited to thick stocky wind-pruned bushes. I had run out of island. I had no option but to return to the herons. It was a good 3 kilometres back into the wind. It took almost an hour and I was irritated by my lack of foresight and this wasted effort. As I approached the herons I saw a bridge and inlet which I had not noticed earlier. I paddled under the bridge and into a large sheltered basin. On one side were a few tasteless modern cabins with flat roofs, but on the other was an old farm, with fields of grass and juniper forest above a muddy beach. It was ideal. I landed and found a campsite beside a large juniper bush. I then noticed some sheep and a very old man tending them. He must have been 90 and walked with difficulty, yet he had overalls on. I approached him and asked if I could camp here. He switched his hearing aid on and said "of course I could". He then herded his sheep down the grassy track to an old barn. I felt a lot of admiration for him, this old man who should have been in a nursing home but refused to give up. I had my tent up in the evening sun, with enough shelter in the juniper bush copse to keep the tent from rustling, and enough of a draft to keep the midges at bay.

Day 225. I found a sheltered place to camp among juniper bushes beside a hidden inlet on the south tip of Vestre Bokn island

It was completely windstill when I woke, which was great for the crossing of Boknafjord, but terrible for the midges in this damp forested glade. As well as the

Day 226. It was pouring with rain but totally calm when I crossed the 10km Boknafjord to the distant Mosterøy hiding in the mist

midges there were also frequent showers, and many of them were heavy. I waited for a pause and then packed the tent and launched, before the plague of midges reached Biblical proportions. Initially, I paddled past the ferry terminal to get out of this ferry route, and then set my sights on the distant island of Mosterøy and the Fjøløy fyr lighthouse at its western tip. The crossing was relatively easy and much quieter than I had anticipated, with very little ship traffic. There were frequent showers, but it remained calm. Indeed, it was so calm I could see the raindrops hitting the water and then exploding into small globules which rode across the surface meniscus of the water, until they merged with it and vanished. After two hours I reached the north west tip of Mosterøy and then followed the western shoreline to the large white lighthouse which was now glistening in the sun. I found a calm rocky inlet near the lighthouse and got out on to the shoreline slabs for a stretch. I had been told there was a medieval abbey near here worth visiting, but it was a slight detour and the monks had gone centuries ago. I had planned to continue all the way to the beaches to the west of Sandnes and camp, and then ring Tom Amundsen to see if he wanted to come over for a beer and chat. It was still some 25-30 kilometres away so I set off quickly for the final fjord crossing. This would take me over the 5-kilometre-wide Byfjord to the Tungenes fyr lighthouse, which was on the northern tip of the peninsula on which the city of Stavanger sprawled. It was a busy crossing, with many freight ships and offshore supply vessels coming in and out of Byfjord and Stavanger harbour. About half way across I thought I heard my phone. I fumbled for it in the day hatch, careful not to drop it into the fjord, and saw it was Tom Amundsen. He was wondering where I was. I told him my plans and he said forget the camping, and suggested I paddle another 10 kilometres to Kvernevik, where I could stay in his brother's empty house. That sounded great. I was really looking forward to meeting Tom, who was usually 10 to 20 days ahead of me down the coast and we had weekly contact on the phone.

Day 226. When I reached Fjøløy fyr lighthouse the sun came out and the wet landscape glistened under the northern light

Day 226. As I paddled towards Tungenes fyr lighthouse marking the entrance to Byfjord and Stavanger harbour Tom Amundsen phoned

I passed Tungenes fyr and was in a world of my own after passing some porpoises, when I suddenly noticed the bow of a kayak beside me. It had crept up behind me silently, without me noticing. I had to do a double take, and right enough, there was a kayak there. Initially, I thought it was Tom, but it was Richard. Naturally we got chatting. It transpired that Richard was a work colleague of Tom in the fire department, and also a kayaking buddy, who by complete chance was returning from his cabin in Byfjord. Not only this, he was actually heading to the very same bay where I had just arranged to meet Tom, and where Tom's brother Øyvind lived. It is not unusual to have social coincidences in Norway. I have often seen someone come into a DNT mountain cabin, or seen someone arrive at a party, and it is only a matter of time before some connection is made to

Day 226. Suddenly there was a kayak beside me as Richard was returning to Sandnes in his self made wooden kayak

someone else there. It is normally something like a cousin married to someone in your street, or an ex-work colleague has moved to your village. Norway is a small world, but meeting Richard out here in the middle of the fjord was really extraordinary. Naturally we paddled together chatting incessantly. Richard was in a beautiful wooden kayak he had made himself, from the drawings of a famous Swedish kayak designer called Björn Thomasson. He had spent about 250 hours building the boat and had made his own Greenland paddle. He was fast and graceful and glided through the water with the minimum of effort. I had to increase my tempo a lot to keep up with him. We rounded the headland at Vistnes and then paddled across the bay to Kvernevik. As we approached the land he pointed out a few things, like the memorial to the Alexander Kielland platform, which was Norway's large offshore tragedy some 30 years ago, when 123 people died as the oilrig capsized. As we approached land in Kvernevik bay I saw someone standing on a high knoll slowly waving a large Norwegian flag. Then I saw the small figure of Tom on the rocks above the water. He was directing us round the corner to a sheltered harbour with a small beach some 200 metres away. By the time we got there, Tom and the rest of the Amundsen's had walked over.

What a reception I got from the Amundsen's. Tom, Øyvind and their father, who was waving the flag a few minutes earlier, had all been reading my blog regularly and felt they knew me. I was quite humbled by the warm welcome, and there was a lot of hand-shaking and banter from this lively family. Then all hands grabbed my fully-loaded boat as if it was a balsa model and carried it up to Øyvind's house some 200 metres away. There was a lot more banter and photographs taken amidst the laughter and back-slapping. The head of the clan, Mr Amundsen, now well into his 70s, had a very welcoming manner and warm personality. He had five children of which Tom, who had just finished paddling the Norwegian coast was one, and Øyvind, whose house we were at was another. Mr Amundsen had been one of the early North Sea saturation divers.

Day 226. I got a fantastic welcome from the Amundsen family and here am I shaking hands with Mr Amundsen as his son Tom cracks a joke.

He was an industrial pioneer in a courageous job. To leave a dive bell at 200 metres depth in the dark, and fumble over the muddy sea-bed to a pipeline and start welding a segment on to it, must have taken a lot of bravery in those early days, 30 years ago. He must have inherited that from his great, great uncle, Roald Amundsen. After a couple of hours the three Amundsen men and Richard all had to return to their families. Tom's and Øyvind's families were at a cabin an hour away, so once they had made sure I was comfortable and had showed me a fridge full of food, the shower and a comfortable bed, they all left leaving me in absolute luxury. It was the most comfortable evening of the year so far. I wrote some of my blog, made a meal from the food Øyvind had kindly bought for me, washed some clothes and relaxed in front of the TV. The weather forecast looked grim for tomorrow, and it gave me a great deal of satisfaction to hear it, as I was staying here and Tom was going to drop by tomorrow for a chat.

Øyvind and his wife Elin had even bought bacon and eggs and put them in the fridge for my breakfast. After I had eaten them I wrote, occasionally looking out of the window at the foul weather. It was pouring rain, the wind was a good force 6 and the bay was full of white caps. I could afford to gloat at my good fortune, as I looked from the comfortable sanctuary of the room out of the window to the misery outside. In the early afternoon Elin arrived with more food, including bacon and eggs for tomorrow's breakfast. Then Tom arrived and we chatted about the paddle and our experiences as Elin listened. There was noise at the door which heralded the arrival of more Amundsens. It was Torild, one of Tom's three sisters and Mr Amundsen. Torild kindly brought fruit for us, and for the first time this year I probably had my daily five fruit or veg. Mr Amundsen brought beer. I was quite overwhelmed by the thoughtfulness of the Amundsens. It was a very cheerful afternoon and everybody stayed for a few hours. There was a lot of laughter, leg-pulling and banter among this large and enthusiastic family, and I felt very included. They were the yardstick of how a family should be. Then, as evening approached, everybody left to return to their homes and cabins, and suddenly the house fell quiet again. I spent the evening processing and loading photos on to my website and watching the television. The weather forecast for tomorrow did not make good viewing, and it looked like I would be here another day.

When I woke the next morning, the weather forecast was spot on, and it was indeed another foul day. The rain was torrential and was bouncing back off the garden furniture. In addition, the wind was at least as strong as yesterday and the tops of the trees were swaying and whipping in the wind. It was not a day for paddling. I had the luxury of having very little to do. The writing and photos on my website were up to date and there was nothing nagging on that topic. Tom had brought some books and I spent the morning reading through them. One was a book by a Swede called Jim Danielsson who paddled the Norwegian coast some 20 years ago, and was perhaps the first to do so. The other was a coffee table type book with masses of aerial photographs from northern Norway and Finnmark in particular. In the afternoon Tom arrived, and he brought my much-travelled and elusive rubberized spraydeck I had spent the last six weeks trying to obtain. He had picked it up from Platou Sports in Sandnes where it had been forwarded. We reminisced a lot about the north of Norway. It was apparent that Tom was most taken by Finnmark province out of all the sections of his trip. In retrospect Finnmark would probably be the most memorable province for me also. It was certainly the most challenging so far. Troms province was perhaps the most spectacular, and Nordland the most idyllic province. The weather let up for a couple of hours so we went for a short walk from the house along the edge of the Hafrsfjord. This was the fjord in which Harald Hårfagre defeated his rivals some 1100 years ago and united Norway. Harald later appointed 12 of his sons as governors to rule the districts he had collected together, but there was some friction between them. His favourite son, Erik Bloodaxe, soon sorted them out by slaughtering many of them. However, he became so despotic that the Norwegians rose up against him and forced him out of Norway, and he fled to England conquering Northumbria. As we walked we soon reached the knoll with a large monument of a broken chain link. This was to commemorate the 123 people who lost their lives when the five-legged semi-submersible 'Alexander Kielland' capsized after a leg broke off. All but one of the anchor chains broke and this kept the rig upright, but listing, for 15 minutes until it too snapped and the rig turned upside down. This happened in 1980, which were the early days of the North Sea oil industry, and there were a lot of skills being exchanged between Scotland and Norway. There was a list of names, and I counted 16 Scottish names on it, but at least half were apparently from the Stavanger region.

We returned to Øyvind's house from this poignant memorial, just as Øyvind, Elin and their two bright children, Lasse and Elena, arrived back from the weekend at their cabin, where they had been with other members of the Amundsen clan. There was a lot more brotherly banter before Tom left. Tom, Øyvind and their three sister's husbands were all part-time tradesmen. So when one needed an extension or modernisation they had relations to help. Tom had recently helped Øyvind with his house, so the banter was affectionate and heartfelt. The pair of them had added another storey, by building a new roof above the old one. When it was finished they removed the original roof and extended the ground floor up to meet the new roof. They had somehow done all this with the family still living here. The new space created upstairs was fantastic, and typically Scandinavian, with big bright windows and large uncluttered spaces. While Tom helped with the carpentry, a brother-in-law did all the electrics. That evening Elin treated everyone to a carry out pizza as there was a lot to get ready for the school week coming up. After the kids were in bed, we chatted for a good few hours', with Øyvind telling me about his time as a UN peacekeeper in Lebanon. It was well after midnight before we realized the time and went to bed.

SECTION 32. South Vestlandet – Bergen to Stavanger
8 days. 204 kilometres. 42.5 hours. 0m ascent. 0m descent.

THE KAYAK: SECTION 33. THE NORTH SEA – STAVANGER TO LINDESNES

THE KAYAK: SECTION 33. THE NORTH SEA – STAVANGER TO LINDESNES

The whole house was up early to go to school and work. Tom arrived soon afterwards and we all had breakfast together. The weather did not look too promising, with a good force 5 and frequent showers. By the time I was packed and ready to go it had improved a bit, so Tom and I carried my boat back to the beach, while Elin took my drybags in a wheelbarrow. After a heartfelt goodbye, I paddled out of the bay, really grateful for the kindness and generosity this large family had shown to me. I paddled across the mouth of Hafrsfjord, negotiated some skerries at the western lip and emerged into the open sea. The wind was now just a force 4 but the force 6 over the last couple of days had left a legacy of a large swell, which was well over two metres. I headed south and paddled down the coast, with the new offices of the oil industry at Tananger and then Sola on my east, and a scattering of flat islands and islets in the North Sea on my west, where a typical 150-year-old Norwegian lighthouse with a white keeper's cottage stood.

Day 229. Leaving Hafrsfjord by Sandnes and paddling out into the North Sea to start heading down the Jæren coast

After I crossed Solavika bay, the islets vanished, allowing the full ocean swell to surge through and I was pitched on to the Jæren coast. Tom had warned me about a feature on this coastline; while the land was flat and shallow, it was actually a vast moraine and provided some of the best farming land in Norway. Over the last 10,000 years the sea had transformed this moraine, washing the sand out from the boulders, creating huge beaches many kilometres long. But between the beaches the boulders became concentrated at each headland. Many of the boulders were vast, as large as houses, and they extended in ridges out from the headlands, very gradually descending into the sea. Even a kilometre out to sea from a boulder-strewn headland, there could be a house-sized boulder lurking a few metres under the swell. The sea might remain dormant when an average swell passes over them, but will suddenly erupt into a towering green claw with white fingertips when the larger swells passes over. With today's swell I had to be constantly on the lookout, scanning the sea in front of me as far as I could see, to locate these sleeping monsters.

Day 229. The wealthy farms in Jæren exploit the fertile soil to raise large herds of dairy cattle for meat and milk production

The first of these ridges was at Ølberg and I had to detour a long way out to sea to avoid the eruptions. Once round Ølberg I stopped in a small inlet at Hellestø to prepare for the next bouldery headland. While taking photos there my camera fell out of my pocket and into a rockpool. It drowned at once, but I had foreseen this and had two of the same.

Before I left I prepared myself for the next section which was Jærens Rev, an infamous stretch of exposed coast peppered with large boulders. I changed paddles to the larger blade, clipped myself into the kayak and attached the paddle leash before heading out into the swell again. There was a roar of breaking surf along the coast here, as this swell dumped on to the beaches. I passed a few shipwrecks along the coast and noticed

Day 229. Along the Jæren coast there are huge glacial boulders which lurk under the surface and only awaken when large waves pass over

Day 229. These huge glacial boulders on the approach to Jærens Rev are the main hazard found on this coast, especially when submerged

they seemed as frequent here as in Finnmark. However, the surf here splashed against their rusty hulls on the shore, while in Finnmark they were high and dry on the rocks where the violent storms had finally tossed them. I approached Jærens Rev with some trepidation, fearful what I might find there. The sea charts marked it as an area with dangerous waves. Initially, I headed down one of the longest beaches in Norway, Borestranda, at nearly 4 kilometres. Eventually, more and more boulders appeared among the sand, until I could see a boulder ridge extending into the sea and the surf where this ridge was submerged. I started paddling out to give it a wide berth, expecting the swell to increase in height. However, contrary to my expectations, the swell did not increase. I kept a kilometre offshore, and while there was a lot of rough and erratic sea with breaking surf nearer the headland, I felt very confident where I was. Before I knew it I was round the worst of it and paddling in a much smaller sea on the south side of the boulder-strewn Jærens Rev. Here, there was another enormous beach, a light beige, almost buttermilk, crescent, stretching right down the coast for another 4 kilometres. This beach, called Orrestranda, was reputedly the longest beach in Norway. Although the swell was now a bit smaller on the south side of Jærens Rev, I could still see the crests of green water starting to curl, and then hear the roar as they thumped on to the beach. I would not have been comfortable landing my fully-laden kayak through them.

All along the hinterland, behind the beaches, sand dunes and the boulders, were the rich farms. Huge barns for the large dairy herds had expensive clay tiles on the roofs. The large wealthy-looking farmhouses were traditional, but with many embellishments, like Swiss-style balconies and rows of dormer windows in the mansard roofs. Around these almost stately farmhouses were lush fields of grass. Farming had made this area wealthy, long before oil was discovered. By the time I got to the end of Orrestranda it was late afternoon and I had started to look for somewhere to camp. But I could not see anywhere to land easily, and more importantly, somewhere which would not trap me if the wind increased in the night, and the surf was too big in the morning. I paddled past the hamlet of Vik, and then Nærland, passing sandy beaches and boulder fields. In the end I had to head out round another of the numerous small boulder headlands to the next bay, when suddenly a calm estuary appeared, where the Håelva river emerged from the fields. The headland I had just paddled past curved around the estuary, enveloping it in a protective embrace. I paddled up the estuary for 200 metres, passing a group of some 20 swans and landed on grass beside a couple of boat sheds. Because the grass went right down to the water, I just hopped out of the kayak and then had the luxury of dragging the fully-loaded kayak straight up the meadow for 30 metres to a camp spot in the lee of a shed. As the evening wore on, a few fly fishermen appeared, hoping to catch a migrating salmon as it instinctively swam up the river to spawn. I did not see any of them catch anything before the darkness fell around 2230 and it started to rain.

Day 229. Looking south down the evening coast from my camp at the Håelva estuary, towards Obrestad fyr lighthouse

I had arranged to meet Tom today. He would paddle north from Egersund, where I had hoped to finish today. With him paddling north, and me south, we should meet around Sirevåg and then we could continue to Egersund together. We had spoken about leaving our starting points around 1000. However, when I got up and looked out at the sea, I had second thoughts. It was a good force 6 and the sea was full of white horses. While I took my

Day 230. The miniature church at Varhaug was dwarfed by the huge barn of the wealthy farm

tent down and packed, the wind did seem to decrease, but it was still a force 5 when I set off, but luckily it was behind me. I paddled past more shipwrecks and many beaches. Separating the beaches were more of the large glacial boulders. There were many more of the wealthy Jæren farms down the coast here, behind the beaches where the loam and silt deposited by the glaciers had left such a fertile hinterland. Many of the barns were over 100 metres in length. Beside one of them at Varhaug was a small chapel. It had the shape and proportions of a typical Lutheran church, but was a miniature version of it. I tried to get a picture of it in the waves and barely succeeded. I paddled on past Vigrestad, where the waves started to grow in size again in this brisk north-west wind, and soon reached Kvassheim fyr lighthouse. I managed to find some lee and phoned Tom. He had just arrived at Sirevåg and would wait, but I still had a good hour to paddle across the wide bay of Ognabukta. There were a lot of tystie in this bay. I was surprised, as their favoured nesting places are in cracks and crevices along rocky shores and there was only sand and dunes here, so they must commute to feed. There were also many eider duck, and this year's male juveniles were already developing the distinctive white patches on their uniform brown markings.

I met Tom just after the massive breakwater at Sirevåg and we paddled south towards the headland. As we went round, the waves suddenly built to around two and a half metres and we were often out of sight of each other. It was just a short piece of rocky coastline, and after a couple of kilometres we reached the shelter of a strip of offshore islets which continued down the coast. I think we both enjoyed the waves here. While they were quite substantial, we both knew that we had paddled alone round many remote headlands in northern Norway in much, much bigger conditions. The

Day 230. There were many shipwrecks along the Jæren coast, but they were all along the shore and none had been thrust high up the beach

beaches and boulders of Jæren were now replaced by craggy rock outcrops and islets rising 20-30 metres out of the sea. Occasionally, the sea surged between the islets and it was possible to surf the odd short lived wave, but by and large it was quite sheltered. It was obviously along here the tystie who had been bobbing about in Ognabukta bay found their nesting places. The next hour was an easy run between these sheltered rocky islets with the wind behind us. We chatted a lot and paddled a little, with the wind giving us an extra few kilometres per hour as we paddled and wove through the islets in the funnel of Nordragabet which narrowed into the picturesque Egersund sound.

Egersund was the Norway I knew and loved. There were lots of beautiful boat sheds, cabins and old small holdings along the sides of the sound, and the green fields on the island of Eigerøy were so lush they were vibrant. Conifers and large deciduous trees covered the steep slopes, and soon the grey, uniform blandness of

Day 230. Tom Amundsen near Sirevåg in his Tahe Marine kayak just after having completed his paddle down the Norwegian coast

Day 230. One of the many idyllic small holdings on Eigerøy along Egersund sound on the approach to Egersund town

the Jæren coastline was forgotten. On the mainland side of the sound was a small waterfall which plummeted right into the sea. We took it in turns to paddle under it. If I was in my drysuit I could have had a shower. Across the sound the island of Eigerøy was one of the very few islands on this North Sea coast and it provided shelter for one of the few really good harbours here. As a consequence, the town has a long fishing history and is home to one of the biggest fishing fleets in Norway. I wanted to find a campsite cabin, as the forecast was foul, so Tom asked a local beside his boat shed where a suitable one was and got directions. We paddled under an old iron bridge and into a wonderful basin with an island, Kjeøya, in it. Kjeøya was like a park, with many massive, exotic, deciduous trees on it, including copper beeches. Along the fringe of the island were a scattering of modest cabins, nestled under the boughs of these great trees. Beside the lawns of the cabins, which went down to the water's edge, were rowan trees, now heavy with their red berries. While Tom went for his van, I sneaked through a narrow channel on the west side of Kjeøya, which just made it into an island. It was just 30 metres long and a few metres wide. After the channel I paddled to the mouth of the big river which poured down some rapids and spilled into the basin. There was no way up to the cabins, just 500 metres above the rapids, so I hid the kayak in the undergrowth and walked up carrying my drybags. As I was settling in, Tom arrived with his sleek kayak on the roof rack. He had to return to Sandnes, so we said our goodbyes, and I settled in.

Day 230. Tom Amundsen takes a shower under a small waterfall on the mainland side of Egersund sound

I spent the whole of the next day at the campsite, as the wind was too strong to paddle. Even here, inland, it was a force 5, so I thought it must be an 8 on the exposed coast beyond Søragabet. It gave me the opportunity to write in the cabin, while gazing out of the window at the rapids roaring down to the basin just below, where I had hidden my kayak yesterday. The couple who ran the campsite were very curious about my journey and tipped off a journalist at the local newspaper. I was writing in the afternoon when there was a knock on the door and in she stepped. We chatted for a good hour in the cabin and I directed her to my website to get some photos and more information if she needed it. After she left I checked the weather forecast again. It would be worse tomorrow, with a strong low pressure passing through and the winds were forecast to be a force 8 with heavy rain to boot. I was resigned to spending another day here, and was a bit concerned that I would only have paddled two days out of six, but still felt I had enough time to reach Oslo in 18 days.

When I woke in the morning there was probably just enough wind for me to justify having another day here. I had planned to rent a bicycle from the campsite and cycle the 3 kilometres into Egersund and explore the

Day 230. The island of Kjeøya in a largely freshwater basin was a parkland paradise just to the north of Egersund

Day 231. A street in the old centre of Egersund which was rebuilt after fire destroyed the even older centre 150 years ago

town. I was going to be a tourist, window shop, sip latte coffees and perhaps have a haircut, I arrived there about midday. There was an old centre with wooden houses in narrow streets which was built around the middle of the 1800s after a fire had destroyed the more medieval town. It was very quaint, well preserved and was laid out in a grid pattern with leafy streets to act as fire breaks. This old part of town was exactly what I was looking for; I could browse the second-hand bookshops, visit a sports and camping shop, sip coffees while reading the paper, and I even found a hairdresser in an old street full of rickety old houses. I also visited an electrical shop, as the 5000 photos I had taken were still all on my original memory cards. If they were to get wet I might lose the lot, so I bought a hard drive to put them on as a backup.

As I explored the town, the skies were getting darker and more ominous by the minute. Just as I was about to cycle back the heavens finally opened. It was like a monsoon and the streets were soon running as the drains could not cope. Water spilled from gutters and people scurried from doorway to doorway and still got soaked. It lasted for two hours, with frequent flashes of lightning, and huge claps of thunder. I hid in a coffee shop and didn't come out until it was spent.

There was a very ancient church in this old quarter which had escaped the fire in the middle 1800s, and parts of it dated from 1620. I did not know what denomination it was, as Egersund was perhaps one of the most devout towns in Norway, with 15 different denominations, from Methodist to Baptist to Presbyterian, and the usual Lutheran. Indeed, I had now entered Norway's so called 'bible belt' which went from here right round to Kristiansand and half way up to Oslo. Egersund was also home to a large fishing fleet and it was perhaps this maritime influence which encouraged the various denominations. This fleet relied heavily on the mackerel at this time of year. However, the mackerel did not come here as usual this year, but carried on up the coast, due to currents and temperatures. As a consequence, the fishing fleet had

Day 232. This old church in the devout town of Egersund escaped the great fire 150 years ago and parts of it dated from 1620

left Egersund and followed the mackerel up past Stavanger to Haugesund for a couple of months. There was no sign of a fishing industry at all in the harbour area, except for the processing plants along the empty quays.

That evening in the cabin I read one of the books I had bought on the area's geology. As Tom and I paddled down the coast and into Egersund a couple of days ago, I noticed there was some mining going on at various places inland, along the rocky mainland coast. There was a white mineral being extracted and loaded on to small ships. I found out that this was an area rich in anorthosite, which is a relatively rare rock on earth, but the moon is made of it. The geological processes that created these anorthosite rich deposits happened about a billion years ago. Huge magma chambers rose up and forced themselves into the surrounding gneiss at a depth of some 20 kilometres below the surface. These vast magma chambers were about 25-40 kilometres in diameter and 7 kilometres deep, and as they melted their way up into the gneiss they lost some of their heat and eventually stopped. As this silica rich magma slowly cooled, the predominant crystals which formed were plagioclase, and it is these which largely constitute the anorthosite rock. When the chambers solidified, over the course of millions of years, the anorthosite was set. These chambers were then thrust upwards by geological upheavals and the 20 kilometres of rocks which had previously covered them was slowly eroded away until the anorthosite was

Day 233. Down the south part of Egersund sound there were a few large industrial concerns, like this one making fishing nets for trawlers

exposed. It was these surface deposits which were now being mined, and I could expect to see more tomorrow near Sokndal and Jøssingfjord, as the weather forecast was much better.

I left Steinsnes camping early, returned to my kayak, launched and paddled across the lovely basin with the pretty island of Kjeøya in the middle of it. It had all the promise of a good day as it was completely still, but a bit overcast. The current from the river exiting the basin took me under the iron bridge and I was back into Egersund sound again which separated the island of Eigerøy from the mainland. The charming little town of Egersund was up a small inlet which branched of this main sound. The inlet was suitable for smaller ships and fishing boats, but not for anything over 1000 tons really. These docked in this sound I was now paddling down which was remarkably industrial. This sound was now the bread and butter of the town and the industries along its sides sustained the place. It allowed the charming old town to remain pristine. There was a large factory making trawling nets, two protein plants probably making fish food, many fish processing plants and also a large shipyard. After 5 kilometres the sound opened up into a funnel, Søragabet, which then widened into the North Sea as Eigerøy island disappeared. There was no shelter here and the winds of the last few days had created quite a large swell. The more I paddled out towards the hamlet of Stapnes, the larger the waves became. When I reached Stapnes and the headland they were about three metres high and the wind had also picked up to a force 3 creating the occasional white cap. All along the coast here were the knobbly, light coloured anorthosite crags and small cliffs rising out of the sea. As this large swell hit the base of the cliffs, some of it crashed upwards in great plumes of spray, while some of it rebounded back and caused some large clapotis and a lively lumpy sea. I set off down the coast, a bit apprehensive it might get worse. I continued past some spectacular outcrops and cliffs along this lonely unsheltered coast for a good 10 kilometres after Stapnes, with

Day 233. As I approached Stapnes the protection afforded by Eigerøy vanished and I was on an exposed coast with very few landing spots

no possibility really of coming ashore except in a dire emergency. Even in the relatively sheltered inlets, the conditions would have crunched fibreglass. It was not until I got to Nesvåg that I managed to surge through a slot with steep waves, between the mainland and islet and into the calm of a basin. I saw a floating jetty and paddled over to it, as I noticed my GPS, a Garmin 60CSx, had stopped working. I was never that convinced about the 'waterproof' rubber caps over the terminals on the back, so put some duct tape over them. However, after three months this tape must have leaked a bit, and water ingressed into the antennae terminal. I stripped all the tape off, removed the cap, dried it out as best as I could, and then angled it into the sun which had just appeared. Remarkably, after half an hour it was working again.

Day 233. The historic town of Sogndal-strand seen from outside the harbour breakwaters, was a well preserved old trading post

While I ate, two elder ladies came down to the jetty from one of the 10 or so cabins above. They were very curious and friendly, and we chatted for a good half hour. They told me about the next village, Sogndal-strand, which was a very well preserved historical trading post and well worth a visit. They also told me about the next fjord I would come to which was called Jøssingfjord. It had been involved in an incident at the start of World War Two, and while Norway was still neutral, in 1940. Apparently a German tanker called the *Altmark* was trying to return to Germany with 300 British prisoners aboard. They had been plucked out of the South Atlantic after the merchant ships they were on had been sunk by the *Graf Spee* battleship. While the *Altmark* was sailing down the Norwegian coast it was boarded and searched three times by the neutral Norwegians, who failed to find the prisoners, despite being tipped off by the British. The British Navy then sent a search flotilla to find the *Altmark* and rescue the 300 merchant seamen. One of the ships in the flotilla, *HMS Cossack,* found the tanker hiding in Jøssingfjord. The officers of *HMS Cossack* were refused permission to board the *Altmark* by the three small escorting Norwegian ships, but under cover of darkness they did so anyway and liberated the 300 prisoners. *HMS Cossack* then left Jøssingfjord, with the Norwegians protesting about the infringement of their neutrality, but unwilling to block *HMS Cossack*. When Hilter heard about this incident he brought forward his invasion of Scandinavia, as he was desperate to control the all-important traffic of Swedish iron ore from northern Sweden and the Norwegian ports. The collaboration government imposed by the Nazis a few months later, and led by Quisling, coined the term 'Jøssing' to derogatorily describe anti-Nazi Norwegians. But this label was soon used by most Norwegians to describe a patriot, while the term 'Quisling' soon came to describe a traitor.

Day 233. Looking into the deep slot of Jøssingfjord where the Altmark incident took place in 1940 at the start of World War Two

With my GPS dried and working again, I left the sunny shelter behind this string of islets and ventured forth into the North Sea again. Within an hour I reached Sogndal-strand, but just poked my nose into the outer harbour of this town. It looked very quaint but I was sure the really old bits are beyond in the inner harbour, however, I wanted to push on down this exposed coast while the weather was good, so did not go in, and continued to Jøssingfjord. When I reached it I could see why the *Altmark* was difficult to find. It was a very deep slot which cut straight into the bare pale rocky mountains. Deep in the fjord I could see some mining activity. There was lots of a white mineral being loaded on to a boat, similar to what I had seen just north of Egersund. This white mineral was titanium dioxide, and it is found in the anorthosite deposits. It was mined just inland from the head of Jøssingfjord. It was soon out of view again as the side of the fjord obscured it. At the mouth of the fjord there was a small hamlet, called Bu, which really clung on to the side of the fjord on a small flat shelf at the foot of the cliffs. It must have once been a fishing hamlet, as there was no possibility to farm in this barren, but spectacular landscape. I paddled on, hoping to reach the sanctuary of Hildra at the end of this barren, exposed coast. As I paddled round the headland on the east side of Jøssingfjord, the waves, clapotis and current must have been conspiring against me, as I was only paddling at 3 kilometres an hour. I passed a very isolated single farm, Reg, on a grassy verdant platform above the sea, surrounded by cliffs. The farm looked well maintained, but was undoubtedly used only as a cabin now, as it was roadless and there was no place to land a boat on the shore. It must have been a goatherd's or shepherd's house once. I approached the mouth of the slot where

Day 233. The lonely farm at Reg surrounded by cliffs was roadless and without a sheltered harbour

the small narrow Ånafjord sliced into the dramatic landscape and then the River Siri continued up the valley from the head of this fjord. The whole valley and fjord was called Åna-Siri. Just off shore from here is a huge shoal called the Siragrunnen. It was about 10 by 3 kilometres in size and only about 10-15 metres deep. It was known for its dangerous waves, as large swells reared up and toppled in here and this was marked on the sea charts and even the road map! However, it is also one of the richest fishing grounds in the North Sea, especially for herring who migrate here to spawn. I thought I could see heaving surf, however, it was 3 kilometres away but there were definitely white caps out there. The skies above it were also very, very dark. As I was looking out to the Siragrunnen a massive bolt of lightning suddenly flashed between the shoals and the black cloud, followed almost immediately by an enormous clap of thunder. It seemed very close and it made me very uneasy. Suddenly there was another, and then another again. What was even more disconcerting were the black clouds coming my way, and the wind which was quickly increasing. I could feel my mouth drying with fear again and anxiously decided to flee into the fjord and abandon all attempt to continue down the coast. It was a near emergency!

As I neared the mouth of the fjord, the wind went from a 4 to a 6 and the sea was covered in white caps as the dark clouds drew closer. The lightning remained as intense but the thunder was getting louder and more frightening. It was as if it was right behind me and I started to paddle furiously. The waves were becoming alarmingly big and steep as I neared the mouth of the fjord, but despite paddling hard I was making very little progress, it was almost as if there was current against me; and I soon realized there was. There was a swift flow out of the narrow mouth of the fjord and it was piling into the large swell at the mouth of the fjord, creating this very turbulent difficult sea which I seemed to be stuck in. Meanwhile, the thunder and lightning was getting closer, and spray was being whipped off the breaking waves. It was all very apocalyptic and I was not content. I had to get in here, as the approaching storm could have made short work of me out on this exposed rugged coast, now fringed with a churning of chaotic surf. For half an hour I paddled for all I was worth and slowly pulled my way past a beacon towards two red navigation lights on a pole. It was less than a kilometre and somehow I managed to stay upright in this wild sea. I was soon past the red lights on the pole and veered to the north side where there was a slight eddy in the current. The thunder and lightning were still creeping up, but beyond the rock buttress which caused the eddy I could see a breakwater and houses. I was now making better progress out of the main current and the sea state was getting much less frightening. After a few more minutes of vigorous paddling I was round the breakwater and heading for the first jetty behind it. There was some grass beside it, almost like a lawn, and I rammed the kayak on to it and hopped out. Just then there was another flash of lightning and a huge rumble of thunder, which I felt shaking my chest, and the heavens opened in a tremendous downpour. The landscape which would have looked dramatic on a still, sunny summer's day, was now like the backdrop for a Wagnerian opera. I was a shaken and it was perhaps the most vivid hour of the whole trip so far. I was looking at the grass working out where to set my tent up, when a figure dashed from a nearby house towards a small boat, carrying a tarpaulin to cover bags of cement in the hull. Once done he ran over to me in the biblical downpour and within 10 seconds had told me to come to his house. We scurried over to the shelter of his porch.

Day 233. Looking up Ånafjord across to the hamlet of Ystebø on the other side from Jan and Gunn Eide's house

Half an hour later I was eating fresh crab with Jan and Gunn Eide, on a wonderfully laid dining table with a cotton tablecloth and napkins, and quality cutlery. The crab was fresh, the bread was fresh, the mayonnaise was just opened, the lemons were juicy and there was masses of it. Meanwhile, the thunderstorm continued outside and rain poured off the roof and obscured the sodden view. After the meal I was invited to stay in their spare room and given a large cognac. It was utter luxury and Gunn even put the washing machine on as we chatted, watched some Olympic games live on the television, and chatted more. They were fascinated with my journey, and with some of the adrenaline from the afternoon still coursing through my veins, I was eager to tell them. Jan and Gunn Eide were retired farmers from Finnøy island, near Stavanger, and this was their cabin. They had grown-up children, and one was married to an Englishman. They asked me about the red lights on the pole and I said there were two. They said I was lucky, because sometimes there are three, and then things really would have been difficult. They explained that the lights were there to warn returning fishing boats what the current was like. The mouth of the fjord was the tail-race for a massive hydro-electric scheme further up the valley. The scheme was part of Norway's biggest hydro-electric development, with huge reservoirs in the interior, some of which I had skied over seven months previously. Just up the valley was the last set of two turbines and a sluice. If one turbine was operating, the current was small, and one red light was lit. If two turbines were operating, then the current was strong, and two lights were lit, as they had been for me. If three lights are lit the current is up to eight knots, as both turbines are operating and the sluice is open. As I nestled in the fresh cotton sheets, after a warm shower, I was thankful three red lights were not showing, as I would probably not have made it in according to Jan. I left the window open – just to hear the rain and revel in the comfort which Jan and Gunn had bestowed on me.

After a wonderful sleep I went down to breakfast when I heard Jan and Gunn were up. They had laid out a typical Norwegian breakfast with a large selection of spreads, many of which were from the sea, to go on different breads, and coffee. After the relaxing breakfast I found I had very little to pack. Although it was calm in the fjord, Jan suggested we should go to the end of the breakwater and look down the narrow mouth of the fjord where it was just possible to see the sea. There were no white caps visible, so we assumed all was fine. Jan and Gunn waved me off at 1000 and I paddled into the river of water surging down the narrow Ånafjord. I zoomed out of the fjord and was doing nearly 10 kilometres per hour without paddling at all. At the end of the fjord I went to the east of a small island on which the light beacon stood, and through a 40 metre wide gap between it and the mainland. The current through here was holding the swell at bay, and when I eventually met it, would give me a taste of what was to come. The waves were huge, probably four metres from trough to crest, and very steep with just the wispiest curl at the top as they teetered on toppling over on top of me. I got swept through them as on some rollercoaster and then the current spilled into the North Sea and carried me with it. Now I could really see what it was like, and it was a lot worse than the view from the breakwater half an hour ago. The wind was a force 4 south-westerly. It would be side on pretty much all the way to the island of Hidra, some 10 kilometres away. I kept about 500 metres out from the steep cliffs to avoid the worst of the rebounding clapotis. The scenery here was like nothing I had seen before. The very steep, light cliffs came straight out of the dark sea as if in a dramatic painting. Here and there was some vegetation but it was mostly bare, smooth, rock slabs. At the base of these cliffs was a line of white surf where the large swell was smashing into the rock. After I had gone a couple of kilometres I noticed the south west sky was darkening. In fact it was very, very dark. The wind was also increasing and it was soon a force 5. As I looked out to sea the sun was illuminating row upon row of white crests on top of the large swell. This looked all the brighter against the black sky which was approaching fast. Last night's nightmare paddle looked like it was going to happen again.

I was still about 6 kilometres from Hidra and needed to get there before this thunderstorm arrived. I sat bolt upright and started paddling hard. The kayak shot along and was launching off some of the spikes of waves caused by the clapotis. The dark clouds got closer and closer, but the lightning and thunder were just occasional. None the less, I was worried about it, and knowing that lightning travelled from the surface up, I kept imagining that I could feel static energy building in my body. I still had a couple of kilometres to go when the thunderstorm arrived. The wind was now up to a force 6, spray was everywhere and it was pouring rain. I had to lean out to sea to keep my balance as I rode up a wave and fell off the back of it into deep holes. All the white caps and spray were now starting to form streaks on the water's surface. I was lucky none of the larger of the white horses with curls of green water under it caught me. It was like a theatrical film set again. Had I

Day 234. In a sheltered basin on the north-west corner of Hidra, after a testing crossing down the exposed coast from Ånafjord

not seen for myself the drama in the landscape and the sea, I would have thought it would have been necessary to have to paint such a vivid image. The imposing cliffs along the coast were hazy in the rain and there was the occasional bolt of lightning and frequent rumblings of thunder. Amongst all this, on a heaving sea with spray flying off the numerous white caps, was a small yellow kayak being tossed from crest to crest. I paddled hard for 2 kilometres and soon was at last approaching the lee of a small island to the north-west of Hidra.

Day 234. The fishing hamlet of Rasvåg was a typical Sørlandsidyll with white houses in well maintained gardens and boathouses over the sea

I decided not to go down the west side of Hidra as there might be nasty surprises lurking and I had had enough of them already today. Instead, I opted to go down the east side, which was a few kilometres longer but much more sheltered. As I started, the weather eased and the sun came out as the thunderstorm passed over and was spending itself on the mainland. I was already committed to the east side by now though and carried on down the almost tranquil Hidrasund. Now I could look at the map without bucking all over the place, I noticed that there was a thread of water dividing Hidra into two. It started in Eie on the north side and finished at Rasvåg on the south side and I was almost at Eie. I found it easily and started to paddle down it. It was a few metres wide and was formed into a canal by the jetties along each side. Old boathouses and fishermen's cottages lined this canal. It was all natural, except for about 50 metres, where it looked like a slot was blasted long ago to link the natural channels of water on each side. I paddled south through this enchanting, deciduous passage until it opened out again, and then I headed over to Rasvåg. This village was a Sørlandsidyll, or a south coast paradise. It was a tidy jumble of well maintained white fishermen's houses which were all clustered round a small harbour. Between the houses were well maintained colourful gardens and neat lawns. Every house had a boat shed, either over the water or very near it, so the fishermen from the bygone romantic era could moor their boats. It was very typical for south Norway and I looked forward to many more of them. As I paddled along the houses, I noticed there was a café among them, so I pulled in for lunch.

Recharged by lunch and lulled into an optimistic glow by the tranquil surroundings of the canal and the sheltered basins around this idyllic old fishing hamlet, I was ready to continue. The next goal was Lista, a broad flat peninsula across the wide Listafjord. I paddled to the south of the sheltered basin and threaded my way past a couple of small islands at the perimeter of this tranquillity. Just the other side of them the surf was roaring as the four metre waves came crashing down on to their pounded shorelines. The wind was a force 4 and almost directly against me. I started across the fjord and was soon in the biggest of waves. I sunk down for five seconds and then climbed up for five seconds to the crest of the next wave. It was a short rough crossing, where I was continually being hit in the chest by white caps. When I reached the rocky far shore I paddled down it in very rough conditions. The kayak was again lurching from side to side and crest to trough. I was beginning to doubt I would get round Lista fyr lighthouse which I could now see at the end of the flat grey land almost lost in the waves. My momentum almost stopped, and despite the huge amount of energy I was using, the landmarks along the shore came and went very slowly. The waves were very large and there was plenty of clapotis and claws of white snapping sea. When I saw the breakwaters at Jølleste I decided to throw in the towel, even though it was just mid afternoon. The last kilometre alone took nearly half an hour and with plenty of facefuls of water. One of the greatest irritations was the sun. I could hardly see where I was going and it was a great relief when it disappeared behind a cloud and I could see the waves approaching. The final run into the harbour was quite tricky, as the small bay was full of reefs with the swell erupting on them. I eventually entered the sanctuary of the small harbour and found a camp spot. There was a stream nearby, so I rinsed all my clothes which were soaked in the salt water and spray of today. I hung them to dry in a deserted bus shelter, which must have hardly ever been occupied in this small and seemingly abandoned hamlet. After my writing was done, I wondered why nobody had warned me about this coast. People had told me about Nordkinn, Nordkapp, Stad, Jæren, and the exaggerated Hustadvika and Sletta, but I never heard Lista mentioned – and it was easily worthy of a mention.

Day 235. The Lista fyr lighthouse was built of stone on a spit of glacial moraine on the south-west corner of the Lista peninsula

When I looked out of my tent the next morning I could hardly believe I was at the same place. What a difference a day makes. I could not hear the sea, and when I peered through the narrow gap in the harbour wall I could see the waves were small. I packed up the tent, dragged my kayak through the grass to the water's edge, loaded it and set off at 0900. Outside the harbour wall it was unrecognizable from yesterday. The gentle waves were barely a metre and none were breaking in the virtually still air. I made good time across the bay towards Lista fyr lighthouse. It was an erect stone building sitting on the moraine spit with a large village next to it. This was not the remote lighthouse of north or west Norway on a wild craggy peninsula, but a lighthouse in a farmer's field on the outskirts of Vestbygd village. The broad grassy spit the lighthouse sat on was protected from the ocean by ranks of boulders on which the North Sea vented its fury. Most were small, but some were truly massive, and the sea could not shift them, but just wear them down over hundreds of years. Just round the spit was Vestbygd, sheltering behind some massive outer breakwaters. Behind them were also some inner breakwaters which was probably the original harbour from long ago. I did not go in but paddled past the outer entrance and on to the start of a glorious section of coast. This was a series of about five beautiful, light beige beaches which extended down the coast for almost 15 kilometres. One beach alone was 4 kilometres. Between the beaches were shallow rocky headlands and behind them, sand dunes covered in green coastal grasses. In the coastal hinterland beyond the dunes and rocky headlands were farms. It seemed very similar to Jæren, except the farms here were smaller and less like the small estates found up there. Beyond this hinterland were the ice-scoured and pine-clad rocky outcrops which rose up to a few hundred metres altitude.

Half way down the largest beach I kept a kilometre offshore and reached the island of Rauna which is a nature reserve. Rauna is only half a kilometre long and about a quarter wide, yet it was full of birds. It seemed that the island was just composed of boulders and I saw no bare rock, so it was probably a moraine deposit. Because of its position in the very south-west of Norway it is an important staging post for the many species of birds which migrate over it. There were also many different species of bird which nested here in the spring and summer, and during this time it is forbidden to land here, or even come within 50 metres of its shoreline. I saw many types of geese on the island and almost every type of gull. Some young gulls could now catch their own food but they were a sitting target for the skuas, who robbed them mercilessly. There was a recent and unseasonal storm here some three weeks ago and this had washed huge piles of kelp on to the foreshore. It was metres deep in places and was now rotting, giving off a foul smell. Insects were swarming over this kelp, munching into the rotting strands, and flocks of Sandpiper type birds were feasting on the insects. Most prominent of these were the turnstones which were already in their winter plumage and perhaps staging to fly over the North Sea to their overwintering areas in Britain. They hopped about the piles of kelp with their white chests before them as if they owned it. The rotting kelp was not washed away or moved by the tides because there were none. The area around Lindesnes has no tide and is an amphidromic point, which is a point which stays the same while the tidal wave oscillates around it, rather like the centre point of a see-saw. In the case of Lindesnes, what happens is the tidal wave which surges across the Atlantic is split into two by the British Isles. One part of this wave is squeezed through the English Channel while the other half flows relatively unimpeded round the north of Scotland. When the remnants of these two influences reach the sea off Lindesnes they are out of sync, as the one which flows through the Channel has been delayed for six hours. As a consequence, they cancel each other out. But there are still currents here, notably the Norwegian Coastal Current, which is an extension of the Baltic Current and flows west along the south coast of Norway and into the North Sea at about a kilometre an hour.

I continued east from Rauna, keeping a kilometre offshore as I paddled past the rest of the beaches until the stretch of coast they were on disappeared into a large inlet. Up this inlet was the hidden town of Farsund, which had an economically troubled aluminium smelter. I cut straight over the inlet making a course for the south

Day 235. The lighthouse at Søndre Katland was built on a small skerry and marked the entrance of the inlet leading to the town of Farsund

end of Langøy island. En route I passed the lighthouse of Søndre Katland. This was is an important lighthouse as it marked the entrance for the shipping route into Farsund. However, like all but one lighthouse in Norway it is now unmanned. The light tower was built on to the keeper's cottage and the keeper's cottage sat on the small skerry. When it was manned, the keepers liked to grow vegetables in the summer, but there was no soil on the skerry as it got washed off by the spray of big waves in winter storms. So the lighthouse keepers used to take soil out with them on boats in the spring and then took the soil back to the mainland in the autumn.

I passed Langøy and now headed over to Kjøpsøy, weaving through the small islands. The wind had now increased to a force 4 and it was directly against me, but I now had the bit between my teeth, and the excitement and adrenaline were starting to flow, as I realized I should reach the very significant Lindesnes fyr lighthouse this evening. I sneaked through a couple of the bare rocky reddish islands around Kjøpsøy, passing well to the south of the charming looking village of Korshavn, and paddled through an old fishing hamlet which was now a collection of cabins. Soon I had passed all the islands here and was now on the edge of Grønsfjord. Just 4 kilometres away, across the other side of this choppy fjord, were three reddish outcrops of bare stone. The very southern one on this knobbly peninsula was where Lindesnes fyr lighthouse stood, although I could not see it from here. By now the wind was a force 5 but I had my sights set on the knoll at the end of the peninsula as I set off across the fjord. I reached the peninsula well before the end and had to paddle south down the base of the crags. I had to stay out a couple of hundred metres as the clapotis was very bouncy and the sea confused with the large swell. I slowly pulled my way against the current and then suddenly the lighthouse appeared above me. There was no time to rejoice just yet as I had to get round the end of the exposed, choppy peninsula. There were many tourists at the lighthouse looking at me and pointing as I bounced round the tip in the rough sea and sneaked into an inlet just after the lighthouse. There was a boat shed at the end of the inlet and I could easily land here.

Day 235. After nearly eight months I was returning to Lindesnes on the far peninsula beyond these islands and across Grønsfjord

I went up to the keeper's cottage. This was the only lighthouse in Norway that still had a keeper. There is a long tradition of all those who start or finish Norge på langs on foot, ski, kayak, or most commonly on bicycle to come here and sign the book. When I set off at New Year there was no one around. Now the keeper, Helge, welcomed me with a tea and the book, and we had a chat before he had to go off and lock up. I pitched my tent in exactly in the same place as New Year. It was a bit easier to get the tent pegs in this time! After that I went up to the lighthouse to have a look around. A lot of things had happened since I last stood here. I had been up to the very north and back, about 6000 kilometres in all, under my own steam. I was very pleased with myself and it would have been cause for a small celebration. However, I still had another 400 kilometres to paddle to complete the second half of this journey, which was the classic Norgeskyst (Norwegian coast) paddle.

For the sake of nostalgia I had camped in a windy place and the force 6 wind was rattling the tent in the morning. The sea was surging into the mouth of the inlet I had paddled into yesterday evening, and beyond it the sea was covered in white horses. It was as the forecast said and it was predicted to last all day. I was going to have a day off and there was no question about feeling guilty, like I had been in Egersund four days previously. As I

Day 235. Lindesnes lighthouse dates from 1656 and is the oldest lighthouse in Norway, marking the most southerly tip of the mainland

was gazing out to sea three men approached. One was Helge, the lighthouse keeper, and the other two, Simen and Ole Jørgen who ran the museum and the tourist attraction here. Helge had obviously told them about me and they came to introduce themselves. The two of them worked in the adjacent building and insisted I come in for a coffee and a shower. They wanted to know more about my trip, and in this weather there was plenty of time to tell them. I had a wonderful shower while the coffee brewed and then chatted with them for almost an hour. They explained they had work to do, but were aware I needed to write, and generously said I could write in their warm office and use their internet connection to upload data. I wrote all morning while they worked at their desks. It was like working in a corporate office and soon I was getting into the camaraderie of it by making coffees for everyone and running an errand for them to the museum shop. The other 200 odd lighthouses are all automatic now, as are the 5000 light beacons up and down this entire coast. Many of the 200 lighthouses are over 100 years old, and show just what a high price the small and then poor Norwegian population were prepared to pay for them. Until recently the coast was the highway in this huge country, and it was much easier and quicker to travel by ship than by road. Even today, it takes three days to drive from Bergen to Kirkenes along the modern road, and yet only five days by the Hurtigruten ferry. This lighthouse here at Lindesnes is the oldest in Norway and has undergone quite a few transformations since the first three storey wooden one was built in 1656 with 30 flickering candles behind a lead glass window.

There was quite a bit of commotion outside around midday; there were film crews with cameras and sound engineers with fluffy microphones on poles. I wondered what was going on. Simen explained that they were making a television series called '71 grader nord' or 'destination 71'. It was an adventure reality show and this was the celebrity edition. The celebrities soon arrived in taxis and they were now huddling together to try and escape from the wind. I recognized a comedian, a chef and an inspirational disabled athlete called Cato Pedersen, but that was all. Then I saw a knot of three women. One was an ex-playboy model from the 70s, one was a Norwegian handball star, who smoked continually, and the third was Kristin Krohn Devold, previously Norway's defence minister and now Secretary General of the DNT. I went over to introduce myself to Kristin. We chatted for 10 minutes

Day 236, Chatting with Kristin Krohn Devold who was the Secretary General of the DNT, which is the main outdoor body in Norway

about the mountains of Norway, the role of the DNT in making the mountains accessible, and their marvellous cabin network I had used at the start of the year. I told her a bit about my trip and how I revelled in the pristine Norwegian nature. Suddenly, the furry microphones and the large movie cameras were on the move again, and the celebrities had to perform. That evening, when the celebrities and the film crew had finished, Simen, Ole Jørgen and the rest of the museum staff had gone home, and the last tourist had seen the sunset, I was on my own again at the spot where it all started. As darkness finally fell I retreated into the tent to get out of the wind, hoping the weather would be less windy tomorrow, as I only had 13 days to get to Oslo now.

SECTION 33. The North Sea – Stavanger to Lindesnes
8 days. 188 kilometres. 42 hours. 0m ascent. 0m descent.

THE KAYAK: SECTION 34. SØRLANDET

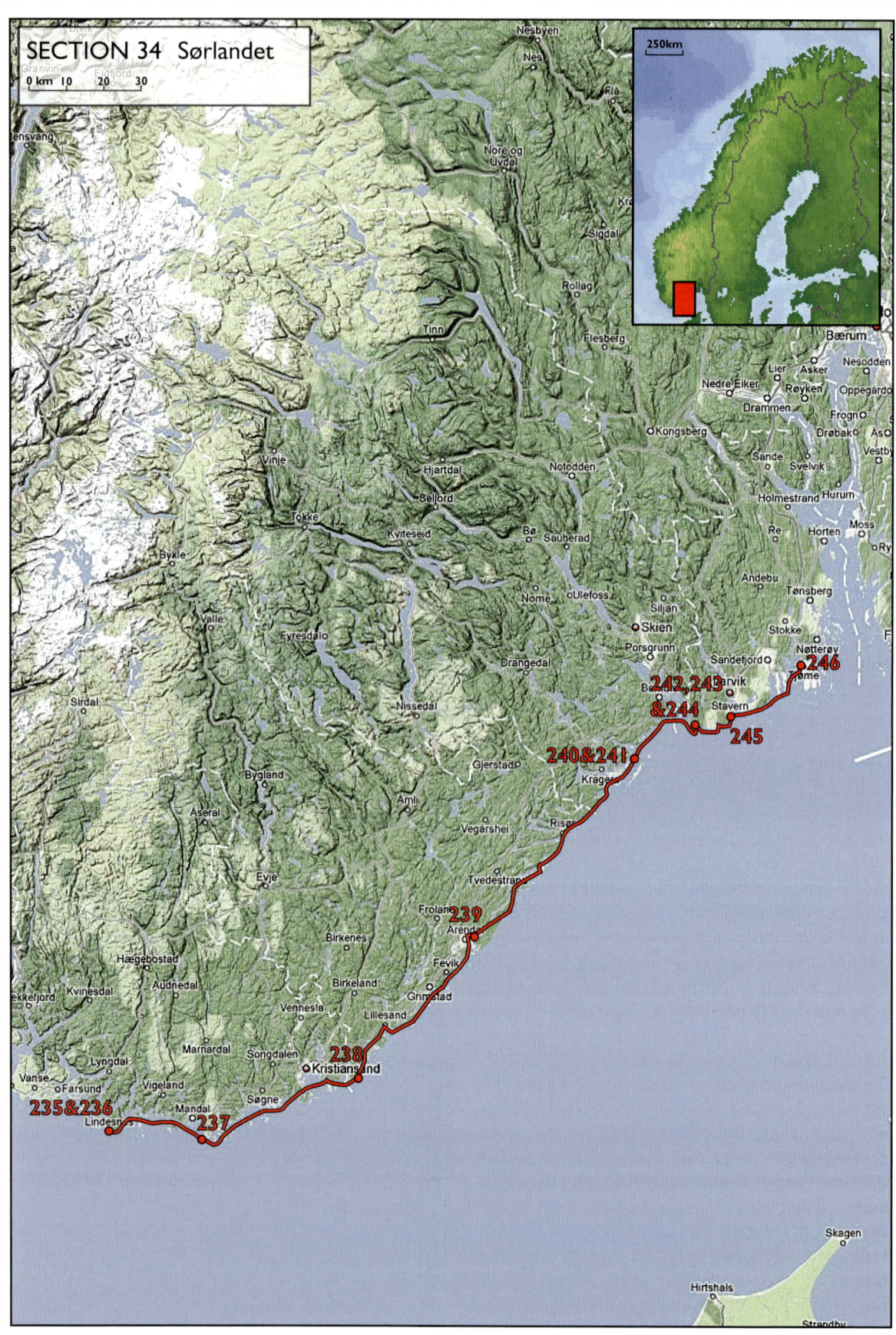

THE KAYAK: SECTION 34. SØRLANDET

Day 237. The calming inlet by Lindesnes fyr lighthouse had been alive with swell and surf just a few hours previously

The good force 6 wind in the night rustled the tent continually on my exposed platform, where I had nostalgically camped in the same place as on the calm night of 31st December, before I started my ski trip north. I was disturbed a few times and did not feel rested in the morning. I popped my head out of the tent and looked down the inlet at the incoming waves. The large south-easterly swell was piling in, crashing over the three metre high rocks in a chaos of surf at the inlet's entrance, before it surged up the inlet itself. The forecast said it would ease with time. Already, by mid-morning, I noticed it had decreased enough for me to start packing up and don my drysuit. I then went over to the lighthouse buildings to say goodbye to the very nice staff. Simen, who managed the visitor attractions, came down to see me off and took some photos. Once I was paddling in the inlet I realized it was not as bad as it looked from land, and I soon punched through the now two-metre swell at the mouth and into the North Sea. But my complacency was short lived, as just round the headland, after the inlet's entrance the wind was being squeezed into a fast jet and it was a good force 7 and directly against me. I was barely moving and the much larger waves were constantly breaking. There was not quite green water on their tops, but it felt uncomfortable. The sea was chaotic, with clapotis everywhere, and a few submerged shoals were erratically exploding with surf. This intense section only lasted for about a kilometre, but this kilometre took nearly an hour until I at last reached the lee of some small islets around Våge. I paused here to let my arms rest before venturing out again for another kilometre until I got to the lee of some larger islands by Lillehavn. By now the force 7 at the tip of the peninsula had diminished to a force 5 and I was making better time, but progress was still horribly slow. After another pause in the lee of these islands I set off again, quite despondent that my efforts were virtually accounting for nothing. In another hour I had only managed a further 3 kilometres to reach the small harbour of Gauksum. In three hard hours Lindesnes fyr lighthouse was just 5 kilometres behind me. However, the headwind was down to a force 4 now and the sea was subsiding the whole time, so I set off for the archipelago of Våre some 5 kilometres across the open sea. I knew it was just a question of making a slow gain until it dropped enough so I could penetrate into the weather more effectively. Slowly but surely Våre approached and before long I was sitting in the lee of it eating my lunch in the kayak. In five hours I had gone less than 10 kilometres.

Day 237. A massive ancient hand-built cairn on a skerry marked the passage for ancient mariners to enter the sanctuary of Hillesund

After lunch, when I went round the island into the wind again, I was delighted to see it was now down to a force 3. I had planned to go round the south of the rocky island of Hille, but now decided to go round the north to get as much protection as possible from the headwind. I paddled across an open bay some 8 kilometres wide, with a few rocky islets scattered across it. To the north was the typical Sørland landscape of rocky outcrops covered in pine forests with the occasional smaller fjord cutting into these lower hills. Like a watched kettle the wind did not really let up at all on the crossing and it was another two-hour slog into the headwind. I had been paddling seven hours now with just 18 kilometres on the clock! Once I reached the north side of Hille, the wind at last died off and I started to make good progress. Soon I was entering a narrow sound between Hille and a small island to its north which opened up into the most delightful basin, around which was the idyllic hamlet of Hillesund. Around its calm waters were about 10 lovely, old wooden cottages with weathered clay roof tiles and small verdant gardens which went right down to the water's edge where there were some small

Day 237. Entering the channel into the sheltered basin around which the old fishing hamlet of Hillesund was built

traditional red boat sheds beside the individual jetties. There were a few flags flying, and in contrast to the morning at Lindesnes where they were snapping in the wind, these flags were almost hanging limply.

I paddled out of this idyllic basin and continued down the north side of Hille. What a difference a few hours made. Not only had the wind dropped right down to a force 2 but it had also swung round to the west and was now in my favour. I did not have a definite goal for the evening, but thought it would be fun to camp on the tiny islet of Pysen to the south of Sandøy. It was Norway's most southerly point. However, as I paddled through the rocky barren islands east of Hille I began to suspect campsites might be few and far between. Every island and islet was a sculpture of knobbly rock, with just the tiniest patches of heather clinging to it. As I emerged from these grey islands I could see Sandøy in the distance, and like every other island around here it was also grey, barren and uninviting. I could easily imagine a scenario of looking for somewhere to pitch my tent and rest my head among the desert of gnarly rock slabs as darkness fell, so I abandoned the idea of camping on Pysen. At the same time, on an adjacent island, the lofty tower of Ryvingen fyr lighthouse appeared on its barren knoll. It was Norway's most southerly lighthouse. I remembered Simen at Lindesnes saying that the lady who managed the old keeper's house was there at the moment and she would probably be pleased if I dropped in. With some mist beginning to roll in off the sea I decided to head for Ryvingen fyr. It stood sentry on some of the most southerly islets in Norway, which lay scattered on this Skagerrak coast. I could not find anywhere to land and paddled round the west side and the entire south side but there was nothing but huge steep bulbous rock slabs which the swell washed. I eventually paddled into a deep inlet on the east side and found a small quay where I could pull myself out.

Day 237. Hillesund comprised of about 10 houses around the basin and would once been the permanent homes of fishing families

The mist was now enveloping the island, and out of it stepped Rita. She had been alerted by Simen at Lindesnes who warned her I might drop in and had spotted me approaching the west side. She worked for Mandal kommune who ran and maintained the entire lighthouse complex, except for the light tower itself. She knew the place intimately as her father had been the last keeper at this lighthouse, and she spent much of her childhood here. She kindly carried some of my stuff the 500 metres to the keeper's cottage. Beside it were other buildings which Mandal kommune hired out to various council departments and even the public. Currently there was a group of about 20 special needs teachers having a celebratory meal and evening at the lighthouse. They volunteered a spare bunk for me in one of the rooms they were using and invited me to their meal, but Rita had already invited me to eat with her and two relations she had staying, who had grown

Day 237. Approaching Ryvingen fyr lighthouse from the north west after which I had to paddle round the south side of the island to land up in Canada. We had a great evening. While my heavily accented Norwegian is pretty fluent and I barely have to think while talking to people it has little of the puns, witticisms and nuances which makes conversation fun. It is more of an exchange of facts, many of which are quite obvious. So, being allowed to run riot in English I took the opportunity, and we had a great evening's chat. Rita was also good friends with Sølvi, who ran the guest house and café at Ulvesund lighthouse, where I stayed four weeks ago, "my lighthouse sister" Rita said. By the time I headed back to the bunk, the three teachers with whom I was sharing the room had moved their celebrations from the polite chatty banter of red wine to the back-slapping, unreserved, pulsing excitement of Aquavit. Both are very Norwegian, but I prefer the latter. They encouraged me to join them and a few of the others around the debris of dinner on the outside tables, but after the long, arduous day I was too tired to join in. Norwegian hospitality was really second to none I thought as I feel asleep soon after.

Day 238. Looking down on the lighthouse keeper's cottage which Rita looks after from the lighthouse where Rita's father once worked

I was up quite early and well before my roommates. A few of the other teachers were up, mostly the women who had tempered their Aquavit consumption, and they invited me over for a coffee and a chat. Then Rita appeared and offered to show me round the lighthouse tower. It was quite a structure with five levels, with the light on the fifth. The whole tower was made out of cast plates measuring a bit less than a metre by two metres and massively reinforced with thick flanges on their internal faces, so each plate must have weighed at least 250 kilos. The flanges round the edge of each plate meant it could be bolted to its neighbour with at least 10 bolts on each of the four sides. The advantage with the plates is they could be transported and assembled quite easily from the foundry where they were cast. These plates had been cast at Bærums Verk foundry which seemed to have cast the plates for quite a few lighthouses. Once the plates were cast they were transported by boat. This tower was assembled in just a couple of months at the end of the 19th Century. From here there was a great view over the island and also the other islands in this archipelago. It was even possible to see the tiny skerry of Pysen, Norway's most southerly point, some 5 kilometres away. I could see it was absolute madness to consider camping on this small wet rock which was constantly washed over by the surf. After the lighthouse tour, the generous Rita came down to the jetty on the east side of the island to see me off, around midday. It was a beautiful day and it was hot in the sun down by the jetty.

Day 238. Looking from the tower down the walkway to the sheltered inlet on the east side of the island and Sandøy in the distance

Day 238. Rita on the jetty for Ryvingen fyr lighthouse which was the only place a boat could land on the island to supply the lighthouse

There was a good force 3 westerly wind which blew me along nicely across the open sea to Pysen. It was so small and flat I could not see it, so I had to head to Odd island which had an obvious cairn on it. Once there

Day 238. Just north of Pysen was the island of Sandøy with a massive cairn on it to warn previous sailors of the dangers nearby

it was easy to see Pysen. It was a tiny, but significant, wet smooth dome of rock measuring no more than 15 metres across and only about 2 metres high. None the less, it was the most southerly part of Norway, and from here it was all north to Oslo. I pressed the left rudder pedal and the kayak's bow swung north-east and I soon entered a fantastic coast with masses of islands and skerries. The wind was pushing me along smoothly, and the islands stopped the waves from building up, which would otherwise have slowed me down. It continued like this for a good 15 kilometres. Some of the islands were just about bare rock, while others had some sparse pine and juniper trees on them. There were goats on one island which had obviously been put out for summer grazing. It was a very nice relaxing paddle through these islands, especially the cluster of Udvår, where the rock was pink, so I assumed it was granite. There were plenty of seagulls here, mostly blackbacks. The juveniles were still whining at their parents to regurgitate some food, although most were probably able to obtain it themselves. It had been a while now since I had seen a sea eagle; I think the last one was north of Bergen.

After this island hopping I reached the islands of Monsøya and Helgøya. Between them was a small sound called Ny Hellesund. It was essentially a waterway through the hamlet of Ny-Hellesund. I think this hamlet was perhaps the most idyllic sight I have seen on the entire coast. Lots of little white cottages, perhaps 30 in all, were arranged along the shore in colourful gardens, squeezed between smooth rocky slabs. The roof tiles were all old and a rusty red with black specks where lichen was growing. Each cottage had an equally quaint boathouse and jetty where there were old boats moored. White picket fences enclosed the jetties, but not the gardens. It looked very old and original and I am sure it was not just kept that way by the people who had expensive cabins here, but also by the others who lived and still fished from here, as perhaps a second or summer job.

Day 238. The small but significant skerry of Pysen was the very southern outpost of Norwegian land with Ryvingen fyr in the distance

There was a real pride in the cultural heritage of this authentic hamlet. The only thing out of place here was a massive cabin cruiser. It was an unsophisticated display of opulent new money, amongst the more confident and modest old money, obvious in the rest of the hamlet with its cultured aesthetic awareness. It was a joy to paddle through Ny-Hellesund and every house had something of interest. However, despite me lingering through the old fishing hamlet, I was soon through it and once more back into the more open waters. The scattering of islands continued for another 6 kilometres, which kept the interesting exploration up and the waves down until I got to Flekkerøya island.

The sound separating Flekkerøya from the mainland was called Vestergapet, and in the days of smaller boats would have been the western entrance to the major

Day 238. The utterly charming and characterful maritime hamlet of Ny-Hellesund was perhaps the prettiest old fishing hamlet I came across

Day 238. The secluded bay on Ramsøya where I sneaked in and camped the night on the lawn in front of the empty houses

port of Kristiansand. However, with today's larger ships the wider Østergapet, on the other side of the island, is the main channel to the port. Flekkerøya island itself was quite built up and was really a suburb of Kristiansand, to which it was connected by a tunnel under Vestergapet. I paddled over the tunnel and emerged into the wide expanse of Østergapet. To my south, each side of the entrance to this waterway was marked by a lighthouse. Grønningen fyr, attached to the keeper's house on its bare skerry on the east side, and the tower of Oksøy fyr sitting on its larger islet on the west side. As I paddled over Østergapet, the city of Kristiansand appeared, unfolded and then hid again as the sides of this fjord revealed and then obscured it. I reached the far side, by Kongshavn, in the sound between the islands of Randsøya and the mainland.

Kongshavn seemed a mix of old fishing hamlet and modern suburb with about 50 new houses and 30 old ones. In tribute to the architect and planning department of Kristiansand kommune the new ones did fit in with the older ones. I weaved through the delightful waterway to the east of Kongshavn for a couple of kilometres until I reached Kvåsefjord. There was quite a swell coming in as I crossed Kvåsefjord as it was open to the south west. With the larger swell I started to wallow more and my speed dropped off as I headed to Indre Ulvøya island. The sun was starting to set now, and the wind which had been a godsend all day started to drop off. I paddled through the Indresund sound and passed under a small bridge to emerge into another small archipelago of small rocky islets and larger pine-clad islands with cabins on. There was still a good half hour's daylight left, but I thought I had better start looking for a place to camp. It would not be easy, as there were many private cabins along the shore. I paddled on for this half hour into the twilight, not seeing anything suitable, until suddenly, I saw three older houses sharing a beach and none had a light on. It was a great campsite, and as the beach was shared there would be no question of intruding. It was on the smaller island of Ramsøya. I paddled over, pulled up my kayak and pitched my tent as it was getting dark. All three houses seemed to be unoccupied. By the time I had finished my cooking and writing chores it was after midnight, and there was a fine drizzle pattering down on to the tent.

I was eager to paddle the 120 kilometres to Kragerø over the next two days, so was up early. It had rained all night, and in my haste to dismantle the heavy, clammy, tent I broke another section of tent pole, but luckily I still had a repair sleeve. My clothes were still wet from last night, so I left on my evening wear of fleece and put my drysuit over them. I was down to my last morsels of food, but knew resupplying would no longer be a problem, and I could pull into a town when hunger got the better of me. I decided to go the slightly longer, but much more scenic route, down a long continuous corridor of small straits and sounds called Blindleia. It did not weave between the islands, but sliced a narrow line right through the middle of them, all the way to the small town of Lillesand. I set off in the drizzle and headed straight to Gamle Hellesund. This was another

Day 239. Swans were confidently trawling the sides of the salt water basin by Gamle Hellesund in the drizzle

coastal hamlet lying in a natural basin surrounded by four islands. It was not as quaint as its namesake yesterday, Ny-Hellesund, but it was still a superb 'Sørlandsidyll', and the drizzle running off the end of my nose was soon forgotten. A group of swans cruised along the sides of the basin in front of the old white fishermen's cottages. These cottages seemed very quiet and empty and I could not smell any wood smoke at all. I left this serene basin and soon entered a maze of forested islets which I had to thread through to reach the start of the Blindleia channel. There were frequent small wooden cabins hidden in secluded bays with the mature conifer

Day 239. The sides of Blindleia were full of small coves, where old idyllic fishermen's cottages sheltered in the surrounding woods

forests enveloping them in a protective embrace. Here and there small rafts of eider duck paddled along the shore and through the fringe of reeds. Frequently I disturbed a heron, which with its cautious nature would laboriously take flight. When I finally entered Blindleia it was enchanting. To the north was the mainland with many small inlets, while to the south was the string of islands separated by small sounds. It was only the seaweed which reminded me I was not paddling a freshwater lake. The scattering of tiny hamlets and cabins continued all the way down the 10-kilometre long channel to Lillesand. Occasionally I smelt smoke, but I did not see anyone on this wet morning. The drizzle continued the whole way but it did little to dampen the beauty, and in fact, perhaps it enhanced it.

The channel passed under a bridge and entered a sheltered basin on the far side of which I could see the town of Lillesand. Its enormous white wooden Lutheran church's high steeple pierced the grey sky. I paddled over towards it, growing increasingly impressed with the waterfront of grand wooden buildings. I found a marina for small boats, pretty much in the heart of the town with a small artificial beach beside it. I pulled the kayak ashore and walked a few blocks to a shop. I bought food for five days and then had a small explore around the centre. People did not seem so friendly here, or maybe I just scared them off with my ragged feral look and drysuit, which, given the rain, seemed the ideal garment. After a good hour's shopping I was back in the kayak again. I had to head out of the basin through a choice of narrow sounds to gain the open sea again, as the idyllic inside passage of Blindleia had finished. I chose to

Day 239. Approaching the town of Lillesand with the great spire of its large Lutheran church piercing the grey wet sky

paddle down the narrow Grunnesund to the sea. It took me through the ranks of wooded islands, then heathery islets and finally, bare skerries, which all protected the superbly located port of Lillesand. I passed the substantial Homborsund fyr lighthouse, with the revolving lens turret attached to the keeper's house. There seemed to be a series of skerries and shoals further out, which broke up the swell, and it was just the residual waves which got through. Occasionally there was a gap in these and the Skagerrak swell came charging in, powered by the wind. The south-westerly force 4 wind was the exact direction and strength I wanted. I went to the outside of Bjorøy, and then the inside of the next larger island of Håøya. The wind helped me tremendously, and my average speed here was about 8 kilometres per hour. I was going so easily and quickly, I barely noticed the town of Grimstad, tucked away in a bay, before I was past it and paddling through the calmer waters on the inside of the wooded island of Hesnesøya.

Day 239. Paddling out of the sheltered harbour down the narrow Grunnesund to reach the outer islands and then the skerries beyond

The coastline along here was typical Sørlandet, with a low lying mainland, riven with numerous inlets. This whole landscape was then covered in pine trees and juniper bushes. There was also a lot of heather now

Day 239. Homborsund fyr lighthouse marked the outer edge of the coastline between Lillesand and Grimstad

which was purple in its autumn grandeur. I also thought I noticed some birch and rowan trees, just showing the first hints of autumn colours. Certainly the rowans were heavy with berry now. On the islets, the juvenile gulls were adult size, but still retained their childhood plumage. They continued to follow their parents and whine constantly for food. There were also many eider duck along the coast here, on the smooth ice-polished rocks of the skerries. They did not seem as shy as the other eider duck I had passed in the summer. With the wind and the lack of wallowing waves I made good progress past bay after bay while protected by a scattering of offshore islets and skerries. The headland at Hasseltangen sped past, and before I knew it I was making the final approach between some islands which marked the southern entrance to Arendal. I had paddled over 30 kilometres in less than four hours, which was in stark contrast to leaving Lindesnes a couple of days ago!

Arendal seemed much bigger than all the other towns on the south except Kristiansand, and more and more of it unfolded as I paddled up Galtesund sound. I crossed over and paddled up the east side along the shore of Tromøya island. For 4 kilometres I paddled past waterfront homes on the steep hillside. Many of these homes were quite bohemian and quirky. Interspersed among them were some older boatyards and wharfs. Just at the top of this sound, it did get more industrial for a while. Across the sound was the main centre of Arendal. It looked an interesting town and seemed a bit more relaxed than the formal Lillesand. Sunset had already been, it was getting dark and I needed somewhere to camp. After the industrial buildings I turned east into Tromøysund and past a grand stately home set in large parkland with huge sweeping lawns. It was the nearest thing I had seen to aristocracy in this egalitarian country. I thought about camping on the lawn along the shore, as the house was empty, but it might have been awkward if a factor arrived later and asked me to move.

Day 239. Havsøya island marked the entrance to the sheltered seas south of Arendal with the sheltered Galtesund leading north from it

Soon afterwards I settled for a spot in an overgrown glade with metre-high grass hidden in the trees. It was virtually dark now and I had to put the tent up with my head torch on. First I had to saw the broken bit off the pole section I had snapped this morning. Then I had to evict a huge and stubborn toad which had somehow got into the erected tent while I was unpacking and securing the boat. I had a cold dinner, directly from a tin, and set the alarm for 0330.

A few hours later, when the alarm sounded, I got up at once without even pausing for a moment to think. I knew any delay would be fatal, as I would rationalize a reason to go back to sleep. Breakfast was a packet of biscuits and a bar of chocolate. I then slid the kayak down the bank into the water, packed it and set off at 0500 all in the dark. I was still in a bit of a daze as I

Day 239. Lobster creels stacked on a jetty on the side of the relatively suburban Galtesund which led north to the large town of Arendal

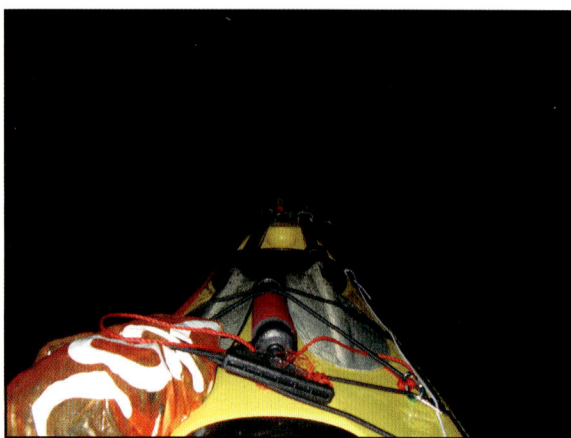

Day 240. Paddling east up Tromøysund and leaving Arendal long before sunrise, at the start of long and exciting day

paddled up Tromøysund feeling very tired and yawning profusely. It was completely wind still which did not help wake me up. I paddled about 2 kilometres to the bridge before the first hint of dawn started to appear. The south shore on Tromøya here seemed to be a sparse string of houses, sometimes bunched into the odd hamlet, but by and large it had a rural feel, while the north side on the mainland was much more urban and had the occasional industrial complex. It was only when I got to the open sea around 0700 did I start to wake up a bit. There was a small wind building, which was directly behind me, and there were many areas where the swell found a way through the scant shoals and skerries to make me more alert. I started to get into my pace now and headed up the east side of Sandøya, where a line of skerries protected me from the swell. At the north of Sandøya I crossed Sandfjord to reach Askerøya island and noticed the wind was swinging from the south west to the south and the first of the rain showers arrived.

At the east end of Askerøya was a very small town called Lyngør. It is one of the pearls of Sørlandet and is built round a sheltered basin where two narrow sounds cross. Lyngør is only accessible by boat and there are no cars there as there are no roads. It claims to be the best preserved town in northern Europe! It is renowned as the most beautiful town on the south coast and had become a favourite place for Norway's ships captains to retire to. When I reached it I could see why it would appeal to wealthy sea dogs as a place to hang their weathered caps. It was like taking a step back 50 years into a bygone era. Both the basin itself and the channels were lined with gorgeous wooden houses and small businesses, and access to all of them was via jetties and quays. The houses were rectangular and white, many were quite grand, and all were very well kept. The main business seemed to be the sail maker, but there were also a few boatyards, which now probably concentrated on maintaining the small boats and yachts which were located here.

Day 240. Some of Skagerrak swell was finding its way through the islands on the south of Askerøya just before the pearl of Lyngør town

I stopped at a jetty beside the shop and levered the kayak on to the wet wood. I needed a coffee and was curious to have a look in the shop. It too was from a bygone era, with all its wares stacked on wide wooden shelves, right up to the ceiling. They did not serve coffee and suggested the café but I did not really have enough time to linger, so returned to the kayak and set off slowly for a tour around the basin. It was raining heavily, so I could not take as many, or as composed, photos as I wanted. There were many working boats moored beside the quays in front on the houses and some older modest wooden sailing yachts. Indeed, it seemed modern cabin cruisers were sparse and outnumbered. I read there were only about 100 people who stay here through the year, and in the summer the population grows to well over 1000, as people come to live in their maritime

Day 240. The sail makers at Lyngør was still a going concern and was sited on the edge of the sheltered basin like every other building

Day 240. The sheltered basin of the historic town of Lyngør was lined with quite grand houses which were only accessible by boat

houses and cabins. With regret, I left before I was ready, and paddled out of the very small channel, lined with old houses, leading out from the north of the basin and into the east end of Lyngørfjord.

As I headed west up the coast and out of Lyngørfjord the islands and skerries started to vanish and I soon found myself in the open sea. The south-westerly wind was up to a force 4 now but it was forecast to increase to an 8 in the evening. There was nothing to stop the increasing waves and when I went round one small peninsula, called Sildodden, they were already two metres and the sea was getting quite confused. It was a short section though and I was soon back into the shelter of the skerries as I paddled up to the end of this peninsula at Fie. Here I had a dilemma; I could either make a detour into the sheltered fjord and go round Furuøya island, or just cut straight cross Stangholmgapet, which would be half an hour quicker. Once on the other side I would reach the protection of a string of islands which sheltered the town of Risør. With the wind now up to a force 5 I decided to make a quick dash across the fjord before it increased more. I surged across this fjord mouth with the kayak bucking under me as waves broke over the stern and got to the other side unscathed. I was now on the lee side of the 7-kilometre string of islands and I was beginning to get quite optimistic about reaching the comforts of Arøy by Kragerø that evening, but I still had 30 kilometres to go and some of it was exposed.

I ate lunch in the kayak with the wind blowing me past Risør. In half an hour I was blown nearly 2 kilometres up the sound with the town drifting past. It was a nice looking town but not in the same league as Lyngør, and it was not as quirky as the much larger Arendal. Indeed, it seemed to have the formal order of Lillesand, but then I was viewing it from a distance through the drizzle. The advantage of the rudder was that I could keep my back to the wind rather than wallowing across the beam. Lunch over, I took up the paddle again and continued behind the lee of the islands for another hour before they gradually petered out just before Gjernestangen. I now had a 10-kilometre stretch of exposed coastline, and both my road map and fiddly GPS showed that there was no sheltered inside passage. Unfortunately, coinciding with my arrival at the start of this coast the weather deteriorated yet another stage. The wind was now a good force 6 and the skies behind me, and downwind, were black. I was worried, but the thought of a warm dry bed and home cooking put me in a predicament. Had I been camping, I would have called it a day here. Tentatively, I decided to continue, and with a nervous knot in my stomach set off. I knew that once I neared the exposed headland I was pretty much committed, as it would not be possible to turn back.

The more I paddled out round the headland, being forced into the open sea, the more worried I became. The waves at the point were three metres, steep and nearly all were curling over at the top. I now wished I had camped a few kilometres back and did not have to face the next 8 kilometres. There was no way I could take my hands off the paddle to check my GPS to see if there was any escape route. From my low position on the crests of the waves, all I could see was a constant line of crashing surf, as these large waves pounded the smooth rocky slabs of the coast. Suddenly there was a blinding flash and a huge clap of thunder. If I was not unnerved enough, this was sufficient to dry my mouth, as fear became very real. With the thunder came a tremendously heavy rain shower. Often, very heavy rain tends to calm the sea, but not this time and it continued to tumble all around me as the wind in this violent squall was at least a force 8. Spray was flying everywhere and the sea's surface was heavily streaked with froth. I could not see any escape through the mayhem along the shore and knew I would have to carry on all the way to Portør. I thought it was perhaps 5 kilometres away by now but it could not come quick enough. The crest of the waves were no longer toppling surf, but great claws of green water, which reared up and toppled on to the wave's face. If one of these reared up behind me, I was over, and I was psyching myself for a capsize and hopefully a roll, at any instant. I was a good kilometre from the land as I had to avoid the numerous shoals which were a chaos of crashing surf. On the crest of every wave I was desperately looking

Day 240. After a very challenging 5km between Gjernes and Portør I managed to find some shelter on the inside of the skerries and islets

for an escape route from this apocalyptic surging sea, and the flashes of lightning and claps, of thunder which were all around. I reckoned only another 4 kilometres to Portør now.

Suddenly I saw a red fishing boat on my right. It was heaving and surging on the waves and was obviously making for land. The fisherman must have called it a day and was heading for shelter. At one stage we were just 100 metres apart and I could see him looking out of the wheelhouse at me disappearing into the troughs and then leaping up on a white crest. He must have been thinking "madman". I knew he would know a route in to sheltered waters, so I followed him the best I could for a kilometre, until he disappeared from sight behind an islet. I knew this was my route and in five minutes I was at last entering calmer waters behind a rank of shoals and islets. I had made it and was now quite prepared to find the nearest campsite and put up the tent. At last I could take my hand off the paddle and take my GPS out of my life jacket pocket. I wedged the kayak between two rocks as another squall hit with more flashes of lightning and the heaviest rain shower I had seen on this entire trip. The droplets were bouncing nearly head height back off the surface, which I could only see for 10 metres before it was a haze of splash. I realized I was at Bruntangen and just a mere 3 kilometres from Portør, and with delight saw on my GPS map that there was in fact a sheltered inside route from here on, and I would not have to venture back into the mayhem. I decided to give it a try, as although the wind was ferocious, it was behind me and in these waters, peppered with islets, there was just no fetch for any sea to build up. The warm bed and home cooking beckoned again. As I sneaked through the skerries the rain ceased and I made good progress in the strong wind. Occasionally I had to go round a headland but it was not difficult as the main violence between the sea and the land was taking place off the coast on the other side of the shoals and it was just the remnants of the rage which got through. Reaching Portør after this sheltered paddle was almost an anticlimax.

I had a surprisingly easy crossing across the kilometre-wide bay to Rapentangen, with the wind pushing me hard but the waves remaining small. Now I just had to cross Kragerøfjord, the last obstacle before I reached the sheltered sanctuary of the extensive Kragerø archipelago. The fjord was just a kilometre wide, but in this force 7 wind I was wary about the waves on the far side, but knew they would be nothing like the rampant ocean waves I had endured just an hour earlier. To the south I could see the whole sea was white where the swell, which had grown suddenly, was toppling on the reefs and exploding on to the skerries. The force 7 wind would then disperse the spray over the whole area, like smoke from burning fields. By the time I reached the island cluster of Vestre Rauane on the far side of Kragerøfjord, the waves were already a metre, having formed in the short one kilometre fetch, and every one was breaking, streaking the sea with surf. I paddled through the shelter of this cluster with the wind whistling through its channels, and then had an easy short crossing into the heart of this archipelago, which was not only protected by its own islands but also by Jomfruland. This long crescent-shaped island, which was composed of boulders on the outside and beaches on the inside shores, was a part of the Ra Moraine. As this huge ice sheet retreated some 10,000 years ago, it occasionally paused during colder spells. During these pauses the margin stood still and the ice sheet dumped debris on the same spot for a few hundred years. The Ra Moraine was the most prominent of these concentric marginal moraines of the ice sheet, and it partially encircles Scandinavia. Jomfruland is part of the ridge of the Ra Moraine which later became flooded by the Skagerrak sea.

I had just 6 kilometres to go now, and all of it sheltered, so I stopped, unwrapped my phone and told my ex mother-in-law, Ingrid, to put the kettle on. I had told her a week ago I might drop in as I knew she would be there, but she was still surprised. The islands around Kragerø have become very fashionable in the last 25 years, for the wealthy of Oslo to build their summer cabins. In some places there are ridiculously opulent palaces of the new rich, and in other places, desperate social climbers have bought a small bare skerry and built a white palace

Day 240. Getting blown through the Kragerø archipelago to my goal at Arøy, with the island and lighthouse of Jomfruland to the bow's right

on top of it, complete with Corinthian pillars. There is little of the magic and charisma of Ny-Hellesund among these newer intrusions. However, there are also some charming small fishing hamlets dotted about on these islands and modest older cabins dating back 50 years. Ingrid had one of these and she spent the entire summer at it enjoying its natural peace. Her delightful cabin was on the very south west tip of Arøy island and I knew it well. I reached her jetty at 1900, after 14 hours and 70 kilometres of paddling. I pulled the kayak up on to the grass and carried my bags up to the collection of cabins and annexes. It was good to be here again and I felt very much at home. I had a shower and had to borrow clothes, as everything I had was filthy or wet, much of it both. Clean and shaved, I had a great meal of king crab and wine and then chatted in front of the crackling fire as the sun went down outside the window, and the lighthouse on Jomfruland began to flash. Perhaps I still had some adrenaline coursing through my arteries after the desperate paddle before Portør, as despite the early start I did not feel tired. We chatted until well after midnight before I went out to my annexe cabin and a bed with clean cotton sheets. I lay in the warm bed with glee, listening to the wind ripping through the birch trees and lashing heavy rain against the window.

I still had another week to paddle the remaining 200 kilometres to Oslo, and had paddled well over that in the last four days, so thought I could afford a rest day here. I also had a few tasks to do which could not wait until the finish at Oslo. There was still a strong wind whipping the hanging branches of the large weeping birch trees, and the sea was full of white horses, so I did not feel anxious about lingering at this peaceful spot, and Ingrid and was keen for me to stay. After breakfast I had a long chat with Ingrid, for a few hours, while she showed me round the cabin and the grounds again. Not much had changed since I was last here some four years ago. I then started some of my tasks. Firstly, I had to repair the expensive 'Epic' paddle. I had to wash it in fresh water, dry it, sand and abrade it and then glue it. It was the second time I have had to repair this poorly-designed paddle. Secondly, I had to repair my tent poles, as a few of them were starting to split. Some of the poles were now probably a good 15 centimetres shorter after I had cut off the broken sections. I also oiled the joints, as most were sticking due to salt corroding them. Thirdly, I had to wash all my clothes. I put them in a large tub to soak, and agitated them after a couple of hours. Water was scarce on these islands, but the wet weather of recent days had filled up a dinghy on the lawn beside the boat shed with fresh water. I used it to rinse my clothes before emptying it and turning the small plastic boat upside down. Finally, I started my writing, and by late afternoon I had managed to catch up with it and process and publish all the necessary photos. If there was one thing above all other I was looking forward

Day 240. Ingrid's boat shed and cabin on the south-west corner of Arøy, where I was to find sanctuary from the wind for a day

Day 241. My small cosy dry cabin for two nights where I managed to clean my clothes, write and repair a few things for the final week

to when finishing this trip, it was not having to constantly catch up with my writing which always seemed to be hanging over me like a dark cloud. All day the sun had shone, but the wind did not let up, and remained around a force 6. The strong wind did not worry me at all and it justified my rest day and dried my clothes in an instant.

Day 241. The view from the cabin, out across the sheltered waters, with the natural barrier of Jomfruland in the distance

That evening, Ingrid made a huge casserole of Fårikål. It was another sure sign summer was coming to an end, as this was the culinary equivalent of the autumn equinox. Fårikål is Norway's national dish; it is a simple rural dish which has now become something of a feast. It is a lamb and cabbage stew. The stew was traditionally made when farmers brought their sheep down from the mountain farms with the onset of colder autumn weather which could mean snow above the treeline. The sheep would return to the limited fields around the farm, and eventually the barns, for the winter when the snow piled up. However, the large lambs, having been fattened up on the lush grasses in the high birch woods all summer, had no place on the farm. The farmer kept a few for his pot and the rest went off to market, where the fate of many was Fårikål. After the meal I gave Jon Westgård a ring, as he lived nearby. I had paddled with Jon for much of the first week after the extraordinary chance meeting on the deserted Finnmark beach in the spring. He took the ferry from Vardø to Tromsø, skipping the exposed Østhavet and Nordishavet coasts before resuming his journey and finishing in Bergen just a few days behind me. Despite the poor weather forecast he was keen to meet me for a paddle the next day and would join me around Langesund.

The next morning, before I set off, I had to do a few small jobs for Ingrid, as she was now preparing to close the cabin and sheds up for winter. It seemed hard to imagine that this warm, lush place, where a decade ago I had once measured the temperature in the sea at 24 degrees, would soon be covered in snow, and the same sea would freeze over, but it would. We then carried everything down to the kayak, where I packed. Ingrid looked on in disbelief as all my possessions disappeared into the small craft, and could barely comprehend that it had come all the way from Grense Jakobselv, some 3000 kilometres to the north, on the Russian border. Eventually at midday everything was packed, I said goodbye and pushed off. Ingrid had kindly phoned a relation of hers, Vava, who owned a cabin some 10 kilometres up the coast on the island of Såstein. He was not there but said I could use it if I wanted. I was keen to push on a bit further than the 10 kilometres, but it was still very windy and Såstein was on the near side of the exposed and renowned Langesundsbukta which might be too difficult to cross, in which case the cabin would be a godsend. I set off round the north side of Arøy and soon phoned Jon, conscious I was delayed. He was already at Langesund and on the water, but he said the sea was rough and was apprehensive about accompanying me over the infamous Langesundsbukta. I said I would paddle up to Såstein island and give him a ring from there. The journey to Såstein was quick and easy, and the string of islands which extended from the north east of Arøy continued nearly all the way and prevented any swell coming through from Skagerrak. At the same time there was a good force 5 directly behind me, which pushed me along quite quickly. In well under two hours I was at Såstein, a smaller beautiful island covered in pine forest. It was actually two islands divided by a very narrow channel just a few metres wide in places. The smaller island was a nature reserve. I paddled round the north of the island and into this channel and noticed a large swell crashing on to the reefs and shoals of the seaward side. I feared this was a taste of things to come. In the sanctuary of the narrow channel I phoned Jon. He was not keen to paddle and was now back on dry land. He said if I was actually going to paddle over he would meet me on the other side, but he advised me to be cautious.

I sat in the channel deliberating, beneath the comfortable looking cabin Vava said I could use. Beyond the entrance to the channel was the significant crossing of Langesundsbukta where there were likely to be difficult conditions. It was only 6 kilometres, an hour, to Fugløya on the far side where I could bail out. Looking at the deteriorating forecast over the next few days I knew I had to do it now, in this force 5, or be stuck here for days. I knew the seas here could be bad, and there was evidence of this all around me and filling my nostrils. Four weeks previously there had been an unseasonal storm here, and a large 30,000 ton bulk carrier, the *Full City* which was anchored nearby, broke its chain anchor in the middle of the night. The inattentive crew had not noticed the ship was drifting until it smashed on to the rocks just 400 metres from where I was now sitting. Many of the holds were flooded and some 250 tons of heavy bunker fuel oil were spilled into the sea. There had been an effective clean-up operation over the last month, and much of this oil had been collected and removed, and the ship had been refloated and towed off for repair. However, there was considerable damage to the environment around Såstein and the adjacent coasts; many sea birds, mostly ducks had been killed. The smell of oil still lingered in the air and I could see many patches, smeared on the rocks, still wreaking havoc with the wildlife. Indeed the smell of the oil partly prompted me to carry on, so I secured my map and GPS and took up my paddle.

Day 242. In the narrow channel on Såstein and just about to cross the 5km Langesundsbukta which I knew had a large swell and fresh wind

As soon as I poked my nose out of the sheltered channel and into the fjord I realized I was in for an exciting ride. The swell was a good two metres immediately outside the channel and I had to weave through shoals where green water was breaking. Once I was clear of these, the swell increased to three metres and on the tops of many of them were small tumbling white horses. The wind was a force 5 and it was coming from the southwest which was almost directly behind me. I was pretty much committed now as I was a kilometre from Såstein and it would be too difficult to return. I had my sights on the south end of Fugløya which was no nearer than it was when I started. I kept a constant eye out to sea, just to make sure no rogue wave was going to surprise me. Despite the wind, the white horses remained quite small and manageable, but the swell was getting bigger and bigger. After an hour, as I neared Fugløya island, I thought some of them must have been four metres from trough to crest and they were like moving hills of water. I could not land here, but could have continued to the far side of the bay and easily have sneaked inside a boulder spit called Mølen, which I learned later was also a glacial deposit from the Ra Moraine. But this would still leave the exposed headland of Oddane to get round, and it was my goal, otherwise I would be stuck on this side of it for the next few days. I paddled the kilometre to Mølen beach which was composed of huge boulders. There would be no chance of landing here, even in an emergency, as the hills of water were surging towards the beach and then rising up and dumping down on to the boulders. It would have made short work of me and my kayak, so I had to continue for what I estimated was another 3 kilometres, but I feared the wind was increasing up to a force 6.

The paddle from Mølen to Oddane was exciting. The swell was a good four metres with some enormous steep mountains of water charging in from the south west. It was shallow enough here to make this ocean swell and form into steep waves, but not so shallow the top part toppled over, except for one skerry called Finsbåane, which was a mayhem of frightening exploding surf, and I gave it a very wide berth. There were still plenty of white caps created by the wind, which was lifting spray off all the crests. For some reason I still had my sun glasses on but I could not afford a spare hand to take them off. They were constantly deluged in spray and impaired my vision and I was hoping they would get swept off into the sea. I was broadside to the oncoming waves, and had a rogue wave come I would not have been able to turn into it quickly enough, so would have

Day 242. The waves crashing on to the boulder beach at Mølen were a few metres high and prohibited any landing here

had to have taken all side on. However, I was getting very confident in the kayak's sea-worthiness and stability. I would have gone over in almost anything else, but this Tiderace Explore X had looked after me very well. While I was perched on top of these large waves I could see people on the boulder beach. Eventually I approached Oddane and saw there was a wide gap between the headland and some islands. I could easily paddle here, but it would mean turning my back on this heaving sea for 300-400 metres. This made me nervous, but I had to do it, as beyond the gap was the reward of sanctuary. As I paddled through, there was the odd unwelcome surprise, as some large waves surged up behind me and lifted me almost violently as they passed beneath me, but I was soon into quieter waters. A little further on, I spotted a beach and some cabins.

I paddled to the beach and landed in the small surf. The woman running the campsite approached me. She had seen me going round the headland at Oddane, and was fascinated that anybody would be out in it, let alone in a kayak. I chatted a bit with her still pumping with adrenaline. She said she was not really open to the public, but she had a spare cabin I could use. I unpacked into the cabin and gave Jon a ring. He had been taking photos of the waves at Mølen and arrived soon after. It was good to see him again. We decided to go for a meal in Nevlunghavn, a short walk to the north. Nevlunghavn seemed a very quaint south coast village with white wooden houses lining narrow twisting streets. White picket fences separated the tidy gardens. We soon reached the harbour which was the heart of the village. There was a shop, a hotel and a few cafés which were closed, as the season was over. With Jon's easy gregarious manner we met many locals near the hotel and chatted with them before going for a meal. We had a lot to reminisce about. Jon had taken a pause a month after leaving Tromsø and during this time I had caught him up and overtaken him. When he resumed, he was just two days behind me, and remained there pretty much all the time until he got to Bergen when he finished his trip. We talked about all the scary bits, like Stad, and both of us waxed lyrically about Helgelandskysten. We walked back through Nevlunghavn in the dark to the cabin and Jon left, allowing me to write about the day's exciting paddling.

The weather the next morning was initially dull, with a stiff breeze and a light drizzle, or Scotch mist. It was perfectly good to paddle in, so I started to pack up and then went to the reception to return the key to Reidun Berg who managed the complex and let me stay. The complex was called Gurvika Camping and it was composed of 22 cabins, a large building for groups, and a central building with a pool of heated sea water and showers. It was not really open to the public, as it was set up by a trust to provide holiday accommodation for handicapped people and their families or carers. It was only because I arrived from the sea in a kayak in a near gale and rain that she took pity on me and let me use a cabin. When I returned to my cabin just a quarter of an hour later to carry my bags to the beach, the weather had quickly deteriorated. The flag in the campsite was cracking in the wind, and even the relatively sheltered bay was full of white caps. The islets beyond were ringed with exploding surf. I stood on the balcony of the cabin, out of the rain, looking at the willow trees whipping in the increasing wind. It would be madness to go, as the forecast predicted this and I would not gain much before I had to seek shelter from the sea and hide in my tent. Just then Reidun arrived to clean the cabin. She said I could stay another day. In fact, she wanted me to meet a local journalist and also come to dinner that evening. She also said I could use the heated salt water swimming pool on the complex. It was manna from heaven. I retreated back to the cabin, delighted to be staying another day.

Day 242. Looking out from Gurvika bay to the islands and skerries which were taking the brunt of the Skagerrak swell

The weather turned out to be worse than the forecast; it was a very wet near gale all day. I stayed in the cabin resting most of the day, smugly looking out of the window at the flag cracking in the raging weather. After a siesta I went for a swim in the heated pool. It was apparently 34 degrees and it felt warm. The swimming pool was also very wheelchair friendly with a long tiled ramp down to the water. The journalist, Roy, arrived with Reidun at 1830. We chatted before Reidun had to go to finish cooking the meal. The interview was very relaxed. We would have supper together so there was no need to make frantic notes. We chatted for an hour before we walked up to Reidun's lovely home, a typical Nevlunghavn white wooden building with its tidy garden and berry bushes. Unfortunately I forgot my camera. The meal was simply amazing, the best I had had all year, and there were huge amounts of it beautifully served on large white plates. Roast pork with crispy crackling, broccoli, carrots, boiled potatoes, caramelized baby potatoes, surkål, cranberry sauce and pepper gravy. I had three helpings, as Reidun would not accept "I am full" as an answer. We all chatted for a few hours. I heard about Roy's work as a professional healer and accomplished amateur journalist. His website 'http://paaneset.no' covered a lot of local issues, especially the recent 'Full City' ship disaster. Full of delicious healthy food, I walked back through the charming town of narrow streets lined by the picturesque houses, in the dark at 2200. I felt like a Lilliputian midget wandering through a collection of the Giant's expensive white doll's houses draped in lace and separated by the white picket fences.

Day 243. The small marina in the pretty town of Nevlunghavn was once a fishing harbour, but most of the boats now are for leisure

When I woke and looked out of the window, the first thing I saw was the large willow bush outside the window thrashing wildly in the wind, but curiously the waves on the beach were not that big. I re-checked the forecast and it said it would be a force 5 in the morning, rising to a force 7 in the afternoon. It seemed the force 7 had already arrived, and I had to resign myself to staying here for another day. It was frustrating, but there was little I could do, other than return to bed. Oslo was still 150 kilometres away, and I now had just five days to do it in, which was perfectly feasible if the wind allowed. During the next 10 kilometres, between here and the harbour of Stavern, I would have to pass the infamous Rakkebåene, one of the most notorious passages on the entire south coast, with many shoals waiting to spring a surprise. Reidun arrived at midday and said Roy, the journalist, was at the bakery in Nevlunghavn and wanted to treat me to lunch there. We wandered over, through the picturesque town to the bakery. It was a 20 year-old family-run business which made bread, cakes and had a café also selling filled rolls and soup. It was doing a roaring trade and many of the locals seemed to come here for lunch and a social catch-up. People even rated the food here better than the hotel. We joined a table with three others and there was a lot of banter for the lively lunch. Both Roy and Reidun had to return to work, so I wandered through Nevlunghavn to pass some time. The winter population of Nevlunghavn was about 500, but in the summer this can rise to 5000. There are a lot of summer houses here which are just used for a few months in the holidays and then closed up for the autumn, and it looked like it was already autumn. All the houses, summer or permanent, were well-kept and many of the gardens had apple or pear trees heavy with fruit. I wondered through the small lanes and around the harbour area for two hours, admiring the buildings and the village. There were a few older men repairing lobster creels for the season, which opens on October 1st. These creels were totally different to the Scottish creels I was very familiar with and are made from slats of wood rather than netting over a wire frame. Nevlunghavn was a nice place to be weather bound in, and the hospitality and friendliness of Reidun and Roy made my stay a happy one.

Day 244. Repairing the lobster creels in Nevlunghavn harbour for the start of the season on October 1st

It was surprisingly still when I woke early. It was the opportunity I had been waiting for to get round the difficult Brunlanes peninsula which lay between Nevlunghavn and Stavern, and if I was really lucky, perhaps the next peninsulas between Larvik and Sandefjord and into Oslofjord. The immediate hazard off Brunlanes was Rakkebåene. This 4-kilometre stretch of shoals extends about 3 kilometres into Skagerrak. In calm weather there is just a current to contend with. But if there is a big swell in Skagerrak, especially a south-westerly one, the seas in this quadrant are dangerous, with erratic breaking waves. Even the sea charts have 'area with dangerous waves' marked on them so I was keen to get it behind me. I quickly had breakfast, packed up, swept the cabin and was off by 0700. The first few kilometres were easy and I was confident I would get to Oslofjord that day. I had the slight wind behind me and the swell was small. I should have realised I was being protected from Skagerrak's anger by the islands extending out from Nevlunghavn, but I did notice the wind picking up and the skies darkening. I paddled past the shoals at Midtbåene, where there were some large breaking waves, past the deep inlet of Hummerbakkfjorden, and started round the convoluted headland to reach the deep bay of Naverfjord. Out to sea I could see Tvistein fyr lighthouse sitting on its small skerry surrounded by a ring of surf, and I could see ahead across the fjord, where just a kilometre away the next headland pushed into the ocean. What I saw unnerved me as there were numerous areas where the large swell was breaking over the shoals at the start of Rakkebåene.

Day 245. Looking to one of the headlands by Rakkebåene where the Skagerrak swell was erratically erupting on the hidden shoals

I was hoping for an inside passage and crossed Naverfjord to the east side. The start of the headland on the east side of Naverfjord proved to be very difficult. The waves were large and confused, there was the occasional swell erupting on unseen shoals and the wind was now at least a force 5. I could not see any inside passage and there was no chance of me taking my hands off the paddle to have a look at my GPS map. I decided to go into an inlet and see, but it was a dead end, so I returned to the start of the headland. After plucking up some courage I starting heading out, but in the force 5 I was just getting nowhere and the sea in front was boiling white. I lost my nerve and decided to call it a day and retreat into Naverfjord where there was a beach, and camp. On the way in there was a tremendous thunderstorm and very heavy rain. The wind had now increased to a force 7 and I was very thankful I was not at the mercy of the Rakkebåene in this tempest. I landed in the small surf and stood under a small shelter while the biblical rain shower passed. I was now cold, wet and miserable and could not find anywhere to camp. As I dithered, the thunderstorm passed, the wind dropped down to a force 5 again and there was even a flash of blue sky to the west. I decided to give the headland and Rakkebåene another go.

I paddled the slow 2 kilometres into the wind out to the headland again. As I approached the headland the south-westerly swell returned, charging in from the sea. I was gazing at this swell when I saw a huge set coming and watched them as they approached rapidly. Suddenly, the first in this series just grew and grew, some 30 metres to my side, until it was a huge pyramid of water at least five metres high. It hung there for a while then this vertical wall of dark green water curled over into a large green tube and came crashing down on the hidden skerry. There was a massive explosion of surf which billowed up into the air for a good ten metres before it was carried off in the wind. Then the next ridge of water charging towards me did the same, as did the next two. Then the fifth and smaller swell just rolled straight over the hidden shoal without so much as a ruffle as did all the following ones. This display of raw power really unsettled me. There was no indication there was a shoal here from the way the sea behaved until this massive set of swells came through. Had I been 30 metres to the east I would have been in the middle of it. Despite the fact I was perpendicular to it, I would have been turned end over end and smashed on to the rock with hundreds of tons of water pummelling me. Even a cabin cruiser or yacht would have been turned over and destroyed by these monsters. I did not want to carry on and was really quite frightened, so paddled towards the rocks and into an inlet to gather my thoughts. I sat watching this area for at least 10 minutes but did not see any huge swells return to reawaken the monsters. I thought about returning to the dull beach, the wet abandoned caravan park, and the two kilometres I paddled into the wind since them, and decided to try again. When I got to the headland there were very choppy seas with many breaking swells. Most seemed to lose a lot of their power on the shoals further out and they were a diminished, but not spent, force by the time they reached the headland. I waited and watched for another 10 minutes, until I was quite confident there was a relatively safe passage. Then I made a dash across the 200 metres of choppy chaotic water to reach an islet I could shelter behind, and a deep inlet I could escape into had I wanted. However, there was another headland to get round and again I waited, watched and made the dash to the next sanctuary. There were about five such headlands, and each one got easier as I went further east. There were also more islands to hide behind as I approached the final headland. Soon, Stavernsodden fyr lighthouse appeared, and a reasonably sheltered channel opened up in front of me as the last headland was an anti-climax. Rakkebåene was behind me.

Day 245. After passing the five small but challenging headlands of Rakkebåene I reached the sanctuary of a channel before Stavern town

I paddled past the lighthouse and down the channel into Stavern with the force 5 blowing me along. I was planning to cross Larviksfjord at once, but saw a shop beside the small boat marina. I paddled up and pulled the boat on to the floating jetty. There were two groups of friendly sailors with whom I started chatting when I landed. I told them I had just come round from Nevlungshavn and they were keen to pick my brains about Rakkebåene, but I told them I sneaked along the coast which they could not hope to do in their yachts. I also told them about the four monster waves which had scared me a lot and they decided to stay put. I bought food and returned to the kayak, but by now the wind was up to a force 6 again and I was apprehensive about leaving. One of the sailing boats' crew suggested a coffee and we chatted as it brewed. I then decided to pitch my tent on the grass nearby and stay in Stavern.

Once I pitched I went for a small walk through this nice town. Back at the jetty, Espen and Sunya, the sailing couple who had made me coffee earlier on, invited me and the other two sailors on board their yacht for fish soup. It was delicious and rich, more like a stew, with at least 10 different ingredients. We had a great evening and I was plied with Aquavit until I was almost exuberant, which did not take much, as my alcohol tolerance was now like a child's again, after months of near abstinence.

A conspiracy of urban ravens started a tremendous racket outside my tent early in the morning and woke me. They carried on for a good hour until I had to get up and chase them off. Espen and Sunya were already up and on their deck and beckoned me over for coffee. After the coffee, I quickly took down the tent and launched, to get as much under my belt as possible before the forecast easterly wind started in earnest this afternoon. As soon as I was out of the harbour, I realized the easterly wind had already started and was now a force 3. Today was going to be a fight. I made it across Larviksfjord to Malmøya island quite quickly. I had to, as Larvik was a busy port and there were a few ferries entering and leaving the fjord as I crossed, and I had to keep out of their way. The wind hampered me a little, but the current I was warned about did not seem

Day 245. Old fishing boats in the small boat marina in Stavern harbour, next to where I pitched my tent for the night under trees

to exist. This is the current which comes out of the Baltic and flows up the Swedish west coast before being forced west down the Norwegian south coast. I continued east past the headland and round a couple of small peninsulas to the bay of Ula. I did not go in but continued to pull myself across the bay to the next headland. There was the odd island or islet to find shelter behind, but by and large it was an exposed coast and I had to

Day 246. Stavern Fort on the islands outside the harbour dates back more than 300 years and has been an important naval base in its time

battle into the relentless wind and smaller waves. By now the wind was a good force 5 and my progress had slowed right down. The spray was coming off each wave and back into my face. I was surprised how warm it was. It felt well over 20 degrees. Slowly but surely I made some hard-fought progress and soon I was round the last headland and heading towards Kjerringholmen, a larger island behind which there was some lee. There is a small village, Kjerringsvik, tucked behind these islands which must have been an old fishing village, as the rocky wooded landscape here was far too rugged for farming.

I had a snack in the lee of the islands while preparing myself for the final two hurdles of the day. I could see the wind whipping the pendant-like flags on a few of the flag posts in the village, and knew I had heavy work ahead. These hurdles were the crossing of two quite narrow fjords, each only 2 kilometres wide, to reach the two headlands of Vesterøya and Østerøya respectively. Although these peninsulas were called islands, they were not, but were thin fingers of land radiating from the large town of Sandefjord. The crossing of the first was relatively easy, after I had waited for the fast ferry from Sandefjord to Sweden to go past. It took less than an hour to reach the other side 2 kilometres away on the southern tip of Vesterøya. The wind by now was a solid force 5 and gusting to 6. I assumed the same effort would get me across the next fjord to the southern tip of Østerøya. However, this was different. The wind was probably a force 6 here and it was coming directly from the north-east. In addition, I thought there was a stronger current here. It took well over an hour of hard paddling to do this kilometre and a half to reach the tip of the peninsula. The warm spray was splashing everywhere from every paddle stroke and from the bow, and my eyes were smarting with salt water. The bare smooth rocks at the end

Day 246. Looking at the village of Kjerringsvik from the lee of islands before I paddled across to the Vesterøya and Østerøya headlands

of this peninsula just did not seem to creep any closer for ages. With straining sinews and aching shoulders I at last pulled level with this headland, called Tønsberg tønne. It had been my goal since leaving Ingrid's five days ago and I thought it would be much easier to get here! It was significant, because I considered it the start of Oslofjord and the end of the Sørlandet.

I thought once I reached Tønsberg tønne it would all be over and I could just cruise up Oslofjord. However, the east side of this sharp peninsula was the hardest part. There was now a definite current against me and the force 6 wind was being deflected and funnelled by the headland into a jetstream against me. I went quite close to the rocks and endured the clapotis from the rebounding waves to try and keep out of the current which was heading south. The buttresses and crevices went past very slowly. Sometimes I was pretty much stationary for five minutes until a burst of temper and some furious paddling saw me inch forwards for 200-

Day 246. About to cross the 2km from Kjerringsvik to the headland on Vesterøya into the rapidly increasing headwind

300 metres until I had to recover again. It probably took an hour to go a single kilometre, but there was no avoiding it. After this very strenuous hour a sheltered bay slowly unfolded with a beach at the head of it. I paddled in here for a breather and to eat something, and most importantly let my wrists, arms and shoulders relax a bit, as they had been straining. It was a remarkable bay with beautiful sand and tall dry reeds rustling under the mixed forest around the edge of the bay. It looked almost tropical and with the water temperature of at least 20 degrees it felt tropical. There were a lot of the evil-looking jelly fish here, but they seemed to have completed their cycle and most were deteriorating and washing up on beaches by now.

Day 246. Paddling into the quiet warm sheltered Strandvika bay after a strenuous paddle round Østerøya headland against wind and current

After a good hour stretching and recuperating on the warm sheltered sand, I reluctantly felt I had to leave Strandvika bay and continue. The wind was still from the north-east and directly against me but I felt it was abating a bit. None the less I decided to paddle over to the large island of Tjøme and try and get some lee along its west shoreline. After an hour I made it to the first of many islands in Tønsbergfjord, but they offered little protection. They were smooth bare low-lying outcrops which had probably just emerged from below sea level in the last few thousand years. It was only when I got to the wooded island of Hui, yet another hour later, did I at last find some shelter. There was a lot of bird life here in the sheltered bays surrounded by forest. Large rafts of eider duck of perhaps 100 birds or more had gathered together. I had last seen this in Varangerfjord, just before the breeding season started and thought perhaps that they are normally gregarious animals and just split up into pairs for the breeding, and then return to smaller rafts for the rearing of young and larger rafts when the ducklings have grown up. There were also quite a few merganser and heron about. As I paddled further into the islands, swans and their fully grown, but still grey, cygnets cruised between the reeds on the fringes of the bays.

As dusk was approaching I passed the town of Tjøme in the middle of the island. I had been before; it was a thriving centre in the summer with many holidaymakers who had cabins in the area, and a cosy community in the winter with the local population. Tjøme island itself and a few islands to the west of it, where I was now paddling, along with the numerous islands to the east of it, are the prime areas in which to have a summer cottage in Norway. Tjøme, and to a lesser extent Kragerø, are the Norwegian 'Riviera'. It sounds slightly amusing, but in the height of summer these areas have a fantastic climate with many hot, dry days under blue skies, which warms the sea to 25 degrees in the sheltered bays. But summer had now passed and it was the cusp of autumn; the area was closing down for the winter. I also noticed that although the wind had almost completely abated now there were dark clouds gathering in the twilight and I needed somewhere to camp, and soon. As I paddled up the coast I passed some lovely quaint older cabins and some modern palaces. Many had very green lawns coming down to artificial beaches. It was tempting to camp on them, but it was too private. However, the more darkness approached, the more brazen I was going to get, and none of the cabins had lights on. I silently paddled over a small inlet, called Glennekilen, and soon afterwards I passed a small isolated lawn on a tiny beach surrounded by pine forest. The house it belonged to was a good 50 metres away through some trees; it was modest and the lights were out. I landed on the beach and pulled the kayak across the small lawn into the woods where there was a lovely sheltered and hidden camp spot among the large pines. As soon as the tent was up and I had unpacked, the dark clouds finally burst in a biblical downpour. Huge rain drops were drumming off the taut ripstop and it was so noisy I could not think to write. It kept up through my dinner and then lulled me into a deep and well-deserved sleep.

SECTION 34. Sørlandet
10 days. 289 kilometres. 62 hours. 0m ascent. 0m descent.

THE KAYAK: SECTION 35. OSLOFJORD

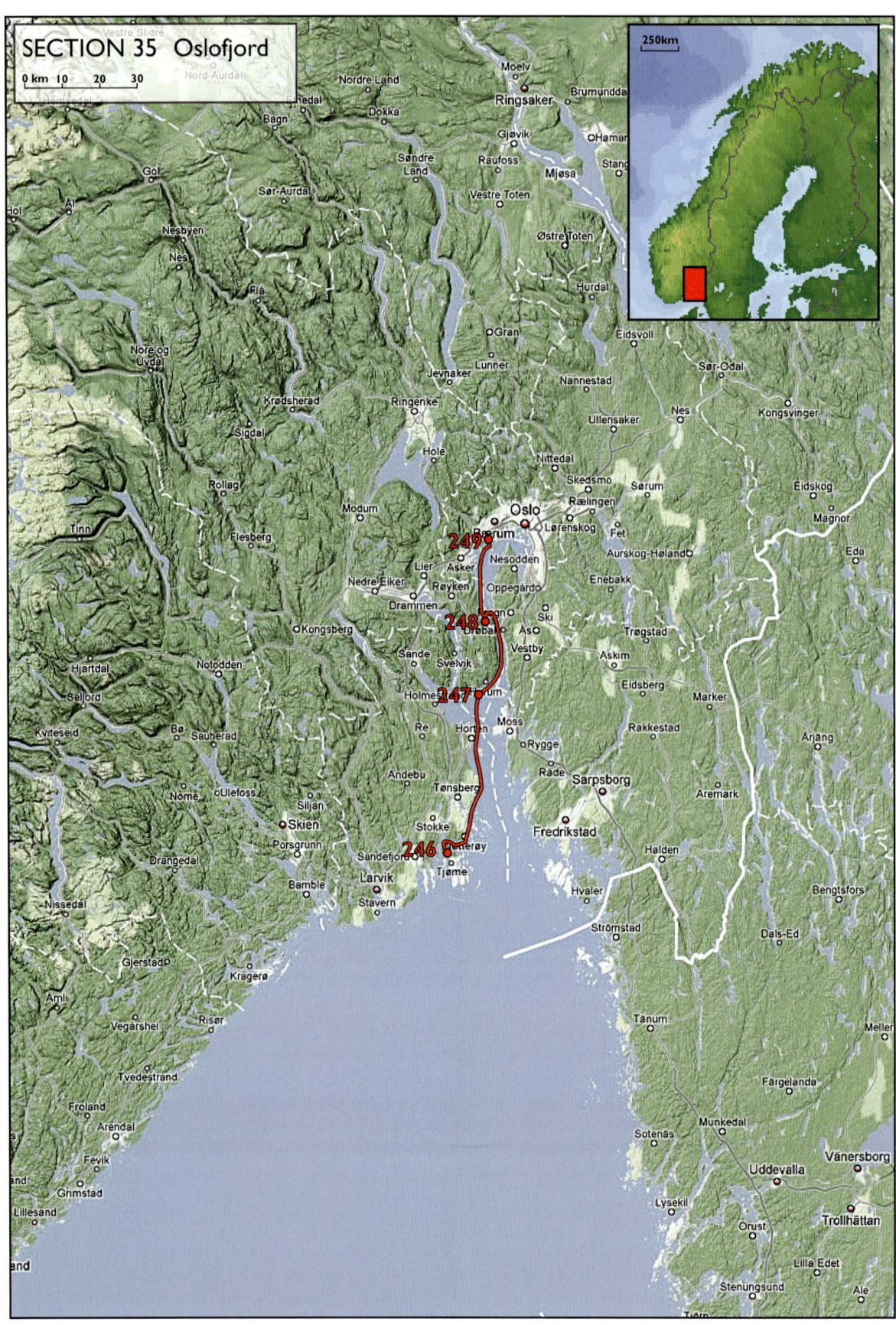

THE KAYAK: SECTION 35. OSLOFJORD

When I woke under the large pines in the morning the rain was still pelting down on to the tent and I was sure it had been doing it all night. Everything I owned, from sleeping bag to head torch batteries had slowly become impregnated with salt crystals over the last three and a half months. It absorbed any dampness in the air, and there was plenty of it this morning, so everything was clammy, except the tent which was soaking with condensation. With an admirable resolve I got up early and packed all the damp stuff away into the damp bags. Then I put my drysuit on in the tent, packed the glistening wet tent into its soaking bag and shaking the droplets off the bags, packed up the hatches and set forth on the final section with the water's surface opaque with the ripples of rain drops. I paddled past pine woods with expensive waterside cabins dotted in the glades along the shore until I got to the arched concrete bridge which connected Tjøme to the adjacent island of Nøtterøy. It was pouring rain and I was surrounded by grey as I paddled under the bridge and entered a sheltered basin surrounded by small boatyards and small offices. I am sure it would usually be a busy thriving place, but today it seemed deserted in the downpour as everybody but me had taken shelter. As I paddled further east down Vrengen I returned to the rural charm with the occasional older farm and some cabins until the sound finished and entered Oslofjord proper.

Day 247. Paddling up Årøysund with Nøtterøy island on the left in the pouring rain, after a very wet night camping on the island of Tjøme

There was a small sound I could paddle north along without going into the fjord. The wind had suddenly built from the south and it quickly blew me up the charming Årøysund with the cabins of Nøtterøy on one side and the quite pristine twin Årøy islands on the other. Before I knew it the wind had already carried me up to the entrance of Tønsberg. Tønsberg is the oldest town in Norway, although its origins are lost in the mists of Viking history. The great Norse chronicler, Snorre Sturlason, claimed Tønsberg already existed as a town at the Battle of Hafrsfjord in 872, which happened just where I stayed with the Amundsen family in Sandsnes a few weeks ago. Two very important Viking ships, the Oseberg ship and the Gokstad ship, were discovered in large burial mounds in the vicinity of Tønsberg. There were also many valuable relics and even skeletons in the mounds, although the really valuable gold and silver were plundered long ago. It is assumed the Oseberg burial mound of 834, belonged to a queen of the ancient dynasty called the 'Yngling' who hailed from this era and two generations later produced Harald Hårfagre, who won this battle of Hafrsfjord and united Norway. The Gokstad ship, from 890, belonged to an Yngling petty king who was Harald Hårfagre's uncle. After this prosperous Viking era Tønsberg became a Hansatic town and flourished. After the demise of the Hansatic league Tønsberg continued as an important fishing and shipping port and then a major whaling centre in the late 19th Century. I had sailed through the characterful Tønsberg on a previous trip and did not have time to make the detour into it now. I was half blown and half paddled past the mouth of its fjord making good progress, but still had 35 kilometres to go to the day's goal, where there was hopefully a public cabin in which I could dry off.

Day 247. Being blown up Oslofjord by the town of Tønsberg with a strong force 5 and increasing wind behind me

North of Tønsberg the islands petered out and I was soon paddling in the exposed Oslofjord with a force 5 wind behind me. The waves were now nearly two metres and quite steep. As I approached the headland at Slagentangen the wind increased to a 6 and I could see the deciduous trees along the boulder shore, especially

Day 247. Paddling up Oslofjord after Tønsberg in poor weather with the Slagentangen headland appearing through the rain

the aspen, swinging widely in the wind. This breezy, lush scene came to an abrupt halt as soon as I was round the headland as an oil refinery appeared, with its ranks of storage tanks and occasional flare. I paddled past, glancing occasionally at its monstrous forms and having to inhale its foul smell. I passed Åsgårdstrand, keeping a couple of kilometres offshore as it lay in a bit of a bay. None the less I could see its pretty winding streets and white houses, but I felt its charm was rather ruined by its evil-smelling neighbour to the south. Åsgårdstrand was the place where Edvard Munch, one of Norway's most famous cultural figures, thrived. He bought a house here in 1897 when he was in his 30s and spent the next 20 summers painting many of his best works. The wind was perhaps a constant force 6 by now and I was getting quite worried about a crossing I had to do later. Even as I approached Bastøy island there was plenty of surf and streaks of froth all over the water in front of me. If I looked ahead, the sea did not look too bad, but when I turned round there were white caps everywhere and some large sets of breakers charging towards me.

Bastøy initially seemed uninhabited and was a nature reserve. As I paddled to the north-west side of it however, a huge farm appeared among the large deciduous trees. This farm looked semi-aristocratic with its large clock towers on the barn and distinctive spires and towers on other buildings. The fields around it looked lush and fertile. I thought it looked quite idyllic and a nice place to live, and it was quite ironic when I found out months later it was actually a prison! From Bastøy I crossed over to Horten. It was still a solid force 6 and I was getting more worried about the imminent longer crossing. This was highlighted by a big ferry crossing Oslofjord from Moss to Horten. It was on the other side of Bastøy in the main channel and each time it hit a wave there were plumes of spray flying high across its large bow. There were obviously big steep waves out there. I was blown past Horten and along the peninsula which extended north from it. I passed a stone church in a hamlet of grand old farm buildings and continued until I was near the island of Vealøs. The rain of the morning had now largely vanished although there was the odd squall. It seemed the wind was abating slightly and it was now down to a force 5. The waves were still large and there were white caps everywhere, but they were not tumbling over the wave crests as much. It was just as well the weather had eased a tad, as I had now run out of coastline and had to make the 10-kilometre crossing across Oslofjord.

From Vealøs I could see the island of Mølen in the middle of the fjord, and on the far side in the grey distance was the barely visible island of Ranvikholmen. Here, I optimistically hoped there would be a cabin run by Oslofjordens Friluftsråd (Outdoor Recreation Council). I had found out about it on my little laptop last night in the rainy tent at Tjøme. The cabin was locked but I had called an automatic answer phone which told me the code for the door, which I wrote down on a soggy piece of paper. It all seemed too good to be true and I was prepared for a big disappointment and a damp night's camping when I reached Ranvikholmen. I decided not to wait until the wind eased further but to head straight over to Mølen, and if it turned nasty I could put my soaking tent up on its lee side, but if it eased I could continue across the fjord to Ranvikholmen.

As I paddled over to Mølen the wind eased yet again so I didn't stop and continued to Ranvikholmen. There was the occasional worrying force 6 gust which very quickly turned the sea light grey and I could hear large tumbling crests catching me up and breaking on the back of the kayak. When I looked behind, the sea was wild with three metre swells and many larger white horses. I kept looking forwards and hoped for the best and pretty quickly the squall passed, the wind dropped to a force 4 and the white caps all but vanished again. I soon reached Ranvikholmen and paddled round the small rocky island to the beach on the north side. Like its neighbour, Tofteholmen, Ranvikholmen is the remains of some magma ducts from the long-eroded Hurum volcano which existed here 250 million years ago. As a consequence the soil is rich in nutrients, and with the mild climate there is a large variety of flora on the lush island. I landed on a small gravel beach surrounded by dripping wet bushes,

Day 247. The fantastic cabin on the rocky but fertile island of Ranvikholmen where I could dry off all my belongings and write

where I could have camped if the cabin did not exist or the code was wrong. There was a path up to the middle of the small island so I followed it for a few hundred metres through wet autumnal woods. Tall pines and rowans, red with berries, made up the forest, while the ground cover was blueberry and grass. As a sign of the oncoming autumn the forest floor was covered in mushrooms, especially the red Russula varieties. The island was a temperate paradise. Soon I got a glimpse of a cabin through the trees and approached the clearing it was in. Nervously I stood on the balcony and punched the number into the lock. It clicked and I could push the door open. It was perfect. There were four bunks with mattresses, a table I could write at, an area where I could cook, and a few candles to make it cosy. It was certainly worth making the extra effort to get here in the foul weather, as I could look forward to a comfortable evening. I returned to the kayak to get my belongings and then made myself at home in the cabin.

I had a fantastic sleep, and by the morning my sleeping bag had completely dried out. For the first time in at least a fortnight it was both calm and sunny outside. My damp clothes hanging on the veranda were also crisp and dry. Summer was trying to make a comeback. I only had another 40 kilometres to the end and nearly all of that was in sheltered waters, so I could afford to relax in the cabin with the door open and do some writing, then go for a small exploration of the island. It was quite a craggy island but there were trees and shrubs growing from every crevice. In the hollows where earth and humus had collected there were thick clusters of heather and blueberry bushes. I lingered so long on this delightful and wild island that I did not finally launch until midday, by which time there was a slight northerly breeze against me and the skies were clouding over again.

Day 247. Looking over the eastern part of Ranvikholmen with the neighbouring island of Tofteholmen in the middle distance

Day 248. Paddling up Drøbaksund with the Tall Ship of Christian Radich sailing south

The first task was to paddle to the bottom of Hurum and the town of Tofte, where there was an enormous paper mill. Barges shuttled back and forth from other parts of Oslofjord where they had picked up wood from the inlets like Drammensfjord. Previously the logs would have floated down the rivers to these coastal towns up the inlets, but now the logs were transported there by lorry and train. At the quay a few ships unloaded their cargos of logs and woodchips, and it looked like some of these had come from abroad. Indeed, there was a boat from Scotland unloading logs as I paddled past. Like the refinery yesterday, this place had an odious smell. It was one of the few industrial complexes in the otherwise rural and quite pristine Oslofjord. It took a while to paddle past the mill with the wind against me and my progress was slow, but surely I gained the narrower part of the fjord called Drøbaksund, which separated Ytre Oslofjord from Indre Oslofjord. I had to paddle up this 12-kilometre sound to gain the large inner sanctuary of Oslofjord where the city of Oslo is spread in a big crescent, enveloping its northern shore. Across the water from me was the small town of Hvitsen and further up the sound I could see the larger town of Drøbak. A sailing ship soon came round the corner. It was the Christian Radich; Norway's other great white swan from a bygone era of sail. Like her counterpart in Bergen, the Statsraad Lehmkuhl, it is now used for sail training and education, and also takes part in many of the Tall Ships races and Trans-Atlantic voyages. It was marginally smaller than the Statsraad Lehmkuhl which I thought was a slightly finer vessel, although both are magnificent sailing ships.

Day 248. Approaching Filtvet fyr lighthouse on the west side of the entrance to narrow Drøbaksund which joins Inner and Outer Oslofjord

Once in Drøbaksund I started looking for a place to eat without losing ground in this wind. I really needed a beach to land on so I would not blow south again. I passed a campsite and nearly stopped there, but it seemed too exposed in this north wind. About half an hour later I arrived at a small cove where there was a man chest deep in the water swinging a hammer. He was repairing his jetty and seemed to be getting deluged by the occasional wave. He came over once he had finished and we chatted. Him in dripping shorts and T-shirt and me in damp fleeces, as my paddling jacket was now porous and almost rotten. He was in his 50s and was a keen paddler. I told him about my voyage and website and he said he would look at it as soon as he had returned to his cabin and was dry. His wife soon arrived and we chatted more, and then before I left they kindly filled my water bottles so I had water for the evening. After I left I had barely gone 100 metres when I noticed my balaclava hat which I had put between my spraydeck and the map loosely attached to it had gone. It must have fallen out at the beach so I returned. The hardy carpenter and I searched but it was gone. Perhaps it had been washed into the water and sunk in the half metre surf. I did not need it now, but it was sentimental as it had been with me on the entire ski and kayak trip.

It was a reasonably quick paddle up the fjord past Drøbak as the wind had abated, and soon I was approaching the fortifications of Oscarsborg. This fort sits on two smaller islands in the middle of the kilometre-wide sound and guards the entrance to inner Oslofjord and Oslo. It has undergone a few rebuilds in the last 300 years to improve the battery; the last major one was in 1890 to 1900 in case the Swedes invaded Norway. Three massive 280mm Krupp guns from Germany were installed in emplacements on the island. In addition to this, Austrian torpedoes were installed in secret batteries and could be launched underwater. These defences were largely in hibernation for 40 years until 9th April 1940 when a flotilla sailed up Oslofjord in the darkness of night. The fortress commander did not know if the boats were friendly or hostile, but decided

Day 248. The Oscarsborg fortifications sitting in the middle of the narrow Drøbaksund was the ideal sea defence for the city of Oslo

to fire on them with the ageing weapons. Luckily for the commander the fleet was indeed hostile, as it was the German invasion flotilla arriving to storm Oslo and capture the King and Government. Also fortunately for him the ancient German guns still worked perfectly and the lead ship in the flotilla, the heavy cruiser called Blücher, was hit twice, virtually disabling it. It sailed on until it was level with the torpedo batteries. Two torpedoes were fired which also hit the Blücher causing fatal damage which led to the battleship sinking. About 700 Germans died, 500 were captured, but 800 made it ashore evading capture, including the top German officers. They

Day 248. The birch trees lining the side of Oslofjord near Oscarsborg were starting to show the first signs of autumn

hijacked a lorry and continued to Oslo, but without the troops they could not surprise and capture the King or Government, who now had time to escape. The rest of the flotilla turned round and landed the remaining troops, who then marched on Oslo, overwhelming it a few days later. That same day German planes bombed Oscarsborg and the Norwegian forces fled as 500 bombs fell on the small island.

Just beyond Oscarsborg the fjord was split into Vestfjord and Østfjord by the larger steep-sided island of Håøya. The main shipping lane went up Østfjord and I was going up Vestfjord where I hoped to find another of Oslofjordens Friluftsråd's cabins. I cruised along the west shore near the lush forest of pines and deciduous trees. I noticed that some of the birch were definitely changing colour now and autumn had started. It was my fourth season of the trip. I paddled along the leafy shore for just a couple of kilometres to reach the very enclosed bay of Sandspollen, which was really a basin of water a kilometre across with a small entrance. It was a wonderful harbour for the yachting fraternity to come and spend the night moored in its sheltered waters. I paddled into the basin and went along the shore until I spotted the waterside cabin. It was lovely and I hoped it was open, but there was great camping beside it. Again I went up nervously ready to pitch my tent and was delighted when it opened up with the same combination as the cabin on Ranvikholmen. It was very cosy inside and the perfect place to spend my last night. The cabin was 100 years old and was initially a fishing cabin. In earlier times this basin was filled with mackerel on a yearly basis and this cabin played a role in harvesting them. It was the first building in the area to get a telephone, so people could be alerted to come and help with the mackerel when they arrived in the bay. I unpacked what I needed and then got my writing

Day 248. The lovely old cabin at Sandspollen was the perfect place for me to spend my last night after a fantastic 8 months

out of the way at once. A few dozen yachts arrived in the evening and anchored in the mirror-calm waters, but none were near the cabin. As I finished my writing at 2000, one of the yachts sounded a bugle or horn, which served to remind people to take in the Norwegian flags flying on the stern of their boats. I am sure many used it as a signal to have a second or third 'ankerdram'. The whole bay fell silent now and in the dusk I lit a few candles in the cosy cabin and enjoyed an evening of total peace and contentment as I reflected on what had been a remarkable pilgrimage for me.

It was easy to get up, as the sun was streaming into the small cabin and I could see it was a beautiful day outside. When I opened the door and looked across Sandspollen it was mirror calm and the all the yachts were sitting motionless on their perfect reflections. It was an absolutely glorious day with just the odd puff of small cloud in the otherwise blue skies and it was completely still. It was not before time as I had endured

Day 248. Inside the simple cosy cabin at Sandspollen I spent the night reflecting on the ebb and flow of nature which I was about to leave

Day 249. Paddling up Vestfjord with Håøya on the right on the magnificent morning of the last day

unseasonably poor weather for the last two weeks. I had a small breakfast, swept out the lovely old cabin and then packed up the boat and launched it. Before I started paddling for the day I capsized a couple of times to practice my roll with the laden kayak. I had not had the need or desire to roll at any time during the trip since my victory roll to Vidar in Mehamn, although I was prepared on a few occasions. I just did a Pawlata roll as the kayak had about 70 kilos in it. One should be able to roll an oil tanker with the Pawlata technique. With the ripples from my rolls spreading out across the silvery Sandspollen bay I set off as a few people were stirring on the yachts. It should just be an easy four-hour paddle up the fjord to the finish at Konglungen bridge in these conditions. I left the bay and paddled up Vestfjord on the west side of Håøya island. Occasionally where there was a stake in the water I could see there was a very slight tide against me as the large basin of Indre Oslofjord had to fall about half a metre to equalize with the level in the Ytre Oslofjord and Skagerrak.

I soon reached the north end of Håøya and the iconic light beacon on the small Sundbyholmen islet, which must be a well-known landmark for sailors. I had passed countless of these iconic navigation beacons and this would be the last one. Across the widening and reunited Oslofjord I could look across to the east side where the large peninsula of Nesodden jutted out so far it almost reached Oslo itself. I kept more to the rural west side, skirting past a few small towns and plenty of forest. It was now late morning and the fjord was coming to life with sailing boats emerging from many marinas around the coast to enjoy one of the last of the warm sunny days. After a couple of hours I could pick out the dark green pine-clad islands in the north of the Oslofjord where I was heading and soon after some of Oslo city started to unfold from behind the Nesodden peninsula.

Day 249. Approaching the well-known landmark of Sundbyholmen with its iconic navigational beacon, which was the last I passed

There can be few cities in the world which have the same situation as Oslo. In front of it is this vast basin of Indre Oslofjord with its peninsulas and wooded islands, many of which are still quite rural. It is an aquatic paradise for sailors and leisure boats. If this was not enough, then beyond the arc of the city around the fjord in every direction are rolling hills and crags covered in pine and spruce. These forests extend for many tens of kilometres in each direction and are peppered with lakes fed by clear streams and becks. There are networks of paths through these vast forests which one could spend days following. Hidden in glades across this forest, and usually beside small tarns are a number of timber cabins to stay in. In the summer it is a paradise for hikers, fishermen and berry pickers and in the winter it is a paradise for cross-country skiers.

Day 249. A leisure fisherman out with the City of Oslo appearing between him and the peninsula of Nesodden on the right of the photo

I paddled past a couple of old wooden boats with families fishing for cod. I stopped to have a chat with them and see if they had caught anything. I was dying to

Day 249. The windmill on the roadless island of Bjerkøya were I had lunch and waited in the kayak for an hour practising my rolls

tell them I was just a few kilometres from the end of a great journey, but thought it would have been too vain. Instead I complimented them on their catch. Before long I passed the landmark towers of the cement factory at Slemmerstad and then the quaint town of Vollen where Øivind had his art studio and gallery, before I reached the lovely pine-clad island of Bjerkøya with its old windmill. My destination of Konglungen was just the other side of this island, some 10 minutes paddle away. I parked the kayak on a sunny beach on the south side of the island and had lunch. I was getting restless, agitated and nervous. I had just been pottering along at my own speed for the last eight months, spending most of the time on my own in the best nature in Europe, immersing myself in it. I felt I had more in common with the world of ptarmigan and eider duck at that moment and I was about to wrench myself from it and tumble back into the banal humdrum of humanity. I was not sure I wanted to leave the ebb and flow of the natural world and it made me nervous. I could not sit still and practised another 10 kayak rolls while I was waiting for the time to come to continue round the island and paddle the last kilometre to the finishing line. The water here was now warm and pleasant, almost refreshing, compared to the icy shock I endured during the roll at Mehamn, which gave me 'ice cream head'. I had said I would cross the line at 1400 hrs and knew there would be a few people and a journalist or two waiting there and this added to my nervousness. Just as I was about to set off my phone rang. It was Hartmut and Øivind on the hunt for me in a boat, so I told them where I was and set off round the east end of Bjerkøya. Soon a boat came whizzing round the corner with six people on board. It was the advance party of my welcome committee. I showed off with a roll before the boat disappeared north to Konglungen Bru, leaving me alone again.

Day 249. The final metres to small Konglungen Bru bridge connecting the Konglungen peninsula to Konglungøya island on the centre right

I was still too early and had to wait another 10 minutes and the nervousness returned. My life of watching the winter snows accumulate and melt, a spring of observing the leaves unfold and a summer of watching ducklings grow was about to end and I would be sad to leave it. Just round the corner was the busy, metropolitan life which really had no connection to the one I was used to and content with. At 1355 hrs with half a kilometre to go I braced myself for the new world and took the first paddle strokes towards the final paddle strokes. I rounded the end of Bjerkøya and the small Konglungen Bru appeared. It was a small bridge just a few metres long and high which connected the small delightful Konglungøya island to the charming rural Konglungen peninsula. It was right beside my good friend Hartmut's house which is where I always made a base on my visits to Norway over the last decade. With about 250 metres to go I heard something familiar yet inexplicable. It was my favourite bagpipe tune. A friend on the Isle of Skye, Jonathan, used to play it on many a rowdy night when I

Day 249. Some of the welcome committee on Konglungen Bru bridge complete with bagpipes and a few kayakers

Day 249. A rather bewildered kayaker about to pass under the bridge and into a whole new world

lived there some 15-18 years ago. It was being played as expertly as Jonathan would play it, so I thought it was a recording, and then I saw a piper. Then I saw a large Scottish flag of the St Andrew's Cross draped over the bridge. As I approached the bridge I saw there were about 40 or 50 people on it and in the vicinity waiting to greet me. I did not feel emotional, only nervous. I paddled up to the bridge, paused a bit, and then went under and into the new world. There was a kayak on the other side with Knut Jorfald in it, who is Øivinds' brother. I veered over to him, like a duckling imprinting, while the crowd above cheered and applauded. After a brief chat with Knut I did a few victory rolls in the warm shallow, clear, water. It would have been embarrassing if one failed, but it went smoothly.

I chatted with a few people from below the bridge, my neck craning and the sun in my eyes. There were now many people I recognized. James, Karoline and family, Ole Bjøråsen, Roy Myrland from Nevlunghavn a week ago, Hartmut's daughter, Jose and her Icelandic husband, Hjalti. There were also many faces I did not recognise and who had been following my website blog and had come along because of Øivind's amusing open invitation. There was one face I recognized, but just could not place and he beckoned me over. When I had paddled under him he dropped my balaclava hat on to my kayak. It was the tough Norwegian who I met repairing his jetty while chest-deep in the waves yesterday. It had washed ashore later in the afternoon and he had looked at my website and found I was finishing here. He then drove up to deliver it. So fantastic is Norway! I then went back under the bridge again and had more time and composure to recognize many of the faces now they were out of the sun. Suddenly there was a lady barking questions from the

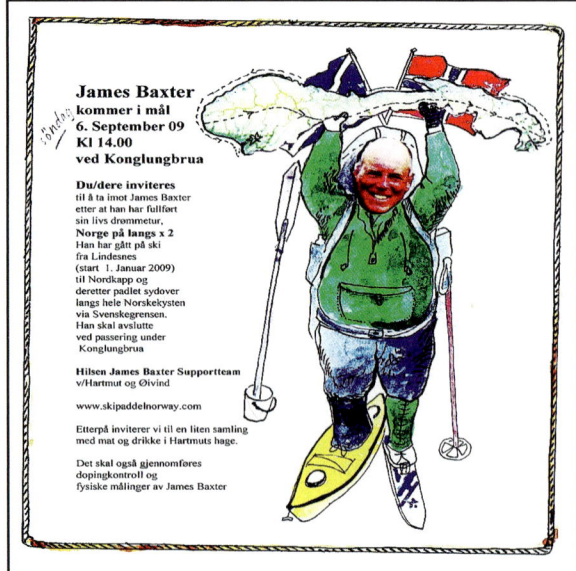

Day 249. The invite to the party drawn by Øivind and posted on my website which allowed the hardy carpenter to return my balaclava

bank. They were the clichéd questions a journalist would ask. What are you feeling right now? What was the most dangerous moment? I was quite short with her and paddled off at the first opportunity back to Knut in his kayak under the bridge and then on another 50 metres where Hartmut had a very narrow strip of beach where I could land and haul the kayak out. As I stepped on to land here I had time to congratulate myself. Whenever I have a daunting project or an arduous journey I always reassure myself that it won't last forever and there will be an end. It seemed a very, very, long time ago when I shouldered my rucksack on the dark, crisp, morning of January 1st at the start of the long journey north, thinking this exact sentiment, when the scale of the journey I was embarking

Day 249. The bagpipes are a very hard instrument to play and I got some notes out of it – but not necessarily in the right order

Day 249. The welcome committee had surpassed themselves and provided copious amounts of champagne

on completely overwhelmed me Now, over eight months and many extraordinary experiences later, the end had indeed come.

I then went back up to chat to everyone on the bridge and was introduced to many people. One person introduced himself as Ragnvald Jacobsen whom I had heard so much about but never met. He was a relation of my ex mother-in-law, Ingrid, who owned the cabin at Såstein and had offered it to me a week ago. He was there with his sons. Then my son, Kenneth, who lives in Oslo, arrived and gave me a congratulatory hug. There was champagne in flutes, more bagpipes and cameras galore. I felt very self-conscious and luckily nobody shouted 'Speech!'. I had a go on the bagpipes and managed to get the right sound out of them but no tune on the chanter. Roy from Nevlunghavn was the only journalist I knew there and was the only one I was prepared to give a small interview to. After a good 20 minutes everybody slowly started to drift up the lane to Hartmut's old and traditional wooden house. As we went past my kayak many hands grabbed each end and the cockpit and we all carried it up to his house where there was more champagne and food. Hartmut is an excellent cook and a charming host and he took the onus off me by introducing everybody to each other and serving large bowls of couscous salads, curried meatballs and delicious snacks. Soon everybody was eating and mingling while the 10 kids looked after themselves. Karoline and James produced a large cake in the shape of Norway

Day 249. Karoline baked a fantastic cake in the shape of Norway which was cut into 40 pieces and devoured soon after

and everybody had a slice and it was soon finished. After a few hours people started to drift off and take their kids home. Kenneth and his girlfriend left in the evening and then there was just Hartmut and one rather bewildered me left. I was exhausted by the occasion. Hartmut and I go back some 30 years, to when I first lived in Norway, so I lay down on his sofa, at last having a chance to relax, while he produced a final bottle of champagne for us. We chatted into the evening while my kayak lay fully laden in the dark garden waiting for another day to be unpacked. It was the end of a fantastic 6213 kilometre adventure and pilgrimage through the best nature in Europe, which I will surely cherish for the rest of my life.

Day 250. The invaluable and self-styled Support Team of Øivind Jorfald and Hartmut Liste took their role very seriously right up to the very end

SECTION 35. Oslofjord
3 days. 93 kilometres. 19.5 hours. 0m ascent. 0m descent.

SECTIONS 1 TO 35 TOTAL:
249 days. 6213 kilometres. 1486 hours. 50,460m ascent. 50,420m descent.

THE EPILOGUE

When I woke up the next morning in Hartmut's house I was bewildered and at a loss. I felt I should get into my drysuit and paddle 40 kilometres in wind and rain as I recently had done but there was nowhere to go now. The first thing I wanted to do was finish writing my blog. It had been a constant issue for the last 250 days and I would be glad to see the back of it. I had about 600 people following the blog from all over the world so I felt a duty to keep it up-to-date, but at last I was about to release the shackle from the millstone and write 'The End' at the bottom of the last page. Despite the fantastic weather outside I opened up my little mini laptop at the comfort of Hartmut's desk and typed away, oblivious of the sun until it was at last done and I had written and published these two long-awaited words.

I also had an interview with a lady called Trude Blåsmo. She was editor of 'Fjell og Vidde' which was the bi-monthly journal of Den Norske Turisforening. She wanted to write a five page article on my expedition and publish it in the January edition of this reasonably prestigious magazine with a readership of almost a tenth of the Norwegian population. I had had about 10 local newspapers publish articles about my trip as I padded through their areas, but the one with 'Fjell of Vidde' would be the most useful and perhaps the best for fundraising for the schools in Limi, Nepal. It would lie around all the DNT cabins in Norway for a decade and weather-bound hikers and skiers would read it as storms raged outside. As arranged, Trude came to Hartmut's on Konglungen that afternoon as I had finished writing everything up from yesterday. We chatted for a couple of hours and she did a small photo shoot and I provided her with a disk of my best 300 photos she could use for her article.

Another photographer came the next day to get some pictures for an interview I had already given. It was for the widely read and prominent American 'Canoe and Kayak' magazine. It was published in December 2009 in a two page article called 'Money Talks' and largely focused on the fact that I was using the kayak trip to raise money for the three Limi schools. Once he had his pictures of me paddling about around Konglungen Bru bridge where I finished, it was time to pack up my kayak and rinse off all the salt which was engrained in all my equipment. A few things were completely knackered by the salt, like the alloy tent poles, the cooking pans and my paddling cagoule and needed to be thrown away, but most things were redeemable and the drysuit looked almost as good as new. There were a few other requests for interviews but I really did not want to answer any more rapid-fire questions barked at me and was content to relax and visit friends in Oslo. Even the BBC phoned up and I just told them what they wanted to hear to get them off the phone. The article she produced 'Adventurer completes Norway trip' was remarkably accurate considering the half-hearted information she received.

After a few days in Oslo it was time to book a flight home and pack up. Norwegian Air were going to allow me a very generous baggage allowance and I booked three 20 kilo bags and a pair of skis for just a slight add-on in price. This allowed me to get everything back except for my kayak. Dave Felton at Tiderace again came to the rescue here and put me in touch with a freight company who would pick it up from Hartmut's house and deliver it to Tiderace in Penrith for around £300. This was perfect, as Dave offered to help with the cost if he could keep the kayak for a couple of months to use at various shows as a display. As soon as it was agreed I phoned the freight company and a lorry came within a few hours. I spent a few more days in Oslo, gently leaving the fantastic outdoor life I had enjoyed for eight months and tentatively dipping my toe back into the turbulent waters of reality again. I finally left Norway about a week after I had finished my expedition.

As usual when I return home from a big trip nothing much had changed. Johanna had done a great job monitoring my business and dealing with a few small crises. The only thing I really had to do was cut the lawn which looked like a wild meadow. Within a month the cherished memories were being overtaken by other events, like a combined homecoming and 50th birthday party. I had been asked to do a few presentations. Firstly, to The Alpine Club in London which I thoroughly enjoyed and who not only looked after me well but also made a very generous donation to the Schools project in Nepal. The second presentation was to the prestigious Kendal Mountain Festival where I was the first speaker to sell out. There must have been at least 300 people at the latter and I think I was more nervous at the start of this talk than kayaking round some of the exposed headlands in the Barents Sea. It had always been in the back of my mind to write a book on the adventure and I spent the next 24 months putting it together until it was ready to go off to the printers. It was perhaps a more laborious feat than the expedition itself and I completely underestimated the time and effort involved.

THE EPILOGUE

Throughout the expedition I have had the pleasure of some exceptional Norwegian hospitality, in addition to the country's wonderful and pristine nature which I had the privilege to immerse myself into. I would especially like to thank;

- Solbjørg Kvålshaugen of Fondsbu for the respite when I was feeling low.
- Lars Erik Støver for the warm evening at Glåmos.
- Elisabeth Green of Skalstugan for giving me shelter and food in a snowstorm.
- Steinar Gaundal of Gaundal for his exceptional hospitality and the scooter tracks and food.
- Bjørn and Regina Klauer for the stay at their Husky farm at Innset.
- The unforgettable Ivar Olsen of Tromsø for the stories and the hjemmebrent.
- Peder Janssen of Bekkarfjord for the meal and evening with his family.
- Stein Are Ulvang and Kimek in Kirkenes for importing my kayak and paying the tax duty.
- James Roe at Grense Jakobselv for transporting my kayak from Kirkenes to the Russian border.
- The Berlevåg male choir for the hearty applause.
- Astor of Måsøy island for the seagulls' eggs, the Lagavulin and the evening in his home.
- The Bergly sisters at Hakkstabben for the great meal and warm bed.
- Cort Buck Rustad who gave me shelter for two nights in the lovely Bergsfjord.
- Frank and Ida Næss at Russelv for taking me into their home for two days at Russelv on Lyngen.
- Bjørn Eines of Bjornskajakk in Tromsø for helping me out throughout my time in the north.
- Arve and Dagmar Johansen of Lavangnes for a great meal with the family.
- Evelynn Brattström and Klara Jansson, Sisters-in-Arms for solidarity.
- William Pedersen and Bent and Inge Skauen at Husvær for hospitality and help.
- Colin and Karen Bruce for the new equipment and some great food at Magnillen.
- Frederik and Sissel Johansen for a great evening on Averøya.
- Johanna Gulestø for letting me sleep in a great cabin on her farm at Gulestøa.
- Richard Lennox for a great meal and a balcony to crash on in Askvoll.
- The entire Amundsen family for hospitality, food, great company and good humour.
- Tom Amundsen, a Brother-in-Arms, for many tips and for setting the pace.
- Jan and Gunn Eide of Ystebø for giving me shelter from the storm and a great evening.
- Simen Phil at Lindesnes for the use of the lighthouse facilities and good humour.
- Rita at Ryvingen fyr for the bed and the meal at her lighthouse.
- Ingrid Bibow for spoiling her ex son-in-law on Arøy island by Kragerø.
- Jon Westgård, a Brother-in-Arms, for his laid-back company around Varangerfjord.
- Reidun Berg of Nevlunghavn for the cabin, good company and great meal.
- Roy Myrland of Nevlunghavn for the good company and photographs.

—o—

I would also like to thank my 'Support Team' of Hartmut Liste and Øivind Jorfald for taking their role seriously. Theirs was a thankless task of sorting out the customs duty, paying the phone bills, posting and receiving numerous packages. I will always be grateful for the superb and memorable welcome committee, complete with bagpipes, great food and champagne, which I am surprised they managed to resist until my arrival.

—o—

I would also like to thank Dave Felton at Tiderace for going out of his way to sort out any problems.

I would also like to thank Richard Cross and Paul Clough for all the advice and work they have put in to maintain and repair my website, and the hours they gave up to bail me out when things went wrong.

Finally, I would like to thank the wonderful country and nature of Norway. As a 'Norgesvenn' I know I will return like a migratory bird to nourish my soul.

LIMI VALLEY NEPAL

The impoverished and very remote village of Nepka in the Take valley in Mugu district is a few day's walk from the nearest school

Doing a journey like this was a good opportunity to raise money for a cause. I had been to Nepal quite a few times over the last 20 years. Most of the time going to the mountainous areas in the centre of the country, which had seen some tourism or development projects by some of the hundreds of NGOs (Non Governmental Organizations). These areas were poor and lacked amenities which we take for granted, like roads, electricity, sewage and running water in every home, but there was usually a rudimentary school and occasional, but very poorly paid, employment. The last two times I went to Nepal I visited the districts of Humla, Mugu, Jumla and Dolpa in the very west of the country. I was quite shocked at the poverty here. No tourists or NGOs ever come here so there is no wealth trickling down and absolutely no employment. There is not enough land to grow sufficient food for the malnourished populations. Most have to rely on the United Nations World Food Programme to top up their meagre diets with erratic rich supplies flown to tiny rustic airstrips. As there is virtually no employment locally, many men leave to find poorly paid manual work in India, often exploited in road construction gangs.

The village houses in the west are medieval hovels. Animals shelter downstairs in a single low dark room and the floor is covered in wet dung which often flows out on to the muddy lane, while the family crowd into a single room upstairs. Disease is rife and many of the children have scabies and helminths. Medical facilities are non-existent outside the few towns and even here they are limited and prohibitively expensive. Village schools, and they hardly ever exist in west Nepal, are virtually useless and very archaic with no facilities, like chairs or paper. The government teachers struggle with the primitive conditions away from their families and are often absent. There are some basic schools in the towns and administrative centres but these could be a few days walk away. In addition many parents simply cannot see the benefit of schooling and need

The houses of Nepka were medieval with animals sheltering below while the family all crammed into the small dark smoky room above

their children to work in the fields. School is a luxury very few rural Nepalese in the west can afford their children the money or time to go to. There is virtually no escape from this cycle of grinding poverty. While trekking through Mugu and Humla, the two poorest districts in Nepal, I could not help wondering how much difference a school would make to the life quality of the villagers. Would education merely aggravate the situation, as people would realize just how desperately impoverished they are, or would it help them so they could read instructions on medicine packets or be aware of the tricks Indian gang masters used to exploit them further. There was no doubt at all that a school would be beneficial. However, to set one up myself was a daunting task; with so many obstacles to overcome it was overwhelming. I just didn't know where to start.

The children of Nepka were happy to see a very rare tourist, but their opportunities in life were hopeless, with no education or medical facility

LIMI VALLEY NEPAL

The 'town' of Simikot is the capital of the vast Humla district. The muddy airstrip here is mostly used to fly in UN sponsored rice supplies

During my last visit to western Nepal my route took me through the hidden valleys of Mugu and then up to the small town of Simikot, which is the administrative centre and the only town in Humla. From here I carried on north out of the ethnically Chhetri hill country into the ethnically Tibetan mountainous border lands. My goal was the hidden Limi Valley, fabled as something of a Shangri-La, a few days and a couple of high passes away. When the Chinese invaded and annexed Tibet in 1950 they started to dismantle the original Tibetan culture and impose their draconian reforms on this vast land. Monasteries and cultural artefacts were destroyed, monks were persecuted, while the unstoppable Chinese swamped Tibet with administrators and settlers. Many of the Tibetan schools of Buddhism and their members eventually sought refuge, largely at Dharamshala, in northern India. The Dalai Lama also had to seek refuge here in 1959 and set up the 'Tibetan Government in Exile'. However, by a quirk of geography, Limi Valley which was part of the Tibetan cultural plateau, lay inside the borders of Nepal. When the Chinese annexed the plateau they did not occupy this remote valley on its fringe as the Nepalese successfully protested its sovereignty. But for the Nepalese Limi is extremely remote, lying on the north side of the Himalayas and on the other side of near 5000-metre passes, and it is also snowbound for a few months each year. There are no resources or taxable income here for the Nepalese Government to take much interest in the valley and they largely ignore it. As a result, the whole of Limi Valley is still culturally the same as it was prior to 1950 and is perhaps the last true remaining, untarnished fragment of Tibetan culture left.

Everything except stone and what is produced in Limi has to be carried in by yak. Here is a caravan getting loaded with building timber

The Limi Valley is so remote that Michael Palin erroneously described it as inaccessible on foot. However, there are two very arduous footpaths into this valley which have been used for centuries. Each footpath takes at least half a week to walk to from Simikot, the capital of Humla district and itself a small very basic town. The inhabitants of Limi Valley live at about 4000 metres and are divided into three villages called Til, Waltse and Zang. Each village has about 50 households with Waltse being slightly larger. The total population of the Limi Valley is about 1700. During the summer months, life in this Shangri-La revolves around cultivating the small terraced barley fields. These fields are planted in May and harvested in October and during this period the whole family, including children must help out. In addition to this, various family members must look after the herds of yak in the high pastures up the side valleys. This is not really suffice to make ends meet so the villagers also trade commodities between China and Nepal using their Tibetan connections. This trade has made the three villages of the Limi Valley much more prosperous than their Chhetri neighbours to the south, over the mountains in Nepal. The houses

The yak caravans have to follow tortuous and precipitous mountain paths which sometimes result in calamity

The yak caravans have to follow the mountain paths over 5000-metre passes for three days to reach Limi Valley

in Limi are more like small stone citadels rather than the Chhetri hovels. During the winter months the valley is snowbound and the fields and pastures are buried under heavy snowfalls. The villagers now retire to the confines of their solid houses from December to March and the village-bound families spend a lot of time maintaining properties, traditional handcrafts, socializing and in prayer. Very few of the wealthier traders even migrate to Kathmandu for the winter months but most remain. Unless it is local or grown in the valley everything must be carried in. This includes all the building materials except for stone. The structural timbers for roofs, pillars, doorways and windows have to be carried in from the forests around Simikot on the backs of yak. The yaks can carry about 70 kilos or two lengths of timber each for the three-day journey over the 5000-metre Nyalu La Pass.

To nearly all the adults and most of the children the concept of academic schooling is totally alien. Education has always been limited to Buddhist teachings and the monastic studying of ancient scripts. This usually happened in the monasteries located in each village. The monastery at Waltse, which is about 800 years old, was the most important one and is the spiritual centre of Limi. Sometimes young monks would leave to study at larger monasteries, previously in Tibet and now in India. Buddhism still plays a pivotal, if not the pivotal, role in Limi culture. Limi Buddhism belongs to the Kagyu or 'oral tradition' of Tibetan Buddhism. The lineage of the Kagyu School prevalent in Limi is the Drikung Kagyu lineage and the spiritual leader of this tradition is HH Drikung Kaybgon Chetsang Rinpoche, who now resides in northern India near Dharamshala.

A yak caravan descending the dry northern slopes of a 5000-metre pass down to the Tibetan Plateau en route to Limi Valley

He is held in the very highest esteem in Limi Valley and a visit by him is a significant and joyous event, around which the whole valley revolves and celebrates for the entire duration of his visit.

The people of Limi Valley are excellent horsemen and can easily pick a handkerchief off the ground at full gallop

The main pastoral and scholarly needs of Limi are looked after by the Limi Tulku who is the Most Venerable Senge Tenzin Rinpoche. His 'Diocese' not only includes the three monasteries of Limi Valley but also the Gongphur Monastery just over the border in Chinese Tibet at Purang. Gongphur Monastery is the spiritual centre of his 'Diocese'. Senge Tenzin Rinpoche also spends a lot of time in Taiwan where he runs two Dharma Centres. His confidante and right-hand man is Khenpo Tashi Kailash who is a distinguished monk scholar and is also from Purang. For the last five years Tashi Kailash has been championing a project to bring academic education to the villages of Limi. His tireless work in this regard took him to Europe and North America. On one visit to America Tashi Kailash was introduced to Deanna Campbell, the CEO of a

Limi Valley viewed from above the impenetrable gorge at the west end, is about 30km long and lies at about 4000 metres altitude

small company. This meeting led to Deanna eventually retiring from the small company as she focused more on the plight of education in Limi. After a few visits to Limi with Tashi, during which the education projects were discussed with the elders of each village, some plans were made. These plans were discussed with the spiritual leader HH Drikung Kaybgon Chetsang Rinpoche and also HH the 17th Karmapa Ogyen Trinley Dorje for their approval. In the wake of these meetings Deanna established Antahkarana Society International, a charitable organization, which promotes education in Limi.

Due to the very remote location of Limi the logistics of setting up a school here for the fledgling Antahkarana Society International was a daunting task for Deanna and Tashi Kailash. Ideally each village needed a school, each school needed a teacher and each teacher needed books and stationery. To make matters even harder, the valley was virtually snowbound from December to March inclusive. The schools could only be built in the summer and the timber and supplies needed for the building could only be brought by numerous yak caravans during these same summer months. Basic provisions would have to be stockpiled and teachers would have to be encouraged to spend the entire winter marooned in the valley, which no Nepali government teacher would ever do. All these logistical problems made the building of schools in Limi prohibitively difficult. So Deanna and Tashi thought the best way to further education in Limi was bring some of the children from the three Limi villages to Kathmandu and educate them there. An old building was acquired in 2006 in the predominantly Tibetan Boudhanath district of Kathmandu. This building was renovated and became the 'Limi Youth Hostel'. In late 2006 some 15 children arrived from Limi Valley to stay in this hostel. Some had to walk for 17 days! Once

Limi has a few side valleys which go up to the 6000m mountains on each and whose glacial streams provide water for the barley fields

at the hostel in Kathmandu the 15 children were educated to a rudimentary level so they were prepared to enrol at the Namgyal Tibetan School. In the spring of 2007 all the 15 children entered Namgyal School and everyone had completed a year's education in spring 2008, with many receiving excellent grades. The Limi Youth Hostel in Kathmandu was expanded significantly to cater for another 15 children who arrived in late 2007 to prepare to go to the Namgyal Tibetan School. In spring 2008, as the first cohort of 15 children were finishing their first year, the second cohort were starting their first year. Again in late 2008 the third cohort of children left Limi for the Hostel in Kathmandu to prepare for their first year at Namgyal School in spring 2009. They started as the 2007 class were finishing their second year and the 2008 class finishing their first year.

The Hostel in Kathmandu is expensive to run. Not only are the children to be fed and looked after but school fees have to be paid, medical and dental emergencies to

Til is one of the three villages in Limi valley and has about 40 houses, a monastery and a population of 400 who live off barley and yak

Zang village has about 40 houses, a monastery and a population of 500 who graze their yaks in the high pastures at the head of the valley

be covered, clothes to be bought etc. All these expenses have to be met by Antahkarana Society International. But the Hostel has developed into a strong Limi Valley community and cultural centre as the children who board here reminisce about their homeland. They developed strong links with the newly founded Limi Youth Society in Kathmandu set up by young people from Limi who wanted to promote and preserve the culture in the valley. However, the ultimate goal of Deanna and Tashi was to set up a primary school in each of the three villages in Limi Valley itself and when I visited here in the summer of 2008 and met Deanna and Tashi these three village schools were just in their infancy. The elders of each village had modified a building to be used as a primary school classroom. The classrooms, however, were very rustic. There was no furniture and the pupils had to sit on the cold earthen floor in rooms with no glass in the windows. There were no school books and the blackboards were old newspapers pinned up on the mud plastered wall. One thing all three schools had was an exceptional enthusiasm. Truancy will not be a word they will have to learn.

Due to the genius of establishing the Hostel in Kathmandu and educating some 15 Limi children a year there, Deanna and Tashi have educated the first teachers for the primary schools in Limi. Each of the three village schools had two teachers, one for first year and one for the second year, recruited from the first cohort of youth who have been to the Hostel and the Namgyal School in Kathmandu. As these teachers are from Limi they will not abandon their posts like government teachers and there is now a solid teaching base for primary education. This means children of Limi can now start their education at the age of 5 or 6 and they can be educated locally for the whole of their primary education up to the age 11 or 12. The winters now need not be wasted as the children can attend classes in the snowbound villages. While in the summer, schools can break for the all important tasks of planting in May and then harvesting in October.

Khenpo Tashi Kailash and Deanna Campbell attend the simple class for older students who want to go to Kathmandu to learn at Namgyal

The pupils at the primary 1 class in Zang have no facilities and have to sit on sacks on the mud floor with cardboard scraps as their jotters

In about two years time, around 2014, these primary school pupils will be ready to go to secondary school. There will be at least 50 pupils in each secondary school class once the primary school in each of the three villages feeds it. It will simply not be feasible or desirable to send them all off to school in Kathmandu. Not feasible because of the expense and not desirable because once many of the pupils have a taste of city culture they would not want to return to their unique valley. It will therefore be necessary to build a secondary school in Limi Valley. This will be expensive to build, maintain and equip, as everything has to be carried in by yak from the small town of Simikot three days away. However, it will mean that the children of Limi can complete their education in the home cradle

Pupils in the primary 2 class at Zang have jotters but still have to sit on the mud floor while they enthusiastically learn from their local teacher

of their culture and enjoying a family life right up to the end of secondary school, using the long winters for education. When I visited the three primary schools with Deanna and Tashi it seemed exactly the sort of project I could endorse and raise money for. Deanna's enthusiasm and her American business acumen would make sure money was not squandered. While the esteem which Tashi was held in Limi by everybody due to his scholarly achievements and religious connections meant the project was approved of by everyone. Tashi's enthusiasm and wisdom would also make him ideal for guiding and steering the education project which he had already spent five years working on. Although the three villages of Limi were not as desperate as some of the impoverished Chhetri villages I had visited in Mugu, I would just not know where to start with developing a school in the latter. Limi, under Deanna's and Tashi's leadership, seemed a very worthwhile project.

I only had about two months to prepare for the trip in Norway. I had to decide what outdoor equipment and clothing I needed for the trip. I had to buy and test all this equipment and clothing. I had to buy a kayak and get it and all my kayaking equipment up to Kirkenes in North Norway. I had to have a rough plan of the ski route and sort out the maps I needed. I had to set up a website so I could upload the daily blogs and some photos. I had to get hardy, lightweight data devices, with a good battery life, so I could upload to this blog and be familiar with it. Once all this was in hand I wrote to Deanna Campbell and asked her if I could raise money for Antahkarana Society International to help with the costs of the Hostel and schooling at Namgyal in Kathmandu and also to help build and equip the schools in Limi. Naturally she was delighted.

Deanna, Tashi and Myself with the pupils at Zang primary school who are taught by the pictured local teachers who had learnt at Namgyal

As Antahkarana Society International is an American 501(c)3 charitable organization I had to set up a donation page on firstgiving.com, which accepts donations from the public and then channels them to Antahkarana. About 20 donations came in before I even started, from friends who must have a lot of faith in my determination. Over the next eight months there was a good trickle of further donations. When I finally finished there was a flood of them. By the time of writing, nearly two years after I took the first step north from Lindesnes lighthouse, 162 people or organisations had made nearly 13,000 dollars worth of donations. My donations page on the website www.firstgiving.com will still be open until 31st December 2015. You can find it by searching for 'Antahkarana Society International' from the search box on the www.firstgiving.com home page.

Deanna Campbell, Tashi Kailash, myself and the people of Limi would again like to thank all those who have already made a donation.

Day 59. The morning after the storm there was a thick blanket of new snow covering the rolling hills of Nord Trøndelag

Day 183. Fjetterstad beach on the west side of the the craggy wild Lundøya was home to a tern colony

Other books published by James Baxter and Scandinavian Publishing:

James Baxter has climbed all the mountains in Scandinavia over 2000 metres. There are altogether 130 in Norway and 7 in Sweden. There is a lot of information about these mountainous areas on his website: www.scandinavianmountains.com As a part of this project he has so far published one guide book on the most challenging and spectacular of these areas, called Hurrungane. This alpine and heavily glaciated area lies on the western side of the mountainous Jotunheimen region and includes 14 mountains over 2000 metres and numerous challenging subsidiary peaks. This hardback book has detailed route descriptions with a few colour photos and a colour map on each of the 14 mountains and its subsidiary peaks. There is also a wealth of practical information about the surrounding area. The book also includes a comprehensive section on the flora and fauna of the area with 58 photos of birds and 138 photos of flowers alone. It is available online via Amazon, where there are independent reviews and some illustrations of the pages. It is hoped further books in this series will be published soon.